A HISTORY OF CARICATURE AND GROTESQUE

In Literature and Art

By

Thomas Wright

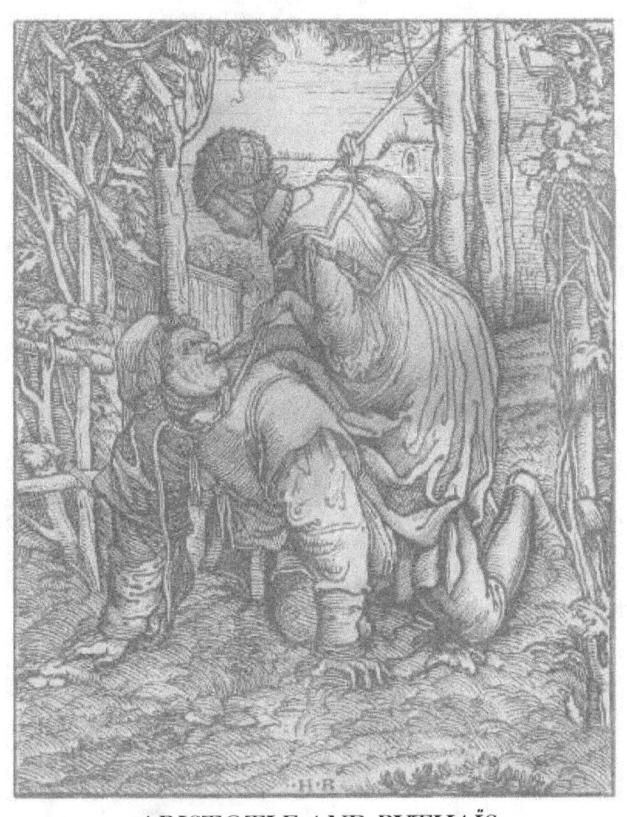

ARISTOTLE AND PYTHAÏS.
From an Engraving by Burgmair (15th cent.)

A HISTORY
OF
CARICATURE AND GROTESQUE

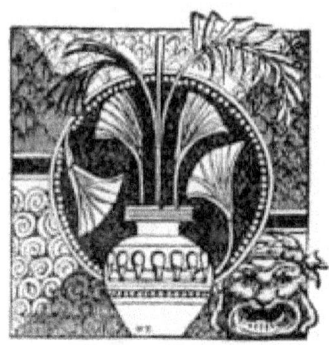

THE ILLUSTRATIONS DRAWN AND ENGRAVED BY

F. W. FAIRHOLT, F.S.A.

London:
CHATTO AND WINDUS, PICCADILLY.
1875.

LONDON:
SAVILL, EDWARDS, AND CO., PRINTERS, CHANDOS STREET,
COVENT GARDEN.

ISBN-13: 978-1721015528

ISBN-10: 1721015523

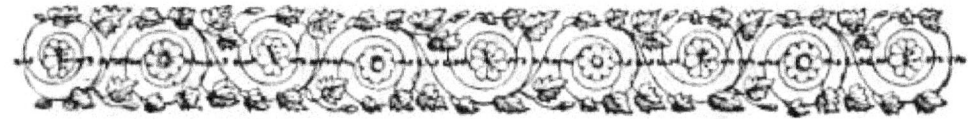

PREFACE.

I have felt some difficulty in selecting a title for the contents of the following pages, in which it was, in fact, my design to give, as far as may be done within such moderate limits, and in as popular a manner as such information can easily be imparted, a general view of the History of Comic Literature and Art. Yet the word comic seems to me hardly to express all the parts of the subject which I have sought to bring together in my book. Moreover, the field of this history is very large, and, though I have only taken as my theme one part of it, it was necessary to circumscribe even that, in some degree; and my plan, therefore, is to follow it chiefly through those branches which have contributed most towards the formation of modern comic and satiric literature and art in our own island.

Thus, as the comic literature of the middle ages to a very great extent, and comic art in a considerable degree also, were founded upon, or rather arose out of, those of the Romans which had preceded them, it seemed desirable to give a comprehensive history of this branch of literature and art as it was cultivated among the peoples of antiquity. Literature and art in the middle ages presented a certain unity of general character, arising, probably, from the uniformity of the influence of the Roman element of society, modified only by its lower degree of intensity at a greater distance from the centre, and by secondary causes attendant upon it. To understand the literature of any one country in Western Europe, especially during what we may term the feudal period—and the remark applies to art equally—it is necessary to make ourselves acquainted with the whole history of literature in Western Europe during that time. The peculiarities in different countries naturally became more marked in the progress of society, and more strongly individualised; but it was not till towards the close of the feudal period that the literature of each of these different countries was becoming more entirely its own. At that period the plan I have formed restricts itself, according to the view stated above. Thus, the satirical literature of the Reformation and pictorial caricature had their cradle in Germany, and, in the earlier half of the sixteenth century, carried their influence largely into France and England; but from that time any influence of German literature on these two countries ceases. Modern satirical literature has its models in France during the sixteenth century, and the direct influence of this literature in France upon English literature continued during that and the succeeding century, but no further. Political caricature rose to importance in France in the sixteenth century, and was transplanted to Holland in the seventeenth century, and until the beginning of the eighteenth century England owed its caricature, indirectly or directly, to the French and the Dutch; but after that time a purely English school of caricature was formed, which was entirely independent of Continental caricaturists.

There are two senses in which the word history may be taken in regard to literature and art. It has been usually employed to signify a chronological account of authors or artists and their works, though this comes more properly under the title of biography and bibliography. But there is another and a very different application of the word, and this is the meaning which I attach to it in the present volume. During the middle ages, and for some period after (in special branches), literature—I mean poetry, satire, and popular literature of all kinds—belonged to society, and not to the individual authors, who were but workmen who gained a living by satisfying society's wants; and its changes in form or character depended all upon the varying progress, and therefore changing necessities, of society itself. This is the reason why, especially in the earlier periods, nearly the whole mass of the popular—I may, perhaps, be allowed to call it the social literature of the middle ages, is anonymous; and it was only at rare intervals that some individual rose and made himself a great name by the superiority of his talents. A certain number of writers of fabliaux put their names to their compositions, probably because they were names of writers who had gained the reputation of telling better or racier stories than many of their fellows. In some branches of literature—as in the satirical literature of the sixteenth century—society still exercised this kind of influence over it; and although its great monuments owe everything to the peculiar genius of their authors, they were produced under the pressure of social circumstances. To trace all these variations in literature connected with society, to describe the influences of society upon literature and of literature upon society, during the progress of the latter, appears to me to be the true meaning of the word history, and it is in this sense that I take it.

This will explain why my history of the different branches of popular literature and art ends at very different periods. The grotesque and satirical sculpture, which adorned the ecclesiastical buildings, ceased with the middle ages. The story-books, as a part of this social literature, came down to the sixteenth century, and the history of the jest-books which arose out of them cannot be considered to extend further than the beginning of the seventeenth; for, to give a list of jest-books since that time would be to compile a catalogue of books made by booksellers for sale, copied from one another, and, till recently, each more contemptible than its predecessor. The school of satirical literature in France, at all events as far as it had any influence in England, lasted no longer than the earlier part of the seventeenth century. England can hardly be said to have had a school of satirical literature, with the exception of its comedy, which belongs properly to the seventeenth century; and its caricature belongs especially to the last century and to the earlier part of the present, beyond which it is not a part of my plan to carry it.

These few remarks will perhaps serve to explain what some may consider to be defects in my book; and with them I venture to trust it to the indulgence of its readers. It is a subject which will have some novelty for the English reader, for I am not aware that we have any previous book devoted to it. At all events, it is not a mere compilation from other people's labours.

Thomas Wright.

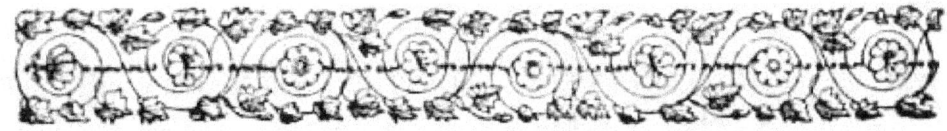

CONTENTS.

CHAPTER V.

EMPLOYMENT OF ANIMALS IN MEDIÆVAL SATIRE—POPULARITY OF FABLES; ODO DE CIRINGTON—REYNARD THE FOX—BURNELLUS AND FAUVEL—THE CHARIVARI—LE MONDE BESTORNÉ—ENCAUSTIC TILES—SHOEING THE GOOSE, AND FEEDING PIGS WITH ROSES—SATIRICAL SIGNS; THE MUSTARD MAKER

CHAPTER VI.

THE MONKEY IN BURLESQUE AND CARICATURE—TOURNAMENTS AND SINGLE COMBATS—MONSTROUS COMBINATIONS OF ANIMAL FORMS—CARICATURES ON COSTUME—THE HAT—THE HELMET—LADIES' HEAD-DRESSES—THE GOWN, AND ITS LONG SLEEVES

CHAPTER VII.

PRESERVATION OF THE CHARACTER OF THE MIMUS AFTER THE FALL OF THE EMPIRE—THE MINSTREL AND JOGELOUR—HISTORY OF POPULAR STORIES— THE FABLIAUX—ACCOUNT OF THEM—THE CONTES DEVOTS

CHAPTER VIII.

CARICATURES OF DOMESTIC LIFE—STATE OF DOMESTIC LIFE IN THE MIDDLE AGES—EXAMPLES OF DOMESTIC CARICATURE FROM THE CARVINGS OF THE MISERERES—KITCHEN SCENES—DOMESTIC BRAWLS—THE FIGHT FOR THE BREECHES—THE JUDICIAL DUEL BETWEEN MAN AND WIFE AMONG THE GERMANS—ALLUSIONS TO WITCHCRAFT—SATIRES ON THE TRADES: THE BAKER, THE MILLER, THE WINE-PEDLAR AND TAVERN KEEPER, THE ALE-WIFE, ETC.

CHAPTER IX.

GROTESQUE FACES AND FIGURES—PREVALENCE OF THE TASTE FOR UGLY AND GROTESQUE FACES—SOME OF THE POPULAR FORMS DERIVED FROM ANTIQUITY: THE TONGUE LOLLING OUT, AND THE DISTORTED MOUTH— HORRIBLE SUBJECTS: THE MAN AND THE SERPENTS—ALLEGORICAL FIGURES: GLUTTONY AND LUXURY—OTHER REPRESENTATIONS OF CLERICAL GLUTTONY AND DRUNKENNESS—GROTESQUE FIGURES OF INDIVIDUALS, AND GROTESQUE GROUPS—ORNAMENTS OF THE BORDERS OF BOOKS— UNINTENTIONAL CARICATURE; THE MOTE AND THE BEAM

CHAPTER XVI.

ORIGIN OF MEDIÆVAL FARCE AND MODERN COMEDY—HROTSVITHA—
MEDIÆVAL NOTIONS OF TERENCE—THE EARLY RELIGIOUS PLAYS—MYSTERIES
AND MIRACLE PLAYS—THE FARCES—THE DRAMA IN THE SIXTEENTH CENTURY

CHAPTER XVII.

DIABLERIE IN THE SIXTEENTH CENTURY—EARLY TYPES OF THE DIABOLICAL
FORMS—ST. ANTHONY—ST. GUTHLAC—REVIVAL OF THE TASTE FOR SUCH
SUBJECTS IN THE BEGINNING OF THE SIXTEENTH CENTURY—THE FLEMISH
SCHOOL OF BREUGHEL—THE FRENCH AND ITALIAN SCHOOLS—CALLOT,
SALVATOR ROSA

CHAPTER XVIII.

CALLOT AND HIS SCHOOL—CALLOT'S ROMANTIC HISTORY—HIS "CAPRICI,"
AND OTHER BURLESQUE WORKS—THE "BALLI" AND THE BEGGARS—
IMITATORS OF CALLOT; DELLA BELLA—EXAMPLES OF DELLA BELLA—ROMAIN
DE HOOGHE

CHAPTER XIX.

THE SATIRICAL LITERATURE OF THE SIXTEENTH CENTURY—PASQUIL—
MACARONIC POETRY—THE EPISTOLÆ OBSCURORUM VIRORUM—RABELAIS—
COURT OF THE QUEEN OF NAVARRE, AND ITS LITERARY CIRCLE;
BONAVENTURE DES PERIERS—HENRI ETIENNE—THE LIGUE, AND ITS SATIRE:
THE "SATYRE MENIPPEE"

CHAPTER XX.

POLITICAL CARICATURE IN ITS INFANCY—THE REVERS DU JEU DES SUYSSES—
CARICATURE IN FRANCE—THE THREE ORDERS—PERIOD OF THE LIGUE;
CARICATURES AGAINST HENRI III.—CARICATURES AGAINST THE LIGUE—
CARICATURE IN FRANCE IN THE SEVENTEENTH CENTURY—GENERAL GALAS—
THE QUARREL OF AMBASSADORS—CARICATURE AGAINST LOUIS XXV.;
WILLIAM OF FURSTEMBERG

CHAPTER XXI.

EARLY POLITICAL CARICATURE IN ENGLAND—THE SATIRICAL WRITINGS AND
PICTURES OF THE COMMONWEALTH PERIOD—SATIRES AGAINST THE
BISHOPS; BISHOP WILLIAMS—CARICATURES ON THE CAVALIERS; SIR JOHN
SUCKLING—THE ROARING BOYS; VIOLENCE OF THE ROYALIST SOLDIERS—
CONTEST BETWEEN THE PRESBYTERIANS AND INDEPENDENTS—GRINDING
THE KING'S NOSE—PLAYING-CARDS USED AS THE MEDIUM FOR CARICATURE;
HASELRIGGE AND LAMBERT—SHROVETIDE

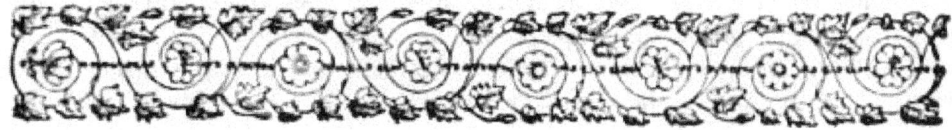

A HISTORY
OF
CARICATURE AND GROTESQUE.

CHAPTER I.

ORIGIN OF CARICATURE AND GROTESQUE.–SPIRIT OF CARICATURE IN EGYPT.–
MONSTERS: PYTHON AND GORGON.–GREECE.–THE DIONYSIAC CEREMONIES,
AND ORIGIN OF THE DRAMA.–THE OLD COMEDY.–LOVE OF PARODY.–
PARODIES ON SUBJECTS TAKEN FROM GRECIAN MYTHOLOGY: THE VISIT TO
THE LOVER: APOLLO AT DELPHI.–THE PARTIALITY FOR PARODY CONTINUED
AMONG THE ROMANS: THE FLIGHT OF ÆNEAS.

It is not my intention in the following pages to discuss the question what constitutes the comic or
the laughable, or, in other words, to enter into the philosophy of the subject; I design only to trace
the history of its outward development, the various forms it has assumed, and its social influence.
Laughter appears to be almost a necessity of human nature, in all conditions of man's existence,
however rude or however cultivated; and some of the greatest men of all ages, men of the most
refined intellects, such as Cicero in the ages of antiquity, and Erasmus among the moderns, have
been celebrated for their indulgence in it. The former was sometimes called by his opponents
scurra consularis, the "consular jester;" and the latter, who has been spoken of as the "mocking-
bird," is said to have laughed so immoderately over the well-known "Epistolæ Obscurorum
Virorum," that he brought upon himself a serious fit of illness. The greatest of comic writers,
Aristophanes, has always been looked upon as a model of literary perfection. An epigram in the
Greek Anthology, written by the divine Plato, tells us how, when the Graces sought a temple which
would not fall, they found the soul of Aristophanes:—

Ἁι χάριτες τέμενός τι λαβεῖν ὅπερ οὐχὶ πεσεῖται
Ζητοῦσαι, ψυχὴν εὗρον Ἀριστοφάνους.

On the other hand, the men who never laughed, the ἀγέλαστοι, were looked upon as the least
respectable of mortals.

A tendency to burlesque and caricature appears, indeed, to be a feeling deeply implanted in human
nature, and it is one of the earliest talents displayed by people in a rude state of society. An
appreciation of, and sensitiveness to, ridicule, and a love of that which is humorous, are found even
among savages, and enter largely into their relations with their fellow men. When, before people
cultivated either literature or art, the chieftain sat in his rude hall surrounded by his warriors, they
amused themselves by turning their enemies and opponents into mockery, by laughing at their
weaknesses, joking on their defects, whether physical or mental, and giving them nicknames in
accordance therewith,—in fact, caricaturing them in words, or by telling stories which were

calculated to excite laughter. When the agricultural slaves (for the tillers of the land were then slaves) were indulged with a day of relief from their labours, they spent it in unrestrained mirth. And when these same people began to erect permanent buildings, and to ornament them, the favourite subjects of their ornamentation were such as presented ludicrous ideas. The warrior, too, who caricatured his enemy in his speeches over the festive board, soon sought to give a more permanent form to his ridicule, which he endeavoured to do by rude delineations on the bare rock, or on any other convenient surface which presented itself to his hand. Thus originated caricature and the grotesque in art. In fact, art itself, in its earliest forms, is caricature; for it is only by that exaggeration of features which belongs to caricature, that unskilful draughtsmen could make themselves understood.

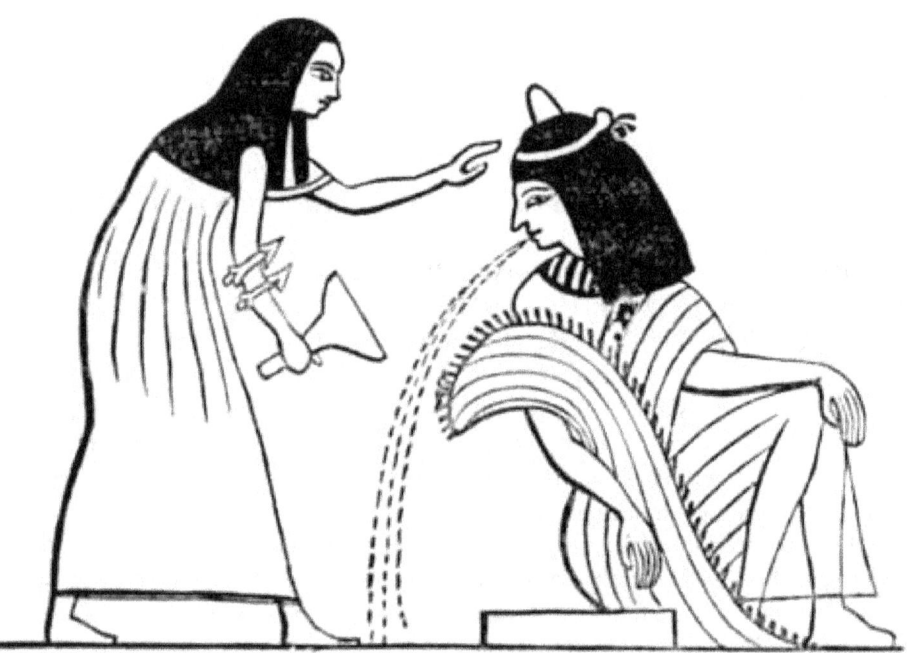

No. 1. An Egyptian Lady at a Feast.

Although we might, perhaps, find in different countries examples of these principles in different states of development, we cannot in any one country trace the entire course of the development itself: for in all the highly civilised races of mankind, we first become acquainted with their history when they had already reached a considerable degree of refinement; and even at that period of their progress, our knowledge is almost confined to their religious, and to their more severely historical, monuments. Such is especially the case with Egypt, the history of which country, as represented by its monuments of art, carries us back to the remotest ages of antiquity. Egyptian art generally presents itself in a sombre and massive character, with little of gaiety or joviality in its designs or forms. Yet, as Sir Gardner Wilkinson has remarked in his valuable work on the "Manners and Customs of the Ancient Egyptians," the early Egyptian artists cannot always conceal their natural tendency to the humorous, which creeps out in a variety of little incidents. Thus, in a series of grave historical pictures on one of the great monuments at Thebes, we find a representation of a wine party, where the company consists of both sexes, and which evidently shows that the ladies were not restricted in the use of the juice of the grape in their entertainments; and, as he adds, "the painters, in illustrating this fact, have sometimes sacrificed their gallantry to a love of caricature." Among the females, evidently of rank, represented in this scene, "some call the servants to support them as they sit, others with difficulty prevent themselves from falling on those behind them, and the faded flower, which is ready to drop from their heated hands, is intended to be characteristic of their own sensations." One group, a lady whose excess has been carried too far, and her servant who comes to her assistance, is represented in our cut No. 1. Sir Gardner observes that "many similar instances of a talent for caricature are observable in the compositions of the Egyptian artists, who executed the paintings of the tombs" at Thebes, which belong to a very early period of the Egyptian annals. Nor is the application of this talent restricted always to secular subjects, but we see it at times intruding into the most sacred mysteries of their religion. I give as a curious example, taken from one of Sir Gardner Wilkinson's engravings, a scene in the representation of a funeral procession crossing the Lake of the Dead (No. 2), that appears in one of these early paintings at Thebes, in which "the love of caricature common to the Egyptians is shown to have been indulged even in this serious subject; and the retrograde movement of the large boat, which has grounded and is pushed off the bank, striking the smaller one with its rudder, has overturned a large table loaded with cakes and other things, upon the rowers seated below, in spite of all the efforts of the prowman, and the earnest vociferations of the alarmed steersman." The accident which thus overthrows and scatters the provisions intended for the funeral feast, and the confusion attendant upon it, form a ludicrous scene in the midst of a solemn picture, that would be worthy of the imagination of a Rowlandson.

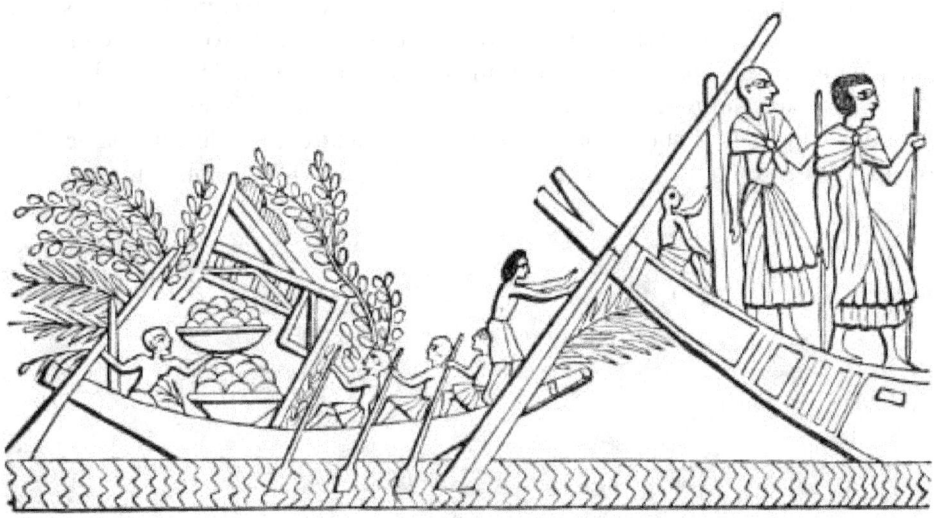

No. 2. Catastrophe in a Funeral Procession.

Another cut (No. 3), taken from one of the same series of paintings, belongs to a class of caricatures which dates from a very remote period. One of the most natural ideas among all people would be to compare men with the animals whose particular qualities they possessed. Thus, one might be as bold as a lion, another as faithful as a dog, or as cunning as a fox, or as swinish as a hog. The name of the animal would thus often be given as a nickname to the man, and in the sequel he would be represented pictorially under the form of the animal. It was partly out of this kind of caricature, no doubt, that the singular class of apologues which have been since distinguished by the name of fables arose. Connected with it was the belief in the metempsychosis, or transmission of the soul into the bodies of animals after death, which formed a part of several of the primitive religions. The earliest examples of this class of caricature of mankind are found on the Egyptian monuments, as in the instance just referred to, which represents "a soul condemned to return to earth under the form of a pig, having been weighed in the scales before Osiris and been found wanting. Being placed in a boat, and accompanied by two monkeys, it is dismissed the sacred precinct." The latter animals, it may be remarked, as they are here represented, are the cynocephali, or dog-headed monkeys (the *simia inuus*), which were sacred animals among the Egyptians, and the peculiar characteristic of which—the dog-shaped head—is, as usual, exaggerated by the artist.

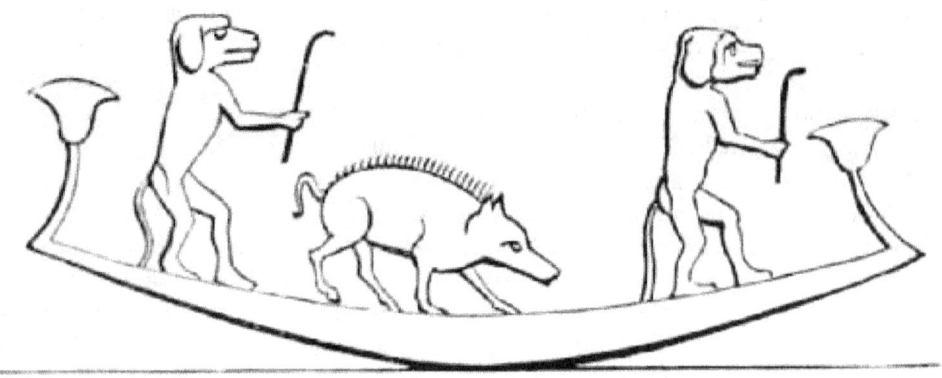

No. 3. An Unfortunate Soul.

The representation of this return of a condemned soul under the repulsive form of a pig, is painted on the left side wall of the long entrance-gallery to the tomb of King Rameses V., in the valley of royal catacombs known as the Biban-el-Molook, at Thebes. Wilkinson gives the date of the accession of this monarch to the throne as 1185 B.C. In the original picture, Osiris is seated on his throne at some distance from the stern of the boat, and is dismissing it from his presence by a wave of the hand. This tomb was open in the time of the Romans, and termed by them the "Tomb of Memnon;" it was greatly admired, and is covered with laudatory inscriptions by Greek and Roman visitors. One of the most interesting is placed beneath this picture, recording the name of a *daduchus*, or torch-bearer in the Eleusinian mysteries, who visited this tomb in the reign of Constantine.

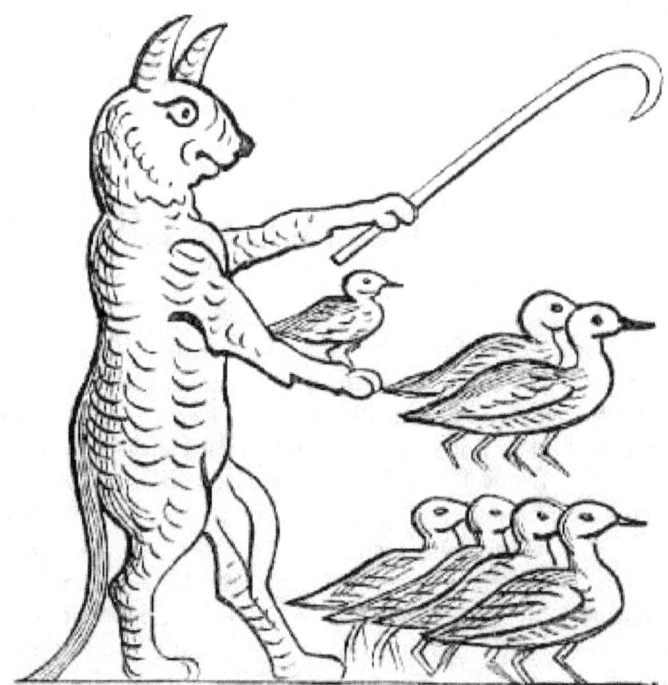

No. 4. The Cat and the Geese.

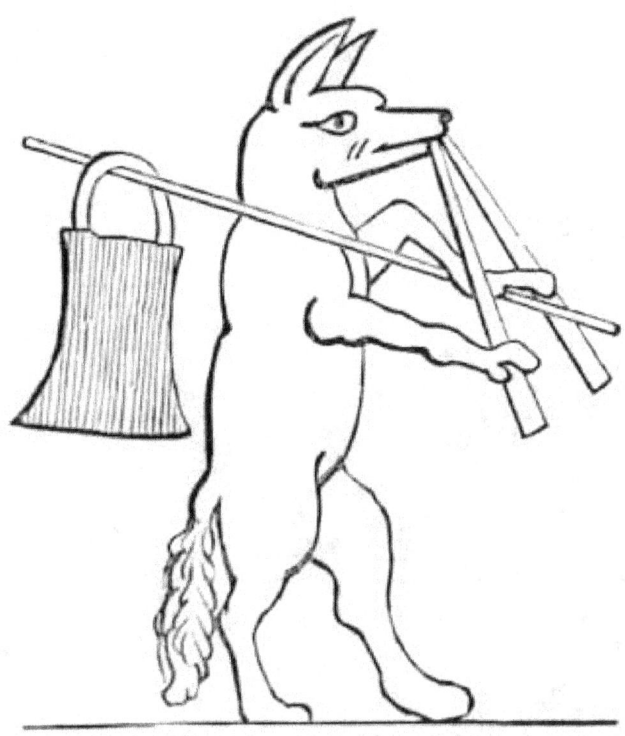

No. 5. The Fox turned Piper.

The practice having been once introduced of representing men under the character of animals, was soon developed into other applications of the same idea—such as that of figuring animals employed in the various occupations of mankind, and that of reversing the position of man and the inferior animals, and representing the latter as treating their human tyrant in the same manner as they are usually treated by him. The latter idea became a very favourite one at a later period, but the other is met with not unfrequently among the works of art which have been saved from the wrecks of antiquity. Among the treasures of the British Museum, there is a long Egyptian picture on papyrus, originally forming a roll, consisting of representations of this description, from which I give three curious examples. The first (see cut No. 4) represents a cat in charge of a drove of geese. It will be observed that the cat holds in her hand the same sort of rod, with a hook at the end, with which the monkeys are furnished in the preceding picture. The second (No. 5) represents a fox carrying a basket by means of a pole supported on his shoulder (a method of carrying burthens frequently represented on the monuments of ancient art), and playing on the well-known double flute, or pipe. The fox soon became a favourite personage in this class of caricatures, and we know what a prominent part he afterwards played in mediæval satire. Perhaps, however, the most popular of all animals in this class of drolleries was the monkey, which appears natural enough when we consider its singular aptitude to mimic the actions of man. The ancient naturalists tell us some curious, though not very credible, stories of the manner in which this characteristic of the monkey tribes was taken advantage of to entrap them, and Pliny (Hist. Nat. lib. viii. c. 80) quotes an older writer, who asserted that they had even been taught to play at draughts. Our third subject from the Egyptian papyrus of the British Museum (No. 6) represents a scene in which the game of draughts—or, more properly speaking, the game which the Romans called the *ludus latrunculorum*, and which is believed to have resembled our draughts—is played by two animals well known to modern heraldry, the lion and the unicorn. The lion has evidently gained the victory, and is fingering the money; and his bold air of swaggering superiority, as well as the look of surprise and disappointment of his vanquished opponent, are by no means ill pictured. This series of caricatures, though Egyptian, belongs to the Roman period.

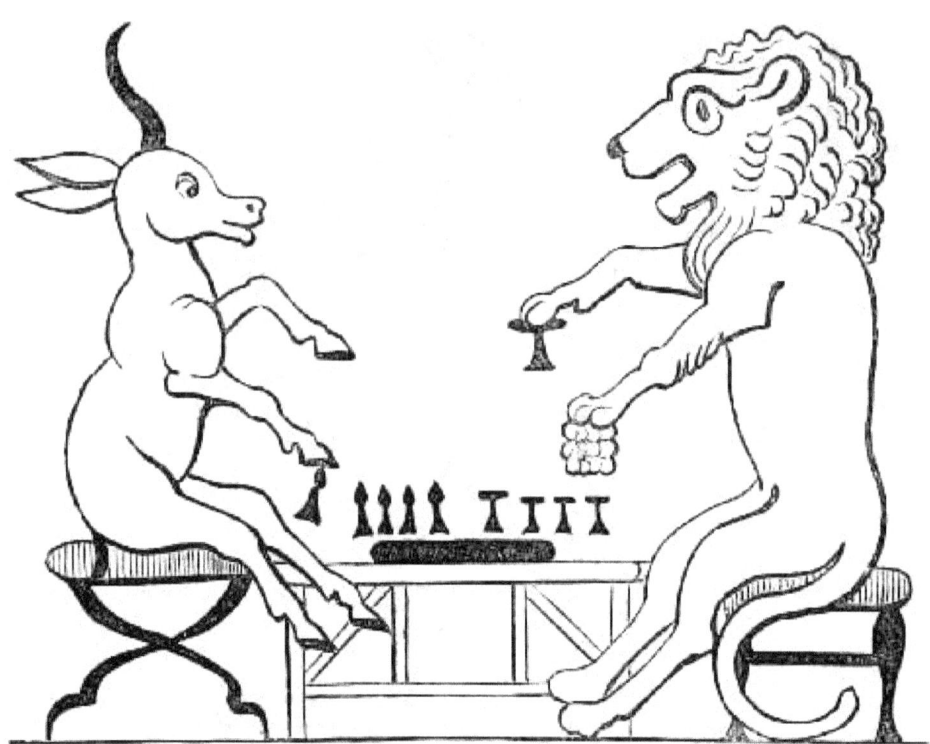

No. 6. The Lion and the Unicorn.

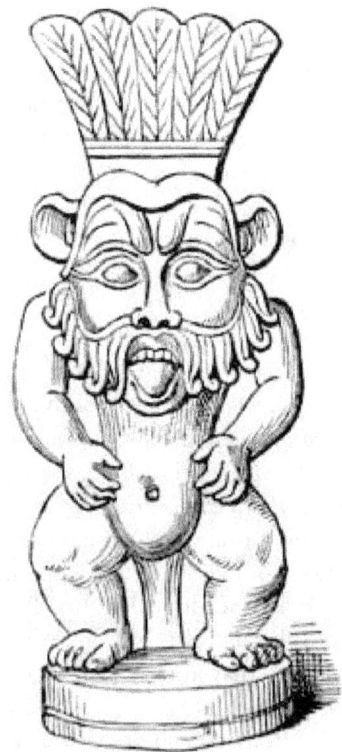

No. 7. Typhon.

The monstrous is closely allied to the grotesque, and both come within the province of caricature, when we take this term in its widest sense. The Greeks, especially, were partial to representations of monsters, and monstrous forms are continually met with among their ornaments and works of art. The type of the Egyptian monster is represented in the accompanying cut (No. 7), taken from the work of Sir Gardner Wilkinson before quoted, and is said to be the figure of the god Typhon. It occurs frequently on Egyptian monuments, with some variation in its forms, but always characterised by the broad, coarse, and frightful face, and by the large tongue lolling out. It is interesting to us, because it is the apparent origin of a long series of faces, or masks, of this form and character, which are continually recurring in the grotesque ornamentation, not only of the Greeks and Romans, but of the middle ages. It appears to have been sometimes given by the Romans to the representations of people whom they hated or despised; and Pliny, in a curious passage of his "Natural History,"[1] informs us that at one time, among the pictures exhibited in the Forum at Rome, there was one in which a Gaul was represented, "thrusting out his tongue in a very unbecoming manner." The Egyptian Typhons had their exact representations in ancient Greece in a figure of frequent occurrence, to which antiquaries have, I know not why, given the name of Gorgon. The example in our cut No. 8, is a figure in terra-cotta, now in the collection of the Royal Museum at Berlin.[2]

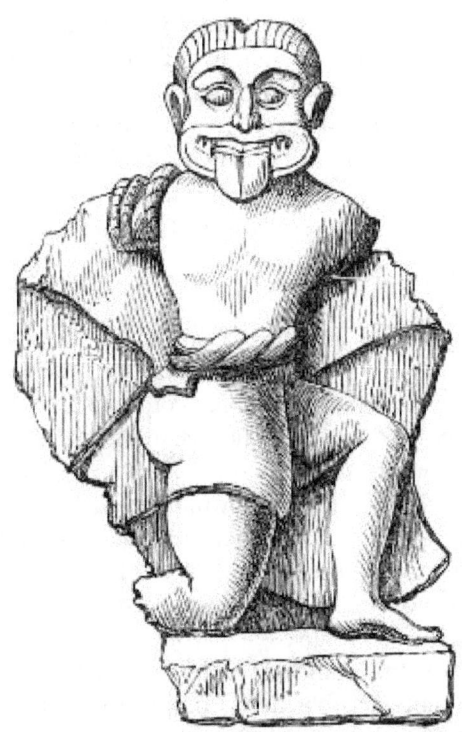

No. 8. Gorgon.

In Greece, however, the spirit of caricature and burlesque representation had assumed a more regular form than in other countries, for it was inherent in the spirit of Grecian society. Among the population of Greece, the worship of Dionysus, or Bacchus, had taken deep root from a very early period—earlier than we can trace back—and it formed the nucleus of the popular religion and superstitions, the cradle of poetry and the drama. The most popular celebrations of the people of Greece, were the Dionysiac festivals, and the phallic rites and processions which accompanied them, in which the chief actors assumed the disguise of satyrs and fawns, covering themselves with goat-skins, and disfiguring their faces by rubbing them over with the lees of wine. Thus, in the guise of noisy bacchanals, they displayed an unrestrained licentiousness of gesture and language, uttering indecent jests and abusive speeches, in which they spared nobody. This portion of the ceremony was the especial attribute of a part of the performers, who accompanied the procession in waggons, and acted something like dramatic performances, in which they uttered an abundance of loose extempore satire on those who passed or who accompanied the procession, a little in the style of the modern carnivals. It became thus the occasion for an unrestrained publication of coarse pasquinades. In the time of Pisistratus, these performances are assumed to have been reduced to a little more order by an individual named Thespis, who is said to have invented masks as a better disguise than dirty faces, and is looked upon as the father of the Grecian drama. There can be no doubt, indeed, that the drama arose out of these popular ceremonies, and it long bore the unmistakable marks of its origin. Even the name of tragedy has nothing tragic in its derivation, for it is formed from the Greek word *tragos* (τράγος), a goat, in the skins of which animal the satyrs clothed themselves, and hence the name was given also to those who personated the satyrs in the processions. A *tragodus* (τραγῳδός) was the singer, whose words accompanied the movements of a chorus of satyrs, and the term *tragodia* was applied to his performance. In the same manner, a *comodus* (κωμῳδός) was one who accompanied similarly, with chants of an abusive or satirical character, a *comus* (κῶμος), or band of revellers, in the more riotous and licentious portion of the performances in the Bacchic festivals. The Greek drama always betrayed its origin by the circumstance that the performances took place annually, only at the yearly festivals in honour of Bacchus, of which in fact they constituted a part. Moreover, as the Greek drama became perfected, it still retained from its origin a triple division, into tragedy, comedy, and the satiric drama; and, being still performed at the Dionysiac festival in Athens, each dramatic author was expected to produce what was called a *trilogy*, that is, a tragedy, a satirical play, and a comedy. So completely was all this identified in the popular mind with the worship of Bacchus, that, long afterwards, when even a tragedy did not please the audience by its subject, the common form of disapproval was, τί ταῦτα πρὸς τὸν Διόνυσον–"What has this to do with Bacchus?" and, οὐδὲν πρὸς τὸν Διόνυσον–"This has nothing to do with Bacchus."

We have no perfect remains of the Greek satiric drama, which was, perhaps, of a temporary character, and less frequently preserved; but the early Greek comedy is preserved in a certain number of the plays of Aristophanes, in which we can contemplate it in all its freedom of character. It represented the waggon-jesting, of the age of Thespis, in its full development. In its form it was burlesque to a wanton degree of extravagance, and its essence was personal vilification, as well as general satire. Individuals were not only attacked by the application to them of abusive epithets, but they were represented personally on the stage as performing every kind of contemptible action, and as suffering all sorts of ludicrous and disgraceful treatment. The drama thus bore marks of its origin in its extraordinary licentiousness of language and costume, and in the constant use of the mask. One of its most favourite instruments of satire was parody, which was employed unsparingly on everything which society in its solemn moments respected–against everything that the satirist considered worthy of being held up to public derision or scorn. Religion itself, philosophy, social manners and institutions–even poetry–were all parodied in their turn. The comedies of Aristophanes are full of parodies on the poetry of the tragic and other writers of his age. He is especially happy in parodying the poetry of the tragic dramatist Euripides. The old comedy of Greece has thus been correctly described as the comedy of caricature; and the spirit, and even the scenes, of this comedy, being transferred to pictorial representations, became entirely identical with that branch of art to which we give the name of caricature in modern times. Under the cover of bacchanalian buffoonery, a serious purpose, it is true, was aimed at; but the general satire was chiefly implied in the violent personal attacks on individuals, and this became so offensive that when such persons obtained greater power in Athens than the populace the old comedy was abolished.

Aristophanes was the greatest and most perfect poet of the Old Comedy, and his remaining comedies are as strongly marked representations of the hostility of political and social parties in his time, as the caricatures of Gillray are of party in the reign of our George III., and, we may add, even more minute. They range through the memorable period of the Peloponnesian war, and the earlier ones give us the regular annual series of these performances, as far as Aristophanes contributed them, during several years. The first of them, "The Acharnians," was performed at the Lenæan feast of Bacchus in the sixth year of the Peloponnesian war, the year 425 B.C., when it gained the first prize. It is a bold attack on the factious prolongation of the war through the influence of the Athenian demagogues. The next, "The Knights," brought out in B.C. 424, is a direct attack upon Cleon, the chief of these demagogues, although he is not mentioned by name; and it is recorded that, finding nobody who had courage enough to make a mask representing Cleon, or to play the character, Aristophanes was obliged to perform it himself, and that he smeared his face with lees of wine, in order to represent the flushed and bloated countenance of the great demagogue, thus returning to the original mode of acting of the predecessors of Thespis. This, too, was the first of the comedies of Aristophanes which he published in his own name. "The Clouds," published in 423, is aimed at Socrates and the philosophers. The fourth, "The Wasps," published in B.C. 422, presents a satire on the litigious spirit of the Athenians. The fifth, entitled "Peace" (Ειρηνη), appeared in the year following, at the time of the peace of Nicias, and is another satire on the bellicose spirit of the Athenian democracy. The next in the list of extant plays comes after an interval of several years, having been published in B.C. 414, the first year of the Sicilian war, and relates to an irreligious movement in Athens, which had caused a great sensation. Two Athenians are represented as leaving Athens, in disgust at the vices and follies of their fellow citizens, and seeking the kingdom of the birds, where they form a new state, by which the communication between the mortals and the immortals is cut off, and is only opened again by an arrangement between all the parties. In the "Lysistrata," believed to have been brought out in 411, when the war was still at its height, the women of Athens are represented as engaging in a cunning and successful plot, by which they gain possession of the government of the state, and compel their husbands to make peace. "The Thesmophoriazusæ," appears to have been published in B.C. 410; it is a satire upon Euripides, whose writings were remarkable for their bitter attacks on the character of the female sex, who, in this comedy, conspire against him to secure his punishment. The comedy of "The Frogs" was brought out in the year 405 B.C., and is a satire on the literature of the day; it is aimed especially at Euripides, and was perhaps written soon after his death, its real subject being the decline of the tragic drama, which Euripides was accused of having promoted. It is perhaps the most witty of the plays of Aristophanes which have been preserved. "The Ecclesiazusæ," published in 392, is a burlesque upon the theories of republican government, which were then started among the philosophers, some of which differed little from our modern communism. The ladies again, by a clever conspiracy, gain the mastery in the estate, and they decree a community of goods and women, with some laws very peculiar to that state of things. The humour of the piece, which is extremely broad, turns upon the disputes and embarrassments resulting from this state of things. The last of his comedies extant, "Plutus," appears to be a work of the concluding years of the active life of Aristophanes; it is the least striking of them all, and is rather a moral than a political satire.

In a comedy brought out in 426, the year before "The Archarnians," under the title of "The Babylonians," Aristophanes appears to have given great offence to the democratic party, a circumstance to which he alludes more than once in the former play. However, his talents and popularity seem to have carried him over the danger, and certainly nothing can have exceeded the bitterness of satire employed in his subsequent comedies. Those who followed him were less fortunate.

One of the latest writers of the Old Comedy was Anaximandrides, who cast a reflection on the state of Athens in parodying a line of Euripides. This poet had said,—

ἡ φύσις ἐβούλεθ' ἦ νόμων οὐδεν μέλει
(Nature has commanded, which cares nothing for the laws);

which Anaximandrides changed to—

ἡ πόλις ἐβούλεθ' ἦ νόμων οὐδεν μέλει
(The state has commanded, which cares nothing for the laws).

Nowhere is oppression exercised with greater harshness than under democratic governments; and Anaximandrides was prosecuted for this joke as a crime against the state, and condemned to death. As may be supposed, liberty of speech ceased to exist in Athens. We are well acquainted with the character of the Old Comedy, in its greatest freedom, through the writings of Aristophanes. What was called the Middle Comedy, in which political satire was prohibited, lasted from this time until the age of Philip of Macedon, when the old liberty of Greece was finally crushed. The last form of Greek comedy followed, which is known as the New Comedy, and was represented by such names as Epicharmus and Menander. In the New Comedy all caricature and parody, and all personal allusions, were entirely proscribed; it was changed entirely into a comedy of manners and domestic life, a picture of contemporary society under conventional names and characters. From this New Comedy was taken the Roman comedy, such as we now have it in the plays of Plautus and Terence, who were professed imitators of Menander and the other writers of the new comedy of the Greeks.

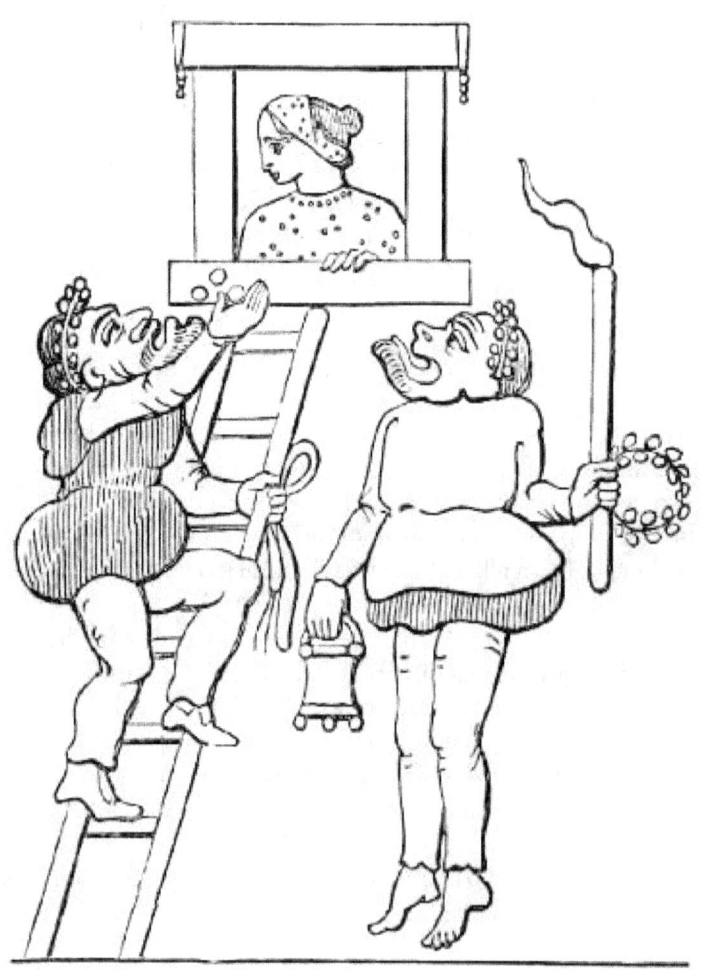

No. 9. A Greek Parody.

Pictorial caricature was, of course, rarely to be seen on the public monuments of Greece or Rome, but must have been consigned to objects of a more popular character and to articles of common use; and, accordingly, modern antiquarian research has brought it to light somewhat abundantly on the pottery of Greece and Etruria, and on the wall-paintings of domestic buildings in Herculaneum and Pompeii. The former contains comic scenes, especially parodies, which are evidently transferred to them from the stage, and which preserve the marks and other attributes—some of which I have necessarily omitted—proving the model from which they were taken. The Greeks, as we know from many sources, were extremely fond of parodies of every description, whether literary or pictorial. The subject of our cut No. 9 is a good example of the parodies found on the Greek pottery; it is taken from a fine Etruscan vase,[3] and has been supposed to be a parody on the visit of Jupiter to Alcmena. This appears rather doubtful, but there can be no doubt that it is a burlesque representation of the visit of a lover to the object of his aspirations. The lover, in the comic mask and costume, mounts by a ladder to the window at which the lady presents herself, who, it must be confessed, presents the appearance of giving her admirer a very cold reception. He tries to conciliate her by a present of what seem to be apples, instead of gold, but without much effect. He is attended by his servant with a torch, to give him light on the way, which shows that it is a night adventure. Both master and servant have wreaths round their heads, and the latter carries a third in his hand, which, with the contents of his basket, are also probably intended as presents to the lady.

A more unmistakable burlesque on the visit of Jupiter to Alcmena is published by Winckelmann from a vase, formerly in the library of the Vatican, and now at St. Petersburg. The treatment of the subject is not unlike the picture just described. Alcmena appears just in the same posture at her chamber window, and Jupiter is carrying his ladder to mount up to her, but has not yet placed it against the wall. His companion is identified with Mercury by the well-known caduceus he carries in his left hand, while with his right hand he holds a lamp up to the window, in order to enable Jupiter to see the object of his amour.

It is astonishing with how much boldness the Greeks parodied and ridiculed sacred subjects. The Christian father, Arnobius, in writing against his heathen opponents, reproached them with this circumstance. The laws, he says, were made to protect the characters of men from slander and libel, but there was no such protection for the characters of the gods, which were treated with the greatest disrespect.[4] This was especially the case in their pictorial representations.

Pliny informs us that Ctesilochus, a pupil of the celebrated Apelles, painted a burlesque picture of Jupiter giving birth to Bacchus, in which the god was represented in a very ridiculous posture.[5] Ancient writers intimate that similar examples were not uncommon, and mention the names of several comic painters, whose works of this class were in repute. Some of these were bitter personal caricatures, like a celebrated work of a painter named Ctesicles, described also by Pliny. It appears that Stratonice, the queen of Seleucus Nicator, had received this painter ill when he visited her court, and in revenge he executed a picture in which she was represented, according to a current scandal, as engaged in an amour with a common fisherman, which he exhibited in the harbour of Ephesus, and then made his escape on ship-board. Pliny adds that the queen admired the beauty and accuracy of the painting more than she felt the insult, and that she forbade the removal of the picture.[6]

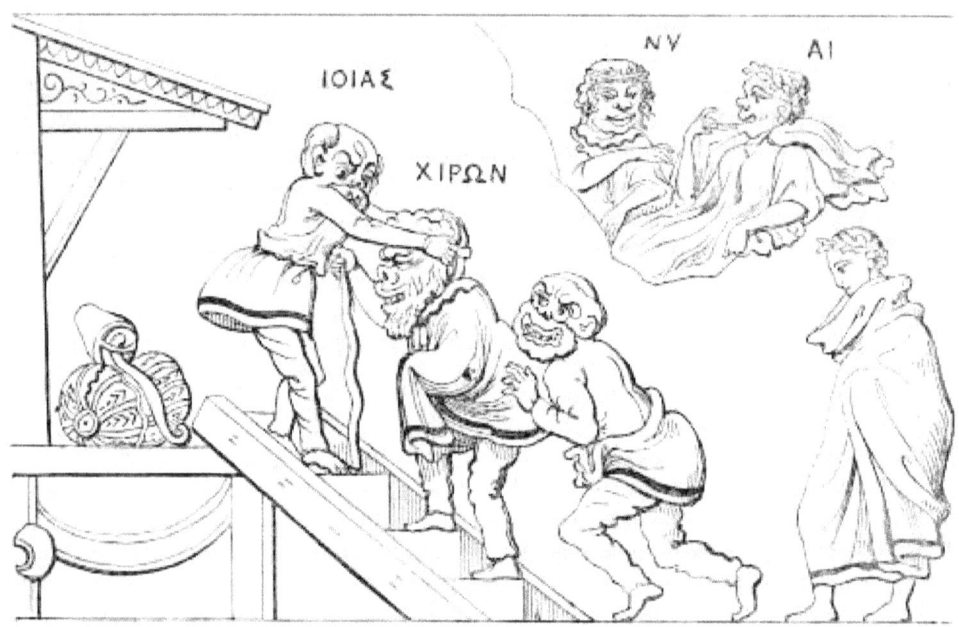

No. 10. Apollo at Delphi.

The subject of our second example of the Greek caricature is better known. It is taken from an oxybaphon which was brought from the Continent to England, where it passed into the collection of Mr. William Hope.[7] The *oxybaphon* (ὀξύβαφον), or, as it was called by the Romans, *acetabulum*, was a large vessel for holding vinegar, which formed one of the important ornaments of the table, and was therefore very susceptible of pictorial embellishment of this description. It is one of the most remarkable Greek caricatures of this kind yet known, and represents a parody on one of the most interesting stories of the Grecian mythology, that of the arrival of Apollo at Delphi. The artist, in his love of burlesque, has spared none of the personages who belonged to the story. The Hyperborean Apollo himself appears in the character of a quack doctor, on his temporary stage, covered by a sort of roof, and approached by wooden steps. On the stage lies Apollo's luggage, consisting of a bag, a bow, and his Scythian cap. Chiron (ΧΙΡΩΝ) is represented as labouring under the effects of age and blindness, and supporting himself by the aid of a crooked staff, as he repairs to the Delphian quack-doctor for relief. The figure of the centaur is made to ascend by the aid of a companion, both being furnished with the masks and other attributes of the comic performers. Above are the mountains, and on them the nymphs of Parnassus (ΝΥΜΦΑΙ), who, like all the other actors in the scene, are disguised with masks, and those of a very grotesque character. On the right-hand side stands a figure which is considered as representing the *epoptes*, the inspector or overseer of the performance, who alone wears no mask. Even a pun is employed to heighten the drollery of the scene, for instead of ΠΥΘΙΑΣ, the Pythian, placed over the head of the burlesque Apollo, it seems evident that the artist had written ΠΕΙΘΙΑΣ, the consoler, in allusion, perhaps, to the consolation which the quack-doctor is administering to his blind and aged visitor.

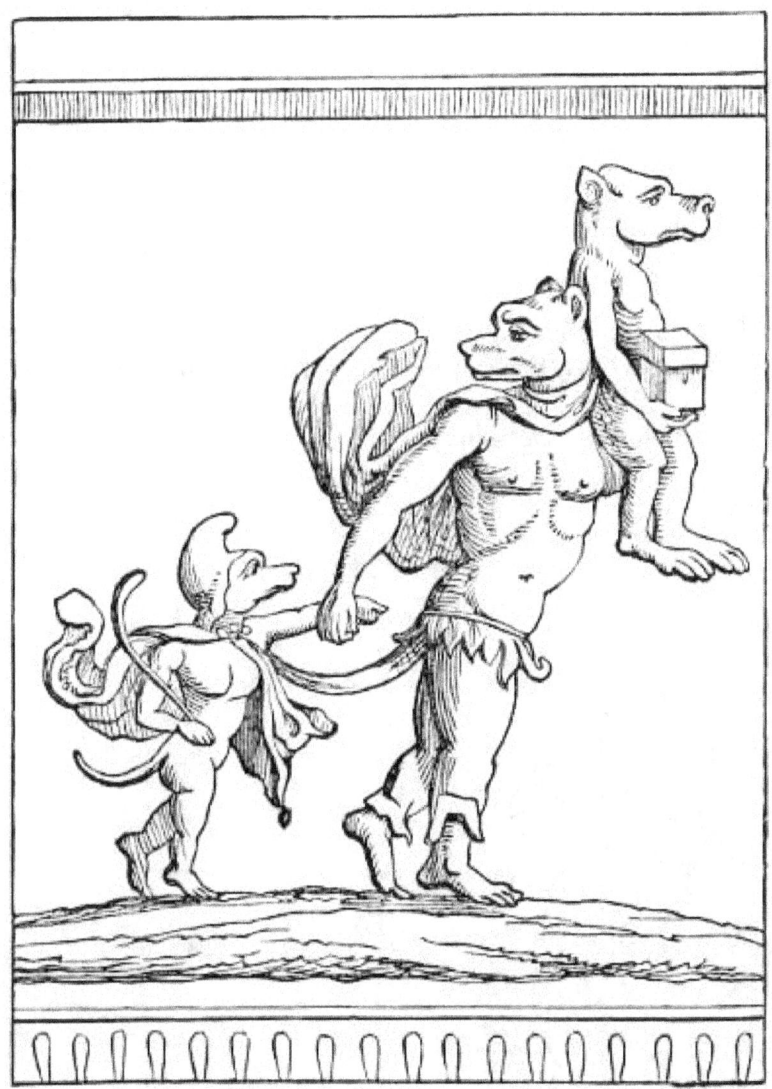

No. 11. The Flight of Æneas from Troy.

The Greek spirit of parody, applied even to the most sacred subjects, however it may have declined in Greece, was revived at Rome, and we find examples of it on the walls of Pompeii and Herculaneum. They show the same readiness to turn into burlesque the most sacred and popular legends of the Roman mythology. The example given (cut No. 11), from one of the wall-paintings, is peculiarly interesting, both from circumstances in the drawing itself, and because it is a parody on one of the favourite national legends of the Roman people, who prided themselves on their descent from Æneas. Virgil has told, with great effect, the story of his hero's escape from the destruction of Troy—or rather has put the story into his hero's mouth. When the devoted city was already in flames, Æneas took his father, Anchises, on his shoulder, and his boy, Iulus, or, as he was otherwise called, Ascanius, by the hand, and thus fled from his home, followed by his wife—

Ergo age, care pater, cervici imponere nostræ;
Ipse subibo humeris, nec me labor iste gravabit.
Quo res cumque cadent, unum et commune periclum,
Una salus ambobus erit. Mihi parvus Iulus
Sit comes, et longe servat vestigia conjux.

—Virg. Æn., lib. ii. l. 707.

Thus they hurried on, the child holding by his father's right hand, and dragging after with "unequal steps,"—

dextræ se parvus Iulus
Implicuit sequiturque patrem non passibus æquis.
—Virg. Æn., lib. ii. 1. 723.

And thus Æneas bore away both father and son, and the penates, or household gods, of his family, which were to be transferred to another country, and become the future guardians of Rome—

Ascanium, Anchisemque patrem, Tencrosque penates.—Ib., 1. 747.

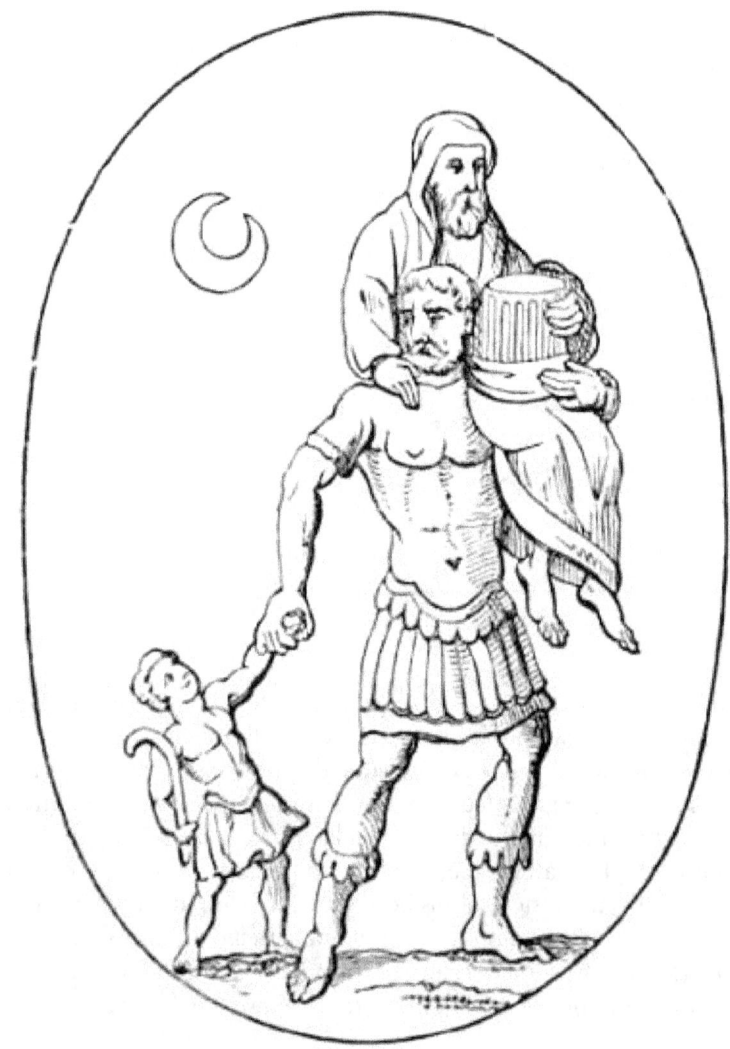

No. 12. The Flight of Æneas.

In this case we know that the design is intended to be a parody, or burlesque, upon a picture which appears to have been celebrated at the time, and of which at least two different copies are found upon ancient intaglios. It is the only case I know in which both the original and the parody have been preserved from this remote period, and this is so curious a circumstance, that I give in the cut on the preceding page a copy of one of the intaglios.[8] It represented literally Virgil's account of the story, and the only difference between the design on the intaglios and the one given in our first cut is, that in the latter the personages are represented under the forms of monkeys. Æneas, personified by the strong and vigorous animal, carrying the old monkey, Anchises, on his left shoulder, hurries forward, and at the same time looks back on the burning city. With his right hand he drags along the boy Iulus, or Ascanius, who is evidently proceeding *non passibus æquis*, and with difficulty keeps up with his father's pace. The boy wears a Phrygian bonnet, and holds in his right hand the instrument of play which we should now call a "bandy"—the pedun. Anchises has charge of the box, which contains the sacred penates. It is a curious circumstance that the monkeys in this picture are the same dog-headed animals, or cynocephali, which are found on the Egyptian monuments.

When this chapter was already given for press, I first became acquainted with an interesting paper, by Panofka, on the "Parodieen und Karikaturen auf Werken der Klassischen Kunst," in the "Abhandlungen der Akademie der Wissenschaften zu Berlin," for the year 1854, and I can only now refer my readers to it.

CHAPTER II.

ORIGIN OF THE STAGE IN ROME.—USES OF THE MASK AMONG THE ROMANS.—
SCENES FROM ROMAN COMEDY.—THE SANNIO AND MIMUS.—THE ROMAN
DRAMA.—THE ROMAN SATIRISTS.—CARICATURE.—ANIMALS INTRODUCED IN
THE CHARACTERS OF MEN.—THE PIGMIES, AND THEIR INTRODUCTION INTO
CARICATURE; THE FARM-YARD; THE PAINTER'S STUDIO; THE PROCESSION.—
POLITICAL CARICATURE IN POMPEII; THE GRAFFITI.

The Romans appear to have never had any real taste for the regular drama, which they merely copied from the Greeks, and from the earliest period of their history we find them borrowing all their arts of this description from their neighbours. In Italy, as in Greece, the first germs of comic literature may be traced in the religious festivals, which presented a mixture of religious worship and riotous festivity, where the feasters danced and sung, and, as they became excited with wine and enthusiasm, indulged in mutual reproaches and abuse. The oldest poetry of the Romans, which was composed in irregular measure, was represented by the *versus saturnini*, said to have been so called from their antiquity (for things of remote antiquity were believed to belong to the age of Saturn). Nævius, one of the oldest of Latin poets, is said to have written in this verse. Next in order of time came the Fescennine verses, which appear to have been distinguished chiefly by their license, and received their name because they were brought from Fescennia, in Etruria, where they were employed originally in the festivals of Ceres and Bacchus. In the year 391 of Rome, or 361 B.C., the city was visited by a dreadful plague, and the citizens hit upon what will appear to us the rather strange expedient of sending for performers (*ludiones*) from Etruria, hoping, by employing them, to appease the anger of the gods. Any performer of this kind appears to have been so little known to the Romans before this, that there was not even a name for him in the language, and they were obliged to adopt the Tuscan word, and call him a *histrio*, because *hister* in that language meant a player or pantomimist. This word, we know, remained in the Latin language. These first Etrurian performers appear indeed to have been mere pantomimists, who accompanied the flute with all sorts of mountebank tricks, gestures, dances, gesticulations, and the like, mixed with satirical songs, and sometimes with the performance of coarse farces. The Romans had also a class of performances rather more dramatic in character, consisting of stories which were named *Fabulæ Atellanæ*, because these performers were brought from Atella, a city of the Osci.

A considerable advance was made in dramatic Art in Rome about the middle of the third century before Christ. It is ascribed to a freedman named Livius Andronicus, a Greek by birth, who is said to have brought out, in the year 240 B.C., the first regular comedy ever performed in Rome. Thus we trace not only the Roman comedy, but the very rudiments of dramatic art in Rome, either direct to the Greeks, or to the Grecian colonies in Italy. With the Romans, as well as with the Greeks, the theatre was a popular institution, open to the public, and the state or a wealthy individual paid for the performance; and therefore the building itself was necessarily of very great extent, and, in both countries open to the sky, except that the Romans provided for throwing an awning over it. As the Roman comedy was copied from the new comedy of the Greeks, and therefore did not admit of the introduction of caricature and burlesque on the stage, these were left especially to the province of the pantomime and farce, which the Romans, as just stated, had received from a still earlier period.

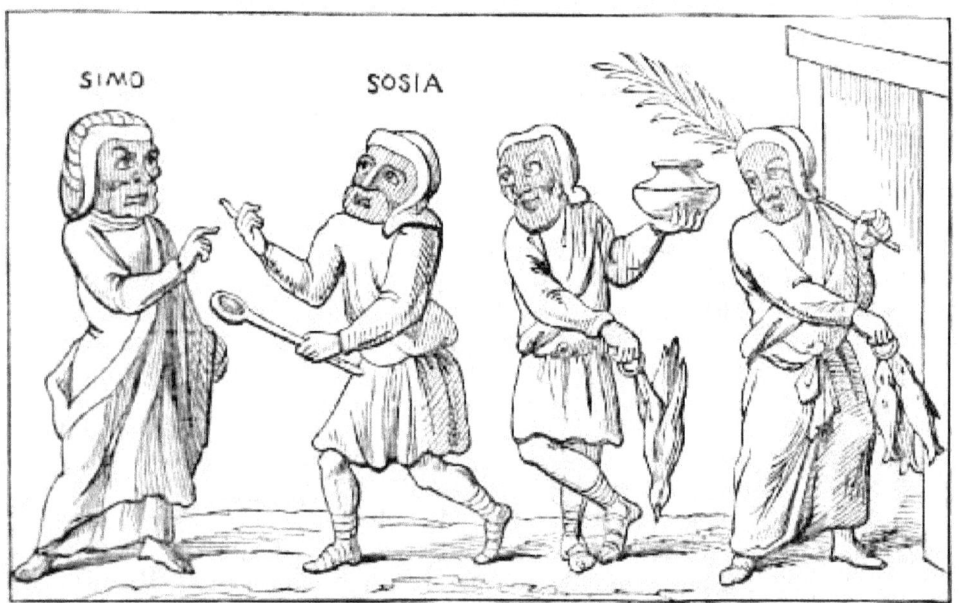

No. 13. A Scene from Terence.

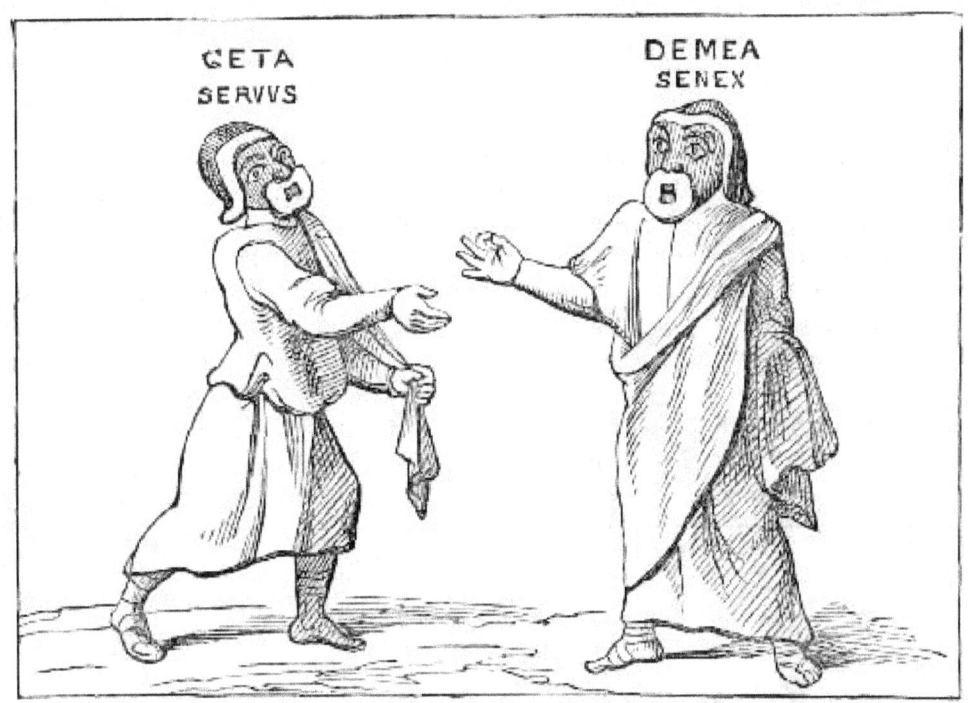

No. 14. Geta and Demea.

Whether the Romans borrowed the mask from the Greeks, or not, is rather uncertain, but it was used as generally in the Roman theatres, whether in comedy or tragedy, as among the Greeks. The Greek actors performed upon stilts, in order to magnify their figures, as the area of the theatre was very large and uncovered, and without this help they were not so well seen at a distance; and one object of utility aimed at by the mask is said to have been to make the head appear proportionate in size to the artificial height of the body. It may be remarked that the mask seems generally to have been made to cover the whole head, representing the hair as well as the face, so that the character of age or complexion might be given complete. Among the Romans the stilts were certainly not in general use, but still the mask, besides its comic or tragic character, is supposed to have served useful purposes. The first improvement upon its original structure is said to have been the making it of brass, or some other sonorous metal, or at least lining the mouth with it, so as to reverberate, and give force to the voice, and also to the mouth of the mask something of the character of a speaking-trumpet.[9] All these accessories could not fail to detract much from the effect of the acting, which must in general have been very measured and formal, and have received most of its importance from the excellence of the poetry, and the declamatory talents of the actors. We have pictures in which scenes from the Roman stage are accurately represented. Several rather early manuscripts of Terence have been preserved, illustrated with drawings of the scenes as represented on the stage, and these, though belonging to a period long subsequent to the age in which the Roman stage existed in its original character, are, no doubt, copied from drawings of an earlier date. A German antiquary of the last century, Henry Berger, published in a quarto volume a series of such illustrations from a manuscript of Terence in the library of the Vatican at Rome, from which two examples are selected, as showing the usual style of Roman comic acting, and the use of the mask. The first (No. 13) is the opening scene in the *Andria*. On the right, two servants have brought provisions, and on the left appear Simo, the master of the household, and his freedman, Sosia, who seems to be entrusted with the charge of his domestic affairs. Simo tells his servants to go away with the provisions, while he beckons Sosia to confer with him in private:—

Si. Vos istæc intro auferte; abite. Sosia,

Adesdum; paucis te volo. So. Dictum puta
Nempe ut curentur recte hæc. Si. Imo aliud.
Terent. Andr., Actus i., Scena 1.

When we compare these words with the picture, we cannot but feel that in the latter there is an unnecessary degree of energy put into the *pose* of the figures; which is perhaps less the case in the other (No. 14), an illustration of the sixth scene of the fifth act of the *Adelphi* of Terence. It represents the meeting of Geta, a rather talkative and conceited servant, and Demea, a countryfied and churlish old man, his acquaintance, and of course superior. To Geta's salutation, Demea asks churlishly, as not at first knowing him, "Who are you?" but when he finds that it is Geta, he changes suddenly to an almost fawning tone:—

G. ... Sed eccum Demeam. Salvus fies.
D. Oh, qui vocare? G. Geta. D. Geta, hominem maximi
Pretii esse te hodie judicavi animo mei.

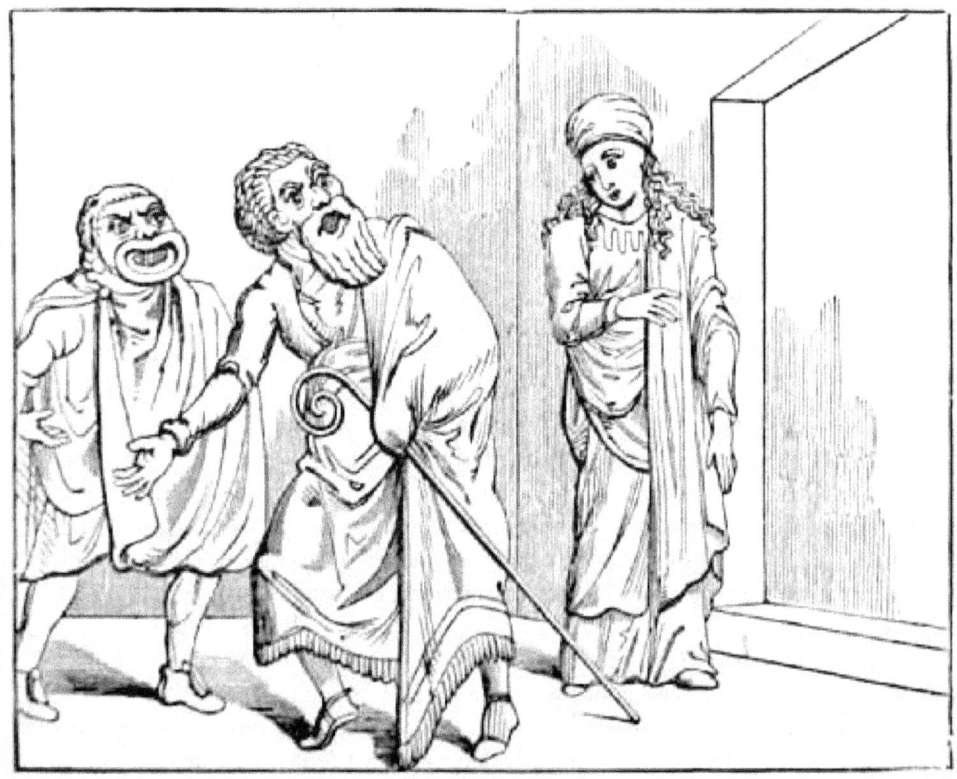

No. 15. Comic Scene from Pompeii.

That these representations are truthful, the scenes in the wall-paintings of Pompeii leave us no room to doubt. One of these is produced in our cut No. 15, which is no doubt taken from a comedy now lost, and we are ignorant whom the characters are intended to represent. The *pose* given to the two comic figures, compared with the example given from Berger, would lead us to suppose that this over-energetic action was considered as part of the character of comic acting.

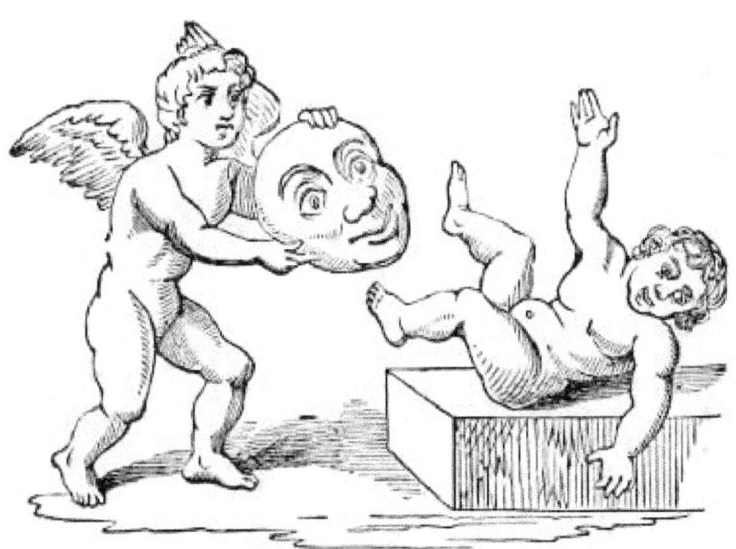

No. 16. Cupids at Play.

The subject of the Roman masks is the more interesting, because they were probably the origin of many of the grotesque faces so often met with in mediæval sculpture. The comic mask was, indeed, a very popular object among the Romans, and appears to have been taken as symbolical of everything that was droll and burlesque. From the comic scenes of the theatre, to which it was first appropriated, it passed to the popular festivals of a public character, such as the Lupercalia, with which, no doubt, it was carried into the carnival of the middle ages, and to our masquerades. Among the Romans, also, the use of the mask soon passed from the public festivals to private supper parties. Its use was so common that it became a plaything among children, and was sometimes used as a bugbear to frighten them. Our cut No. 16, taken from a painting at Resina, represents two cupids playing with a mask, and using it for this latter purpose, that is, to frighten one another; and it is curious that the mediæval gloss of Ugutio explains *larva*, a mask, as being an image, "which was put over the face to frighten children."[10] The mask thus became a favourite ornament, especially on lamps, and on the antefixa and gargoyls of Roman buildings, to which were often given the form of grotesque masks, monstrous faces, with great mouths wide open, and other figures, like those of the gargoyls of the mediæval architects.

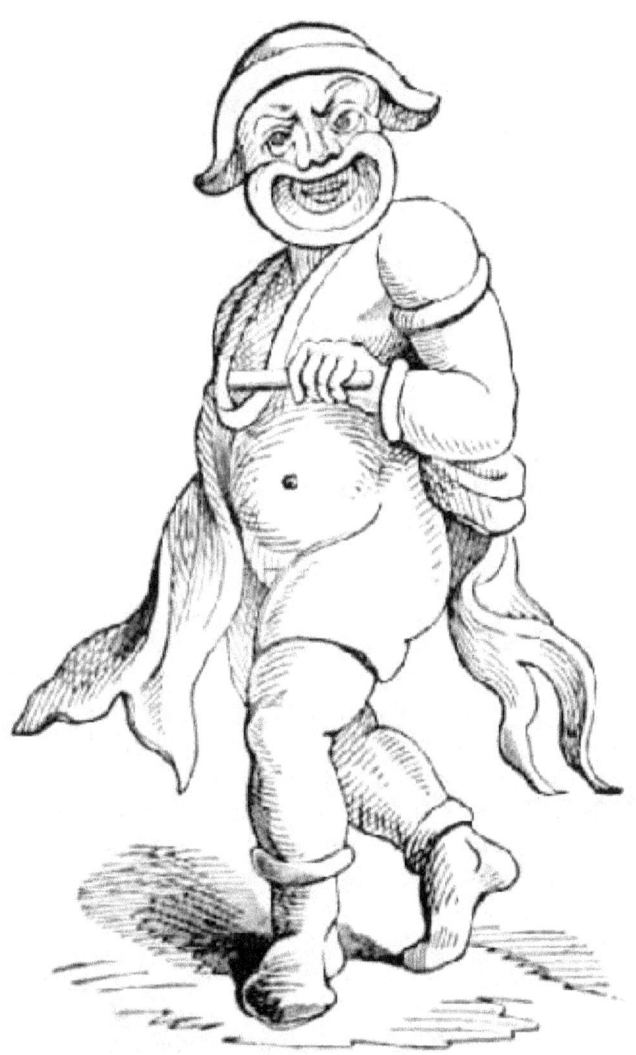

No. 17. The Roman Sannio, or Buffoon.

While the comic mask was used generally in the burlesque entertainments, it also became distinctive of particular characters. One of these was the *sannio*, or buffoon, whose name was derived from the Greek word σάννος, "a fool," and who was employed in performing burlesque dances, making grimaces, and in other acts calculated to excite the mirth of the spectator. A representation of the *sannio* is given in our cut No. 17, copied from one of the engravings in the "Dissertatio de Larvis Scenicis," by the Italian antiquary Ficoroni, who took it from an engraved gem. The sannio holds in his hand what is supposed to be a brass rod, and he has probably another in the other hand, so that he could strike them together. He wears the *soccus*, or low shoe peculiar to the comic actors. This buffoon was a favourite character among the Romans, who introduced him constantly into their feasts and supper parties. The *manducus* was another character of this description, represented with a grotesque mask, presenting a wide mouth and tongue lolling out, and said to have been peculiar to the Atellane plays. A character in Plautus (Rud., ii. 6, 51) talks of hiring himself as a *manducus* in the plays.

" *Quid si aliquo ad ludos me pro manduco locem?* "

The mediæval glosses interpret *manducus* by *joculator*, "a jogelor," and add that the characteristic from which he took his name was the practice of making grimaces like a man gobbling up his food in a vulgar and gluttonous manner.

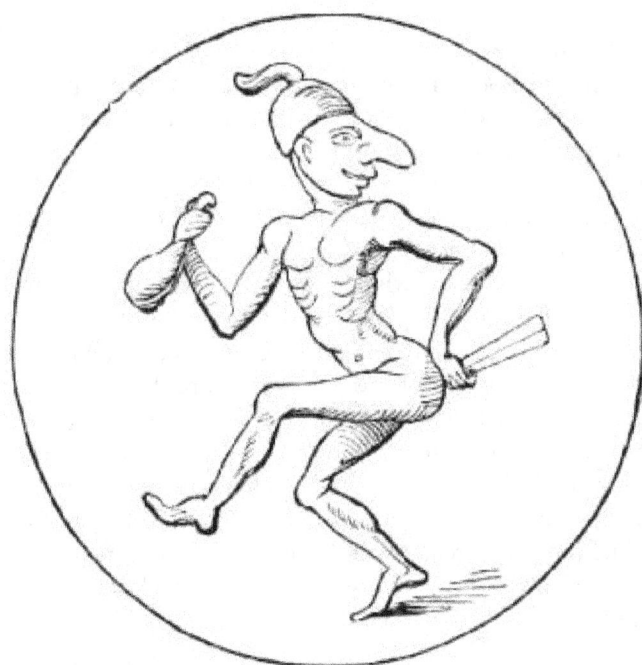

No. 18. Roman Tom Fool.

Ficoroni gives, from an engraved onyx, a figure of another burlesque performer, copied in our cut No. 18, and which he compares to the Catanian dancer of his time (his book was published in 1754), who was called a *giangurgolo*. This is considered to represent the Roman *mimus*, a class of performers who told with mimicry and action scenes taken from common life, and more especially scandalous and indecent anecdotes, like the jogelors and performers of farces in the middle ages. The Romans were very much attached to these performances, so much so, that they even had them at their funeral processions and at their funeral feasts. In our figure, the *mimus* is represented naked, masked (with an exaggerated nose), and wearing what is perhaps intended as a caricature of the Phrygian bonnet. In his right hand he holds a bag, or purse, full of objects which rattle and make a noise when shaken, while the other holds the *crotalum*, or castanets, an instrument in common use among the ancients. One of the statues in the Barberini Palace represents a youth in a Phrygian cap playing on the *crotalum*. We learn, from an early authority, that it was an instrument especially used in the satirical and burlesque dances which were so popular among the Romans.

As I have remarked before, the Romans had no taste for the regular drama, but they retained to the last their love for the performances of the popular *mimi*, or *comædi* (as they were often called), the players of farces, and the dancers. These performed on the stage, in the public festivals, in the streets, and were usually introduced at private parties.[11] Suetonius tells us that on one occasion, the emperor Caligula ordered a poet who composed the Atellanes (*Attellanæ poetam*) to be burnt in the middle of the amphitheatre, for a pun. A more regular comedy, however, did flourish, to a certain degree, at the same time with these more popular compositions. Of the works of the earliest of the Roman comic writers, Livius Andronicus and Nævius, we know only one or two titles, and a few fragments quoted in the works of the later Roman writers. They were followed by Plautus, who died B.C. 184, and nineteen of whose comedies are preserved and well known; by several other writers, whose names are almost forgotten, and whose comedies are all lost; and by Terence, six of whose comedies are preserved. Terence died about the year 159 B.C. About the same time with Terence lived Lucius Afranius and Quinctius Atta, who appear to close the list of the Roman writers of comedy.

But another branch of comic literature had sprung out of the satire of the religious festivities. A year after Livius Andronicus produced the first drama at Rome, in the year 239 B.C., the poet Ennius was born at Rudiæ, in Magna Græcia. The satirical verse, whether Saturnine or Fescennine, had been gradually improving in its form, although still very rude, but Ennius is said to have given at least a new polish, and perhaps a new metrical shape, to it. The verse was still irregular, but it appears to have been no longer intended for recitation, accompanied by the flute. The Romans looked upon Ennius not only as their earliest epic poet, but as the father of satire, a class of literary composition which appears to have originated with them, and which they claimed as their own.[12] Ennius had an imitator in M. Terentius Varro. The satires of these first writers are said to have been very irregular compositions, mixing prose with verse, and sometimes even Greek with Latin; and to have been rather general in their aim than personal. But soon after this period, and rather more than a century before Christ, came Caius Lucilius, who raised Roman satirical literature to its perfection. Lucilius, we are told, was the first who wrote satires in heroic verse, or hexameters, mixing with them now and then, though rarely, an iambic or trochaic line. He was more refined, more pointed, and more personal, than his predecessors, and he had rescued satire from the street performer to make it a class of literature which was to be read by the educated, and not merely listened to by the vulgar. Lucilius is said to have written thirty books of satires, of which, unfortunately, only some scattered lines remain.

Lucilius had imitators, the very names of most of whom are now forgotten, but about forty years after his death, and sixty-five years before the birth of Christ, was born Quintus Horatius Flaccus, the oldest of the satirists whose works we now possess, and the most polished of Roman poets. In the time of Horace, the satire of the Romans had reached its highest degree of perfection. Of the two other great satirists whose works are preserved, Juvenal was born about the year 40 of the Christian era, and Persius in 43. During the period through which these writers flourished, Rome saw a considerable number of other satirists of the same class, whose works have perished.

In the time of Juvenal another variety of the same class of literature had already sprung up, more artificial and somewhat more indirect than the other, the prose satiric romance. Three celebrated writers represent this school. Petronius, who, born about the commencement of our era, died in A.D. 65, is the earliest and most remarkable of them. He compiled a romance, designed as a satire on the vices of the age of Nero, in which real persons are supposed to be aimed at under fictitious names, and which rivals in license, at least, anything that could have been uttered in the Atellanes or other farces of the *mimi*. Lucian, of Samosata, who died an old man in the year 200, and who, though he wrote in Greek, may be considered as belonging to the Roman school, composed several satires of this kind, in one of the most remarkable of which, entitled "Lucius, or the Ass," the author describes himself as changed by sorcery into the form of that animal, under which he passes through a number of adventures which illustrate the vices and weaknesses of contemporary society. Apuleius, who was considerably the junior of Lucian, made this novel the groundwork of his "Golden Ass," a much larger and more elaborate work, written in Latin. This work of Apuleius was very popular through subsequent ages.

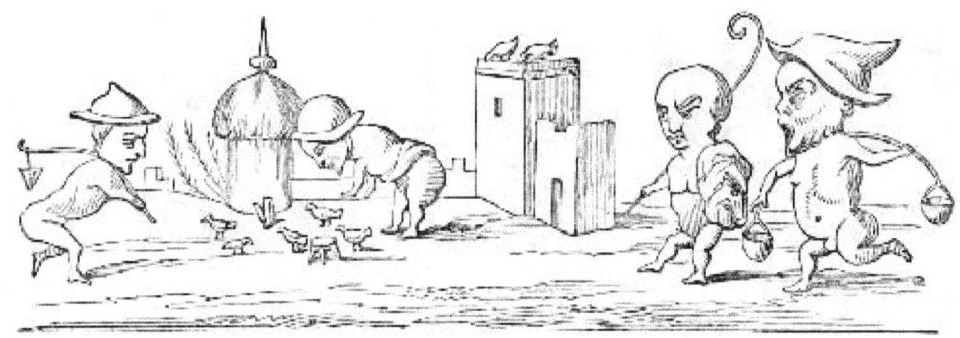

No. 19. The Farm-yard in Burlesque.

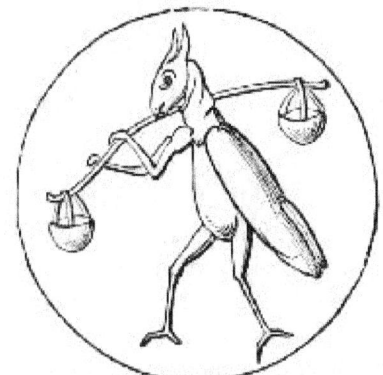

No. 20. An Asilla-Bearer.

Let us return to Roman caricature, one form of which seems to have been especially a favourite among the people. It is difficult to imagine how the story of the pigmies and of their wars with the cranes originated, but it is certainly of great antiquity, as it is spoken of in Homer, and it was a very popular legend among the Romans, who eagerly sought and purchased dwarfs to make domestic pets of them. The pigmies and cranes occur frequently among the pictorial ornamentations of the houses of Pompeii and Herculaneum; and the painters of Pompeii not only represented them in their proper character, but they made use of them for the purpose of caricaturing the various occupations of life—domestic and social scenes, grave conferences, and many other subjects, and even personal character. In this class of caricatures they gave to the pigmies, or dwarfs, very large heads, and very small legs and arms. I need hardly remark that this is a class of caricature which is very common in modern times. Our first group of these pigmy caricatures (No. 19) is taken from a painting on the walls of the Temple of Venus, at Pompeii, and represents the interior of a farm-yard in burlesque. The structure in the background is perhaps intended for a hayrick. In front of it, one of the farm servants is attending on the poultry. The more important-looking personage with the pastoral staff is possibly the overseer of the farm, who is visiting the labourers, and this probably is the cause why their movements have assumed so much activity. The labourer on the right is using the *asilla*, a wooden yoke or pole, which was carried over the shoulder, with the *corbis*, or basket, suspended at each end. This was a common method of carrying, and is not unfrequently represented on Roman works of art. Several examples might be quoted from the antiquities of Pompeii. Our cut No. 20, from a gem in the Florentine Museum, and illustrating another class of caricature, that of introducing animals performing the actions and duties of men, represents a grasshopper carrying the *asilla* and the *corbes*.

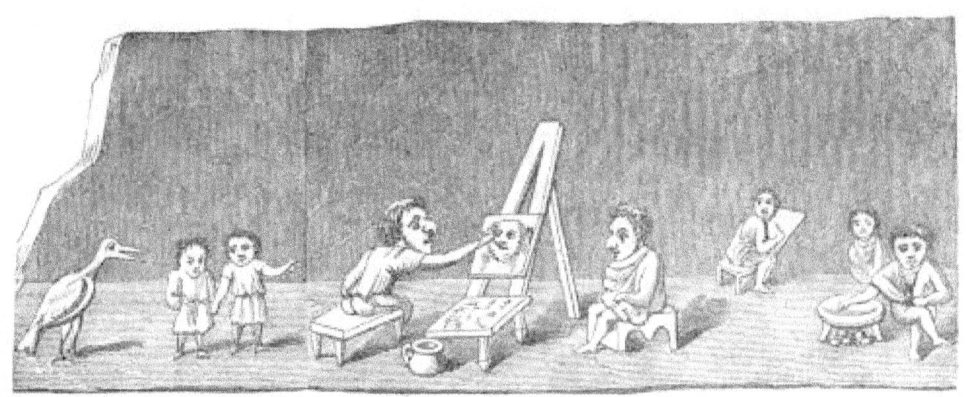

No. 21. A Painter's Studio.

A private house in Pompeii furnished another example of this style of caricature, which is given in our cut No. 21. It represents the interior of a painter's studio, and is extremely curious on account of the numerous details of his method of operation with which it furnishes us. The painter, who is, like most of the figures in these pigmy caricatures, very scantily clothed, is occupied with the portrait of another, who, by the rather exaggerated fulness of the gathering of his toga, is evidently intended for a dashing and fashionable patrician, though he is seated as bare-legged and bare-breeched as the artist himself. Both are distinguished by a large allowance of nose. The easel here employed resembles greatly the same article now in use, and might belong to the studio of a modern painter. Before it is a small table, probably formed of a slab of stone, which serves for a palette, on which the painter spreads and mixes his colours. To the right a servant, who fills the office of colour-grinder, is seated by the side of a vessel placed over hot coals, and appears to be preparing colours, mixed, according to the directions given in old writers, with punic wax and oil. In the background is seated a student, whose attention is taken from his drawing by what is going on at the other side of the room, where two small personages are entering, who look as if they were amateurs, and who appear to be talking about the portrait. Behind them stands a bird, and when the painting was first uncovered there were two. Mazois, who made the drawing from which our cut is taken, before the original had perished—for it was found in a state of decay—imagined that the birds typified some well-known singers or musicians, but they are, perhaps, merely intended for cranes, birds so generally associated with the pigmies.

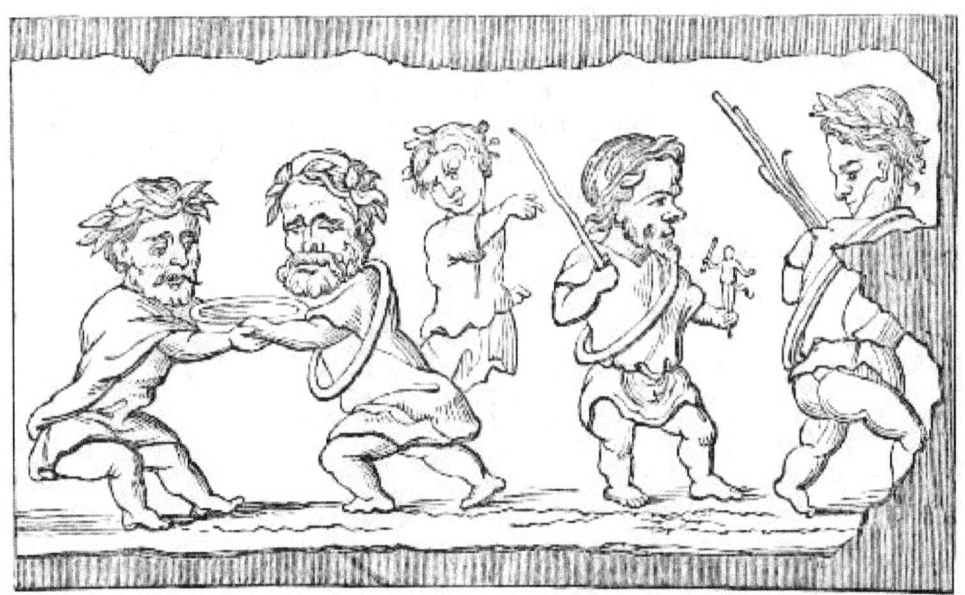

No. 22. Part of a Triumphal Procession.

According to an ancient writer, combats of pigmies were favourite representations on the walls of taverns and shops;[13] and, curiously enough, the walls of a shop in Pompeii have furnished the picture represented in our cut No. 22, which has evidently been intended for a caricature, probably a parody. All the pigmies in this picture are crowned with laurel, as though the painter intended to turn to ridicule some over-pompous triumph, or some public, perhaps religious, ceremony. The two figures to the left, who are clothed in yellow and green garments, appear to be disputing the possession of a bowl containing a liquid. One of these, like the two figures on the right, has a hoop thrown over his shoulder. The first of the latter personages wears a violet dress, and holds in his right hand a rod, and in his left a statuette, apparently of a deity, but its attributes are not distinguishable. The last figure to the right has a robe, or mantle, of two colours, red and green, and holds in his hand a branch of a lily, or some similar plant; the rest of the picture is lost. Behind the other figure stands a fifth, who appears younger and more refined in character than the others, and seems to be ordering or directing them. His dress is red.

We can have no doubt that political and personal caricature flourished among the Romans, as we have some examples of it on their works of art, chiefly on engraved stones, though these are mostly of a character we could not here conveniently introduce; but the same rich mine of Roman art and antiquities, Pompeii, has furnished us with one sample of what may be properly considered as a political caricature. In the year 59 of the Christian era, at a gladiatorial exhibition in the amphitheatre of Pompeii, where the people of Nuceria were present, the latter expressed themselves in such scornful terms towards the Pompeians, as led to a violent quarrel, which was followed by a pitched battle between the inhabitants of the two towns, and the Nucerians, being defeated, carried their complaints before the reigning emperor, Nero, who gave judgment in their favour, and condemned the people of Pompeii to suspension from all theatrical amusements for ten years. The feelings of the Pompeians on this occasion are displayed in the rude drawing represented in our cut No. 23, which is scratched on the plaster of the external wall of a house in the street to which the Italian antiquarians have given the name of the street of Mercury. A figure, completely armed, his head covered with what might be taken for a mediæval helmet, is descending what appear to be intended for the steps of the amphitheatre. He carries in his hand a palm-branch, the emblem of victory. Another palm-branch stands erect by his side, and underneath is the inscription, in rather rustic Latin, "CAMPANI VICTORIA VNA CVM NVCERINIS

PERISTIS"—"O Campanians, you perished in the victory together with the Nucerians." The other side of the picture is more rudely and hastily drawn. It has been supposed to represent one of the victors dragging a prisoner, with his arms bound, up a ladder to a stage or platform, on which he was perhaps to be exhibited to the jeers of the populace. Four years after this event, Pompeii was greatly damaged by an earthquake, and sixteen years later came the eruption of Vesuvius, which buried the town, and left it in the condition in which it is now found.

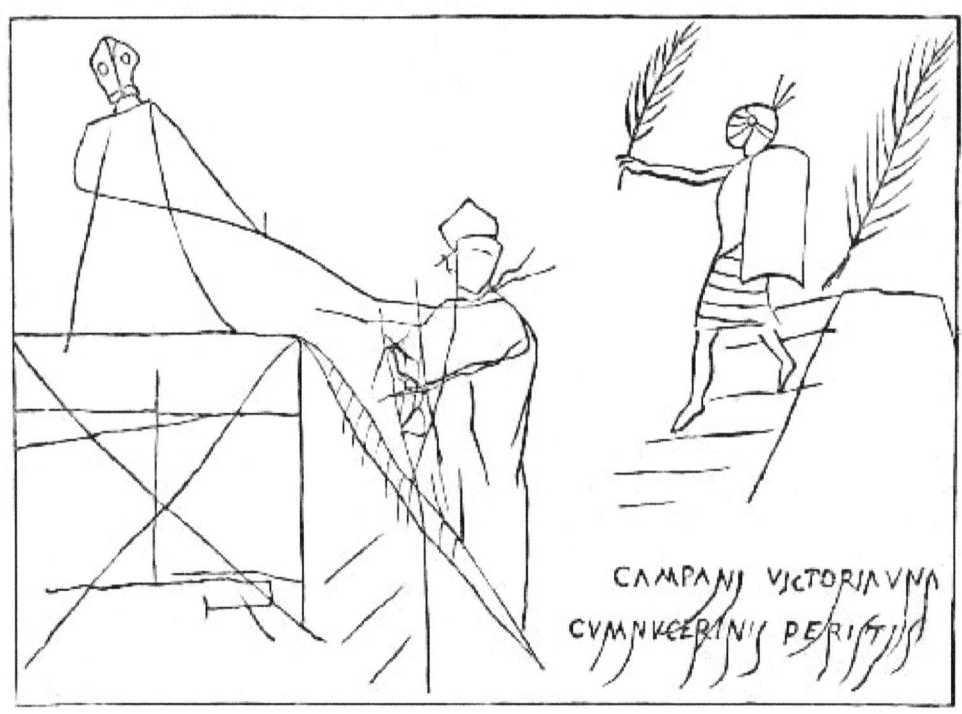

No. 23. A Popular Caricature.

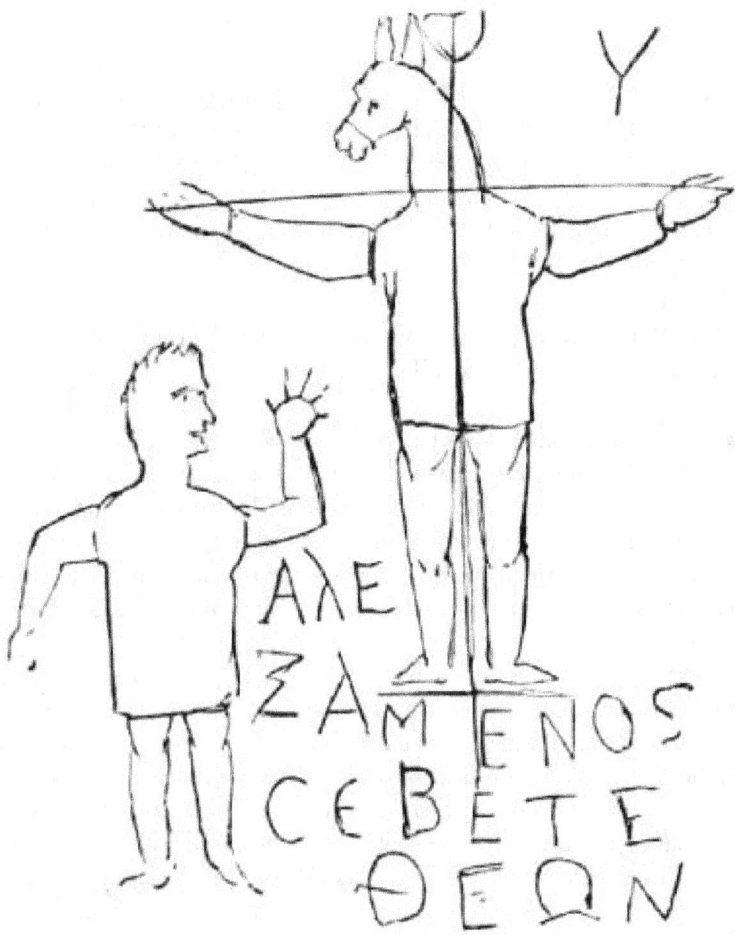

No. 24. Early Caricature upon a Christian.

This curious caricature belongs to a class of monuments to which archæologists have given technically the Italian name of *graffiti*, scratches or scrawls, of which a great number, consisting chiefly of writing, have been found on the walls of Pompeii. They also occur among the remains on other Roman sites, and one found in Rome itself is especially interesting. During the alterations and extensions which were made from time to time in the palace of the Cæsars, it had been found necessary to build across a narrow street which intersected the Palatine, and, in order to give support to the structure above, a portion of the street was walled off, and remained thus hermetically sealed until about the year 1857, when some excavations on the spot brought it to view. The walls of the street were found to be covered with these *graffiti*, among which one attracted especial attention, and, having been carefully removed, is now preserved in the museum of the Collegio Romano. It is a caricature upon a Christian named Alexamenos, by some pagan who despised Christianity. The Saviour is represented under the form of a man with the head of an ass, extended upon a cross, the Christian, Alexamenos, standing on one side in the attitude of worship of that period. Underneath we read the inscription, ΑΛΕΞΑΜΕΝΟΣ ΣΕΒΕΤΕ (for σεβεται) ΘΕΟΝ, "Alexamenos worships God." This curious figure, which may be placed among the most interesting as well as early evidences of the truth of Gospel history, is copied in our cut No. 24. It was drawn when the prevailing religion at Rome was still pagan, and a Christian was an object of contempt.

CHAPTER III.

THE PERIOD OF TRANSITION FROM ANTIQUITY TO THE MIDDLE AGES.—THE ROMAN MIMI CONTINUED TO EXIST.—THE TEUTONIC AFTER-DINNER ENTERTAINMENTS.—CLERICAL SATIRES; ARCHBISHOP HERIGER AND THE DREAMER; THE SUPPER OF THE SAINTS.—TRANSITION FROM ANCIENT TO MEDIÆVAL ART.—TASTE FOR MONSTROUS ANIMALS, DRAGONS, ETC.; CHURCH OF SAN FEDELE, AT COMO.—SPIRIT OF CARICATURE AND LOVE OF GROTESQUE AMONG THE ANGLO-SAXONS.—GROTESQUE FIGURES OF DEMONS.—NATURAL TENDENCY OF THE EARLY MEDIÆVAL ARTISTS TO DRAW IN CARICATURE.— EXAMPLES FROM EARLY MANUSCRIPTS AND SCULPTURES.

The transition from antiquity to what we usually understand by the name of the middle ages was long and slow; it was a period during which much of the texture of the old society was destroyed, while at the same time a new life was gradually given to that which remained. We know very little of the comic literature of this period of transition; its literary remains consist chiefly of a mass of heavy theology and of lives of saints. The stage in its perfectly dramatic form—theatre and amphitheatre— had disappeared. The pure drama, indeed, appears never to have had great vitality among the Romans, whose tastes lay far more among the vulgar performances of the mimics and jesters, and among the savage scenes of the amphitheatre. While probably the performance of comedies, such as those of Plautus and Terence, soon went out of fashion, and tragedies, like those of Seneca, were only written as literary compositions, imitations of the similar works which formed so remarkable a feature in the literature of Greece, the Romans of all ranks loved to witness the loose attitudes of their *mimi*, or listen to their equally loose songs and stories. The theatre and the amphitheatre were state institutions, kept up at the national expense, and, as just stated, they perished with the overthrow of the western empire; and the sanguinary performances of the amphitheatre, if the amphitheatre itself continued to be used (which was perhaps the case in some parts of western Europe), and they gave place to the more harmless exhibitions of dancing bears and other tamed animals,[14] for deliberate cruelty was not a characteristic of the Teutonic race. But the mimi, the performers who sung songs and told stories, accompanied with dancing and music, survived the fall of the empire, and continued to be as popular as ever. St. Augustine, in the fourth century, calls these things *nefaria*, detestable things, and says that they were performed at night.[15] We trace in the capitularies the continuous existence of these performances during the ages which followed the empire, and, as in the time of St. Augustine, they still formed the amusement of nocturnal assemblies. The capitulary of Childebert proscribes those who passed their nights with drunkenness, jesting, and songs.[16] The council of Narbonne, in the year 589, forbade people to spend their nights "with dancings and filthy songs."[17] The council of Mayence, in 813, calls these songs "filthy and licentious" (*turpia atque luxuriosa*); and that of Paris speaks of them as "obscene and filthy" (*obscæna et turpia*); while in another they are called "frivolous and diabolic." From the bitterness with which the ecclesiastical ordinances are expressed, it is probable that these performances continued to preserve much of their old paganism; yet it is curious that they are spoken of in these capitularies and acts of the councils as being still practised in the religious festivals, and even in the churches, so tenaciously did the old sentiments of the race keep their possession of the minds of the populace, long after they had embraced Christianity. These "songs," as they are called, continued also to consist not only of general, but of personal satire, and contained scandalous stories of persons living, and well known to those who heard them. A capitulary of the Frankish king Childeric III., published in the year 744, is directed against those who compose and sing songs in defamation of others (*in blasphemiam alterius*, to use the rather energetic language of the original); and it is evident that this offence was a very common one, for it is not unfrequently repeated in later records of this character in the same words or in words to the same purpose. Thus one result of the overthrow of the Roman empire was to leave comic literature almost in the same condition in which it was found by Thespis in Greece and by Livius Andronicus in Rome. There was nothing in it which would be contrary to the feelings of the new races who had now planted themselves in the Roman provinces.

The Teutonic and Scandinavian nations had no doubt their popular festivals, in which mirth and frolic bore sway, though we know little about them; but there were circumstances in their domestic manners which implied a necessity for amusement. After the comparatively early meal, the hall of the primitive Teuton was the scene—especially in the darker months of winter—of long sittings over the festive board, in which there was much drinking and much talking, and, as we all know, such talking could not preserve long a very serious tone. From Bede's account of the poet Cædmon, we learn that it was the practice of the Anglo-Saxons in the seventh century, at their entertainments, for all those present to sing in their turns, each accompanying himself with a musical instrument. From the sequel of the story we are led to suppose that these songs were extemporary effusions, probably mythic legends, stories of personal adventure, praise of themselves, or vituperation of their enemies. In the chieftain's household there appears to have been usually some individual who acted the part of the satirist, or, as we should perhaps now say, the comedian. Hunferth appears as holding some such position in Beowulf; in the later romances, Sir Kay held a similar position at the court of king Arthur. At a still later period, the place of these heroes was occupied by the court fool. The Roman *mimus* must have been a welcome addition to the entertainments of the Teutonic hall, and there is every reason to think that he was cordially received. The performances of the hall were soon delegated from the guests to such hired actors, and we have representations of them in the illuminations of Anglo-Saxon manuscripts.[18] Among the earliest amusements of the Anglo-Saxon table were riddles, which in every form present some of the features of the comic, and are capable of being made the source of much laughter. The saintly Aldhelm condescended to write such riddles in Latin verse, which were, of course, intended for the tables of the clergy. In primitive society, verse was the ordinary form of conveying ideas. A large portion of the celebrated collection of Anglo-Saxon poetry known as the "Exeter Book," consists of riddles, and this taste for riddles has continued to exist down to our own times. But other forms of entertainment, if they did not already exist, were soon introduced. In a curious Latin poem, older than the twelfth century, of which fragments only are preserved, and have been published under the title of "Ruodlieb," and which appears to have been a translation of a much earlier German romance, we have a curious description of the post-prandial entertainments after the dinner of a great Teutonic chieftain, or king. In the first place there was a grand distribution of rich presents, and then were shown strange animals, and among the rest tame bears. These bears stood upon their hind legs, and performed some of the offices of a man; and when the minstrels (*mimi*) came in, and played upon their musical instruments, these animals danced to the music, and performed all sorts of strange tricks.

Et pariles ursi....
Qui vas tollebant, ut homo, bipedesque gerebant.
Mimi quando fides digitis tangunt modulantes,
Illi saltabant, neumas pedibus variabant.
Interdum saliunt, seseque super jaciebant.
Alterutrum dorso se portabant residendo,
Amplexando se, luctando deficiunt se.

Then followed dancing-girls, and exhibitions of other kinds.[19]

Although these performances were proscribed by the ecclesiastical laws, they were not discountenanced by the ecclesiastics themselves, who, on the contrary, indulged as much in after-dinner amusements as anybody. The laws against the profane songs are often directed especially at the clergy; and it is evident that among the Anglo-Saxons, as well as on the Continent, not only the priests and monks, but the nuns also, in their love of such amusements, far transgressed the bounds of decency.[20] These entertainments were the cradle of comic literature, but, as this literature in the early ages of its history was rarely committed to writing, it has almost entirely perished. But, at the tables of the ecclesiastics, these stories were sometimes told in Latin verse, and as Latin was not so easily carried in the memory as the vernacular tongue, in this language they were sometimes committed to writing, and thus a few examples of early comic literature have fortunately been preserved. These consist chiefly of popular stories, which were among the favourite amusements of mediæval society—stories many of which are derived from the earliest period of the history of our race, and are still cherished among our peasantry. Such are the stories of the Child of Snow, and of the Mendacious Hunter, preserved in a manuscript of the eleventh century.[21] The first of these was a very popular story in the middle ages. According to this early version, a merchant of Constance, in Switzerland, was detained abroad for several years, during which time his wife made other acquaintance, and bore a child. On his return, she excused her fault by telling him that on a cold wintry day she had swallowed snow, by which she had conceived; and, in revenge, the husband carried away the child, and sold it into slavery, and returning, told its mother, that the infant which had originated in snow, had melted away under a hotter sun. Some of these stories originated in the different collections of fables, which were part of the favourite literature of the later Roman period. Another is rather a ridiculous story of an ass belonging to two sisters in a nunnery, which was devoured by a wolf.[22] curious how soon the mediæval clergy began to imitate their pagan predecessors in parodying religious subjects and forms, of which we have one or two very curious examples. Visits to purgatory, hell, and paradise, in body or spirit, were greatly in fashion during the earlier part of the middle ages, and afforded extremely good material for satire. In a metrical Latin story, preserved in a manuscript of the eleventh century, we are told how a "prophet," or visionary, went to Heriger, archbishop of Mayence from 912 to 926, and told him that he had been carried in a vision to the regions below, and described them as a place surrounded by thick woods. It was the Teutonic notion of hell, and indeed of all settlements of peoples; and Heriger replied with a sneer that he would send his herdsmen there with his lean swine to fatten them. Each "mark," or land of a family or clan, in the early Teutonic settlements, was surrounded by woodland, which was common to all members of the clan for fattening their swine and hunting. The false dreamer added, that he was afterwards carried to heaven, where he saw Christ sitting at the table and eating. John the Baptist was butler, and served excellent wine round to the saints, who were the Lord's guests. St. Peter was the chief cook. After some remarks on the appointments to these two offices, archbishop Heriger asked the informant how he was received in the heavenly hall, where he sat, and what he eat. He replied that he sat in a corner, and stole from the cooks a piece of liver, which he eat, and then departed. Instead of rewarding him for his information, Heriger took him on his own confession for the theft, and ordered him to be bound to a stake and flogged, which, for the offence, was rather a light punishment.

Heriger illum
jussit ad palum
loris ligari,
scopisque cedi,
sermone duro
hunc arguendo.

These lines will serve as a specimen of the popular Latin verse in which these monkish after-dinner stories were written; but the most remarkable of these early parodies on religious subjects, is one which may be described as the supper of the saints; its title is simply *Cœna*. It is falsely ascribed to St. Cyprian, who lived in the third century; but it is as old as the tenth century, as a copy was printed by professor Endlicher from a manuscript of that period at Vienna. It was so popular, that it is found and known to have existed in different forms in verse and in prose. It is a sort of drollery, founded upon the wedding feast at which the Saviour changed water into wine, though that miracle is not at all introduced into it. It was a great king of the East, named Zoel, who held his nuptial feast at Cana of Galilee. The personages invited are all scriptural, beginning with Adam. Before the feast, they wash in the river Jordan, and the number of the guests was so great, that seats could not be provided for them, and they took their places as they could. Adam took the first place, and seated himself in the middle of the assembly, and next to him Eve sat upon leaves (*super folia*),—fig-leaves, we may suppose. Cain sat on a plough, Abel on a milk-pail, Noah on an ark, Japhet on tiles, Abraham on a tree, Isaac on an altar, Lot near the door, and so with a long list of others. Two were obliged to stand—Paul, who bore it patiently, and Esau, who grumbled—while Job lamented bitterly because he was obliged to sit on a dunghill. Moses, and others, who came late, were obliged to find seats out of doors. When the king saw that all his guests had arrived, he took them into his wardrobe, and there, in the spirit of mediæval generosity, distributed to them dresses, which had all some burlesque allusion to their particular characters. Before they were allowed to sit down to the feast, they were obliged to go through other ceremonies, which, as well as the eating, are described in the same style of caricature. The wines, of which there was great variety, were served to the guests with the same allusions to their individual characters; but some of them complained that they were badly mixed, although Jonah was the butler. In the same manner are described the proceedings which followed the dinner, the washing of hands, and the dessert, to the latter of which Adam contributed apples, Samson honey; while David played on the harp and Mary on the tabor; Judith led the round dance; Jubal played on the psalter; Asael sung songs, and Herodias acted the part of the dancing-girl:—

Tunc Adam poma ministrat, Samson favi dulcia.
David cytharum percussit, et Maria tympana.
Judith choreas ducebat, et Jubal psalteria.
Asael metra canebat, saltabat Herodias.

Mambres entertained the company with his magical performances; and the other incidents of a mediæval festival followed, throughout which the same tone of burlesque is continued; and so the story continues, to the end.[23] We shall find these incipient forms of mediæval comic literature largely developed as we go on.

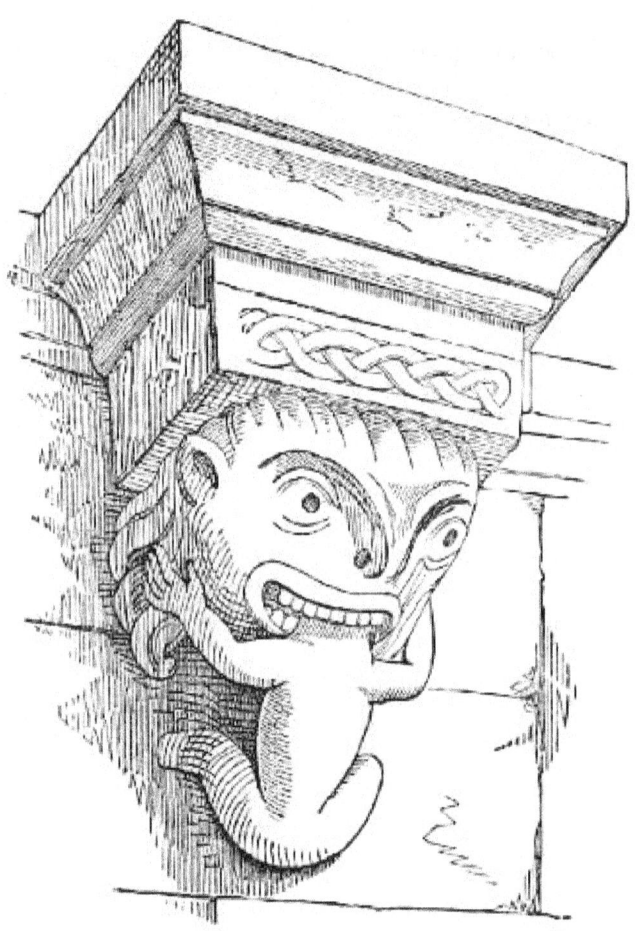

No. 25. Saturn Devouring his Child.

The period between antiquity and the middle ages was one of such great and general destruction, that the gulf between ancient and mediæval art seems to us greater and more abrupt than it really was. The want of monuments, no doubt, prevents our seeing the gradual change of one into the other, but nevertheless enough of facts remain to convince us that it was not a sudden change. It is now indeed generally understood that the knowledge and practice of the arts and manufactures of the Romans were handed onward from master to pupil after the empire had fallen; and this took place especially in the towns, so that the workmanship which had been declining in character during the later periods of the empire, only continued in the course of degradation afterwards. Thus, in the first Christian edifices, the builders who were employed, or at least many of them, must have been pagans, and they would follow their old models of ornamentation, introducing the same grotesque figures, the same masks and monstrous faces, and even sometimes the same subjects from the old mythology, to which they had been accustomed. It is to be observed, too, that this kind of iconographical ornamentation had been encroaching more and more upon the old architectural purity during the latter ages of the empire, and that it was employed more profusely in the later works, from which this taste was transferred to the ecclesiastical and to the domestic architecture of the middle ages. After the workmen themselves had become Christians, they still found pagan emblems and figures in their models, and still went on imitating them, sometimes merely copying, and at others turning them to caricature or burlesque. And this tendency continued so long, that, at a much later date, where there still existed remains of Roman buildings, the mediæval architects adopted them as models, and did not hesitate to copy the sculpture, although it might be evidently pagan in character. The accompanying cut (No. 25) represents a bracket in the church of Mont Majour, near Nismes, built in the tenth century. The subject is a monstrous head eating a child, and we can hardly doubt that it was really intended for a caricature on Saturn devouring one of his children.

Sometimes the mediæval sculptors mistook the emblematical designs of the Romans, and misapplied them, and gave an allegorical meaning to that which was not intended to be emblematical or allegorical, until the subjects themselves became extremely confused. They readily employed that class of parody of the ancients in which animals were represented performing the actions of men, and they had a great taste for monsters of every description, especially those which were made up of portions of incongruous animals joined together, in contradiction to the precept of Horace:—

Humano capiti cervicem pictor equinam
Jungere si velit, et varias inducere plumas,
Undique collatis membris, ut turpiter atrum
Desinet in piscem mulier formosa superne;
Spectatum admissi risum teneatis, amici?

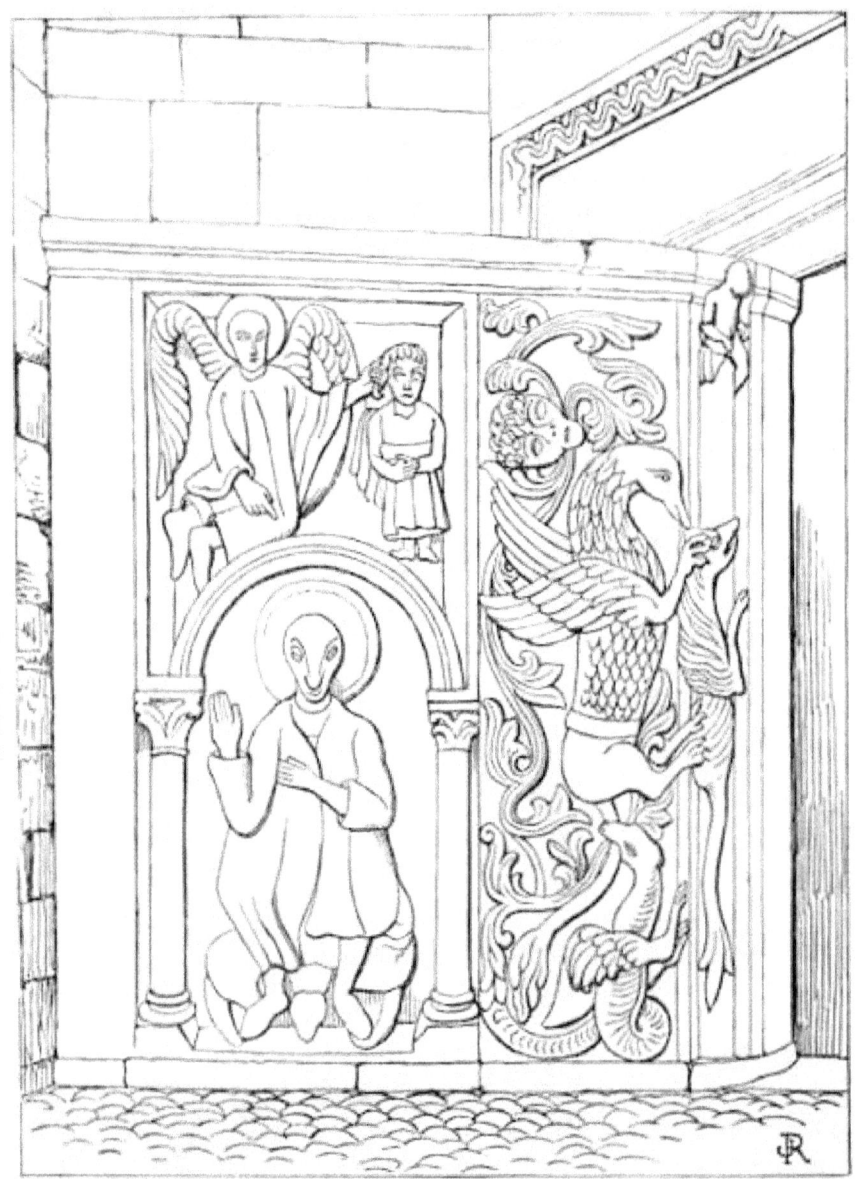

No. 26. Sculpture from San Fedele, at Como.

The mediæval architects loved such representations, always and in all parts, and examples are abundant. At Como, in Italy, there is a very ancient and remarkable church dedicated to San Fedele (Saint Fidelis); it has been considered to be of so early a date as the fifth century. The sculptures that adorn the doorway, which is triangular-headed, are especially interesting. On one of these, represented in our cut No. 26, in a compartment to the left, appears a figure of an angel, holding in one hand a dwarf figure, probably intended for a child, by a lock of his hair, and with the other hand directing his attention to a seated figure in the compartment below. This latter figure has apparently the head of a sheep, and as the head is surrounded with a large nimbus, and the right hand is held out in the attitude of benediction, it may be intended to represent the Lamb. This personage is seated on something which is difficult to make out, but which looks somewhat like a crab-fish. The boy in the compartment above carries a large basin in his arms. The adjoining compartment to the right contains the representation of a conflict between a dragon, a winged serpent, and a winged fox. On the opposite side of the door, two winged monsters are represented devouring a lamb's head. I owe the drawing from which this and the preceding engraving were made to my friend Mr. John Robinson, the architect, who made the sketches while travelling with the medal of the Royal Academy. Figures of dragons, as ornaments, were great favourites with the peoples of the Teutonic race; they were creatures intimately wrapped up in their national mythology and romance, and they are found on all their artistic monuments mingled together in grotesque forms and groups. When the Anglo-Saxons began to ornament their books, the dragon was continually introduced for ornamental borders and in forming initial letters. One of the latter, from an Anglo-Saxon manuscript of the tenth century (the well-known manuscript of Cædmon, where it is given as an initial V), is represented in our cut on the next page, No. 27.

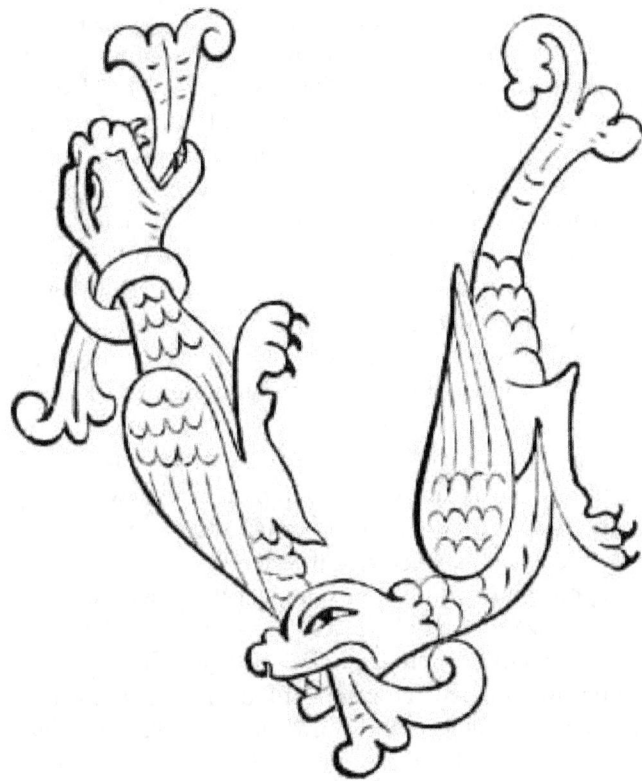

No. 27. Anglo-Saxon Dragons.

Caricature and burlesque are naturally intended to be heard and seen publicly, and would therefore be figured on such monuments as were most exposed to popular gaze. Such was the case, in the earlier periods of the middle ages, chiefly with ecclesiastical buildings, which explains how they became the grand receptacles of this class of Art. We have few traces of what may be termed comic literature among our Anglo-Saxon forefathers, but this is fully explained by the circumstance that very little of the popular Anglo-Saxon literature has been preserved. In their festive hours the Anglo-Saxons seem to have especially amused themselves in boasting of what they had done, and what they could do; and these boasts were perhaps often of a burlesque character, like the *gabs* of the French and Anglo-Norman romancers of a later date, or so extravagant as to produce laughter. The chieftains appear also to have encouraged men who could make jokes, and satirise and caricature others; for the company of such men seems to have been cherished, and they are not unfrequently introduced in the stories. Such a personage, as I have remarked before, is Hunferth in Beowulf; such was the Sir Kay of the later Arthurian romances; and such too was the Norman minstrel in the history of Hereward, who amused the Norman soldiers at their feasts by mimicry of the manners of their Anglo-Saxon opponents. The too personal satire of these wits often led to quarrels, which ended in sanguinary brawls. The Anglo-Saxon love of caricature is shown largely in their proper names, which were mostly significant of personal qualities their parents hoped they would possess; and in these we remark the proneness of the Teutonic race, as well as the peoples of antiquity, to represent these qualities by the animals supposed to possess them, the animals most popular being the wolf and the bear. But it is not to be expected that the hopes of the parents in giving the name would always be fulfilled, and it is not an uncommon thing to find individuals losing their original names to receive in their place nicknames, or names which probably expressed qualities they did possess, and which were given to them by their acquaintances. These names, though often not very complimentary, and even sometimes very much the contrary, completely superseded the original name, and were even accepted by the individuals to whom they applied. The second names were indeed so generally acknowledged, that they were used in signing legal documents. An Anglo-Saxon abbess of rank, whose real name was Hrodwaru, but who was known universally by the name Bugga, the Bug, wrote this latter name in signing charters. We can hardly doubt that such a name was intended to ascribe to her qualities of a not agreeable character, and very different to those implied by the original name, which perhaps meant, a dweller in heaven. Another lady gained the name of the Crow. It is well known that surnames did not come into use till long after the Anglo-Saxon period, but appellatives, like these nicknames, were often added to the name for the purpose of distinction, or at pleasure, and these, too, being given by other people, were frequently satirical. Thus, one Harold, for his swiftness, was called Hare-foot; a well-known Edith, for the elegant form of her neck, was called Swan-neck; and a Thurcyl, for a form of his head, which can hardly have been called beautiful, was named Mare's-head. Among many other names, quite as satirical as the last-mentioned, we find Flat-nose, the Ugly Squint-eye, Hawk-nose, &c.

Of Anglo-Saxon sculpture we have little left, but we have a few illuminated manuscripts which present here and there an attempt at caricature, though they are rare. It would seem, however, that the two favourite subjects of caricature among the Anglo-Saxons were the clergy and the evil one. We have abundant evidence that, from the eighth century downwards, neither the Anglo-Saxon clergy nor the Anglo-Saxon nuns were generally objects of much respect among the people; and their character and the manner of their lives sufficiently account for it. Perhaps, also, it was increased by the hostility between the old clergy and the new reformers of Dunstan's party, who would no doubt caricature each other. A manuscript psalter, in the University Library, Cambridge (Ff. 1, 23), of the Anglo-Saxon period, and apparently of the tenth century, illustrated with rather grotesque initial letters, furnishes us with the figure of a jolly Anglo-Saxon monk, given in our cut No. 28, and which it is hardly necessary to state represents the letter Q. As we proceed, we shall see the clergy continuing to furnish a butt for the shafts of satire through all the middle ages.

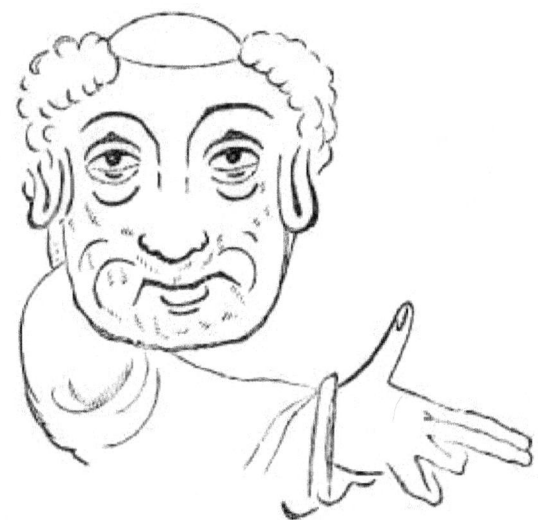

No. 28. A Jolly Monk.

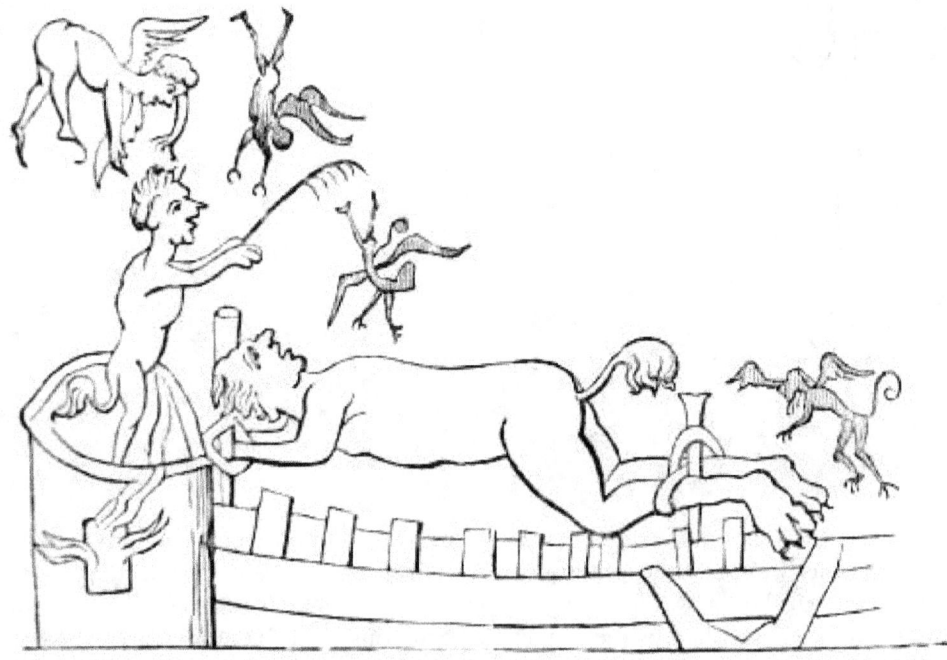

No. 29. Satan in Bonds.

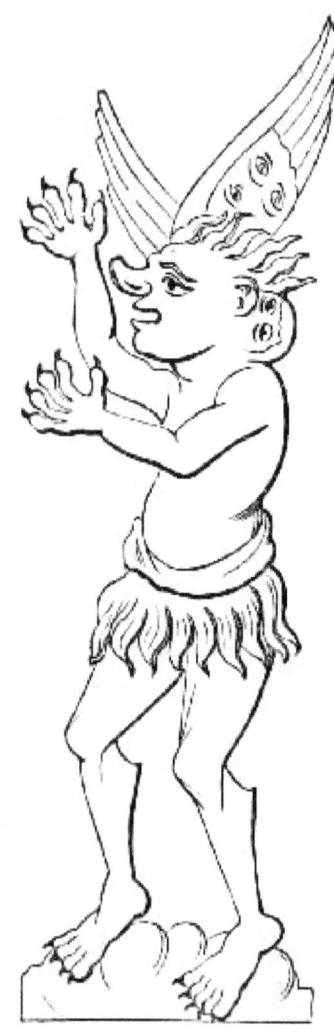

No. 30. Satan.

The inclination to give to the demons (the middle ages always looked upon them as innumerable) monstrous forms, which easily ran into the grotesque, was natural, and the painter, indeed, prided himself on drawing them ugly; but he was no doubt influenced in so generally caricaturing them, by mixing up this idea with those furnished by the popular superstitions of the Teutonic race, who believed in multitudes of spirits, representatives of the ancient satyrs, who were of a playfully malicious description, and went about plaguing mankind in a very droll manner, and sometimes appeared to them in equally droll forms. They were the Pucks and Robin Goodfellows of later times; but the Christian missionaries to the west taught their converts to believe, and probably believed themselves, that all these imaginary beings were real demons, who wandered over the earth for people's ruin and destruction. Thus the grotesque imagination of the converted people was introduced into the Christian system of demonology. It is a part of the subject to which we shall return in our next chapter; but I will here introduce two examples of the Anglo-Saxon demons. To explain the first of these, it will be necessary to state that, according to the mediæval notions, Satan, the arch demon, who had fallen from heaven for his rebellion against the Almighty, was not a free agent who went about tempting mankind, but he was himself plunged in the abyss, where he was held in bonds, and tormented by the demons who peopled the infernal regions, and also issued thence to seek their prey upon God's newest creation, the earth. The history of Satan's fall, and the description of his position (No. 29), form the subject of the earlier part of the Anglo-Saxon poetry ascribed to Cædmon, and it is one of the illuminations to the manuscript of Cædmon (which is now preserved at Oxford), which has furnished us with our cut, representing Satan in his bonds. The fiend is here pictured bound to stakes, over what appears to be a gridiron, while one of the demons, rising out of a fiery furnace, and holding in his hand an instrument of punishment, seems to be exulting over him, and at the same time urging on the troop of grotesque imps who are swarming round and tormenting their victim. The next cut, No. 30, is also taken from an Anglo-Saxon manuscript, preserved in the British Museum (MS. Cotton., Tiberius, C. vi.), which belongs to the earlier half of the eleventh century, and contains a copy of the psalter. It gives us the Anglo-Saxon notion of the demon under another form, equally characteristic, wearing only a girdle of flames, but in this case the especial singularity of the design consists in the eyes in the fiend's wings.

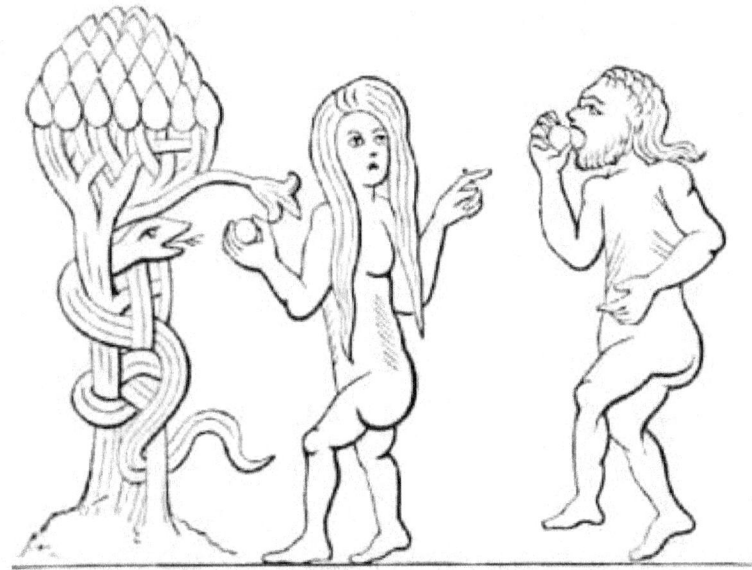

No. 31. The Temptation.

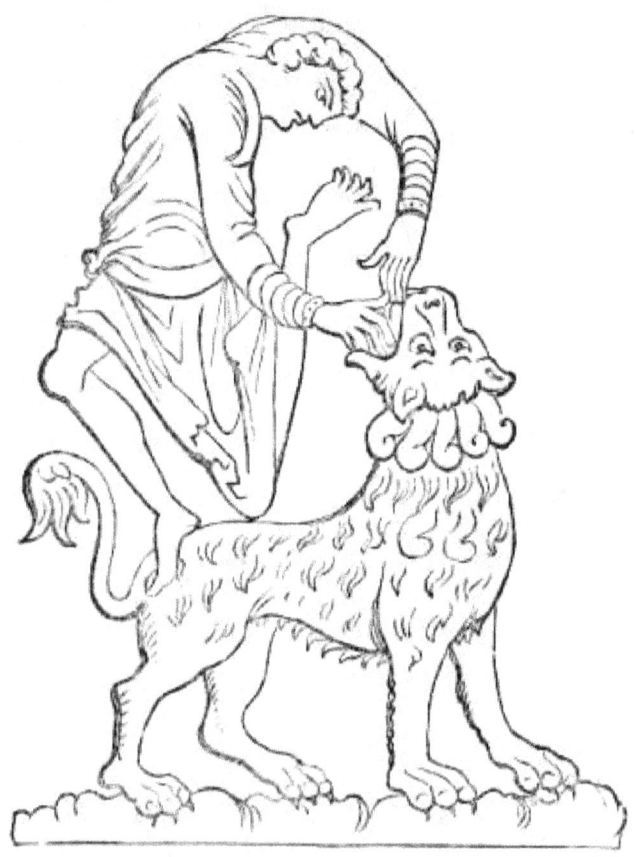

No. 32. David and the Lion.

Another circumstance had no doubt an influence on the mediæval taste for grotesque and caricature—the natural rudeness of early mediæval art. The writers of antiquity tell us of a remote period of Grecian art when it was necessary to write under each figure of a picture the name of what it was intended to represent, in order to make the whole intelligible—"this is a horse," "this is a man," "this is a tree." Without being quite so rude as this, the early mediæval artists, through ignorance of perspective, want of knowledge of proportion, and of skill in drawing, found great difficulty in representing a scene in which there was more than one figure, and in which it was necessary to distinguish them from each other; and they were continually trying to help themselves by adopting conventional forms or conventional positions, and by sometimes adding symbols that did not exactly represent what they meant. The exaggeration in form consisted chiefly in giving an undue prominence to some characteristic feature, which answered the same purpose as the Anglo-Saxon nickname and distinctive name, and which is, in fact, one of the first principles of all caricature. Conventional positions partook much of the character of conventional forms, but gave still greater room for grotesque. Thus the very first characteristics of mediæval art implied the existence of caricature, and no doubt led to the taste for the grotesque. The effect of this influence is apparent everywhere, and in innumerable cases serious pictures of the gravest and most important subjects are simply and absolutely caricatures. Anglo-Saxon art ran much into this style, and is often very grotesque in character. The first example we give (cut No. 31) is taken from one of the illustrations to Alfric's Anglo-Saxon version of the Pentateuch, in the profusely illuminated manuscript in the British Museum (MS. Cotton., Claudius B iv.), which was written at the end of the tenth, or beginning of the eleventh, century. It represents the temptation and fall of man; and the subject is treated, as will be seen, in a rather grotesque manner. Eve is evidently dictating to her husband, who, in obeying her, shows a mixture of eagerness and trepidation. Adam is no less evidently going to swallow the apple whole, which is, perhaps, in accordance with the mediæval legend, according to which the fruit stuck in his throat. It is hardly necessary to remark that the tree is entirely a conventional one; and it would be difficult to imagine how it came to bear apples at all. The mediæval artists were extremely unskilful in drawing trees; to these they usually gave the forms of cabbages, or some such plants, of which the form was simple, or often of a mere bunch of leaves. Our next example (cut No. 32) is also Anglo-Saxon, and is furnished by the manuscript in the British Museum already mentioned (MS. Cotton., Tiberius C vi.) It probably represents young David killing the lion, and is remarkable not only for the strange posture and bad proportions of the man, but for the tranquillity of the animal and the exaggerated and violent action of its slayer. This is very commonly the case in the mediæval drawings and sculptures, the artists apparently possessing far less skill in representing action in an animal than in man, and therefore more rarely attempting it. These illustrations are both taken from illuminated manuscripts. The two which follow are furnished by sculptures, and are of a rather later date than the preceding. The abbey of St. George of Boscherville, in the diocese of Auxerre (in Normandy), was founded by Ralph de Tancarville, one of the ministers of William the Conqueror, and therefore in the latter half of the eleventh century. A history of this religious house was published by a clever local antiquary—M. Achille Deville—from whose work we take our cut No. 33, one of a few rude sculptures on the abbey church, which no doubt belonged to the original fabric. It is not difficult to recognise the subject as Joseph taking the Virgin Mary with her Child into Egypt; but there is something exceedingly droll in the unintentional caricature of the faces, as well as in the whole design. The Virgin Mary appears without a nimbus, while the nimbus of the Infant Jesus is made to look very like a bonnet. It may be remarked that this subject of the flight into Egypt is by no means an uncommon one in mediæval art; and a drawing of the same subject, copied in my "History of Domestic Manners and Sentiments" (p. 115), presents a remarkable illustration of the contrast of the skill of a Norman sculptor and of an almost contemporary Anglo-Norman illuminator. Our cut also furnishes us with evidence of the error of the old opinion that ladies rode astride in the middle ages. Even one, who by his style of art must have been an obscure local carver on stone, when he represented a female on horseback, placed her in the position which has always been considered suitable to the sex.

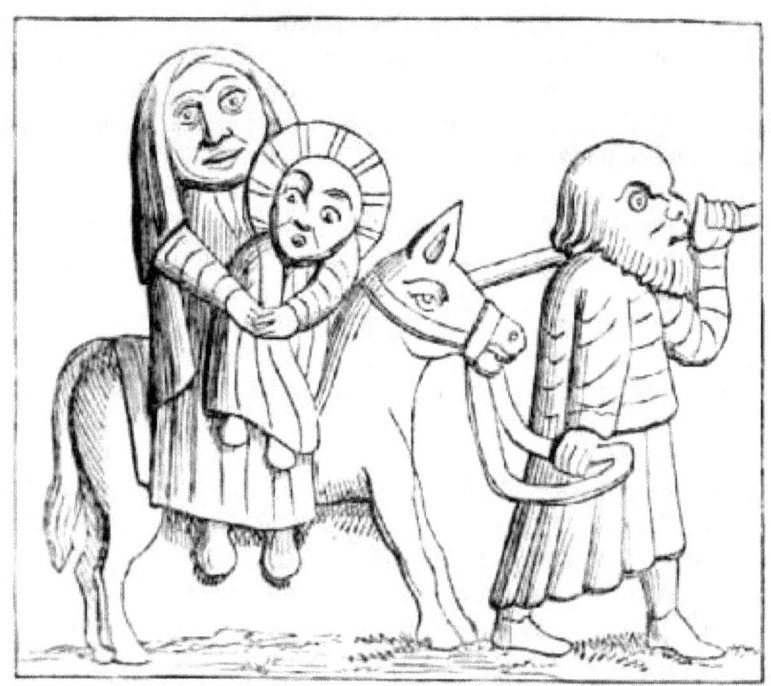

No. 33. The flight into Egypt.

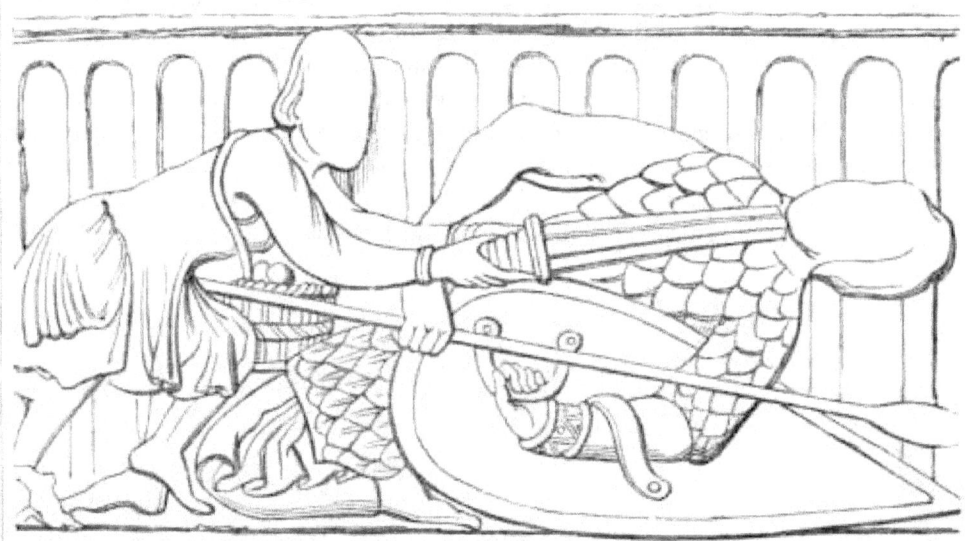

No. 34. David and Goliah.

For the drawing of the other sculpture to which I allude, I am indebted to Mr. Robinson. It is one of the subjects carved on the façade of the church of St. Gilles, near Nismes, and is a work of the twelfth century. It appears to represent the young David slaying the giant Goliah, the latter fully armed in scale armour, and with shield and spear, like a Norman knight; while to David the artist has given a figure which is feminine in its forms. What we might take at first sight for a basket of apples, appears to be meant for a supply of stones for the sling which the young hero carries suspended from his neck. He has slain the giant with one of these, and is cutting off his head with his own sword.

CHAPTER IV.

THE DIABOLICAL IN CARICATURE.—MEDIÆVAL LOVE OF THE LUDICROUS.—
CAUSES WHICH MADE IT INFLUENCE THE NOTIONS OF DEMONS.—STORIES OF
THE PIOUS PAINTER AND THE ERRING MONK.—DARKNESS AND UGLINESS
CARICATURED.—THE DEMONS IN THE MIRACLE PLAYS.—THE DEMON OF NOTRE
DAME.

As I have already stated in the last chapter, there can be no doubt that the whole system of the demonology of the middle ages was derived from the older pagan mythology. The demons of the monkish legends were simply the elves and hobgoblins of our forefathers, who haunted woods, and fields, and waters, and delighted in misleading or plaguing mankind, though their mischief was usually of a rather mirthful character. They were represented in classical mythology by the fauns and satyrs who had, as we have seen, much to do with the birth of comic literature among the Greeks and Romans; but these Teutonic elves were more ubiquitous than the satyrs, as they even haunted men's houses, and played tricks, not only of a mischievous, but of a very familiar character. The Christian clergy did not look upon the personages of the popular superstitions as fabulous beings, but they taught that they were all diabolical, and that they were so many agents of the evil one, constantly employed in enticing and entrapping mankind. Hence, in the mediæval legends, we frequently find demons presenting themselves under ludicrous forms or in ludicrous situations; or performing acts, such as eating and drinking, which are not in accordance with their real character; or at times even letting themselves be outwitted or entrapped by mortals in a very undignified manner. Although they assumed any form they pleased, their natural form was remarkable chiefly for being extremely ugly; one of them, which appeared in a wild wood, is described by Giraldus Cambrensis, who wrote at the end of the twelfth century, as being hairy, shaggy, and rough, and monstrously deformed.[24] According to a mediæval story, which was told in different forms, a great man's cellar was once haunted by these demons, who drank all his wine, while the owner was totally at a loss to account for its rapid disappearance. After many unsuccessful attempts to discover the depredators, some one, probably suspecting the truth, suggested that he should mark one of the barrels with holy water, and next morning a demon, much resembling the description given by Giraldus, was found stuck fast to the barrel. It is told also of Edward the Confessor, that he once went to see the tribute called the Danegeld, and it was shown to him all packed up in great barrels ready to be sent away—for this appears to have been the usual mode of transporting large quantities of money. The saintly king had the faculty of being able to see spiritual beings—a sort of spiritual second-sight—and he beheld seated on the largest barrel, a devil, who was "black and hideous."

Vit un déable saer desus
Le tresor, noir et hidus.—Life of S. Edward, l. 944.

An early illuminator, in a manuscript preserved in the library of Trinity College, Cambridge (MS. Trin. Col., B x. 2), has left us a pictorial representation of this scene, from which I copy his notion of the form of the demon in cut No. 35. The general idea is evidently taken from the figure of the goat, and the relationship between the demon and the classical satyr is very evident.

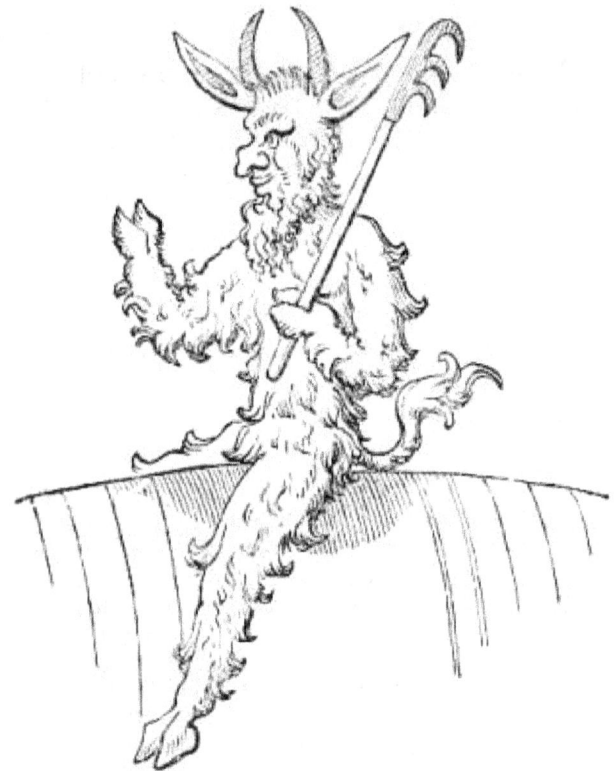

No. 35. The Demon of the Treasure.

Ugliness was an essential characteristic of the demons, and, moreover, their features have usually a mirthful cast, as though they greatly enjoyed their occupation. There is a mediæval story of a young monk, who was sacristan to an abbey, and had the directions of the building and ornamentation. The carvers of stone were making admirable representations of hell and paradise, in the former of which the demons "seemed to take great delight in well tormenting their victims"—

Qui par semblant se delitoit
En ce que bien les tormentoit.

The sacristan, who watched the sculptors every day, was at last moved by pious zeal to try and imitate them, and he set to work to make a devil himself, with such success, that his fiend was so black and ugly that nobody could look at it without terror.

Tant qu'un déable à fere emprist;
Si i mist sa poine et sa cure,
Que la forme fu si oscure
Et si laide, que cil doutast
Que entre deus oilz l'esgardast.

The sacristan, encouraged by his success—for it must be understood that his art was a sudden inspiration (as he had not been an artist before)—continued his work till it was completed, and then "it was so horrible and so ugly, that all who saw it affirmed upon their oaths that they had never seen so ugly a figure either in sculpture or in painting, or one which had so repulsive an appearance, or a devil which was a better likeness than the one this monk had made for them"—

Si horribles fu et si lez,
Que trestouz cels que le véoient
Seur leur serement afermoient
C'onques mès si laide figure,
Ne en taille ne en peinture,
N'avoient à nul jor véue,
Qui si éust laide véue,
Ne déable miex contrefet
Que cil moines leur avoit fet.
—Meon's Fabliaux, tom. ii. p. 414.

The demon himself now took offence at the affront which had been put upon him, and appearing the night following to the sacristan, reproached him with having made him so ugly, and enjoined him to break the sculpture, and execute another representing him better looking, on pain of very severe punishment; but, although this visit was repeated thrice, the pious monk refused to comply. The evil one now began to work in another way, and, by his cunning, he drew the sacristan into a disgraceful amour with a lady of the neighbourhood, and they plotted not only to elope together by night, but to rob the monastery of its treasure, which was of course in the keeping of the sacristan. They were discovered, and caught in their flight, laden with the treasure, and the unfaithful sacristan was thrown into prison. The fiend now appeared to him, and promised to clear him out of all his trouble on the mere condition that he should break his ugly statue, and make another representing him as looking handsome—a bargain to which the sacristan acceded without further hesitation. It would thus appear that the demons did not like to be represented ugly. In this case, the fiend immediately took the form and place of the sacristan, while the latter went to his bed as if nothing had happened. When the other monks found him there next morning, and heard him disclaim all knowledge of the robbery or of the prison, they hurried to the latter place, and found the devil in chains, who, when they attempted to exorcise him, behaved in a very turbulent manner, and disappeared from their sight. The monks believed that it was all a deception of the evil one, while the sacristan, who was not inclined to brave his displeasure a second time, performed faithfully his part of the contract, and made a devil who did not look ugly. In another version of the story, however, it ends differently. After the third warning, the monk went in defiance of the devil, and made his picture uglier than ever; in revenge for which the demon came unexpectedly and broke the ladder on which he was mounted at his work, whereby the monk would undoubtedly have been killed. But the Virgin, to whom he was much devoted, came to his assistance, and, seizing him with her hand, and holding him in the air, disappointed the devil of his purpose. It is this latter *dénouement* which is represented in the cut No. 36, taken from the celebrated manuscript in the British Museum known as "Queen Mary's Psalter" (MS. Reg. 2 B vii.). The two demons employed here present, well defined, the air of mirthful jollity which was evidently derived from the popular hobgoblins.

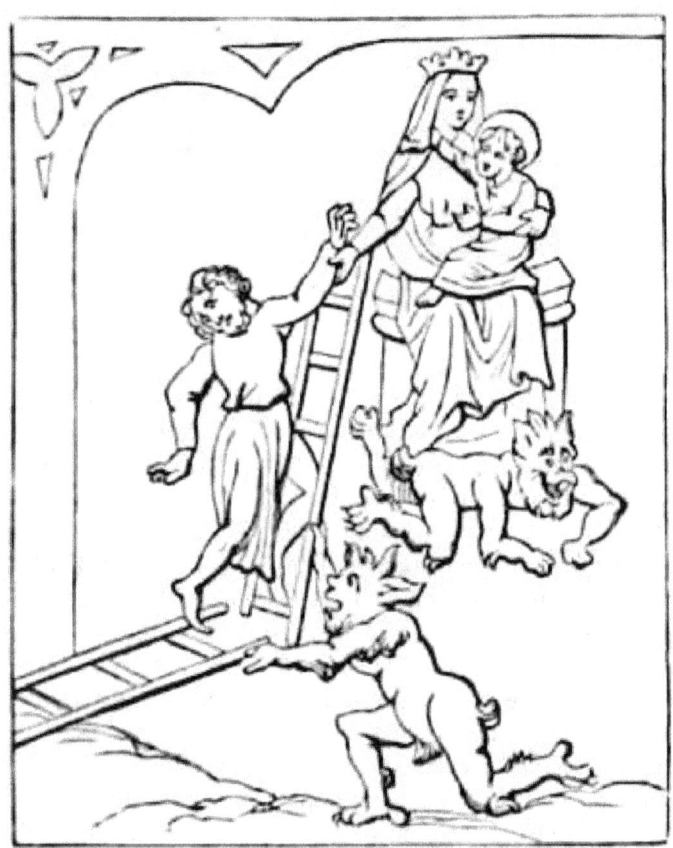

No. 36. The Pious Sculptor.

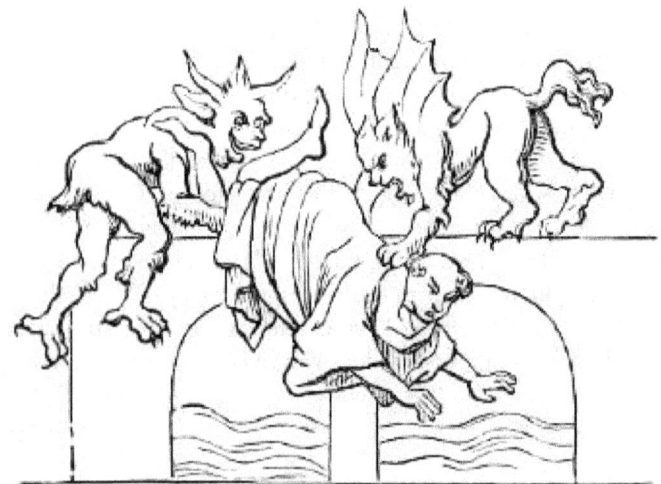

No. 37. The Monk's Disaster.

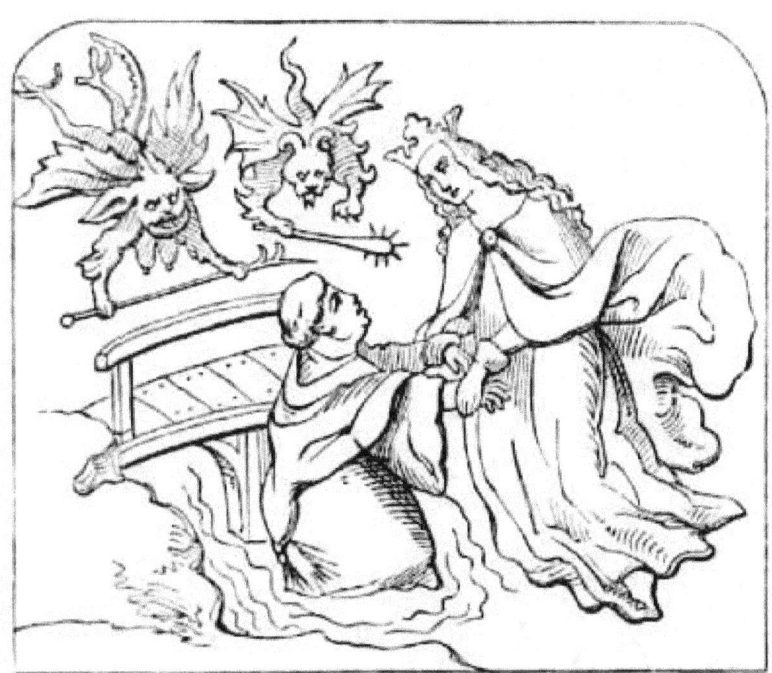

No. 38. The Demons Disappointed.

There was another popular story, which also was told under several forms. The old Norman historians tell it of their duke Richard Sans-Peur. There was a monk of the abbey of St. Ouen, who also held the office of sacristan, but, neglecting the duties of his position, entered into an intrigue with a lady who dwelt in the neighbourhood, and was accustomed at night to leave the abbey secretly, and repair to her. His place as sacristan enabled him thus to leave the house unknown to the other brethren. On his way, he had to pass the little river Robec, by means of a plank or wooden bridge, and one night the demons, who had been watching him on his errand of sin, caught him on the bridge, and threw him over into the water, where he was drowned. One devil seized his soul, and would have carried it away, but an angel came to claim him on account of his good actions, and the dispute ran so high, that duke Richard, whose piety was as great as his courage, was called in to decide it. The same manuscript from which our last cut was taken has furnished our cut No. 37, which represents two demons tripping up the monk, and throwing him very unceremoniously into the river. The body of one of the demons here assumes the form of an animal, instead of taking, like the other, that of a man, and he is, moreover, furnished with a dragon's wings. There was one version of this story, in which it found its place among the legends of the Virgin Mary, instead of those of duke Richard. The monk, in spite of his failings, had been a constant worshipper of the Virgin, and, as he was falling from the bridge into the river, she stepped forward to protect him from his persecutors, and taking hold of him with her hand, saved him from death. One of the compartments of the rather early wall-paintings in Winchester Cathedral represents the scene according to this version of the story, and is copied in our cut No. 38. The fiends here take more fantastic shapes than we have previously seen given to them. They remind us already of the infinitely varied grotesque forms which the painters of the age of the Renaissance crowded together in such subjects as "The Temptation of St. Anthony." In fact these strange notions of the forms of the demons were not only preserved through the whole period of the middle ages, but are still hardly extinct. They appear in almost exaggerated forms in the illustrations to books of a popular religious character which appeared in the first ages of printing. I may quote, as an example, one of the cuts of an early and very rare block-book, entitled the *Ars Moriendi*, or "Art of Dying," or, in a second title, *De Tentationibus Morientium*, on the temptations to which dying men are exposed. The scene, of which a part is given in the annexed cut (No. 39), is in the room of the dying man, whose bed is surrounded by three demons, who are come to tempt him, while his relatives of both sexes are looking on quite unconscious of their presence. The figures of these demons are particularly grotesque, and their ugly features betray a degree of vulgar cunning which adds not a little to this effect. The one leaning over the dying man suggests to him the words expressed in the label issuing from his mouth, *Provideas amicis*, "provide for your friends;" while the one whose head appears to the left whispers to him, *Yntende thesauro*, "think of your treasure." The dying man seems grievously perplexed with the various thoughts thus suggested to him.

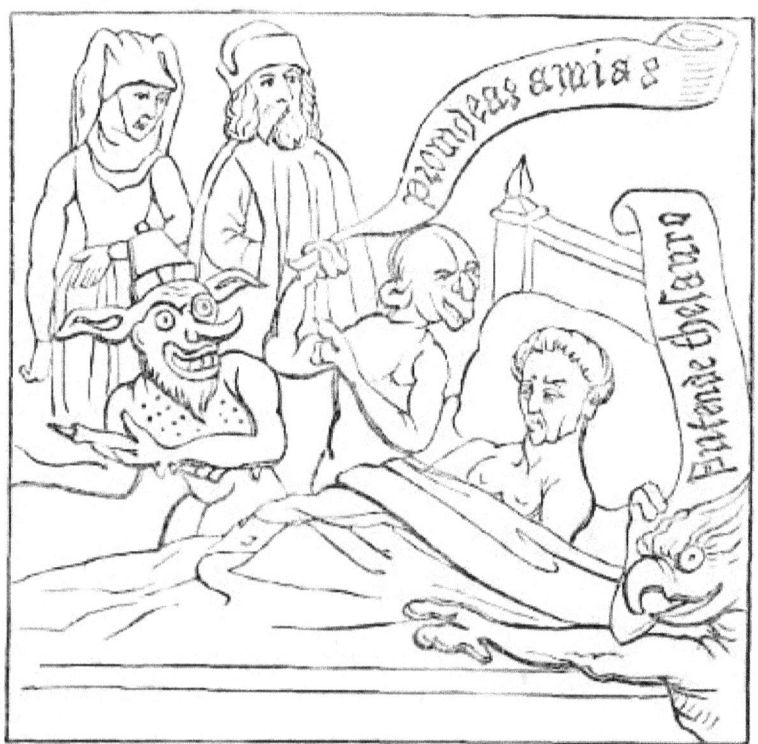

No. 39. A Mediæval Death-bed.

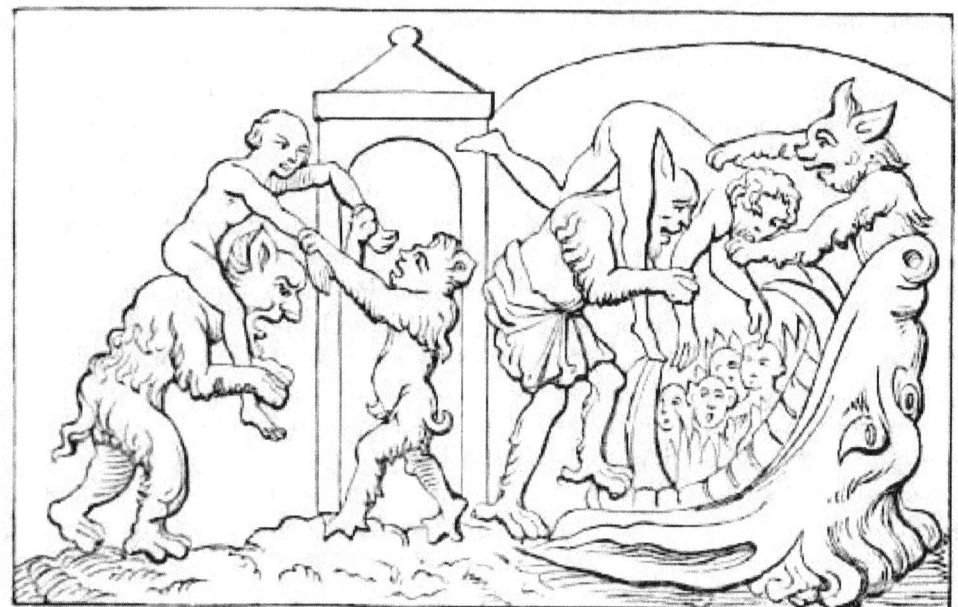

No. 40. Condemned Souls carried to their Place of Punishment.

Why did the mediæval Christians think it necessary to make the devils black and ugly? The first reply to this question which presents itself is, that the characteristics intended to be represented were the blackness and ugliness of sin. This, however, is only partially the explanation of the fact; for there can be no doubt that the notion was a popular one, and that it had previously existed in the popular mythology; and, as has been already remarked, the ugliness exhibited by them is a vulgar, mirthful ugliness, which makes you laugh instead of shudder. Another scene, from the interesting drawings at the foot of the pages in "Queen Mary's Psalter," is given in our cut No. 40. It represents that most popular of mediæval pictures, and, at the same time, most remarkable of literal interpretations, hell mouth. The entrance to the infernal regions was always represented pictorially as the mouth of a monstrous animal, where the demons appeared leaving and returning. Here they are seen bringing the sinful souls to their last destination, and it cannot be denied that they are doing the work right merrily and jovially. In our cut No. 41, from the manuscript in the library of Trinity College, Cambridge, which furnished a former subject, three demons, who appear to be the guardians of the entrance to the regions below—for it is upon the brow above the monstrous mouth that they are standing—present varieties of the diabolical form. The one in the middle is the most remarkable, for he has wings not only on his shoulders, but also on his knees and heels. All three have horns; in fact, the three special characteristics of mediæval demons were horns, hoofs—or, at least, the feet of beasts,—and tails, which sufficiently indicate the source from which the popular notions of these beings were derived. In the cathedral of Treves, there is a mural painting by William of Cologne, a painter of the fifteenth century, which represents the entrance to the shades, the monstrous mouth, with its keepers, in still more grotesque forms. Our cut No. 42 gives but a small portion of this picture, in which the porter of the regions of punishment is sitting astride the snout of the monstrous mouth, and is sounding with a trumpet what may be supposed to be the call for those who are condemned. Another minstrel of the same stamp, spurred, though not booted, sits astride the tube of the trumpet, playing on the bagpipes; and the sound which issues from the former instrument is represented by a host of smaller imps who are scattering themselves about.

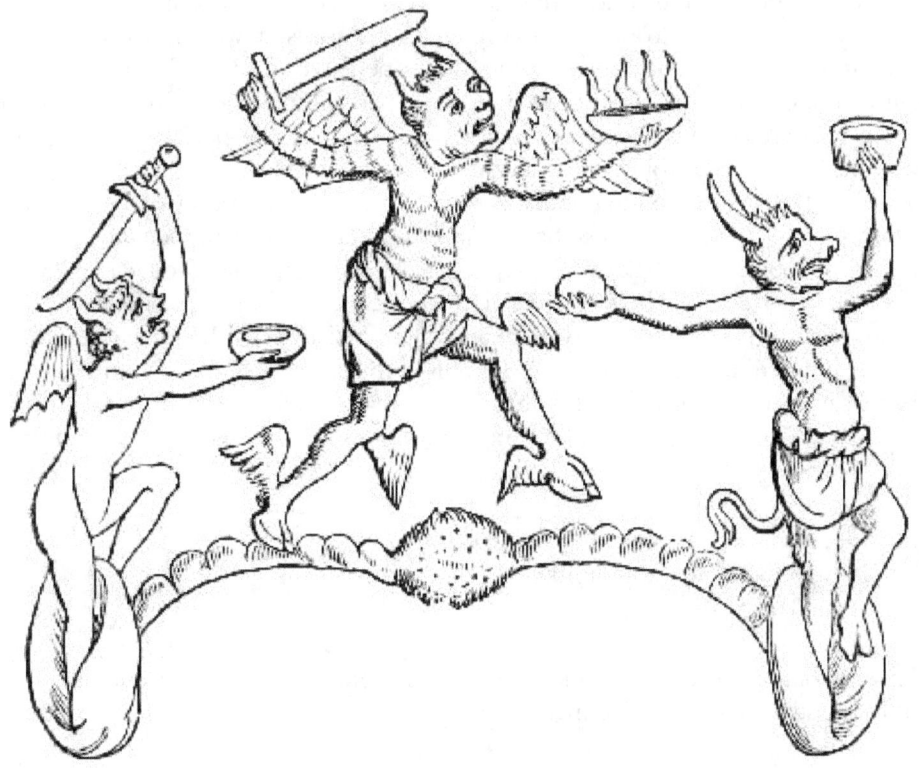

No. 41. The Guardians of Hell Mouth.

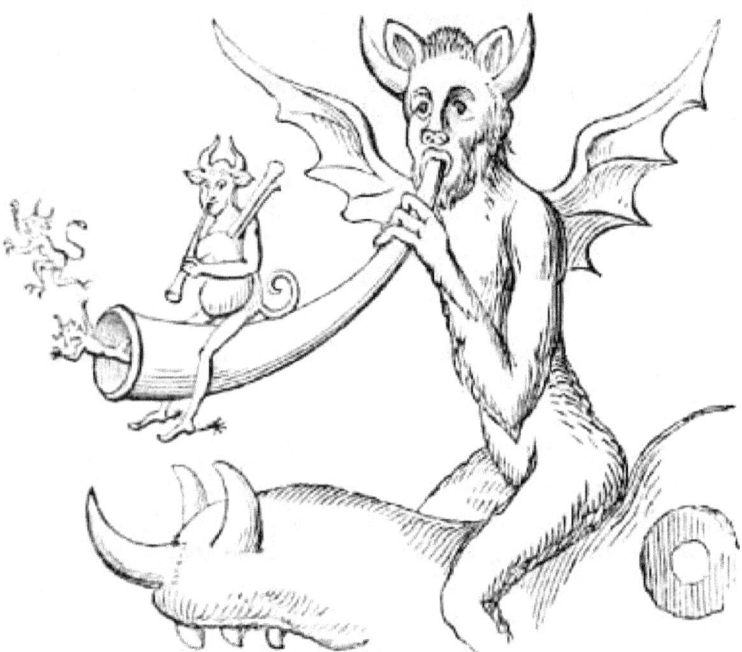

No. 42. The Trumpeter of Evil.

It must not be supposed that, in subjects like these, the drollery of the scene was accidental; but, on the contrary, the mediæval artists and popular writers gave them this character purposely. The demons and the executioners—the latter of whom were called in Latin *tortores*, and in popular old English phraseology the "tormentours"—were the comic characters of the time, and the scenes in the old mysteries or religious plays in which they were introduced were the comic scenes, or farce, of the piece. The love of burlesque and caricature was, indeed, so deeply planted in the popular mind, that it was found necessary to introduce them even in pious works, in which such scenes as the slaughter of the innocents, where the "knights" and the women abused each other in vulgar language, the treatment of Christ at the time of His trial, some parts of the scene of the crucifixion, and the day of judgment, were essentially comic. The last of these subjects, especially, was a scene of mirth, because it often consisted throughout of a coarse satire on the vices of the age, especially on those which were most obnoxious to the populace, such as the pride and vanity of the higher ranks, and the extortions and frauds of usurers, bakers, taverners, and others. In the play of "Juditium," or the day of doom, in the "Towneley Mysteries," one of the earliest collections of mysteries in the English language, the whole conversation among the demons is exactly of that joking kind which we might expect from their countenances in the pictures. When one of them appears carrying a bag full of different offences, another, his companion, is so joyful at this circumstance, that he says it makes him laugh till he is out of breath, or, in other words, till he is ready to burst; and, while asking if anger be not among the sins he had collected, proposes to treat him with something to drink—

Primus dæmon. Peasze, I pray the, be stille; I laghe that I kynke.
Is oghte ire in thi bille? and then salle thou drynke.
—Towneley Mysteries, p. 309.

And in the continuation of the conversation, one telling of the events which had preceded the announcement of Doomsday says, rather jeeringly, and somewhat exultingly, "Souls came so thick now of late to hell, that our porter at hell gate is ever held so close at work, up early and down late, that he never rests"—

Saules cam so thyk now late unto helle,
As ever
Oure porter at helle gate
Is halden so strate,
Up erly and downe late,
He rystys never.—Ib., p. 314.

With such popular notions on the subject, we have no reason to be surprised that the artists of the middle ages frequently chose the figures of demons as objects on which to exercise their skill in burlesque and caricature, that they often introduced grotesque figures of their heads and bodies in the sculptured ornamentation of building, and that they presented them in ludicrous situations and attitudes in their pictures. They are often brought in as secondary actors in a picture in a very singular manner, of which an excellent example is furnished by the beautifully illuminated manuscript known as "Queen Mary's Psalter," which is copied in our cut No. 43. Nothing is more certain than that in this instance the intention of the artist was perfectly serious. Eve, under the influence of a rather singularly formed serpent, having the head of a beautiful woman and the body of a dragon, is plucking the apples and offering them to Adam, who is preparing to eat one, with evident hesitation and reluctance. But three demons, downright hobgoblins, appear as secondary actors in the scene, who exercise an influence upon the principals. One is patting Eve on the shoulder, with an air of approval and encouragement, while a second, with wings, is urging on Adam, and apparently laughing at his apprehensions; and a third, in a very ludicrous manner, is preventing him from drawing back from the trial.

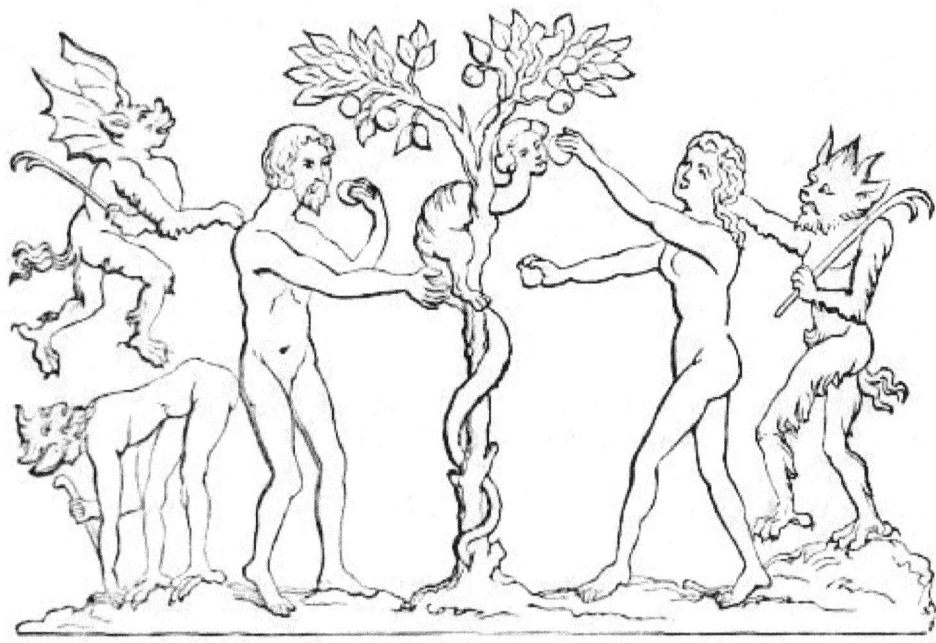

No. 43. The Fall of Man.

In all the delineations of demons we have yet seen, the ludicrous is the spirit which chiefly predominates, and in no one instance have we had a figure which is really demoniacal. The devils are droll but not frightful; they provoke laughter, or at least excite a smile, but they create no horror. Indeed, they torment their victims so good-humouredly, that we hardly feel for them. There is, however, one well-known instance in which the mediæval artist has shown himself fully successful in representing the features of the spirit of evil. On the parapet of the external gallery of the cathedral church of Notre Dame in Paris, there is a figure in stone, of the ordinary stature of a man, representing the demon, apparently looking with satisfaction upon the inhabitants of the city as they were everywhere indulging in sin and wickedness. We give a sketch of this figure in our cut No. 44. The unmixed evil—horrible in its expression in this countenance—is marvellously portrayed. It is an absolute Mephistophiles, carrying in his features a strange mixture of hateful qualities—malice, pride, envy—in fact, all the deadly sins combined in one diabolical whole.

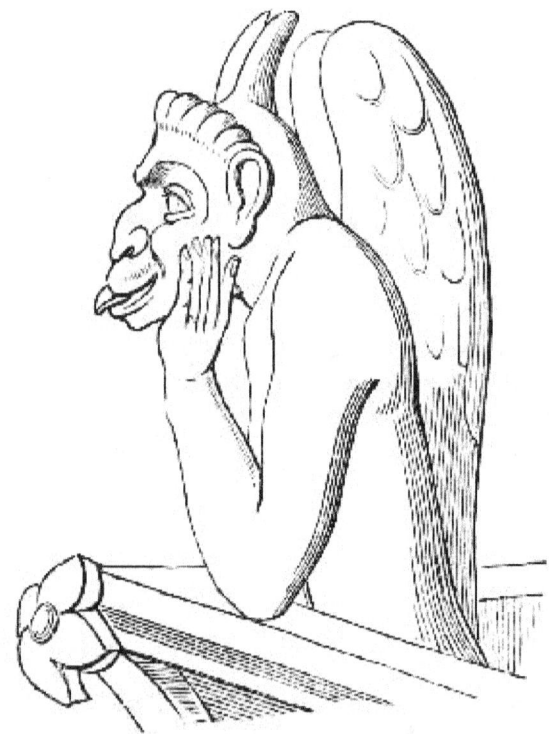

No. 44. The Spirit of Evil.

CHAPTER V.

EMPLOYMENT OF ANIMALS IN MEDIÆVAL SATIRE.—POPULARITY OF FABLES; ODO DE CIRINGTON.—REYNARD THE FOX.—BURNELLUS AND FAUVEL.—THE CHARIVARI.—LE MONDE BESTORNÉ.—ENCAUSTIC TILES.—SHOEING THE GOOSE, AND FEEDING PIGS WITH ROSES.—SATIRICAL SIGNS; THE MUSTARD MAKER.

The people of the middle ages appear to have been great admirers of animals, to have observed closely their various characters and peculiarities, and to have been fond of domesticating them. They soon began to employ their peculiarities as means of satirising and caricaturing mankind; and among the literature bequeathed to them by the Romans, they received no book more eagerly than the "Fables of Æsop," and the other collections of fables which were published under the empire. We find no traces of fables among the original literature of the German race; but the tribes who took possession of the Roman provinces no sooner became acquainted with the fables of the ancients, than they began to imitate them, and stories in which animals acted the part of men were multiplied immensely, and became a very important branch of mediæval fiction.

Among the Teutonic peoples especially, these fables often assumed very grotesque forms, and the satire they convey is very amusing. One of the earliest of these collections of original fables was composed by an English ecclesiastic named Odo de Cirington, who lived in the time of Henry II. and Richard I. In Odo's fables, we find the animals figuring under the same popular names by which they were afterwards so well known, such as Reynard for the Fox, Isengrin for the wolf, Teburg for the cat, and the like. Thus the subject of one of them is "Isengrin made Monk" (*de Isengrino monacho*). "Once," we are told, "Isengrin desired to be a monk. By dint of fervent supplications, he obtained the consent of the chapter, and received the tonsure, the cowl, and the other insignia of monachism. At length they put him to school, and he was to learn the 'Paternoster,' but he always replied, 'lamb' (*agnus*) or 'ram' (*aries*). The monks taught him that he ought to look upon the crucifix and upon the sacrament, but he ever directed his eyes to the lambs and rams." The fable is droll enough, but the moral, or application is still more grotesque. "Such is the conduct of many of the monks, whose only cry is 'aries,' that is, good wine, and who have their eyes always fixed on fat flesh and their platter;" whence the saying in English—

They thou the vulf hore
hod to preste,
they thou him to skole sette
salmes to lerne,
hevere bet hise geres
to the grove grene

Though thou the hoary wolf
consecrate to a priest,
though thou put him to school
to learn Psalms,
ever are his ears turned
to the green grove.

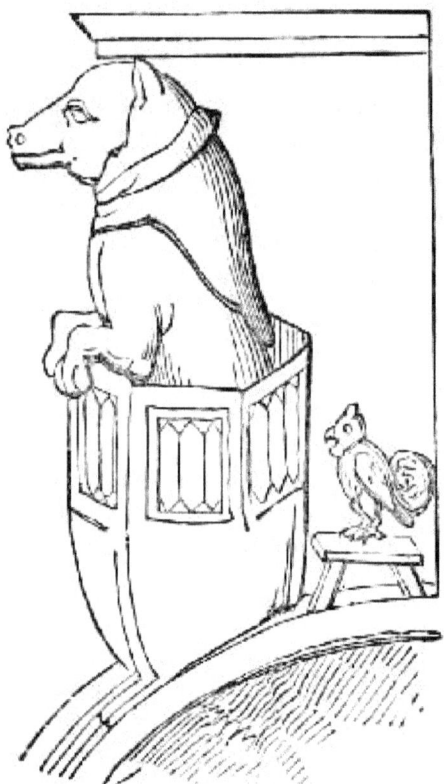

No. 45. The Fox in the Pulpit.

These lines are in the alliterative verse of the Anglo-Saxons, and show that such fables had already found their place in the popular poetry of the English people. Another of these fables is entitled "Of the Beetle (*serabo*) and his Wife." "A beetle, flying through the land, passed among most beautiful blooming trees, through orchards and among roses and lilies, in the most lovely places, and at length threw himself upon a dunghill among the dung of horses, and found there his wife, who asked him whence he came. And the beetle said, 'I have flown all round the earth and through it; I have seen the flowers of almonds, and lilies, and roses, but I have seen no place so pleasant as this,' pointing to the dunghill." The application is equally droll with the former and equally uncomplimentary to the religious part of the community. Odo de Cirington tells us that, "Thus many of the clergy, monks, and laymen listen to the lives of the fathers, pass among the lilies of the virgins, among the roses of the martyrs, and among the violets of the confessors, yet nothing ever appears so pleasant and agreeable as a strumpet, or the tavern, or a singing party, though it is but a stinking dunghill and congregation of sinners."

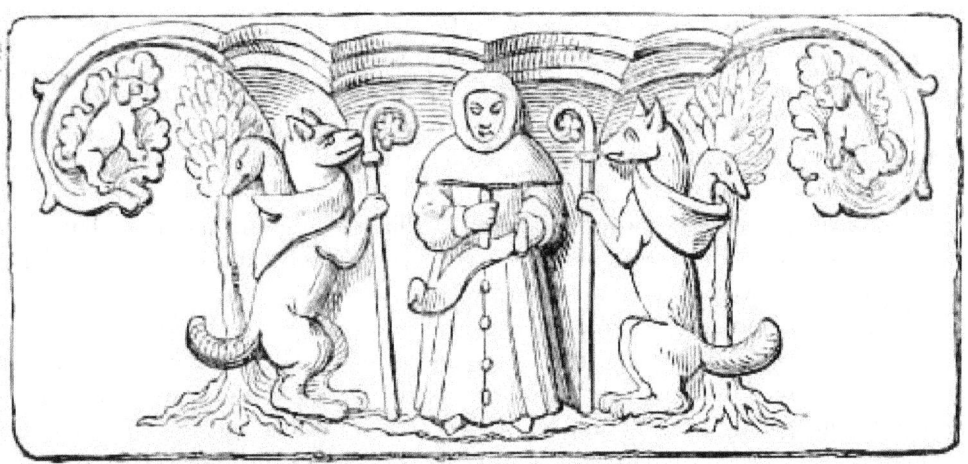

No. 46. Ecclesiastical Sincerity.

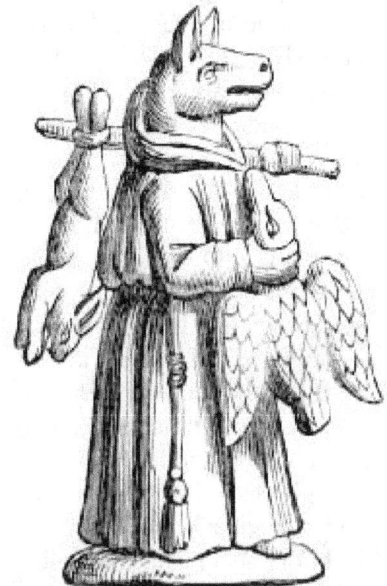

No. 47. Reynard turned Monk.

Popular sculpture and painting were but the translation of popular literature, and nothing was more common to represent, in pictures and carvings, than individual men under the forms of the animals who displayed similar characters or similar propensities. Cunning, treachery, and intrigue were the prevailing vices of the middle ages, and they were those also of the fox, who hence became a favourite character in satire. The victory of craft over force always provoked mirth. The fabulists, or, we should perhaps rather say, the satirists, soon began to extend their canvas and enlarge their picture, and, instead of single examples of fraud or injustice, they introduced a variety of characters, not only foxes, but wolves, and sheep, and bears, with birds also, as the eagle, the cock, and the crow, and mixed them up together in long narratives, which thus formed general satires on the vices of contemporary society. In this manner originated the celebrated romance of "Reynard the Fox," which in various forms, from the twelfth century to the eighteenth, has enjoyed a popularity which was granted probably to no other book. The plot of this remarkable satire turns chiefly on the long struggle between the brute force of Isengrin the Wolf, possessed only with a small amount of intelligence, which is easily deceived—under which character is presented the powerful feudal baron—and the craftiness of Reynard the Fox, who represents the intelligent portion of society, which had to hold its ground by its wits, and these were continually abused to evil purposes.

Reynard is swayed by a constant impulse to deceive and victimise everybody, whether friends or enemies, but especially his uncle Isengrin. It was somewhat the relationship between the ecclesiastical and baronial aristocracy. Reynard was educated in the schools, and intended for the clerical order; and at different times he is represented as acting under the disguise of a priest, of a monk, of a pilgrim, or even of a prelate of the church. Though frequently reduced to the greatest straits by the power of Isengrin, Reynard has generally the better of it in the end: he robs and defrauds Isengrin continually, outrages his wife, who is half in alliance with him, and draws him into all sorts of dangers and sufferings, for which the latter never succeeds in obtaining justice. The old sculptors and artists appear to have preferred exhibiting Reynard in his ecclesiastical disguises, and in these he appears often in the ornamentation of mediæval architectural sculpture, in wood-carvings, in the illuminations of manuscripts, and in other objects of art. The popular feeling against the clergy was strong in the middle ages, and no caricature was received with more favour than those which exposed the immorality or dishonesty of a monk or a priest. Our cut No. 45 is taken from a sculpture in the church of Christchurch, in Hampshire, for the drawing of which I am indebted to my friend, Mr. Llewellynn Jewitt. It represents Reynard in the pulpit preaching; behind, or rather perhaps beside him, a diminutive cock stands upon a stool—in modern times we should be inclined to say he was acting as clerk. Reynard's costume consists merely of the ecclesiastical hood or cowl. Such subjects are frequently found on the carved seats, or misereres, in the stalls of the old cathedrals and collegiate churches. The painted glass of the great window of the north cross-aisle of St. Martin's church in Leicester, which was destroyed in the last century, represented the fox, in the character of an ecclesiastic, preaching to a congregation of geese, and addressing them in the words—*Testis est mihi Deus, quam cupiam vos omnes visceribus meis* (God is witness, how I desire you all in my bowels), a parody on the words of the New Testament.[25] Our cut No. 46 is taken from one of the misereres in the church of St. Mary, at Beverley, in Yorkshire. Two foxes are represented in the disguise of ecclesiastics, each furnished with a pastoral staff, and they appear to be receiving instructions from a prelate or personage of rank—perhaps they are undertaking a pilgrimage of penance. But their sincerity is rendered somewhat doubtful by the geese concealed in their hoods. In one of the incidents of the romance of Reynard, the hero enters a monastery and becomes a monk, in order to escape the wrath of King Noble, the lion. For some time he made an outward show of sanctity and self-privation, but unknown to his brethren he secretly helped himself freely to the good things of the monastery. One day he observed, with longing lips, a messenger who brought four fat capons as a present from a lay neighbour to the abbot. That night, when all the monks had retired to rest, Reynard obtained admission to the larder, regaled himself with one of the capons, and as soon as he had eaten it, trussed the three others on his back, escaped secretly from the abbey, and, throwing away his monastic garment, hurried home with his prey. We might almost imagine our cut No. 47, taken from one of the stalls of the church of Nantwich, in Cheshire, to have been intended to represent this incident, or, at least, a similar one. Our next cut, No. 48, is taken from a stall in the church of Boston, in Lincolnshire. A prelate, equally false, is seated in his chair, with a mitre on his head, and the pastoral staff in his right hand. His flock are represented by a cock and hens, the former of which he holds securely with his right hand, while he appears to be preaching to them.

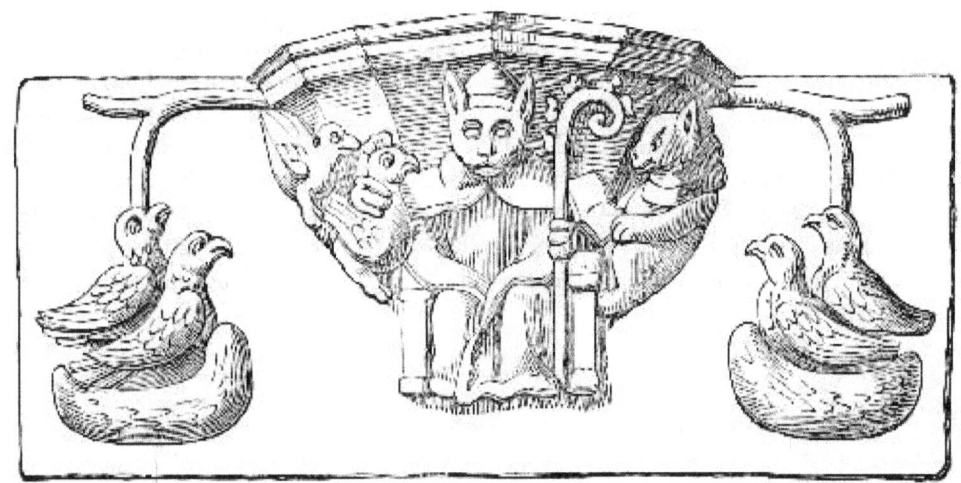

No. 48. The Prelate and his Flock.

Another mediæval sculpture has furnished events for a rather curious history, at the same time that it is a good illustration of our subject. Odo de Cirington, the fabulist, tells us how, one day, the wolf died, and the lion called the animals together to celebrate his exequies. The hare carried the holy water, hedgehogs bore the candles, the goats rang the bells, the moles dug the grave, the foxes carried the corpse on the bier. Berengarius, the bear, celebrated mass, the ox read the gospel, and the ass the epistle. When the mass was concluded, and Isengrin buried, the animals made a splendid feast out of his goods, and wished for such another funeral. Our satirical ecclesiastic makes an application of this story which tells little to the credit of the monks of his time. "So it frequently happens," he says, "that when some rich man, an extortionist or a usurer, dies, the abbot or prior of a convent of beasts, *i.e.* of men living like beasts, causes them to assemble. For it commonly happens that in a great convent of black or white monks (Benedictines or Augustinians) there are none but beasts—lions by their pride, foxes by their craftiness, bears by their voracity, stinking goats by their incontinence, asses by their sluggishness, hedgehogs by their asperity, hares by their timidity, because they were cowardly where there was no fear, and oxen by their laborious cultivation of their land."[26]

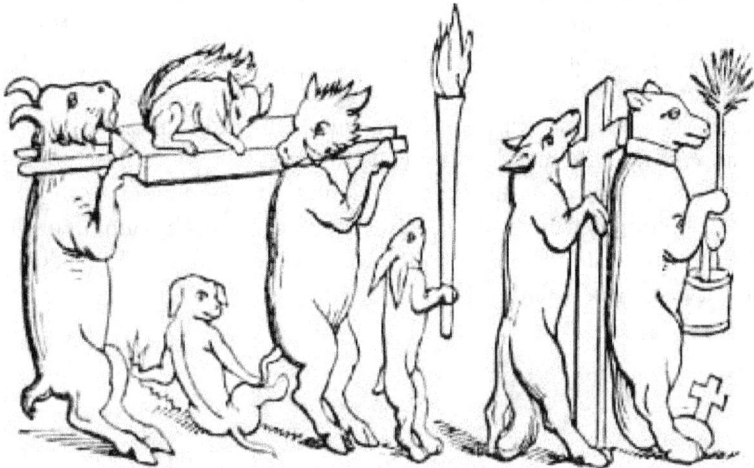

No. 49. The Funeral of the Fox.

A scene closely resembling that here described by Odo, differing only in the distribution of the characters, was translated from some such written story into the pictorial language of the ancient sculptured ornamentation of Strasburg Cathedral, where it formed, apparently, two sides of the capital or entablature of a column near the chancel. The deceased in this picture appears to be a fox, which was probably the animal intended to be represented in the original, although, in the copy of it preserved, it looks more like a squirrel. The bier is carried by the goat and the boar, while a little dog underneath is taking liberties with the tail of the latter. Immediately before the bier, the hare carries the lighted taper, preceded by the wolf, who carries the cross, and the bear, who holds in one hand the holy-water vessel and in the other the aspersoir. This forms the first division of the subject, and is represented in our cut No. 49. In the next division (cut No. 50), the stag is represented celebrating mass, and the ass reads the Gospel from a book which the cat supports with its head.

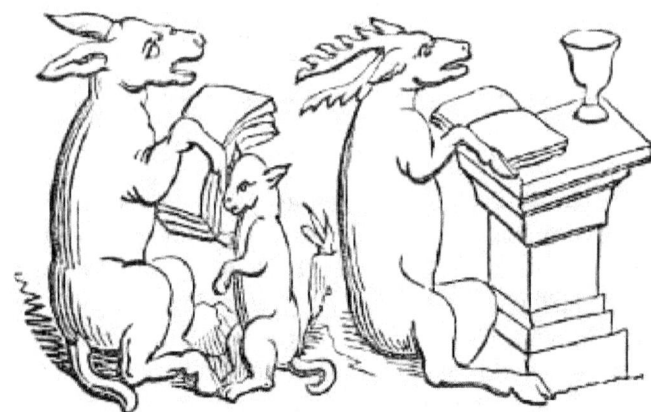

No. 50. The Mass for the Fox.

This curious sculpture is said to have been of the thirteenth century. In the fifteenth century it attracted the attention of the reformers, who looked upon it as an ancient protest against the corruptions of the mass, and one of the more distinguished of them, John Fischart, had it copied and engraved on wood, and published it about the year 1580, with some verses of his own, in which it was interpreted as a satire upon the papacy. This publication gave such dire offence to the ecclesiastical authorities of Strasburg, that the Lutheran bookseller who had ventured to publish it, was compelled to make a public apology in the church, and the wood-engraving and all the impressions were seized and burnt by the common hangman. A few years later, however, in 1608, another engraving was made, and published in a large folio with Fischart's verses; and it is from the diminished copy of this second edition—given in Flögel's "Geschichte des Komisches Literatur"— that our cuts are taken. The original Sculpture was still more unfortunate. Its publication and explanation by Fischart was the cause of no little scandal among the Catholics, who tried to retort upon their opponents by asserting that the figures in this funeral celebration were intended to represent the ignorance of the Protestant preachers; and the sculpture in the church continued to be regarded by the ecclesiastical authorities with dissatisfaction until the year 1685, when, to take away all further ground of scandal, it was entirely defaced.

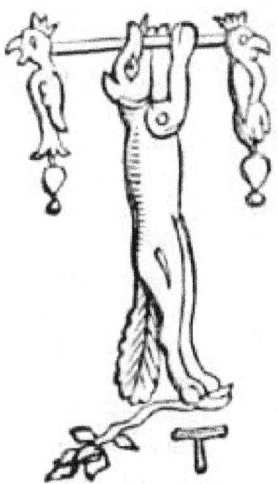

No. 51. The Fox Provided.

Reynard's mediæval celebrity dates certainly from a rather early period. Montflaucon has given an alphabet of ornamental initial letters, formed chiefly of figures of men and animals, from a manuscript which he ascribes to the ninth century, among which is the one copied in our cut No. 51, representing a fox walking upon his hind legs, and carrying two small cocks, suspended at the ends of a cross staff. It is hardly necessary to say that this group forms the letter T. Long before this, the Frankish historian Fredegarius, who wrote about the middle of the seventh century, introduces a fable in which the fox figures at the court of the lion. The same fable is repeated by a monkish writer of Bavaria, named Fromond, who flourished in the tenth century, and by another named Aimoinus, who lived about the year 1,000. At length, in the twelfth century, Guibert de Nogent, who died about the year 1124, and who has left us his autobiography (*de Vita sua*), relates an anecdote in that work, in explanation of which he tells us that the wolf was then popularly designated by the name of Isengrin; and in the fables of Odo, as we have already seen, this name is commonly given to the wolf, Reynard to the fox, Teburg to the cat, and so on with the others. This only shows that in the fables of the twelfth century the various animals were known by these names, but it does not prove that what we know as the romance of Reynard existed. Jacob Grimm argued from the derivation and forms of these names, that the fables themselves, and the romance, originated with the Teutonic peoples, and were indigenous to them; but his reasons appear to me to be more specious than conclusive, and I certainly lean to the opinion of my friend Paulin Paris, that the romance of Reynard was native of France,[27] and that it was partly founded upon old Latin legends perhaps poems. Its character is altogether feudal, and it is strictly a picture of society, in France primarily, and secondly in England and the other nations of feudalism, in the twelfth century. The earliest form in which this romance is known is in the French poem—or rather poems, for it consists of several branches or continuations—and is supposed to date from about the middle of the twelfth century. It soon became so popular, that it appeared in different forms in all the languages of Western Europe, except in England, where there appears to have existed no edition of the romance of Reynard the Fox until Caxton printed his prose English version of the story. From that time it became, if possible, more popular in England than elsewhere, and that popularity had hardly diminished down to the commencement of the present century.

The popularity of the story of Reynard caused it to be imitated in a variety of shapes, and this form of satire, in which animals acted the part of men, became altogether popular. In the latter part of the twelfth century, an Anglo-Latin poet, named Nigellus Wireker, composed a very severe satire in elegiac verse, under the title of *Speculum Stultorum*, the "Mirror of Fools." It is not a wise animal like the fox, but a simple animal, the ass, who, under the name of Brunellus, passes among the various ranks and classes of society, and notes their crimes and vices. A prose introduction to this poem informs us that its hero is the representative of the monks in general, who were always longing for some new acquisition which was inconsistent with their profession. In fact, Brunellus is absorbed with the notion that his tail was too short, and his great ambition is to get it lengthened. For this purpose he consults a physician, who, after representing to him in vain the folly of his pursuit, gives him a receipt to make his tail grow longer, and sends him to the celebrated medical school of Salerno to obtain the ingredients. After various adventures, in the course of which he loses a part of his tail instead of its being lengthened, Brunellus proceeds to the University of Paris to study and obtain knowledge; and we are treated with a most amusingly satirical account of the condition and manners of the scholars of that time. Soon convinced of his incapacity for learning, Brunellus abandons the university in despair, and he resolves to enter one of the monastic orders, the character of all which he passes in review. The greater part of the poem consists of a very bitter satire on the corruptions of the monkish orders and of the Church in general. While still hesitating which order to choose, Brunellus falls into the hands of his old master, from whom he had run away in order to seek his fortune in the world, and he is compelled to pass the rest of his days in the same humble and servile condition in which he had begun them.

A more direct imitation of "Reynard the Fox" is found in the early French romance of "Fauvel," the hero of which is neither a fox nor an ass, but a horse. People of all ranks and classes repair to the court of Fauvel, the horse, and furnish abundant matter for satire on the moral, political, and religious hypocrisy which pervaded the whole frame of society. At length the hero resolves to marry, and, in a finely illuminated manuscript of this romance, preserved in the Imperial Library in Paris, this marriage furnishes the subject of a picture, which gives the only representation I have met with of one of the popular burlesque ceremonies which were so common in the middle ages.

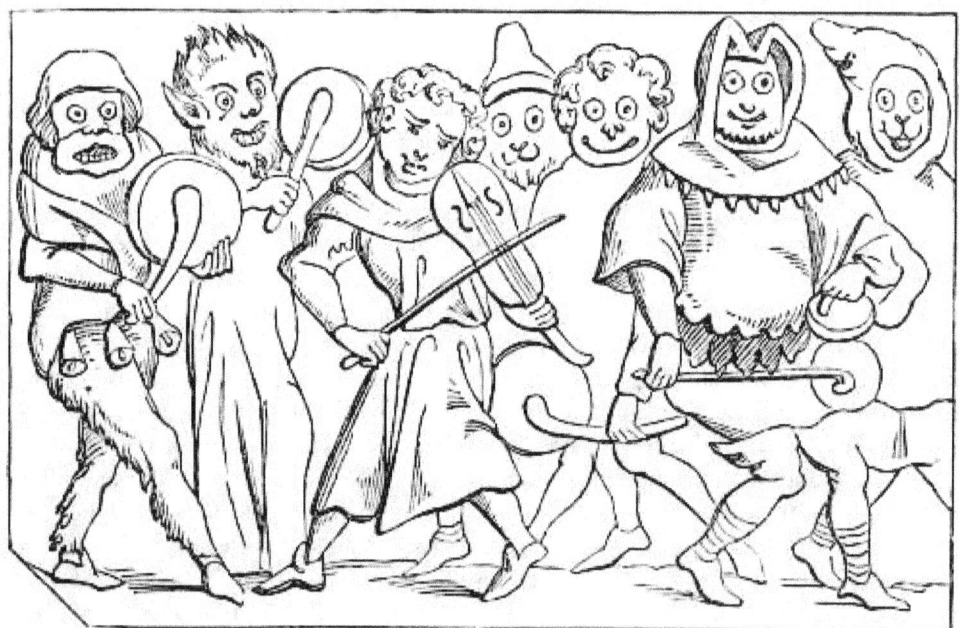

No. 52. A Mediæval Charivari.

Among other such ceremonies, it was customary with the populace, on the occasion of a man's or woman's second marriage, or an ill-sorted match, or on the espousals of people who were obnoxious to their neighbours, to assemble outside the house, and greet them with discordant music. This custom is said to have been practised especially in France, and it was called a *charivari*. There is still a last remnant of it in our country in the music of marrow-bones and cleavers, with which the marriages of butchers are popularly celebrated; but the derivation of the French name appears not to be known. It occurs in old Latin documents, for it gave rise to such scandalous scenes of riot and licentiousness, that the Church did all it could, though in vain, to suppress it. The earliest mention of this custom, furnished in the *Glossarium* of Ducange, is contained in the synodal statutes of the church of Avignon, passed in the year 1337, from which we learn that when such marriages occurred, people forced their way into the houses of the married couple, and carried away their goods, which they were obliged to pay a ransom for before they were returned, and the money thus raised was spent in getting up what is called in the statute relating to it a *Chalvaricum*. It appears from this statute, that the individuals who performed the *charivari* accompanied the happy couple to the church, and returned with them to their residence, with coarse and indecent gestures and discordant music, and uttering scurrilous and indecent abuse, and that they ended with feasting. In the statutes of Meaux, in 1365, and in those of Hugh, bishop of Beziers, in 1368, the same practice is forbidden, under the name of *Charavallium*, and it is mentioned in a document of the year 1372, also quoted by Ducange, under that of *Carivarium*, as then existing at Nîmes. Again, in 1445, the Council of Tours made a decree, forbidding, under pain of excommunication, "the insolences, clamours, sounds, and other tumults practised at second and third nuptials, called by the vulgar a *Charivarium*, on account of the many and grave evils arising out of them."[28] It will be observed that these early allusions to the *charivari* are found almost solely in documents coming from the Roman towns in the south of France, so that this practice was probably one of the many popular customs derived directly from the Romans. When Cotgrave's "Dictionary" was published (that is, in 1632) the practice of the *charivari* appears to have become more general in its existence, as well as its application; for he describes it as "a public defamation, or traducing of; a foule noise made, blacke santus rung, to the shame and disgrace of another; hence an infamous (or infaming) ballad sung, by an armed troupe, under the window of an old dotard, married the day before unto a yong wanton, in mockerie of them both." And, again, a *charivaris de poelles* is explained as "the carting of an infamous person, graced with the harmonie of tinging kettles and frying-pan musicke."[29] The word is now generally used in the sense of a great tumult of discordant music, produced often by a number of persons playing different tunes on different instruments at the same time.

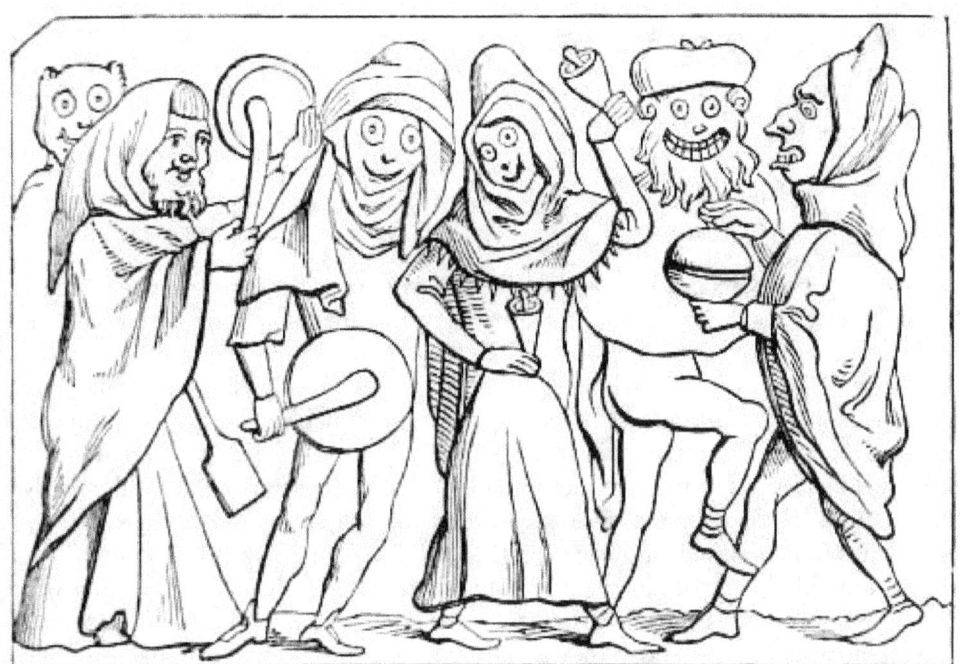

No. 53. Continuation of the Charivari.

As I have stated above, the manuscript of the romance of "Fauvel" is in the Imperial Library in Paris. A copy of this illumination is engraved in Jaime's "Musée de la Caricature," from which our cuts Nos. 52 and 53 are taken. It is divided into three compartments, one above another, in the uppermost of which Fauvel is seen entering the nuptial chamber to his young wife, who is already in bed. The scene in the compartment below, which is copied in our cut No. 52, represents the street outside, and the mock revellers performing the *charivari*, and this is continued in the third, or lowest, compartment, which is represented in our cut No. 53. Down each side of the original illumination is a frame-work of windows, from which people, who have been disturbed by the noise, are looking out upon the tumult. It will be seen that all the performers wear masks, and that they are dressed in burlesque costume. In confirmation of the statement of the ecclesiastical synods as to the licentiousness of these exhibitions, we see one of the performers here disguised as a woman, who lifts up his dress to expose his person while dancing. The musical instruments are no less grotesque than the costumes, for they consist chiefly of kitchen utensils, such as frying-pans, mortars, saucepans, and the like.

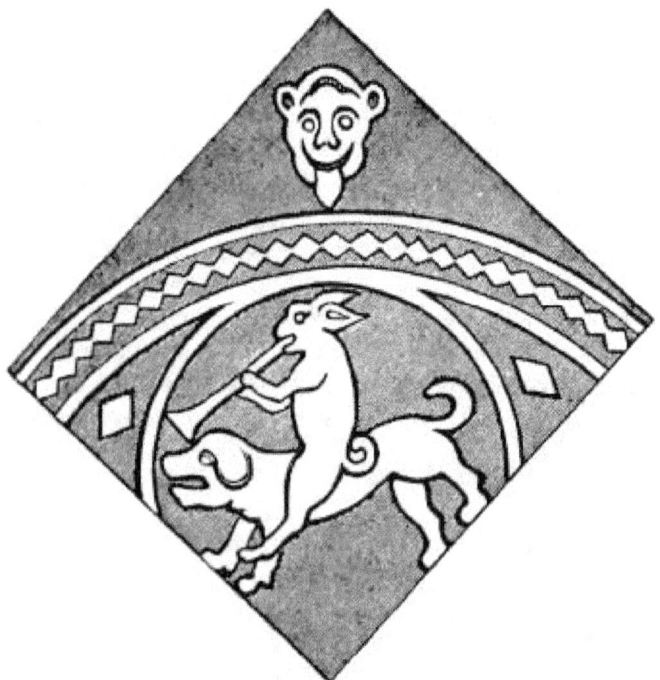

No. 54. The Tables Turned.

There was another series of subjects in which animals were introduced as the instruments of satire. This satire consisted in reverting the position of man with regard to the animals over which he had been accustomed to tyrannise, so that he was subjected to the same treatment from the animals which, in his actual position, he uses towards them. This change of relative position was called in old French and Anglo-Norman, *le monde bestorné*, which was equivalent to the English phrase, "the world turned upside down." It forms the subject of rather old verses, I believe, both in French and English, and individual scenes from it are met with in pictorial representation at a rather early date. During the year 1862, in the course of accidental excavations on the site of the Friary, at Derby, a number of encaustic tiles, such as were used for the floors of the interiors of churches and large buildings, were found.[30] The ornamentation of these tiles, especially of the earlier ones, is, like all mediæval ornamentations, extremely varied, and even these tiles sometimes present subjects of a burlesque and satirical character, though they are more frequently adorned with the arms and badges of benefactors to the church or convent. The tiles found on the site of the priory at Derby are believed to be of the thirteenth century, and one pattern, a diminished copy of which is given in our cut No. 54, presents a subject taken from the *monde bestorné*. The hare, master of his old enemy, the dog, has become hunter himself, and seated upon the dog's back he rides vigorously to the chace, blowing his horn as he goes. The design is spiritedly executed, and its satirical intention is shown by the monstrous and mirthful face, with the tongue lolling out, figured on the outer corner of the tile. It will be seen that four of these tiles are intended to be joined together to make the complete piece. In an illumination in a manuscript of the fourteenth century in the British Museum (MS. Reg. 10 E iv.), the hares are taking a still more severe vengeance on their old enemy. The dog has been caught, brought to trial for his numerous murders, and condemned, and they are represented here (cut No. 55) conducting him in the criminal's cart to the gallows. Our cut No. 56, the subject of which is furnished by one of the carved stalls in Sherborne Minster (it is here copied from the engraving in Carter's "Specimens of Ancient Sculpture"), represents another execution scene, similar in spirit to the former. The geese have seized their old enemy, Reynard, and are hanging him on a gallows, while two monks, who attend the execution, appear to be amused at the energetic manner in which the geese perform their task. Mr. Jewitt mentions two other subjects belonging to this series, one of them taken from an illuminated manuscript; they are, the mouse chasing the cat, and the horse driving the cart—the former human carter in this case taking the place of the horse between the shafts.

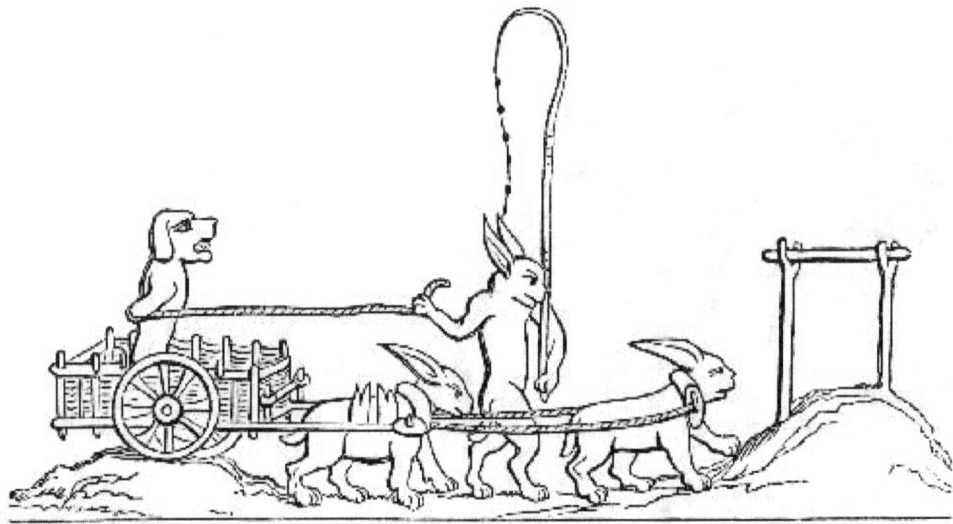

No. 55. Justice in the Hands of the Persecuted.

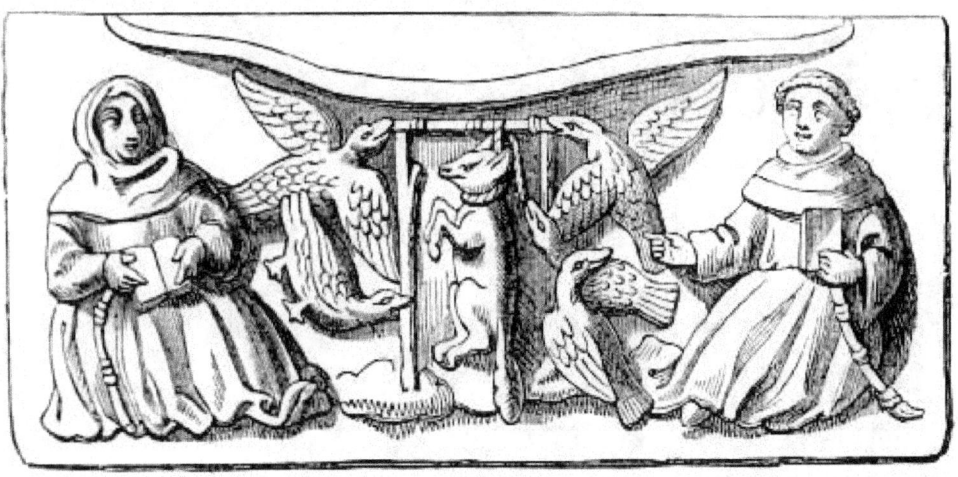

No. 56. Reynard brought to Account at Last.

"The World turned upside down; or, the Folly of Man," has continued amongst us to be a popular chap-book and child's book till within a very few years, and I have now a copy before me printed in London about the year 1790. It consists of a series of rude woodcuts, with a few doggrel verses under each. One of these, entitled "The Ox turned Farmer," represents two men drawing the plough, driven by an ox. In the next, a rabbit is seen turning the spit on which a man is roasting, while a cock holds a ladle and bastes. In a third, we see a tournament, in which the horses are armed and ride upon the men. Another represents the ox killing the butcher. In others we have birds netting men and women; the ass, turned miller, employing the man-miller to carry his sacks; the horse turned groom, and currying the man; and the fishes angling for men and catching them.

In a cleverly sculptured ornament in Beverley Minster, represented in our cut No. 57, the goose herself is represented in a grotesque situation, which might almost give her a place in "The World turned upside down," although it is a mere burlesque, without any apparent satirical aim. The goose has here taken the place of the horse at the blacksmith's, who is vigorously nailing the shoe on her webbed foot.

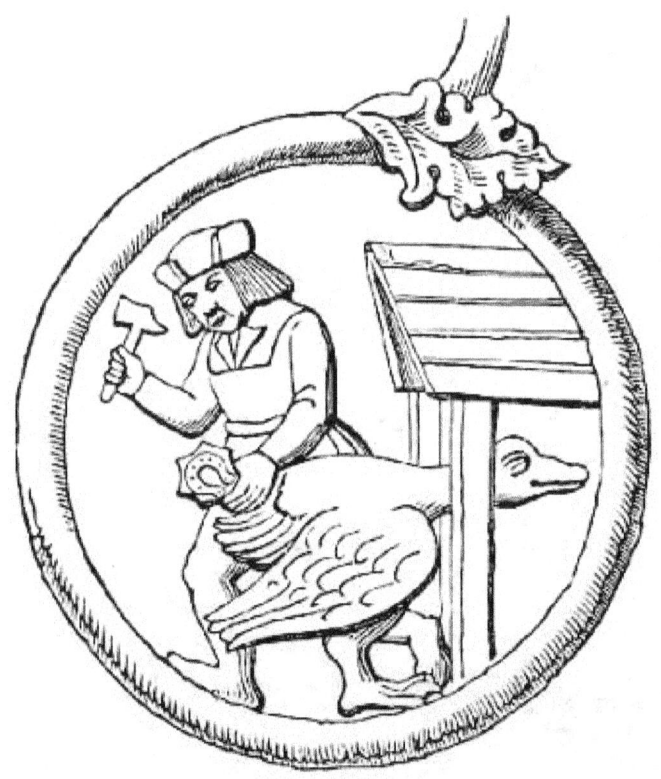

No. 57. Shoeing the Goose.

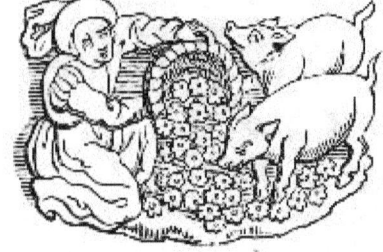

No. 58. Food for Swine.

Burlesque subjects of this description are not uncommon, especially among architectural sculpture and wood-carving, and, at a rather later period, on all ornamental objects. The field for such subjects was so extensive, that the artist had an almost unlimited choice, and therefore his subjects might be almost infinitely varied, though we usually find them running on particular classes. The old popular proverbs, for instance, furnished a fruitful source for drollery, and are at times delineated in an amusingly literal or practical manner. Pictorial proverbs and popular sayings are sometimes met with on the carved misereres. For example, in one of those at Rouen, in Normandy, represented in our cut No. 58, the carver has intended to represent the idea of the old saying, in allusion to misplaced bounty, of throwing pearls to swine, and has given it a much more picturesque and pictorially intelligible form, by introducing a rather dashing female feeding her swine with roses, or rather offering them roses for food, for the swine display no eagerness to feed upon them.

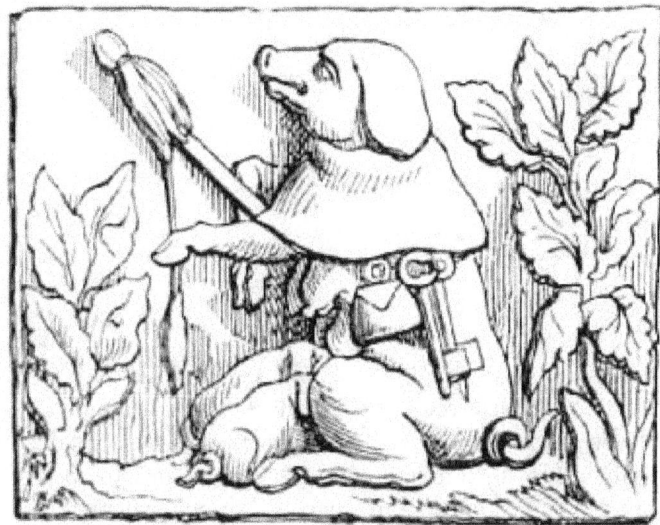

No. 59. The Industrious Sow.

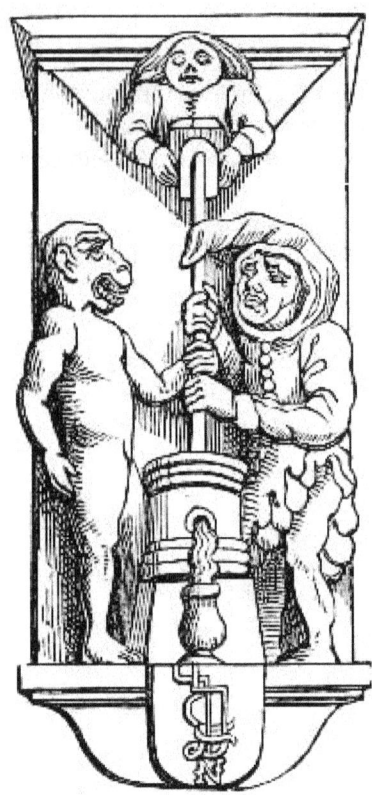

No. 60. Adulteration.

We meet with such subjects as these scattered over all mediæval works of art, and at a somewhat later period they were transferred to other objects, such as the signs of houses. The custom of placing signs over the doors of shops and taverns, was well known to the ancients, as is abundantly manifested by their frequent occurrence in the ruins of Pompeii; but in the middle ages, the use of signs and badges was universal, and as—contrary to the apparent practice in Pompeii, where certain badges were appropriated to certain trades and professions—every individual was free to choose his own sign, the variety was unlimited. Many still had reference, no doubt, to the particular calling of those to whom they belonged, while others were of a religious character, and indicated the saint under whose protection the householder had placed himself. Some people took animals for their signs, others monstrous or burlesque figures; and, in fact, there were hardly any of the subjects of caricature or burlesque familiar to the mediæval sculptor and illuminator which did not from time to time appear on these popular signs. A few of the old signs still preserved, especially in the quaint old towns of France, Germany, and the Netherlands, show us how frequently they were made the instruments of popular satire. A sign not uncommon in France was *La Truie qui file* (the sow spinning). Our cut No. 59 represents this subject as treated on an old sign, a carving in bas-relief of the sixteenth century, on a house in the Rue du Marché-aux-Poirées, in Rouen. The sow appears here in the character of the industrious housewife, employing herself in spinning at the same time that she is attending to the wants of her children. There is a singularly satirical sign at Beauvais, on a house which was formerly occupied by an *épicier-moutardier*, or grocer who made mustard, in the Rue du Châtel. In front of this sign, which is represented in our cut No. 60, appears a large mustard-mill, on one side of which stands Folly with a staff in her hand, with which she is stirring the mustard, while an ape with a sort of sardonic grin, throws in a seasoning, which may be conjectured by his posture.[31] The trade-mark of the individual who adopted this strange device, is carved below.

CHAPTER VI.

THE MONKEY IN BURLESQUE AND CARICATURE.—TOURNAMENTS AND SINGLE COMBATS.—MONSTROUS COMBINATIONS OF ANIMAL FORMS.—CARICATURES ON COSTUME.—THE HAT.—THE HELMET.—LADIES' HEAD-DRESSES.—THE GOWN, AND ITS LONG SLEEVES.

The fox, the wolf, and their companions, were introduced as instruments of satire, on account of their peculiar characters; but there were other animals which were also favourites with the satirist, because they displayed an innate inclination to imitate; they formed, as it were, natural parodies upon mankind. I need hardly say that of these the principal and most remarkable was the monkey. This animal must have been known to our Anglo-Saxon forefathers from a remote period, for they had a word for it in their own language—*apa*, our *ape*. Monkey is a more modern name, and seems to be equivalent with maniken, or a little man. The earliest *Bestiaries*, or popular treatises on natural history, give anecdotes illustrative of the aptness of this animal for imitating the actions of men, and ascribe to it a degree of understanding which would almost raise it above the level of the brute creation. Philip de Thaun, an Anglo-Norman poet of the reign of Henry I., in his *Bestiary*, tells us that "the monkey, by imitation, as books say, counterfeits what it sees, and mocks people:"—

Li singe par figure, si cum dit escripture,
Ceo que il vait contrefait, de gent escar hait.[32]

/He goes on to inform us, as a proof of the extraordinary instinct of this animal, that it has more affection for some of its cubs than for others, and that, when running away, it carried those which it liked before it, and those it disliked behind its back. The sketch from the illuminated manuscript of the Romance of the Comte d'Artois, of the fifteenth century, which forms our cut No. 61, represents the monkey, carrying, of course, its favourite child before it in its flight, and what is more, it is taking that flight mounted on a donkey. A monkey on horseback appears not to have been a novelty, as we shall see in the sequel.

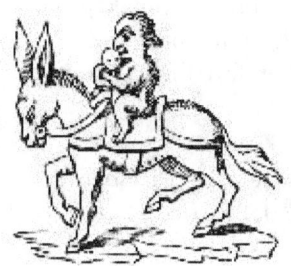

No. 61. A Monkey Mounted.

Alexander Neckam, a very celebrated English scholar of the latter part of the twelfth century, and one of the most interesting of the early mediæval writers on natural history, gives us many anecdotes, which show us how much attached our mediæval forefathers were to domesticated animals, and how common a practice it was to keep them in their houses. The baronial castle appears often to have presented the appearance of a menagerie of animals, among which some were of that strong and ferocious character that rendered it necessary to keep them in close confinement, while others, such as monkeys, roamed about the buildings at will. One of Neckam's stories is very curious in regard to our subject, for it shows that the people in those days exercised their tamed animals in practically caricaturing contemporary weaknesses and fashions. This writer remarks that "the nature of the ape is so ready at acting, by ridiculous gesticulations, the representations of things it has seen, and thus gratifying the vain curiosity of worldly men in public exhibitions, that it will even dare to imitate a military conflict. A jougleur (*histrio*) was in the habit of constantly taking two monkeys to the military exercises which are commonly called tournaments, that the labour of teaching might be diminished by frequent inspection. He afterwards taught two dogs to carry these apes, who sat on their backs, furnished with proper arms. Nor did they want spurs, with which they strenuously urged on the dogs. Having broken their lances, they drew out their swords, with which they spent many blows on each other's shields. Who at this sight could refrain from laughter?" [33]

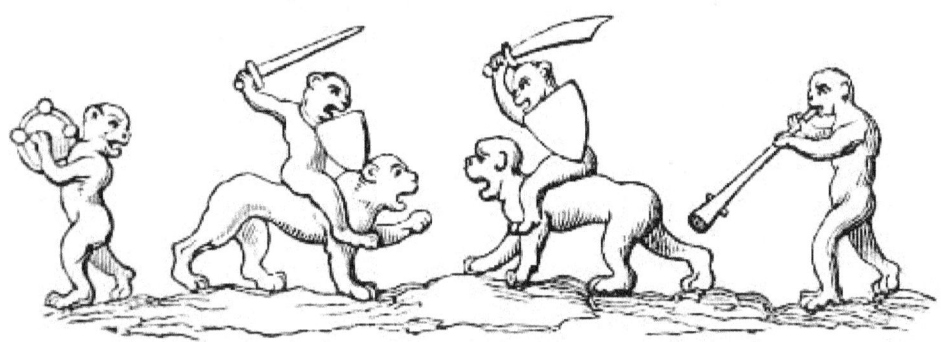

No. 62. A Tournament.

Such contemporary caricatures of the mediæval tournament, which was in its greatest fashion during the period from the twelfth to the fourteenth century, appear to have been extremely popular, and are not unfrequently represented in the borders of illuminated manuscripts. The manuscript now so well known as "Queen Mary's Psalter" (MS. Reg. 2 B vii.), and written and illuminated very early in the fourteenth century, contains not a few illustrations of this description. One of these, which forms our cut No. 62, represents a tournament not much unlike that described by Alexander Neckam, except that the monkeys are here riding upon other monkeys, and not upon dogs. In fact, all the individuals here engaged are monkeys, and the parody is completed by the introduction of the trumpeter on one side, and of minstrelsy, represented by a monkey playing on the tabor, on the other; or, perhaps, the two monkeys are simply playing on the pipe and tabor, which were looked upon as the lowest description of minstrelsy, and are therefore the more aptly introduced into the scene.

The same manuscript has furnished us with the cut No. 63. Here the combat takes place between a monkey and a stag, the latter having the claws of a griffin. They are mounted, too, on rather nondescript animals—one having the head and body of a lion, with the forefeet of an eagle; the other having a head somewhat like that of a lion, on a lion's body, with the hind parts of a bear. This subject may, perhaps, be intended as a burlesque on the mediæval romances, filled with combats between the Christians and the Saracens; for the ape—who, in the moralisations which accompany the *Bestiaries*, is said to represent the devil—is here armed with what are evidently intended for the sabre and shield of a Saracen, while the flag carries the shield and lance of a Christian knight.

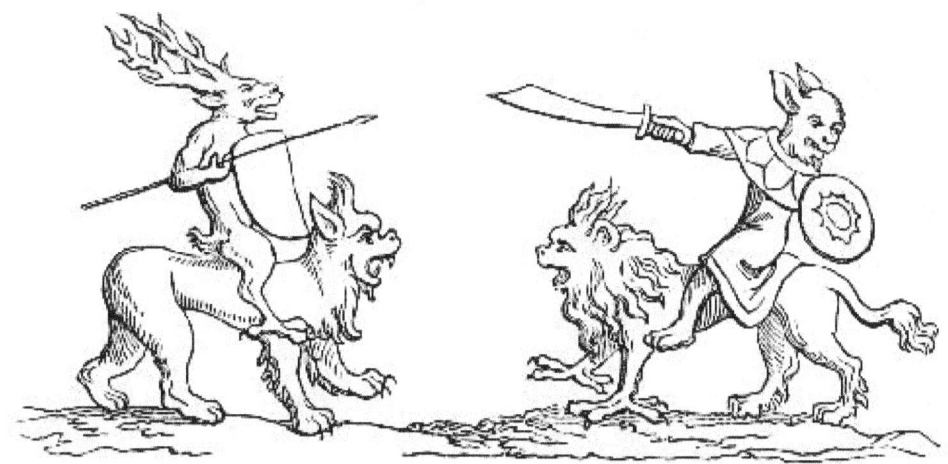

No. 63. A Feat of Arms.

The love of the mediæval artists for monstrous figures of animals, and for mixtures of animals and men, has been alluded to in a former chapter. The combatants in the accompanying cut (No. 64), taken from the same manuscript, present a sort of combination of the rider and the animal, and they again seem to be intended for a Saracen and a Christian. The figure to the right, which is composed of the body of a satyr, with the feet of a goose and the wings of a dragon, is armed with a similar Saracenic sabre; while that to the left, which is on the whole less monstrous, wields a Norman sword. Both have human faces below the navel as well as above, which was a favourite idea in the grotesque of the middle ages. Our mediæval forefathers appear to have had a decided taste for monstrosities of every description, and especially for mixtures of different kinds of animals, and of animals and men. There is no doubt, to judge by the anecdotes recorded by such writers as Giraldus Cambrensis, that a belief in the existence of such unnatural creatures was widely entertained. In his account of Ireland, this writer tells us of animals which were half ox and half man, half stag and half cow, and half dog and half monkey.[34] It is certain that there was a general belief in such animals, and nobody could be more credulous than Giraldus himself.

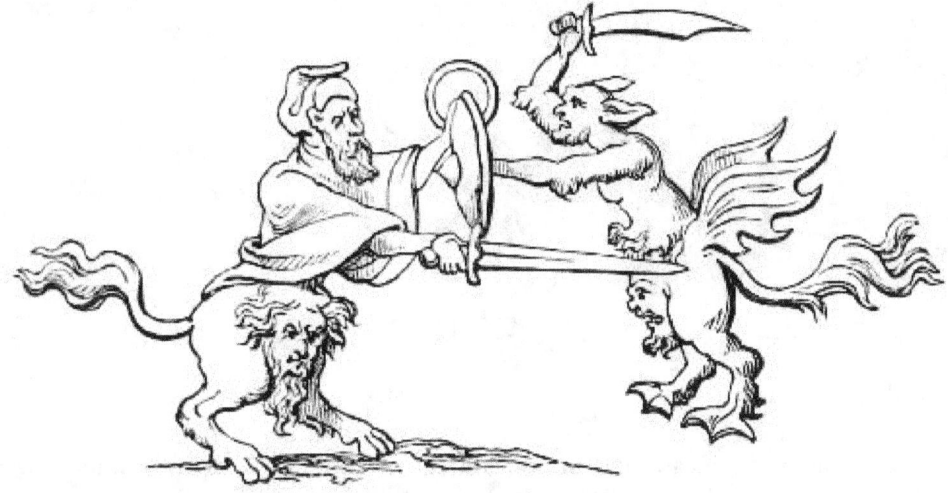

No. 64. A Terrible Combat.

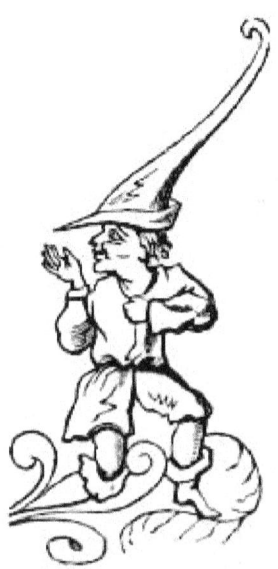

No. 65. Fashionable Dress.

The design to caricature, which is tolerably evident in the subjects just given, is still more apparent in other grotesques that adorn the borders of the mediæval manuscripts, as well as in some of the mediæval carvings and sculpture. Thus, in our cut No. 65, taken from one of the borders in the Romance of the Comte d'Artois, a manuscript of the fifteenth century, we cannot fail to recognise an attempt at turning to ridicule the contemporary fashions in dress. The hat is only an exaggerated form of one which appears to have been commonly used in France in the latter half of the fifteenth century, and which appears frequently in illuminated manuscripts executed in Burgundy; and the boot also belongs to the same period. The latter reappeared at different times, until at length it became developed into the modern top-boots. In cut No. 66, from the same manuscript, where it forms the letter T, we have the same form of hat, still more exaggerated, and combined at the same time with grotesque faces.

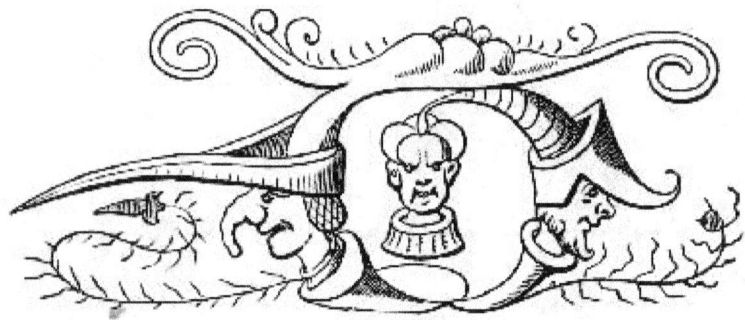

No. 66. Heads and Hats.

Caricatures on costume are by no means uncommon among the artistic remains of the middle ages, and are not confined to illuminated manuscripts. The fashionable dresses of those days went into far more ridiculous excesses of shape than anything we see in our times—at least, so far as we can believe the drawings in the manuscripts; but these, however seriously intended, were constantly degenerating into caricature, from circumstances which are easily explained, and which have, in fact, been explained already in their influence on other parts of our subject. The mediæval artists in general were not very good delineators of form, and their outlines are much inferior to their finish. Conscious of this, though perhaps unknowingly, they sought to remedy the defect in a spirit which has always been adopted in the early stages of art-progress—they aimed at making themselves understood by giving a special prominence to the peculiar characteristics of the objects they wished to represent. These were the points which naturally attracted people's first attention, and the resemblance was felt most by people in general when these points were put forward in excessive prominence in the picture. The dresses, perhaps, hardly existed in the exact forms in which we see them in the illuminations, or at least those were only exceptions to the generally more moderate forms; and hence, in using these pictorial records as materials for the history of costume, we ought to make a certain allowance for exaggeration—we ought, indeed, to treat them almost as caricatures. In fact, much of what we now call caricature, was then characteristic of serious art, and of what was considered its high development. Many of the attempts which have been made of late years to introduce ancient costume on the stage, would probably be regarded by the people who lived in the age which they were intended to represent, as a mere design to turn them into ridicule. Nevertheless, the fashions in dress were, especially from the twelfth century to the sixteenth, carried to a great degree of extravagance, and were not only the objects of satire and caricature, but drew forth the indignant declamations of the Church, and furnished a continuous theme to the preachers. The contemporary chronicles abound with bitter reflections on the extravagance in costume, which was considered as one of the outward signs of the great corruption of particular periods; and they give us not unfrequent examples of the coarse manner in which the clergy discussed them in their sermons. The readers of Chaucer will remember the manner in which this subject is treated in the "Parson's Tale." In this respect the satirists of the Church went hand in hand with the pictorial caricaturists of the illuminated manuscripts, and of the sculptures with which we sometimes meet in contemporary architectural ornamentation. In the latter, this class of caricature is perhaps less frequent, but it is sometimes very expressive. The very curious *misereres* in the church of Ludlow, in Shropshire, present the caricature reproduced in our cut No. 67. It represents an ugly, and, to judge by the expression of the countenance, an ill-tempered old woman, wearing the fashionable head-dress of the earlier half of the fifteenth century, which seems to have been carried to its greatest extravagance in the beginning of the reign of Henry VI. It is the style of coiffure known especially as the horned head-dress, and the very name carries with it a sort of relationship to an individual who was notoriously horned—the spirit of evil. This dashing dame of the olden time appears to have struck terror into two unfortunates who have fallen within her influence, one of whom, as though he took her for a new Gorgon, is attempting to cover himself with his buckler, while the other, apprehending danger of another kind, is prepared to defend himself with his sword. The details of the head-dress in this figure are interesting for the history of costume.

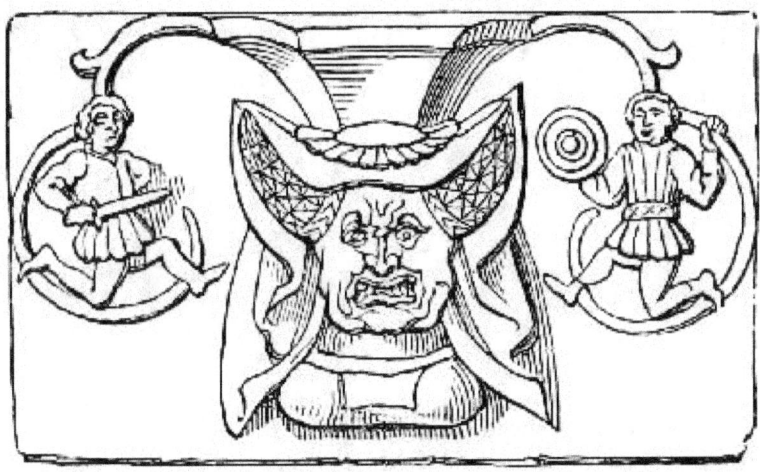

No. 67. A Fashionable Beauty.

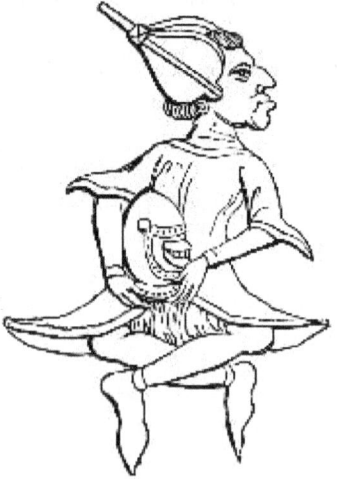

No. 68. A Man of War.

Our next cut, No. 68, is taken from a manuscript in private possession, which is now rather well known among antiquaries by the name of the "Luttrell Psalter," and which belongs to the fourteenth century. It seems to involve a satire on the aristocratic order of society—on the knight who was distinguished by his helmet, his shield, and his armour. The individual here represented presents a type which is anything but aristocratic. While he holds a helmet in his hand to show the meaning of the satire, his own helmet, which he wears on his head, is simply a bellows. He may be a knight of the kitchen, or perhaps a mere *quistron*, or kitchen lad.

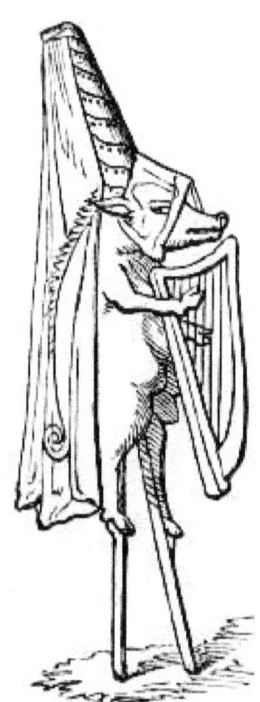

No. 69. A Lady's Head-dress.

We have just seen a caricature of one of the ladies' head-dresses of the earlier half of the fifteenth century, and our cut No. 69, from an illuminated manuscript in the British Museum of the latter half of the same century (MS. Harl., No. 4379), furnishes us with a caricature of a head-dress of a different character, which came into fashion in the reign of our Edward IV. The horned head-dress of the previous generation had been entirely laid aside, and the ladies adopted in its place a sort of steeple-shaped head-dress, or rather of the form of a spire, made by rolling a piece of linen into the form of a long cone. Over this lofty cap was thrown a piece of fine lawn or muslin, which descended almost to the ground, and formed, as it were, two wings. A short transparent veil was thrown over the face, and reached not quite to the chin, resembling rather closely the veils in use among our ladies of the present day (1864). The whole head-dress, indeed, has been preserved by the Norman peasantry; for it may be observed that, during the feudal ages, the fashions in France and England were always identical. These steeple head-dresses greatly provoked the indignation of the clergy, and zealous preachers attacked them roughly in their sermons. A French monk, named Thomas Conecte, distinguished himself especially in this crusade, and inveighed against the head-dress with such effect, that we are assured that many of the women threw down their head-dresses in the middle of the sermon, and made a bonfire of them at its conclusion. The zeal of the preacher soon extended itself to the populace, and, for a while, when ladies appeared in this head-dress in public, they were exposed to be pelted by the rabble. Under such a double persecution it disappeared for a moment, but when the preacher was no longer present, it returned again, and, to use the words of the old writer who has preserved this anecdote, "the women who, like snails in a fright, had drawn in their horns, shot them out again as soon as the danger was over." The caricaturist would hardly overlook so extravagant a fashion, and accordingly the manuscript in the British Museum, just mentioned, furnishes us with the subject of our cut No. 69. In those times, when the passions were subjected to no restraint, the fine ladies indulged in such luxury and licentiousness, that the caricaturist has chosen as their fit representative a sow, who wears the objectionable head-dress in full fashion. The original forms one of the illustrations of a copy of the historian Froissart, and was, therefore, executed in France, or, more probably, in Burgundy.

The sermons and satires against extravagance in costume began at an early period. The Anglo-Norman ladies, in the earlier part of the twelfth century, first brought in vogue in our island this extravagance in fashion, which quickly fell under the lash of satirist and caricaturist. It was first exhibited in the robes rather than in the head-dress. These Anglo-Norman ladies are understood to have first introduced stays, in order to give an artificial appearance of slenderness to their waists; but the greatest extravagance appeared in the forms of their sleeves. The robe, or gown, instead of being loose, as among the Anglo-Saxons, was laced close round the body, and the sleeves, which fitted the arm tightly till they reached the elbows, or sometimes nearly to the wrist, then suddenly became larger, and hung down to an extravagant length, often trailing on the ground, and sometimes shortened by means of a knot. The gown, also, was itself worn very long. The clergy preached against these extravagances in fashion, and at times, it is said, with effect; and they fell under the vigorous lash of the satirist. In a class of satires which became extremely popular in the twelfth century, and which produced in the thirteenth the immortal poem of Dante—the visions of purgatory and of hell—these contemporary extravagances in fashion are held up to public detestation, and are made the subject of severe punishment. They were looked upon as among the outward forms of pride. It arose, no doubt, from this taste—from the darker shade which spread over men's minds in the twelfth century—that demons, instead of animals, were introduced to personify the evil-doers of the time. Such is the figure (cut No. 70) which we take from a very interesting manuscript in the British Museum (MS. Cotton. Nero, C iv.). The demon is here dressed in the fashionable gown with its long sleeves, of which one appears to have been usually much longer than the other. Both the gown and sleeve are shortened by means of knots, while the former is brought close round the waist by tight lacing. It is a picture of the use of stays made at the time of their first introduction.

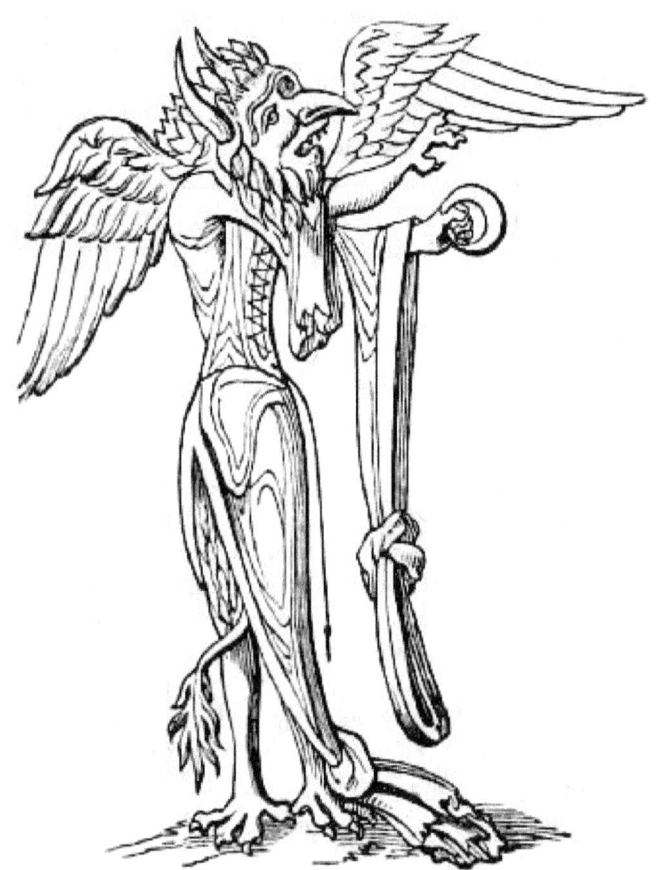

No. 70. Sin in Satins.

This superfluity of length in the different parts of the dress was a subject of complaint and satire at various and very distant periods, and contemporary illuminations of a perfectly serious character show that these complaints were not without foundation.

CHAPTER VII.

PRESERVATION OF THE CHARACTER OF THE MIMUS AFTER THE FALL OF THE EMPIRE.—THE MINSTREL AND JOGELOUR.—HISTORY OF POPULAR STORIES.— THE FABLIAUX.—ACCOUNT OF THEM.—THE CONTES DEVOTS.

I have already remarked that, upon the fall of the Roman empire, the popular institutions of the Romans were more generally preserved to the middle ages than those of a higher and more refined character. This is understood without difficulty, when we consider that the lower class of the population—in the towns, what we might perhaps call the lower and middle classes—continued to exist much the same as before, while the barbarian conquerors came in and took the place of the ruling classes. The drama, which had never much hold upon the love of the Roman populace, was lost, and the theatres and the amphitheatres, which had been supported only by the wealth of the imperial court and of the ruling class, were abandoned and fell into ruin; but the *mimus*, who furnished mirth to the people, continued to exist, and probably underwent no immediate change in his character. It will be well to state again the chief characteristics of the ancient *mimus*, before we proceed to describe his mediæval representative.

The grand aim of the *mimus* was to make people laugh, and he employed generally every means he knew of for effecting this purpose, by language, by gestures or motions of the body, or by dress. Thus he carried, strapped over his loins, a wooden sword, which was called *gladius histricus* and *clunaculum*, and wore sometimes a garment made of a great number of small pieces of cloth of different colours, which was hence called *centunculus*, or the hundred-patched dress.[35] These two characteristics have been preserved in the modern harlequin. Other peculiarities of costume may conveniently be left undescribed; the female mimæ sometimes exhibited themselves unrestricted by dress. They danced and sung; repeated jokes and told merry stories; recited or acted farces and scandalous anecdotes; performed what we now call mimicry, a word derived from the name of mimus; and they put themselves in strange postures, and made frightful faces. They sometimes acted the part of a fool or zany (*morio*), or of a madman. They added to these performances that of the conjurer or juggler (*præstigiator*), and played tricks of sleight of hand. The mimi performed in the streets and public places, or in the theatres, and especially at festivals, and they were often employed at private parties, to entertain the guests at a supper.

We trace the existence of this class of performers during the earlier period of the middle ages by the expressions of hostility towards them used from time to time by the ecclesiastical writers, and the denunciations of synods and councils, which have been quoted in a former chapter.[36] Nevertheless, it is evident from many allusions to them, that they found their way into the monastic houses, and were in great favour not only among the monks, but among the nuns also; that they were introduced into the religious festivals; and that they were tolerated even in the churches. It is probable that they long continued to be known in Italy and the countries near the centre of Roman influence, and where the Latin language was continued, by their old name of *mimus*. The writers of the mediæval vocabularies appear all to have been much better acquainted with the meaning of this word than of most of the Latin words of the same class, and they evidently had a class of performers existing in their own times to whom they considered that the name applied. The Anglo-Saxon vocabularies interpret the Latin *mimus* by *glig-mon*, a gleeman. In Anglo-Saxon, *glig* or *gliu* meant mirth and game of every description, and as the Anglo-Saxon teachers who compiled the vocabularies give, as synonyms of *mimus*, the words *scurra*, *jocista*, and *pantomimus*, it is evident that all these were included in the character of the gleeman, and that the latter was quite identical with his Roman type. It was the Roman *mimus* introduced into Saxon England. We have no traces of the existence of such a class of performers among the Teutonic race before they became acquainted with the civilisation of imperial Rome. We know from drawings in contemporary illuminated manuscripts that the performances of the gleeman did include music, singing, and dancing, and also the tricks of mountebanks and jugglers, such as throwing up and catching knives and balls, and performing with tamed bears, &c.[37]

But even among the peoples who preserved the Latin language, the word *mimus* was gradually exchanged for others employed to signify the same thing. The word *jocus* had been used in the signification of a jest, playfulness, *jocari* signified to jest, and *joculator* was a word for a jester; but, in the debasement of the language, *jocus* was taken in the signification of everything which created mirth. It became, in the course of time the French word *jeu*, and the Italian *gioco*, or *giuoco*. People introduced a form of the verb, *jocare*, which became the French *juer*, to play or perform. *Joculator* was then used in the sense of *mimus*. In French the word became *jogléor*, or *jougléor*, and in its later form *jougleur*. I may remark that, in mediæval manuscripts, it is almost impossible to distinguish between the *u* and the *n*, and that modern writers have misread this last word as *jongleur*, and thus introduced into the language a word which never existed, and which ought to be abandoned. In old English, as we see in Chaucer, the usual form was *jogelere*. The mediæval joculator, or jougleur, embraced all the attributes of the Roman *mimus*,[38] and perhaps more. In the first place he was very often a poet himself, and composed the pieces which it was one of his duties to sing or recite. These were chiefly songs, or stories, the latter usually told in verse, and so many of them are preserved in manuscripts that they form a very numerous and important class of mediæval literature. The songs were commonly satirical and abusive, and they were made use of for purposes of general or personal vituperation. Out of them, indeed, grew the political songs of a later period. There were female jougleurs, and both sexes danced, and, to create mirth among those who encouraged them, they practised a variety of performances, such as mimicking people, making wry and ugly faces, distorting their bodies into strange postures, often exposing their persons in a very unbecoming manner, and performing many vulgar and indecent acts, which it is not necessary to describe more particularly. They carried about with them for exhibition tame bears, monkeys, and other animals, taught to perform the actions of men. As early as the thirteenth century, we find them including among their other accomplishments that of dancing upon the tight-rope. Finally, the jougleurs performed tricks of sleight of hand, and were often conjurers and magicians. As, in modern times, the jougleurs of the middle ages gradually passed away, sleight of hand appears to have become their principal accomplishment, and the name only was left in the modern word *juggler*. The jougleurs of the middle ages, like the mimi of antiquity, wandered about from place to place, and often from country to country, sometimes singly and at others in companies, exhibited their performances in the roads and streets, repaired to all great festivals, and were employed especially in the baronial hall, where, by their songs, stories, and other performances, they created mirth after dinner.

This class of society had become known by another name, the origin of which is not so easily explained. The primary meaning of the Latin word *minister* was a servant, one who ministers to another, either in his wants or in his pleasures and amusements. It was applied particularly to the cup-bearer. In low Latinity, a diminutive of this word was formed, *minestellus*, or *ministrellus*, a petty servant, or minister. When we first meet with this word, which is not at a very early date, it is used as perfectly synonymous with *joculator*, and, as the word is certainly of Latin derivation, it is clear that it was from it the middle ages derived the French word *menestrel* (the modern *ménétrier*), and the English *minstrel*. The mimi or jougleurs were perhaps considered as the petty ministers to the amusements of their lord, or of him who for the time employed them. Until the close of the middle ages, the minstrel and the jougleur were absolutely identical. Possibly the former may have been considered the more courtly of the two names. But in England, as the middle ages disappeared, and lost their influence on society sooner than in France, the word minstrel remained attached only to the musical part of the functions of the old mimus, while, as just observed, the juggler took the sleight of hand and the mountebank tricks. In modern French, except where employed technically by the antiquary, the word *ménétrier* means a fiddler.

The jougleurs, or minstrels, formed a very numerous and important, though a low and despised, class of mediæval society. The dulness of every-day life in a feudal castle or mansion required something more than ordinary excitement in the way of amusement, and the old family bard, who continually repeated to the Teutonic chief the praises of himself and his ancestors, was soon felt to be a wearisome companion. The mediæval knights and their ladies wanted to laugh, and to make them laugh sufficiently it required that the jokes, or tales, or comic performances, should be broad, coarse, and racy, with a good spicing of violence and of the wonderful. Hence the jougleur was always welcome to the feudal mansion, and he seldom went away dissatisfied. But the subject of the present chapter is rather the literature of the jougleur than his personal history, and, having traced his origin to the Roman mimus, we will now proceed to one class of his performances.

It has been stated that the mimus and the jougleurs told stories. Of those of the former, unfortunately, none are preserved, except, perhaps, in a few anecdotes scattered in the pages of such writers as Apuleius and Lucian, and we are obliged to guess at their character, but of the stories of the jougleurs a considerable number has been preserved. It becomes an interesting question how far these stories have been derived from the mimi, handed down traditionally from mimus to jougleur, how far they are native in our race, or how far they were derived at a later date from other sources. And in considering this question, we must not forget that the mediæval jougleurs were not the only representatives of the mimi, for among the Arabs of the East also there had originated from them, modified under different circumstances, a very important class of minstrels and story-tellers, and with these the jougleurs of the west were brought into communication at the commencement of the crusades. There can be no doubt that a very large number of the stories of the jougleurs were borrowed from the East, for the evidence is furnished by the stories themselves; and there can be little doubt also that the jougleurs improved themselves, and underwent some modification, by their intercourse with Eastern performers of the same class.

On the other hand, we have traces of the existence of these popular stories before the jougleurs can have had communication with the East. Thus, as already mentioned, we find, composed in Germany, apparently in the tenth century, in rhythmical Latin, the well-known story of the wife of a merchant who bore a child during the long absence of her husband, and who excused herself by stating that her pregnancy had been the result of swallowing a flake of snow in a snow-storm. This, and another of the same kind, were evidently intended to be sung. Another poem in popular Latin verse, which Grimm and Schmeller, who edited it,[39] believe may be of the eleventh century, relates a very amusing story of an adventurer named Unibos, who, continually caught in his own snares, finishes by getting the better of all his enemies, and becoming rich, by mere ingenious cunning and good fortune. This story is not met with among those of the jougleurs, as far as they are yet known, but, curiously enough, Lover found it existing orally among the Irish peasantry, and inserted the Irish story among his "Legends of Ireland." It is a curious illustration of the pertinacity with which the popular stories descend along with peoples through generations from the remotest ages of antiquity. The same story is found in an oriental form among the tales of the Tartars published in French by Guenlette.

The people of the middle ages, who took their word *fable* from the Latin *fabula*, which they appear to have understood as a mere term for any short narration, included under it the stories told by the mimi and jougleurs; but, in the fondness of the middle ages for diminutives, by which they intended to express familiarity and attachment, applied to them more particularly the Latin *fabella*, which in the old French became *fablel*, or, more usually, *fabliau*. The fabliaux of the jougleurs form a most important class of the comic literature of the middle ages. They must have been wonderfully numerous, for a very large quantity of them still remain, and these are only the small portion of what once existed, which have escaped perishing like the others by the accident of being written in manuscripts which have had the fortune to survive; while manuscripts containing others have no doubt perished, and it is probable that many were only preserved orally, and never written down at all.[40] The recital of these fabliaux appears to have been the favourite employment of the jougleurs, and they became so popular that the mediæval preachers turned them into short stories in Latin prose, and made use of them as illustrations in their sermons. Many collections of these short Latin stories are found in manuscripts which had served as note-books to the preachers,[41] and out of them was originally compiled that celebrated mediæval book called the "Gesta Romanorum."

It is to be regretted that the subjects and language of a large portion of these fabliaux are such as to make it impossible to present them before modern readers, for they furnish singularly interesting and minute pictures of mediæval life in all classes of society. Domestic scenes are among those most frequent, and they represent the interior of the mediæval household in no favourable point of view. The majority of these tell loose stories of husbands deceived by their fair spouses, or of tricks played upon unsuspecting damsels. In some instances the treatment of the husband is perhaps what may be called of a less objectionable character, as in the fabliau of La Vilain Mire (the clown doctor), printed in Barbazan (iii. 1), which was the origin of Molière's well-known comedy of "Le Médecin malgré lui." A rich peasant married the daughter of a poor knight; it was of course a marriage of ambition on his part, and of interest on hers—one of those ill-sorted matches which, according to feudal sentiments, could never be happy, and in which the wife was considered as privileged to treat her husband with all possible contempt. In this instance the lady hit upon an ingenious mode of punishing her husband for his want of submission to her ill-treatment. Messengers from the king passed that way, seeking a skilful doctor to cure the king's daughter of a dangerous malady. The lady secretly informed these messengers that her husband was a physician of extraordinary talent, but of an eccentric temper, for he would never acknowledge or exercise his art until first subjected to a severe beating. The husband is seized, bound, and carried by force to the king's court, where, of course, he denies all knowledge of the healing art, but a severe beating obliges him to compliance, and he is successful by a combination of impudence and chance. This is only the beginning of the poor man's miseries. Instead of being allowed to go home, his fame has become so great that he is retained at court for the public good, and, with a rapid succession of patients, fearful of the results of his conscious ignorance, he refuses them all, and is subjected in every case to the same ill-treatment to force his compliance. The examples in which the husband, on the other hand, outwits the wife are few. A fabliau by a poet who gives himself the name of Cortebarbe, printed also by Barbazan (iii. 398), relates how three blind beggars were deceived by a clerc, or scholar, of Paris, who met them on the road near Compiègne. The clerk pretended to give the three beggars a bezant, which was then a good sum of money, and they hastened joyfully to the next tavern, where they ordered a plentiful supper, and feasted to their hearts' content. But, in fact, the clerk had not given them a bezant at all, although, as he said he did so, and they could only judge by their hearing, they imagined that they had the coin, and each thought that it was in the keeping of one of his companions. Thus, when the time of paying came, and the money was not forthcoming, in the common belief that one of the three had received the bezant and intended to keep it and cheat the others, they quarrelled violently, and from abuse soon came to blows. The landlord, drawn to the spot by the uproar, and informed of the state of the case, accused the three blind men of a conspiracy to cheat him, and demanded payment with great threats. The clerk of Paris, who had followed them to the inn, and taken his lodging there in order to witness the result, delivered the blind men by an equally ingenious trick which he plays upon the landlord and the priest of the parish.

Some of these stories have for their subject tricks played among thieves. In one printed by Méon (i. 124), we have the story of a rich but simple villan, or countryman, named Brifaut, who is robbed at market by a cunning sharper, and severely corrected by his wife for his carelessness. Robbery, both by force and by sleight of hand and craft, prevailed to an extraordinary degree during the middle ages. The plot of the fabliau of Barat and Haimet, by Jean de Boves (Barbazan, iv. 233), turns upon a trial of skill among three robbers to determine who shall commit the cleverest act of thievery, and the result is, at least, an extremely amusing story. It may be mentioned as an example of the numerous stories which the jougleurs certainly obtained from the East, that the well-known story of the Hunchback in the "Arabian Nights" appears among them in two or three different forms.

The social vices of the middle ages, their general licentiousness, the prevalence of injustice and extortion, are very fully exposed to view in these compositions, in which no class of society is spared. The villan, or peasant, is always treated very contemptuously; he formed the class from which the jougleur received least benefit. But the aristocracy, the great barons, the lords of the soil, come in for their full share of satire, and they no doubt enjoyed the ridiculous pictures of their own order. I will not venture to introduce the reader to female life in the baronial castle, as it appears in many of these stories, and as it is no doubt truly painted, although, of course, in many instances, much exaggerated. We have already seen how in the story of Reynard, the character of mediæval society was represented by the long struggle between brute force represented by the wolf, the emblem of the aristocratic class, and the low astuteness of the fox, or the unaristocratic class. The success of the craft of the human fox over the force of his lordly antagonist is often told in the fabliaux in ludicrous colours. In that of Trubert, printed by Méon (i. 192), the "duke" of a country, with his wife and family, become repeatedly the dupes of the gross deceptions of a poor but impudent peasant. These satires upon the aristocracy were no doubt greatly enjoyed by the good *bourgeoisie*, who, in their turn, furnished abundance of stories, of the drollest description, to provoke the mirth of the lords of the soil, between whom and themselves there was a kind of natural antipathy. Nor are the clergy spared. The priest is usually described as living with a concubine—his order forbade marrying—and both are considered as fair game to the community; while the monk figures more frequently as the hero of gallant adventures. Both priest and monk are usually distinguished by their selfishness and love of indulgence. In the fabliau Du Bouchier d'Abbeville, in Barbazan (iv. 1), a butcher, on his way home from the fair, seeks a night's lodging at the house of an inhospitable priest, who refuses it. But when the former returns, and offers, in exchange for his hospitality, one of his fat sheep which he has purchased at the fair, and not only to kill it for their supper, but to give all the meat they do not eat to his host, he is willingly received into the house, and they make an excellent supper. By the promise of the skin of the sheep, the guest succeeds in seducing both the concubine and the maid-servant, and it is only after his departure the following morning, in the middle of a domestic uproar caused by the conflicting claims of the priest, the concubine, and the maid, to the possession of the skin, that it is discovered that the butcher had stolen the sheep from the priest's own flock.

The fabliaux, as remarked before, form the most important class of the extensive mass of the popular literature of the middle ages, and the writers, confident in their strong hold upon public favour, sometimes turn round and burlesque the literature of other classes, especially the long heavy monotony of style of the great romances of chivalry and the extravagant adventures they contained, as though conscious that they were gradually undermining the popularity of the romance writers. One of these poems, entitled "De Audigier," and printed in Barbazan (iv. 217), is a parody on the romance writers and on their style, not at all wanting in spirit or wit, but the satire is coarse and vulgar. Another printed in Barbazan (iv. 287), under the title "De Berengier," is a satire upon a sort of knight-errantry which had found its way into mediæval chivalry. Berengier was a knight of Lombardy, much given to boasting, who had a beautiful lady for his wife. He used to leave her alone in his castle, under pretext of sallying forth in search of chivalrous adventures, and, after a while, having well hacked his sword and shield, he returned to vaunt the desperate exploits he had performed. But the lady was shrewd as well as handsome, and, having some suspicions of his truthfulness as well as of his courage, she determined to make trial of both. One morning, when her husband rode forth as usual, she hastily disguised herself in a suit of armour, mounted a good steed, and hurrying round by a different way, met the boastful knight in the middle of a wood, where he no sooner saw that he had to encounter a real assailant, than he displayed the most abject cowardice, and his opponent exacted from him an ignominious condition as the price of his escape. On his return home at night, boasting as usual of his success, he found his lady taking her revenge upon him in a still less respectful manner, but he was silenced by her ridicule.

The *trouvères*, or poets, who wrote the fabliaux—I need hardly remark that *trouvère* is the same word as *trobador*, but in the northern dialect of the French language—appear to have flourished chiefly from the close of the twelfth century to the earlier part of the fourteenth. They all composed in French, which was a language then common to England and France, but some of their compositions bear internal evidence of having been composed in England, and others are found in contemporary manuscripts written in this island. The scene of a fabliau, printed by Méon (i. 113), is laid at Colchester; and that of La Male Honte, printed in Barbazan (iii. 204), is laid in Kent. The latter, however, was written by a trouvère named Hugues de Cambrai. No objection appears to have been entertained to the recital of these licentious stories before the ladies of the castle or of the domestic circle, and their general popularity was so great, that the more pious clergy seem to have thought necessary to find something to take their place in the post-prandial society of the monastery, and especially of the nunnery; and religious stories were written in the same form and metre as the fabliaux. Some of these have been published under the title of "Contes Devots," and, from their general dulness, it may be doubted if they answered their purpose of furnishing amusement so well as the others.

CHAPTER VIII.

CARICATURES OF DOMESTIC LIFE.—STATE OF DOMESTIC LIFE IN THE MIDDLE AGES.—EXAMPLES OF DOMESTIC CARICATURE FROM THE CARVINGS OF THE MISERERES.—KITCHEN SCENES.—DOMESTIC BRAWLS.—THE FIGHT FOR THE BREECHES.—THE JUDICIAL DUEL BETWEEN MAN AND WIFE AMONG THE GERMANS.—ALLUSIONS TO WITCHCRAFT.—SATIRES ON THE TRADES; THE BAKER, THE MILLER, THE WINE-PEDLAR AND TAVERN-KEEPER, THE ALE-WIFE, ETC.

The influence of the jougleurs over people's minds generally, with their stories and satirical pieces, their grimaces, their postures, and their wonderful performances, was very considerable, and may be easily traced in mediæval manners and sentiments. This influence would naturally be exerted upon inventive art, and when a painter had to adorn the margin of a book, or the sculptor to decorate the ornamental parts of a building, we might expect the ideas which would first present themselves to him to be those suggested by the jougleur's performance, for the same taste had to be indulged in the one as in the other. The same wit or satire would pervade them both.

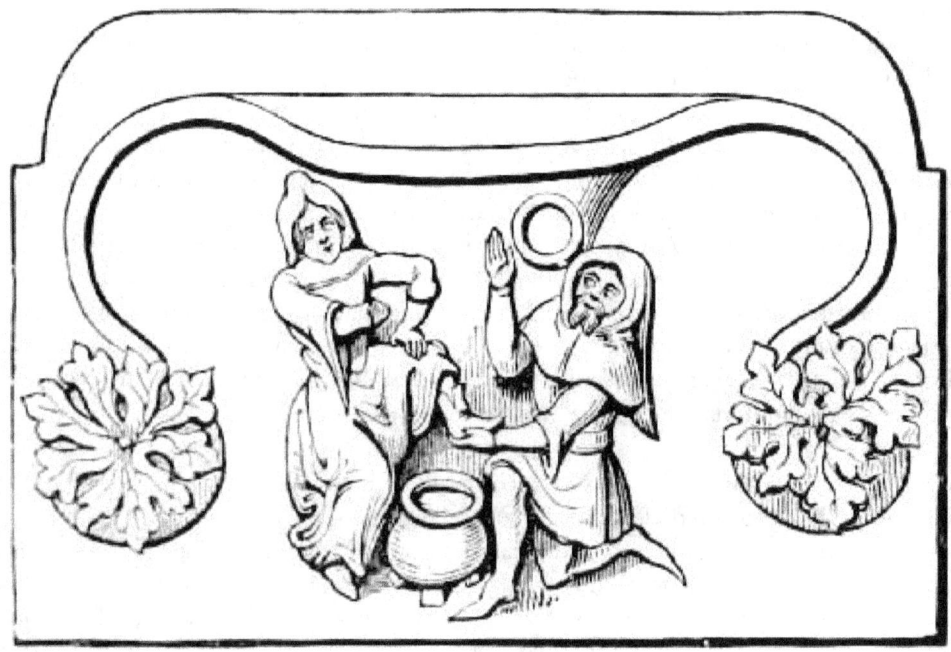

No. 71. A Mediæval Kitchen Scene.

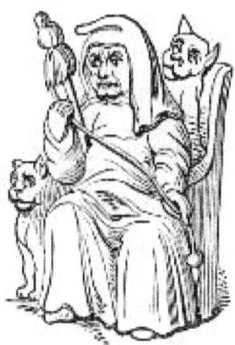

No. 72. An Old Lady and her Friends.

Among the most popular subjects of satire during the middle ages, were domestic scenes. Domestic life at that period appears to have been in its general character coarse, turbulent, and, I should say, anything but happy. In all its points of view, it presented abundant subjects for jest and burlesque. There is little room for doubt that the Romish Church, as it existed in the middle ages, was extremely hostile to domestic happiness among the middle and lower classes, and that the interference of the priest in the family was only a source of domestic trouble. The satirical writings of the period, the popular tales, the discourses of those who sought reform, even the pictures in the manuscripts and the sculptures on the walls invariably represent the female portion of the family as entirely under the influence of the priests, and that influence as exercised for the worst of purposes. They encouraged faithlessness as well as disobedience in wives, and undermined the virtue of daughters, and were consequently regarded with anything but kindly feeling by the male portion of the population. The priest, the wife, and the husband, form the usual leading characters in a mediæval farce. Subjects of this kind are not very unfrequent in the illuminations of manuscripts, and more especially in the sculptures of buildings, and those chiefly ecclesiastical, in which monks or priests are introduced in very equivocal situations. This part of the subject, however, is one into which we shall not here venture, as we find the mediæval caricaturists drawing plenty of materials from the less vicious shades of contemporary life; and, in fact, some of their most amusing pictures are taken from the droll, rather than from the vicious, scenes of the interior of the household. Such scenes are very frequent on the misereres of the old cathedrals and collegiate churches. Thus, in the stalls at Worcester Cathedral, there is a droll figure of a man seated before a fire in a kitchen well stored with flitches of bacon, he himself occupied in attending to the boiling pot, while he warms his feet, for which purpose he has taken off his shoes. In a similar carving in Hereford Cathedral, a man, also in the kitchen, is seen attempting to take liberties with the cook maid, who throws a platter at his head. A copy of this curious subject is given in cut No. 71, and the cut No. 72 is taken from a similar miserere in Minster Church, in the Isle of Thanet. It represents an old lady seated, occupied industriously in spinning, and accompanied by her cats.

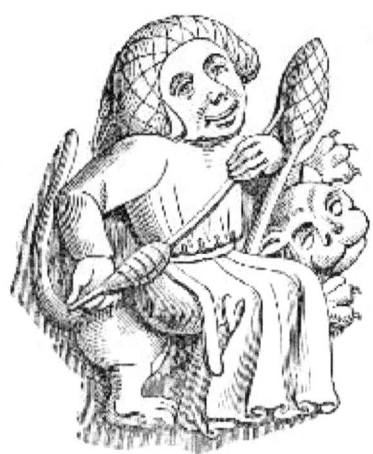

No. 73. The Lady and her Cat.

We might easily add other examples of similar subjects from the same sources, such as the scene in our cut No. 73, taken from one of the stalls of Winchester Cathedral, which seems to be intended to represent a witch riding away upon her cat, an enormous animal, whose jovial look is only outdone by that of its mistress. The latter has carried her distaff with her, and is diligently employed in spinning. A stall in Sherborne Minster, given in our cut No. 74, represents a scene in a school, in which an unfortunate scholar is experiencing punishment of a rather severe description, to the great alarm of his companions, on whom his disgrace is evidently acting as a warning. The flogging scene at school appears to have been rather a favourite subject among the early caricaturists, for the scourge was looked upon in the middle ages as the grand stimulant to scholarship. In those good old times, when a man recalled to memory his schoolboy days, he did not say, "When I was at school," but, "When I was under the rod."

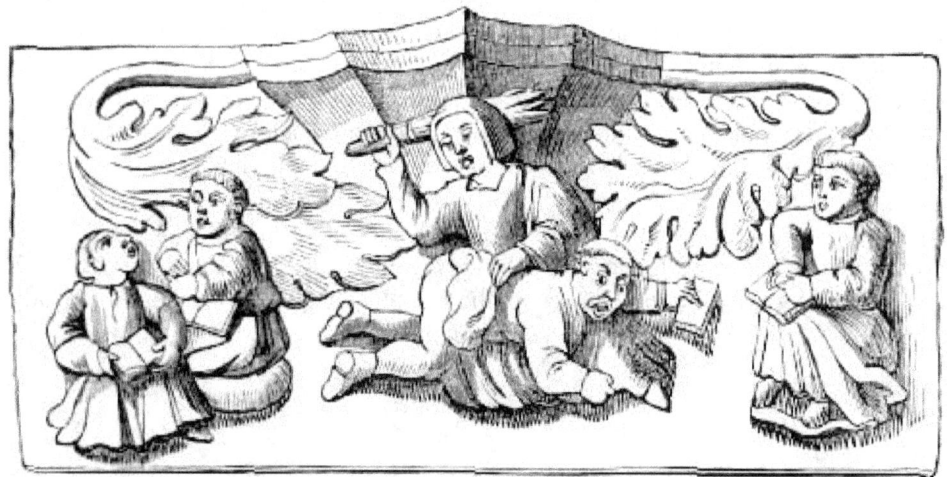

No. 74. Scholastic Discipline.

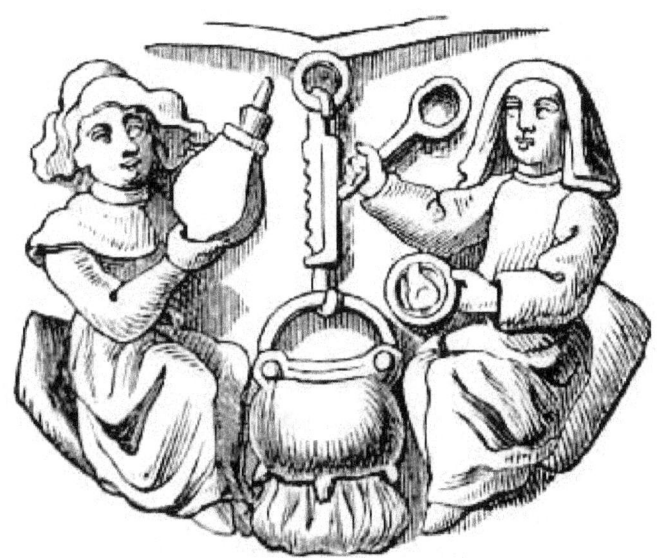

No. 75. A Point in Dispute.

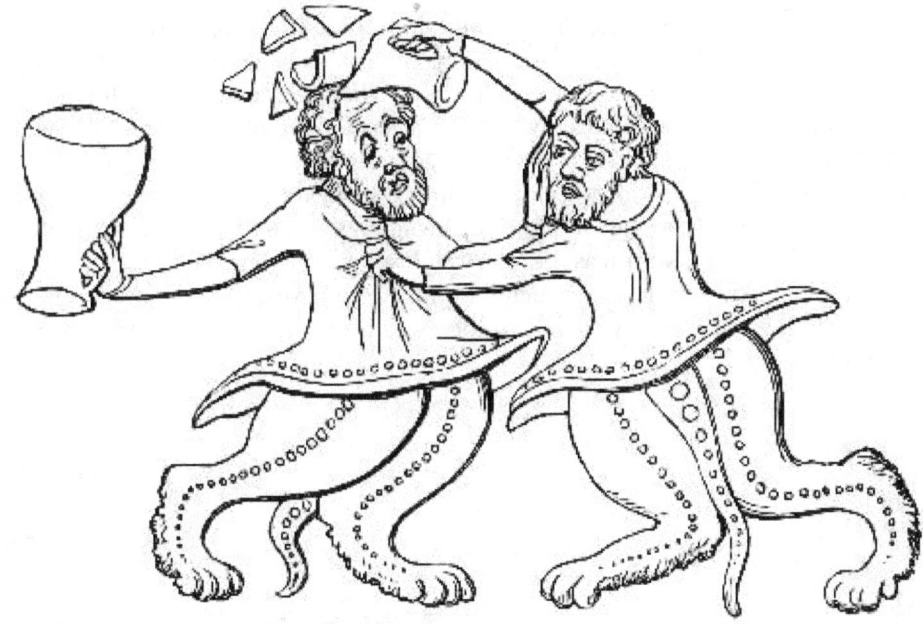

No. 76. Want of Harmony over the Pot.

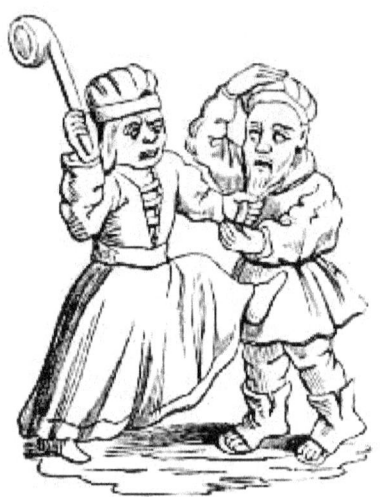

No. 77. Domestic Strife.

An extensive field for the study of this interesting part of our subject will be found in the architectural gallery in the Kensington Museum, which contains a large number of calls from stalls and other sculptures, chiefly selected from the French cathedrals. One of these, engraved in our cut No. 75, represents a couple of females, seated before the kitchen fire. The date of this sculpture is stated to be 1382. To judge by their looks and attitude, there is a disagreement between them, and the object in dispute seems to be a piece of meat, which one has taken out of the pot and placed on a dish. This lady wields her ladle as though she were prepared to use it as a weapon, while her opponent is armed with the bellows. The ale-pot was not unfrequently the subject of pictures of a turbulent character, and among the grotesque and monstrous figures in the margins of the noble manuscript of the fourteenth century, known as the "Luttrell Psalter," one represents two personages not only quarrelling over their pots, which they appear to have emptied, but actually fighting with them. One of them has literally broken his pot over his companion's head. The scene is copied in our cut No. 76.

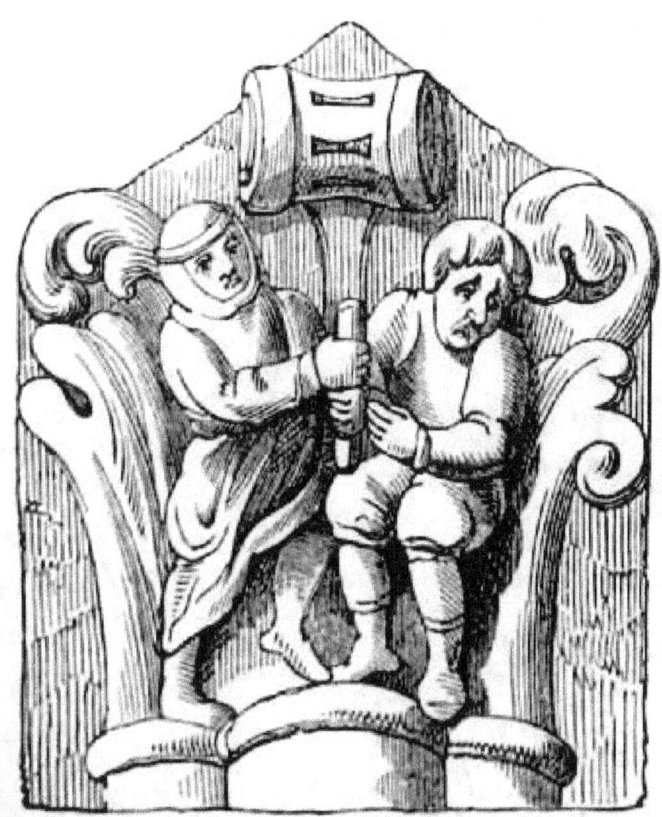

No. 78. A Struggle for the Mastery.

It must be stated, however, that the more common subjects of these homely scenes are domestic quarrels, and that the man, or his wife, enjoying their fireside, or similar bits of domestic comfort, only make their appearance at rare intervals. Domestic quarrels and combats are much more frequent. We have already seen, in the cut No. 75, two dames of the kitchen evidently beginning to quarrel over their cookery. A stall in the church of Stratford-upon-Avon gives us the group represented in our cut No. 77. The battle has here become desperate, but whether the male combatant be an oppressed husband or an impertinent intruder, is not clear. The quarrel would seem to have arisen during the process of cooking, as the female, who has seized her opponent by the beard, has evidently snatched up the ladle as the readiest weapon at hand. The anger appears to be mainly on her side, and the rather tame countenance of her antagonist contrasts strangely with her inflamed features. Our next cut, No. 78, is taken from the sculpture of a column in Ely Cathedral, here copied from an engraving in Carter's "Specimens of Ancient Sculpture." A man and wife, apparently, are struggling for the possession of a staff, which is perhaps intended to be the emblem of mastery. As is generally represented to be the case in these scenes of domestic strife, the woman shows more energy and more strength than her opponent, and she is evidently overcoming him. The mastery of the wife over the husband seems to have been a universally acknowledged state of things. A stall in Sherborne Minster, in Dorset, which has furnished the subject of our cut No. 79, might almost be taken as the sequel of the last cut. The lady has possessed herself of the staff, has overthrown her husband, and is even striking him on the head with it when he is down. In our next cut, No. 80, which is taken from one of the casts of stalls in the French cathedrals exhibited in the Kensington Museum, it is not quite clear which of the two is the offender, but, perhaps, in this case, the archer, as his profession is indicated by his bow and arrows, has made a gallant assault, which, although she does not look much displeased at it, the offended dame certainly resists with spirit.

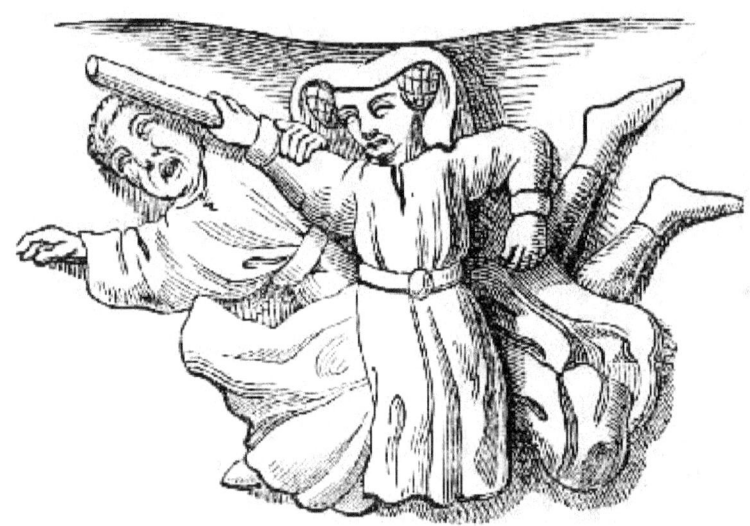

No. 79. The Wife in the Ascendant.

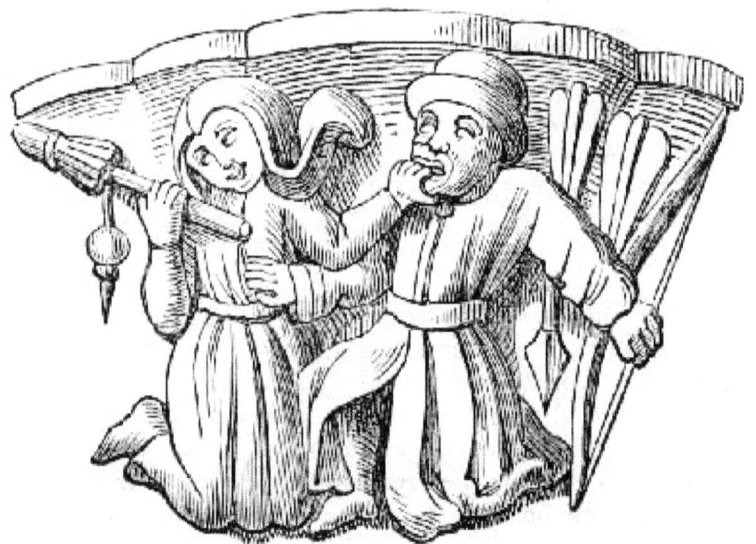

No. 80. Violence Resisted.

One idea connected with this picture of domestic antagonism appears to have been very popular from a rather early period. There is a proverbial phrase to signify that the wife is master in the household, by which it is intimated that "she wears the breeches." The phrase is, it must be confessed, an odd one, and is only half understood by modern explanations; but in mediæval story we learn how "she" first put in her claim to wear this particular article of dress, how it was first disputed and contested, how she was at times defeated, but how, as a general rule, the claim was enforced. There was a French poet of the thirteenth century, Hugues Piaucelles, two of whose *fabliaux*, or metrical tales, entitled the "Fabliau d'Estourmi," and the "Fabliau de Sire Hains et de Dame Anieuse," are preserved in manuscript, and have been printed in the collection of Barbazan. The second of these relates some of the adventures of a mediæval couple, whose household was not the best regulated in the world. The name of the heroine of this story, Anieuse, is simply an old form of the French word *ennuyeuse*, and certainly dame Anieuse was sufficiently "ennuyeuse" to her lord and husband. "Sire Hains," her husband, was, it appears, a maker of "cottes" and mantles, and we should judge also, by the point on which the quarrel turned, that he was partial to a good dinner. Dame Anieuse was of that disagreeable temper, that whenever Sire Hains told her of some particularly nice thing which he wished her to buy for his meal, she bought instead something which she knew was disagreeable to him. If he ordered boiled meat, she invariably roasted it, and further contrived that it should be so covered with cinders and ashes that he could not eat it. This would show that people in the middle ages (except, perhaps, professional cooks) were very unapt at roasting meat. This state of things had gone on for some time, when one day Sire Hains gave orders to his wife to buy him fish for his dinner. The disobedient wife, instead of buying fish, provided nothing for his meal but a dish of spinage, telling him falsely that all the fish stank. This leads to a violent quarrel, in which, after some fierce wrangling, especially on the part of the lady, Sire Hains proposes to decide their difference in a novel manner. "Early in the morning," he said, "I will take off my breeches and lay them down in the middle of the court, and the one who can win them shall be acknowledged to be master or mistress of the house."

Le matinet, sans contredire,
Voudrai mes braies deschaucier,
Et enmi nostre cort couchier;
Et qui conquerre les porra,
Par bone reson mousterra
Qu'il ert sire ou dame du nostre.
Barbazan, Fabliaux, tome iii. p. 383.

Dame Anieuse accepted the challenge with eagerness, and each prepared for the struggle. After due preparation, two neighbours, friend Symon and Dame Aupais, having been called in as witnesses, and the object of dispute, the breeches, having been placed on the pavement of the court, the battle began, with some slight parody on the formalities of the judicial combat. The first blow was given by the dame, who was so eager for the fray that she struck her husband before he had put himself on his guard; and the war of tongues, in which at least Dame Anieuse had the best of it, went on at the same time as the other battle. Sire Hains ventured a slight expostulation on her eagerness for the fray, in answer to which she only threw in his teeth a fierce defiance to do his worst. Provoked at this, Sire Hains struck at her, and hit her over the eyebrows, so effectively, that the skin was discoloured; and, over-confident in the effect of this first blow, he began rather too soon to exult over his wife's defeat. But Dame Anieuse was less disconcerted than he expected, and recovering quickly from the effect of the blow, she turned upon him and struck him on the same part of his face with such force, that she nearly knocked him over the sheepfold. Dame Anieuse, in her turn, now sneered over him, and while he was recovering from his confusion, her eyes fell upon the object of contention, and she rushed to it, and laid her hands upon it to carry it away. This movement roused Sire Hains, who instantly seized another part of the article of his dress of which he was thus in danger of being deprived, and began a struggle for possession, in which the said article underwent considerable dilapidation, and fragments of it were scattered over the court. In the midst of this struggle the actual fight recommenced, by the husband giving his wife so heavy a blow on the teeth that her mouth was filled with blood. The effect was such that Sire Hains already reckoned on the victory, and proclaimed himself lord of the breeches.

Hains fiert sa fame enmi les denz
Tel cop, que la bouche dedenz
Li a toute emplie de sancz.
"Tien ore," dist Sire Hains, "anc,
Je cuit que je t'ai bien atainte,
Or t'ai-je de deux colors tainte—
J'aurai les braies toutes voies."

But the immediate effect on Dame Anieuse was only to render her more desperate. She quitted her hold on the disputed garment, and fell upon her husband with such a shower of blows that he hardly knew which way to turn. She was thus, however, unconsciously exhausting herself, and Sire Hains soon recovered. The battle now became fiercer than ever, and the lady seemed to be gaining the upper hand, when Sire Hains gave her a skilful blow in the ribs, which nearly broke one of them, and considerably checked her ardour. Friend Symon here interposed, with the praiseworthy aim of restoring peace before further harm might be done, but in vain, for the lady was only rendered more obstinate by her mishap; and he agreed that it was useless to interfere until one had got a more decided advantage over the other. The fight therefore went on, the two combatants having now seized each other by the hair of the head, a mode of combat in which the advantages were rather on the side of the male. At this moment, one of the judges, Dame Aupais, sympathising too much with Dame Anieuse, ventured some words of encouragement, which drew upon her a severe rebuke from her colleague, Symon, who intimated that if she interfered again there might be two pairs of combatants instead of one. Meanwhile Dame Anieuse was becoming exhausted, and was evidently getting the worst of the contest, until at length, staggering from a vigorous push, she fell back into a large basket which lay behind her. Sire Hains stood over her exultingly, and Symon, as umpire, pronounced him victorious. He thereupon took possession of the disputed article of raiment, and again invested himself with it, while the lady accepted faithfully the conditions imposed upon her, and we are assured by the poet that she was a good and obedient wife during the rest of her life. In this story, which affords a curious picture of mediæval life, we learn the origin of the proverb relating to the possession and wearing of the breeches. Hugues Piaucelles concludes his *fabliau* by recommending every man who has a disobedient wife to treat her in the same manner; and mediæval husbands appear to have followed his advice, without fear of laws against the ill-treatment of women.

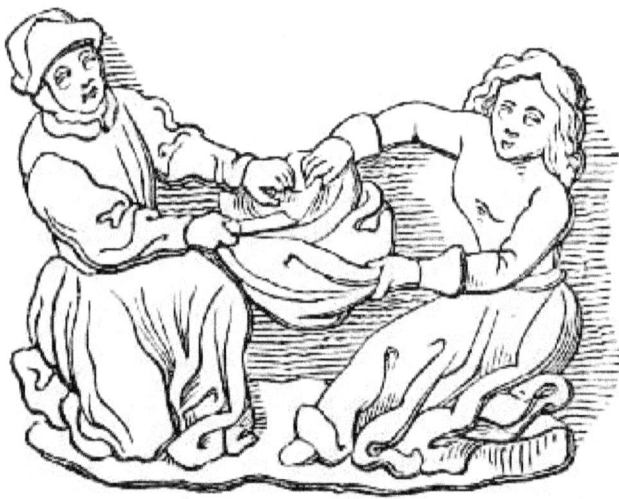

No. 81. The Fight for the Breeches.

A subject like this was well fitted for the burlesques on the stalls, and accordingly we find on one of those in the cathedral at Rouen, the group given in our cut No. 81, which seems to represent the part of the story in which both combatants seize hold of the disputed garment, and struggle for possession of it. The husband here grasps a knife in his hand, with which he seems to be threatening to cut it to pieces rather than give it up. The *fabliau* gives the victory to the husband, but the wife was generally considered as in a majority of cases carrying off the prize. In an extremely rare engraving by the Flemish artist Van Mecken, dated in 1480, of which I give a copy in our cut No. 82. the lady, while putting on the breeches, of which she has just become possessed, shows an inclination to lord it rather tyrannically over her other half, whom she has condemned to perform the domestic drudgery of the mansion.

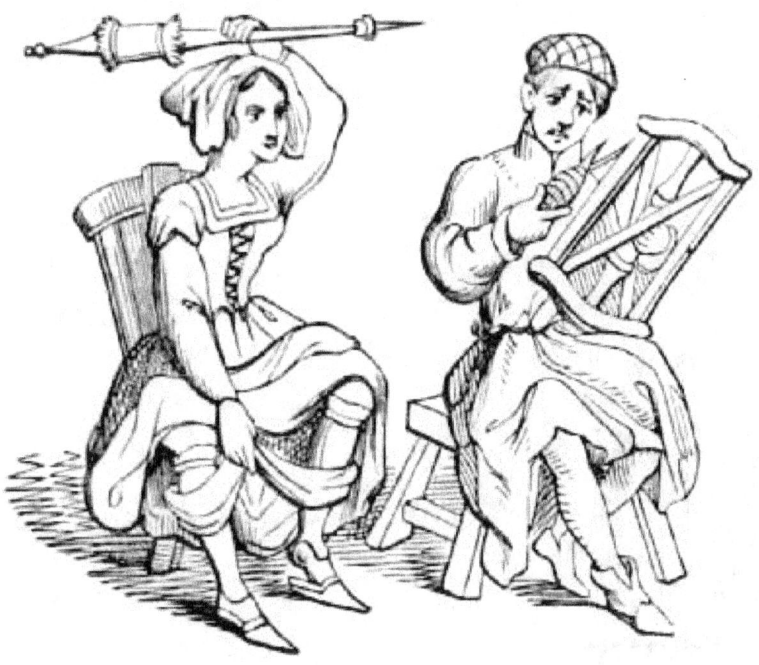

No. 82. The Breeches Won.

In Germany, where there was still more roughness in mediæval life, what was told in England and France as a good story of domestic doings, was actually carried into practice under the authority of the laws. The judicial duel was there adopted by the legal authorities as a mode of settling the differences between husband and wife. Curious particulars on this subject are given in an interesting paper entitled "Some observations on Judicial Duels as practised in Germany," published in the twenty-ninth volume of the Archæologia of the Society of Antiquaries (p. 348). These observations are chiefly taken from a volume of directions, accompanied with drawings, for the various modes of attack and defence, compiled by Paulus Kall, a celebrated teacher of defence at the court of Bavaria about the year 1400. Among these drawings we have one representing the mode of combat between husband and wife. The only weapon allowed the female, but that a very formidable one, was, according to these directions, a heavy stone wrapped up in an elongation of her chemise, while her opponent had only a short staff, and he was placed up to the waist in a pit formed in the ground. The following is a literal translation of the directions given in the manuscript, and our cut No. 83 is a copy of the drawing which illustrates it:—"The woman must be so prepared, that a sleeve of her chemise extend a small ell beyond her hand, like a little sack; there indeed is put a stone weighing three pounds; and she has nothing else but her chemise, and that is bound together between the legs with a lace. Then the man makes himself ready in the pit over against his wife. He is buried therein up to the girdle, and one hand is bound at the elbow to the side." At this time the practice of such combats in Germany seems to have been long known, for it is stated that in the year 1200 a man and his wife fought under the sanction of the civic authorities at Bâle, in Switzerland. In a picture of a combat between man and wife, from a manuscript resembling that of Paulus Kall, but executed nearly a century later, the man is placed in a tub instead of a pit, with his left arm tied to his side as before, and his right holding a short heavy staff; while the woman is dressed, and not stripped to the chemise, as in the former case. The man appears to be holding the stick in such a manner that the sling in which the stone was contained would twist round it, and the woman would thus be at the mercy of her opponent. In an ancient manuscript on the science of defence in the library at Gotha, the man in the tub is represented as the conqueror of his wife, having thus dragged her head-foremost into the tub, where she appears with her legs kicking up in the air.

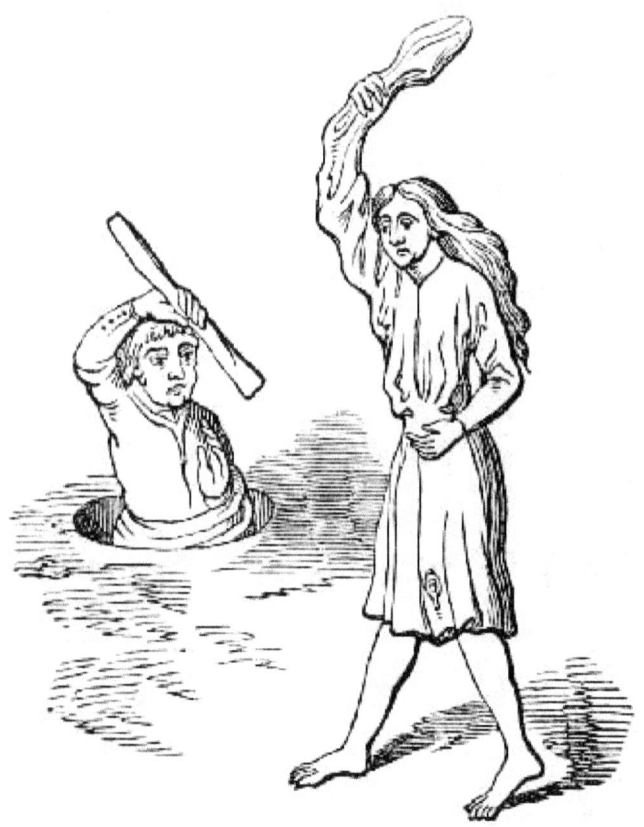

No. 83. A Legal Combat.

This was the orthodox mode of combat between man and wife, but it was sometimes practised under more sanguinary forms. In one picture given from these old books on the science of defence by the writer of the paper on the subject in the Archæologia, the two combatants, naked down to the waist, are represented fighting with sharp knives, and inflicting upon each other's bodies frightful gashes.

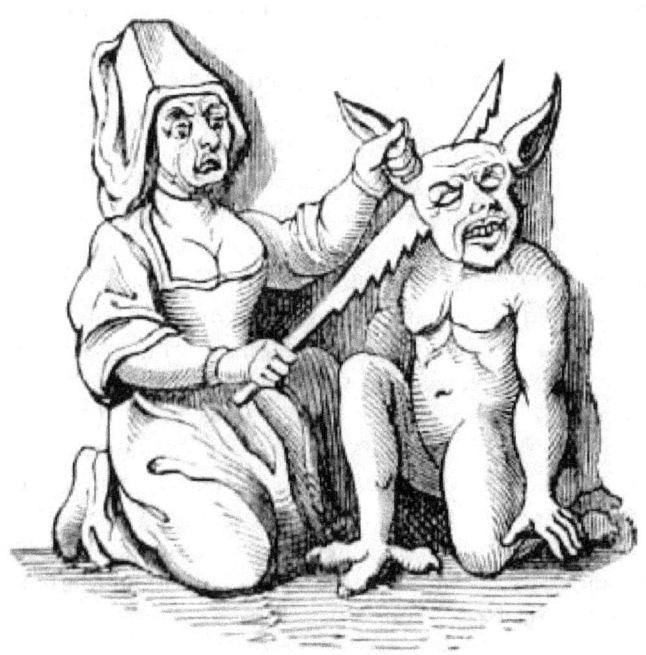

No. 84. The Witch and the Demon.

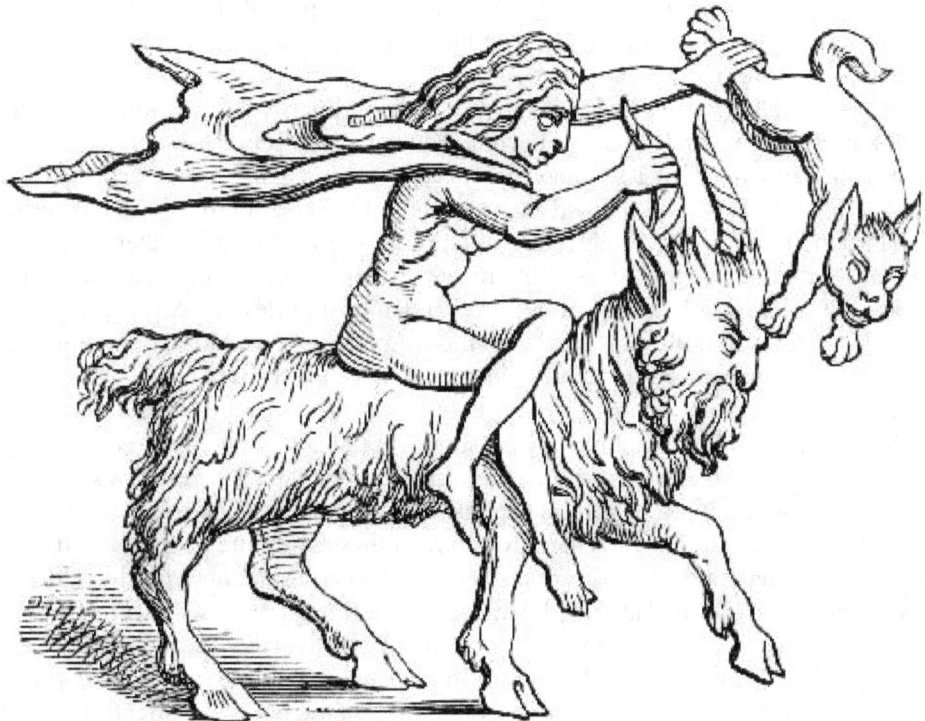

No. 85. The Witch and her Victim.

A series of stall carvings at Corbeil, near Paris, of which more will be said a little farther on in this chapter, has furnished the curious group represented in our cut No. 84, which is one of the rather rare pictorial allusions to the subject of witchcraft. It represents a woman who must, by her occupation, be a witch, for she has so far got the mastery of the demon that she is sawing off his head with a very uncomfortable looking instrument. Another story of witchcraft is told in the sculpture of a stone panel at the entrance of the cathedral of Lyons, which is represented in our cut

No. 85. One power, supposed to be possessed by witches, was that of transforming people to animals at will. William of Malmesbury, in his Chronicle, tells a story of two witches in the neighbourhood of Rome, who used to allure travellers into their cottage, and there transform them into horses, pigs, or other animals, which they sold, and feasted themselves with the money. One day a young man, who lived by the profession of a jougleur, sought a night's lodging at their cottage, and was received, but they turned him into an ass, and, as he retained his understanding and his power of acting, they gained much money by exhibiting him. At length a rich man of the neighbourhood, who wanted him for his private amusement, offered the two women a large sum for him, which they accepted, but they warned the new possessor of the ass that he should carefully restrain him from going into the water, as that would deprive him of his power of performing. The man who had purchased the ass acted upon this advice, and carefully kept him from water, but one day, through the negligence of his keeper, the ass escaped from his stable, and, rushing to a pond at no great distance, threw himself into it. Water—and running water especially—was believed to destroy the power of witchcraft or magic; and no sooner was the ass immersed in the water, than he recovered his original form of a young man. He told his story, which soon reached the ears of the pope, and the two women were seized, and confessed their crimes. The carving from Lyons Cathedral appears to represent some such scene of sorcery. The naked woman, evidently a witch, is, perhaps, seated on a man whom she has transformed into a goat, and she seems to be whirling the cat over him in such a manner that it may tear his face with its claws.

There was still another class of subjects for satire and caricature which belongs to this part of our subject—I mean that of the trader and manufacturer. We must not suppose that fraudulent trading, that deceptive and imperfect workmanship, that adulteration of everything that could be adulterated, are peculiar to modern times. On the contrary, there was no period in the world's history in which dishonest dealing was carried on to such an extraordinary extent, in which there was so much deception used in manufactures, or in which adulteration was practised on so shameless a scale, as during the middle ages. These vices, or, as we may, perhaps, more properly describe them, these crimes, are often mentioned in the mediæval writers, but they were not easily represented pictorially, and therefore we rarely meet with direct allusions to them, either in sculpture, on stone or wood, or in the paintings of illuminated manuscripts. Representations of the trades themselves are not so rare, and are sometimes droll and almost burlesque. A curious series of such representations of arts and trades was carved on the *misereres* of the church of St. Spire, at Corbeil, near Paris, which only exist now in Millin's engravings, but they seem to have been works of the fifteenth century. Among them the first place is given to the various occupations necessary for the production of bread, that article so important to the support of life. Thus we see, in these carvings at Corbeil, the labours of the reaper, cutting the wheat and forming it into sheaves, the miller carrying it away to be ground into meal, and the baker thrusting it into the oven, and drawing it out in the shape of loaves. Our cut No. 86, taken from one of these sculptures, represents the baker either putting in or taking out the bread with his peel; by the earnest manner in which he looks at it, we may suppose that it is the latter, and that he is ascertaining if it be sufficiently baked. We have an earlier representation of a mediæval oven in our cut No. 87, taken from the celebrated illuminated manuscript of the "Romance of Alexandre," in the Bodleian Library at Oxford, which appears to belong to an early period of the fourteenth century. Here the baker is evidently going to take a loaf out of the oven, for his companion holds a dish for the purpose of receiving it.

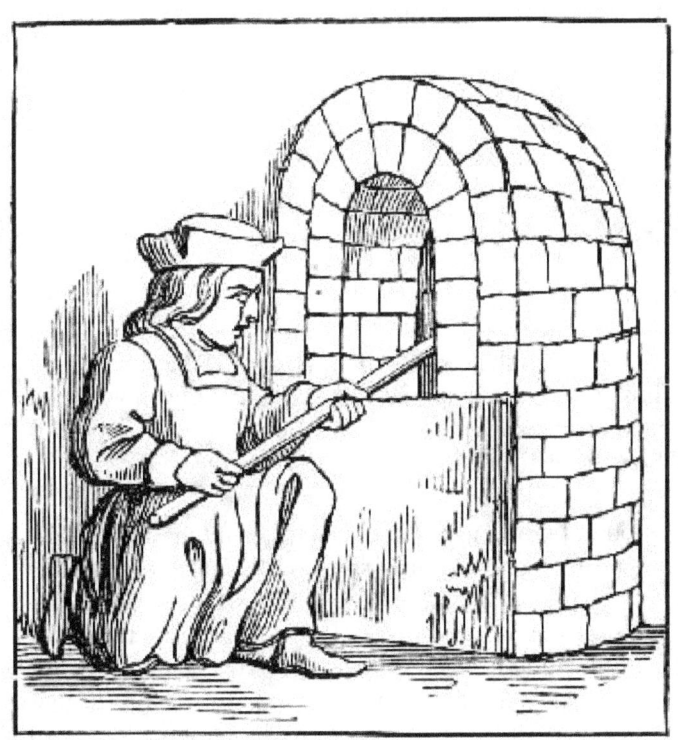

No. 86. A Baker of the Fifteenth Century.

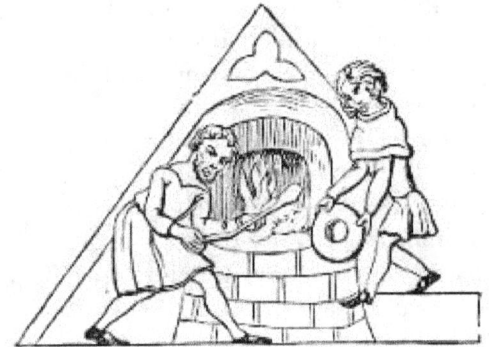

No. 87. A Mediæval Baker.

In nothing was fraud and adulteration practised to so great an extent as in the important article of bread, and the two occupations especially employed in making it were objects of very great dislike and of scornful satire. The miller was proverbially a thief. Every reader of Chaucer will remember his character so admirably drawn in that of the miller of Trumpington, who, though he was as proud and gay "as eny pecok," was nevertheless eminently dishonest.

A theef he was for soth of corn and mele,
And that a sleigh (sly), and usyng (practised) for to stele.
Chaucer's Reeves Tale.

This practice included a large college then existing in Cambridge, but now forgotten, the Soler Hall, which suffered greatly by his depredations.

And on a day it happed in a stounde,

Syk lay the mauncyple on a maledye,
Men wenden wisly that he schulde dye;
For which this meller stal bothe mele and corn
A thousend part more than byforn.
For ther biforn he stal but curteysly;
But now he is a theef outrageously.
For which the wardeyn chidde and made fare,
But therof sette the meller not a tare;
He crakked boost, and swor it was nat so.

Two of the scholars of this college resolved to go with the corn to the mill, and by their watchfulness prevent his depredations. Those who are acquainted with the story know how the scholars succeeded, or rather how they failed; how the miller stole half a bushel of their flour and caused his wife to make a cake of it; and how the victims had their revenge and recovered the cake.

As already stated, the baker had in these good old times no better character than the miller, if not worse. There was an old saying, that if three persons of three obnoxious professions were put together in a sack and shaken up, the first who came out would certainly be a rogue, and one of these was a baker. Moreover, the opinion concerning the baker was so strong that, as in the phrase taken from the old legends of the witches, who in their festivals sat thirteen at a table, this number was popularly called a devil's dozen, and was believed to be unlucky—so, when the devil's name was abandoned, perhaps for the sake of euphony, the name substituted for it was that of the baker, and the number thirteen was called "a baker's dozen." The makers of nearly all sorts of provisions for sale were, in the middle ages, tainted with the same vice, and there was nothing from which society in general, especially in the towns where few made bread for themselves, suffered so much. This evil is alluded to more than once in that curious educational treatise, the "Dictionarius" of John de Garlande, printed in my "Volume of Vocabularies." This writer, who wrote in the earlier half of the thirteenth century, insinuates that the makers of pies (*pastillarii*), an article of food which was greatly in repute during the middle ages, often made use of bad eggs. The cooks, he says further, sold, especially in Paris to the scholars of the university, cooked meats, sausages, and such things, which were not fit to eat; while the butchers furnished the meat of animals which had died of disease. Even the spices and drugs sold by the apothecaries, or *épiciers*, were not, he says, to be trusted. John de Garlande had evidently an inclination to satire, and he gives way to it not unfrequently in the little book of which I am speaking. He says that the glovers of Paris cheated the scholars of the university, by selling them gloves made of bad materials; that the women who gained their living by winding thread (*devacuatrices*, in the Latin of the time), not only emptied the scholars' purses, but wasted their bodies also (it is intended as a pun upon the Latin word); and the hucksters sold them unripe fruit for ripe. The drapers, he says, cheated people not only by selling bad materials, but by measuring them with false measures; while the hawkers, who went about from house to house, robbed as well as cheated.

M. Jubinal has published in his curious volume entitled "Jongleurs et Trouvères," a rather jocular poem on the bakers, written in French of, perhaps, the thirteenth century, in which their art is lauded as much better and more useful than that of the goldsmith's. The millers' depredations on the corn sent to be ground at the mill, are laid to the charge of the rats, which attack it by night, and the hens, which find their way to it by day; and he explains the diminution the bakings experienced in the hands of the baker as arising out of the charity of the latter towards the poor and needy, to whom they gave the meal and paste before it had even been put into the oven. The celebrated English poet, John Lydgate, in a short poem preserved in a manuscript in the Harleian Library in the British Museum (MS. Harl. No. 2,255, fol. 157, v°, describes the pillory, which he calls their Bastile, as the proper heritage of the miller and the baker:—

Put out his hed, lyst nat for to dare,
But lyk a man upon that tour to abyde,
For cast of eggys wil not oonys spare,
Tyl he be quallyd body, bak, and syde.
His heed endooryd, and of verray pryde
Put out his armys, shewith abrood his face;
The fenestrallys be made for hym so wyde,
Claymyth to been a capteyn of that place.
The bastyle longith of verray dewe ryght
To fals bakerys, it is trewe herytage
Severalle to them, this knoweth every wyght,
Be kynde assygned for ther sittyng stage;
Wheer they may freely shewe out ther visage,
Whan they tak oonys their possessioun,
Owthir in youthe or in myddyl age;
Men doon hem wrong yif they take hym down.
Let mellerys and bakerys gadre hem a gilde,
And alle of assent make a fraternité,
Undir the pillory a letil chapelle bylde,
The place amorteyse, and purchase lyberté,
For alle thos that of ther noumbre be;
What evir it coost afftir that they wende,
They may clayme, be just auctorité,
Upon that bastile to make an ende.

The wine-dealer and the publican formed another class in mediæval society who lived by fraud and dishonesty, and were the objects of satire. The latter gave both bad wine and bad measure, and he often also acted as a pawnbroker, and when people had drunk more than they could pay for, he would take their clothes as pledges for their money. The tavern, in the middle ages, was the resort of very miscellaneous company; gamblers and loose women were always on the watch there to lead more honest people into ruin, and the tavern-keeper profited largely by their gains; and the more vulgar minstrel and "jogelour" found employment there; for the middle classes of society, and even their betters, frequented the tavern much more generally than at the present day. In the carved stalls of the church of Corbeil, the liquor merchant is represented by the figure of a man wheeling a hogshead in a barrow, as shown in our cut No. 88. The graveness and air of importance with which he regards it would lead us to suppose that the barrel contains wine; and the cup and jug on the shelf above show that it was to be sold retail. The wine-sellers called out their wines from their doors, and boasted of their qualities, in order to tempt people in; and John de Garlande assures us that when they entered, they were served with wine which was not worth drinking. "The criers of wine," he says, "proclaim with extended throat the diluted wine they have in their taverns, offering it at four pennies, at six, at eight, and at twelve, fresh poured out from the gallon cask into the cup, to tempt people." ("Volume of Vocabularies," p. 126.) The ale-wife was an especial subject of jest and satire, and is not unfrequently represented on the pictorial monuments of our forefathers. Our cut No. 89 is taken from one of the misereres in the church of Wellingborough, in Northamptonshire; the ale-wife is pouring her liquor from her jug into a cup to serve a rustic, who appears to be waiting for it with impatience.

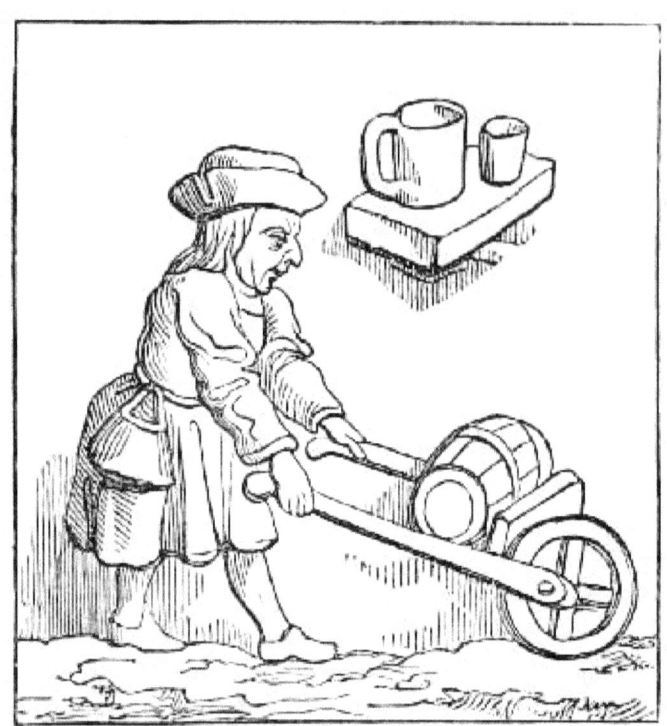

No. 88. The Wine Dealer.

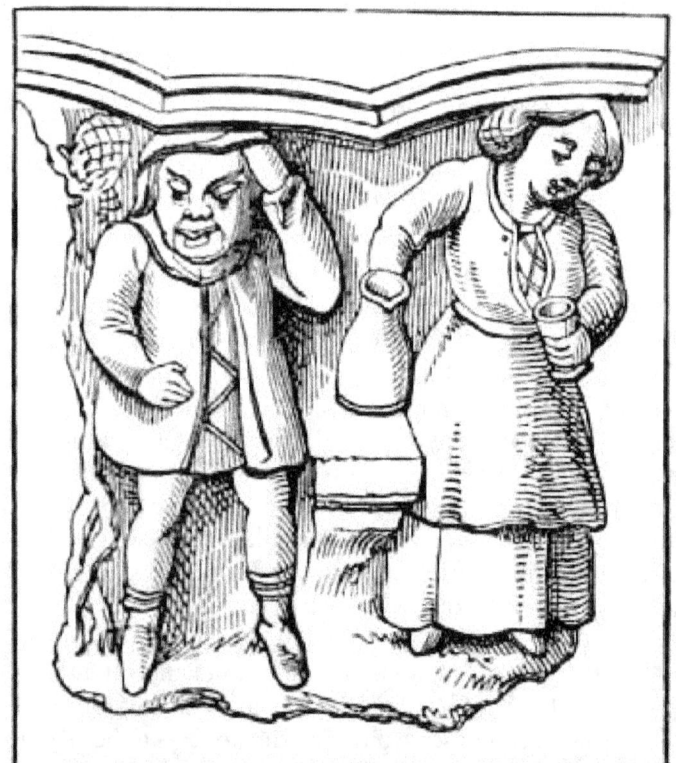

No. 89. The Ale-Wife.

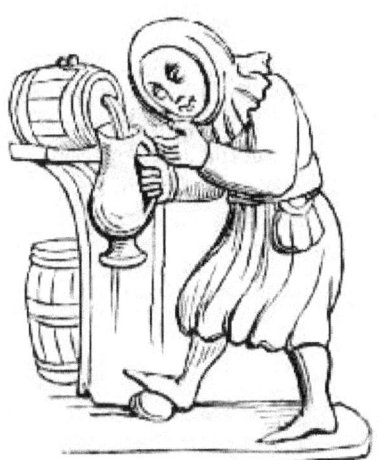

No. 90. The Ale-Drawer.

The figure of the ale-drawer, No. 90, is taken from one of the misereres in the parish church of Ludlow, in Shropshire. The size of his jug is somewhat disproportionate to that of the barrel from which he obtains the ale. The same misereres of Ludlow Church furnish the next scene, cut No. 91, which represents the end of the wicked ale-wife. The day of judgment is supposed to have arrived, and she has received her sentence. A demon, seated on one side, is reading a list of the crimes she has committed, which the magnitude of the parchment shows to be a rather copious one. Another demon (whose head has been broken off in the original) carries on his back, in a very irreverent manner, the unfortunate lady, in order to throw her into hell-mouth, on the other side of the picture. She is naked with the exception of the fashionable head-gear, which formed one of her vanities in the world, and she carries with her the false measure with which she cheated her customers. A demon bagpiper welcomes her on her arrival. The scene is full of wit and humour.

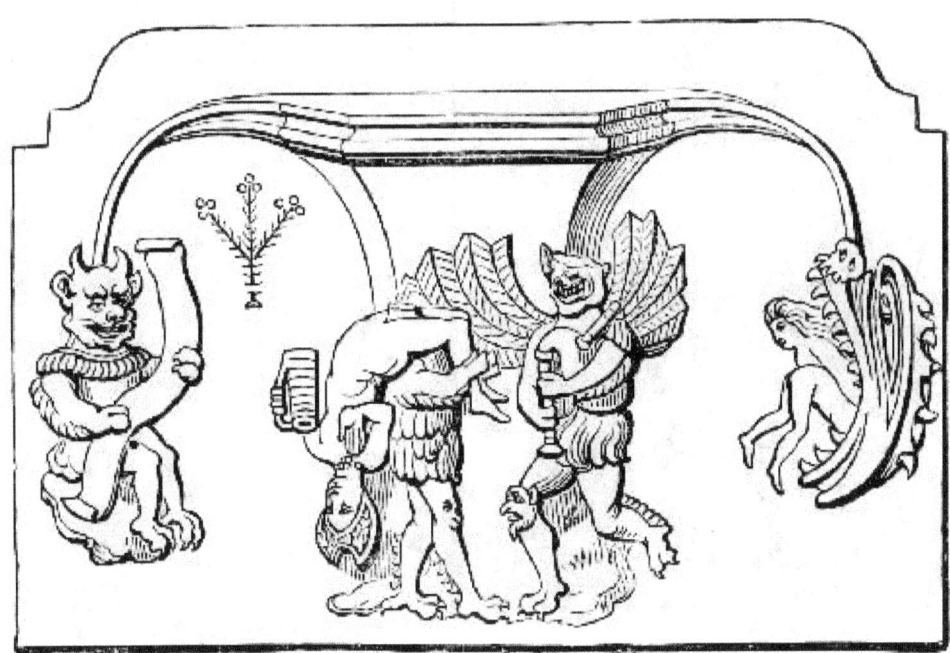

No. 91. The Ale-Wife's End.

The rustic classes, and instances of their rusticity, are not unfrequently met with in these interesting carvings. The stalls of Corbeil present several agricultural scenes. Our cut No. 92 is taken from those of Gloucester cathedral, of an earlier date, and represents the three shepherds, astonished at the appearance of the star which announced the birth of the Saviour of mankind. Like the three kings, the shepherds to whom this revelation was made were always in the middle ages represented as three in number. In our drawing from the miserere in Gloucester cathedral, the costume of the shepherds is remarkably well depicted, even to the details, with the various implements appertaining to their profession, most of which are suspended to their girdles. They are drawn with much spirit, and even the dog is well represented as an especially active partaker in the scene.

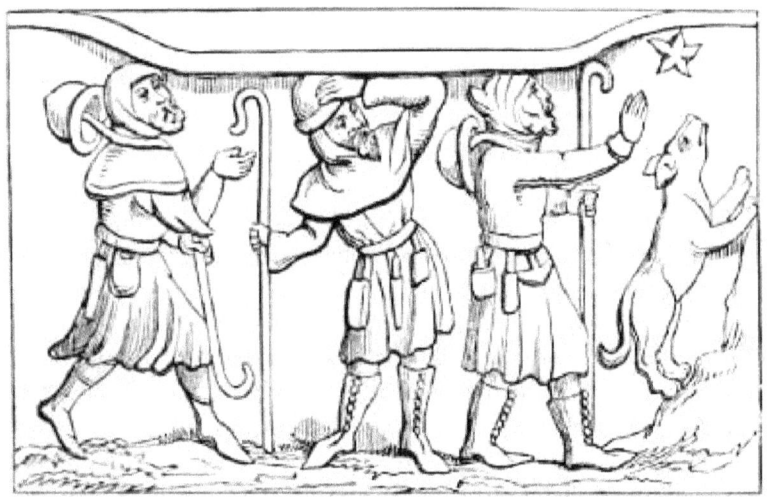

No. 92. The Shepherds of the East.

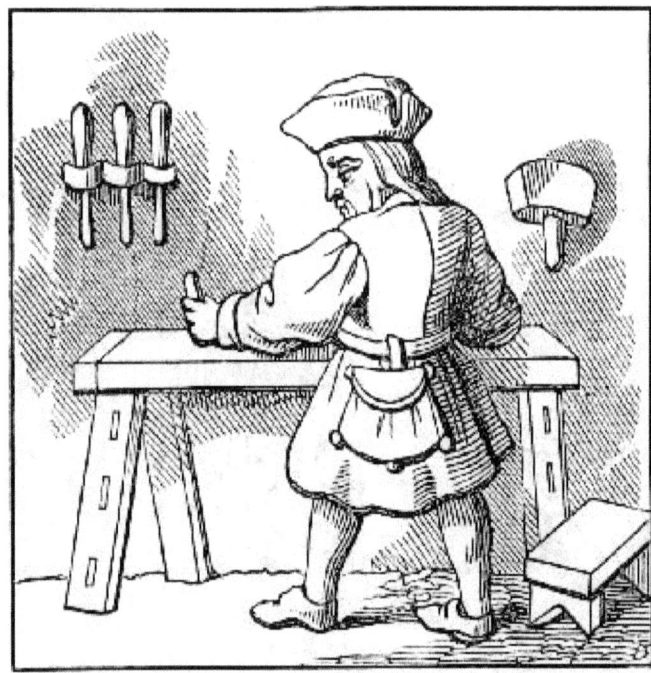

No. 93. The Carpenter.

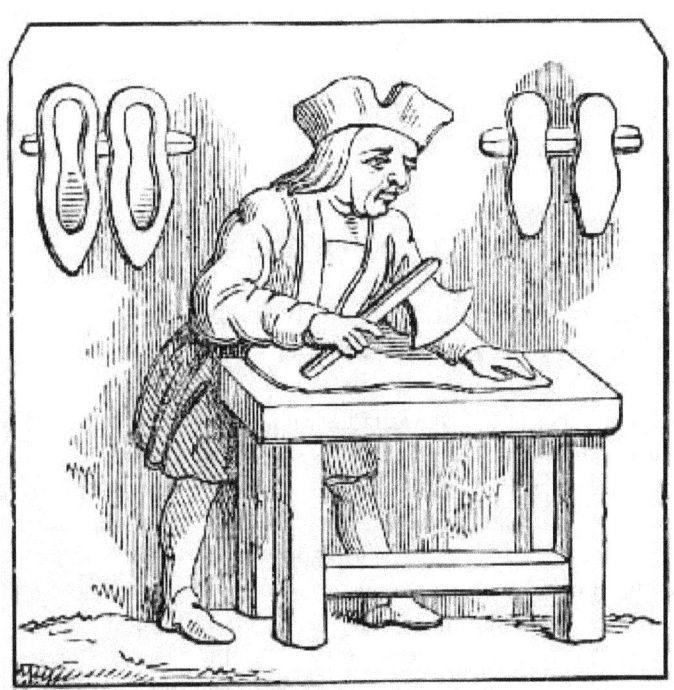

No. 94. The Shoemaker.

Of the two other examples we select from the misereres of Corbeil, the first represents the carpenter, or, as he was commonly called by our Anglo-Saxon and mediæval forefathers, the *wright*, which signifies simply the "maker." The application of this higher and more general term—for the Almighty himself is called, in the Anglo-Saxon poetry, *ealra gesceafta wyrhta*, the Maker, or Creator, of all things—shows how important an art that of the carpenter was considered in the middle ages. Everything made of wood came within his province. In the Anglo-Saxon "Colloquy" of archbishop Alfric, where some of the more useful artisans are introduced disputing about the relative value of their several crafts, the "wright" says, "Who of you can do without my craft, since I make houses and all sorts of vessels (*vasa*), and ships for you all?" ("Volume of Vocabularies," p. 11.) And John de Garlande, in the thirteenth century, describes the carpenter as making, among other things, tubs, and barrels, and wine-cades. The workmanship of those times was exercised, before all other materials, on wood and metals, and the wright, or worker in the former material, was distinguished by this circumstance from the smith, or worker in metal. The carpenter is still called a wright in Scotland. Our last cut (No. 94), taken also from one of the misereres at Corbeil, represents the shoemaker, or as he was then usually called, the cordwainer, because the leather which he chiefly used came from Cordova in Spain, and was thence called *cordewan*, or *cordewaine*. Our shoemaker is engaged in cutting a skin of leather with an instrument of a rather singular form. Shoes, and perhaps forms for making shoes, are suspended on pegs against the wall.

CHAPTER IX.

GROTESQUE FACES AND FIGURES.—PREVALENCE OF THE TASTE FOR UGLY AND GROTESQUE FACES.—SOME OF THE POPULAR FORMS DERIVED FROM ANTIQUITY; THE TONGUE LOLLING OUT, AND THE DISTORTED MOUTH.—HORRIBLE SUBJECTS: THE MAN AND THE SERPENTS.—ALLEGORICAL FIGURES: GLUTTONY AND LUXURY.—OTHER REPRESENTATIONS OF CLERICAL GLUTTONY AND DRUNKENNESS.—GROTESQUE FIGURES OF INDIVIDUALS, AND GROTESQUE GROUPS.—ORNAMENTS OF THE BORDERS OF BOOKS.—UNINTENTIONAL CARICATURE; THE MOTE AND THE BEAM.

The grimaces and strange postures of the jougleurs seem to have had great attractions for those who witnessed them. To unrefined and uneducated minds no object conveys so perfect a notion of mirth as an ugly and distorted face. Hence it is that among the common peasantry at a country fair few exhibitions are more satisfactory than that of grinning through a horse-collar. This sentiment is largely exemplified in the sculpture especially of the middle ages, a long period, during which the general character of society presented that want of refinement which we now observe chiefly in its least cultivated classes. Among the most common decorations of our ancient churches and other mediæval buildings, are grotesque and monstrous heads and faces. Antiquity, which lent us the types of many of these monstrosities, saw in her Typhons and Gorgons a signification beyond the surface of the picture, and her grotesque masks had a general meaning, and were in a manner typical of the whole field of comic literature. The mask was less an individual grotesque to be laughed at for itself, than a personification of comedy. In the middle ages, on the contrary, although in some cases certain forms were often regarded as typical of certain ideas, in general the design extended no farther than the forms which the artist had given to it; the grotesque features, like the grinning through the horse-collar, gave satisfaction by their mere ugliness. Even the applications, when such figures were intended to have one, were coarsely satirical, without any intellectuality, and, where they had a meaning beyond the plain text of the sculpture or drawing, it was not far-fetched, but plain and easily understood. When the Anglo-Saxon drew the face of a bloated and disfigured monk, he no doubt intended thereby to proclaim the popular notion of the general character of monastic life, but this was a design which nobody could misunderstand, an interpretation which everybody was prepared to give to it. We have already seen various examples of this description of satire, scattered here and there among the immense mass of grotesque sculpture which has no such meaning. A great proportion, indeed, of these grotesque sculptures appears to present mere variations of a certain number of distinct types which had been handed down from a remote period, some of them borrowed, perhaps involuntarily, from antiquity. Hence we naturally look for the earlier and more curious examples of this class of art to Italy and the south of France, where the transition from classical to mediæval was more gradual, and the continued influence of classical forms is more easily traced. The early Christian masons appear to have caricatured under the form of such grotesques the personages of the heathen mythology, and to this practice we perhaps owe some of the types of the mediæval monsters. We have seen in a former chapter a grotesque from the church of Monte Majour, near Nismes, the original type of which had evidently been some burlesque figure of Saturn eating one of his children. The classical mask doubtless furnished the type for those figures, so common in mediæval sculpture, of faces with disproportionately large mouths; just as another favourite class of grotesque faces, those with distended mouths and tongues lolling out, were taken originally from the Typhons and Gorgons of the ancients. Many other popular types of faces rendered artificially ugly are mere exaggerations of the distortions produced on the features by different operations, such, for instance, as that of blowing a horn.

The practice of blowing the horn, is, indeed, peculiarly calculated to exhibit the features of the face to disadvantage, and was not overlooked by the designers of the mediæval decorative sculpture. One of the large collection of casts of sculptures from French cathedrals exhibited in the museum at South Kensington, has furnished the two subjects given in our cut No. 95. The first is represented as blowing a horn, but he is producing the greatest possible distortion in his features, and especially in his mouth, by drawing the horn forcibly on one side with his left hand, while he pulls his beard in the other direction with the right hand. The force with which he is supposed to be blowing is perhaps represented by the form given to his eyes. The face of the lower figure is in at least comparative repose. The design of representing general distortion in the first is further shown by the ridiculously unnatural position of the arms. Such distortion of the members was not unfrequently introduced to heighten the effect of the grimace in the face; and, as in these examples, it was not uncommon to introduce as a further element of grotesque, the bodies, or parts of the bodies, of animals, or even of demons.

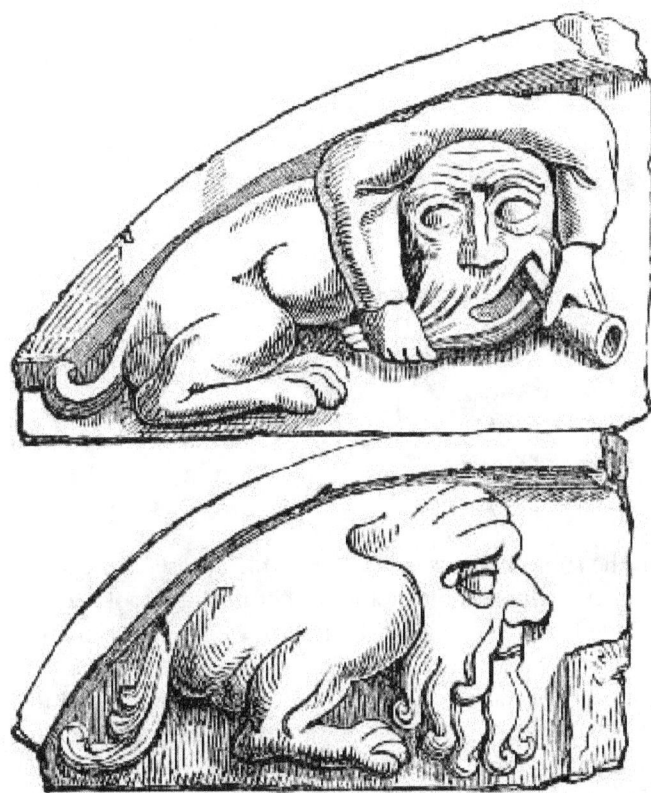

No. 95. Grotesque Monsters.

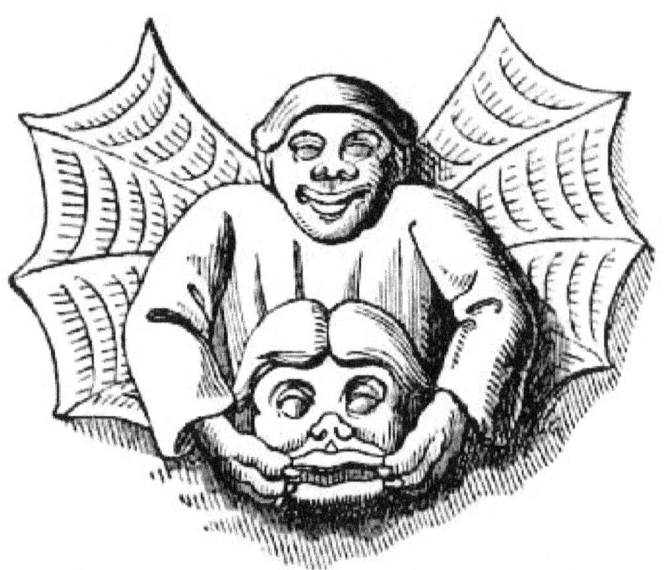

No. 96. Diabolical Mirth.

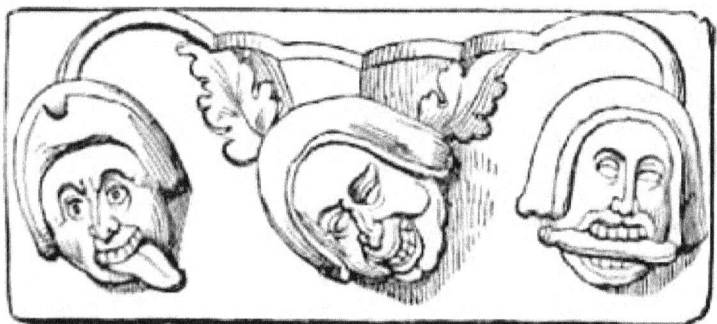

No. 97. Making Faces.

Another cast in the Kensington Museum is the subject of our cut No. 96, which presents the same idea of stretching the mouth. The subject is here exhibited by another rather mirthful looking individual, but whether the exhibitor is intended to be a goblin or demon, or whether he is merely furnished with the wings and claws of a bat, seems rather uncertain. The bat was looked upon as an unpropitious if not an unholy animal; like the owl, it was the companion of the witches, and of the spirits of darkness. The group in our cut No. 97 is taken from one of the carved stalls in the church of Stratford-upon-Avon, and represents a trio of grimacers. The first of these three grotesque faces is lolling out the tongue to an extravagant length; the second is simply grinning; while the third has taken a sausage between his teeth to render his grimace still more ridiculous. The number and variety of such grotesque faces, which we find scattered over the architectural decoration of our old ecclesiastical buildings, are so great that I will not attempt to give any more particular classification of them. All this church decoration was calculated especially to produce its effect upon the middle and lower classes, and mediæval art was, perhaps more than anything else, suited to mediæval society, for it belonged to the mass and not to the individual. The man who could enjoy a match at grinning through horse-collars, must have been charmed by the grotesque works of the mediæval stone sculptor and wood carver; and we may add that these display, though often rather rude, a very high degree of skill in art, a great power of producing striking imagery.

These mediæval artists loved also to produce horrible objects as well as laughable ones, though even in their horrors they were continually running into the grotesque. Among the adjuncts to these sculptured figures, we sometimes meet with instruments of pain, and very talented attempts to exhibit this on the features of the victims. The creed of the middle ages gave great scope for the indulgence of this taste in the infinitely varied terrors of purgatory and hell; and, not to speak of the more crude descriptions that are so common in mediæval popular literature, the account to which these descriptions might be turned by the poet as well as the artist are well known to the reader of Dante. Coils of serpents and dragons, which were the most usual instruments in the tortures of the infernal regions, were always favourite objects in mediæval ornamentation, whether sculptured or drawn, in the details of architectural decoration, or in the initial letters and margins of books. They are often combined in forming grotesque tracery with the bodies of animals or of human beings, and their movements are generally hostile to the latter. We have already seen, in previous chapters, examples of this use of serpents and dragons, dating from the earliest periods of mediæval art; and it is perhaps the most common style of ornamentation in the buildings and illuminated manuscripts in our island from the earlier Saxon times to the thirteenth century. This ornamentation is sometimes strikingly bold and effective. In the cathedral of Wells there is a series of ornamental bosses, formed by faces writhing under the attacks of numerous dragons, who are seizing upon the lips, eyes, and cheeks of their victims. One of these bosses, which are of the thirteenth century, is represented in our cut No. 98. A large, coarsely featured face is the victim of two dragons, one of which attacks his mouth, while the other has seized him by the eye. The expression of the face is strikingly horrible.

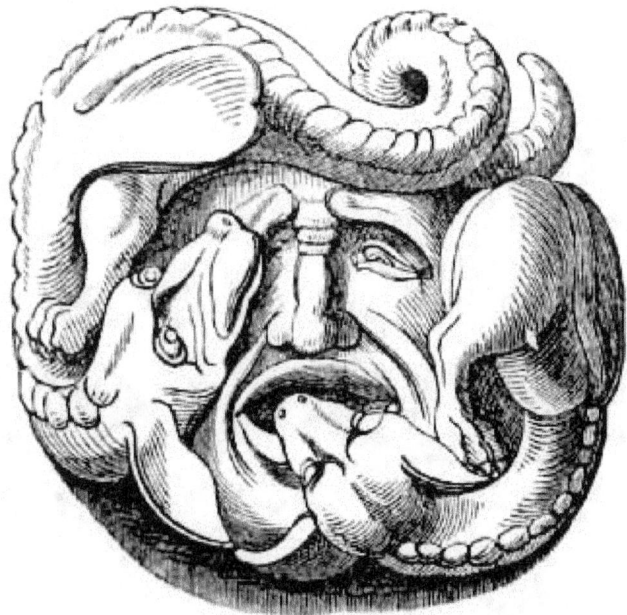

No. 98. Horror.

The higher mind of the middle ages loved to see inner meanings through outward forms; or, at least, it was a fashion which manifested itself most strongly in the latter half of the twelfth century, to adapt these outward forms to inward meanings by comparisons and moralisations; and under the effect of this feeling certain figures were at times adopted, with a view to some other purpose than mere ornament, though this was probably an innovation upon mediæval art. The tongue lolling out, taken originally, as we have seen, from the imagery of classic times, was accepted rather early in the middle ages as the emblem or symbol of luxury; and, when we find it among the sculptured ornaments of the architecture especially of some of the larger and more important churches, it implied probably an allusion to that vice—at least the face presented to us was intended to be that of a voluptuary. Among the remarkable series of sculptures which crown the battlements of the cloisters of Magdalen College, Oxford, executed a very few years after the middle of the fifteenth century, amid many figures of a very miscellaneous character, there are several which were thus, no doubt, intended to be representatives of vices, if not of virtues. I give two examples of these curious sculptures.

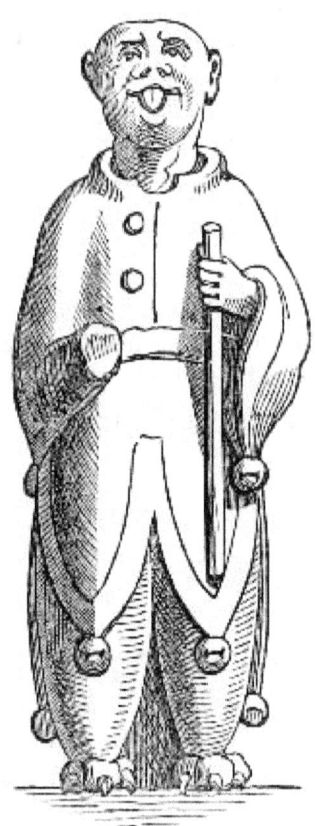

No. 99. Gluttony.

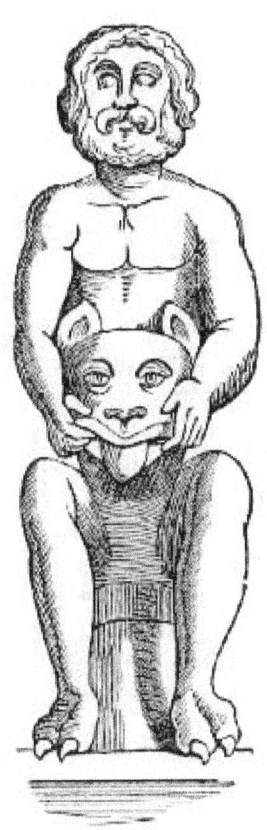

No. 100. Luxury.

The first, No. 99, is generally considered to represent gluttony, and it is a remarkable circumstance that, in a building the character of which was partly ecclesiastical, and which was erected at the expense and under the directions of a great prelate, Bishop Wainflete, the vice of gluttony, with which the ecclesiastical order was especially reproached, should be represented in ecclesiastical costume. It is an additional proof that the detail of the work of the building was left entirely to the builders. The coarse, bloated features of the face, and the "villainous" low forehead, are characteristically executed; and the lolling tongue may perhaps be intended to intimate that, in the lives of the clergy, luxury went hand in hand with its kindred vice. The second of our examples, No. 100, appears by its different characteristics (some of which we have been unable to introduce in our woodcut) to be intended to represent luxury itself. Sometimes qualities of the individual man, or even the class of society, are represented in a manner far less disguised by allegorical clothing, and therefore much more plainly to the understanding of the vulgar. Thus in an illuminated manuscript of the fourteenth century, in the British Museum (MS. Arundel, No. 91), gluttony is represented by a monk devouring a pie alone and in secret, except that a little cloven-footed imp holds up the dish, and seems to enjoy the prospect of monastic indulgence. This picture is copied in our cut No. 101. Another manuscript of the same date (MS. Sloane, No. 2435) contains a scene, copied in our cut No. 102, representing drunkenness under the form of another monk, who has obtained the keys and found his way into the cellar of his monastery, and is there indulging his love for good ale in similar secrecy. It is to be remarked that here, again, the vices are laid to the charge of the clergy. Our cut No. 103, from a bas-relief in Ely Cathedral, given in Carter's "Specimens of Ancient Sculpture," represents a man drinking from a horn, and evidently enjoying his employment, but his costume is not sufficiently characteristic to betray his quality.

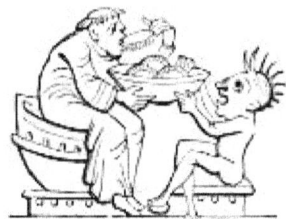

No. 101. Monkish Gluttony.

The subject of grotesque faces and heads naturally leads us to that of monstrous and grotesque bodies and groups of bodies, which has already been partly treated in a former chapter, where we have noticed the great love shown in the middle ages for monstrous animated figures, not only monsters of one nature, but, and that especially, of figures formed by joining together the parts of different, and entirely dissimilar, animals, of similar mixtures between animals and men. This, as stated above, was often effected by joining the body of some nondescript animal to a human head and face; so that, by the disproportionate size of the latter, the body, as a secondary part of the picture, became only an adjunct to set off still further the grotesque character of the human face. More importance was sometimes given to the body combined with fantastic forms, which baffle any attempt at giving an intelligible description. The accompanying cut, No. 104, represents a winged monster of this kind; it is taken from one of the casts from French churches exhibited in the Kensington Museum.

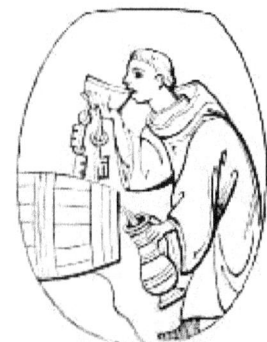

No. 102. The Monastic Cellarer.

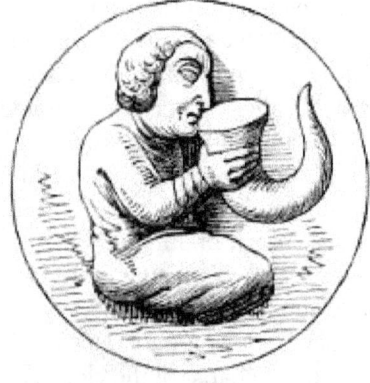

No. 103. Drunkenness.

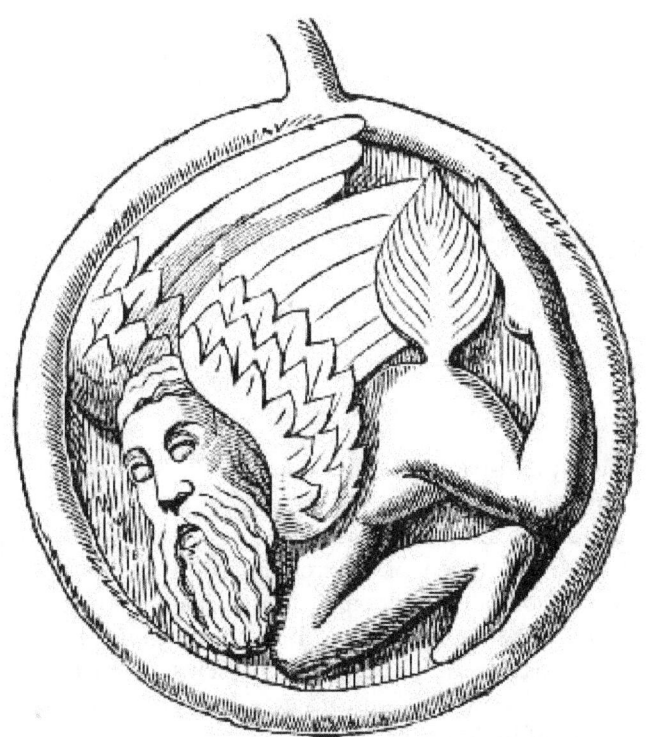

No. 104. A Strange Monster.

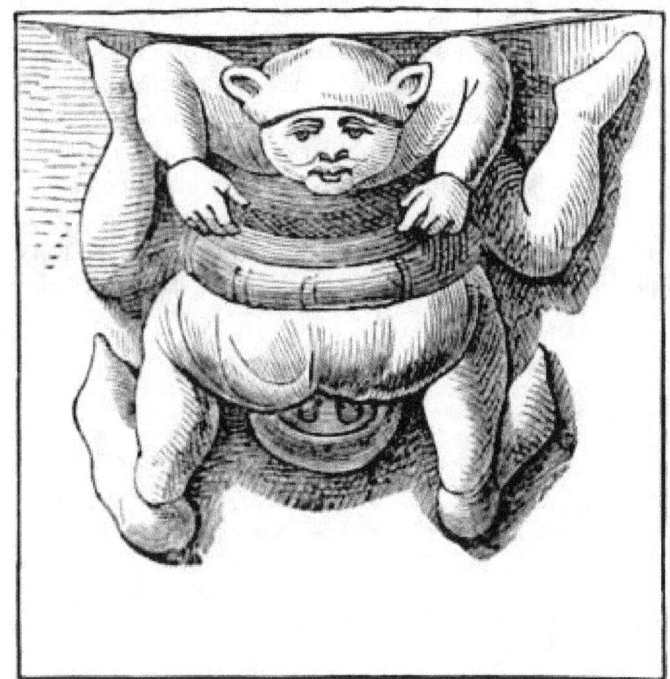

No. 105. Rolling Topsy Turvy.

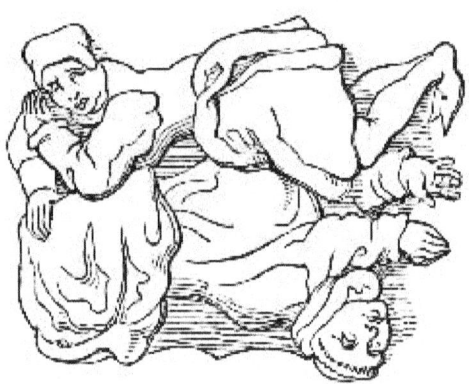

No. 106. A Continuous Group.

Sometimes the mediæval artist, without giving any unusual form to his human figures, placed them in strange postures, or joined them in singular combinations. These latter are commonly of a playful character, or sometimes they represent droll feats of skill, or puzzles, or other subjects, all of which have been published pictorially and for the amusement of children down to very recent times. There were a few of these groups which are of rather frequent occurrence, and they were evidently favourite types. One of these is given in the annexed cut, No. 105. It is taken from one of the carved misereres of the stalls in Ely cathedral, as given in Carter, and represents two men who appear to be rolling over each other. The upper figure exhibits animal's ears on his cap, which seem to proclaim him a member of the fraternity of fools: the ears of the lower figure are concealed from view. This group is not a rare one, especially on similar monuments in France, where the architectural antiquaries have a technical name for it; and this shows us how even the particular forms of art in the middle ages were not confined to any particular country, but more or less, and with exceptions, they pervaded all those which acknowledged the ecclesiastical supremacy of the church of Rome; whatever peculiarity of style it took in particular countries, the same forms were spread through all western Europe. Our next cut, No. 106, gives another of these curious groups, consisting, in fact, of two individuals, one of which is evidently an ecclesiastic. It will be seen that, as we follow this round, we obtain, by means of the two heads, four different figures in so many totally different positions. This group is taken from one of the very curious seats in the cathedral of Rouen in Normandy, which were engraved and published in an interesting volume by the late Monsieur E. H. Langlois.

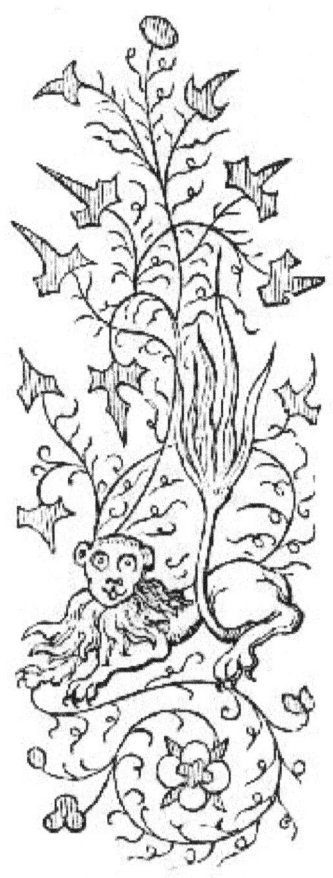

No. 107. Border Ornament.

Among the most interesting of the mediæval burlesque drawings are those which are found in such abundance in the borders of the pages of illuminated manuscripts. During the earlier periods of the mediæval miniatures, the favourite objects for these borders were monstrous animals, especially dragons, which could easily be twined into grotesque combinations. In course of time, the subjects thus introduced became more numerous, and in the fifteenth century they were very varied. Strange animals still continued to be favourites, but they were more light and elegant in their forms, and were more gracefully designed. Our cut No. 107, taken from the beautifully-illuminated manuscript of the romance of the "Comte d'Artois," of the fifteenth century, which has furnished us previously with several cuts, will illustrate my meaning. The graceful lightness of the tracery of the foliage shown in this design is found in none of the earlier works of art of this class. This, of course, is chiefly to be ascribed to the great advance which had been made in the art of design since the thirteenth century. But, though so greatly improved in the style of art, the same class of subjects continued to be introduced in this border ornamentation long after the art of printing, and that of engraving, which accompanied it, had been introduced. The revolution in the ornamentation of the borders of the pages of books was effected by the artists of the sixteenth century, at which time people had become better acquainted with, and had learnt to appreciate, ancient art and Roman antiquities, and they drew their inspiration from a correct knowledge of what the middle ages had copied blindly, but had not understood. Among the subjects of burlesque which the monuments of Roman art presented to them, the stumpy figures of the pigmies appear to have gained special favour, and they are employed in a manner which reminds us of the pictures found in Pompeii. Jost Amman, the well-known artist, who exercised his profession at Nüremberg in the latter half of the sixteenth century, engraved a set of illustrations to Ovid's Metamorphoses, which were printed at Lyons in 1574, and each cut and page of which is enclosed in a border of very fanciful and neatly-executed burlesque. The pigmies are introduced in these borders very freely, and are grouped with great spirit. I select as an example, cut No. 108, a scene which represents a triumphal procession—some pigmy Alexander returning from his conquests. The hero is seated on a throne carried by an elephant, and before him a bird, perhaps a vanquished crane, proclaims loudly his praise. Before them a pigmy attendant marches proudly, carrying in one hand the olive branch of peace, and leading in the other a ponderous but captive ostrich, as a trophy of his master's victories. Before him again a pigmy warrior, heavily armed with battle-axe and falchion, is mounting the steps of a stage, on which a nondescript animal, partaking somewhat of the character of a sow, but perhaps intended as a burlesque on the strange animals which, in mediæval romance, Alexander was said to have encountered in Egypt, blows a horn, to celebrate or announce the return of the conqueror. A snail, also advancing slowly up the stage, implies, perhaps, a sneer at the whole scene.

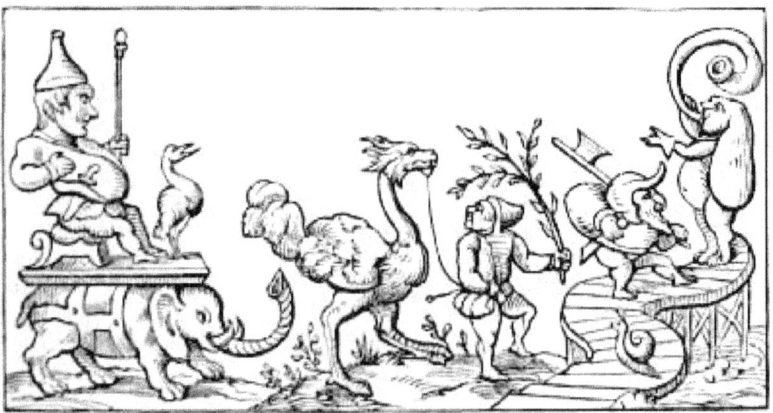

No. 108. A Triumphal Procession.

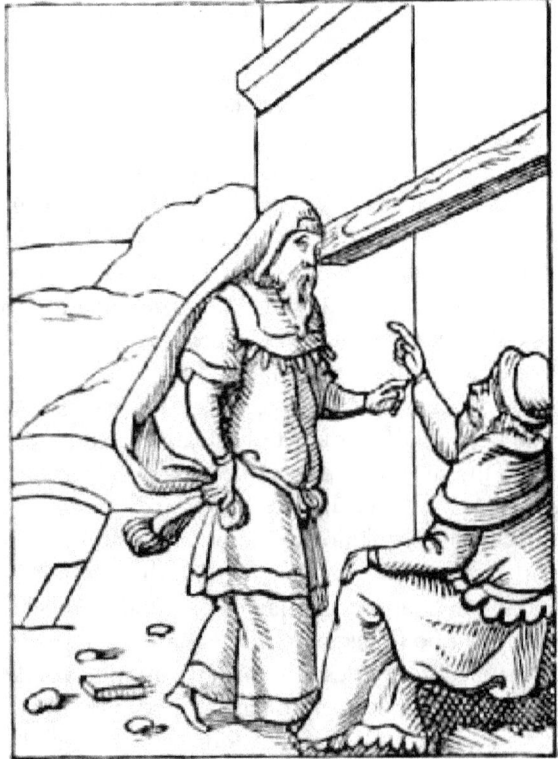

No. 109. The Mote and the Beam.

Nevertheless, these old German, Flemish, and Dutch artists were still much influenced by the mediæval spirit, which they displayed in their coarse and clumsy imagination, in their neglect of everything like congruity in their treatment of the subject with regard to time and place, and their *naïve* exaggerations and blunders. Extreme examples of these characteristics are spoken of, in which the Israelites crossing the Red Sea are armed with muskets, and all the other accoutrements of modern soldiers, and in which Abraham is preparing to sacrifice his son Isaac by shooting him with a matchlock. In delineating scriptural subjects, an attempt is generally made to clothe the figures in an imaginary ancient oriental costume, but the landscapes are filled with the modern castles and mansion houses, churches, and monasteries of western Europe. These half-mediæval artists, too, like their more ancient predecessors, often fall into unintentional caricature by the exaggeration or simplicity with which they treat their subjects. There was one subject which the artists of this period of regeneration of art seemed to have agreed to treat in a very unimaginative manner. In the beautiful Sermon on the Mount, our Saviour, in condemning hasty judgments of other people's actions, says (Matt. vii. 3-5), "And why beholdest thou the mote that is in thy brother's eye, but considerest not the beam that is in thine own eye? Or how wilt thou say to thy brother, Let me pull out the mote out of thine eye, and, behold, a beam is in thine own eye? Thou hypocrite, first cast out the beam out of thine own eye, and then shalt thou see clearly to cast out the mote out of thy brother's eye." Whatever be the exact nature of the beam which the man was expected to overlook in his "own eye," it certainly was not a large beam of timber. Yet such was the conception of it by artists of the sixteenth century. One of them, named Solomon Bernard, designed a series of woodcuts illustrating the New Testament, which were published at Lyons in 1553; and the manner in which he treated the subject will be seen in our cut No. 109, taken from one of the illustrations to that book. The individual seated is the man who has a mote in his eye, which the other, approaching him, points out; and he retorts by pointing to the "beam," which is certainly such a massive object as could not easily have been overlooked. About thirteen years before this, an artist of Augsburg, named Daniel Hopfer, had published a large copper-plate engraving of this same subject, a reduced copy of which is given in the cut No. 110. The individual who sees the mote in his brother's eye, is evidently treating it in the character of a physician or surgeon. It is only necessary to add that the beam in his own eye is of still more extraordinary dimensions than the former, and that, though it seems to escape the notice both of himself and his patient, it is evident that the group in the distance contemplate it with astonishment. The building accompanying this scene appears to be a church, with paintings of saints in the windows.

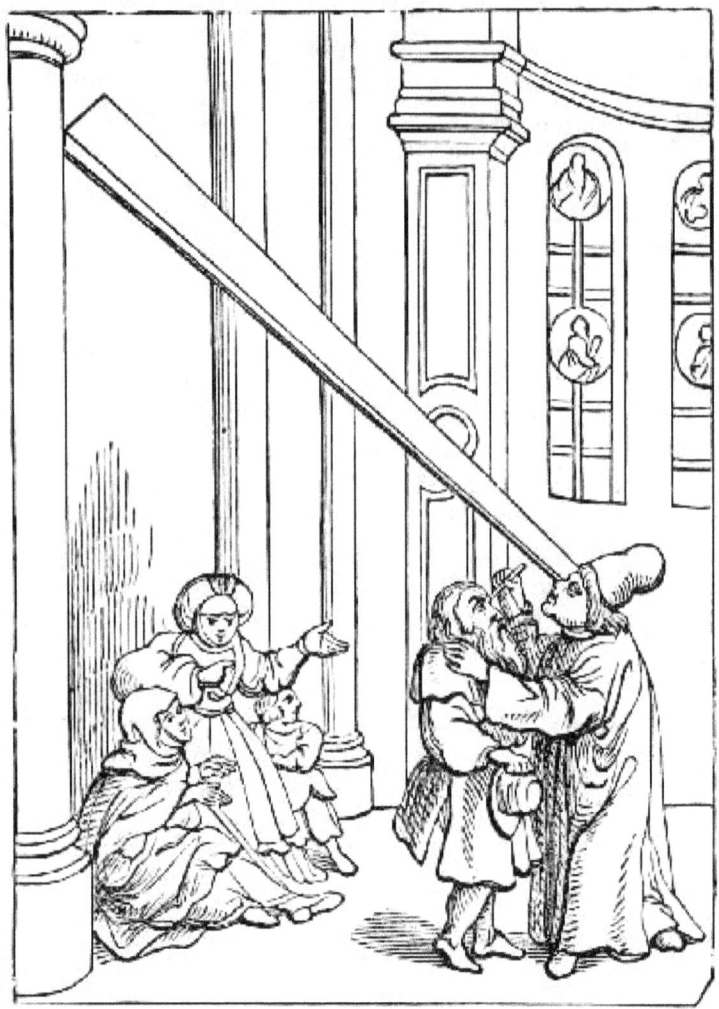

No. 110. The Mote and the Beam—Another Treatment.

CHAPTER X.

SATIRICAL LITERATURE IN THE MIDDLE AGES.—JOHN DE HAUTEVILLE AND ALAN DE LILLE.—GOLIAS AND THE GOLIARDS.—THE GOLIARDIC POETRY.—TASTE FOR PARODY.—PARODIES ON RELIGIOUS SUBJECTS.—POLITICAL CARICATURE IN THE MIDDLE AGES.—THE JEWS OF NORWICH.—CARICATURE REPRESENTATIONS OF COUNTRIES.—LOCAL SATIRE.—POLITICAL SONGS AND POEMS.

In a previous chapter I have spoken of a class of satirical literature which was entirely popular in its character. Not that on this account it was original among the peoples who composed mediæval society, for the intellectual development of the middle ages came almost all from Rome through one medium or other, although we know so little of the details of the popular literature of the Romans that we cannot always trace it. The mediæval literature of western Europe was mostly modelled upon that of France, which was received, like its language, from Rome. But when the great university system became established, towards the end of the eleventh century, the scholars of western Europe became more directly acquainted with the models of literature which antiquity had left them; and during the twelfth century these found imitators so skilful that some of them almost deceive us into accepting them for classical writers themselves. Among the first of these models to attract the attention of mediæval scholars, were the Roman satirists, and the study of them produced, during the twelfth century, a number of satirical writers in Latin prose and verse, who are remarkable not only for their boldness and poignancy, but for the elegance of their style. I may mention among those of English birth, John of Salisbury, Walter Mapes, and Giraldus Cambrensis, who all wrote in prose, and Nigellus Wireker, already mentioned in a former chapter, and John de Hauteville, who wrote in verse. The first of these, in his "Polycraticus," Walter Mapes, in his book "De Nugis Curialium," and Giraldus, in his "Speculum Ecclesiæ," and several other of his writings, lay the lash on the corruptions and vices of their contemporaries with no tender hand. The two most remarkable English satirists of the twelfth century were John de Hauteville and Nigellus Wireker. The former wrote, in the year 1184, a poem in nine books of Latin hexameters, entitled, after the name of its hero, "Architrenius," or the Arch-mourner. Architrenius is represented as a youth, arrived at years of maturity, who sorrows over the spectacle of human vices and weaknesses, until he resolves to go on a pilgrimage to Dame Nature, in order to expostulate with her for having made him feeble to resist the temptations of the world, and to entreat her assistance. On his way, he arrives successively at the court of Venus and at the abode of Gluttony, which give him the occasion to dwell at considerable length on the license and luxury which prevailed among his contemporaries. He next reaches Paris, and visits the famous mediæval university, and his satire on the manners of the students and the fruitlessness of their studies, forms a remarkable and interesting picture of the age. The pilgrim next arrives at the Mount of Ambition, tempting by its beauty and by the stately palace with which it was crowned, and here we are presented with a satire on the manners and corruptions of the court. Near to this was the Hill of Presumption, which was inhabited by ecclesiastics of all classes, great scholastic doctors and professors, monks, and the like. It is a satire on the manners of the clergy. As Architrenius turns from this painful spectacle, he encounters a gigantic and hideous monster named Cupidity, is led into a series of reflections upon the greediness and avarice of the prelates, from which he is roused by the uproar caused by a fierce combat between the prodigals and the misers. He is subsequently carried to the island of far-distant Thule, which he finds to be the resting-place of the philosophers of ancient Greece, and he listens to their declamations against the vices of mankind. After this visit, Architrenius reaches the end of his pilgrimage. He finds Nature in the form of a beautiful woman, dwelling with a host of attendants in the midst of a flowery plain, and meats with a courteous reception, but she begins by giving him a long lecture on natural philosophy. After this is concluded, Dame Nature listens to his complaints, and, to console him, gives him a handsome woman, named Moderation, for a wife, and dismisses him with a chapter of good counsels on the duties of married life. The general moral intended to be inculcated appears to be that the retirement of domestic happiness is to be preferred to the vain and heartless turmoils of active life in all its phases. It will be seen that the kind of allegory which subsequently produced the "Pilgrim's Progress," had already made its appearance in mediæval literature.

Another of the celebrated satirists of the scholastic ages was named Alanus de Insulis, or Alan of Lille, because he is understood to have been born at Lille in Flanders. He occupied the chair of theology for many years in the university of Paris with great distinction, and his learning was so extensive that he gained the name of *doctor universalis*, the universal doctor. In one of his books, which is an imitation of that favourite book in the middle ages "Boethius de Consolatione Philosophiæ," Dame Nature, in the place of Philosophy—not, as in John de Hauteville, as the referee, but as the complainant—is introduced bitterly lamenting over the deep depravity of the thirteenth century, especially displayed in the prevalence of vices of a revolting character. This work, which, like Boethius, consists of alternate chapters in verse and prose, is entitled "De Planctu Naturæ," the lamentation of nature. I will not, however, go on here to give a list of the graver satirical writers, but we will proceed to another class of satirists which sprang up among the mediæval scholars, more remarkable and more peculiar in their character—I mean peculiar to the middle ages.

The satires of the time show us that the students in the universities in the twelfth and thirteenth centuries, who enjoyed a great amount of independence from authority, were generally wild and riotous, and, among the vast number of youths who then devoted themselves to a scholastic life, we can have no doubt that the habit of dissipation became permanent. Among these wild students there existed, probably, far more wit and satirical talent than among their steadier and more laborious brethren, and this wit, and the manner in which it was displayed, made its possessors welcome guests at the luxurious tables of the higher and richer clergy, at which Latin seems to have been the language in ordinary use. In all probability it was from this circumstance (in allusion to the Latin word *gula*, as intimating their love of the table) that these merry scholars, who displayed in Latin some of the accomplishments which the jougleurs professed in the vulgar tongue, took or received the name of *goliards* (in the Latin of that time, *goliardi*, or *goliardenses*).[42] The name at least appears to have been adopted towards the end of the twelfth century. In the year 1229, during the minority of Louis IX., and while the government of France was in the hands of the queen-mother, troubles arose in the university of Paris through the intrigues of the papal legate, and the turbulence of the scholars led to their dispersion and to the temporary closing of the schools; and the contemporary historian, Matthew Paris, tells us how "some of the servants of the departing scholars, or those whom we used to call goliardenses," composed an indecent epigram on the rumoured familiarities between the legate and the queen. But this is not the first mention of the goliards, for a statute of the council of Treves, in 1227, forbade "all priests to permit truants, or other wandering scholars, or goliards, to sing verses or *Sanctus* and *Angelus Dei* in the service of the mass."[43] This probably refers to parodies on the religious service, such as those of which I shall soon have to speak. From this time the goliards are frequently mentioned. In ecclesiastical statutes published in the year 1289, it is ordered that the clerks or clergy (*clerici*, that is, men who had their education in the university) "should not be jougleurs, goliards, or buffoons;"[44] and the same statute proclaims a heavy penalty against those *clerici* "who persist in the practice of goliardy or stage performance during a year,"[45] which shows that they exercised more of the functions of the jougleur than the mere singing of songs.

These vagabond clerks made for themselves an imaginary chieftain, or president of their order, to whom they gave the name of Golias, probably as a pun on the name of the giant who combated against David, and, to show further their defiance of the existing church government, they made him a bishop—*Golias episcopus*. Bishop Golias was the burlesque representative of the clerical order, the general satirist, the reformer of eclesiastical and all other corruptions. If he was not a doctor of divinity, he was a master of arts, for he is spoken of as *Magister Golias*. But above all he was the father of the Goliards, the "ribald clerks," as they are called, who all belonged to his household,[46] and they are spoken of as his children.

Summa salus omnium, filius Mariæ,
Pascat, potat, vestiat pueros Golyæ![47]

"May the Saviour of all, the Son of Mary, give food, drink, and clothes to the children of Golias!" Still the name was clothed in so much mystery, that Giraldus Cambrensis, who flourished towards the latter end of the twelfth century, believed Golias to be a real personage, and his contemporary. It may be added that Golias not only boasts of the dignity of bishop, but he appears sometimes under the title of *archipoeta*, the archpoet or poet-in-chief.

Cæsarius of Heisterbach, who completed his book of the miracles of his time in the year 1222, tells us a curious anecdote of the character of the wandering clerk. In the year before he wrote, he tells us, "It happened at Bonn, in the diocese of Cologne, that a certain wandering clerk, named Nicholas, of the class they call archpoet, was grievously ill, and when he supposed that he was dying, he obtained from our abbot, through his own pleading, and the intercession of the canons of the same church, admission into the order. What more? He put on the tunic, as it appeared to us, with much contrition, but, when the danger was past, he took it off immediately, and, throwing it down with derision, took to flight." We learn best the character of the goliards from their own poetry, a considerable quantity of which is preserved. They wandered about from mansion to mansion, probably from monastery to monastery, just like the jougleurs, but they seem to have been especially welcome at the tables of the prelates of the church, and, like the jougleurs, besides being well feasted, they received gifts of clothing and other articles. In few instances only were they otherwise than welcome, as described in the rhyming epigram printed in my "Latin Poems attributed to Walter Mapes." "I come uninvited," says the goliard to the bishop, "ready for dinner; such is my fate, never to dine invited." The bishop replies, "I care not for vagabonds, who wander among the fields, and cottages, and villages; such guests are not for my table. I do not invite you, for I avoid such as you; yet without my will you may eat the bread you ask. Wash, wipe, sit, dine, drink, wipe, and depart."

Goliardus.
Non invitatus venio prandere paratus;
Sic sum fatatus, nunquam prandere vocatus.
Episcopus.
Non ego curo vagos, qui rura, mapalia, pagos
Perlustrant, tales non vult mea mensa sodales.
Te non invito, tibi consimiles ego vito;
Me tamen invito potieris pane petito.
Ablue, terge, sede, prande, bibe, terge, recede.

In another similar epigram, the goliard complains of the bishop who had given him as his reward nothing but an old worn-out mantle. Most of the writers of the goliardic poetry complain of their poverty, and some of them admit that this poverty arose from the tavern and the love of gambling. One of them alleges as his claim to the liberality of his host, that, as he was a scholar, he had not learnt to labour, that his parents were knights, but he had no taste for fighting, and that, in a word, he preferred poetry to any occupation. Another speaks still more to the point, and complains that he is in danger of being obliged to sell his clothes. "If this garment of vair which I wear," he says, "be sold for money, it will be a great disgrace to me; I would rather suffer a long fast. A bishop, who is the most generous of all generous men, gave me this cloak, and will have for it heaven, a greater reward than St. Martin has, who only gave half of his cloak. It is needful now that the poet's want be relieved by your liberality [addressing his hearers]; let noble men give noble gifts—gold, and robes, and the like."

Si vendatur propter denarium
Indumentum quod porto varium,
Grande mihi fiet opprobrium;
Malo diu pati jejunium.
Largissimus largorum omnium
Prœsul dedit mihi hoc pallium,
Majus habens in cælis præmium
Quam Martinus, qui dedit medium.
Nunc est opus ut vestra copia
Sublevetur vatis inopia;
Dent nobiles dona nobilia,—

Aurum, vestes, et his similia.

There has been some difference of opinion as to the country to which this poetry more especially belongs. Giraldus Cambrensis, writing at the end of the twelfth or the beginning of the thirteenth century, evidently thought that Golias was an Englishman; and at a later date the goliardic poetry was almost all ascribed to Giraldus's contemporary and friend, the celebrated humourist, Walter Mapes. This was, no doubt, an error. Jacob Grimm seemed inclined to claim them for Germany; but Grimm, on this occasion, certainly took a narrow view of the question. We shall probably be more correct in saying that they belonged in common to all the countries over which university learning extended; that in whatever country a particular poem of this class was composed, it became the property of the whole body of these scholastic jougleurs, and that it was thus carried from one land to another, receiving sometimes alterations or additions to adapt it to each. Several of these poems are found in manuscripts written in different countries with such alterations and additions, as, for instance, that in the well-known "Confession," in the English copies of which we have, near the conclusion, the line—

Præsul Coventrensium, parce confitenti;

an appeal to the bishop of Coventry, which is changed, in a copy in a German manuscript, to

Electe Coloniæ, parce pœnitenti,

"O elect of Cologne, spare me penitent." From a comparison of what remains of this poetry in manuscripts written in different countries, it appears probable that the names Golias and goliard originated in the university of Paris, but were more especially popular in England, while the term *archipoeta* was more commonly used in Germany.

In 1841 I collected all the goliardic poetry which I could then find in English manuscripts, and edited it, under the name of Walter Mapes, as one of the publications of the Camden Society.[48] At a rather later date I gave a chapter of additional matter of the same description in my "Anecdota Literaria."[49] All the poems I have printed in these two volumes are found in manuscripts written in England, and some of them are certainly the compositions of English writers. They are distinguished by remarkable facility and ease in versification and rhyme, and by great pungency of satire. The latter is directed especially against the clerical order, and none are spared, from the pope at the summit of the scale down to the lowest of the clergy. In the "Apocalypsis Goliæ," or Golias's Revelations, which appears to have been the most popular of all these poems,[50] the poet describes himself as carried up in a vision to heaven, where the vices and disorders of the various classes of the popish clergy are successively revealed to him. The pope is a devouring lion; in his eagerness for pounds, he pawns books; at the sight of a mark of money, he treats Mark the Evangelist with disdain; while he sails aloft, money alone is his anchoring-place. The original lines will serve as a specimen of the style of these curious compositions, and of the love of punning which was so characteristic of the literature of that age:—

Est leo pontifex summus, qui devorat,
Qui libras sitiens, libros impignorat;
Marcam respiciet, Marcum dedecorat;
In summis navigans, in nummis anchorat.

The bishop is in haste to intrude himself into other people's pastures, and fills himself with other people's goods. The ravenous archdeacon is compared to an eagle, because he has sharp eyes to see his prey afar off, and is swift to seize upon it. The dean is represented by an animal with a man's face, full of silent guile, who covers fraud with the form of justice, and by the show of simplicity would make others believe him to be pious. In this spirit the faults of the clergy, of all degrees, are minutely criticised through between four and five hundred lines; and it must not be forgotten that it was the English clergy whose character was thus exposed.

Tu scribes etiam, forma sed alia,
Septem ecclesiis quæ sunt in Anglia.

Others of these pieces are termed Sermons, and are addressed, some to the bishops and dignitaries of the church, others to the pope, others to the monastic orders, and others to the clergy in general. The court of Rome, we are told, was infamous for its greediness; there all right and justice were put up for sale, and no favour could be had without money. In this court money occupies everybody's thoughts; its cross—i. e. the mark on the reverse of the coin—its roundness, and its whiteness, all please the Romans; where money speaks law is silent.

Nummis in hac curia non est qui non vacet;
Crux placet, rotunditas, et albedo placet,
Et cum totum placeat, et Romanis placet,
Ubi nummus loquitur, et lex omnis tacet.

Perhaps one of the most curious of these poems is the "Confession of Golias," in which the poet is made to satirise himself, and he thus gives us a curious picture of the goliard's life. He complains that he is made of light material, which is moved by every wind; that he wanders about irregularly, like the ship on the sea or the bird in the air, seeking worthless companions like himself. He is a slave to the charms of the fair sex. He is a martyr to gambling, which often turns him out naked to the cold, but he is warmed inwardly by the inspiration of his mind, and he writes better poetry than ever. Lechery and gambling are two of his vices, and the third is drinking. "The tavern," he says, "I never despised, nor shall I ever despise it, until I see the holy angels coming to sing the eternal requiem over my corpse. It is my design to die in the tavern; let wine be placed to my mouth when I am expiring, that when the choirs of angels come, they may say, 'Be God propitious to this drinker!' The lamp of the soul is lighted with cups; the heart steeped in nectar flies up to heaven; and the wine in the tavern has for me a better flavour than that which the bishop's butler mixes with water.... Nature gives to every one his peculiar gift: I never could write fasting; a boy could beat me in composition when I am hungry; I hate thirst and fasting as much as death."

Tertio capitulo memoro tabernam:
Illam nullo tempore sprevi, neque spernam,
Donec sanctos angelos venientes cernam,
Cantantes pro mortuo requiem æternam.
Meum est propositum in taberna mori;
Vindum sit appositum morientis ori,
Ut dicant cum venerint angelorum chori,
'Deus sit propitius huic potatori!'
Poculis accenditur animi lucerna;
Cor imbutum nectare volat ad superna:
Mihi sapit dulcius vinum in taberna,
Quam quod aqua miscuit præsulis pincerna.
Unicuique proprium dat natura munus:
Ego nunquam potui scribere jejunus;
Me jejunum vincere posset puer unus;

Sitim et jejunium odi tanquam funus.[51]

Another of the more popular of these goliardic poems was the advice of Golias against marriage, a gross satire upon the female sex. Contrary to what we might perhaps expect from their being written in Latin, many of these metrical satires are directed against the vices of the laity, as well as against those of the clergy.

In 1844 the celebrated German scholar, Jacob Grimm, published in the "Transactions of the Academy of Sciences at Berlin" a selection of goliardic verses from manuscripts in Germany, which had evidently been written by Germans, and some of them containing allusions to German affairs in the thirteenth century.[52] They present the same form of verse and the same style of satire as those found in England, but the name of Golias is exchanged for *archipoeta*, the archpoet. Some of the stanzas of the "Confession of Golias" are found in a poem in which the archpoet addresses a petition to the archchancellor for assistance in his distress, and confesses his partiality for wine. A copy of the Confession itself is also found in this German collection, under the title of the "Poet's Confession."

The Royal Library at Munich contains a very important manuscript of this goliardic Latin poetry, written in the thirteenth century. It belonged originally to one of the great Benedictine abbeys in Bavaria, where it appears to have been very carefully preserved, but still with an apparent consciousness that it was not exactly a book for a religious brotherhood, which led the monks to omit it in the catalogue of their library, no doubt as a book the possession of which was not to be proclaimed publicly. When written, it was evidently intended to be a careful selection of the poetry of this class then current. One part of it consists of poetry of a more serious character, such as hymns, moral poems, and especially satirical pieces. In this class there are more than one piece which are also found in the manuscripts written in England. A very large portion of the collection consists of love songs, which, although evidently treasured by the Benedictine monks, are sometimes licentious in character. A third class consists of drinking and gambling songs (*potatoria et lusoria*). The general character of this poetry is more playful, more ingenious and intricate in its metrical structure, in fact, more lyric than that of the poetry we have been describing; yet it came, in all probability, from the same class of poets—the clerical jougleurs. The touches of sentiment, the descriptions of female beauty, the admiration of nature, are sometimes expressed with remarkable grace. Thus, the green wood sweetly enlivened by the joyous voices of its feathered inhabitants, the shade of its branches, the thorns covered with flowers, which, says the poet, are emblematical of love, which pricks like a thorn and then soothes like a flower, are tastefully described in the following lines:—

Cantu nemus avium
Lascivia canentium
Suave delinitur,
Fronde redimitur,
Vernant spinæ floribus
Micantibus,
Venerem signantibus
Quia spina pungit, flos blanditur.

And the following scrap of the description of a beautiful damsel shows no small command of language and versification—

Allicit dulcibus

Verbis et osculis,
Labellulis
Castigate tumentibus,
Roseo nectareus
Odor infusus ori;
Pariter eburneus
Sedat ordo dentium
Par niveo candori.

The whole contents of this manuscript were printed in 1847, in an octavo volume, issued by the Literary Society at Stuttgard.[53] I had already printed some examples of such amatory Latin lyric poetry in 1838, in a volume of "Early Mysteries and Latin Poems;"[54] but this poetry does not belong properly to the subject of the present volume, and I pass on from it.

The goliards did not always write in verse, for we have some of their prose compositions, and these appear especially in the form of parodies. We trace a great love for parody in the middle ages, which spared not even things the most sacred, and the examples brought forward in the celebrated trial of William Hone, were mild in comparison to some which are found scattered here and there in mediæval manuscripts. In my Poems, attributed to Walter Mapes,[55] I have printed a satire in prose entitled "*Magister Golyas de quodam abbate*" (i.e., Master Golias's account of a certain abbot), which has somewhat the character of a parody upon a saint's legend. The voluptuous life of the superior of a monastic house is here described in a tone of banter which nothing could excel. Several parodies, more direct in their character, are printed in the two volumes of the "Reliquæ Antiquæ."[56] One of these (vol. ii. p. 208) is a complete parody on the service of the mass, which is entitled in the original, "*Missa de Potatoribus*," the Mass of the Drunkard. In this extraordinary composition, even the pater-noster is parodied. A portion of this, with great variations, is found in the German collection of the Carmina Burana, under the title of *Officium Lusorum*, the Office of the Gamblers. In the "Reliquæ Antiquæ" (ii. 58) we have a parody on the Gospel of St. Luke, beginning with the words, *Initium fallacis Evangelii secundum Lupum*, this last word being, of course, a sort of pun upon Lucam. Its subject also is Bacchus, and the scene having been laid in a tavern in Oxford, we have no difficulty in ascribing it to some scholar of that university in the thirteenth century. Among the Carmina Burana we find a similar parody on the Gospel of St. Mark, which has evidently belonged to one of these burlesques on the church service; and as it is less profane than the others, and at the same time pictures the mediæval hatred towards the church of Rome, I will give a translation of it as an example of this singular class of compositions. It is hardly necessary to remind the reader that a mark was a coin of the value of thirteen shillings and fourpence:—

"The beginning of the holy gospel according to Marks of silver. At that time the pope said to the Romans: 'When the son of man shall come to the seat of our majesty, first say, Friend, for what hast thou come? But if he should persevere in knocking without giving you anything, cast him out into utter darkness.' And it came to pass, that a certain poor clerk came to the court of the lord the pope, and cried out, saying, 'Have pity on me at least, you doorkeepers of the pope, for the hand of poverty has touched me. For I am needy and poor, and therefore I seek your assistance in my calamity and misery.' But they hearing this were highly indignant, and said to him: 'Friend, thy poverty be with thee in perdition; get thee backward, Satan, for thou dost not savour of those things which have the savour of money. Verily, verily, I say unto thee, Thou shalt not enter into the joy of thy lord, until thou shalt have given thy last farthing.'

"Then the poor man went away, and sold his cloak and his gown, and all that he had, and gave it to the cardinals, and to the doorkeepers, and to the chamberlains. But they said, 'And what is this among so many?' And they cast him out of the gates, and going out he wept bitterly, and was without consolation. After him there came to the court a certain clerk who was rich, and gross, and fat, and large, and who in a tumult had committed manslaughter. He gave first to the doorkeeper, secondly to the chamberlain, third to the cardinals. But they judged among themselves, that they were to receive more. Then the lord the pope, hearing that the cardinals and officials had received many gifts from the clerk, became sick unto death. But the rich man sent him an electuary of gold and silver, and he was immediately made whole. Then the lord the pope called before him the cardinals and officials, and said to them: 'Brethren, see that no one deceive you with empty words. For I give you an example, that, as I take, so take ye also.'"

This mediæval love of parody was not unfrequently displayed in a more popular form, and in the language of the people. In the *Reliquæ Antiquæ* (i. 82) we have a very singular parody in English on the sermons of the Catholic priesthood, a good part of which is so written as to present no consecutive sense, which circumstance itself implies a sneer at the preachers. Thus our burlesque preacher, in the middle of his discourse, proceeds to narrate as follows (I modernise the English):—

"Sirs, what time that God and St. Peter came to Rome, Peter asked Adam a full great doubtful question, and said, 'Adam, Adam, why ate thou the apple unpared?' 'Forsooth,' quod he, 'for I had no wardens (pears) fried.' And Peter saw the fire, and dread him, and stepped into a plum-tree that hanged full of ripe red cherries. And there he saw all the parrots in the sea. There he saw steeds and stockfish pricking 'swose' (?) in the water. There he saw hens and herrings that hunted after harts in hedges. There he saw eels roasting larks. There he saw haddocks were done on the pillory for wrong roasting of May butter; and there he saw how bakers baked butter to grease with old monks' boots. There he saw how the fox preached," &c.

The same volume contains some rather clever parodies on the old English alliterative romances, composed in a similar style of consecutive nonsense. It is a class of parody which we trace to a rather early period, which the French term a *coq-à-l'âne*, and which became fashionable in England in the seventeenth century in the form of songs entitled "Tom-a-Bedlams." M. Jubinal has printed two such poems in French, perhaps of the thirteenth century,[57] and others are found scattered through the old manuscripts. There is generally so much coarseness in them that it is not easy to select a portion for translation, and in fact their point consists in going on through the length of a poem of this kind without imparting a single clear idea. Thus, in the second of those published by Jubinal, we are told how, "The shadow of an egg carried the new year upon the bottom of a pot; two old new combs made a ball to run the trot; when it came to paying the scot, I, who never move myself, cried out, without saying a word, 'Take the feather of an ox, and clothe a wise fool with it.'"—

Li ombres d'un oef
Portoit l'an reneuf
Sur la fonz d'un pot;
Deus viez pinges neuf
Firent un estuef
Pour courre le trot;
Quant vint au paier l'escot,
Je, qui onques ne me muef,
M'escriai, si ne dis mot:—
'Prenés la plume d'un buef,
S'en vestez un sage sot.'—Jubinal, Nouv. Rec., ii. 217.

The spirit of the goliards continued to exist long after the name had been forgotten; and the mass of bitter satire which they had left behind them against the whole papal system, and against the corruptions of the papal church of the middle ages, were a perfect godsend to the reformers of the sixteenth century, who could point to them triumphantly as irresistible evidence in their favour. Such scholars as Flacius Illyricus, eagerly examined the manuscripts which contained this goliardic poetry, and printed it, chiefly as good and effective weapons in the great religious strife which was then convulsing European society. To us, besides their interest as literary compositions, they have also a historical value, for they introduce us to a more intimate acquaintance with the character of the great mental struggle for emancipation from mediæval darkness which extended especially through the thirteenth century, and which was only overcome for a while to begin more strongly and more successfully at a later period. They display to us the gross ignorance, as well as the corruption of manners, of the great mass of the mediæval clergy. Nothing can be more amusing than the satire which some of these pieces throw on the character of monkish Latin. I printed in the "Reliquæ Antiquæ," under the title of "The Abbot of Gloucester's Feast," a complaint supposed to issue from the mouth of one of the common herd of the monks, against the selfishness of their superiors, in which all the rules of Latin grammar are entirely set at defiance. The abbot and prior of Gloucester, with their whole convent, are invited to a feast, and on their arrival, "the abbot," says the complainant, "goes to sit at the top, and the prior next to him, but I stood always in the back place among the low people."

Abbas ire sede sursum,
Et prioris juxta ipsum;
Ego semper stavi dorsum
inter rascalilia.

The wine was served liberally to the prior and the abbot, but "nothing was give to us poor folks—everything was for the rich."

Vinum venit sanguinatis
Ad prioris et abbatis;
Nihil nobis paupertatis,
sed ad dives omnia.

When some dissatisfaction was displayed by the poor monks, which the great men treated with contempt, "said the prior to the abbot, 'They have wine enough; will you give all our drink to the poor? What does their poverty regard us? they have little, and that is enough, since they came uninvited to our feast.'"

Prior dixit ad abbatis,
'Ipsi habent vinum satis;
Vultis dare paupertatis
noster potus omnia?
Quid nos spectat paupertatis?
Postquam venit non vocatis
ad noster convivia.'

Thus through several pages this amusing poem goes on to describe the gluttony and drunkenness of the abbot and prior, and the ill-treatment of their inferiors. This composition belongs to the close of the thirteenth century. A song very similar to it in character, but much shorter, is found in a manuscript of the middle of the fifteenth century, and printed with the other contents of this manuscript in a little volume issued by the Percy Society.[58] The writer complains that the abbot and prior drunk good and high-flavoured wine, while nothing but inferior stuff was usually given to the convent; "But," he says, "it is better to go drink good wine at the tavern, where the wines are of the best quality, and money is the butler."

Bonum vinum cum sapore
Bibit abbas cum priore;
Sed conventus de pejore
semper solet bibere.
Bonum vinum in taberna,
Ubi vina sunt valarna (for Falerna),
Ubi nummus est pincerna,
Ibi prodest bibere.

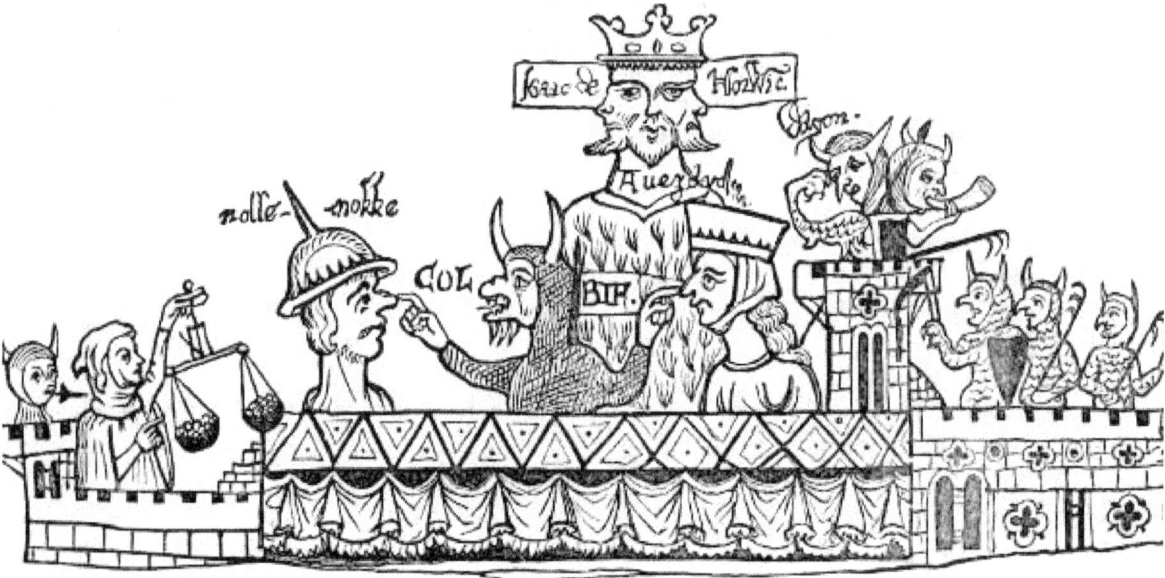

No. 111. Caricature upon the Jews at Norwich.

Partly out of the earnest, though playful, satire described in this chapter, arose political satire, and at a later period political caricature. I have before remarked that the period we call the middle ages was not that of political or personal caricature, because it wanted that means of circulating quickly and largely which is necessary for it. Yet, no doubt, men who could draw, did, in the middle ages, sometimes amuse themselves in sketching caricatures, which, in general, have perished, because nobody cared to preserve them; but the fact of the existence of such works is proved by a very curious example, which has been preserved, and which is copied in our cut No. 111. It is a caricature on the Jews of Norwich, which some one of the clerks of the king's courts in the thirteenth century has drawn with a pen, on one of the official rolls of the Pell office, where it has been preserved. Norwich, as it is well known, was one of the principal seats of the Jews in England at this early period, and Isaac of Norwich, the crowned Jew with three faces, who towers over the other figures, was no doubt some personage of great importance among them. Dagon, as a two-headed demon, occupies a tower, which a party of demon knights is attacking. Beneath the figure of Isaac there is a lady, whose name appears to be Avezarden, who has some relation or other with a male figure named Nolle-Mokke, in which another demon, named Colbif, is interfering. As this latter name is written in capital letters, we may perhaps conclude that he is the most important personage in the scene; but, without any knowledge of the circumstances to which it relates, it would be in vain to attempt to explain this curious and rather elaborate caricature.

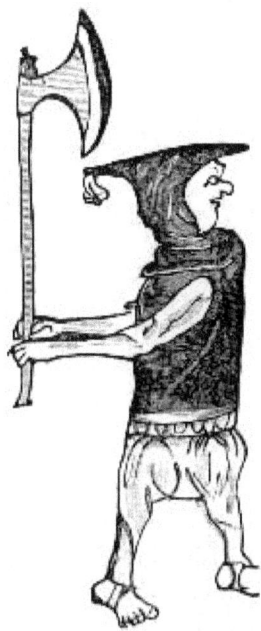

No. 112. An Irishman.

Similar attempts at caricature, though less direct and elaborate, are found in others of our national records. One of these, pointed out to me by an excellent and respected friend, the Rev. Lambert B. Larking, is peculiarly interesting, as well as amusing. It belongs to the Treasury of the Exchequer, and consists of two volumes of vellum called Liber A and Liber B, forming a register of treaties, marriages, and similar documents of the reign of Edward I., which have been very fully used by Rymer. The clerk who was employed in writing it, seems to have been, like many of these official clerks, somewhat of a wag, and he has amused himself by drawing in the margin figures of the inhabitants of the provinces of Edward's crown to which the documents referred. Some of these are evidently designed for caricature. Thus, the figure given in our cut No. 112 was intended to represent an Irishman. One trait, at least, in this caricature is well known from the description given by Giraldus Cambrensis, who speaks with a sort of horror of the formidable axes which the Irish were accustomed to carry about with them. In treating of the manner in which Ireland ought to be governed when it had been entirely reduced to subjection, he recommends that, "in the meantime, they ought not to be allowed in time of peace, on any pretence or in any place, to use that detestable instrument of destruction, which, by an ancient but accursed custom, they constantly carry in their hands instead of a staff." In a chapter of his "Topography of Ireland," Giraldus treats of this "ancient and wicked custom" of always carrying in their hand an axe, instead of a staff, to the danger of all persons who had any relations with them. Another Irishman, from a drawing in the same manuscript, given in our cut No. 113, carries his axe in the same threatening attitude. The costume of these figures answers with sufficient accuracy to the description given by Giraldus Cambrensis. The drawings exhibit more exactly than that writer's description the "small close-fitting hoods, hanging a cubit's length (half-a-yard) below the shoulders," which, he tells us, they were accustomed to wear. This small hood, with the flat cap attached to it, is shown better perhaps in the second figure than in the first. The "breeches and hose of one piece, or hose and breeches joined together," are also exhibited here very distinctly, and appear to be tied over the heel, but the feet are clearly naked, and evidently the use of the "brogues" was not yet general among the Irish of the thirteenth century.

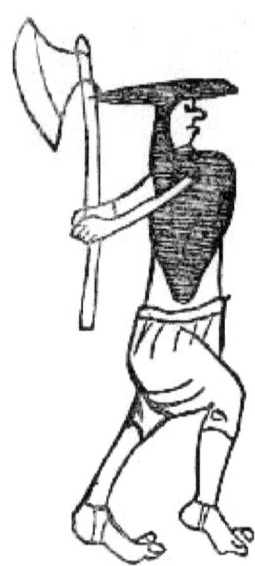

No. 113. Another Irishman.

If the Welshman of this period was somewhat more scantily clothed than the Irishman, he had the advantage of him, to judge by this manuscript, in wearing at least one shoe. Our cut No. 114, taken from it, represents a Welshman armed with bow and arrow, whose clothing consists apparently only of a plain tunic and a light mantle. This is quite in accordance with the description by Giraldus Cambrensis, who tells us that in all seasons their dress was the same, and that, however severe the weather, "they defended themselves from the cold only by a thin cloak and tunic." Giraldus says nothing of the practice of the Welsh in wearing but one shoe, yet it is evident that at the time of this record that was their practice, for in another figure of a Welshman, given in our cut No. 115, we see the same peculiarity, and in both cases the shoe is worn on the left foot. Giraldus merely says that the Welshmen in general, when engaged in warfare, "either walked bare-footed, or made use of high shoes, roughly made of untanned leather." He describes them as armed sometimes with bows and arrows, and sometimes with long spears; and accordingly our first example of a Welshman from this manuscript is using the bow, while the second carries the spear, which he apparently rests on the single shoe of his left foot, while he brandishes a sword in his left hand. Both our Welshmen present a singularly grotesque appearance.

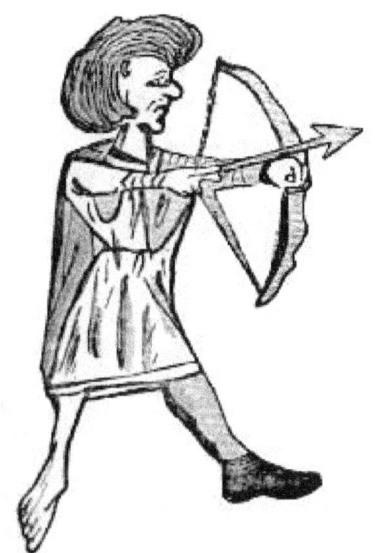

No. 114. A Welsh Archer.

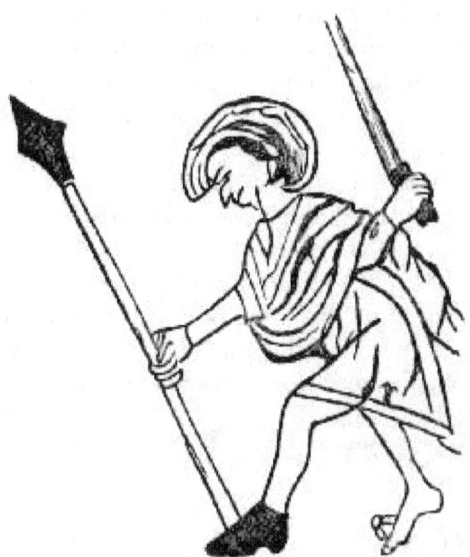

No. 115. A Welshman with his Spear.

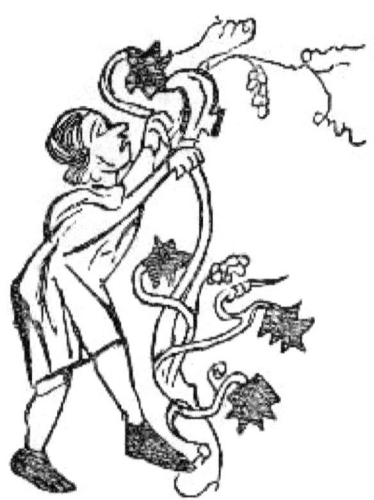

No. 116. A Gascon at his Vine.

The Gascon is represented with more peaceful attributes. Gascony was the country of vineyards, from whence we drew our great supply of wines, a very important article of consumption in the middle ages. When the official clerk who wrote this manuscript came to documents relating to Gascony, his thoughts wandered naturally enough to its rich vineyards and the wine they supplied so plentifully, and to which, according to old reports, clerks seldom showed any dislike, and accordingly, in the sketch, which we copy in our cut No. 116, we have a Gascon occupied diligently in pruning his vine-tree. He, at least, wears two shoes, though his clothing is of the lightest description. He is perhaps the *vinitor* of the mediæval documents on this subject, a serf attached to the vineyard. Our second sketch, cut No. 117, presents a more enlarged scene, and introduces us to the whole process of making wine. First we see a man better clothed, with shoes (or boots) of much superior make, and a hat on his head, carrying away the grapes from the vineyard to the place where another man, with no clothing at all, is treading out the juice in a large vat. This is still in some of the wine countries the common method of extracting the juice from the grape. Further to the left is the large cask in which the juice is put when turned into wine.

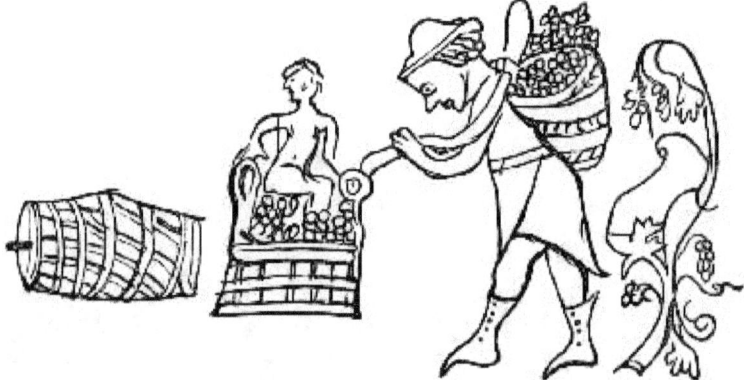

No. 117. The Wine Manufacturer.

Satires on the people of particular localities were not uncommon during the middle ages, because local rivalries and consequent local feuds prevailed everywhere. The records of such feuds were naturally of a temporary character, and perished when the feuds and rivalries themselves ceased to exist, but a few curious satires of this kind have been preserved. A monk of Peterborough, who lived late in the twelfth or early in the thirteenth century, and for some reason or other nourished an unfriendly feeling to the people of Norfolk, gave vent to his hostility in a short Latin poem in what we may call goliardic verse. He begins by abusing the county itself, which, he says, was as bad and unfruitful as its inhabitants were vile; and he suggests that the evil one, when he fled from the anger of the Almighty, had passed through it and left his pollution upon it. Among other anecdotes of the simplicity and folly of the people of this county, which closely resemble the stories of the wise men of Gotham of a later date, he informs us that one day the peasantry of one district were so grieved by the oppressions of their feudal lord, that they subscribed together and bought their freedom, which he secured to them by formal deed, ratified with a ponderous seal. They adjourned to the tavern, and celebrated their deliverance by feasting and drinking until night came on, and then, for want of a candle, they agreed to burn the wax of the seal. Next day their former lord, informed of what had taken place, brought them before a court, where the deed was judged to be void for want of the seal, and they lost all their money, were reduced to their old position of slavery, and treated worse than ever. Other stories, still more ridiculous, are told of these old Norfolkians, but few of them are worth repeating. Another monk, apparently, who calls himself John de St. Omer, took up the cudgels for the people of Norfolk, and replied to the Peterborough satirist in similar language.[59] I have printed in another collection,[60] a satirical poem against the people of a place called Stockton (perhaps Stockton-on-Tees in Durham), by the monk of a monastic house, of which they were serfs. It appeared that they had risen against the tyranny of their lord, but had been unsuccessful in defending their cause in a court of law, and the ecclesiastical satirist exults over their defeat in a very uncharitable tone. There will be found in the "Reliquæ Antiquæ,"[61] a very curious satire in Latin prose directed against the inhabitants of Rochester, although it is in truth aimed against Englishmen in general, and is entitled in the manuscript, which is of the fourteenth century, "Proprietates Anglicorum" (the Peculiarities of Englishmen). In the first place, we are told, that the people of Rochester had tails, and the question is discussed, very scholastically, what species of animals these Rocestrians were. We are then told that the cause of their deformity arose from the insolent manner in which they treated St. Augustine, when he came to preach the Gospel to the heathen English. After visiting many parts of England, the saint came to Rochester, where the people, instead of listening to him, hooted at him through the streets, and, in derision, attached tails of pigs and calves to his vestments, and so turned him out of the city. The vengeance of Heaven came upon them, and all who inhabited the city and the country round it, and their descendants after them, were condemned to bear tails exactly like those of pigs. This story of the tails was not an invention of the author of the satire, but was a popular legend connected with the history of St. Augustine's preaching, though the scene of the legend was laid in Dorsetshire. The writer of this singular composition goes on to describe the people of Rochester as seducers of other people, as men without gratitude, and as traitors. He proceeds to show that Rochester being situated in England, its vices had tainted the whole nation, and he illustrates the baseness of the English character by a number of anecdotes of worse than doubtful authenticity. It is, in fact, a satire on the English composed in France, and leads us into the domains of political satire.

Political satire in the middle ages appeared chiefly in the form of poetry and song, and it was especially in England that it flourished, a sure sign that there was in our country a more advanced feeling of popular independence, and greater freedom of speech, than in France or Germany.[62] M. Leroux de Lincy, who undertook to make a collection of this poetry for France, found so little during the mediæval period that came under the character of political, that he was obliged to substitute the word "historical" in the title of his book.[63] Where feudalism was supreme, indeed, the songs which arose out of private or public strife, which then were almost inseparable from society, contained no political sentiment, but consisted chiefly of personal attacks on the opponents of those who employed them. Such are the four short songs written in the time of the revolt of the French during the minority of St. Louis, which commenced in 1226; they are all of a political character which M. Leroux de Lincy has been able to collect previous to the year 1270, and they consist merely of personal taunts against the courtiers by the dissatisfied barons who were out of power. We trace a similar feeling in some of the popular records of our baronial wars of the reign of Henry III., especially in a song, in the baronial language (Anglo-Norman), preserved in a small roll of vellum, which appears to have belonged to the minstrel who chanted it in the halls of the partisans of Simon de Montfort. The fragment which remains consists of stanzas in praise of the leaders of the popular party, and in reproach of their opponents. Thus of Roger de Clifford, one of earl Simon's friends, we are told that "the good Roger de Clifford behaved like a noble baron, and exercised great justice; he suffered none, either small or great, or secretly or openly, to do any wrong."

Et de Cliffort ly bon Roger
Se contint cum noble ber,
Si fu de grant justice;
Ne suffri pas petit ne grant,
Ne arère ne par devant,
Fere nul mesprise.

On the other hand, one of Montfort's opponents, the bishop of Hereford, is treated rather contemptuously. We are told that he "learnt well that the earl was strong when he took the matter in hand; before that he (the bishop) was very fierce, and thought to eat up all the English; but now he is reduced to straits."

Ly eveske de Herefort
Sout bien que ly quens fu fort,
Kant il prist l'affère;
Devant ce esteit mult fer,
Les Englais quida touz manger,
Mès ore ne set que fere.

This bishop was Peter de Aigueblanche, one of the foreign favourites, who had been intruded into the see of Hereford, to the exclusion of a better man, and had been an oppressor of those who were under his rule. The barons seized him, threw him into prison, and plundered his possessions, and at the time this song was written, he was suffering under the imprisonment which appears to have shortened his life.

The universities and the clerical body in general were deeply involved in these political movements of the thirteenth century; and our earliest political songs now known are composed in Latin, and in that form and style of verse which seems to have been peculiar to the goliards, and which I venture to call goliardic. Such is a song against the three bishops who supported king John in his quarrel with the pope about the presentation to the see of Canterbury, printed in my Political Songs. Such, too, is the song of the Welsh, and one or two others, in the same volume. And such, above all, is that remarkable Latin poem in which a partisan of the barons, immediately after the victory at Lewes, set forth the political tenets of his party, and gave the principles of English liberty nearly the same broad basis on which they stand at the present. It is an evidence of the extent to which these principles were now acknowledged, that in this great baronial struggle our political songs began to be written in the English language, an acknowledgment that they concerned the whole English public.

We trace little of this class of literature during the reign of Edward I.; but, when the popular feelings became turbulent again under the reign of his son and successor, political songs became more abundant, and their satire was directed more even than formerly against measures and principles, and was less an instrument of mere personal abuse. One satirical poem of this period, which I had printed from an imperfect copy in a manuscript at Edinburgh, but of which a more complete copy was subsequently found in a manuscript in the library of St. Peter's College, Cambridge,[64] is extremely curious as being the earliest satire of this kind written in English that we possess. It appears to have been written in the year 1320. The writer of this poem begins by telling us that his object is to explain the cause of the war, ruin, and manslaughter which then prevailed throughout the land, and why the poor were suffering from hunger and want, the cattle perished in the field, and the corn was dear. These he ascribes to the increasing wickedness of all orders of society. To begin with the church, Rome was the head of all corruptions, at the papal court false-hood and treachery only reigned, and the door of the pope's palace was shut against truth. During the twelfth and following centuries these complaints, in terms more or less forcible, against the corruptions of Rome, are continually repeated, and show that the evil must have been one under which everybody felt oppressed. The old charge of Romish simony is repeated in this poem in very strong terms. "The clerk's voice shall be little heard at the court of Rome, were he ever so good, unless he bring silver with him; though he were the holiest man that ever was born, unless he bring gold or silver, all his time and anxiety are lost. Alas! why love they so much that which is perishable?"

Voys of clerk shall lytyl be heard at the court of Rome,
Were he never so gode a clerk, without silver and he come;
Though he were the holyst man that ever yet was ibore,
But he bryng gold or sylver, al hys while is forlore
And his thowght.
Allas! whi love thei that so much that schal turne to nowght?

When, on the contrary, a wicked man presented himself at the pope's court, he had only to carry plenty of money thither, and all went well with him. According to our satirist, the bishops were "fools," and the other dignitaries and officials of the church were influenced chiefly by the love of money and self-indulgence. The parson began humbly, when he first obtained his benefice, but no sooner had he gathered money together, than he took "a wenche" to live with him as his wife, and rode a hunting with hawks and hounds like a gentleman. The priests were men with no learning, who preached by rote what they neither understood nor appreciated. "Truely," he says, "it fares by our unlearned priests as by a jay in a cage, who curses himself: he speaks good English, but he knows not what it means. No more does an unlearned priest know his gospel that he reads daily. An unlearned priest, then, is no better than a jay."

Certes at so hyt fareth by a prest that is lewed,
As by a jay in a cage that hymself hath beshrewed:
Gode Englysh he speketh, but he not never what.
No more wot a lewed prest hys gospel wat he rat
By day.
Than is a lewed prest no better than a jay.

Abbots and priors were remarkable chiefly for their pride and luxury, and the monks naturally followed their examples. Thus was religion debased everywhere. The character of the physician is treated with equal severity, and his various tricks to obtain money are amusingly described. In this manner the songster presents to view the failings of the various orders of lay society also, the selfishness and oppressive bearing of the knights and aristocracy, and their extravagance in dress and living, the neglect of justice, the ill-management of the wars, the weight of taxation, and all the other evils which then afflicted the state. This poem marks a period in our social history, and led the way to that larger work of the same character, which came about thirty years later, the well-known "Visions of Piers Ploughman,"[65] one of the most remarkable satires, as well as one of the most remarkable poems, in the English language.

We will do no more than glance at the further progress of political satire which had now taken a permanent footing in English literature. We see less of it during the reign of Edward III., the greater part of which was occupied with foreign wars and triumphs, but there appeared towards the close of his reign, a very remarkable satire, which I have printed in my "Political Poems and Songs." It is written in Latin, and consists of a pretended prophecy in verse by an inspired monk named John of Bridlington, with a mock commentary in prose—in fact, a parody on the commentaries in which the scholastics of that age displayed their learning, but in this case the commentary contains a bold though to us rather obscure criticism on the whole policy of Edward's reign. The reign of Richard II. was convulsed by the great struggle for religious reform, by the insurrections of the lower orders, and by the ambition and feuds of the nobles, and produced a vast quantity of political and religious satire, both in prose and verse, but especially the latter. We must not overlook our great poet Chaucer, as one of the powerful satirists of this period. Political song next makes itself heard loudly in the wars of the Roses. It was the last struggle of feudalism in England, and the character of the song had fallen back to its earlier characteristics, in which all patriotic feelings were abandoned to make place for personal hatred.

CHAPTER XI.

MINSTRELSY A SUBJECT OF BURLESQUE AND CARICATURE.—CHARACTER OF THE MINSTRELS.—THEIR JOKES UPON THEMSELVES AND UPON ONE ANOTHER.—VARIOUS MUSICAL INSTRUMENTS REPRESENTED IN THE SCULPTURES OF THE MEDIÆVAL ARTISTS.—SIR MATTHEW GOURNAY AND THE KING OF PORTUGAL.—DISCREDIT OF THE TABOR AND BAGPIPES.—MERMAIDS.

One of the principal classes of the satirists of the middle ages, the minstrels, or jougleurs, were far from being unamenable to satire themselves. They belonged generally to a low class of the population, one that was hardly acknowledged by the law, which merely administered to the pleasures and amusements of others, and, though sometimes liberally rewarded, they were objects rather of contempt than of respect. Of course there were minstrels belonging to a class more respectable than the others, but these were comparatively few; and the ordinary minstrel seems to have been simply an unprincipled vagabond, who hardly possessed any settled resting-place, who wandered about from place to place, and was not too nice as to the means by which he gained his living—perhaps fairly represented by the street minstrel, or mountebank, of the present day. One of his talents was that of mocking and ridiculing others, and it is not to be wondered at, therefore, if he sometimes became an object of mockery and ridicule himself. One of the well-known minstrels of the thirteenth century, Rutebeuf, was, like many of his fellows, a poet also, and he has left several short pieces of verse descriptive of himself and of his own mode of life. In one of these he complains of his poverty, and tells us that the world had in his time—the reign of St. Louis—become so degenerate, that few people gave anything to the unfortunate minstrel. According to his own account, he was without food, and in a fair way towards starvation, exposed to the cold without sufficient clothing, and with nothing but straw for his bed.

Je touz de froit, de fain baaille,
Dont je suis mors et maubailliz,

Je suis sanz coutes et sans liz;
N'a si povre jusqu'à Senliz.
Sire, si ne sai quel part aille;
Mes costeiz connoit le pailliz,
Et liz de paille n'est pas liz,
Et en mon lit n'a fors la paille.
—Œuvres de Rutebeuf, vol. i. p. 3.

In another poem, Rutebeuf laments that he has rendered his condition still more miserable by marrying, when he had not wherewith to keep a wife and family. In a third, he complains that in the midst of his poverty, his wife has brought him a child to increase his domestic expenses, while his horse, on which he was accustomed to travel to places where he might exercise his profession, had broken its leg, and his nurse was dunning him for money. In addition to all these causes of grief, he had lost the use of one of his eyes.

Or a d'enfant géu ma fame;
Mon cheval a brisié la jame
A une lice;
Or veut de l'argent ma norrice,
Qui m'en destraint et me pélice,
For l'enfant pestre.

Throughout his complaint, although he laments over the decline of liberality among his contemporaries, he nevertheless turns his poverty into a joke. In several other pieces of verse he speaks in the same way, half joking and half lamenting over his condition, and he does not conceal that the love of gambling was one of the causes of it. "The dice," he says, "have stripped me entirely of my robe; the dice watch and spy me; it is these which kill me; they assault and ruin me, to my grief."

Li dé que li détier ont fet,
M'ont de ma robe tout desfet;
Li dé m'ocient.
Li dé m'aguetent et espient;
Li dé m'assaillent et dessient,
Ce poise moi.—Ib., vol. i. p. 27.

And elsewhere he intimates that what the minstrels sometimes gained from the lavish generosity of their hearers, soon passed away at the tavern in dice and drinking.

One of Rutebeuf's contemporaries in the same profession, Colin Muset, indulges in similar complaints, and speaks bitterly of the want of generosity displayed by the great barons of his time. In addressing one of them who had treated him ungenerously, he says, "Sir Count, I have fiddled before you in your hostel, and you neither gave me a gift, nor paid me my wages. It is discreditable behaviour. By the duty I owe to St. Mary, I cannot continue in your service at this rate. My purse is ill furnished, and my wallet is empty."

Sire quens, j'ai vielé
Devant vos en vostre ostel;
Si ne m'avez riens donné,
Ne mes gages acquitez,

C'est vilanie.
Foi que doi sainte Marie,
Ensi ne vos sieurré-je mie.
M'aumosnière est mal garnie,
Et ma male mal farsie.

He proceeds to state that when he went home to his wife (for Colin Muset also was a married minstrel), he was ill received if his purse and wallet were empty; but it was very different when they were full. His wife then sprang forward and threw her arms round his neck; she took his wallet from his horse with alacrity, while his lad conducted the animal cheerfully to the stable, and his maiden killed a couple of capons, and prepared them with piquant sauce. His daughter brought a comb for his hair. "Then," he exclaims, "I am master in my own house."

Ma fame va destroser
Ma male sans demorer;
Mon garçon va abuvrer
Men cheval et conreer;
Ma pucele va tuer
Deux chapons por deporter
A la sause aillie.
Ma fille m'aporte un pigne
En sa main par cortoisie.
Lors sui de mon ostel sire.

When the minstrels could thus joke upon themselves, we need not be surprised if they satirised one another. In a poem of the thirteenth century, entitled "Les deux Troveors Ribauz," two minstrels are introduced on the stage abusing and insulting one another, and while indulging in mutual accusations of ignorance in their art, they display their ignorance at the same time by misquoting the titles of the poems which they profess to be able to recite. One of them boasts of the variety of instruments on which he could perform:—

Je suis jugleres de viele,
Si sai de muse et frestele,
Et de harpes et de chifonie,
De la gigue, de l'armonie,
De l'salteire, et en la rote
Sai-ge bien chanter une note.

It appears, however, that among all these instruments, the viol, or fiddle, was the one most generally in use.

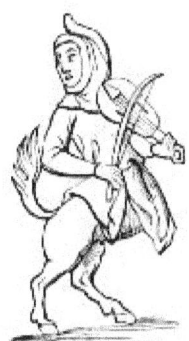

No. 118. A Charming Fiddler.

The mediæval monuments of art abound with burlesques and satires on the minstrels, whose instruments of music are placed in the hands sometimes of monsters, and at others in those of animals of a not very refined character. Our cut No. 118 is taken from a manuscript in the British Museum (MS. Cotton, Domitian A. ii.), and represents a female minstrel playing on the fiddle; she has the upper part of a lady, and the lower parts of a mare, a combination which appears to have been rather familiar to the imagination of the mediæval artists. In our cut No. 119, which is taken from a copy made by Carter of one of the misereres in Ely Cathedral, it is not quite clear whether the performer on the fiddle be a monster or merely a cripple; but perhaps the latter was intended. The instrument, too, assumes a rather singular form. Our cut No. 120, also taken from Carter, was furnished by a sculpture in the church of St. John, at Cirencester, and represents a man performing on an instrument rather closely resembling the modern hurdy-gurdy, which is evidently played by turning a handle, and the music is produced by striking wires or strings inside. The face is evidently intended to be that of a jovial companion.

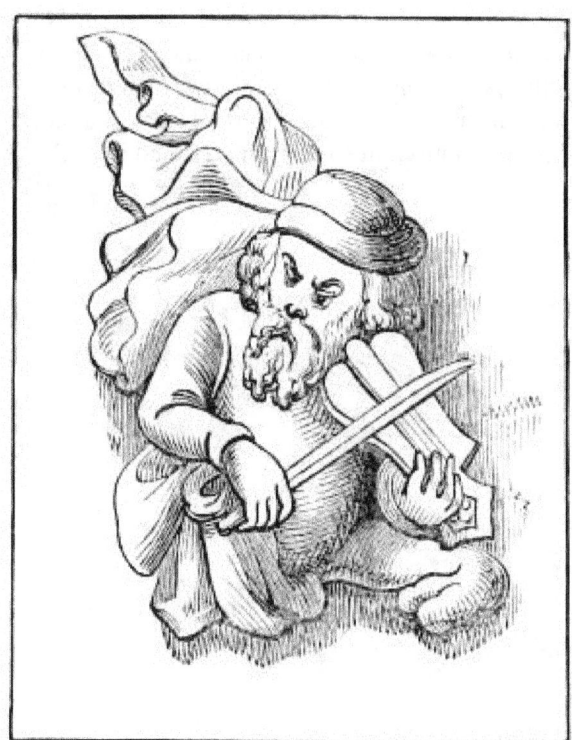

No. 119. A Crippled Minstrel.

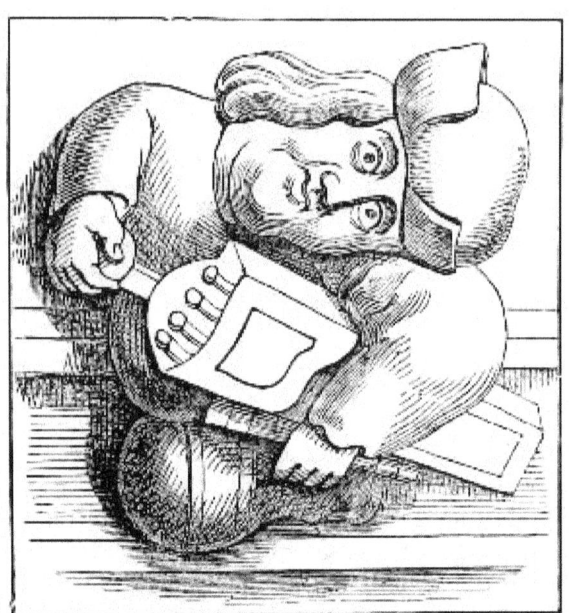

No. 120. The Hurdy-Gurdy.

Gluttony was an especial characteristic of that class of society to which the minstrel belonged, and perhaps this was the idea intended to be conveyed in the next picture, No. 121, taken from one of the stalls in Winchester Cathedral, in which a pig is performing on the fiddle, and appears to be accompanied by a juvenile of the same species of animal. One of the same stalls, copied in our cut No. 122, represents a sow performing on another sort of musical instrument, which is not at all uncommon in mediæval delineations. It is the double pipe or flute, which was evidently borrowed from the ancients. Minstrelsy was the usual accompaniment of the mediæval meal, and perhaps this picture is intended to be a burlesque on that circumstance, as the mother is playing to her brood while they are feeding. They all seem to listen quietly, except one, who is evidently much more affected by the music than his companions. The same instrument is placed in the hands of a rather jolly-looking female in one of the sculptures of St. John's Church in Cirencester, copied in our cut No. 123.

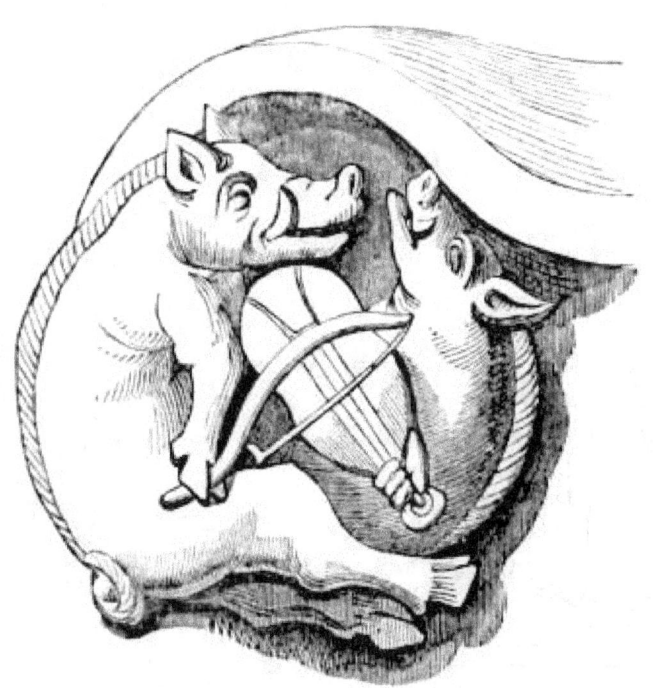

No. 121. A Swinish Minstrel.

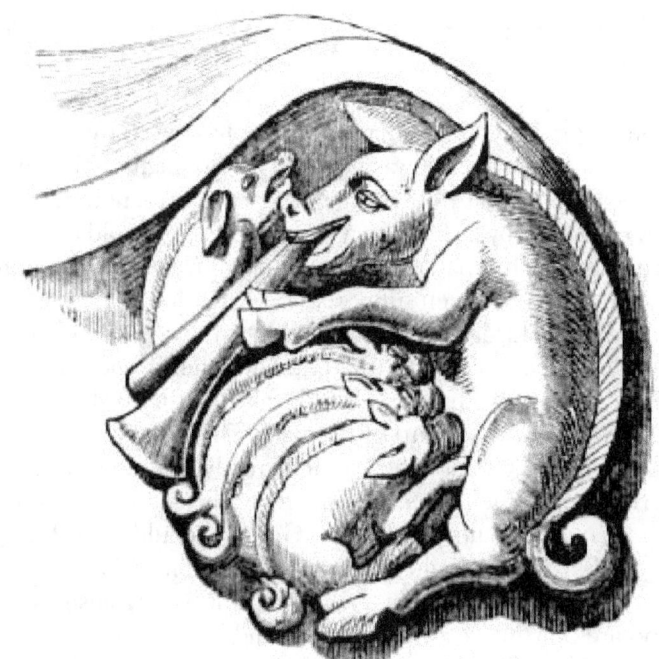

No. 122. A Musical Mother.

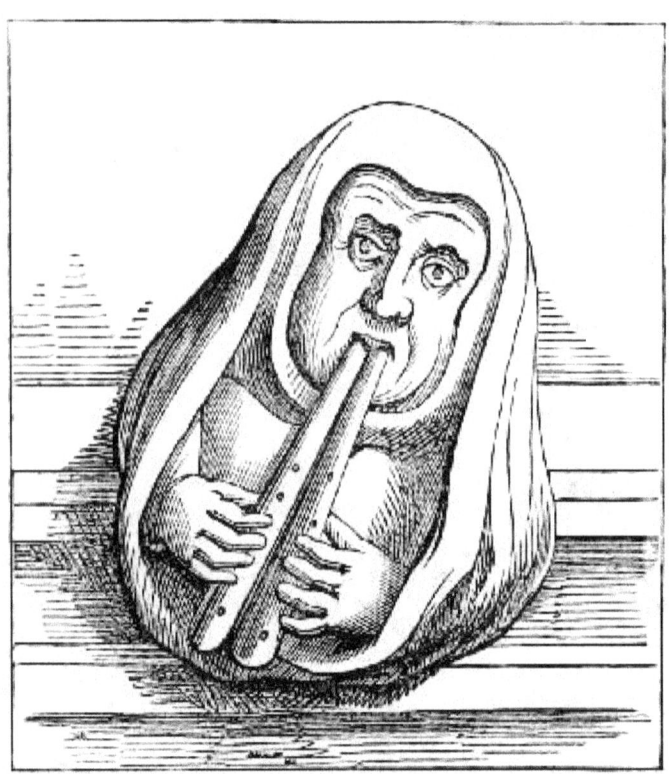

No. 123. The Double Flute.

Although this instrument is rather frequently represented in mediæval works of art, we have no account of or allusion to it in mediæval writers; and perhaps it was not held in very high estimation, and was used only by a low class of performers. As in many other things, the employment of particular musical instruments was guided, no doubt, by fashion, new ones coming in as old ones went out. Such was the case with the instrument which is named in one of the above extracts, and in some other mediæval writers, a *chiffonie*, and which has been supposed to be the dulcimer, that had fallen into discredit in the fourteenth century. This instrument is introduced in a story which is found in Cuvelier's metrical history of the celebrated warrior Bertrand du Gueselin. In the course of the war for the expulsion of Pedro the Cruel from the throne of Castile, an English knight, Sir Matthew Gournay, was sent as a special ambassador to the court of Portugal. The Portuguese monarch had in his service two minstrels whose performances he vaunted greatly, and on whom he let great store, and he insisted on their performing in the presence of the new ambassador. It turned out that they played on the instrument just mentioned, and Sir Matthew Gournay could not refrain from laughing at the performance. When the king pressed him to give his opinion, he said, with more regard for truth than politeness, "in France and Normandy, the instruments your minstrels play upon are regarded with contempt, and are only in use among beggars and blind people, so that they are popularly called beggar's instruments." The king, we are told, took great offence at the bluntness of his English guest.

The fiddle itself appears at this time to have been gradually sinking in credit, and the poets complained that a degraded taste for more vulgar musical instruments was introducing itself. Among these we may mention especially the pipe and tabor. The French antiquary, M. Jubinal, in a very valuable collection of early popular poetry, published under the title of "Jongleurs et Trouvères," has printed a curious poem of the thirteenth or fourteenth century, intended as a protest against the use of the tabor and the bagpipes, which he characterises as properly the musical instruments of the peasantry. Yet people then, he says, were becoming so besotted on such instruments, that they introduced them in places where better minstrelsy would be more suitable. The writer thinks that the introduction of so vulgar an instrument as the tabor into grand festivals could be looked upon in no other light than as one of the signs which might be expected to be the precursors of the coming of Antichrist. "If such people are to come to grand festivals as carry a bushel [*i.e.* a tabor made in the form of a bushel measure, on the end of which they beat], and make such a terrible noise, it would seem that Antichrist must now be being born; people ought to break the head of each of them with a staff."

Déussent itiels genz venir à bele feste
Qui portent un boissel, qui mainent tel tempeste,
Il samble que Antecrist doie maintenant nestre;
L'en duroit d'un baston chascun brisier la teste.

This satirist adds, as a proof of the contempt in which the Virgin Mary held such instruments, that she never loved a tabor, or consented to hear one, and that no tabor was introduced among the minstrelsy at her espousals. "The gentle mother of God," he says, "loved the sound of the fiddle," and he goes on to prove her partiality for that instrument by citing some of her miracles.

Onques le mère Dieu, qui est virge honorée,
Et est avoec les angles hautement coronée,
N'ama onques tabour, ne point ne li agrée,
N'onques tabour n'i ot quant el fu espousée.
La douce mère Dieu ama son de viele.

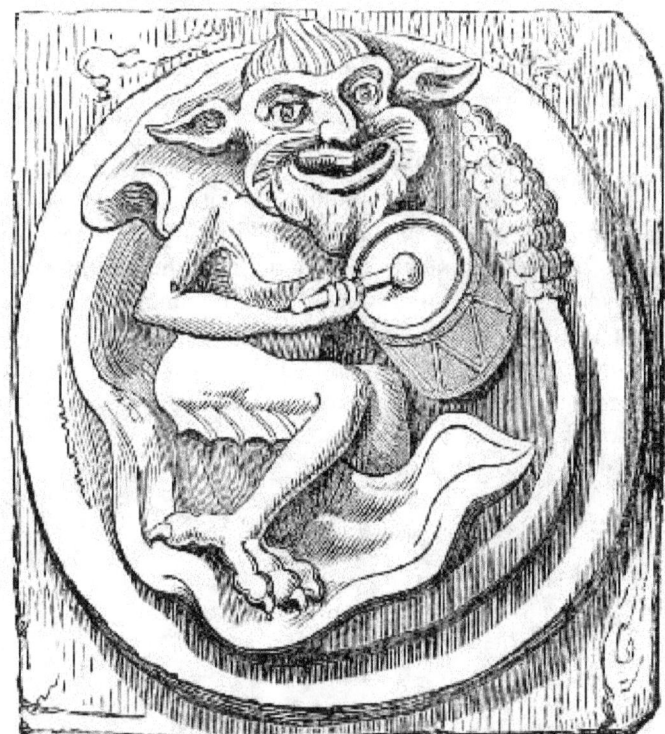

No. 124. The Tabor, or Drum.

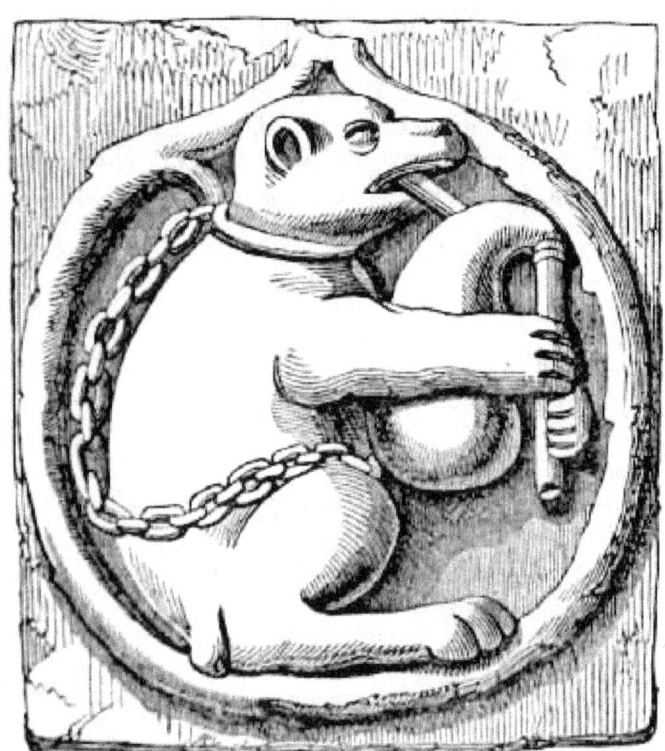

No. 125. Bruin turned Piper.

The artist who carved the curious stalls in Henry VII.'s Chapel at Westminster, seems to have entered fully into the spirit displayed by this satirist, for in one of them, represented in our cut No. 124, he has introduced a masked demon playing on the tabor, with an expression apparently of derision. This tabor presents much the form of a bushel measure, or rather, perhaps, of a modern drum. It may be remarked that the drum is, in fact, the same instrument as the tabor, or, at least, is derived from it, and they were called by the same names, *tabor* or *tambour*. The English name *drum*, which has equivalents in the later forms of the Teutonic dialects, perhaps means simply something which makes a noise, and is not, as far as I know, met with before the sixteenth century. Another carving of the same series of stalls at Westminster, copied in our cut No. 125, represents a tame bear playing on the bagpipes. This is perhaps intended to be at the same time a satire on the instrument itself, and upon the strange exhibitions of animals domesticated and taught various singular performances, which were then so popular.

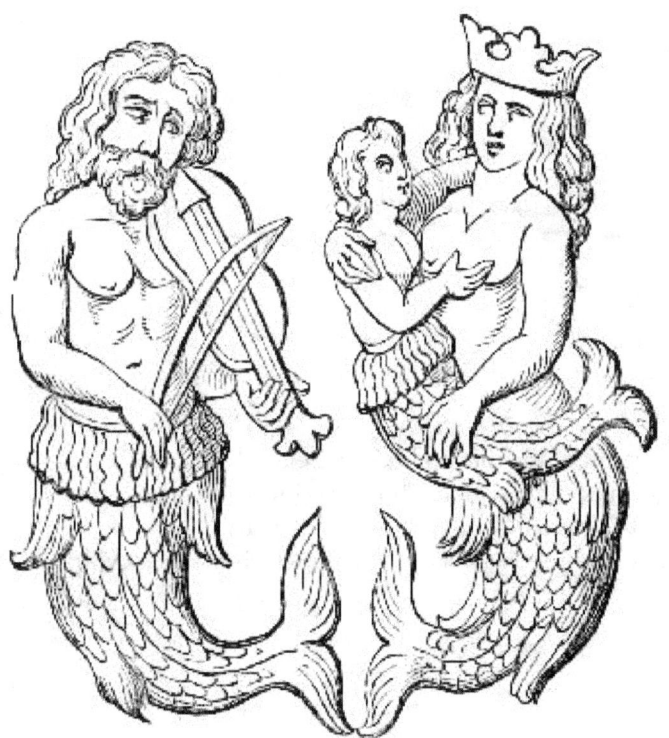

No. 126. Royal Minstrelsy.

In our cut No. 126 we come to the fiddle again, which long sustained its place in the highest rank of musical instruments. It is taken from one of the sculptures on the porch of the principal entrance to the Cathedral of Lyons in France, and represents a mermaid with her child, listening to the music of the fiddle. She wears a crown, and is intended, no doubt, to be one of the queens of the sea, and the introduction of the fiddle under such circumstances can leave no doubt how highly it was esteemed.

The mermaid is a creature of the imagination, which appears to have been at all times a favourite object of poetry and legend. It holds an important place in the mediæval bestiaries, or popular treatises on natural history, and it has only been expelled from the domains of science at a comparatively recent date. It still retains its place in popular legends of our sea-coasts, and more especially in the remoter parts of our islands. The stories of the merrow, or Irish fairy, hold a prominent place among my late friend Crofton Croker's "Fairy Legends of the South of Ireland." The mermaid is also introduced not unfrequently in mediæval sculpture and carving. Our cut No. 127, representing a mermaid and a merman, is copied from one of the stalls of Winchester Cathedral. The usual attributes of the mermaid are a looking-glass and comb, by the aid of which she is dressing her hair; but here she holds the comb alone. Her companion, the male, holds a fish, which he appears to have just caught, in his hand.

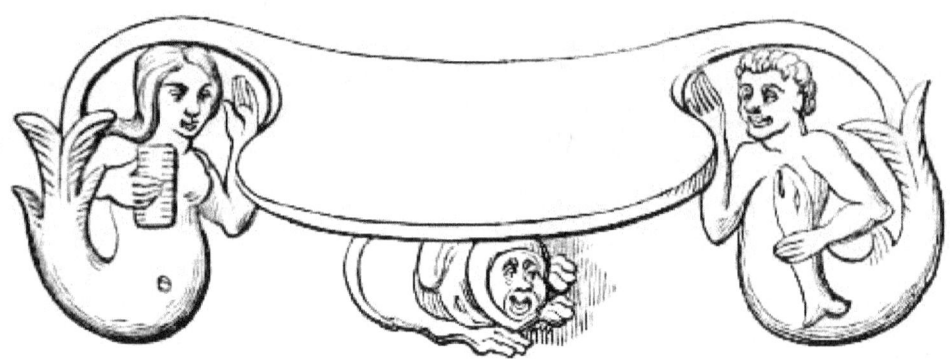

No. 127. Mermaids.

While, after the fifteenth century the profession of the minstrel became entirely degraded, and he was looked upon more than ever as a rogue and vagabond, the fiddle accompanied him, and it long remained, as it still remains in Ireland, the favourite instrument of the peasantry. The blind fiddler, even at the present day, is not unknown in our rural districts. It has always been in England the favourite instrument of minstrelsy.

CHAPTER XII.

THE COURT FOOL.—THE NORMANS AND THEIR GABS.—EARLY HISTORY OF COURT FOOLS.—THEIR COSTUME.—CARVINGS IN THE CORNISH CHURCHES.— THE BURLESQUE SOCIETIES OF THE MIDDLE AGES.—THE FEASTS OF ASSES, AND OF FOOLS.—THEIR LICENCE.—THE LEADEN MONEY OF THE FOOLS.—THE BISHOP'S BLESSING.

From the employment of minstrels attached to the family, probably arose another and well-known character of later times, the court fool, who took the place of satirist in the great households. I do not consider what we understand by the court fool to be a character of any great antiquity.

It is somewhat doubtful whether what we call a jest, was really appreciated in the middle ages. Puns seem to have been considered as elegant figures of speech in literary composition, and we rarely meet with anything like a quick and clever repartee. In the earlier ages, when a party of warriors would be merry, their mirth appears to have consisted usually in ridiculous boasts, or in rude remarks, or in sneers at enemies or opponents. These jests were termed by the French and Normans *gabs* (*gabæ*, in mediæval Latin), a word supposed to have been derived from the classical Latin word *cavilla*, a mock or taunt; and a short poem in Anglo-Norman has been preserved which furnishes a curious illustration of the meaning attached to it in the twelfth century. This poem relates how Charlemagne, piqued by the taunts of his empress on the superiority of Hugh the Great, emperor of Constantinople, went to Constantinople, accompanied by his *douze pairs* and a thousand knights, to verify the truth of his wife's story. They proceeded first to Jerusalem, where, when Charlemagne and his twelve peers entered the Church of the Holy Sepulchre, they looked so handsome and majestic, that they were taken at first for Christ and his twelve apostles, but the mystery was soon cleared up, and they were treated by the patriarch with great hospitality during four months. They then continued their progress till they reached Constantinople, where they were equally well received by the emperor Hugo. At night the emperor placed his guests in a chamber furnished with thirteen splendid beds, one in the middle of the room, and the other twelve distributed around it, and illuminated by a large carbuncle, which gave a light as bright as that of day. When Hugh left them in their quarters for the night, he lent them wine and whatever was necessary to make them comfortable; and, when alone, they proceeded to amuse themselves with *gabs*, or jokes, each being expected to say his joke in his turn. Charlemagne took the lead, and boasted that if the emperor Hugh would place before him his strongest "bachelor," in full armour, and mounted on his good steed, he would, with one blow of his sword, cut him through from the head downwards, and through the saddle and horse, and that the sword should, after all this, sink into the ground to the handle. Charlemagne then called upon Roland for his *gab*, who boasted that his breath was so strong, that if the emperor Hugh would lend him his horn, he would take it out into the fields and blow it with such force, that the wind and noise of it would shake down the whole city of Constantinople. Oliver, whose turn came next, boasted of exploits of another description if he were left alone with the beautiful princess, Hugh's daughter. The rest of the peers indulged in similar boasts, and when the *gabs* had gone round, they went to sleep. Now the emperor of Constantinople had very cunningly, and rather treacherously, made a hole through the wall, by which all that passed inside could be seen and heard, and he had placed a spy on the outside, who gave a full account of the conversation of the distinguished guests to his imperial master. Next morning Hugh called his guests before him, told them what he had heard by his spy, and declared that each of them should perform his boast, or, if he failed, be put to death. Charlemagne expostulated, and represented that it was the custom in France when people retired for the night to amuse themselves in that manner. "Such is the custom in France," he said, "at Paris, and at Chartres, when the French are in bed they amuse themselves and make jokes, and say things both of wisdom and of folly."

Si est tel custume en France, à Paris e à Cartres,
Quand Franceis sunt culchiez, que se giuunt e gabent,
E si dient ambure e saver e folage.

But Charlemagne expostulated in vain, and they were only saved from the consequence of their imprudence by the intervention of so many miracles from above.[66]

In such trials of skill as this, an individual must continually have arisen who excelled in some at least of the qualities needful for raising mirth and making him a good companion, by showing himself more brilliant in wit, or more biting in sarcasms, or more impudent in his jokes, and he would thus become the favourite mirth-maker of the court, the boon companion of the chieftain and his followers in their hours of relaxation. We find such an individual not unusually introduced in the early romances and in the mythology of nations, and he sometimes unites the character of court orator with the other. Such a personage was the Sir Kay of the cycle of the romances of king Arthur. I have remarked in a former chapter that Hunferth, in the Anglo-Saxon poem of Beowulf, is described as holding a somewhat similar position at the court of king Hrothgar. To go farther back in the mythology of our forefathers, the Loki of Scandinavian fable appears sometimes to have performed a similar character in the assembly of his fellow deities; and we know that, among the Greeks, Homer on one occasion introduces Vulcan acting the part of joker (γελωτοποιὸς) to the gods of Olympus. But all these have no relationship whatever to the court-fool of modern times.

The German writer Flögel, in his "History of Court Fools,"[67] has thrown this subject into much confusion by introducing a great mass of irrelevant matter; and those who have since compiled from Flögel, have made the confusion still greater. Much of this confusion has arisen from the misunderstanding and confounding of names and terms. The mimus, the joculator, the ministrel, or whatever name this class of society went by, was not in any respects identical with what we understand by a court fool, nor does any such character as the latter appear in the feudal household before the fourteenth century, as far as we are acquainted with the social manners and customs of the olden time. The vast extent of the early French *romans de geste*, or Carlovingian romances, which are filled with pictures of courts both of princes and barons, in which the court fool must have been introduced had he been known at the time they were composed, that is, in the twelfth and thirteenth centuries, contains, I believe, no trace of such personage; and the same may be said of the numerous other romances, fabliaux, and in fact all the literature of that period, one so rich in works illustrative of contemporary manners in their most minute detail. From these facts I conclude that the single brief charter published by M. Rigollot from a manuscript in the Imperial Library in Paris, is either misunderstood or it presents a very exceptional case. By this charter, John, king of England, grants to his *follus*, William Picol, or Piculph (as he is called at the close of the document), an estate in Normandy named in the document Fons Ossanæ (Menil-Ozenne in Mortain), with all its appurtenances, "to have and to hold, to him and to his heirs, by doing there-for to us once a year the service of one *follus*, as long as he lives; and after his death his heirs shall hold it of us, by the service of one pair of gilt spurs to be rendered annually to us."[68] The service (*servitium*) here enjoined means the annual payment of the obligation of the feudal tenure, and therefore if *follus* is to be taken as signifying "a fool," it only means that Picol was to perform that character on one occasion in the course of the year. In this case, he may have been some fool whom king John had taken into his special favour; but it certainly is no proof that the practice of keeping court fools then existed. It is not improbable that this practice was first introduced in Germany, for Flögel speaks, though rather doubtfully, of one who was kept at the court of the emperor Rudolph I. (of Hapsburg), whose reign lasted from 1273 to 1292. It is more certain, however, that the kings of France possessed court fools before the middle of the fourteenth century, and from this time anecdotes relating to them begin to be common. One of the earliest and most curious of these anecdotes, if it be true, relates to the celebrated victory of Sluys gained over the French fleet by our king Edward III. in the year 1340. It is said that no one dared to announce this disaster to the French king, Philippe VI., until a court fool undertook the task. Entering the king's chamber, he continued muttering to himself, but loud enough to be heard, "Those cowardly English! the chicken-hearted Britons!" "How so, cousin?" the king inquired. "Why," replied the fool, "because they have not courage enough to jump into the sea, like your French soldiers, who went over headlong from their ships, leaving those to the enemy who showed no inclination to follow them." Philippe thus became aware of the full extent of his calamity. The institution of the court fool was carried to its greatest degree of perfection during the fifteenth century; it only expired in the age of Louis XIV.

It was apparently with the court fool that the costume was introduced which has ever since been considered as the characteristic mark of folly. Some parts of this costume, at least, appear to have been borrowed from an earlier date. The *gelotopœi* of the Greeks, and the *mimi* and *moriones* of the Romans, shaved their heads; but the court fools perhaps adopted this fashion as a satire upon the clergy and monks. Some writers professed to doubt whether the fools borrowed from the monks, or the monks from the fools; and Cornelius Agrippa, in his treatise on the Vanity of Sciences, remarks that the monks had their heads "all shaven like fools" (*raso toto capite ut fatui*). The cowl, also, was perhaps adopted in derision of the monks, but it was distinguished by the addition of a pair of asses' ears, or by a cock's head and comb, which formed its termination above, or by both. The court fool was also furnished with a staff or club, which became eventually his bauble. The bells were another necessary article in the equipment of a court fool, perhaps also intended as a satire on the custom of wearing small bells in the dress, which prevailed largely during the fourteenth and fifteenth centuries, especially among people who were fond of childish ostentation. The fool wore also a party-coloured, or motley, garment, probably with the same aim—that of satirising one of the ridiculous fashions of the fourteenth century.

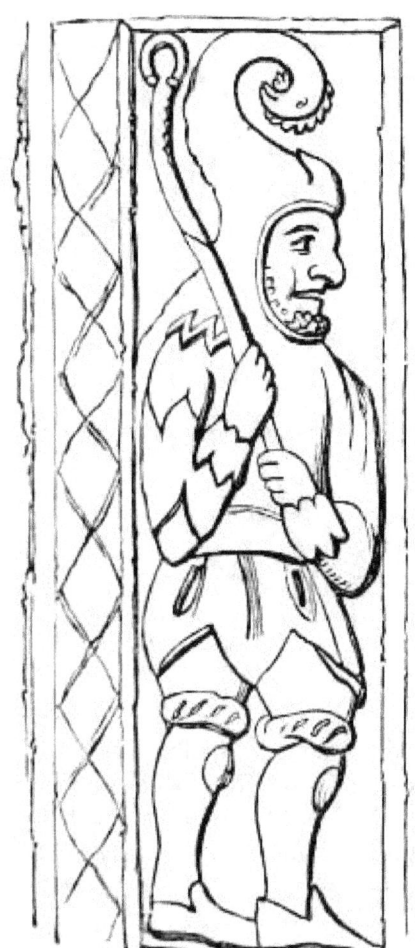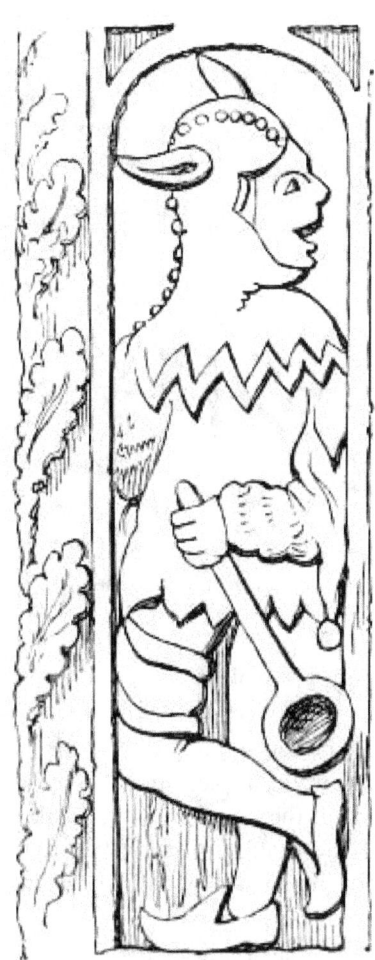

No. 127a. Court Fools.

It is in the fifteenth century that we first meet with the fool in full costume in the illuminations or manuscripts, and towards the end of the century this costume appears continually in engravings. It is also met with at this time among the sculptures of buildings and the carvings of wood-work. The two very interesting examples given in our cut No. 127a are taken from carvings of the fifteenth century, in the church of St. Levan, in Cornwall, near the Land's End. They represent the court fool in two varieties of costume; in the first, the fool's cowl, or cap, ends in the cock's head; in the other, it is fitted with asses' ears. There are variations also in other parts of the dress; for the second only has bells to his sleeves, and the first carries a singularly formed staff, which may perhaps be intended for a strap or belt, with a buckle at the end; while the other has a ladle in his hand. As one possesses a beard, and presents marks of age in his countenance, while the other is beardless and youthful, we may consider the pair as an old fool and a young fool.

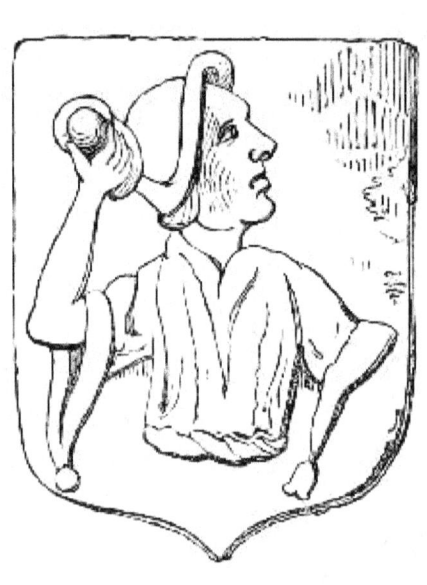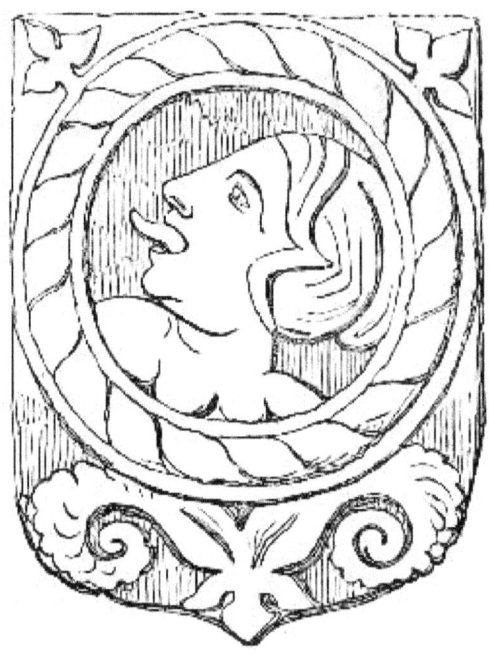

No. 128. A Fool and a Grimace-maker.

The Cornish churches are rather celebrated for their early carved wood-work, chiefly of the fifteenth century, of which two examples are given in our cut, No. 128, taken from bench pannels in the church of St. Mullion, on the Cornish coast, a little to the north of the Lizard Point. The first has bells hanging to the sleeves, and is no doubt intended to represent folly in some form; the other appears to be intended for the head of a woman making grimaces.[69]

The fool had long been a character among the people before he became a court fool, for Folly—or, as she was then called, "Mother Folly"—was one of the favourite objects of popular worship in the middle ages, and, where that worship sprang up spontaneously among the people, it grew with more energy, and presented more hearty joyousness and bolder satire than under the patronage of the great. Our forefathers in those times were accustomed to form themselves into associations or societies of a mirthful character, parodies of those of a more serious description, especially ecclesiastical, and elected as their officers mock popes, cardinals, archbishops and bishops, kings, &c They held periodical festivals, riotous and licentious carnivals, which were admitted into the churches, and even taken under the especial patronage of the clergy, under such titles as "the feast of fools," "the feast of the ass," "the feast of the innocents," and the like. There was hardly a Continental town of any account which had not its "company of fools," with its mock ordinances and mock ceremonies. In our own island we had our abbots of misrule and of unreason. At their public festivals satirical songs were sung and satirical masks and dresses were worn; and in many of them, especially at a later date, brief satirical dramas were acted. These satires assumed much of the functions of modern caricature; the caricature of the pictorial representations, which were mostly permanent monuments and destined for future generations, was naturally general in its character, but in the representations of which I am speaking, which were temporary, and designed to excite the mirth of the moment, it became personal, and, often, even political, and it was constantly directed against the ecclesiastical order. The scandal of the day furnished it with abundant materials. A fragment of one of their songs of an early date, sung at one of these "feasts" at Rouen, has been preserved, and contains the following lines, written in Latin and French:—

De asino bono nostro,

Meliori et optimo,
Debemus faire fête.
En revenant de Gravinaria,
Un gros chardon reperit in via,
Il lui coupa la tête.
Vir monachus in mense Julio
Egressus est e monasterio,
C'est dom de la Bucaille;
Egressus est sine licentia,
Pour aller voir dona Venissia,
Et faire la ripaille.

TRANSLATION.

For our good ass,
The better and the best,
We ought to rejoice.
In returning from Gravinière,
A great thistle he found in the way,
He cut off its head.
A monk in the month of July
Went out of his monastery,
It is dom de la Bucaille;
He went out without license,
To pay a visit to the dame de Venisse,
And make jovial cheer.

It appears that De la Bucaille was the prior of the abbey of St. Taurin, at Rouen, and that the dame de Venisse was prioress of St. Saviour, and these lines, no doubt, commemorate some great scandal of the day relating to the private relations between these two individuals.

These mock religious ceremonies are supposed to have been derived from the Roman Saturnalia; they were evidently of great antiquity in the mediæval church, and were most prevalent in France and Italy. Under the name of "the feast of the sub-deacons" they are forbidden by the acts of the council of Toledo, in 633; at a later period, the French punned on the word *sous-diacres*, and called them *Saouls-diacres* (Drunken Deacons), words which had nearly the same sound. The "feast of the ass" is said to be traced back in France as far as the ninth century. It was celebrated in most of the great towns in that country, such as Rouen, Sens, Douai, &c, and the service for the occasion is actually preserved in some of the old church books. From this it appears that the ass was led in procession to a place in the middle of the church, which had been decked out to receive it, and that the procession was led by two clerks, who sung a Latin song in praise of the animal. This song commences by telling us how "the ass came from the east, handsome and very strong, and most fit for carrying burthens":—

Orientis partibus
Adventavit asinus,
Pulcher et fortissimus,
Sarcinis aptissimus.

The refrain or burthen of the song is in French, and exhorts the animal to join in the uproar—"Eh! sir ass, chant now, fair mouth, bray, you shall have hay enough, and oats in abundance:"—

Hez, sire asnes, car chantez,
Belle bouche, rechignez,
Vous aurez du foin assez,
Et de l'avoine à plantez.

In this tone the chant continues through nine similar stanzas, describing the mode of life and food of the ass. When the procession reached the altar, the priest began a service in prose. Beleth, one of the celebrated doctors of the university of Paris, who flourished in 1182, speaks of the "feast of fools" as in existence in his time; and the acts of the council of Paris, held in 1212, forbid the presence of archbishops and bishops, and more especially of monks and nuns, at the feasts of fools, "in which a staff was carried."[70] We know the proceedings of this latter festival rather minutely from the accounts given in the ecclesiastical censures. It was in the cathedral churches that they elected the archbishop or bishop of fools, whose election was confirmed, and he was consecrated, with a multitude of buffooneries. He then entered upon his pontifical duties wearing the mitre and carrying the crosier before the people, on whom he bestowed his solemn benediction. In the exempt churches, or those which depended immediately upon the Holy See, they elected a pope of fools (*unum papam fatuorum*), who wore similarly the ensigns of the papacy. These dignitaries were assisted by an equally burlesque and licentious clergy, who uttered and performed a mixture of follies and impieties during the church service of the day, which they attended in disguises and masquerade dresses. Some wore masks, or had their faces painted, and others were dressed in women's clothing, or in ridiculous costumes. On entering the choir, they danced and sang licentious songs. The deacons and sub-deacons ate black puddings and sausages on the altar while the priest was celebrating; others played at cards or dice under his eyes; and others threw bits of old leather into the censer in order to raise a disagreeable smell. After the mass was ended, the people broke out into all sorts of riotous behaviour in the church, leaping, dancing, and exhibiting themselves in indecent postures, and some went as far as to strip themselves naked, and in this condition they were drawn through the streets with tubs full of ordure and filth, which they threw about at the mob. Every now and then they halted, when they exhibited immodest postures and actions, accompanied with songs and speeches of the same character. Many of the laity took part in the procession, dressed as monks and nuns. These disorders seem to have been carried to their greatest degree of extravagance during the fourteenth and fifteenth centuries.[71]

Towards the fifteenth century, lay societies, having apparently no connection with the clergy or the church, but of just the same burlesque character, arose in France. One of the earliest of these was formed by the clerks of the Bazoche, or lawyers' clerks of the Palais de Justice in Paris, whose president was a sort of king of misrule. The other principal society of this kind in Paris took the rather mirthful name of *Enfans sans Souci* (Careless Boys); it consisted of young men of education, who gave to their president or chieftain the title of *Prince des Sots* (the Prince of Fools). Both these societies composed and performed farces, and other small dramatic pieces. These farces were satires on contemporary society, and appear to have been often very personal.

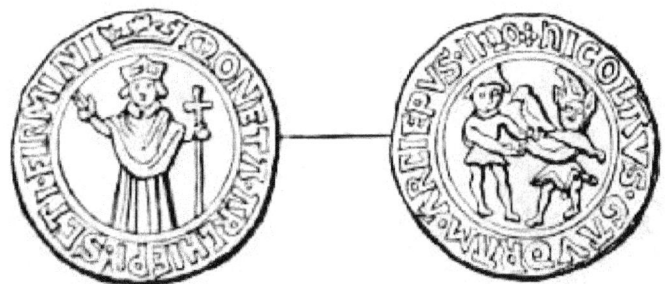

No. 129. Money of the Archbishop of the Innocents.

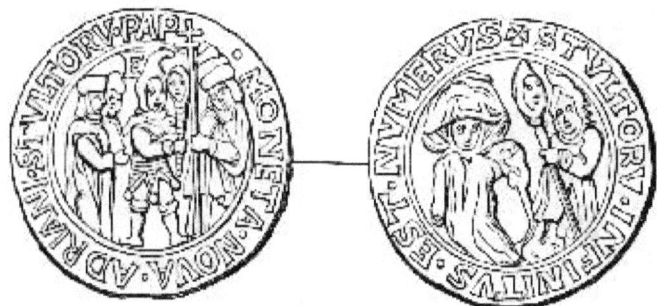

No. 130. Money of the Pope of Fools.

Almost the only monuments of the older of these societies consist of coins, or tokens, struck in lead, and sometimes commemorating the names of their mock dignitaries. A considerable number of these have been found in France, and an account of them, with engravings, was published by Dr. Rigollot some years ago.[72] Our cut No. 129 will serve as an example. It represents a leaden token of the Archbishop of the Innocents of the parish of St. Firmin, at Amiens, and is curious as bearing a date. On one side the archbishop of the Innocents is represented in the act of giving his blessing to his flock, surrounded by the inscription, MONETA · ARCHIEPI · SCTI · FIRMINI. On the other side we have the name of the individual who that year held the office of archbishop, NICOLAVS · GAVDRAM · ARCHIEPVS · 1520, surrounding a group consisting of two men, one of whom is dressed as a fool, holding between them a bird, which has somewhat the appearance of a magpie. Our cut No. 130 is still more curious; it is a token of the *pope* of fools. On one side appears the pope with his tiara and double cross, and a fool in full costume, who approaches his bauble to the pontifical cross. It is certainly a bitter caricature on the papacy, whether that were the intention or not. Two persons behind, dressed apparently in scholastic costume, seem to be merely spectators. The inscription is, MONETA · NOVA · ADRIANI · STVLTORV [M]· PAPE (the last E being in the field of the piece), "new money of Adrian, the pope of fools." The inscription on the other side of the token is one frequently repeated on these leaden medals, STVLTORV [M] · INFINITVS · EST · NVMERVS, "the number of fools is infinite." In the field we see Mother Folly holding up her bauble, and before her a grotesque figure in a cardinal's hat, apparently kneeling to her. It is rather surprising that we find so few allusions to these burlesque societies in the various classes of pictorial records from which the subject of these chapters has been illustrated; but we have evidence that they were not altogether overlooked. Until the latter end of the last century, the misereres of the church of St. Spire, at Corbeil, near Paris, were remarkable for the singular carvings with which they were decorated, and which have since been destroyed, but fortunately they were engraved by Millin. One of them, copied in our cut No. 131, evidently represents the bishop of fools conferring his blessing; the fool's bauble occupies the place of the pastoral staff.

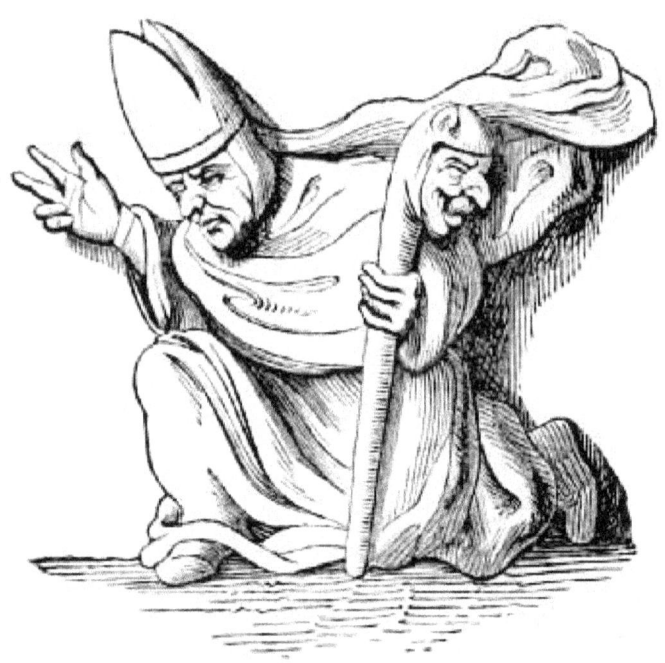

No. 131. The Bishop of Fools.

CHAPTER XIII.

THE DANCE OF DEATH.—THE PAINTINGS IN THE CHURCH OF LA CHAISE DIEU.—
THE REIGN OF FOLLY.—SEBASTIAN BRANDT; THE "SHIP OF FOOLS."—
DISTURBERS OF CHURCH SERVICE.—TROUBLESOME BEGGARS.—GEILER'S
SERMONS.—BADIUS, AND HIS SHIP OF FOOLISH WOMEN.—THE PLEASURES OF
SMELL.—ERASMUS; THE "PRAISE OF FOLLY."

There is still one cycle of satire which almost belongs to the middle ages, though it only became developed at their close, and became most popular after they were past. There existed, at least as early as the beginning of the thirteenth century, a legendary story of an interview between three living and three dead men, which is usually told in French verse, and appears under the title of "Des trois vifs et des trois morts." According to some versions of the legend, it was St. Macarius, the Egyptian recluse, who thus introduced the living to the dead. The verses are sometimes accompanied with figures, and these have been found both sculptured and painted on ecclesiastical buildings. At a later period, apparently early in the fifteenth century, some one extended this idea to all ranks of society, and pictured a skeleton, the emblem of death, or even more than one, in communication with an individual of each class; and this extended scene, from the manner of the grouping—in which the dead appeared to be wildly dancing off with the living—became known as the "Dance of Death." As the earlier legend of the three dead and the three living was, however, still often introduced at the beginning of it, the whole group was most generally known—especially during the fifteenth century—as the "Danse Macabre," or Dance of Macabre, this name being considered as a mere corruption of Macarius. The temper of the age—in which death in every form was constantly before the eyes of all, and in which people sought to regard life as a mere transitory moment of enjoyment—gave to this grim idea of the fellowship of death and life great popularity, and it was not only painted on the walls of churches, but it was suspended in tapestry around people's chambers. Sometimes they even attempted to represent it in masquerade, and we are told that in the month of October, 1424, the "Danse Macabre" was publicly danced by living people in the cemetery of the Innocents, in Paris—a fit place for so lugubrious a performance—in the presence of the Duke of Bedford and the Duke of Burgundy, who came to Paris after the battle of Verneuil. During the rest of the century we find not unfrequently allusions to the "Danse Macabre." The English poet Lydgate wrote a series of stanzas to accompany the figures, and it was the subject of some of the earliest engravings on wood. In the posture and accompaniments of the figures representing the different classes of society, and in the greater or less reluctance with which the living accept their not very attractive partners, satire is usually implied, and it is in some cases accompanied with drollery. The figure representing death has almost always a grimly mirthful countenance, and appears to be dancing with good will. The most remarkable early representation of the "Danse Macabre" now preserved, is that painted on the wall of the church of La Chaise Dieu, in Auvergne, a beautiful fac-simile of which was published a few years ago by the well-known antiquary M. Jubinal. This remarkable picture begins with the figures of Adam and Eve, who are introducing death into the world in the form of a serpent with a death's head. The dance is opened by an ecclesiastic preaching from a pulpit, towards whom death is leading first in the dance the pope, for each individual takes his precedence strictly according to his class—alternately an ecclesiastic and a layman. Thus next after the pope comes the emperor, and the cardinal is followed by the king. The baron is followed by the bishop, and the grim partner of the latter appears to pay more intention to the layman than to his own priest, so that two dead men appear to have the former in charge. The group thus represented by the nobleman and the two deaths, is copied in our cut No. 132, and will serve as an example of the style and grouping of this remarkable painting. After a few other figures, perhaps less striking, we come to the merchant, who receives the advances of his partner with a thoughtful air; while immediately after him another death is trying to make himself more acceptable to the bashful nun by throwing a cloak over his nakedness. In another place two deaths armed with bows and arrows are scattering their shafts rather dangerously. Soon follow some of the more gay and youthful members of society. Our cut No. 133 represents the musician, who appears also to attract the attentions of two of the persecutors. In his dismay he is treading under foot his own viol. The dance closes with the lower orders of society, and is concluded by a group which is not so easily understood. Before the end of the fifteenth century, there had appeared in Paris several editions of a series of bold engravings on wood, in a small folio size, representing the same dance, though somewhat differently treated. France, indeed, appears to have been the native country of the "Danse Macabre." But in the century following the beautiful set of drawings by the great artist Hans Holbein, first published at Lyons in 1538, gave to the Dance of Death a still greater and wider celebrity. From this time the subjects of this dance were commonly introduced in initial letters, and in the engraved borders of pages, especially in books of a religious character.

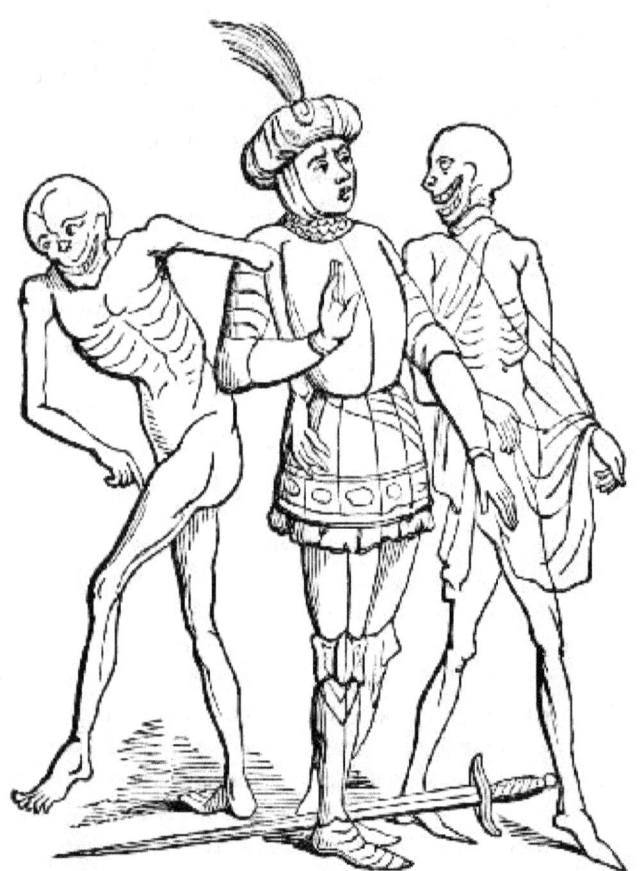

No. 132. The Knight in the Dance of Death.

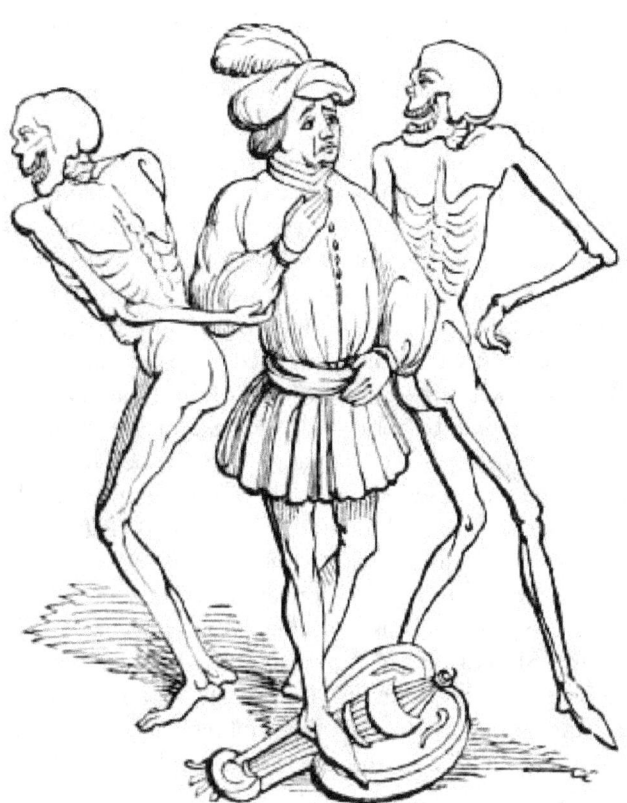

No. 133. The Musician in Death's Hands.

Death may truly be said to have shared with Folly that melancholy period—the fifteenth century. As society then presented itself to the eye, people might easily suppose that the world was running mad, and folly, in one shape or other, seemed to be the principle which ruled most men's actions. The jocular societies, described in my last chapter, which multiplied in France during the fifteenth century, initiated a sort of mock worship of Folly. That sort of inauguration of death which was performed in the "Danse Macabre," was of French growth, but the grand crusade against folly appears to have originated in Germany. Sebastian Brandt was a native of Strasburg, born in 1458. He studied in that city and in Bâle, became a celebrated professor in both those places, and died at the former in 1520. The "Ship of Fools," which has immortalised the name of Sebastian Brandt, is believed to have been first published in the year 1494. The original German text went through numerous editions within a few years; a Latin translation was equally popular, and it was afterwards edited and enlarged by Jodocus Badius Ascensius. A French text was no less successful; an English translation was printed by Richard Pynson in 1509; a Dutch version appeared in 1519. During the sixteenth century, Brandt's "Ship of Fools" was the most popular of books. It consists of a series of bold woodcuts, which form its characteristic feature, and of metrical explanations, written by Brandt, and annexed to each cut. Taking his text from the words of the preacher, "Stultorum numerus est infinitus," Brandt exposes to the eye, in all its shades and forms, the folly of his contemporaries, and bares to view its roots and causes. The cuts are especially interesting as striking pictures of contemporary manners. The "Ship of Fools" is the great ship of the world, into which the various descriptions of fatuity are pouring from all quarters in boat-loads. The first folly is that of men who collected great quantities of books, not for their utility, but for their rarity, or beauty of execution, or rich bindings, so that we see that bibliomania had already taken its place among human vanities. The second class of fools were interested and partial judges, who sold justice for money, and are represented under the emblem of two fools throwing a boar into a caldron, according to the old Latin proverb, *Agere aprum in lebetem*. Then come the various follies of misers, fops, dotards, men who are foolishly indulgent to their children, mischief-makers, and despisers of good advice; of nobles and men in power; of the profane and the improvident; of foolish lovers; of extravagant eaters and drinkers, &c, &c Foolish talking, hypocrisy, frivolous pursuits, ecclesiastical corruptions, impudicity, and a great number of other vices as well as follies, are duly passed in review, and are represented in various forms of satirical caricature, and sometimes in simpler unadorned pictures. Thus the foolish valuers of things are represented by a fool holding a balance, one scale of which contains the sun, moon, and stars, to represent heaven and heavenly things, and the other a castle and fields, to represent earthly things, the latter scale overweighing the other; and the procrastinator is pictured by another fool, with a parrot perched on his head, and a magpie on each hand, all repeating *cras, cras, cras* (to-morrow). Our cut No. 134 represents a group of disturbers of church service. It was a common practice in former days to take to church hawks (which were constantly carried about as the outward ensign of the gentleman) and dogs. The fool has here thrown back his fool's-cap to exhibit more fully the fashionable "gent" of the day; he carries his hawk on his hand, and wears not only a fashionable pair of shoes, but very fashionable clogs also. These gentlemen *à la mode, turgentes genere et natalibus altis*, we are told, were the persons who disturbed the church service by the creaking of their shoes and clogs, the noise made by their birds, the barking and quarrelling of their dogs, by their own whisperings, and especially with immodest women, whom they met in church as in a convenient place of assignation. All these forms of the offence are expressed in the picture. Our second example cut No. 135, which forms the fifty-ninth title or subject in the "Ship of Fools," represents a party of the beggars with which, either lay or ecclesiastical, the country was then overrun. In the explanation, these wicked beggars are described as indulging in idleness, in eating, drinking, rioting, and sleep, while they levy contributions on the charitable feelings of the honest and industrious, and, under cover of begging, commit robbery wherever they find the opportunity. The beggar, who appears to be only a deceptive cripple, leads his donkey laden with children, whom he is bringing up in the same profession, while his wife lingers behind to indulge in her bibulous propensities. These cuts will give a tolerable notion of the general character of the whole, which amount in number to a hundred and twelve, and therefore present a great variety of subjects relative to almost every class and profession of life.

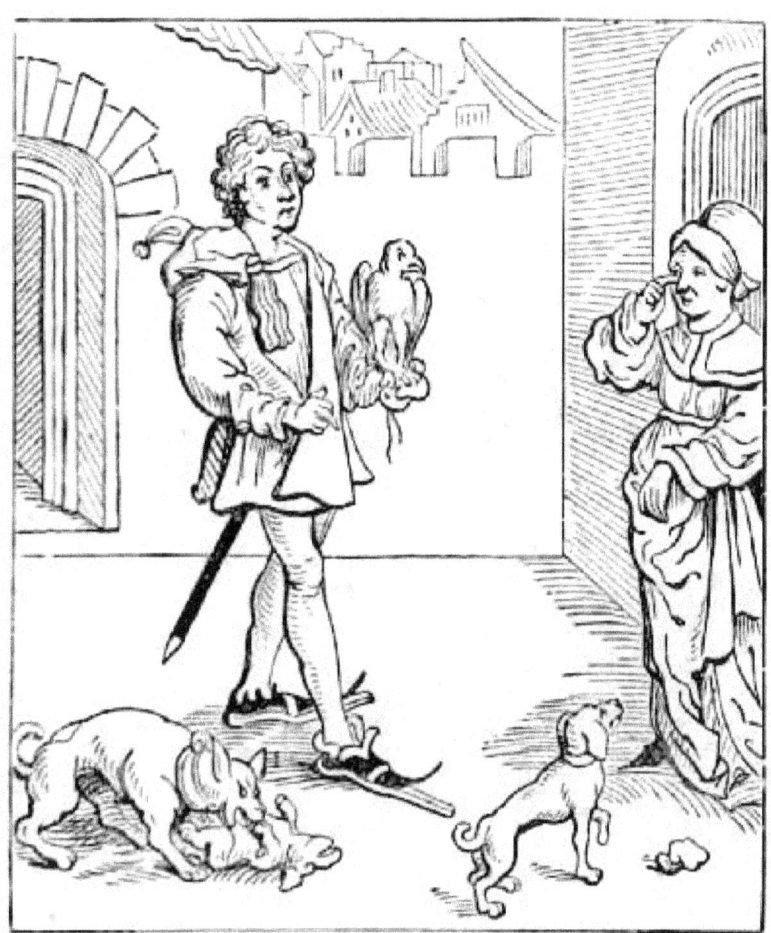

No. 134. Disturbers of Church Service.

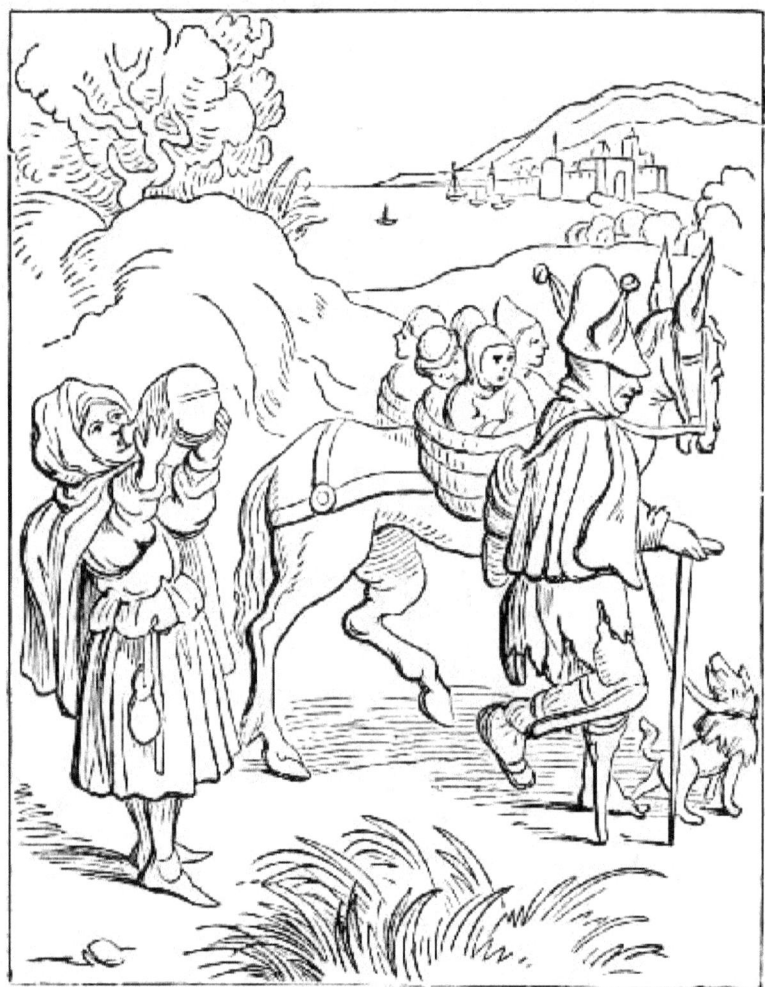

No. 135. Mendicants on their Travels.

We may remark, however, that after Folly had thus run through all the stages of society, until it had reached the lowest of all, the ranks of mendicity, the gods themselves became alarmed, the more so as this great movement was directed especially against Minerva, the goddess of wisdom, and they held a conclave to provide against it. The result is not told, but the course of Folly goes on as vigorously as ever. Ignorant fools who set up for physicians, fools who cannot understand jokes, unwise mathematicians, astrologers, of the latter of which the moraliser says, in his Latin verse—

Siqua voles sortis prænoscere damna futuræ,
Et vitare malum, sol tibi signa dabit.
Sed tibi, stulte, tui cur non dedit ille furoris
Signa? aut, si dederit, cur tanta mala subis?
Nondum grammaticæ callis primordia, et audes
Vim cœli radio supposuisse tuo.

The next cut is a very curious one, and appears to represent a dissecting-house of this early period. Among other chapters which afford interesting pictures of that time, and indeed of all times, we may instance those of litigious fools, who are always going to law, and who confound blind justice, or rather try to unbind her eyes; of filthy-tongued fools, who glorify the race of swine; of ignorant scholars; of gamblers; of bad and thievish cooks; of low men who seek to be high, and of high who are despisers of poverty; of men who forget that they will die; of irreligious men and blasphemers; of the ridiculous indulgence of parents to children, and the ungrateful return which was made to them for it; and of women's pride. Another title describes the ruin of Christianity: the pope, emperor, king, cardinals, &c, are receiving willingly from a suppliant fool the cap of Folly, while two other fools are looking derisively upon them from an adjoining wall. It need hardly be said that this was published on the eve of the Reformation.

In the midst of the popularity which greeted the appearance of the work of Sebastian Brandt, it attracted the special attention of a celebrated preacher of the time named Johann Geiler. Geiler was born at Schaffhausen, in Switzerland, in 1445, but having lost his father when only three years of age, he was educated by his grandfather, who lived at Keysersberg, in Alsace, and hence he was commonly called Geiler of Keysersberg. He studied in Freiburg and Bâle, obtained a great reputation for learning, was esteemed a profound theologian, and was finally settled in Strasburg, where he continued to shine as a preacher until his death in 1510. He was a bold man, too, in the cause of truth, and declaimed with earnest zeal against the corruptions of the church, and especially against the monkish orders, for he compared the black monks to the devil, the white monks to his dam, and the others he said were their chickens. On another occasion he said that the qualities of a good monk were an almighty belly, an ass's back, and a raven's mouth. He told his congregation from the pulpit that a great reformation was at hand, that he did not expect to live to see it himself, but that many of those who heard him would live to see it. As may be supposed, the monks hated him, and spoke of him with contempt. They said, that in his sermons he took his texts, not from the Scriptures, but from the "Ship of Fools" of Sebastian Brandt; and, in fact, during the year 1498, Geiler preached at Strasburg a series of sermons on the follies of his time, which were evidently founded upon Brandt's book, for the various follies were taken in the same order. They were originally compiled in German, but one of Geiler's scholars, Jacob Other, translated them into Latin, and published them, in 1501, under the title of "Navicula sive Speculum Fatuorum præstantissimi sacrarum literarum doctoris Johannis Geiler." Within a few years this work went through several editions both in Latin and in German, some of them illustrated by woodcuts. The style of preaching is quaint and curious, full of satirical wit, which is often coarse, according to the manner of the time, sometimes very indelicate. Each sermon is headed by the motto, "Stultorum infinitus est numerus." Geiler takes for his theme in each sermon one of the titles of Brandt's "Ship of Fools," and he separates them into subdivisions, or branches, which he calls the bells (*nolas*) from the fool's-cap.

The other scholar who did most to spread the knowledge of Brandt's work, was Jodocus Badius, who assumed the additional name of Ascensius because he was born at Assen, near Brussels, in 1462. He was a very distinguished scholar, but is best known for having established a celebrated printing establishment in Paris, where he died in 1535. I have already stated that Badius edited the Latin translation of the "Ship of Fools" of Sebastian Brandt, with additional explanations of his own, but he was one of the first of Brandt's imitators. He seems to have thought that Brandt's book was not complete—that the weaker sex had not received its fair share of importance; and apparently in 1498, while Geiler was turning the "Stultifera Navis" into sermons, Badius compiled a sort of supplement to it (*additamentum*), to which he gave the title of *"Stultiferæ naviculæ, seu Scaphæ, Fatuarum Mulierum,"* the Boats of Foolish Women. As far as can be traced, the first edition appears to have been printed in 1502. The first cut represents the ship carrying Eve alone of the female race, whose folly involved the whole world. The book is divided into five chapters, according to the number of the five senses, each sense represented by a boat carrying its particular class of foolish women to the great ship of foolish women, which lies off at anchor. The text consists of a dissertation on the use and abuse of the particular sense which forms the substance of the chapter, and it ends with Latin verses, which are given as the boatman's *celeusma*, or boat song. The first of these boats is the *scapha stultæ visionis ad stultiferam navem perveniens*—the boat of foolish seeing proceeding to the ship of fools. A party of gay ladies are taking possession of the boat, carrying with them their combs, looking-glasses, and all other implements necessary for making them fair to be looked upon. The second boat is the *scapha auditionis fatuæ*, the boat of foolish hearing, in which the ladies are playing upon musical instruments. The third is the *scapha olfactionis stultæ*, the boat of foolish smell, and the pictorial illustration to it is partly copied in our cut No. 136. In the original some of the ladies are gathering sweet-smelling flowers before they enter the boat, while on board a pedlar is vending his perfume. One *folle femme*, with her fool's cap on her head, is buying a pomander, or, as we should perhaps now say, a scent-ball, from the itinerant dealer. Figures of pomanders are extremely rare, and this is an interesting example; in fact, it is only recently that our Shakspearian critics really understood the meaning of the word. A pomander was a small globular vessel, perforated with holes, and filled with strong perfumes, as it is represented in our woodcut. The fourth of these boats is that of foolish tasting, *scapha gustationis fatuæ*, and the ladies have their well-furnished table on board the boat, and are largely indulging in eating and drinking. In the last of these boats, the *scapha contactionis fatuæ*, or boat of foolish feeling, the women have men on board, and are proceeding to great liberties with them; one of the gentle damsels, too, is picking the pocket of her male companion in a very unlady-like manner.

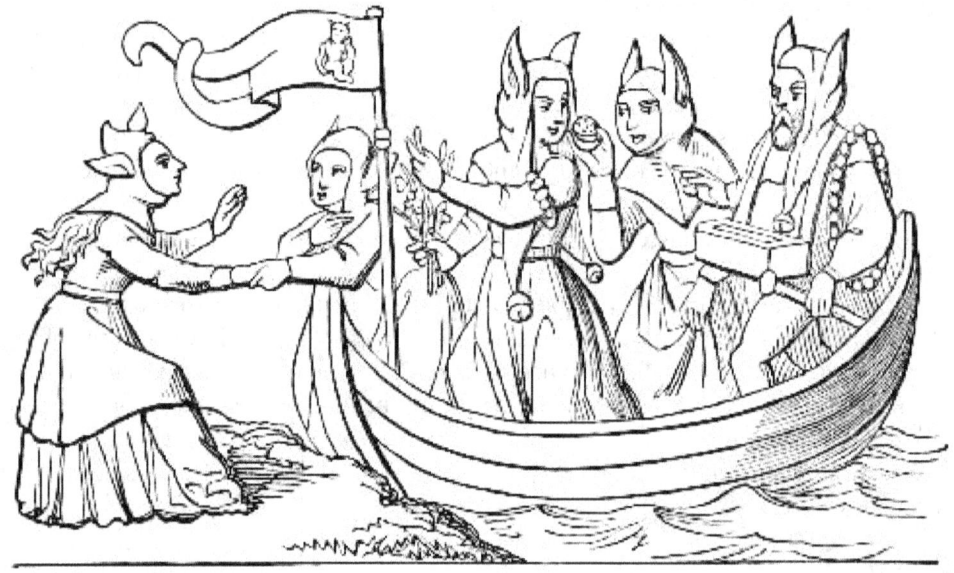

No. 136. The Boat of Pleasant Odours.

Two ideas combined in this peculiar field of satiric literature, that of the ship and that of the fools, now became popular, and gave rise to a host of imitators. There appeared ships of health, ships of penitence, ships of all sorts of things, on the one hand; and on the other, folly was a favourite theme of satire from many quarters. One of the most remarkable of the personages involved in this latter warfare, was the great scholar Desiderius Erasmus, of Rotterdam, who was born in that city in 1467. Like most of these satirists, Erasmus was strongly imbued with the spirit of the Reformation, and he was the acquaintance and friend of those to whom the Reformation owed a great part of its success. In 1497, when the "Ship of Fools" of Sebastian Brandt was in the first full flush of its popularity, Erasmus came to England, and was so well received, that from that time forward his literary life seemed more identified with our island than with any other country. His name is still a sort of household word in our universities, especially in that of Cambridge. He made here the friendly acquaintance of the great Sir Thomas More, himself a lover of mirth, and one of those whose names are celebrated for having kept a court fool. In the earlier years of the sixteenth century, Erasmus visited Italy, and passed two or three years there. He returned thence to England, as appears, early in the year 1508. It is not easy to decide whether his experience of society in Italy had convinced him more than ever that folly was the presiding genius of mankind, or what other feeling influenced him, but one of the first results of his voyage was the Μωρίας Ἐγκώμιον (*Moriæ Encomium*), or "Praise of Folly." Erasmus dedicated this little jocular treatise to Sir Thomas More as a sort of pun upon his name, although he protests that there was a great contrast between the two characters. Erasmus takes much the same view of folly as Brandt, Geiler, Badius, and the others, and under this name he writes a bold satire on the whole frame of contemporary society. The satire is placed in the mouth of Folly herself (the Mère Folie of the jocular clubs), who delivers from her pulpit a declamation in which she sets forth her qualities and praises. She boasts of the greatness of her origin, claims as her kindred the sophists, rhetoricians, and many of the pretentious scholars and wise men, and describes her birth and education. She claims divine affinity, and boasts of her influence over the world, and of the beneficent manner in which it was exercised. All the world, she pretends, was ruled under her auspices, and it was only in her presence that mankind was really happy. Hence the happiest ages of man are infancy, before wisdom has come to interfere, and old age, when it has passed away. Therefore, she says, if men would remain faithful to her, and avoid wisdom altogether, they would pass a life of perpetual youth. In this long discourse of the influence of folly, written by a man of the known sentiments of Erasmus, it would be strange if the Romish church, with its monks and ignorant priesthood, its saints, and relics, and miracles, did not find a place. Erasmus intimates that the superstitious follies had become permanent, because they were profitable. There are some, he tells us, who cherished the foolish yet pleasant persuasion, that if they fixed their eyes devoutly on a figure of St. Christopher, carved in wood or painted on the wall, they would be safe from death on that day; with many other examples of equal credulity. Then there are your pardons, your measures of purgatory, which may be bought off at so much the hour, or the day, or the month, and a multitude of other absurdities. Ecclesiastics, scholars, mathematicians, philosophers, all come in for their share of the refined satire of this book, which, like the "Ship of Fools," has gone through innumerable editions, and has been translated into many languages.

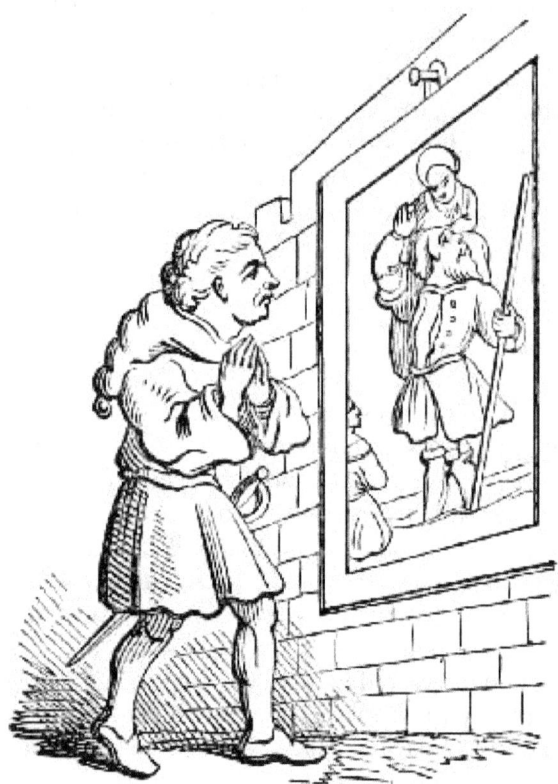

No. 137. Superstition.

In an early French translation, the text of this work of Erasmus is embellished with some of the woodcuts belonging to Brandt's "Ship of Fools," which, it need hardly be remarked, are altogether inappropriate, but the "Praise of Folly" was detained to receive illustrations from a more distinguished pencil. A copy of the book came into the hands of Hans Holbein—it may possibly have been presented to him by the author—and Holbein took so much interest in it, that he amused himself with drawing illustrative sketches with a pen in the margins. This book afterwards passed into the library of the University of Bâle, where it was found in the latter part of the seventeenth century, and these drawings have since been engraved and added to most of the subsequent editions. Many of these sketches are very slight, and some have not a very close connection with the text of Erasmus, but they are all characteristic, and show the spirit—the spirit of the age—in which Holbein read his author. I give two examples of them, taken almost haphazard, for it would require a longer analysis of the book than can be given here to make many of them understood. The first of these, our cut No. 137, represents the foolish warrior, who has a sword long enough to trust to it for defence, bowing with trembling superstition before a painting of St. Christopher crossing the water with the infant Christ on his shoulder, as a more certain security for his safety during that day. The other, our cut No. 138, represents the preacher, Lady Folly, descending from her pulpit, after she has concluded her sermon.

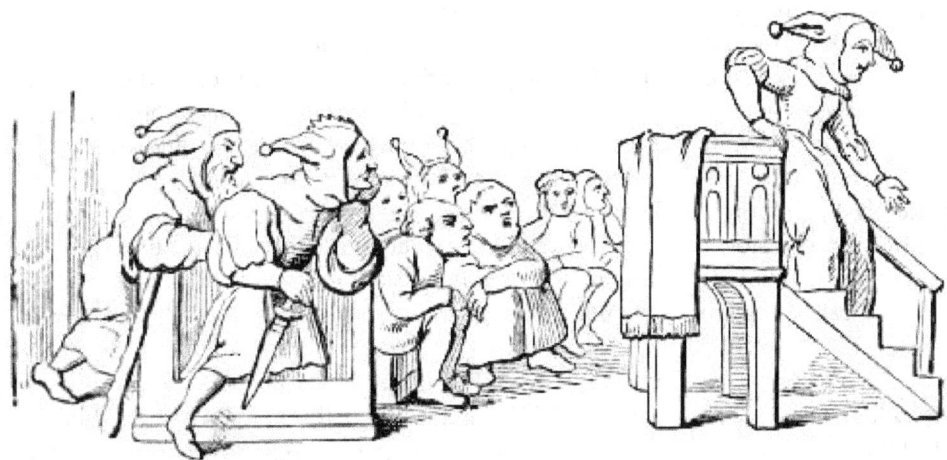

No. 138. Preacher Folly ending her Sermon.

CHAPTER XIV.

POPULAR LITERATURE AND ITS HEROES; BROTHER RUSH, TYLL EULENSPIEGEL,
THE WISE MEN OF GOTHAM.–STORIES AND JEST-BOOKS.–SKELTON, SCOGIN,
TARLTON, PEELE.

The people in the middle ages, as well as its superiors, had its comic literature and legend. Legend
was the literature especially of the peasant, and in it the spirit of burlesque and satire manifested
itself in many ways. Simplicity, combined with vulgar cunning, and the circumstances arising out of
the exercise of these qualities, presented the greatest stimulants to popular mirth. They produced
their popular heroes, who, at first, were much more than half legendary, such as the familiar spirit,
Robin Goodfellow, whose pranks were a source of continual amusement rather than of terror to
the simple minds which listened to those who told them. These stories excited with still greater
interest as their spiritual heroes became incarnate, and the auditors were persuaded that the
perpetrators of so many artful acts of cunning and of so many mischievous practical jokes, were but
ordinary men like themselves. It was but a sign or symbol of the change from the mythic age to that
of practical life. One of the earliest of these stories of mythic comedy transformed into, or at least
presented under the guise of, humanity, is that of Brother Ruth. Although the earliest version of
this story with which we are acquainted dates only from the beginning of the sixteenth century,[73]
there is no reason for doubt that the story itself was in existence at a much more remote period.

Rush was, in truth, a spirit of darkness, whose mission it was to wander on the earth tempting and
impelling people to do evil. Perceiving that the internal condition of a certain abbey was well suited
to his purpose, he presented himself at its gates in the disguise of a youth who wanted employment,
and was received as an assistant in the kitchen, but he pleased the monks best by the skill with
which he furnished them all with fair companions. At length he quarrelled with the cook, and threw
him into the boiling caldron, and the monks, assuming that his death was accidental, appointed
Rush to be cook in his place. After a service of seven years in the kitchen—which appears to have
been considered a fair apprenticeship for the new honour which was to be conferred upon him—
the abbot and convent rewarded him by making him a monk. He now followed still more earnestly
his design for the ruin of his brethren, both soul and body, and began by raising a quarrel about a
woman, which led, through his contrivance, to a fight, in which the monks all suffered grievous
bodily injuries, and in which Brother Rush was especially active. He went on in this way until at last

his true character was accidentally discovered. A neighbouring farmer, overtaken by night, took shelter in a hollow tree. It happened to be the night appointed by Lucifer to meet his agents on earth, and hear from them the report of their several proceedings, and he had selected this very oak as the place of rendezvous. There Brother Rush appeared, and the farmer, in his hiding-place, heard his confession from his own lips, and told it to the abbot, who, being as it would appear a magician, conjured him into the form of a horse, and banished him. Rush hurried away to England, where he laid aside his equine form, and entered the body of the king's daughter, who suffered great torments from his possession. At length some of the great doctors from Paris came and obliged the spirit to confess that nobody but the abbot of the distant monastery had any power over him. The abbot came, called him out of the maiden, and conjured him more forcibly than ever into the form of a horse.

Such is, in mere outline, the story of Brother Rush, which was gradually enlarged by the addition of new incidents. But the people wanted a hero who presented more of the character of reality, who, in fact, might be recognised as one of themselves; and such heroes appear to have existed at all times. They usually represented a class in society, and especially that class which consisted of idle sharpers, who lived by their wits, and which was more numerous and more familiarly known in the middle ages than at the present day. Folly and cunning combined presented a never-failing subject of mirth. This class of adventurers first came into print in Germany, and it is there that we find its first popular hero, to whom they gave the name of Eulenspiegel, which means literally "the owl's mirror," and has been since used in German in the sense of a merry fool. Tyll Eulenspiegel, and his story, are supposed to have belonged to the fourteenth century, though we first know them in the printed book of the commencement of the sixteenth, which is believed to have come from the pen of the well-known popular writer, Thomas Murner, of whom I shall have to speak more at length in another chapter. The popularity of this work was very great, and it was quickly translated into French, English, Latin, and almost every other language of Western Europe. In the English version the name also was translated, and appears under the form of Owleglass, or, as it often occurs with the superfluous aspirate, Howleglass.[74] According to the story, Tyll Eulenspiegel was the son of a peasant, and was born at a village called Kneitlingen, in the land of Brunswick. The story of his birth may be given in the words of the early English version, as a specimen of its quaint and antiquated language:—

"Yn the lande of Sassen, in the vyllage of Ruelnige, there dwelleth a man that was named Nicholas Howleglas, that had a wife named Wypeke, that lay a childbed in the same wyllage, and that chylde was borne to christening; and named Tyell Howleglass. And than the chyld was brought into a taverne, where the father was wyth his gosseppes and made good chere. Whan the mydwife had wel dronke, she toke the childe to bere it home, and in the wai was a litle bridg over a muddy water. And as the mydwife would have gone over the lytle brydge, she fel into the mudde with the chylde, for she had a lytel dronk to much wyne, for had not helpe come quickly, the had both be drowned in the mudde. And whan she came home with the childe, the made a kettle of warm water to be made redi, and therin they washed the child clen of the mudde. And thus was Howleglas thre tymes in one dai cristened, once at the churche, once in the mudde, and once in the warm water."

It will be seen that the English translator was not very correct in his geography or in his names. The child, having thus escaped destruction, grew rapidly, and displayed an extraordinary love of mischief, with various other evil propensities, as well as a cunning beyond his age, in escaping the risks to which these exposed him. At a very early age, he displayed a remarkable talent for setting the other children by the ears, and this was his favourite amusement during life. His mother, who was now a widow, contemplating the extraordinary cunning of her child, which, as she thought, must necessarily ensure his advancement in the world, resolved that he should no longer remain idle, and put him apprentice to a baker; but his wicked and restless disposition defeated all the good intentions of his parent, and Eulenspiegel was obliged to leave his master in consequence of his mal-practices. One day his mother took him to a church-dedication, and the child drank so much at the feast on that occasion, that he crept into an empty beehive and fell asleep, while his mother, thinking he had gone home, returned without him. In the night-time two thieves came into the garden to steal the bees, and they agreed to take first the hive which was heaviest. This, as may be supposed, proved to be the hive in which Eulenspiegel was hidden, and they fixed it on a pole which they carried on their shoulders, one before and one behind, the hive hanging between them. Eulenspiegel, awakened by the movement, soon discovered the position in which he was placed, and hit upon a plan for escaping. Gently lifting the lid of the hive, he put out his arm and plucked the hair of the man before, who turned about and accused his companion of insulting him. The other asserted that he had not touched him, and the first, only half satisfied, continued to bear his share of the burthen, but he had not advanced many steps when a still sharper pull at his hair excited his great anger, and from wrathful words the two thieves proceeded to blows. While they were fighting, Eulenspiegel crept out of the hive and ran away.

After leaving the baker, Eulenspiegel became a wanderer in the world, gaining his living by his trickery and deception, and engaging himself in all sorts of strange and ludicrous adventures. He ended everywhere by creating discord and strife. He became at different times a blacksmith, a shoemaker, a tailor, a cook, a drawer of teeth, and assumed a variety of other characters, but remained in each situation only long enough to make it too hot for him, and to be obliged to secure his retreat. He intruded himself into all classes of society, and invariably came to similar results. Many of his adventures, indeed, are so droll that we can easily understand the great popularity they once enjoyed. But they are not merely amusing—they present a continuous satire upon contemporary society, upon a social condition in which every pretender, every reckless impostor, every private plunderer or public depredator, saw the world exposed to him in its folly and credulity as an easy prey.

The middle ages possessed another class of these popular satirical histories, which were attached to places rather than to persons. There were few countries which did not possess a town or a district, the inhabitants of which were celebrated for stupidity, or for roguery, or for some other ridiculous or contemptible quality. We have seen, in a former chapter, the people of Norfolk enjoying this peculiarity, and, at a later period, the inhabitants of Pevensey in Sussex, and more especially those of Gotham in Nottinghamshire, were similarly distinguished. The inhabitants of many places in Germany bore this character, but their grand representatives among the Germans were the Schildburgers, a name which appears to belong entirely to the domain of fable. Schildburg, we are told, was a town "in Misnopotamia, beyond Utopia, in the kingdom of Calecut." The Schildburgers were originally so renowned for their wisdom, that they were continually invited into foreign countries to give their advice, until at length not a man was left at home, and their wives were obliged to assume the charge of the duties of their husbands. This became at length so onerous, that the wives held a council, and resolved on despatching a solemn message in writing to call the men home. This had the desired effect; all the Schildburgers returned to their own town, and were so joyfully received by their wives that they resolved upon leaving it no more. They accordingly held a council, and it was decided that, having experienced the great inconvenience of a reputation of wisdom, they would avoid it in future by assuming the character of fools. One of the first evil results of their long neglect of home affairs was the want of a council-hall, and this want they now resolved to supply without delay. They accordingly went to the hills and woods, cut down the timber, dragged it with great labour to the town, and in due time completed the erection of a handsome and substantial building. But, when they entered their new council-hall, what was their consternation to find themselves in perfect darkness! In fact, they had forgotten to make any windows. Another council was held, and one who had been among the wisest in the days of their wisdom, gave his opinion very oracularly; the result of which was that they should experiment on every possible expedient for introducing light into the hall, and that they should first try that which seemed most likely to succeed. They had observed that the light of day was caused by sunshine, and the plan proposed was to meet at mid-day when the sun was brightest, and fill sacks, hampers, jugs, and vessels of all kinds, with sunshine and daylight, which they proposed afterwards to empty into the unfortunate council-hall. Next day, as the clock struck one, you might see a crowd of Schildburgers before the council-house door, busily employed, some holding the sacks open, and others throwing the light into them with shovels and any other appropriate implements which came to hand. While they were thus labouring, a stranger came into the town of Schildburg, and, hearing what they were about, told them they were labouring to no purpose, and offered to show them how to get the daylight into the hall. It is unnecessary to say more than that this new plan was to make an opening in the roof, and that the Schildburgers witnessed the effect with astonishment, and were loud in their gratitude to their new comer.

The Schildburgers met with further difficulties before they completed their council-hall. They sowed a field with salt, and when the salt-plant grew up next year, after a meeting of the council, at which it was stiffly disputed whether it ought to be reaped, or mowed, or gathered in in some other manner, it was finally discovered that the crop consisted of nothing but nettles. After many accidents of this kind, the Schildburgers are noticed by the emperor, and obtain a charter of incorporation and freedom, but they profit little by it. In trying some experiments to catch mice, they set fire to their houses, and the whole town is burnt to the ground, upon which, in their sorrow, they abandon it altogether, and become, like the Jews of old, scattered over the world, carrying their own folly into every country they visit.

The earliest known edition of the history of the Schildburgers was printed in 1597,[75] but the story itself is no doubt older. It will be seen at once that it involves a satire upon the municipal towns of the middle ages. A similar series of adventures, only a little more clerical, bore the title of "Der Pfarrherrn vom Kalenberg," or the Parson of Kalenberg, and was first, as far as we know, published in the latter half of the sixteenth century. The first known edition, printed in 1582, is in prose. Von der Hagen, who reprinted a subsequent edition in verse, in a volume already quoted, seems to think that in its first form the story belongs to the fourteenth century.

The Schildburgers of Germany were represented in England by the wise men of Gotham. Gotham is a village and parish about seven miles to the south-west of Nottingham, and, curiously enough, a story is told according to which the folly of the men of Gotham, like that of the Schildburgers, was at first assumed. It is pretended that one day king John, on his way to Nottingham, intended to pass through the village of Gotham, and that the Gothamites, under the influence of some vague notion that his presence would be injurious to them, raised difficulties in his way which prevented his visit. The men of Gotham were now apprehensive of the king's vengeance, and they resolved to try and evade it by assuming the character of simpletons. When the king's officers came to Gotham to inquire into the conduct of the inhabitants, they found them engaged in the most extraordinary pursuits, some of them seeking to drown an eel in a pond of water, others making a hedge round a tree to confine a cuckoo which had settled in it, and others employing themselves in similar futile pursuits. The commissioners reported the people of Gotham to be no better than fools, and by this stratagem they escaped any further persecution, but the character they assumed remained attached to them.

This explanation is, of course, very late and very apocryphal; but there can be little doubt that the character of the wise men of Gotham is one of considerable antiquity. The story is believed to have been drawn up in its present form by Andrew Borde, an English writer of the reign of Henry VIII. It was reprinted a great number of times under the form of those popular books called chap-books, because they were hawked about the country by itinerant booksellers or chap-men. The acts of the

Gothamites displayed a greater degree of simplicity even than those of the Schildburgers, but they are less connected. Here is one anecdote told in the unadorned language of the chap-books, in explanation of which it is only necessary to state that the men of Gotham admired greatly the note of the cuckoo. "On a time the men of Gotham fain would have pinn'd in the cuckow, that she might sing all the year; and, in the midst of the town, they had a hedge made round in compass, and got a cuckow and put her into it, and said, 'Sing here, and you shall lack neither meat nor drink all the year.' The cuckow, when she perceived herself encompassed with the hedge, flew away. 'A vengeance on her,' said these wise men, 'we did not make our hedge high enough.'" On another occasion, having caught a large eel which offended them by its voracity, they assembled in council to deliberate on an appropriate punishment, which ended in a resolution that it should be drowned, and the criminal was ceremoniously thrown into a great pond. One day twelve men of Gotham went a-fishing, and on their way home they suddenly discovered that they had lost one of their number, and each counted in his turn, and could find only eleven. In fact, each forgot to count himself. In the midst of their distress—for they believed their companion to be drowned—a stranger approached, and learnt the cause of their sorrow. Finding they were not to be convinced of their mistake by mere argument, he offered, on certain conditions, to find the lost Gothamite, and he proceeded as follows. He took one by one each of the twelve Gothamites, struck him a hard blow on the shoulder, which made him scream, and at each cry counted one, two, three, &c When it came to twelve, they were all satisfied that the lost Gothamite had returned, and paid the man for the service he had rendered them.

As a chap-book, this history of the men of Gotham became so popular, that it gave rise to a host of other books of similar character, which were compiled at a later period under such titles—formerly well known to children—as, "The Merry Frolicks, or the Comical Cheats of Swalpo;" "The Witty and Entertaining Exploits of George Buchanan, commonly called the King's Fool;" "Simple Simon's Misfortunes;" and the like. Nor must it be forgotten that the history of Eulenspiegel was the prototype of a class of popular histories of larger dimensions, represented in our own literature by "The English Rogue," the work of Richard Head and Francis Kirkman, in the reign of Charles II., and various other "rogues" belonging to different countries, which appeared about that time, or not long afterwards. The earliest of these books was "The Spanish Rogue, or Life of Guzman de Alfarache," written in Spanish by Mateo Aleman in the latter part of the sixteenth century. Curiously enough, some Englishman, not knowing apparently that the history of Eulenspiegel had appeared in English under the name of Owlglass, took it into his head to introduce him among the family of rogues which had thus come into fashion, and, in 1720, published as "Made English from the High Dutch," what he called "The German Rogue, or the Life and Merry Adventures, Cheats, Stratagems, and Contrivances of Tiel Eulespiegle."

The fifteenth century was the period during which mediæval forms generally were changing into forms adapted to another state of society, and in which much of the popular literature which has been in vogue during modern times took its rise. In the fourteenth century, the fabliaux of the jougleurs were already taking what we may perhaps term a more literary form, and were reduced into prose narratives. This took place especially in Italy, where these prose tales were called *novelle*, implying some novelty in their character, a word which was transferred into the French language under the form of *nouvelles*, and was the origin of our modern English *novel*, applied to a work of fiction. The Italian novelists adopted the Eastern plan of stringing these stories together on the slight framework of one general plot, in which are introduced causes for telling them and persons who tell them. Thus the Decameron of Boccaccio holds towards the fabliaux exactly the same position as that of the "Arabian Nights" to the older Arabian tales. The Italian novelists became numerous and celebrated throughout Europe, from the time of Boccaccio to that of Straparola, at the commencement of the sixteenth century, and later. The taste for this class of literature appears to have been introduced into France at the court of Burgundy, where, under duke Philippe le Bon, a well-known courtier and man of letters named Antoine de La Sale, who had, during a sojourn in Italy, become acquainted with one of the most celebrated of the earlier Italian collections, the "Cento Novello," or the Hundred Novels, compiled a collection in French in imitation of them, under the title of "Les Cent Nouvelles Nouvelles," or the Hundred new Novels, one of the purest examples of the French language in the fifteenth century.[76] The later French story-books, such as the Heptameron of the queen of Navarre, and others, belong chiefly to the sixteenth century. These collections of stories can hardly be said to have ever taken root in this island as a part of English literature.

But there arose partly out of these stories a class of books which became greatly multiplied, and were, during a long period, extremely popular. With the household fool, or jester, instead of the old jougleur, the stories had been shorn of their detail, and sank into the shape of mere witty anecdotes, and at the same time a taste arose for what we now class under the general term of jests, clever sayings, what the French call *bons mots*, and what the English of the sixteenth century termed "quick answers." The word *jest* itself arose from the circumstance that the things designated by it arose out of the older stories, for it is a mere corruption of gestes, the Latin *gesta*, in the sense of narratives of acts or deeds, or tales. The Latin writers, who first began to collect them into books, included them under the general name of *facetiæ*. The earlier of these collections of facetiæ were written in Latin, and of the origin of the first with which we are acquainted, that by the celebrated scholar Poggio of Florence, a curious anecdote is told. Some wits of the court of pope Martin V., elected to the papacy in 1417, among whom were the pope's two secretaries, Poggio and Antonio Lusco, Cincio of Rome, and Ruzello of Bologna, appropriated to themselves a private corner in the Vatican, where they assembled to chat freely among themselves. They called it their *buggiale*, a word which signifies in Italian, a place of recreation, where they tell stories, make jests, and amuse themselves with discussing satirically the doings and characters of everybody. This was the way in which Poggio and his friends entertained themselves in their buggiale, and we are assured that in their talk they neither spared the church nor the pope himself or his government. The facetiæ of Poggio, in fact, which are said to be a selection of the good things said in these meetings, show neither reverence for the church of Rome nor respect for decency, but they are mostly stories which had been told over and over again, long before Poggio came into the world. It was perhaps this satire upon the church and upon the ecclesiastics which gave much of their popularity to these facetiæ at a time when a universal agitation of men's minds on religious affairs prevailed, which was the great harbinger of the Reformation; and the next Latin books of facetiæ came from men such as Henry Bebelius, who were zealous reformers themselves.

Many of the jests in these Latin collections are put into the mouths of jesters, or domestic fools, *fatui*, or *moriones*, as they are called in the Latin; and in England, where these jest-books in the vernacular tongue became more popular perhaps than in any other country, many of them were published under the names of celebrated jesters, as the "Merie Tales of Skelton," "The Jests of Scogin," "Tarlton's Jests," and "The Jests of George Peele."

John Skelton, poet-laureat of his time, appears to have been known in the courts of Henry VII. and Henry VIII. quite as much in the character of a jester as in that of a poet. Poet-laureat was then a title or degree given in the university of Oxford. His "Merye Tales" are all personal of himself, and we should be inclined to say that his jests and his poetry are equally bad. The former picture him as holding a place somewhere between Eulenspiegel and the ordinary court-fool. We may give as a sample of the best of them the tale No. 1.—

"*How Skelton came home late to Oxford from Abington.*

"Skelton was an Englysheman borne as Skogyn was, and hee was educated and broughte up in Oxfoorde, and there was he made a poete lauriat. And on a tyme he had ben at Abbington to make mery, wher that he had eate salte meates, and hee did com late home to Oxforde, and he did lye in an ine named the Tabere, whyche is now the Angell, and hee dyd drynke, and went to bed. About midnight he was so thyrstie or drye that he was constrained to call to the tapster for drynke, and the tapster harde him not. Then hee cryed to hys oste and hys ostes, and to the ostler, for drinke, and no man would here hym. Alacke, sayd Skelton, I shall peryshe for lacke of drynke! What reamedye? At the last he dyd crie out and sayd, Fyer, fyer, fyer! When Skelton hard every man bustle hymselfe upward, and some of them were naked, and some were halfe asleepe and amased, and Skelton dyd crye, Fier, fier! styll, that everye man knewe not whether to resorte. Skelton did go to bed, and the oste and ostis, and the tapster, with the ostler, dyd runne to Skeltons chamber with candles lyghted in theyr handes, saying, Where, where, where is the fyer? Here, here, here, said Skelton, and poynted hys fynger to hys mouth, saying, Fetch me some drynke to quenche the fyer and the heate and the drinesse in my mouthe. And so they dyd."

Another of these "Merye Tales" of Skelton contains a satire upon the practice which prevailed in the sixteenth and early part of the seventeenth centuries of obtaining letters-patent of monopoly from the crown, and also on the bibulous propensities of Welshmen—

"*How the Welshman dyd desyre Skelton to ayde hym in hys sute to the kynge for a patent to sell drynke.*

"Skelton, when he was in London, went to the kynges courte, where there did come to hym a Welshman, saying, Syr, it is so, that manye dooth come upp of my country to the kynges court, and some doth get of the kyng by patent a castell, and some a parke, and some a forest, and some one fee and some another, and they dooe lyve lyke honest men; and I shoulde lyve as honestly as the best, if I myght have a patyne for good dryncke, wherefore I dooe praye yow to write a fewe woords for mee in a lytle byll to geve the same to the kynges handes, and I wil geve you well for your laboure. I am contented, sayde Skelton. Syt downe then, sayde the Welshman, and write. What shall I wryte? sayde Skelton. The Welshman sayde wryte *dryncke*. Nowe, sayde the Welshman, write *more dryncke*. What now? sayde Skelton. Wryte nowe, *a great deale of dryncke*. Nowe, sayd the Welshman, putte to all thys dryncke *a littell crome of breade*, and *a great deale of drynke* to it, and reade once agayne. Skelton dyd reade, *Dryncke, more dryncke, and a great deale of dryncke, and a lytle crome of breade, and a great deale of dryncke to it.* Than the Welshman sayde, Put oute *the litle crome of breade*, and sette in, *all dryncke and no breade*. And if I myght have thys sygned of the kynge, sayde the Welshman, I care for no more, as longe as I dooe lyve. Well then, sayde Skelton, when you have thys signed of the kyng, then wyll I labour for a patent to have bread, that you wyth your drynke and I with the bread may fare well, and seeke our livinge with bagge and staffe."

These two tales are rather favourable specimens of the collection published under the name of Skelton, which, as far as we know, was first printed about the middle of the sixteenth century. The collection of the jests of Scogan, or, as he was popularly called, Scogin, which is said to have been compiled by Andrew Borde, was probably given to the world a few years before, but no copies of the earlier editions are now known to exist. Scogan, the hero of these jests, is described as occupying at the court of Henry VII. a position not much different from that of an ordinary court-fool. Good old Holinshed the chronicler says of him, perhaps a little too gently, that he was "a learned gentleman and student for a time in Oxford, of a pleasant wit, and bent to merrie devices, in respect whereof he was called into the court, where, giving himselfe to his naturall inclination of mirth and pleasant pastime, he plaied manie sporting parts, although not in such uncivil manner as hath beene of him reported." This allusion refers most probably to the jests, which represent him as leading a life of low and coarse buffoonery, in the course of which he displayed a considerable share of the dishonest and mischievous qualities of the less real Eulenspiegel. He is even represented as personally insulting the king and queen, and as being consequently banished over the Channel, to show no more respect to the majesty of the king of France. Scogin's jests, like Skelton's, consist in a great measure of those practical jokes which appear in all former ages to have been the delight of the Teutonic race. Many of them are directed against the ignorance and worldliness of the clergy. Scogin is described as being at one time himself a teacher in the university, and on one occasion, we are told, a husbandman sent his son to school to him that he might be made a priest. The whole story, which runs through several chapters, is an excellent caricature on the way in which men vulgarly ignorant were intruded into the priesthood before the Reformation. At length, after much blundering, the scholar came to be ordained, and his examination is reported as follows:—

"How the scholler said Tom Miller of Oseney was Jacob's father.

"After this, the said scholler did come to the next orders, and brought a present to the ordinary from Scogin, but the scholler's father paid for all. Then said the ordinary to the scholler, I must needes oppose you, and for master Scogin's sake, I will oppose you in a light matter. Isaac had two sons, Esau and Jacob. Who was Jacob's father? The scholler stood still, and could not tell. Well, said the ordinary, I cannot admit you to be priest untill the next orders, and then bring me an answer. The scholler went home with a heavy heart, bearing a letter to master Scogin, how his scholler could not answer to this question: Isaac had two sons, Esau and Jacob; who was Jacob's father? Scogin said to his scholler, Thou foole and asse-head! Dost thou not know Tom Miller of Oseney? Yes, said the scholler! Then, said Scogin, thou knowest he had two sonnes, Tom and Jacke; who is Jacke's father? The scholler said, Tom Miller. Why, said Scogin, thou mightest have said that Isaac was Jacob's father. Then said Scogin, Thou shalt arise betime in the morning, and carry a letter to the ordinary, and I trust he will admit thee before the orders shall be given. The scholler rose up betime in the morning, and carried the letter to the ordinary. The ordinary said, For Master Scogin's sake I will oppose you no farther than I did yesterday. Isaac had two sons, Esau and Jacob; who was Jacob's father? Marry, said the scholler, I can tell you now that was Tom Miller of Oseney. Goe, foole, goe, said the ordinary, and let thy master send thee no more to me for orders, for it is impossible to make a foole a wise man."

Scogin's scholar was, however, made a priest, and some of the stories which follow describe the ludicrous manner in which he exercised the priesthood. Two other stories illustrate Scogin's supposed position at court:—

"How Scogin told those that mocked him that he had a wall-eye.

"Scogin went up and down in the king's hall, and his hosen hung downe, and his coat stood awry, and his hat stood a boonjour, so every man did mocke Scogin. Some said he was a proper man, and did wear his rayment cleanly; some said the foole could not put on his owne rayment; some said one thing, and some said another. At last Scogin said, Masters, you have praised me wel, but you did not espy one thing in me. What is that, Tom? said the men. Marry, said Scogin, I have a wall-eye. What meanest thou by that? said the men. Marry, said Scogin, I have spyed a sort of knaves that doe mocke me, and are worse fooles themselves."

"How Scogin drew his sonne up and downe the court.

"After this Scogin went from the court, and put off his foole's garments, and came to the court like an honest man, and brought his son to the court with him, and within the court he drew his sonne up and downe by the heeles. The boy cried out, and Scogin drew the boy in every corner. At last every body had pity on the boy, and said, Sir, what doe you meane, to draw the boy about the court? Masters, said Scogin, he is my sonne, and I doe it for this cause. Every man doth say, that man or child which is drawne up in the court shall be the better as long as hee lives; and therefore I will every day once draw him up and downe the court, after that hee may come to preferment in the end."

The appreciation of a good joke cannot at this time have been very great or very general, for Scogin's jests were wonderfully popular during at least a century, from the first half of the sixteenth century. They passed through many editions, and are frequently alluded to by the writers of the Elizabethan age. The next individual whose name appears at the head of a collection of his jests, was the well-known wit, Richard Tarlton, who may be fairly considered as court fool to Queen Elizabeth. His jests belong to the same class as those of Skelton and Scogin, and if possible, they present a still greater amount of dulness. Tarlton's jests were soon followed by the "merrie conceited jests" of George Peele, the dramatist, who is described in the title as "gentleman, sometimes student in Oxford;" and it is added that in these jests "is shewed the course of his life, how he lived; a man very well knowne in the city of London and elsewhere." In fact, Peele's jests are chiefly curious for the striking picture they give us of the wilder shades of town life under the reigns of Elizabeth and James I.

During the period which witnessed the publication in England of these books, many other jest-books appeared, for they had already become an important class of English popular literature. Most of them were published anonymously, and indeed they are mere compilations from the older collections in Latin and French. All that was at all good, even in the jests of Skelton, Scogin, Tarlton, and Peele, had been repeated over and over again by the story-tellers and jesters of former ages. Two of the earlier English collections have gained a greater celebrity than the rest, chiefly through adventitious circumstances. One of these, entitled "A Hundred Merry Tales," has gained distinction among Shakespearian critics as the one especially alluded to by the great poet in "Much Ado about Nothing," (Act ii., Sc. 1), where Beatrice complains that somebody had said "that I had my good wit out of the Hundred Merry Tales." The other collection alluded to was entitled "Mery Tales, Wittie Questions, and Quicke Answeres, very pleasant to be readde," and was printed in 1567. Its modern fame appears to have arisen chiefly from the circumstance that, until the accidental discovery of the unique and imperfect copy of the "Hundred Merry Tales," it was supposed to be the book alluded to by Shakespeare. Both these collections are mere compilations from the "Cent Nouvelles Nouvelles," "Poggio," "Straparola," and other foreign works.[77] The words put into the mouth of Beatrice are correctly descriptive of the use made of these jest-books. It had become fashionable to learn out of them jests and stories, in order to introduce them into polite conversation, and especially at table; and this practice continued to prevail until a very recent period. The number of such jest-books published during the sixteenth, seventeenth, and eighteenth centuries, was quite extraordinary. Many of these were given anonymously; but many also were put forth under names which possessed temporary celebrity, such as Hobson the carrier, Killigrew the jester, the friend of Charles II., Ben Jonson, Garrick, and a multitude of others. It is, perhaps, unnecessary to remind the reader that the great modern representative of this class of literature is the illustrious Joe Miller.

CHAPTER XV.

THE AGE OF THE REFORMATION.—THOMAS MURNER; HIS GENERAL SATIRES.—
FRUITFULNESS OF FOLLY.—HANS SACHS.—THE TRAP FOR FOOLS.—ATTACKS ON
LUTHER.—THE POPE AS ANTICHRIST.—THE POPE-ASS AND THE MONK-CALF.—
OTHER CARICATURES AGAINST THE POPE.—THE GOOD AND BAD SHEPHERDS.

The reign of Folly did not pass away with the fifteenth century—on the whole the sixteenth century can hardly be said to have been more sane than its predecessor, but it was agitated by a long and fierce struggle to disengage European society from the trammels of the middle ages. We have entered upon what is technically termed the *renaissance*, and are approaching the great religious reformation. The period during which the art of printing began first to spread generally over Western Europe, was peculiarly favourable to the production of satirical books and pamphlets, and a considerable number of clever and spirited satirists and comic writers appeared towards the end of the fifteenth century, especially in Germany, where circumstances of a political character had at an early period given to the intellectual agitation a more permanent strength than it could easily or quickly gain in the great monarchies. Among the more remarkable of these satirists was Thomas Murner, who was born at Strasburg, in 1475. The circumstances even of his childhood are singular, for he was born a cripple, or became one in his earliest infancy, though he was subsequently healed, and it was so universally believed that this malady was the effect of witchcraft, that he himself wrote afterwards a treatise upon this subject under the title of "De Phitonico Contractu." The school in which he was taught may at least have encouraged his satirical spirit, for his master was Jacob Locher, the same who translated into Latin verse the "Ship of Fools" of Sebastian Brandt. At the end of the century Murner had become a master of arts in the University of Paris, and had entered the Franciscan order. His reputation as a German popular poet was so great, that the emperor Maximilian[ ]I., who died in 1519, conferred upon him the crown of poetry, or, in other words, made him poet-laureat. He took the degree of doctor in theology in 1509. Still Murner was known best as the popular writer, and he published several satirical poems, which were remarkable for the bold woodcuts that illustrated them, for engraving on wood flourished at this period. He exposed the corruptions of all classes of society, and, before the Reformation broke out, he did not even spare the corruptions of the ecclesiastical state, but soon declared himself a fierce opponent of the Reformers. When the Lutheran revolt against the Papacy became strong, our king, Henry VIII., who took a decided part against Luther, invited Murner to England, and on his return to his own country, the satiric Franciscan became more bitter against the Reformation than ever. He advocated the cause of the English monarch in a pamphlet, now very rare, in which he discussed the question whether Henry VIII. or Luther was the liar—"Antwort dem Murner uff seine frag, ob der künig von Engllant ein Lügner sey oder Martinus Luther." Murner appears to have divided the people of his age into rogues and fools, or perhaps he considered the two titles as identical. His "Narrenbeschwerung," or Conspiracy of Fools, in which Brandt's idea was followed up, is supposed to have been published as early as 1506, but the first printed edition with a date, appeared in 1512. It became so popular, that it went through several editions during subsequent years; and that which I have before me was printed at Strasburg in 1518. It is, like Brandt's "Ship of Fools," a general satire against society, in which the clergy are not spared, for the writer had not yet come in face of Luther's Reformation. The cuts are superior to those of Brandt's book, and some of them are remarkable for their design and execution. In one of the earliest of them, copied in the cut No. 139, Folly is introduced in the garb of a husbandman, scattering his feed over the earth, the result of which is a very quick and flourishing crop, the fool's heads rising above ground, almost instantaneously, like so many turnips. In a subsequent engraving, represented in our cut No. 140, Folly holds out, as an object of emulation, the fool's cap, and people of all classes, the pope himself, and the emperor, and all the great dignitaries of this world, press forward eagerly to seize upon it.

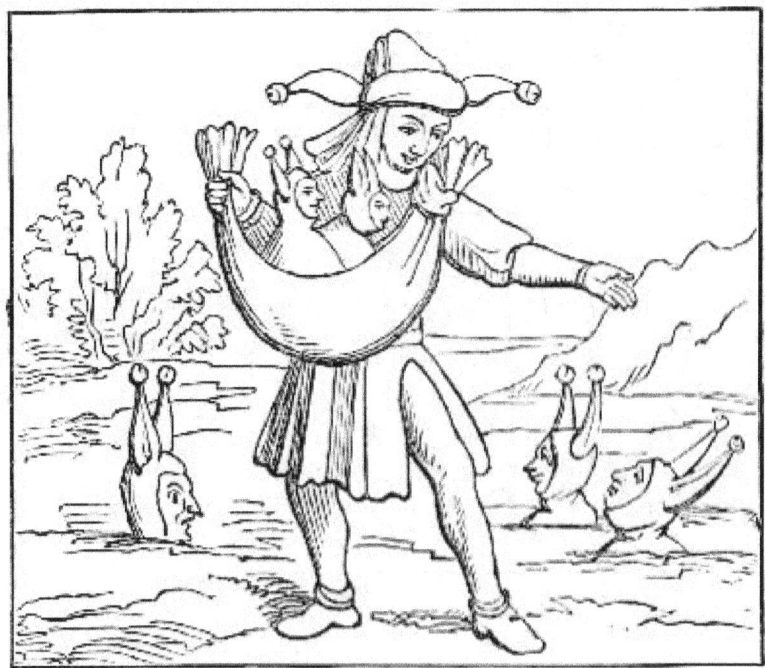

No. 139. Sowing a Fruitful Crop.

The same year (1512) witnessed the appearance of another poetical, or at least metrical, satire by Murner, entitled "Schelmenzunft," or the Confraternity of Rogues, similarly illustrated with very spirited engravings on wood. It is another demonstration of the prevailing dominion of folly under its worst forms, and the satire is equally general with the preceding. Murner's satire appears to have been felt not only generally, but personally; and we are told that he was often threatened with assassination, and he raised up a number of literary opponents, who treated him with no little rudeness; in fact, he had got on the wrong side of politics, or at all events on the unpopular side, and men who had more talents and greater weight appeared as his opponents—men like Ulrich von Utten, and Luther himself.

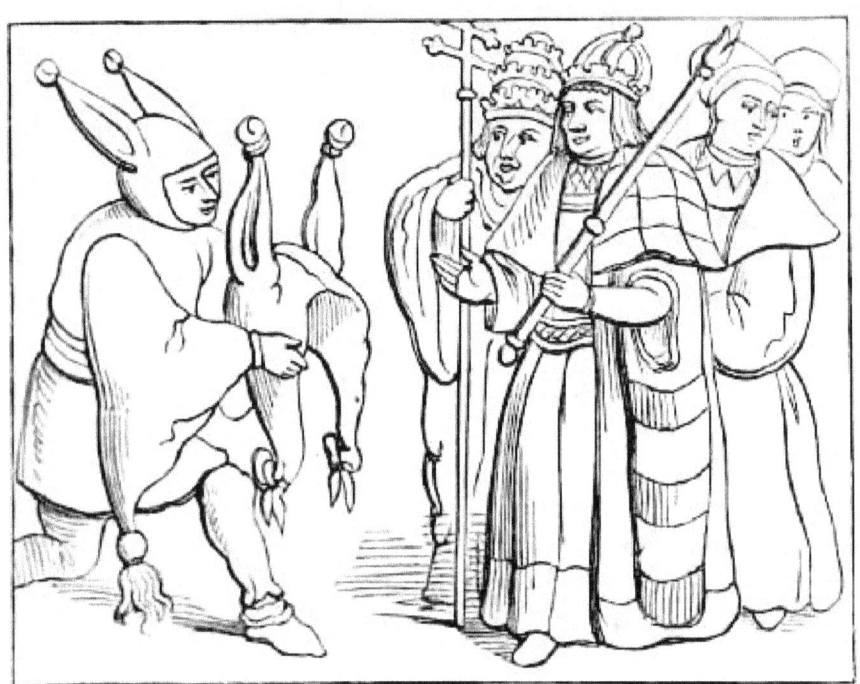

No. 140. An Acceptable Offering.

Among the satirists who espoused the cause to which Murner was opposed, we must not overlook a man who represented in its strongest features, though in a rather debased form, the old spontaneous poetry of the middle ages. His name was Hans Sachs, at least that was the name under which he was known, for his real name is said to have been Loutrdorffer. His spirit was entirely that of the old wandering minstrel, and it was so powerful in him, that, having been apprenticed to the craft of a weaver, he was no sooner freed from his indentures, than he took to a vagabond life, and wandered from town to town, gaining his living by singing the verses he composed upon every occasion which presented itself. In 1519, he married and settled in Nüremberg, and his compositions were then given to the public through the press. The number of these was quite extraordinary—songs, ballads, satires, and dramatic pieces, rude in style, in accordance with the taste of the time, but full of cleverness. Many of them were printed on broadsides, and illustrated with large engravings on wood. Hans Sachs joined in the crusade against the empire of Folly, and one of his broadsides is illustrated with a graceful design, the greater part of which is copied in our cut No. 141. A party of ladies have set a bird-trap to catch the fools of the age, who are waiting to be caught. One fool is taken in the trap, while another is already secured and pinioned, and others are rushing into the snare. A number of people of the world, high in their dignities and stations, are looking on at this remarkable scene.

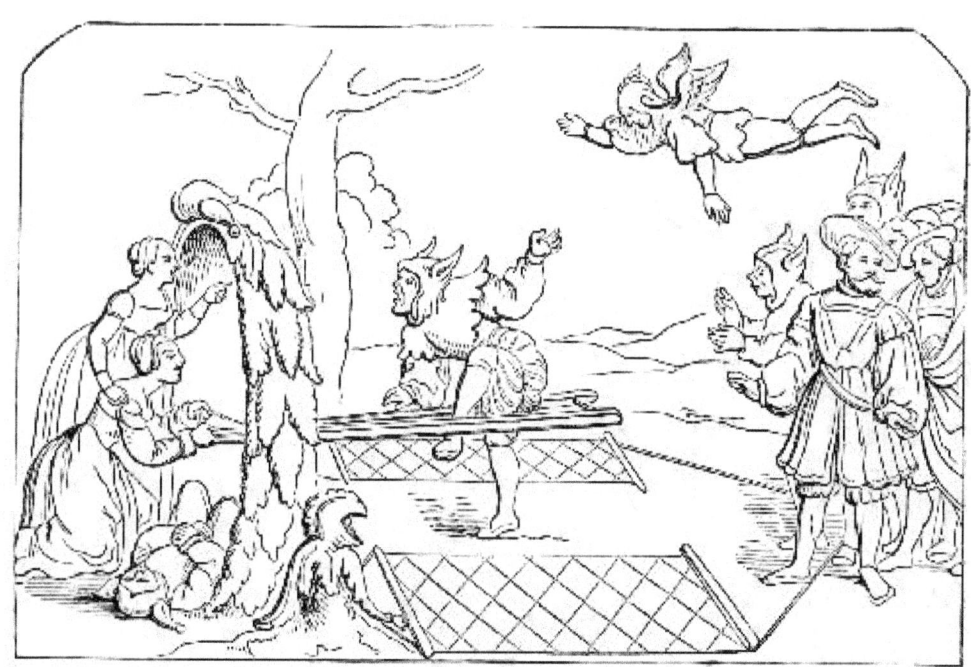

No. 141. Bird-Traps.

The evil influence of the female sex was at this time proverbial, and, in fact, it was an age of extreme licentiousness. Another poet-laureat of the time, Henricus Bebelius, born in the latter half of the fifteenth century, and rather well known in the literature of his time, published, in 1515, a satirical poem in Latin, under the title of "Triumphus Veneris," which was a sort of exposition of the generally licentious character of the age in which he lived. It is distributed into six books, in the third of which the poet attacks the whole ecclesiastical state, not sparing the pope himself, and we are thereby perfectly well initiated into the weaknesses of the clergy. Bebelius had been preceded by another writer on this part of the subject, and we might say by many, for the incontinence of monks and nuns, and indeed of all the clergy, had long been a subject of satire. But the writer to whom I especially allude was named Paulus Olearius, his name in German being Oelschlägel. He published, about the year 1500, a satirical tract, under the title of "De Fide Concubinarum in Sacerdotes." It was a bitter attack on the licentiousness of the clergy, and was rendered more effective by the engravings which accompanied it. We give one of these as a curious picture of contemporary manners; the individual who comes within the range of the lady's attractions, though he may be a scholar, has none of the characteristics of a priest. She presents a nosegay, which we may suppose to represent the influence of perfume upon the senses; but the love of the ladies for pet animals is especially typified in the monkey, attached by a chain. A donkey appears to show by his heels his contempt for the lover.

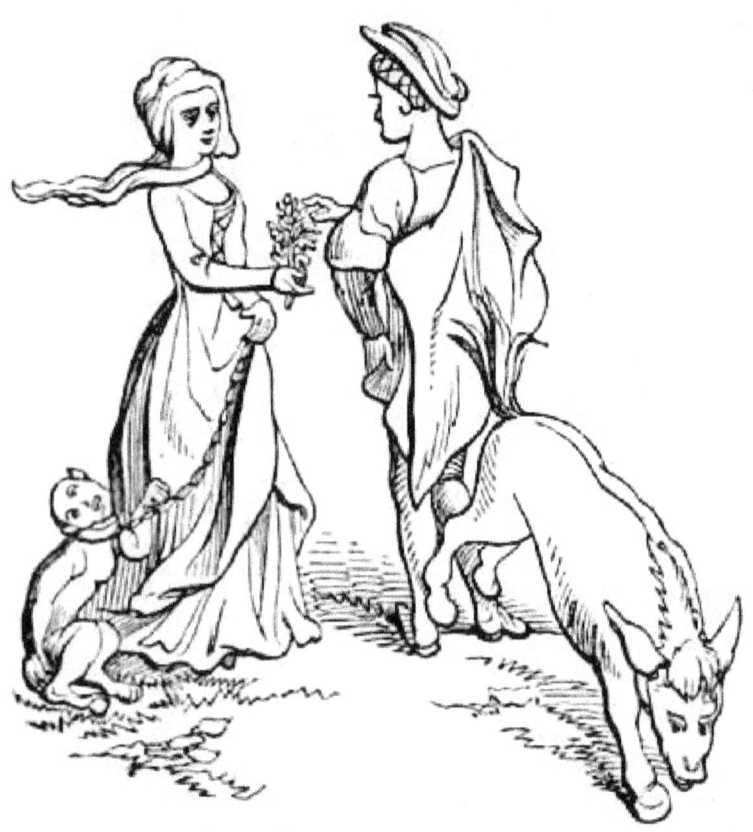

No. 142. Courtship.

From an early period, the Roman church had been accustomed to treat contemptuously, as well as cruelly, all who dissented from its doctrines, or objected to its government, and this feeling was continued down to the age of the Reformation, in spite of the tone of liberalism which was beginning to shine forth in the writings of some of its greatest ornaments. Some research among the dusty, because little used, records of national archives and libraries would no doubt bring to light more than one singular caricature upon the "heretics" of the middle ages, and my attention has been called to one which is possessed of peculiar interest. There is, among the imperial archives of France, in Paris, among records relating to the country of the Albigeois in the thirteenth century, a copy of the bull of pope Innocent IV. giving directions for the proceedings against dissenters from Romanism, on the back of which the scribe, as a mark of his contempt for these arch-heretics of the south, has drawn a caricature of a woman bound to a stake over the fire which is to burn her as an open opponent of the church of Rome. The choice of a woman for the victim was perhaps intended to show that the proselytism of heresy was especially successful among the weaker sex, or that it was considered as having some relation to witchcraft. It is, by a long period, the earliest known pictorial representation of the punishment of burning inflicted on a heretic.

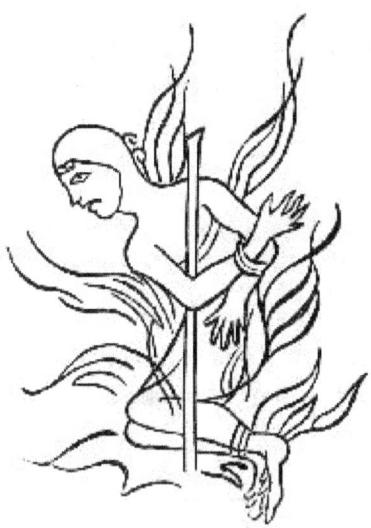

No. 143. Burning a Heretic.

The shafts of satire were early employed against Luther and his new principles, and men like Murner, already mentioned, Emser, Cochlæus, and others, signalised themselves by their zeal in the papal cause. As already stated, Murner distinguished himself as the literary ally of our king Henry VIII. The taste for satirical writings had then become so general, that Murner complains in one of his satires that the printers would print nothing but abusive or satirical works, and neglected his more serious writings.

Da sindt die trucker schuld daran,
Die trucken als die Gauchereien,
Und lassen mein ernstliche bücher leihen.

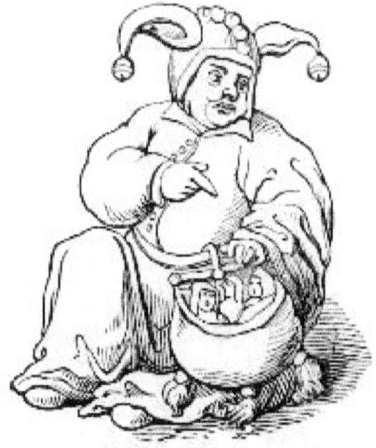

No. 144. Folly in Monastic Habit.

Some of Murner's writings against Luther, most of which are now very rare, are extremely violent, and they are generally illustrated with satirical woodcuts. One of these books, printed without name of place or date, is entitled, "Of the great Lutheran Fool, how Doctor Murner has exorcised him" (*Von dem grossen Lutherisschen Narren, wie in Doctor Murner beschworen hat*). In the woodcuts to this book Murner himself is introduced, as is usually the case in these satirical engravings, under the character of a Franciscan friar, with the head of a cat, while Luther appears as a fat and jolly monk, wearing a fool's cap, and figuring in various ridiculous circumstances. In one of the first woodcuts, the cat Franciscan is drawing a rope so tight round the great Lutheran fool's neck, that he compels him to disgorge a multitude of smaller fools. In another the great Lutheran fool has his purse, or pouch, full of little fools suspended at his girdle. This latter figure is copied in the cut No. 144, as an example of the form under which the great reformer appears in these satirical representations.

In a few other caricatures of this period which have been preserved, the apostle of the Reformation is attacked still more savagely. The one here given (Fig. 145), taken from a contemporary engraving on wood, presents a rather fantastic figure of the demon playing on the bagpipes. The instrument is formed of Luther's head, the pipe through which the devil blows entering his ear, and that through which the music is produced forming an elongation of the reformer's nose. It was a broad intimation that Luther was a mere tool of the evil one, created for the purpose of bringing mischief into the world.

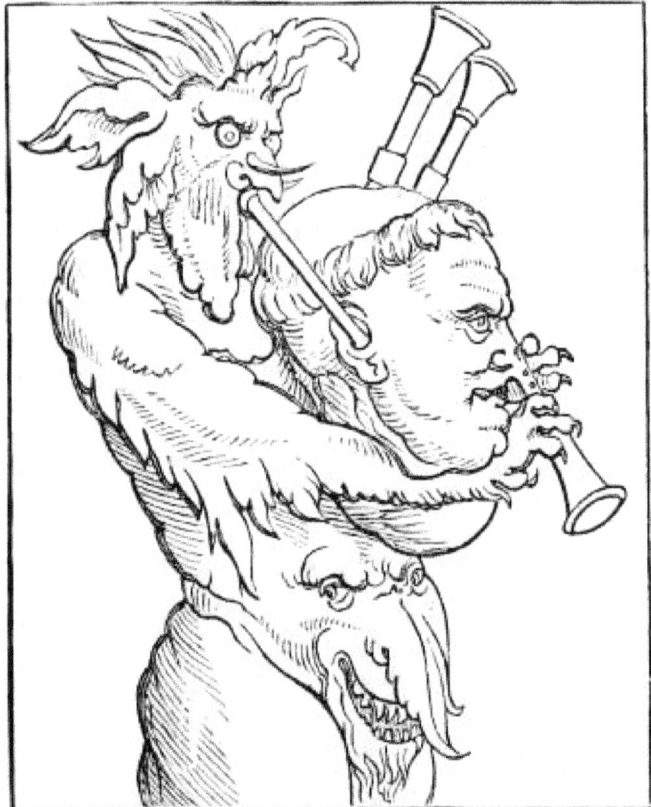

No. 145. The Music of the Demon.

The reformers, however, were more than a match for their opponents in this sort of warfare. Luther himself was full of comic and satiric humour, and a mass of the talent of that age was ranged on his side, both literary and artistic. After the reformer's marriage, the papal party quoted the old legend, that Antichrist was to be born of the union of a monk and a nun, and it was intimated that if Luther himself could not be directly identified with Antichrist, he had, at least, a fair chance of becoming his parent. But the reformers had resolved, on what appeared to be much more conclusive evidence, that Antichrist was only emblematical of the papacy, that under this form he had been long dominant on earth, and that the end of his reign was then approaching. A remarkable pamphlet, designed to place this idea pictorially before the public, was produced from the pencil of Luther's friend, the celebrated painter, Lucas Cranach, and appeared in the year 1521 under the title of "The Passionale of Christ and Antichrist" (*Passional Christi und Antichristi*). It is a small quarto, each page of which is nearly filled by a woodcut, having a few lines of explanation in German below. The cut to the left represents some incident in the life of Christ, while that facing it to the right gives a contrasting fact in the history of papal tyranny. Thus the first cut on the left represents Jesus in His humility, refusing earthly dignities and power, while on the adjoining page we see the pope, with his cardinals and bishops, supported by his hosts of warriors, his cannon, and his fortifications, in his temporal dominion over secular princes. When we open again we see on one side Christ crowned with thorns by the insulting soldiery, and on the other the pope, enthroned in all his worldly glory, exacting the worship of his courtiers. On another we have Christ washing the feet of His disciples, and in contrast the pope compelling the emperor to kiss his toe. And so on, through a number of curious illustrations, until at last we come to Christ's ascension into heaven, in contrast with which a troop of demons, of the most varied and singular forms, have seized upon the papal Antichrist, and are casting him down into the flames of hell, where some of his own monks wait to receive him. This last picture is drawn with so much spirit, that I have copied it in the cut No. 146.

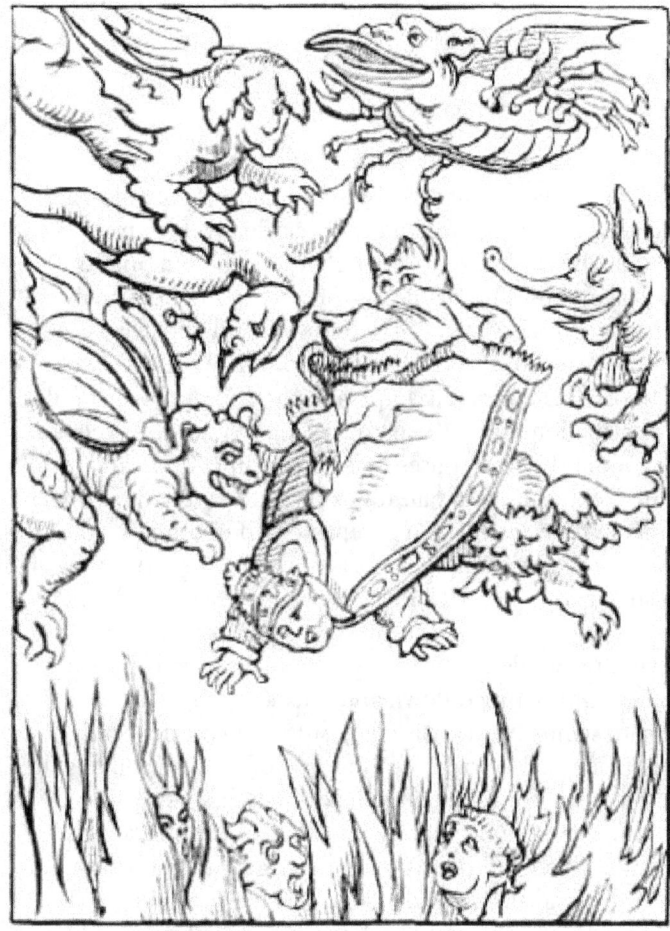

No. 146. The Descent of the Pope.

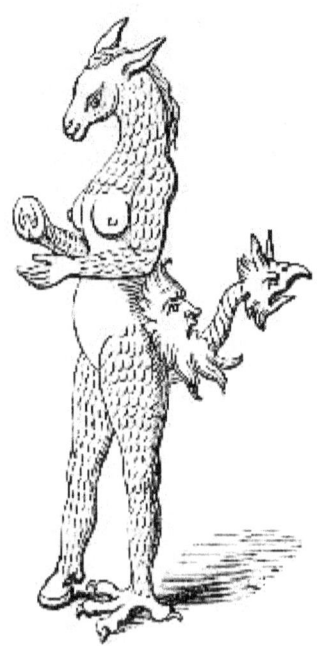

No. 147. The Pope-ass.

The monstrous figures of animals which had amused the sculptors and miniaturists of an earlier period came in time to be looked upon as realities, and were not only regarded with wonder as physical deformities, but were objects of superstition, for they were believed to be sent into the world as warnings of great revolutions and calamities. During the age preceding the Reformation, the reports of the births or discoveries of such monsters were very common, and engravings of them were no doubt profitable articles of merchandise among the early book-hawkers. Two of these were very celebrated in the time of the Reformation, the Pope-ass and the Monk-calf, and were published and republished with an explanation under the names of Luther and Melancthon, which made them emblematical of the Papacy and of the abuses of the Romish church, and, of course, prognostications of their approaching exposure and fall. It was pretended that the Pope-ass was found dead in the river Tiber, at Rome, in the year 1496. It is represented in our cut No. 147, taken from an engraving preserved in a very curious volume of broadside Lutheran caricatures, in the library of the British Museum, all belonging to the year 1545, though this design had been published many years before. The head of an ass, we are told, represented the pope himself, with his false and carnal doctrines. The right hand resembled the foot of an elephant, signifying the spiritual power of the pope, which was heavy, and stamped down and crushed people's consciences. The left hand was that of a man, signifying the worldly power of the pope, which grasped at universal empire over kings and princes. The right foot was that of an ox, signifying the spiritual ministers of the papacy, the doctors of the church, the preachers, confessors, and scholastic theologians, and especially the monks and nuns, those who aided and supported the pope in oppressing people's bodies and souls. The left foot was that of a griffin, an animal which, when it once seizes its prey, never lets it escape, and signified the canonists, the monsters of the pope's temporal power, who grasped people's temporal goods, and never returned them. The breast and belly of this monster were those of a woman, and signified the papal body, the cardinals, bishops, priests, monks, &c, who spent their lives in eating, drinking, and incontinence; and this part of the body was naked, because the popish clergy were not ashamed to expose their vices to the public. The legs, arms, and neck, on the contrary, were clothed with fishes' scales; these signified the temporal princes and lords, who were mostly in alliance with the papacy. The old man's head behind the monster, meant that the papacy had become old, and was approaching its end; and the head of a dragon, vomiting flames, which served for a tail, was significative of the great threats, the venomous horrible bulls and blasphemous writings, which the pontiff and his ministers, enraged at seeing their end approach, were launching into the world against all who opposed them. These explanations were supported by apt quotations from the Scriptures, and were so effective, and became so popular, that the picture was published in various shapes, and was seen adorning the walls of the humblest cottages. I believe it is still to be met with in a similar position in some parts of Germany. It was considered at the time to be a masterly piece of satire. The picture of the Monk-calf, which is represented in our cut No. 148, was published at the same time, and usually accompanies it. This monster is said to have been born at Freyburg, in Misnia, and is simply a rather coarse emblem of the monachal character.

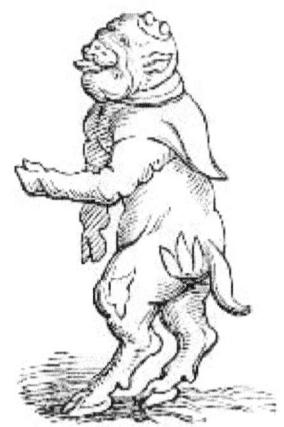

No. 148. The Monk-Calf.

The volume of caricatures just mentioned contains several satires on the pope, which are all very severe, and many of them clever. One has a movable leaf, which covers the upper part of the picture; when it is down, we have a representation of the pope in his ceremonial robes, and over it the inscription ALEX · VI · PONT · MAX. Pope Alexander VI. was the infamous Roderic Borgia, a man stained with all the crimes and vices which strike most horror into men's minds. When the leaf is raised, another figure joins itself with the lower part of the former, and represents a papal demon, crowned, the cross being transformed into an instrument of infernal punishment. This figure is represented in our cut No. 149. Above it are inscribed the words EGO · SVM · PAPA, "I am the Pope." Attached to it is a page of explanation in German, in which the legend of that pope's death is given, a legend that his wicked life appeared sufficient to sanction. It was said that, distrusting the success of his intrigues to secure the papacy for himself, he applied himself to the study of the black art, and sold himself to the Evil One. He then asked the tempter if it were his destiny to be pope, and received an answer in the affirmative. He next inquired how long he should hold the papacy, but Satan returned an equivocal and deceptive answer, for Borgia understood that he was to be pope fifteen years, whereas he died at the end of eleven. It is well known that Pope Alexander VI. died suddenly and unexpectedly through accidentally drinking the poisoned wine he had prepared with his own hand for the murder of another man.

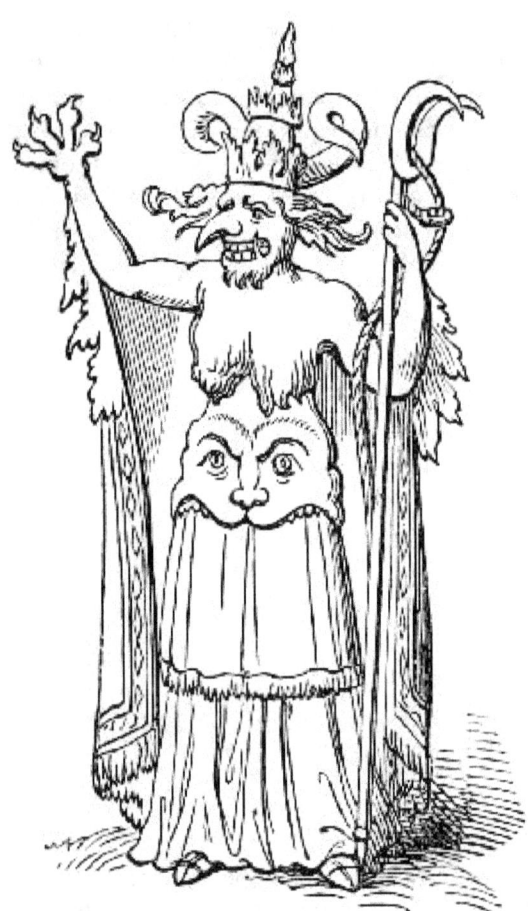

No. 149. The Head of the Papacy.

An Italian theatine wrote a poem against the Reformation, in which he made Luther the offspring of Megæra, one of the furies, who is represented as having been sent from hell into Germany to be delivered of him. This sarcasm was thrown back upon the pope with much greater effect by the Lutheran caricaturists. One of the plates in the above-mentioned volume represents the "birth and origin of the pope" (*ortus et origo papæ*), making the pope identical with Antichrist. In different groups, in this rather elaborate design, the child is represented as attended by the three furies, Megæra acting as his wet-nurse, Alecto as nursery-maid, and Tisiphone in another capacity, &c The name of Martin Luther is added to this caricature also.

Hie wird geborn der Widerchrist.
Megera sein Seugamme ist;
Alecto sein Keindermeidlin,
Tisiphone die gengelt in.—M. Luth., D. 1545.

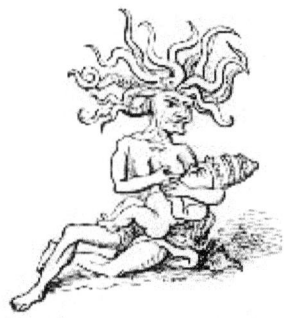

No. 150. The Pope's Nurse.

One of the groups in this plate, representing the fury Megæra, a becoming foster-mother, suckling the pope-infant, is given in our cut, No. 150.

In another of these caricatures the pope is represented trampling on the emperor, to show the manner in which he usurped and tyrannised over the temporal power. Another illustrates "the kingdom of Satan and the Pope" (*regnum Satanæ et Papæ*), and the latter is represented as presiding over hell-mouth in all his state. One, given in our cut No. 151, represents the pope under the form of an ass playing on the bagpipes, and is entitled *Papa doctor theologiæ et magister fidei.* Four lines of German verse beneath the engraving state how "the pope can alone expound Scripture and purge error, just as the ass alone can pipe and touch the notes correctly."

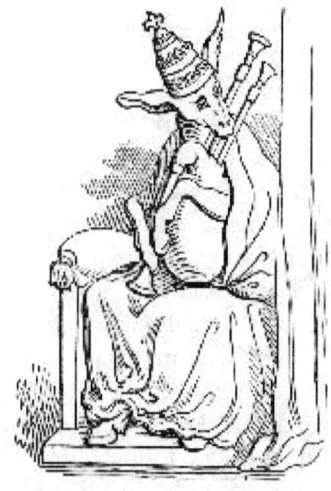

No. 151. The Pope giving the Tune.
Der Bapst kan allein auslegen
Die Schrifft, und irthum ausfegen;
Wie der esel allein pfeiffen
Kan, und die noten recht greiffen.—1545.

This was the last year of Luther's active labours. At the commencement of the year following he died at Eissleben, whither he had gone to attend the council of princes. These caricatures may perhaps be considered as so many proclamations of satisfaction and exultation in the final triumph of the great reformer.

Books, pamphlets, and prints of this kind were multiplied to an extraordinary degree during the age of the Reformation, but the majority of them were in the interest of the new movement. Luther's opponent, Eckius, complained of the infinite number of people who gained their living by wandering over all parts of Germany, and selling Lutheran books.[78] Among those who administered largely to this circulation of polemic books was the poet of farces, comedies, and ballads, Hans Sachs, already mentioned. Hans Sachs had in one poem, published in 1535, celebrated Luther under the title of "the Wittemberg Nightingale:"—

Die Wittembergisch' Nachtigall,
Die man jetzt höret überall;

and described the effects of his song over all the other animals; and he published, also in verse, what he called a Monument, or Lament, on his death ("Ein Denkmal oder Klagred' ob der Leiche Doktors Martin Luther"). Among the numerous broadsides published by Hans Sachs, one contains the very clever caricature of which we give a copy in our cut No. 152. It is entitled "Der gut Hirt und böss Hirt," the good shepherd and bad shepherd, and has for its text the opening verses of the tenth chapter of the gospel of St. John. The good and bad shepherds are, as may be supposed, Christ and the pope. The church is here pictured as a not very stately building; the entrance, especially, is a plain structure of timber. Jesus said to the Pharisees, "He that entereth not by the door into the sheepfold, but climbeth up some other way, the same is a thief and a robber. But he that entereth in by the door is the shepherd of the flock." In the engraving, the pope, as the hireling shepherd, sits on the roof of the stateliest part of the building, pointing out to the Christian flock the wrong way, and blessing the climbers. Under him two men of worldly distinction are making their way into the church through a window; and on a roof below a friar is pointing to the people the way up. At another window a monk holds out his arms to invite people up; and one in spectacles, no doubt emblematical of the doctors of the church, is looking out from an opening over the entrance door to watch the proceedings of the Good Shepherd. To the right, on the papal side of the church, the lords and great men are bringing the people under their influence, till they are stopped by the cardinals and bishops, who prevent them from going forward to the door and point out very energetically the way up the roof. At the door stands, the Saviour, as the good shepherd, who has knocked, and the porter has opened it with his key. Christ's true teachers, the evangelists, show the way to the solitary man of worth who comes by this road, and who listens with calm attention to the gospel teachers, while he opens his purse to bestow his charity on the poor man by the road side. In the original engraving, in the distance on the left, the Good Shepherd is seen followed by his flock, who are obedient to his voice; on the right, the bad shepherd, who has ostentatiously drawn up his sheep round the image of the cross, is abandoning them, and taking to flight on the approach of the wolf. "He that entereth in by the door is the shepherd of the sheep. To him the porter openeth; and the sheep hear his voice, and he calleth his own sheep by name, and leadeth them out. And when he putteth forth his own sheep he goeth before them, and the sheep follow him, for they know his voice.... But he that is an hireling, and not the shepherd, whose own the sheep are not, seeth the wolf coming, and leaveth the sheep, and fleeth; and the wolf catcheth them, and scattereth the sheep." (John x. 2–4, 12.)

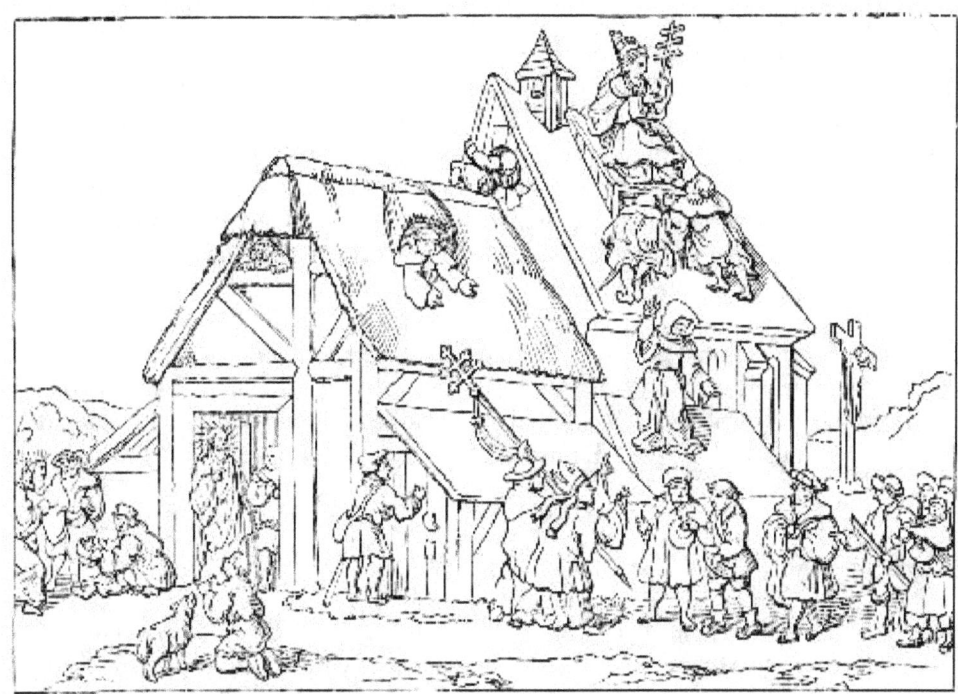

No. 152. The Two Shepherds.

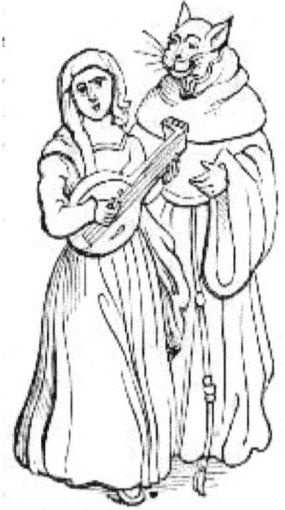

No. 153. Murner and Luther's Daughter.

The triumph of Luther is the subject of a rather large and elaborate caricature, which is an engraving of great rarity, but a copy of it is given in Jaime's "Musée de Caricature." Leo X. is represented seated on his throne upon the edge of the abyss, into which his cardinals are trying to prevent his falling; but their efforts are rendered vain by the appearance of Luther on the other side supported by his principal adherents, and wielding the Bible as his weapon, and the pope is overthrown, in spite of the support he receives from a vast host of popish clergy, doctors, &c.

The popish writers against Luther charged him with vices for which there was probably no foundation, and invented the most scandalous stories against him. They accused him, among other things, of drunkenness and licentiousness. and there may, perhaps, be some allusion to the latter charge in our cut No. 153, which is taken from one of the comic illustrations to Murner's book,

"Von dem grossen Lutherischen Narren," which was published in 1522; but, at all events, it will serve as a specimen of these illustrations, and of Murner's fancy of representing himself with the head of a cat. In 1525, Luther married a nun who had turned Protestant and quitted her convent, named Catherine de Bora, and this became the signal to his opponents for indulging in abusive songs, and satires, and caricatures, most of them too coarse and indelicate to be described in these pages. In many of the caricatures made on this occasion, which are usually woodcut illustrations to books written against the reformer, Luther is represented dancing with Catherine de Bora, or sitting at table with a glass in his hand. An engraving of this kind, which forms one of the illustrations to a work by Dr. Konrad Wimpina, one of the reformer's violent opponents, represents Luther's marriage. It is divided into three compartments; to the left, Luther, whom the Catholics always represented in the character of a monk, gives the marriage ring to Catherine de Bora, and above them, in a sort of aureole, is inscribed the word *Vovete*; on the right appears the nuptial bed, with the curtains drawn, and the inscription *Reddite*; and in the middle the monk and nun are dancing joyously together, and over their heads we read the words—

Discedat ab aris
Cui tulit hesterna gaudia nocte Venus.

While Luther was heroically fighting the great fight of reform in Germany, the foundation of religious reform was laid in France by John Calvin, a man equally sincere and zealous in the cause, but of a totally different temper, and he espoused doctrines and forms of church government which a Lutheran would not admit. Literary satire was used with great effect by the French Calvinists against their popish opponents, but they have left us few caricatures or burlesque engravings of any kind; at least, very few belonging to the earlier period of their history. Jaime, in his "Musée de Caricature," has given a copy of a very rare plate, representing the pope struggling with Luther and Calvin, as his two assailants. Both are tearing the pope's hair, but it is Calvin who is here armed with the Bible, with which he is striking at Luther, who is pulling him by the beard. The pope has his hands upon their heads. This scene takes place in the choir of a church, but I give here (cut No. 154) only the group of the three combatants, intended to represent how the two great opponents to papal corruptions were hostile at the same time to each other.

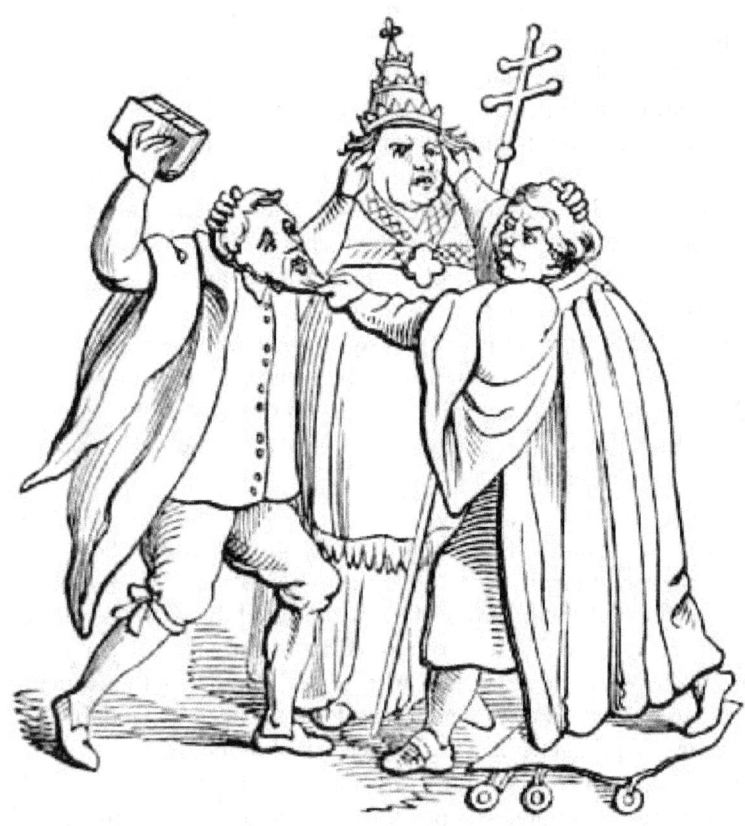

No. 154. Luther and Calvin.

CHAPTER XVI.

ORIGIN OF MEDIÆVAL FARCE AND MODERN COMEDY.—HROTSVITHA.—
MEDIÆVAL NOTIONS OF TERENCE.—THE EARLY RELIGIOUS PLAYS.—MYSTERIES
AND MIRACLE PLAYS.—THE FARCES.—THE DRAMA IN THE SIXTEENTH CENTURY.

There is still another branch of literature which, however it may have been modified, has
descended to us from the middle ages. It has been remarked more than once in the course of this
book, that the theatre of the Romans perished in the transition from the empire to the middle ages;
but something in the shape of theatrical performances appears to be inseparable from society even
in its most barbarous state, and we soon trace among the peoples who had settled upon the ruins of
the empire of Rome an approach towards a drama. It is worthy of remark, too, that the mediæval
drama originated exactly in the same way as that of ancient Greece, that is, from religious
ceremonies.

Such was the ignorance of the ancient stage in the middle ages, that the meaning of the word
comœdia was not understood. The Anglo-Saxon glossaries interpret the word by *racu*, a narrative,
especially an epic recital, and this was the sense in which it was generally taken until late in the
fourteenth or the fifteenth century. It is the sense in which it is used in the title of Dante's great
poem, the "Divina Commedia." When the mediæval scholars became acquainted in manuscripts
with the comedies of Terence, they considered them only as fine examples of a particular sort of
literary composition, as metrical narratives in dialogue, and in this feeling they began to imitate

them. One of the first of these mediæval imitators was a lady. There lived in the tenth century a maiden of Saxony, named Hrotsvitha—a rather unfortunate name for one of her sex, for it means simply "a loud noise of voices," or, as she explains it herself, in her Latin, *clamor validus*. Hrotsvitha, as was common enough among the ladies of those days, had received a very learned education, and her Latin is very respectable. About the middle of the tenth century, she became a nun in the very aristocratic Benedictine abbey of Gandesheim, in Saxony, the abbesses of which were all princesses, and which had been founded only a century before. She wrote in Latin verse a short history of that religious house, but she is best known by seven pieces, which are called comedies (*comœdiæ*), and which consist simply of legends of saints, told dialogue-wise, some in verse and some in prose. As may be supposed, there is not much of real comedy in these compositions, although one of them, the Dulcitius, is treated in a style which approaches that of farce. It is the story of the martyrdom of the three virgin saints—Agape, Chione, and Irene—who excite the lust of the persecutor Dulcitius; and it may be remarked, that in this "comedy," and in that of Callimachus and one or two of the others, the lady Hrotsvitha displays a knowledge of love-making and of the language of love, which was hardly to be expected from a holy nun.[79]

Hrotsvitha, in her preface, complains that, in spite of the general love for the reading of the Scriptures, and contempt for everything derived from ancient paganism, people still too often read the "fictions" of Terence, and thus, seduced by the beauties of his style, soiled their minds with the knowledge of the criminal acts which are described in his writings. A rather early manuscript has preserved a very curious fragment illustrative of the manner in which the comedies of the Romans were regarded by one class of people in the middle ages, and it has also a further meaning. Its form is that of a dialogue in Latin verse between Terence and a personage called in the original *delusor*, which was no doubt intended to express a performer of some kind, and may be probably considered as synonymous with *jougleur*. It is a contention between the new jouglerie of the middle ages and the old jouglerie of the schools, somewhat in the same style as the fabliau of "Les deux Troveors Ribauz," described in a former chapter.[80] We are to suppose that the name of Terence has been in some way or other brought forward in laudatory terms, upon which the jougleur steps forward from among the spectators and expresses himself towards the Roman writer very contemptuously. Terence then makes his appearance to speak in his own defence, and the two go on abusing one another in no very measured language. Terence asks his assailant who he is? to which the other replies, "If you ask who I am, I reply, I am better than thee. Thou art old and broken with years; I am a tyro, full of vigour, and in the force of youth. You are but a barren trunk, while I am a good and fertile tree. If you hold your tongue, old fellow, it will be much better for you."

Si rogitas quis sum, respondeo: te melior sum.
Tu vetus atque senex; ego tyro, valens, adulescens.
Tu sterilis truncus; ego fertilis arbor, opimus.
Si taceas, o vetule, lucrum tibi quæris enorme.

Terence replies:—"What sense have you left? Are you, think you, better than me? Let me see you, young as you are, compose what I, however old and broken, will compose. If you be a good tree, show us some proofs of your fertility. Although I may be a barren trunk, I produce abundance of better fruit than thine."

Quis tibi sensus inest? numquid melior me es?
Nunc vetus atque senex quæ fecero fac adolescens.
Si bonus arbor ades, qua fertilitate redundas?
Cum sim truncus iners, fructu meliore redundo.

And so the dispute continues, but unfortunately the latter part has been lost with a leaf or two of the manuscript. I will only add that I think the age of this curious piece has been overrated.[81]

Hrotsvitha is the earliest example we have of mediæval writers in this particular class of literature. We find no other until the twelfth century, when two writers flourished named Vital of Blois (*Vitalis Blesensis*) and Matthew of Vendôme (*Matthæus Vindocinensis*), the authors of several of the mediæval poems distinguished by the title of *comœdiæ*, which give us a clearer and more distinct idea of what was meant by the word. They are written in Latin Elegiac verse, a form of composition which was very popular among the mediæval scholars, and consist of stories told in dialogue. Hence Professor Osann, of Giessen, who edited two of those of Vital of Blois, gives them the title of eclogues (*eclogæ*). The name comedy is, however, given to them in manuscripts, and it may perhaps admit of the following explanation. These pieces seem to have been first mere abridgments of the plots of the Roman comedies, especially those of Plautus, and the authors appear to have taken the Latin title of the original as applied to the plot, in the sense of a narrative, and not to its dramatic form. Of the two "comedies" by Vital of Blois, one is entitled "Geta," and is taken from the "Amphytrio" of Plautus, and the other, which in the manuscripts bears the title of "Querulus," represents the "Aulularia" of the same writer. Independent of the form of composition, the scholastic writer has given a strangely mediæval turn to the incidents of the classic story of Jupiter and Alcmena. Another similar "comedy," that of Babio, which I first printed from the manuscripts, is still more mediæval in character. Its plot, perhaps taken from a fabliau, for the mediæval writers rarely invented stories, is as follows, although it must be confessed that it comes out rather obscurely in the dialogue itself. Babio, the hero of the piece, is a priest, who, as was still common at that time (the twelfth century), has a wife, or, as the strict religionists would then say, a concubine, named Pecula. She has a daughter named Viola, with whom Babio is in love, and he pursues his design upon her, of course unknown to his wife. Babio has also a man-servant named Fodius, who is engaged in a secret intrigue with his mistress, Pecula, and also seeks to seduce her daughter, Viola. To crown the whole, the lord of the manor, a knight named Croceus, is also in love with Viola, though with more honourable designs. Here is surely intrigue enough and a sufficient absence of morality to satisfy a modern French novelist of the first water. At the opening of the piece, amid some by-play between the four individuals who form the household of Babio, it is suddenly announced that Croceus is on his way to visit him, and a feast is hastily prepared for his reception. It ends in the knight carrying away Viola by force. Babio, after a little vain bluster, consoles himself for the loss of the damsel with reflections on the virtue of his wife, Pecula, and the faithfulness of his man, Fodius, when, at this moment, Fame carries to his ear reports which excite his suspicions against them. He adopts a stratagem very frequently introduced in the mediæval stories, surprises the two lovers under circumstances which leave no room for doubting their guilt, and then forgives them, enters a monastery, and leaves them to themselves. In form, these "comedies" are little more than scholastic exercises; but, at a later period, we shall see the same stories adopted as the subjects of farces.[82]

Already, however, by the side of these dramatic poems, a real drama—the drama of the middle ages—was gradually developing itself. As stated before, it arose, like the drama of the Greeks, out of the religious ceremonies. We know nothing of the existence of anything approaching to dramatic forms which may have existed among the religious rites of the peoples of the Teutonic race before their conversion to Christianity, but the Christian clergy felt the necessity of keeping up festive religious ceremonies in some form or other, and also of impressing upon people's imagination and memory by means of rude scenical representations some of the broader facts of scriptural and ecclesiastical history. These performances at first consisted probably in mere dumb show, or at the most the performers may have chanted the scriptural account of the transaction they were representing. In this manner the choral boys, or the younger clergy, would, on some special Saint's day, perform some striking act in the life of the saint commemorated, or, on particular festivals of the church, those incidents of gospel history to which the festival especially related. By degrees, a rather more imposing character was given to these performances by the addition of a continuous dialogue, which, however, was written in Latin verse, and was no doubt chanted. This incipient drama in Latin, as far as we know it, belongs to the twelfth century, and is represented by a tolerably large number of examples still preserved in mediæval manuscripts. Some of the earliest of these have for their author a pupil of the celebrated Abelard, named Hilarius, who lived in the first half of the twelfth century, and is understood to have been by birth an Englishman. Hilarius appears before us as a playful Latin poet, and among a number of short pieces, which may be almost called lyric, he has left us three of these religious plays. The subject of the first of these is the raising of Lazarus from the dead, the chief peculiarity of which consists of the songs of lamentation placed in the mouths of the two sisters of Lazarus, Mary and Martha. The second represents one of the miracles attributed to St. Nicholas; and the third, the history of Daniel. The latter is longer and more elaborate than the others, and at its conclusion, the stage direction tells us that, if it were performed at matins, Darius, king of the Medes and Persians, was to chant *Te Deum Laudamus*, but if it were at vespers, the great king was to chant *Magnificat anima mea Dominum*.[83]

That this mediæval drama was not derived from that of the Roman is evident from the circumstance that entirely new terms were applied to it. The western people in the middle ages had no words exactly equivalent with the Latin *comœdia*, *tragœdia*, *theatrum*, &c; and even the Latinists, to designate the dramatic pieces performed at the church festivals, employed the word *ludus*, a play. The French called them by a word having exactly the same meaning, *jeu* (from *jocus*). Similarly in English they were termed *plays*. The Anglo-Saxon glossaries present as the representative of the Latin *theatrum*, the compounded words *plege-stow*, or *pleg-stow*, a play-place, and *pleg-hus*, a play-house. It is curious that we Englishmen have preferred to the present time the Anglo-Saxon words in *play*, *player*, and *play-house*. Another Anglo-Saxon word with exactly the same signification, *lac*, or *gelac*, play, appears to have been more in use in the dialect of the Northumbrians, and a Yorkshireman still calls a play a *lake*, and a player a *laker*. So also the Germans called a dramatic performance a *spil*, *i.e.* a play, the modern *spiel*, and a theatre, a *spil-hus*. One of the pieces of Hilarius is thus entitled "Ludus super iconia sancti Nicolai," and the French *jeu* and the English *play* are constantly used in the same sense. But besides this general term, words gradually came into use to characterise different sorts of plays. The church plays consisted of two descriptions of subjects, they either represented the miraculous acts of certain saints, which had a plain meaning, or some incident taken from the Holy Scriptures, which was supposed to have a hidden mysterious signification as well as an apparent one, and hence the one class of subject was usually spoken of simply as *miraculum*, a miracle, and the other as *mysterium*, a mystery. *Mysteries* and *miracle-plays* are still the names usually given to the old religious plays by writers on the history of the stage.

We have a proof that the Latin religious plays, and the festivities in which they were employed, had become greatly developed in the twelfth century, in the notice taken of them in the ecclesiastical councils of that period, for they were disapproved by the stricter church disciplinarians. So early as the papacy of Gregory VIII., the pope urged the clergy to "extirpate" from their churches theatrical plays, and other festive practices which were not quite in harmony with the sacred character of these buildings.[84] Such performances are forbidden by a council held at Treves in 1227.[85] We learn from the annals of the abbey of Corbei, published by Leibnitz, that the younger monks at Heresburg performed on one occasion a "sacred comedy" (*sacram comœdiam*) of the selling into captivity and the exaltation of Joseph, which was disapproved by the other heads of the order.[86] Such performances are included in a proclamation of the bishop of Worms, in 1316, against the various abuses which had crept into the festivities observed in his diocese at Easter and St. John's tide.[87] Similar prohibitions of the acting of such plays in churches are met with at subsequent periods.

While these performances were thus falling under the censure of the church authorities, they were taken up by the laity, and under their management both the plays and the machinery for acting them underwent considerable extension. The municipal guilds contained in their constitution a considerable amount of religious spirit. They were great benefactors of the churches in cities and municipal towns, and had usually some parts of the sacred edifice appropriated to them, and they may, perhaps, have taken a part in these performances, while they were still confined to the church. These guilds, and subsequently the municipal corporations, took them entirely into their own hands. Certain annual religious festivals, and especially the feast of *Corpus Christi*, were still the occasions on which the plays were acted, but they were taken entirely from the churches, and the performances took place in the open streets. Each guild had its particular play, and they acted on movable stages, which were dragged along the streets in the procession of the guild. These stages appear to have been rather complicated. They were divided into three floors, that in the middle, which was the principal stage, representing this world, while the upper division represented heaven, and that at the bottom hell. The mediæval writers in Latin called this machinery a *pegma*, from the Greek word πῆγμα, a scaffold; and they also applied to it, for a reason which is not is easily seen, unless the one word arose out of a corruption of the other, that of *pagina*, and from a further corruption of these came into the French and English languages the word *pageant*, which originally signified one of these movable stages, though it has since received secondary meanings which have a much wider application. Each guild in a town had its pageant and its own actors, who performed in masks and costumes, and each had one of a series of plays, which were performed at places where they halted in the procession. The subjects of these plays were taken from Scripture, and they usually formed a regular series of the principal histories of the Old and New Testaments. For this reason they were generally termed *mysteries*, a title already explained; and among the few series of these plays still preserved, we have the "Coventry Mysteries," which were performed by the guilds of that town, the "Chester Mysteries," belonging to the guilds in the city of Chester, and the "Towneley Mysteries," so called from the name of the possessor of the manuscript, but which probably belonged to the guilds of Wakefield in Yorkshire.

During these changes in the method of performance, the plays themselves had also been considerably modified. The simple Latin phrases, even when in rhyme, which formed the dialogue of the earlier *ludi*—as in the four miracles of St. Nicholas, and the six Latin mysteries taken from the New Testament, printed in my volume of "Early Mysteries and other Latin Poems"—must have been very uninteresting to the mass of the spectators, and an attempt was made to enliven them by introducing among the Latin phrases popular proverbs, or even sometimes a song in the vulgar tongue. Thus in the play of "Lazarus" by Hilarius, the Latin of the lamentations of his two sisters is intermixed with French verses. Such is the case also with the play of "St. Nicholas" by the same writer, as well as with the curious mystery of the Foolish Virgins, printed in my "Early Mysteries" just alluded to, in which latter the Latin is intermingled with Provençal verse. A much greater advance was made when these performances were transferred to the guilds. The Latin was then discarded altogether, and the whole play was written in French, or English, or German, as the case might be, the plot was made more elaborate, and the dialogue greatly extended. But now that the whole institution had become secularised, the want of something to amuse people—to make them laugh, as people liked to laugh in the middle ages—was felt more than ever, and this want was supplied by the introduction of droll and ludicrous scenes, which are often very slightly, if at all, connected with the subject of the play. In one of the earliest of the French plays, that of "St. Nicholas," by Jean Bodel, the characters who form the burlesque scene are a party of gamblers in a tavern. In others, robbers, or peasants, or beggars form the comic scene, or vulgar women, or any personages who could be introduced acting vulgarly and using coarse language, for these were great incitements to mirth among the populace.

In the English plays now remaining, these scenes are, on the whole, less frequent, and they are usually more closely connected with the general subject. The earliest English collection that has been published is that known as the "Towneley Mysteries," the manuscript of which belongs to the fifteenth century, and the plays themselves may have been composed in the latter part of the fourteenth. It contains thirty-two plays, beginning with the Creation, and ending with the Ascension and the Day of Judgment, with two supplementary plays, the "Raising of Lazarus" and the "Hanging of Judas." The play of "Cain and Abel" is throughout a vulgar drollery, in which Cain, who exhibits the character of a blustering ruffian, is accompanied by a *garcio*, or lad, who is the very type of a vulgar and insolent horse-boy, and the conversation of these two worthies reminds us a little of that between the clown and his master in the open-air performances of the old wandering mountebanks. Even the death of Abel by the hand of his brother is performed in a manner calculated to provoke great laughter. In the old mirthful spirit, to hear two persons load each other with vulgar abuse, was as good as seeing them grin through a horse-collar, if not better. Hence the droll scene in the play of "Noah" is a domestic quarrel between Noah and his wife, who was proverbially a shrew, and here gives a tolerable example of abusive language, as it might then come from a woman's tongue. The quarrel arises out of her obstinate refusal to go into the ark. In the New Testament series the play of "The Shepherds" was one of those most susceptible of this sort of embellishment. There are two plays of the Shepherds in the "Towneley Mysteries," the first of which is amusing enough, as it represents, in clever burlesque, the acts and conversation of a party of mediæval shepherds guarding their flocks at night; but the second play of the Shepherds is a much more remarkable example of a comic drama. The shepherds are introduced at the opening of the piece conversing very satirically on the corruptions of the time, and complaining how the people were impoverished by over-taxation, to support the pride and vanity of the aristocracy. After a good deal of very amusing talk, the shepherds, who, as usual, are three in number, agree to sing a song, and it is this song, it appears, which brings to them a fourth, named Mak, who proves to be a sheep-stealer; and, in fact, no sooner have the shepherds resigned themselves to sleep for the night, than Mak chooses one of the best sheep in their flocks, and carries it home to his hut. Knowing that he will be suspected of the theft, and that he will soon be pursued, he is anxious to conceal the plunder, and is only helped out of his difficulty by his wife, who suggests that the carcase shall be laid at the bottom of her cradle, and that she shall lie upon it and groan, pretending to be in labour. Meanwhile the shepherds awake, discover the loss of a sheep, and perceiving that Mak has disappeared also, they naturally suspect him to be the depredator, and pursue him. They find everything very cunningly prepared in the cottage to deceive them, but, after a large amount of roundabout inquiry and research, and much drollery, they discover that the boy of which Mak's wife pretends to have been just delivered, is nothing else but the sheep which had been stolen from their flocks. The wife still asserts that it is her child, and Mak sets up as his defence that the baby had been "forspoken," or enchanted, by an elf at midnight, and that it had thus been changed into the appearance of a sheep; but the shepherds refuse to be satisfied with this explanation. The whole of this little comedy is carried out with great skill, and with infinite drollery. The shepherds, while still wrangling with Mak and his wife, are seized with drowsiness, and lie down to sleep; but they are aroused by the voice of the angel, who proclaims the birth of the Saviour. The next play in which the drollery is introduced, is that of "Herod and the Slaughter of the Innocents." Herod's bluster and bombast, and the vulgar abuse which passes between the Hebrew mothers and the soldiers who are murdering their children, are wonderfully laughable. The plays which represented the arrest, trial, and execution of Jesus, are all full of drollery, for the grotesque character which had been given to the demons in the earlier middle ages, appears to have been transferred to the executioners, or, as they were called, the "tormentors," and the language and manner in which they executed their duties, must have kept the audience in a continual roar of laughter. In the play of "Doomsday," the fiends retained their old character, and the manner in which they joke over the distress of the sinful souls, and the details they give of their sinfulness, are equally mirth-provoking. The "Coventry Mysteries" are also printed from a manuscript of the middle of the fifteenth century, and are, perhaps, as old as the "Towneley

Mysteries." They consist of forty-two plays, but they contain, on the whole, fewer droll scenes than those of the Towneley collection. But a very remarkable example is furnished in the play of the "Trial of Joseph and Mary," which is a very grotesque picture of the proceedings in a mediæval consistory court. The sompnour, a character so well known by Chaucer's picture of him, opens the piece by reading from his book a long list of offenders against chastity. At its conclusion, two "detractors" make their appearance, who repeat various scandalous stories against the Virgin Mary and her husband Joseph, which are overheard by some of the high officers of the court, and Mary and Joseph are formally accused and placed upon their trial. The trial itself is a scene of low ribaldry, which can only have afforded amusement to a very vulgar audience. There is a certain amount of the same kind of indelicate drollery in the play of "The Woman taken in Adultery," in this collection. The "Chester Mysteries" are still more sparing of such scenes, but they are printed from manuscripts written after the Reformation, which had, perhaps, gone through the process of expurgation, in which such excrescences had been lopped off. However, in the play of "Noah's Flood," we have the old quarrel between Noah and his wife, which is carried so far that the latter actually beats her husband in the presence of the audience. There is a little drollery in the play of "The Shepherds," a considerable amount of what may be called "Billingsgate" language in the play of the "Slaughter of the Innocents," but less than the usual amount of insolence in the tormentors and demons.[88] It is probable, however, that these droll scenes were not always considered an integral part of the play in which they were introduced, but that they were kept as separate subjects, to be introduced at will, and not always in the same play, and therefore that they were not copied with the play in the manuscripts.

In the Coventry play of "Noah's Flood," when Noah has received the directions from an angel for the building of the ark, he leaves the stage to proceed to this important work. On his departure, Lamech comes forward, blind and led by a youth, who directs his hand to shoot at a beast concealed in a bush. Lamech shoots, and kills Cain, upon which, in his anger, he beats the youth to death, and laments the misfortune into which the latter has led him. This was the legendary explanation of the passage in the fourth chapter of Genesis: "And Lamech said ... I have slain a man to my wounding, and a young man to my hurt; if Cain shall be avenged seven-fold, truly Lamech seventy and seven-fold." It is evident that this is a piece of scriptural story which has nothing to do with Noah's flood, and accordingly, in the Coventry play, we are told in the stage directions, that it was introduced in the place of the "interlude,"[89] as if there were a place in the machinery of the pageant where the episode, which was not an integral part of the subject, was performed, and that this part of the performance was called an interlude, or play introduced in the interval of the action of the main subject. The word *interlude* remained long in our language as applied to such short and simple dramatic pieces as we may suppose to have formed the drolleries of the mysteries. But they had another name in France which has had a greater and more lulling celebrity. In one of the early French miracle-plays, that of "St. Fiacre," an interlude of this kind is introduced, containing five personages—a brigand or robber, a peasant, a sergeant, and the wives of the two latter. The brigand, meeting the peasant on the highway, asks the way to St. Omer, and receives a clownish answer, which is followed by one equally rude on a second question. The brigand, in revenge, steals the peasant's capon, but the sergeant comes up at this moment and, attempting to arrest the thief, receives a blow from the latter which is supposed to break his right arm. The brigand thus escapes, and the peasant and the sergeant quit the scene, which is immediately occupied by their wives. The sergeant's wife is informed by the other of the injury sustained by her husband, and she exults over it because it will deprive him of the power of beating her. They then proceed to a tavern, call for wine, and make merry, the conversation turning upon the faults of their respective husbands, who are not spared. In the midst of their enjoyments, the two husbands return, and show, by beating their wives, that they are not very greatly disabled. In the manuscript of the miracle-play of "St. Fiacre," in which this amusing episode is introduced, a marginal stage direction is expressed in the following words, "*cy est interposé une farsse*" (here a farce is introduced). This is one of the earliest instances of the application of the term *farce* to these short dramatic facetiæ. Different opinions have been expressed as to the origin of the word, but it seems most probable that it is derived from an old French verb, *farcer*, to jest, to make merry, whence the modern word *farceur* for a joker, and that it thus means merely a drollery or merriment.

I have just suggested as a reason for the absence of these interludes, or farces, in the mysteries as they are found in the manuscripts, that they were probably not looked upon as parts of the mysteries themselves, but as separate pieces which might be used at pleasure. When we reach a certain period in their history, we find that not only was this the case, but that these farces were performed separately and altogether independently of the religious plays. It is in France that we find information which enables us to trace the gradual revolution in the mediæval drama. A society was formed towards the close of the fourteenth century under the title of *Confrères de la Passion*, who, in 1398, established a regular theatre at St. Maur-des-Fossés, and subsequently obtained from Charles VI. a privilege to transport their theatre into Paris, and to perform in it mysteries and miracle-plays. They now rented of the monks of Hermières a hall in the hospital of the Trinity, outside of the Porte St. Denis, performing there regularly on Sundays and saints' days, and probably making a good thing of it, for, during a long period, they enjoyed great popularity. Gradually, however, this popularity was so much diminished, that the *confrères* were obliged to have recourse to expedients for reviving it. Meanwhile other similar societies had arisen into importance. The clerks of the Bazoche, or lawyers' clerks of the Palais de Justice, had thus associated together, it is said, as early as the beginning of the fourteenth century, and they distinguished themselves by composing and performing farces, for which they appear to have obtained a privilege. Towards the close of the fourteenth century, there arose in Paris another society, which took the name of *Enfans sans souci*, or Careless Boys, who elected a president or chief with the title of *Prince des Sots*, or King of the Fools, and who composed a sort of dramatic satires which they called *Sotties*. Jealousies soon arose between these two societies, either because the sotties were made sometimes to resemble too closely the farces, or because each trespassed too often on the territories of the other. Their differences were finally arranged by a compromise, whereby the Bazochians yielded to their rivals the privilege of performing farces, and received in return the permission to perform sotties. The Bazochians, too, had invented a new class of dramatic pieces which they called *Moralities*, and in which allegorical personages were introduced. Thus three dramatic societies continued to exist in France through the fifteenth century, and until the middle of the sixteenth.

These various pieces, under the titles of farces, sotties, moralities, or whatever other names might be given to them, had become exceedingly popular at the beginning of the sixteenth century, and a very considerable number of them were printed, and many of them are still preserved, but they are books of great rarity, and often unique.[90] Of these the farces form the most numerous class. They consist simply of the tales of the older jougleurs or story-tellers represented in a dramatic form, but they often display great skill in conducting the plot, and a considerable amount of wit. The story of the sheep-stealer in the Towneley play of "The Shepherds," is a veritable farce. As in the fabliaux, the most common subjects of these farces are love intrigues, carried on in a manner which speaks little for the morality of the age in which they were written. Family quarrels frequently form the subject of a farce, and the weaknesses and vices of women. The priests, as usual, are not spared, but are introduced as the seducers of wives and daughters. In one the wives have found a means of re-modelling their husbands and making them young again, which they put in practice with various ludicrous circumstances. Tricks of servants are also common subjects for these farces. One is the story of a boy who does not know his own father, and some of the subjects are of a still more trivial character, as that of the boy who steals a tart from the pastrycook's shop. Two hungry boys, prowling about the streets, come to the shop door just as the pastrycook is giving directions for sending an eel-pie after him. By an ingenious deception the boys gain possession of the pie and eat it, and they are both caught and severely chastised. This is the whole plot of the farce. A dull schoolboy examined by his master in the presence of his parents, and the mirth produced by his blunders and their ignorance, formed also a favourite subject among these farces. One or two examples are preserved, and, from a companion of them, we might be led to suspect that Shakespeare took the idea of the opening scene in the fourth act of the "Merry Wives of Windsor" from one of these old farces.

The sotties and moralities were more imaginative and extravagant than the farces, and were filled with allegorical personages. The characters introduced in the former have generally some relation to the kingdom of folly. Thus, in one of the sotties, the king of fools (*le roy des sotz*) is represented as holding his court, and consulting with his courtiers, whose names are Triboulet, Mitouflet, Sottinet, Coquibus, and Guippelin. Their conversation, as may be supposed, is of a satirical character. Another is entitled "The Sottie of the Deceivers," or cheats. Sottie—another name for mother Folly—opens the piece with a proclamation or address to fools of all descriptions, summoning them to her presence. Two, named Teste-Verte and Fine-Mine, obey the call, and they are questioned as to their own condition, and their proceedings, but their conversation is interrupted by the sudden intrusion of another personage named Everyone (*Chascun*), who, on examination, is found to be as perfect a fool as any of them. They accordingly fraternise, and join in a song. Finally, another character, The Time (*le Temps*), joins them, and they agree to submit to his directions. Accordingly he instructs them in the arts of flattery and deceiving, and the other similar means by which men of that time sought to thrive. Another is the Sottie of Foolish Ostentation (*de folle bobance*). This lady similarly opens the scene with an address to all the fools who hold allegiance to her, and three of these make their appearance. The first fool is the gentleman, the second the merchant, the fourth the peasant, and their conversation is a satire on contemporary society. The personification of abstract principles is far bolder. The three characters who compose one of these moralities are Everything (*tout*), Nothing (*rien*), and Everyone (*chascun*). How the personification of Nothing was to be represented, we are not told. The title of another of these moralities will be enough to give the reader a notion of their general title; it is, "A New Morality of the Children of Now-a-Days (*Maintenant*), who are the Scholars of Once-good (*Jabien*), who shows them how to play at Cards and at Dice, and to entertain Luxury, whereby one comes to Shame (*Honte*), and from Shame to Despair (*Desespoir*), and from Despair to the gibbet of Perdition, and then turns himself to Good-doing." The characters in this play are Now-a-Days, Once-good, Luxury, Shame, Despair, Perdition, and Good-doing.

The three dramatic societies which produced all these farces, sotties, and moralities, continued to flourish in France until the middle of the sixteenth century, at which period a great revolution in dramatic literature took place in that country. The performance of the Mysteries had been forbidden by authority, and the Bazochians themselves were suppressed. The petty drama represented by the farces and sotties went rapidly out of fashion, in the great change through which the mind of society was at this time passing, and in which the taste for classical literature overcame all others. The old drama in France had disappeared, and a new one, formed entirely upon an imitation of the classical drama, was beginning to take its place. This incipient drama was represented in the sixteenth century by Etienne Jodel, by Jacques Grevin, by Rémy Belleau, and especially by Pierre de Larivey, the most prolific, and perhaps the most talented, of the earlier French regular dramatic authors.

These French dramatic essays, the farces, the sotties, and the moralities, were imitated, and sometimes translated, in English, and many of them were printed; for the further our researches are carried into the early history of printing, the more we are astonished at the extreme activity of the press, even in its infancy, in multiplying literature of a popular character. In England, as in France, the farces had been, at a rather early period, detached from the mysteries and miracle-plays, but the word *interludes* had been adopted here as the general title for them, and continued in use even after the establishment of the regular drama. Perhaps this name owed its popularity to the circumstance that it seemed more appropriate to its object, when it became so fashionable in England to act these plays at intervals in the great festivals and entertainments given at court, or in the households of the great nobles. At all events, there can be no doubt that this fashion had a great influence on the fate of the English stage. The custom of performing plays in the universities, great schools, and inns of court, had also the effect of producing a number of very clever dramatic writers; for when this literature was so warmly patronised by princes and nobles, people of the highest qualifications sought to excel in it. Hence we find from books of household expenses and similar records of the period, that there was, during the sixteenth century, an immense number of such plays compiled in England which were never printed, and of which, therefore, very few are preserved.

The earliest known plays of this description in the English language belong to the class which were called in France moralities. They are three in number, and are preserved in a manuscript in the possession of Mr. Hudson Gurney, which I have not seen, but which is said to be of the reign of our king Henry VI. Several words and allusions in them seem to me to show that they were translated, or adapted, from the French. They contain exactly the same kind of allegorical personages. The allegory itself is a simple one, and easily understood. In the first, which is entitled the "Castle of Perseverance," the hero is *Humanum Genus* (Mankynd), for the names of the parts are all given in Latin. On the birth of this personage, a good and a bad angel offer themselves as his protectors and guides, and he chooses the latter, who introduces him to *Mundus* (the World), and to his friends, *Stultitia* (Folly), and *Voluptas* (Pleasure). These and some other personages bring him under the influence of the seven deadly sins, and *Humanum Genus* takes for his bedfellow a lady named *Luxuria*. At length *Confessio* and *Pœnitentia* succeed in reclaiming *Humanum Genus*, and they conduct him for security to the Castle of Perseverance, where the seven cardinal virtues attend upon him. He is besieged in this castle by the seven deadly sins, who are led to the attack by Belial, but are defeated. *Humanum Genus* has now become aged, and is exposed to the attacks of another assailant. This is *Avaritia*, who enters the Castle stealthily by undermining the wall, and artfully persuades *Humanum Genus* to leave it. He thus comes again under the influence of *Mundus*, until *Mors* (Death) arrives, and the bad angel carries off the victim to the domains of Satan. This, however, is not the end of the piece. God appears, seated on His throne, and Mercy, Peace, Justice, and Truth appear before Him, the two former pleading for, and the latter against, *Humanum Genus*, who, after some discussion, is saved. This allegorical picture of human life was, in one form or other, a favourite subject of the moralisers. I may quote as examples the interludes of "Lusty Juventus," reprinted in Hawkins's "Origin of the English Drama," and the "Disobedient Child," and "Trial of Treasure," reprinted by the Percy Society.

The second of the moralities ascribed to the reign of Henry VI., has for its principal characters Mind, Will, and Understanding. These are assailed by Lucifer, who succeeds in alluring them to vice, and they change their modest raiment for the dress of gay gallants. Various other characters are introduced in a similar strain of allegory, until they are reclaimed by Wisdom. Mankind is again the principal personage of the third of these moralities, and some of the other characters in the play, such as Nought, New-guise, and Now-a-days, remind us of the similar allegorical personages in the French moralities described above.

These interludes bring us into acquaintance with a new comic character. The great part which folly acted in the social destinies of mankind, had become an acknowledged fact; and as the court and almost every great household had its professed fool, so it seems to have been considered that a play also was incomplete without a fool. But, as the character of the fool was usually given to one of the most objectionable characters in it, so, for this reason apparently, the fool in a play was called the *Vice*. Thus, in "Lusty Juventus," the character of Hypocrisy is called the Vice; in the play of "All for Money," it is Sin; in that of "Tom Tyler and his Wife," it is Desire; in the "Trial of Treasure" it is Inclination; and in some instances the Vice appears to be the demon himself. The Vice seems always to have been dressed in the usual costume of a court fool, and he perhaps had other duties besides his mere part in the plot, such as making jests of his own, and using other means for provoking the mirth of the audience in the intervals of the action.

A few of our early English interludes were, in the strict sense of the word, farces. Such is the "mery play" of "John the Husband, Tyb the Wife, and Sir John the Priest," written by John Heywood, the plot of which presents the same simplicity as those of the farces which were so popular in France. John has a shrew for his wife, and has good causes for suspecting an undue intimacy between her and the priest; but they find means to blind his eyes, which is the more easily done, because he is a great coward, except when he is alone. Tyb, the wife, makes a pie, and proposes that the priest shall be invited to assist in eating it. The husband is obliged, very unwillingly, to be the bearer of the invitation, and is not a little surprised when the priest refuses it. He gives as his reason, that he was unwilling to intrude himself into company where he knew he was disliked, and persuaded John that he had fallen under the wife's displeasure, because, in private interviews with her, he had laboured to induce her to bridle her temper, and treat her husband with more gentleness. John, delighted at the discovery of the priest's honesty, insists on his going home with him to feast upon the pie. There the guilty couple contrive to put the husband to a disagreeable penance, while they eat the pie, and treat him otherwise very ignominiously, in consequence of which the married couple fight. The priest interferes, and the fight thus becomes general, and is only ended by the departure of Tyb and the priest, leaving the husband alone.

The popularity of the moralities in England is, perhaps, to be explained by peculiarities in the condition of society, and the greater pre-occupation of men's minds in our country at that time with the religious and social revolution which was then in progress. The Reformers soon saw the use which might be made of the stage, and compiled and caused to be acted interludes in which the old doctrines and ceremonies were turned to ridicule, and the new ones were held up in a favourable light. We have excellent examples of the success with which this plan was carried out in the plays of the celebrated John Bale. His play of "Kyng Johan," an edition of which was published by the Camden Society, is not only a remarkable work of a very remarkable man, but it may be considered as the first rude model of the English historical drama. The stage became now a political instrument in England, almost as it had been in ancient Greece, and it thus became frequently the object of particular as well as general persecution. In 1543, the vicar of Yoxford, in Suffolk, drew upon himself the violent hostility of the other clergy in that county by composing and causing to be performed plays against the pope's counsellors. Six years afterwards, in 1549, a royal proclamation prohibited for a time the performance of interludes throughout the kingdom, on the ground that they contained "matter tendyng to sedicion and contempnyng of sundery good orders and lawes, whereupon are growen daily, and are likely to growe, muche disquiet, division, tumultes, and uproares in this realme." From this time forward we begin to meet with laws for the regulation of stage performances, and proceedings in cases of supposed infractions of them, and it became customary to obtain the approval of a play by the privy council before it was allowed to be acted. Thus gradually arose the office of a dramatic censor.

With Bale and with John Heywood, the English plays began to approach the form of a regular drama, and the two now rather celebrated pieces, "Ralph Roister Doister," and "Gammer Gurton's Needle," which belong to the middle of the sixteenth century, may be considered as comedies rather than as interludes. The former, written by a well-known scholar of that time, Nicholas Udall, master of Eton, is a satirical picture of some phases of London life, and relates the ridiculous adventures of a weak-headed and vain-glorious gallant, who believes that all the women must be in love with him, and who is led by a needy and designing parasite named Matthew Merygreeke. Rude as it is as a dramatic composition, it displays no lack of talent, and it is full of genuine humour. The humour in "Gammer Gurton's Needle" is none the less rich because it is of coarser and rather broader cast. The good dame of the piece, Gammer Gurton, during an interruption in the process of mending the breeches of her husband, Hodge, has lost her needle, and much lamentation follows a misfortune so great at a time when needles appear to have been rare and valuable articles in the rural household. In the midst of their trouble appears Diccon, who is described in the *dramatis personæ* as "Diccon the Bedlam," meaning that he was an idiot, and who appears to hold the position of Vice in the play. Diccon, however, though weak-minded, is a cunning fellow, and especially given to making mischief, and he accuses a neighbour, Dame Chat, of stealing the needle. At the same time, the same mischievous individual tells Dame Chat that Gammer Gurton's cock had been stolen in the night from the henroost, and that she, Dame Chat, was accused of being the thief. Amid the general misunderstanding which results from Diccon's successful endeavours, they send for the parson of the parish, Dr. Rat, who appears to unite in himself the three parts of preacher, physician, and conjurer, in order to have advantage of his experience in finding the needle. Diccon now contrives a new piece of mischief. He persuades Dame Chat that Hodge intends to hide himself in a certain hole in the premises, in order, that night, to creep out and kill all her hens; and at the same time he informs Dr. Rat, that if he will hide in the same hole, he will give him ocular demonstration of Dame Chat's guilt of stealing the needle. The consequence is that Dame Chat attacks by surprise, and somewhat violently, the supposed depredator in the hole, and that Dr. Rat gets a broken head. Dame Chat is brought before "Master Bayly" for the assault, and the proceedings in the trial bring to light the deceptions which have been played upon them all, and Diccon stands convicted as the wicked perpetrator. In fact, the "bedlam" confesses it all, and it is finally decided by "Master Bayly" that there shall be a general reconciliation, and that Diccon shall take a solemn oath on Hodge's breech, that he will do his best to find the lost needle. Diccon has still the spirit of mischief in him, and instead of laying his hand quietly on Hodge's breech, he gives him a sharp blow, which is responded to by an unexpected scream. The needle, indeed, which has never quitted the breeches, is driven rather deep into the fleshy part of Hodge's body, and the general joy at having found it again overruling all other considerations, they all agree to be friends over a jug of "drink."

We cannot but feel astonished at the short period which it required to develop rude attempts at dramatic composition like this into the wonderful creations of a Shakespeare; and it can only be explained by the fact that it was an age remarkable for producing men of extraordinary genius in every branch of intellectual development. Hitherto, the literature of the stage had represented the intelligence of the mass; it became individualised in Shakespeare, and this fact marks an entirely new era in the history of the drama. In the writings of our great bard, nearly all the peculiarities of the older national drama are preserved, even some which may be perhaps considered as its defects, but carried to a degree of perfection which they had never attained before. The drollery, which, as we have seen, could not be dispensed with even in the religious mysteries and miracle-plays, had become so necessary, that it could not be dispensed with in tragedy. Its omission belonged to a later period, when the foreign dramatists became objects of imitation in England. But in the earlier drama, these scenes of drollery seem frequently to have no connection whatever with the general plot, while Shakespeare always interweaves them skilfully with it, and they seem to form an integral and necessary part of it.

CHAPTER XVII.

DIABLERIE IN THE SIXTEENTH CENTURY.—EARLY TYPES OF THE DIABOLICAL FORMS.—ST. ANTHONY.—ST. GUTHLAC.—REVIVAL OF THE TASTE FOR SUCH SUBJECTS IN THE BEGINNING OF THE SIXTEENTH CENTURY.—THE FLEMISH SCHOOL OF BREUGHEL.—THE FRENCH AND ITALIAN SCHOOLS, CALLOT, SALVATOR ROSA.

We have seen how the popular demonology furnished materials for the earliest exercise of comic art in the middle ages, and how the taste for this particular class of grotesque lasted until the close of the mediæval period. After the "renaissance" of art and literature, this taste took a still more remarkable form, and the school of grotesque *diablerie* which flourished during the sixteenth century, and the first half of the seventeenth, justly claims a chapter to itself.

The birthplace of this demonology, as far as it belongs to Christianity, must probably be sought in the deserts of Egypt. It spread thence over the east and the west, and when it reached our part of the world, it grafted itself, as I have remarked in a former chapter, on the existing popular superstitions of Teutonic paganism. The playfully burlesque, which held so great a place in these superstitions, no doubt gave a more comic character to this Christian demonology than it had possessed before the mixture. Its primitive representative was the Egyptian monk, St. Anthony, who is said to have been born at a village called Coma, in Upper Egypt, in the year 251. His history was written in Greek by St. Athanasius, and was translated into Latin by the ecclesiastical historian Evagrius. Anthony was evidently a fanatical visionary, subject to mental illusions, which were fostered by his education. To escape from the temptations of the world, he sold all his property, which was considerable, gave it to the poor, and then retired into the desert of the Thebaid, to live a life of the strictest asceticism. The evil one persecuted him in his solitude, and sought to drive him back into the corruptions of worldly life. He first tried to fill his mind with regretful reminiscences of his former wealth, position in society, and enjoyments; when this failed, he disturbed his mind with voluptuous images and desires, which the saint resisted with equal success. The persecutor now changed his tactics, and presenting himself to Anthony in the form of a black and ugly youth, confessed to him, with apparent candour, that he was the spirit of uncleanness, and acknowledged that he had been vanquished by the extraordinary merits of Anthony's sanctity. The saint, however, saw that this was only a stratagem to stir up in him the spirit of pride and self-confidence, and he met it by subjecting himself to greater mortifications than ever, which of course made him still more liable to these delusions. Now he sought greater solitude by taking up his residence in a ruined Egyptian sepulchre, but the farther he withdrew from the world, the more he became the object of diabolical persecution. Satan broke in upon his privacy with a host of attendants, and during the night beat him to such a degree, that one morning the attendant who brought him food found him lying senseless in his cell, and had him carried to the town, where his friends were on the point of burying him, believing him to be dead, when he suddenly revived, and insisted on being taken back to his solitary dwelling. The legend tells us that the demons appeared to him in the forms of the most ferocious animals, such as lions, bulls, wolves, asps, serpents, scorpions, panthers, and bears, each attacking him in the manner peculiar to its species, and with its peculiar voice, thus making together a horrible din. Anthony left his tomb to retire farther into the desert, where he made a ruined castle his residence; and here he was again frightfully persecuted by the demons, and the noise they made was so great and horrible that it was often heard at a vast distance. According to the narrative, Anthony reproached the demons in very abusive language, called them hard names, and even spat in their faces; but his most effective weapon was always the cross. Thus the saint became bolder, and sought a still more lonely abode, and finally established himself on the top of a high mountain in the upper Thebaid. The demons still continued to persecute him, under a great variety of forms; on one occasion their chief appeared to him under the form of a man, with the lower members of an ass.

The demons which tormented St. Anthony became the general type for subsequent creations, in which these first pictures were gradually, and in the sequel, greatly improved upon. St. Anthony's persecutors usually assumed the shapes of *bonâ fide* animals, but those of later stories took monstrous and grotesque forms, strange mixtures of the parts of different animals, and of others which never existed. Such were seen by St. Guthlac, the St. Anthony of the Anglo-Saxons, among the wild morasses of Croyland. One night, which he was passing at his devotions in his cell, they poured in upon him in great numbers; "and they filled all the house with their coming, and they poured in on every side, from above and from beneath, and everywhere. They were in countenance horrible, and they had great heads, and a long neck, and lean visage; they were filthy and squalid in their beards, and they had rough ears, and distorted face, and fierce eyes, and foul mouths; and their teeth were like horses' tusks, and their throats were filled with flame, and they were grating in their voice; they had crooked shanks, and knees big and great behind, and distorted toes, and shrieked hoarsely with their voices; and they came with such immoderate noises and immense horror, that it seemed to him that all between heaven and earth resounded with their dreadful cries." On another similar occasion, "it happened one night, when the holy man Guthlac fell to his prayers, he heard the howling of cattle and various wild beasts. Not long after he saw the appearance of animals and wild beasts and creeping things coming in to him. First he saw the visage of a lion that threatened him with his bloody tusks, also the likeness of a bull, and the visage of a bear, as when they are enraged. Also he perceived the appearance of vipers, and a hog's grunting, and the howling of wolves, and croaking of ravens, and the various whistlings of birds, that they might, with their fantastic appearance, divert the mind of the holy man."

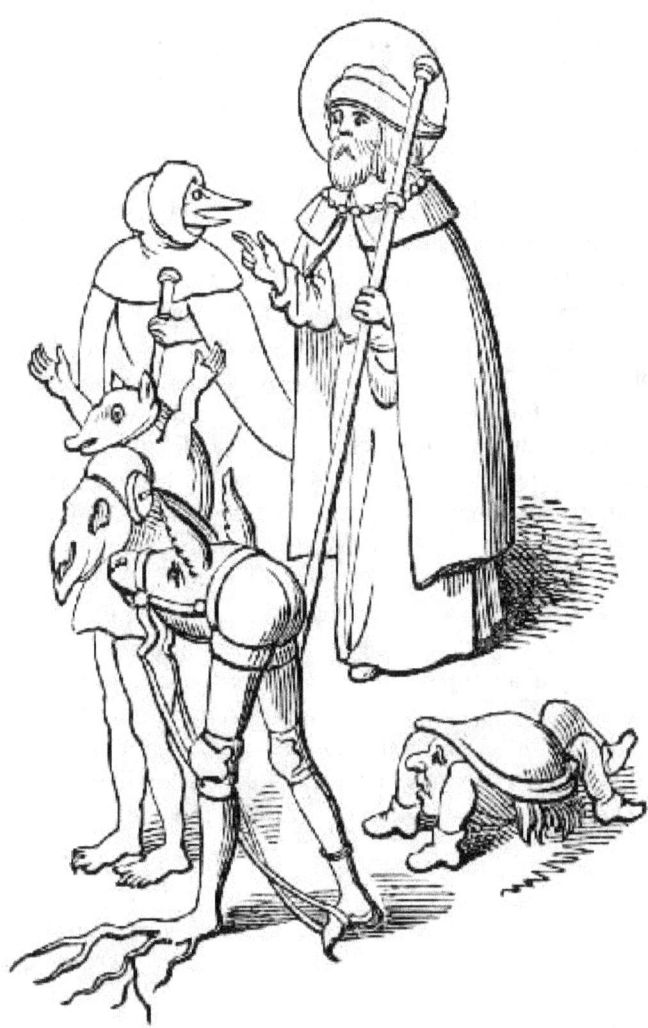

No. 155. St. James and his Persecutors.

Such were the suggestions on which the mediæval sculptors and illuminators worked with so much effect, as we have seen repeatedly in the course of our preceding chapters. After the revival of art in western Europe in the fifteenth century, this class of legends became great favourites with painters and engravers, and soon gave rise to the peculiar school of *diablerie* mentioned above. At that time the story of the Temptation of St. Anthony attracted particular attention, and it is the subject of many remarkable prints belonging to the earlier ages of the art of engraving. It employed the pencils of such artists as Martin Schongauer, Israel van Mechen, and Lucas Cranach. Of the latter we have two different engravings on the same subject—St. Anthony carried into the air by the demons, who are represented in a great variety of grotesque and monstrous forms. The most remarkable of the two bears the date of 1506, and was, therefore, one of Cranach's earlier works. But the great representative of this earlier school of *diablerie* was Peter Breughel, a Flemish painter who flourished in the middle of the sixteenth century. He was born at Breughel, near Breda, and lived some time at Antwerp, but afterwards established himself at Brussels. So celebrated was he for the love of the grotesque displayed in his pictures, that he was known by the name of Peter the Droll. Breughel's "Temptation of St. Anthony," like one or two others of his subjects of the same class, was engraved in a reduced form by J. T. de Bry. Breughel's demons are figures of the most fantastic description—creations of a wildly grotesque imagination; they present incongruous and laughable mixtures of parts of living things which have no relation whatever to one another. Our cut

No. 155 represents a group of these grotesque demons, from a plate by Breughel, engraved in 1565, and entitled *Divus Jacobus diabolicis præstigiis ante magnum sistitur* (St. James is arrested before the magician by diabolical delusions). The engraving is full of similarly grotesque figures. On the right is a spacious chimney, and up it witches, riding on brooms, are making their escape, while in the air are seen other witches riding away upon dragons and a goat. A kettle is boiling over the fire, around which a group of monkeys are seen sitting and warming themselves. Behind these a cat and a toad are holding a very intimate conversation. In the background stands and boils the great witches' caldron. On the right of the picture the *magus*, or magician, is seated, reading his *grimoire*; with a frame before him supporting the pot containing his magical ingredients. The saint occupies the middle of the picture, surrounded by the demons represented in our cut and by many others; and as he approaches the magician, he is seen raising his right hand in the attitude of pronouncing a benediction, the apparent consequence of which is a frightful explosion of the magician's pot, which strikes the demons with evident consternation. Nothing can be more *bizarre* than the horse's head upon human legs in armour, the parody upon a crawling spider behind it, the skull (apparently of a horse) supported upon naked human legs, the strangely excited animal behind the latter, and the figure furnished with pilgrim's hood and staff, which appears to be mocking the saint. Another print—a companion to the foregoing—represents the still more complete discomfiture of the *magus*. The saint here occupies the right-hand side of the picture, and is raising his hand higher, with apparently a greater show of authority. The demons have all turned against their master the magician, whom they are beating and hurling headlong from his chair. They seem to be proclaiming their joy at his fall by all sorts of playful attitudes. It is a sort of demon fair. Some of them, to the left of the picture, are dancing and standing upon their heads on a tight-rope. Near them another is playing some game like that which we now call the thimble-rig. The monkeys are dancing to the tune of a great drum. A variety of their mountebank tricks are going on in different parts of the scene. Three of these playful actors are represented in our cut No. 156.

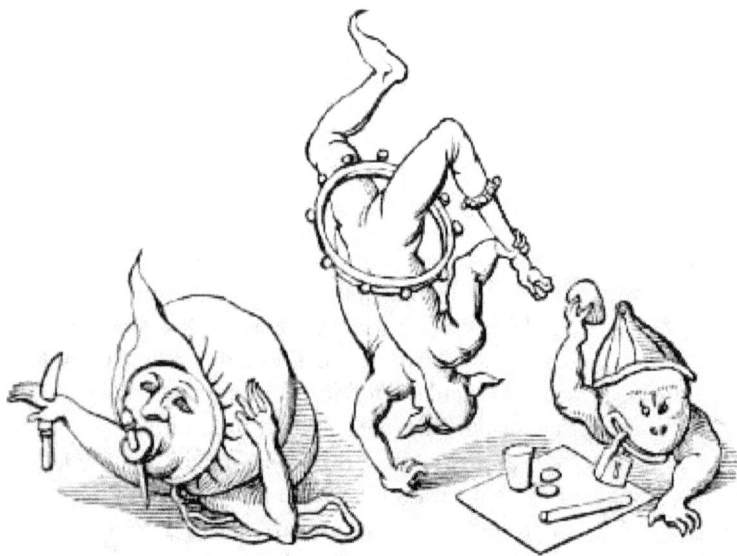

No. 156. Strange Demons.

Breughel also executed a series of similarly grotesque engravings, representing in this same fantastic manner the virtues and vices, such as Pride (*superbia*), Courage (*fortitudo*), Sloth (*desidia*), &c These bear the date of 1558. They are crowded with figures equally grotesque with those just mentioned, but a great part of which it would be almost impossible to describe. I give two examples from the engraving of "Sloth," in the accompanying cut (No. 157).

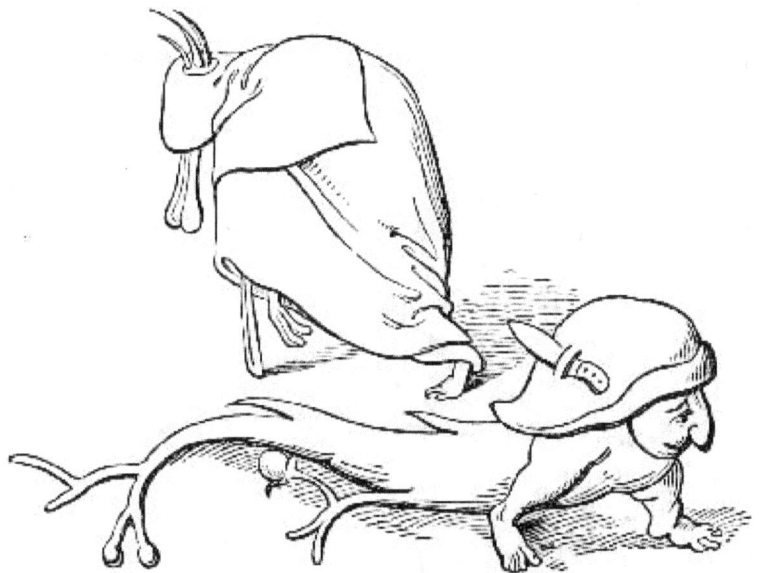

No. 157. Imps of Sloth.

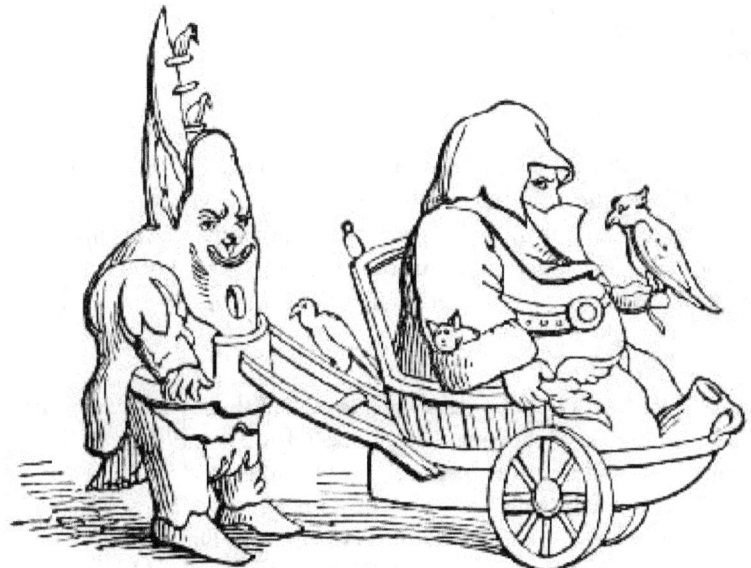

No. 158. The Folly of Hunting.

From making up figures from parts of animals, this early school of grotesque proceeded to create animated figures out of inanimate things, such as machines, implements of various kinds, household utensils, and other such articles. A German artist, of about the same time as Breughel, has left us a singular series of etchings of this description, which are intended as an allegorical satire on the follies of mankind. The allegory is here of such a singular character, that we can only guess at the meaning of these strange groups through four lines of German verse which are attached to each of them. In this manner we learn that the group represented in our cut, No. 158, which is the second in this series, is intended as a satire upon those who waste their time in hunting, which, the verses tell us, they will in the sequel lament bitterly; and they are exhorted to cry loud and continually to God, and to let that serve them in the place of hound and hawk.

Die zeit die du verleurst mit jagen,

Die wirstu zwar noch schmertzlich klagen;
Ruff laut zu Gott gar oft und vil,
Das sey dein hund und federspil.

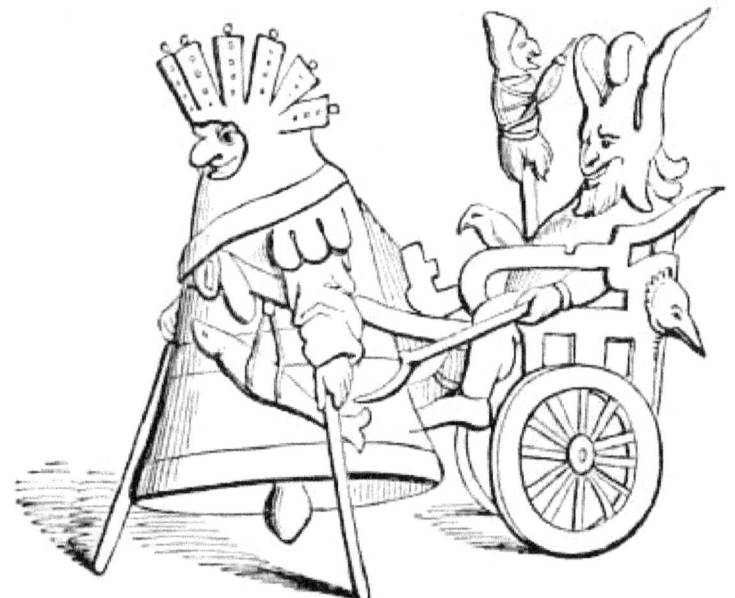

No. 159. The Wastefulness of Youth.

The next picture in the series, which is equally difficult to describe, is aimed against those who fail in attaining virtue or honour through sluggishness. Others follow, but I will only give one more example. It forms our cut No. 159, and appears, from the verses accompanying it, to be aimed against those who practice wastefulness in their youth, and thus become objects of pity and scorn in old age. Whatever may be the point of the allegory contained in the engraving, it is certainly far-fetched, and not very apparent.

This German-Flemish school of grotesque does not appear to have outlived the sixteenth century, or at least it had ceased to flourish in the century following. But the taste for the *diablerie* of the Temptation scenes passed into France and Italy, in which countries it assumed a much more refined character, though at the same time one equally grotesque and imaginative. These artists, too, returned to the original legend, and gave it forms of their own conception. Daniel Rabel, a French artist, who lived at the end of the sixteenth century, published a rather remarkable engraving of the "Temptation of St. Anthony," in which the saint appears on the right of the picture, kneeling before a mound on which three demons are dancing. On the right hand of the saint stands a naked woman, sheltering herself with a parasol, and tempting the saint with her charms. The rest of the piece is filled with demons in a great variety of forms and postures. Another French artist, Nicholas Cochin, has left us two "Temptations of St. Anthony," in rather spirited etching, of the earlier part of the seventeenth century. In the first, the saint is represented kneeling before a crucifix, surrounded by demons. The youthful and charming temptress is here dressed in the richest garments, and the highest style of fashion, and displays all her powers of seduction. The body of the picture is, as usual, occupied by multitudes of diabolical figures, in grotesque forms. In Cochin's other picture of the Temptation of St. Anthony, the saint is represented as a hermit engaged in his prayers; the female figure of voluptuousness (*voluptas*) occupies the middle of the picture, and behind the saint is seen a witch with her besom.

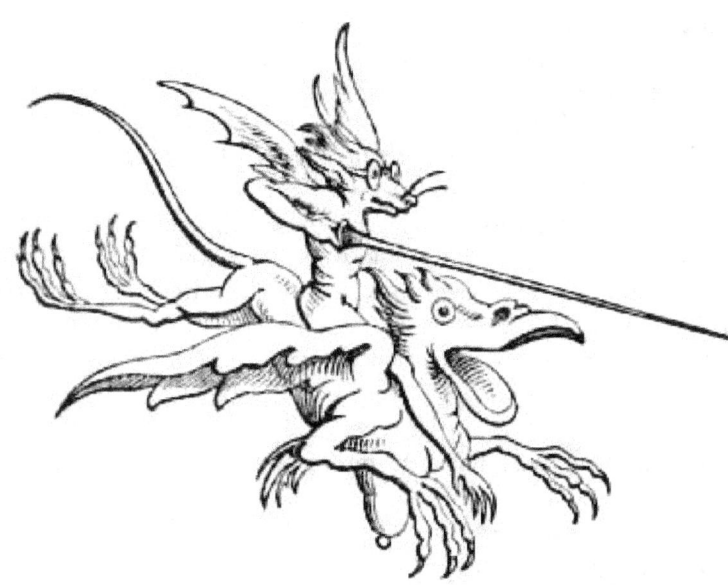

No. 160. The Demon Tilter (Callot).

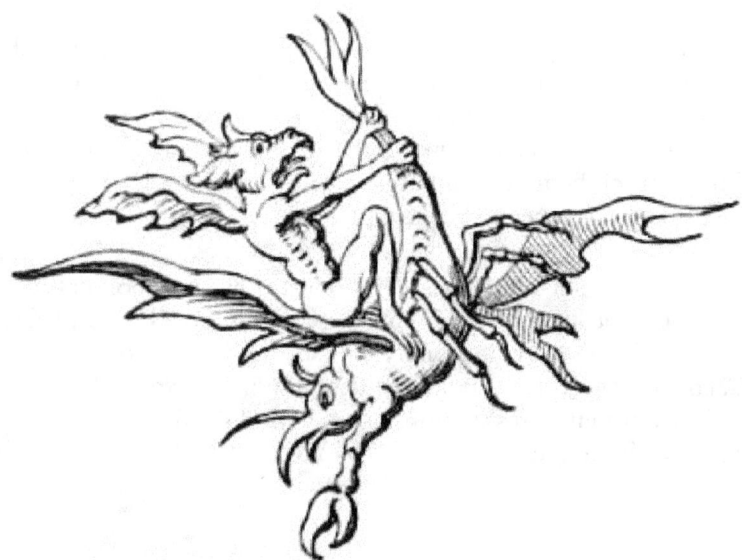

No. 161. Uneasy Riding (Callot).

But the artist who excelled in this subject at the period at which we now arrive, was the celebrated Jacques Callot, who was born at Nancy, in Brittany, in 1593, and died at Florence on the 24th of March, 1635, which, according to the old style of calculating, may mean March, 1636. Of Callot we shall have to speak in another chapter. He treated the subject of the Temptation of St. Anthony in two different plates, which are considered as ranking among the most remarkable of his works, and to which, in fact, he appears to have given much thought and attention. He is known, indeed, to have worked diligently at it. They resemble those of the older artists in the number of diabolical figures introduced into the picture, but they display an extraordinary vivid imagination in the forms, postures, physiognomies, and even the equipments, of the chimerical figures, all equally droll and burlesque, but which present an entire contrast to the more coarse and vulgar conceptions of the German-Flemish school. This difference will be understood best by an example. One of Callot's demons is represented in our cut No. 160. Many of them are mounted on nondescript animals, of the most extraordinary demoniacal character, and such is the case of the demon in our cut, who is running a tilt at the saint with his tilting spear in his hand, and, to make more sure, his eyes well furnished with a pair of spectacles. In our next cut, No. 161, we give a second example of the figures in Callot's peculiar *diablerie*. The demon in this case is riding very uneasily, and, in fact, seems in danger of being thrown. The steeds of both are of an anomalous character; the first is a sort of dragon-horse; the second a mixture of a lobster, a spider, and a craw-fish. Mariette, the art-collector and art-writer of the reign of Louis XV. as well as artist, considers this grotesque, or, as he calls it, "fantastic and comic character," as almost necessary to the pictures of the Temptation of St. Anthony, which he treats as one of Callot's especially *serious* subjects. "It was allowable," he says, "to Callot, to give a flight to his imagination. The more his fictions were of the nature of dreams, the more they were fitted to what he had to express. For the demon intending to torment St. Anthony, it is to be supposed that he must have thought of all the forms most hideous, and most likely to strike terror."

Callot's first and larger print of the Temptation of St. Anthony is rare. It is filled with a vast number of figures. Above is a fantastic being who vomits thousands of demons. The saint is seen at the entrance of a cavern, tormented by some of these. Others are scattered about in different occupations. On one side, a demoniacal party are drinking together, and pledging each other in their glasses; here, a devil is playing on the guitar; there, others are occupied in a dance; all such grotesque figures as our two examples would lead the reader to expect. In the second of Callot's "Temptations," which is dated in 1635, and must therefore have been one of his latest works, the same figure vomiting the demons occupies the upper part of the plate, and the field is covered with a prodigious number of imps, more hideous in their forms, and more varied in their extraordinary attitudes, than in the same artist's first design. Below, a host of demons are dragging the saint to a place where new torments are prepared for him. Callot's prints of the Temptation of St. Anthony gained so great a reputation, that imitations of them were subsequently published, some of which so far approached his style, that they were long supposed to be genuine.

Callot, though a Frenchman, studied and flourished in Italy, and his style is founded upon Italian art. The last great artist whose treatment of the Temptation I shall quote, is Salvator Rosa, an Italian by birth, who flourished in the middle of the seventeenth century. His style, according to some opinions, is refined from that of Callot; at all events, it is bolder in design. Our cut No. 162 represents St. Anthony protecting himself with the cross against the assaults of the demon, as represented by Salvator Rosa. With this artist the school of *diablerie* of the sixteenth century may be considered to have come to its end.

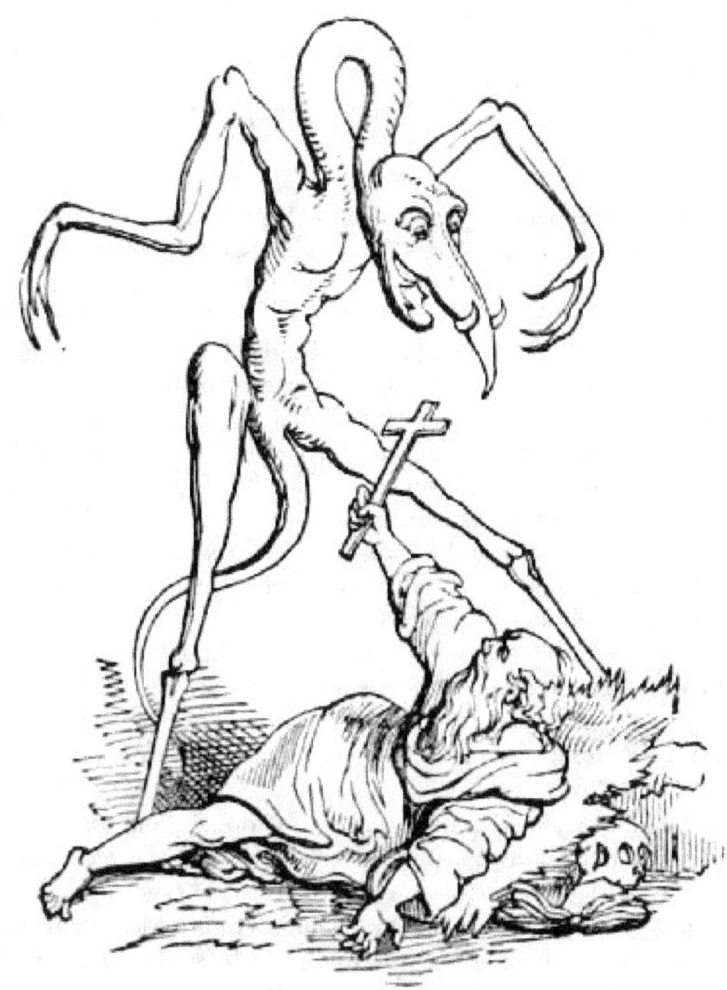

No. 162. St. Anthony and his Persecutor.

CHAPTER XVIII.

CALLOT AND HIS SCHOOL.—CALLOT'S ROMANTIC HISTORY.—HIS "CAPRICI,"
AND OTHER BURLESQUE WORKS.—THE "BALLI" AND THE BEGGARS.—
IMITATORS OF CALLOT; DELLA BELLA.—EXAMPLES OF DELLA BELLA.—ROMAIN
DE HOOGHE.

The art of engraving on copper, although it had made rapid advances during the sixteenth century, was still very far from perfection; but the close of that century witnessed the birth of a man who was destined not only to give a new character to this art, but also to bring in a new style of caricature and burlesque. This was the celebrated Jacques Callot, a native of Lorraine, and descended from a noble Burgundian family. His father, Jean Callot, held the office of herald of Lorraine. Jacques was born in the year 1592,[91] at Nancy, and appears to have been destined for the church, with a view to which his early education was regulated. But the early life of Jacques Callot presents a romantic episode in the history of art aspirations. While yet hardly more than an infant, he seized every opportunity of neglecting more serious studies to practise drawing, and he displayed especially a very precocious taste for satire, for his artistic talent was shown principally in caricaturing all the people he knew. His father, and apparently all his relatives, disapproved of his love for drawing, and did what they could to discourage it; but in vain, for he still found means of indulging it. Claude Henriet, the painter to the court of Lorraine, gave him lessons, and his son, Israel Henriet, formed for him a boy's friendship. He also learnt the elements of the art of engraving of Demange Crocq, the engraver to the duke of Lorraine.

About this time, the painter Bellange, who had been a pupil of Claude Henriet, returned from Italy, and gave young Callot an exciting account of the wonders of art to be seen in that country; and soon afterwards Claude Henriet dying, his son Israel went to Rome, and his letters from thence had no less effect on the mind of the young artist at Nancy, than the conversation of Bellange. Indeed the passion of the boy for art was so strong, that, finding his parents obstinately opposed to all his longings in this direction, he left his father's house secretly, and, in the spring of 1604, when he had only just entered his thirteenth year, he set out for Italy on foot, without introductions and almost without money. He was even unacquainted with the road, but after proceeding a short distance, he fell in with a band of gipsies, and, as they were going to Florence, he joined their company. His life among the gipsies, which lasted seven or eight weeks, appears to have furnished food to his love of burlesque and caricature, and he has handed down to us his impressions, in a series of four engravings of scenes in gipsy life, admirably executed at a rather later period of his life, which are full of comic humour. When they arrived at Florence, Jacques Callot parted company with the gipsies, and was fortunate enough to meet with an officer of the grand duke's household, who listened to his story, and took so much interest in him, that he obtained him admission to the studio of Remigio Canta Gallina. This artist gave him instructions in drawing and engraving, and sought to correct him of his taste for the grotesque by keeping him employed upon serious subjects.

After studying for some months under Canta Gallina, Jacques Callot left Florence, and proceeded to Rome, to seek his old friend Israel Henriet; but he had hardly arrived, when he was recognised in the streets by some merchants from Nancy, who took him, and in spite of his tears and resistance, carried him home to his parents. He was now kept to his studies more strictly than ever, but nothing could overcome his passion for art, and, having contrived to lay by some money, after a short interval he again ran away from home. This time he took the road to Lyons, and crossed Mont Cenis, and he had reached Turin when he met in the street of that city his elder brother Jean, who again carried him home to Nancy. Nothing could now repress young Callot's ardour, and soon after this second escapade, he engraved a copy of a portrait of Charles III., duke of Lorraine, to which he put his name and the date 1607, and which, though it displays little skill in engraving, excited considerable interest at the time. His parents were now persuaded that it was useless to thwart any longer his natural inclinations, and they not only allowed him to follow them, but they yielded to his wish to return to Italy. The circumstances of the moment were especially favourable. Charles III., duke of Lorraine, was dead, and his successor, Henry II., was preparing to send an embassy to Rome to announce his accession. Jean Callot, by his position of herald, had sufficient interest to obtain for his son an appointment in the ambassador's retinue, and Jacques Callot started for Rome on the 1st of December, 1608, under more favourable auspices than those which had attended his former visits to Italy.

Callot reached Rome at the beginning of the year 1609, and now at length he joined the friend of his childhood, Israel Henriet, and began to throw all his energy into his art-labours. It is more than probable that he studied under Tempesta, with Henriet, who was a pupil of that painter, and another Lorrainer, Claude Dervet. After a time, Callot began to feel the want of money, and obtained employment of a French engraver, then residing in Rome, named Philippe Thomassin, with whom he worked nearly three years, and became perfect in handling the graver. Towards the end of the year 1611, Callot went to Florence, to place himself under Julio Parigi, who then flourished there as a painter and engraver. Tuscany was at this time ruled by its duke Cosmo de'

Medicis, a great lover of the arts, who took Callot under his patronage, giving him the means to advance himself. Hitherto his occupation had been principally copying the works of others, but under Parigi he began to practise more in original design, and his taste for the grotesque came upon him stronger than ever. Although Parigi blamed it, he could not help admiring the talent it betrayed. In 1615, the grand duke gave a great entertainment to the prince of Urbino, and Callot was employed to make engravings of the festivities; it was his first commencement in a class of designs by which he afterwards attained great celebrity. In the year following, his engagement with Parigi ended, and he became his own master. He now came out unfettered in his own originality. The first fruits were seen in a new kind of designs, to which he gave the name of "Caprices," a series of which appeared about the year 1617, under the title of "Caprici di varie Figure." Callot re-engraved them at Nancy in later years, and in the new title they were stated to have been originally engraved in 1616. In a short preface, he speaks of these as the first of his works on which he set any value. They now strike us as singular examples of the fanciful creations of a most grotesque imagination, but they no doubt preserve many traits of the festivals, ceremonies, and manners of that land of masquerade, which must have been then familiar to the Florentines; and these engravings would, doubtless, be received by them with absolute delight. One is copied in our cut No. 163; it represents a cripple supporting himself on a short crutch, with his right arm in a sling. Our cut No. 164 is another example from the same set, and represents a masked clown, with his left hand on the hilt of his dagger, or perhaps of a wooden sword. From this time, although he was very industrious and produced much, Callot engraved only his own designs.

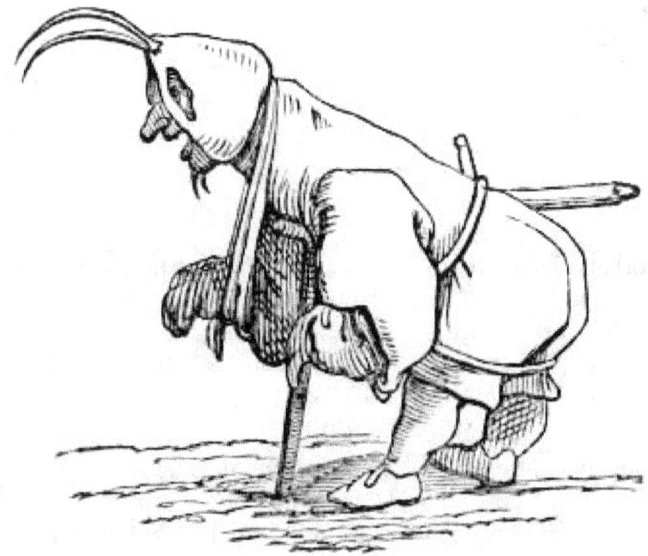

No. 163. A Cripple.

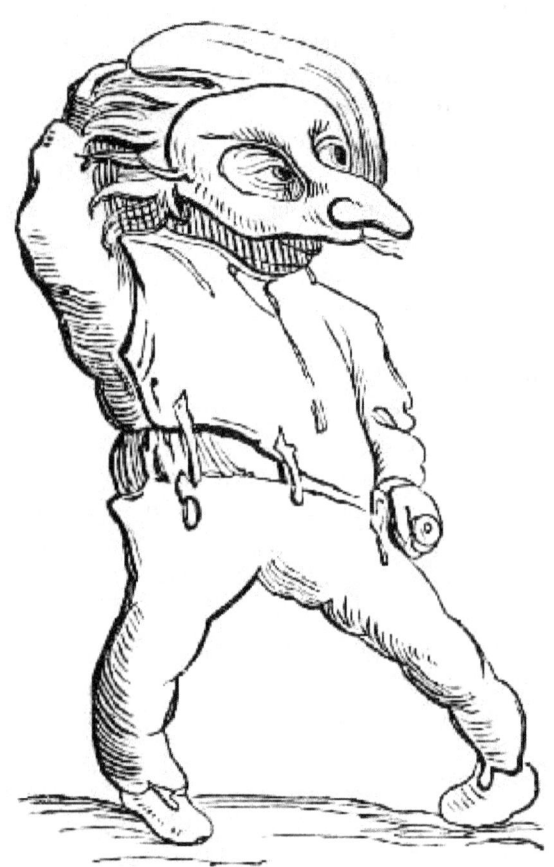

No. 164. A Grotesque Masker.

While employed for others, Callot had worked chiefly with the graver, but now that he was his own master, he laid aside that implement, and devoted himself almost entirely to etching, in which he attained the highest proficiency. His work is remarkable for the cleanness and ease of his lines, and for the life and spirit he gave to his figures. His talent lay especially in the extraordinary skill with which he grouped together great numbers of diminutive figures, each of which preserved its proper and full action and effect. The great annual fair of the Impruneta was held with extraordinary festivities, and attended by an immense concourse of people of all classes on St. Luke's Day, the 18th of October, in the outskirts of Florence. Callot engraved a large picture of this fair, which is absolutely wonderful. The picture embraces an extensive space of ground, which is covered with hundreds of figures, all occupied, singly or in groups, in different manners, conversing, masquerading, buying and selling, playing games, and performing in various ways; each group or figure is a picture in itself. This engraving produced quite a sensation, and it was followed by other pictures of fairs, and, after his final return to Nancy, Callot engraved it anew. It was this talent for grouping large masses of persons which caused the artist to be so often employed in drawing great public ceremonies, sieges, and other warlike operations.

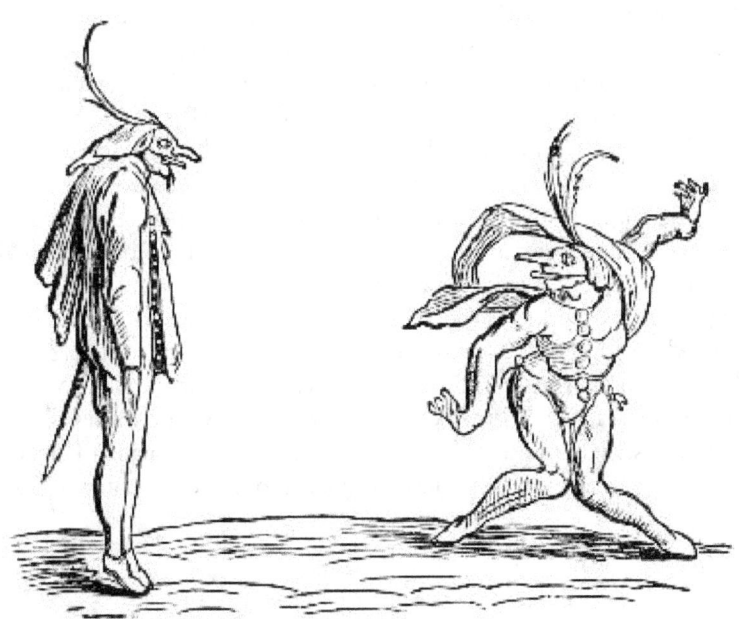

No. 165. Smaraolo Cornuto.—Ratsa di Boio.

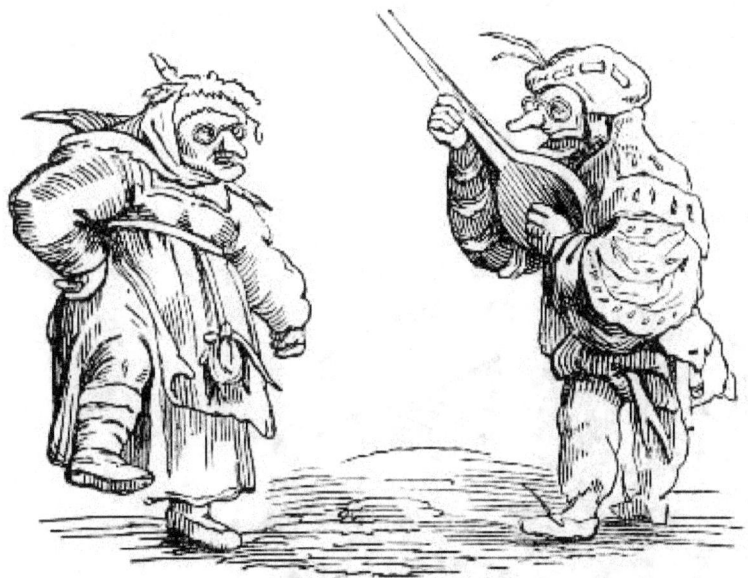

No. 166. A Caprice.

By the duke of Florence, Cosmo II., Callot was liberally patronised and loaded with benefits, but on his death the government had to be placed in the hands of a regency, and art and literature no longer met with the same encouragement. In this state of things, Callot was found by Charles of Lorraine, afterwards duke Charles IV., and persuaded to return to his native country. He arrived at Nancy in 1622, and began to work there with greater activity even than he had displayed before. It was not long after this that he produced his sets of grotesques, the Balli (or dancers), the Gobbi (or hunchbacks), and the Beggars. The first of these sets, called in the title *Balli*, or *Cucurucu*,[92] consists of twenty-four small plates, each of them containing two comic characters in grotesque attitudes, with groups of smaller figures in the distance. Beneath the two prominent figures are their names, now unintelligible, but at that time no doubt well known on the comic stage at Florence. Thus, in the couple given in our cut No. 165, which is taken from the fourth plate of the series, the personage to the left is named Smaraolo Cornuto, which means simply Smaraolo the cuckold; and the one on the right is called Ratsa di Boio. In the original the background is occupied by a street, full of spectators, looking on at a dance of pantaloons, round one who is mounted on stilts and playing on the tabour. The couple in our cut No. 166, represents another of Callot's "Caprices," from a set differing from the first "Caprices," or the Balli. The Gobbi, or hunchbacks, form a set of twenty-one engravings; and the set of the Gipsies, already alluded to, which was also executed at Nancy, was included in four plates, the subjects of which were severally—1, the gipsies travelling; 2, the avant-guard; 3, the halt; and 4, the preparations for the feast. Nothing could be more truthful, and at the same time more comic, than this last set of subjects. We give, as an example of the set of the Baroni, or beggars, Callot's figure of one of that particular class—for beggars and rogues of all kinds were classified in those days—whose part it was to appeal to charity by wounds and sores artificially represented. In the English slang of the seventeenth century, these artificial sores were called *clymes*, and a curious account of the manner in which they were made will be found in that singular picture of the vicious classes of society in this country at that period, the "English Rogue," by Head and Kirkman. The false cripple in our cut is holding up his leg to make a display of his pretended infirmity.

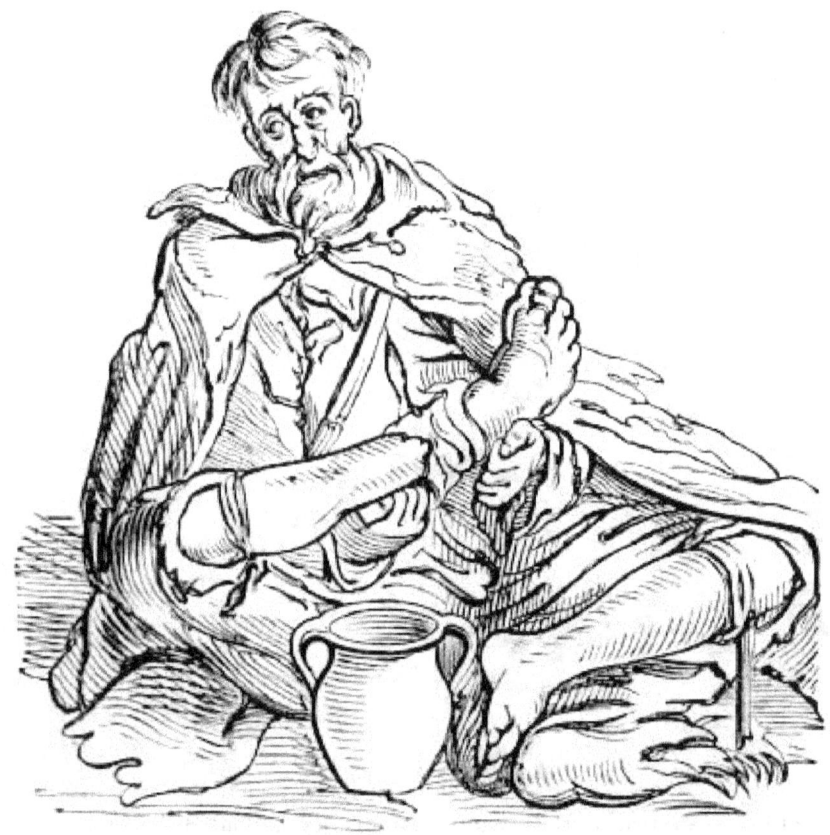

No. 167. The False Cripple.

Callot remained at Nancy, with merely temporary absences, during the remainder of his life. In 1628, he was employed at Brussels in drawing and engraving the "Siege of Breda," one of the most finished of his works, and he there made the personal acquaintance of Vandyck. Early in 1629, he was called to Paris to execute engravings of the siege of La Rochelle, and of the defence of the Isle of Rhé, but he returned to Nancy in 1630. Three years afterwards his native country was invaded by the armies of Louis XIII., and Nancy surrendered to the French on the 25th of September, 1633.

Callot was required to make engravings to celebrate the fall of his native town; but, although he is said to have been threatened with violence, he refused; and afterwards he commemorated the evils brought upon his country by the French invasion in those two immortal sets of prints, the lesser and greater "Misères de la Guerre." About two years after this, Callot died, in the prime of life, on the 24th of March, 1635.

The fame of Callot was great among his contemporaries, and his name is justly respected as one of the most illustrious in the history of French art. He had, as might be expected, many imitators, and the Caprices, the Balli, and the Gobbi, became very favourite subjects. Among these imitators, the most successful and the most distinguished was Stephano Della Bella; and, indeed, the only one deserving of particular notice. Della Bella was born at Florence, on the 18th of May, 1610;[93] his father, dying two years afterwards, left him an orphan, and his mother in great poverty. As he grew up, he showed, like Callot himself, precocious talents in art, and of the same kind. He eagerly attended all public festivals, games, &c, and on his return from them made them the subject of grotesque sketches. It was remarked of him, especially, that he had a curious habit of always beginning to draw a human figure from the feet, and proceeding upwards to the head. He was struck at a very early period of his pursuit of art by the style of Callot, of which, at first, he was a servile imitator, but he afterwards abandoned some of its peculiarities, and adopted a style which was more his own, though still founded upon that of Callot. He almost rivalled Callot in his success in grouping multitudes of figures together, and hence he also was much employed in producing engravings of sieges, festive entertainments, and such elaborate subjects. As Callot's aspirations had been directed towards Italy, those of Della Bella were turned towards France, and when in the latter days of the ministry of Cardinal Richelieu, the grand duke of Florence sent Alexandro del Nero as his resident ambassador in Paris, Della Bella was permitted to accompany him. Richelieu was occupied in the siege of Arras, and the engraving of that event was the foundation of Della Bella's fame in France, where he remained about ten years, frequently employed on similar subjects. He subsequently visited Flanders and Holland, and at Amsterdam made the acquaintance of Rembrandt. He returned to Florence in 1650, and died there on the 23rd of July, 1664.

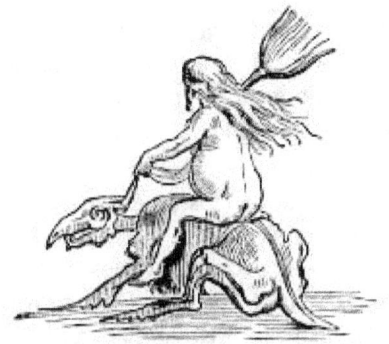

No. 168. A Witch Mounted.

While still in Florence, Della Bella executed four prints of dwarfs quite in the grotesque style of Callot. In 1637, on the occasion of the marriage of the grand duke Ferdinand II., Della Bella published engravings of the different scenes represented, or performed, on that occasion. These were effected by very elaborate machinery, and were represented in six engravings, the fifth of which (*scena quinta*) represents hell (*d'Inferno*), and is filled with furies, demons, and witches, which might have found a place in Callot's "Temptation of St. Anthony."

A specimen of these is given in our cut No. 168—a naked witch seated upon a skeleton of an animal that might have been borrowed from some far distant geological period. In 1642, Della Bella executed a set of small "Caprices," consisting of thirteen plates, from the eighth of which we take our cut No. 169. It represents a beggar-woman, carrying one child on her back, while another is stretched on the ground. In this class of subjects Della Bella imitated Callot, but the copyist never succeeded in equalling the original. His best style, as an original artist of burlesque and caricature, is shown in a set of five plates of Death carrying away people of different ages, which he executed in 1648. The fourth of this set is copied in our cut No. 170, and represents Death carrying off, on his shoulder, a young woman, in spite of her struggles to escape from him.

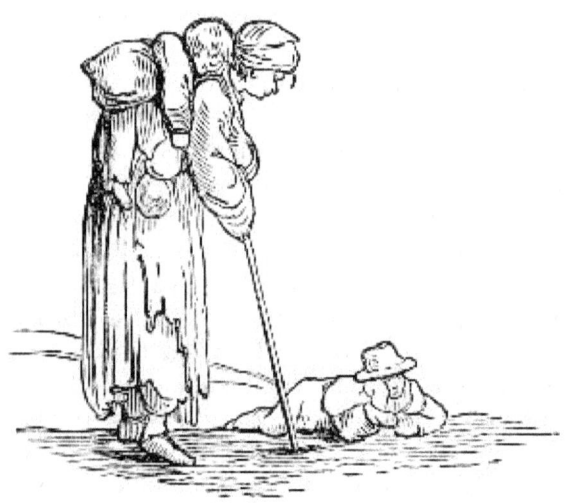

No. 169. Beggary.

With the close of the seventeenth century these "Caprices" and masquerade scenes began to be no longer in vogue, and caricature and burlesque assumed new forms; but Callot and Della Bella had many followers, and their examples had a lasting influence upon art.

We must not forget that a celebrated artist, in another country, at the end of the same century, the well-known Romain de Hooghe, was produced from the school of Callot, in which he had learnt, not the arts of burlesque and caricature, but that of skilfully grouping multitudes of figures, especially in subjects representing episodes of war, tumults, massacres, and public processions.

Of Romain de Hooghe we shall have to speak again in a subsequent chapter. In his time the art of engraving had made great advance on the Continent, and especially in France, where it met with more encouragement than elsewhere. In England this art had, on the whole, made much less progress, and was in rather a low condition, one branch only excepted, that of portraits. Of the two distinguished engravers in England during the seventeenth century, Hollar was a Bohemian, and Faithorne, though an Englishman, learnt his art in France. We only began to have an English school when Dutch and French engravers came in with King William to lay the groundwork.

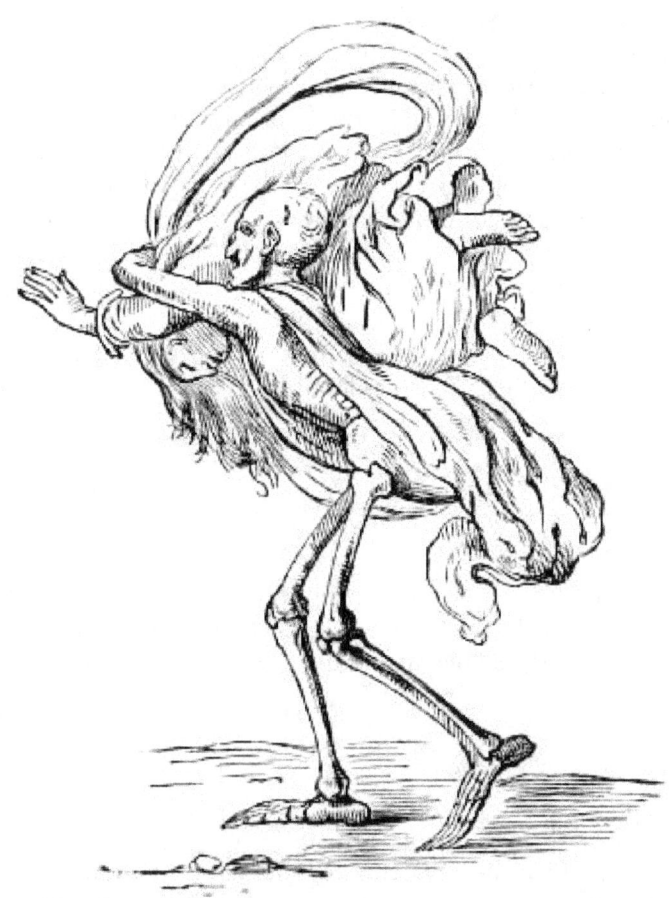

No. 170. Death carrying off his Prey.

CHAPTER XIX.

THE SATIRICAL LITERATURE OF THE SIXTEENTH CENTURY.—PASQUIL.—
MACARONIC POETRY.—THE EPISTOLÆ OBSURORUM VIRORUM.—RABELAIS.—
COURT OF THE QUEEN OF NAVARRE, AND ITS LITERARY CIRCLE;
BONAVENTURE DES PERIERS.—HENRI ETIENNE.—THE LIGUE, AND ITS SATIRE:
THE "SATYRE MÉNIPPÉE."

The sixteenth century, especially on the Continent, was a period of that sort of violent agitation which is most favourable to the growth of satire. Society was breaking up, and going through a course of decomposition, and it presented to the view on every side spectacles which provoked the mockery, perhaps more than the indignation, of lookers-on. Even the clergy had learnt to laugh at themselves, and almost at their own religion; and people who thought or reflected were gradually separating into two classes—those who cast all religion from them, and rushed into a jeering scepticism, and those who entered seriously and with resolution into the work of reformation. The latter found most encouragement among the Teutonic nations, while the sceptical element appears to have had its birth in Italy, and even in Rome itself, where, among popes and cardinals, religion had degenerated into empty forms.

At some period towards the close of the fifteenth century, a mutilated ancient statue was accidentally dug up in Rome, and it was erected on a pedestal in a place not far from the Ursini Palace. Opposite it stood the shop of a shoemaker, named Pasquillo, or Pasquino, the latter being the form most commonly adopted at a later period. This Pasquillo was notorious as a facetious fellow, and his shop was usually crowded by people who went there to tell tales and hear news; and, as no other name had been invented for the statue, people agreed to give it the name of the shoemaker, and they called it Pasquillo. It became a custom, at certain seasons, to write on pieces of paper satirical epigrams, sonnets, and other short compositions in Latin or Italian, mostly of a personal character, in which the writer declared whatever he had seen or heard to the discredit of somebody, and these were published by depositing them with the statue, whence they were taken and read. One of the Latin epigrams which pleads against committing these short personal satires to print, calls the time at which it was usual to compose them Pasquil's festival:—

Jam redit illa dies in qua Romana juventus
Pasquilli festum concelebrabit ovans.
Sed versus impressos obsecro ut edere omittas,
Ne noceant iterum quæ nocuere semel.

The festival was evidently a favourite one, and well celebrated. "The soldiers of Xerxes," says another epigram, placed in Pasquil's mouth, "were not so plentiful as the paper bestowed upon me; I shall soon become a bookseller"—

Armigerûm Xerxi non copia tanta papyri
Quanta mihi: fiam bibliopola statim.

The name of Pasquil was soon given to the papers which were deposited with the statue, and eventually a *pasquil*, or *pasquin*, was only another name for a lampoon or libel. Not far from this statue stood another, which was found in the forum of Mars (*Martis forum*), and was thence popularly called Marforio. Some of these satirical writings were composed in the form of dialogues between Pasquil and Marforio, or of messages from one to the other.

A collection of these pasquils was published in 1544 in two small volumes.[94] Many of them are extremely clever, and they are sharply pointed. The popes are frequent objects of bitterest satire. Thus we are reminded in two lines upon pope Alexander VI. (*sextus*), the infamous Borgia, that Tarquin had been a Sextus, and Nero also, and now another Sextus was at the head of the Romans, and told that Rome was always ruined under a Sextus—

De Alexandro VI. Pont.
Sextus Tarquinius, Sextus Nero, Sextus et iste:
Semper sub Sextis perdita Roma fuit.

The following is given for an epitaph on Lucretia Borgia, pope Alexander's profligate daughter:—

Hoc tumulo dormit Lucretia nomine, sed re
Thais, Alexandri filia, sponsa, nurus.

In another of a rather later date, Rome, addressing herself to Pasquil, is made to complain of two successive popes, Clement VII. (Julio de Medicis, 1523--1534) and Paul III. (Alexandro Farnese, 1534-1549), and also of Leo X. (1513-1521). "I am," Rome says, "sick enough with the physician (*Medicus*, as a pun on the Medicis), I was also the prey of the lion (*Leo*), now, Paul, you tear my vitals like a wolf. You, Paul, are not a god to me, as I thought in my folly, but you are a wolf, since you tear the food from my mouth"—

Sum Medico satis ægra, fui quoque præda Leonis,
Nunc mea dilaceras viscera, Paule, lupus.
Non es, Paule, mihi numen, ceu stulta putabam,
Sed lupus es, quoniam subtrahis ore cibum.

Another epigram, addressed to Rome herself, involves a pun in Greek (in the words *Paulos*, Paul, and *Phaulos*, wicked). "Once, Rome," it says, "lords of lords were thy subjects, now thou in thy wretchedness art subject to the serfs of serfs; once you listened to the oracles of St. Paul, but now you perform the abominable commands of the wicked"—

Quondam, Roma, tibi suberant domini dominorum,
Servorum servis nunc miseranda subes;
Audisti quondam divini oracula Παύλου,
At nunc των φαύλων jussa nefanda facis.

The idea, of course, is the contrast of Rome in her Pagan glory, with Rome in her Christian debasement, very much the same as that which struck Gibbon, and gave birth to his great history of Rome's "decline and fall."[95]

The pasquils formed a body of satire which struck indiscriminately at everybody within its range, but satirists were now rising who took for their subjects special cases of the general disorder. Rotten at the heart, society presented an external glossiness, a mixture of pedantry and affectation, which offered subjects enough for ridicule in whatever point of view it was taken. The ecclesiastical body was in a state of fermentation, out of which new feelings and new doctrines were about to rise. The old learning and literature of the middle ages remained in form after their spirit had passed away, and they were now contending clumsily and unsuccessfully against new learning and literature of a more refined and healthier character. Feudalism itself had fallen, or it was struggling vainly against new political principles, yet the aristocracy clung to feudal forms and feudal assumptions, with an exaggeration which was meant for an appearance of strength. Among the literary affectations of this false feudalism, was the fashion for reading the long, dry, old romances of chivalry; while the churchmen and schoolmen were corrupting the language in which mediæval learning had been expressed, into a form the most barbarous, or introducing words compounded from the later into the vernacular tongue. These peculiarities were among the first to provoke literary satire. Italy, where this class of satire originated, gave it its name also, though it appears still to be a matter of doubt why it was called *macaronic*, or in its Italian form *maccharonea*. Some have considered this name to have been taken from the article of food called *macaroni*, to which the Italians were, and still are, so much attached; while others pretend that it was derived from an old Italian word *macarone*, which meant a lubberly fellow. Be this, however, as it may, what is called macaronic composition, which consists in giving a Latin form to words taken from the vulgar tongue, and mixing them with words which are purely Latin, was introduced in Italy at the close of the fifteenth century.

Four Italian writers in macaronic verse are known to have lived before the year 1500.[96] The first of these was named Fossa, and he tells us that he composed his poem entitled "Vigonce," on the second day of May, 1494. It was printed in 1502. Bassano, a native of Mantua, and the author of a macaronic which bears no title, was dead in 1499; and another, a Paduan named Fifi degli Odassi, was born about the year 1450. Giovan Georgio Allione, of Asti, who is believed also to have written during the last ten years of the fifteenth century, is a name better known through the edition of his French works, published by Monsieur J. C. Brunet in 1836. All these present the same coarseness and vulgarity of sentiment, and the same licence in language and description, which appear to have been taken as necessary characteristics of macaronic composition. Odassi appears to give support to the derivation of the name from macaroni, by making the principal character of his poem a fabricator of that article in Padua—

Est unus in Padua natus speciale cusinus,
In maccharonea princeps bonus atque magister.

But the great matter of macaronic poetry was Teofilo Folengo, of whose life we know just sufficient to give us a notion of the personal character of these old literary caricaturists. Folengo was descended from a noble family, which had its seat at the village of Cipada, near Mantua, where he was born on the 8th of November, 1491, and baptised by the name of Girolamo. He pursued his studies, first in the university of Ferrara, under the professor Visago Cocaio, and afterwards in that of Bologna, under Pietro Pomponiazzo; or rather, he ought to have pursued them, for his love of poetry, and his gaiety of character, led him to neglect them, and at length his irregularities became so great, that he was obliged to make a hasty flight from Bologna. He was ill received at home, and he left it also, and appears to have subsequently led a wild life, during part of which he adopted the profession of a soldier, until at length he took refuge in a Benedictine convent near Brescia, in 1507, and became a monk. The discipline of this house had become entirely relaxed, and the monks appear to have lived very licentiously; and Folengo, who, on his admission to the order, had exchanged his former baptismal name for Teofilo, readily conformed to their example. Eventually he abandoned the convent and the habit, ran away with a lady named Girolama Dedia, and for some years he led a wandering, and, it would seem, very irregular life. Finally, in 1527, he returned to his old profession of a monk, and remained in it until his death, in the December of 1544. He is said to have been extremely vain of his poetical talents, and a story is told of him which, even if it were invented, illustrates well the character which was popularly given to him. It is said that when young, he aspired to excel in Latin poetry, and that he wrote an epic which he himself believed to be *superior* to the Æneid. When, however, he had communicated the work to his friend the bishop of Mantua, and that prelate, intending to compliment him, told him that he had equalled Virgil, he was so mortified, that he threw the manuscript on the fire, and from that time devoted his talents entirely to the composition of macaronic verse.

Such was the man who has justly earned the reputation of being the first of macaronic poets. When he adopted this branch of literature, while he was in the university of Bologna, he assumed in writing it the name of Merlinus Cocaius, or Coccaius, probably from the name of his professor at Ferrara. Folengo's printed poems consist of—1. The Zanitonella, a pastoral in seven eclogues, describing the love of Tonellus for Zanina; 2, the macaronic romance of Baldus, Folengo's principal and most remarkable work; 3, the Moschæa, or dreadful battle between the flies and the ants; and 4, a book of Epistles and Epigrams.

The first edition of the Baldus appeared in 1517. It is a sort of parody on the romances of chivalry, and combines a jovial satire upon everything, which, as has been remarked, spares neither religion nor politics, science nor literature, popes, kings, clergy, nobility, or people. It consists of twenty-five cantos, or, as they are termed in the original, *phantasiæ*, fantasies. In the first we are told of the origin of Baldus. There was at the court of France a famous knight named Guy, descended from that memorable paladin Renaud of Montauban. The king, who showed a particular esteem for Guy, had also a daughter of surpassing beauty, named Balduine, who had fallen in love with Guy, and he was equally amorous of the princess. In the sequel of a grand tournament, at which Guy has distinguished himself greatly, he carries off Balduine, and the two lovers fly on foot, in the disguise of beggars, reach the Alps in safety, and cross them into Italy. At Cipada, in the territory of Brescia, they are hospitably entertained by a generous peasant named Berte Panade, with whom the princess Balduine, who approaches her time of confinement, is left; while her lover goes forth to conquer at least a marquisate for her. After his departure she gives birth to a fine boy, which is named Baldus. Such, as told in the second canto, is the origin of Folengo's hero, who is destined to perform marvellous acts of chivalry. The peasant Berte Panade has also a son named Zambellus, by a mother who had died in childbirth of him. Baldus passes for the son of Berte also, so that the two are supposed to be brothers. Baldus is successively led through a series of extraordinary adventures, some low and vulgar, others more chivalrous, and some of them exhibiting a wild fertility of imagination, which are too long to enable me to take my readers through them, until at length he is left by the poet in the country of Falsehood and Charlatanism, which is inhabited by astrologers, necromancers, and poets. Thus is the hero Baldus dragged through a great number of marvellous accidents, some of them vulgar, many of them ridiculous, and some, again, wildly poetical, but all of them presenting, in one form or other, an opportunity for satire upon some of the follies, or vices, or corruptions of his age. The hybrid language in which the whole is written, gives it a singularly grotesque appearance; yet from time to time we have passages which show that the author was capable of writing true poetry, although it is mixed with a great amount of coarse and licentious ideas, expressed no less coarsely and licentiously. What we may term the filth, indeed, forms a large proportion of the Italian macaronic poetry. The pastoral of Zanitonella presents, as might be expected, more poetic beauty than the romance of Balbus. As an example of the language of the latter, and indeed of that of the Italian macaronics in general, I give a few lines of a description of a storm at sea, from the twelfth canto, with a literal translation:—

Jam gridor æterias hominum concussit abyssos,
Sentiturque ingens cordarum stridor, et ipse
Pontus habet pavidos vultus, mortisque colores.
Nunc Sirochus habit palmam, nunc Borra superchiat;
Irrugit pelagus, tangit quoque fluctibus astra,
Fulgure flammigero creber lampezat Olympus;
Vela forata micant crebris lacerata balottis;
Horrendam mortem nautis ea cuncta minazzant.
Nunc sbalzata ratis celsum tangebat Olympum,
Nunc subit infernam unda sbadacchiante paludem.
TRANSLATION
Now the clamour of the men shook the ethereal abysses,
And the mighty crashing of the ropes is felt, and the very
Sea has pale looks, and the hue of death.
Now the Sirocco has the palm, now Eurus exults over it;
The sea roars, and touches the stars with its waves,
Olympus continually blazes out with flaming thunder,
The pierced sails glitter torn with frequent thunderbolts;
All these threaten frightful death to the sailors.
Now the ship tossed up touched the top of Olympus,
Now, the wave yawning, it sinks into the infernal lake.

Teofilo Folengo was followed by a number of imitators, of whom it will be sufficient to state that he stands in talent as far above his followers as above those who preceded him. One of these minor Italian macaronic writers, named Bartolommeo Bolla, of Bergamo, who flourished in the latter half of the sixteenth century, had the vanity to call himself, in the title of one of his books, "the Apollo of poets, and the Cocaius of this age;" but a modern critic has remarked of him that he is as far removed from his model Folengo, as his native town Bergamo is distant from Siberia. An earlier poet, named Guarino Capella, a native of the town of Sarsina, in the country of Forli, on the borders of Tuscany, approached far nearer in excellence to the prince of macaronic writers. His work also is a mock romance, the history of "Cabrinus, king of Gagamagoga," in six books or cantos, which was printed at Arimini in 1526, and is now a book of excessive rarity.

The taste for macaronics passed rather early, like all other fashions in that age, from Italy into France, where it first brought into literary reputation a man who, if he had not the great talent of Folengo, possessed a very considerable amount of wit and gaiety. Antoine de la Sable, who Latinised his name into Antonius de Arena, was born of a highly respectable family at Soliers, in the diocese of Toulon, about the year 1500, and, being destined from his youth to follow the profession of the law, studied under the celebrated jurisconsult Alciatus. He had only arrived at the simple dignity of *juge*, at St. Remy, in the diocese of Arles, when he died in the year 1544. In fact, he appears to have been no very diligent student, and we gather from his own confessions that his youth had been rather wild. The volume containing his macaronics, the second edition of which (as far as the editions are known) was printed in 1529, bears a title which will give some notion of the character of its contents,—"*Provencalis de bragardissima villa de Soleriis, ad suos compagnones qui sunt de persona friantes, bassas dansas et branlas practicantes novellas, de guerra Romana, Neapolitana, et Genuensi mandat; una cum epistola ad falotissimam suam garsam, Janam Rosæam, pro passando tempora*"—(*i.e.* a Provençal of the most swaggering town of Soliers, sends this to his companions, who are dainty of their persons, practising basse dances and new brawls, concerning the war of Rome, Naples, and Genoa; with an epistle to his most merry wench, Jeanne Rosée, for pastime). In the first of these poems Arena traces in his burlesque verse, which is an imitation of Folengo, his own adventures and sufferings in the war in Italy which led to the sack of Rome, in 1527, and in the subsequent expeditions to Naples and Genoa. From the picture of the horrors of war, he passes very willingly to describe the joyous manners of the students in Provençal universities, of whom he tells us, that they are all fine gallants, and always in love with the pretty girls.

Gentigalantes sunt omnes instudiantes,
Et bellas garsas semper amare solent.

He goes on to describe the scholars as great quarrellers, as well as lovers of the other sex, and after dwelling on their gaiety and love of the dance, he proceeds to treat in the same burlesque style on the subject of dancing; but I pass over this to speak of Arena's principal piece, the satirical description of the invasion of Provence by the emperor Charles V. in 1536. This curious poem, which is entitled "Meygra Enterprisa Catoloqui imperatoris," and which extends to upwards of two thousand lines, opens with a laudatory address to the king of France, François I., and with a sneer at the pride of the emperor, who, believing himself to be the master of the whole world, had foolishly thought to take away France and the cities of Provence from their rightful monarch. It was Antonio de Leyva, the boaster, who had put this project into the emperor's head, and they had already pillaged and ravaged a good part of Provence, and were dividing the plunder, when, harassed continually by the peasantry, the invaders were brought to a stand by the difficulty of subsisting in a devastated country, and by the diseases to which this difficulty gave rise. Nevertheless, the Spaniards and their allies committed terrible devastation, which is described by Arena in strong language. He commemorates the valiant resistance of his native town of Soliers, which, however, was taken and sacked, and he lost in it his house and property. Arles held the imperialists at bay, while the French, under the constable Montmorency, established themselves firmly at Avignon. At length disease gained possession of Antonio de Leyva himself, and the emperor, who had been making an unsuccessful demonstration against Marseilles, came to him in his sickness. The first lines of the description of this interview, will serve as a specimen of the language of the French macaronics:—

Sed de Marsella bragganti quando retornat,
Fort male contentus, quando repolsat eum,
Antonium Levam trobavit forte maladum,
Cui mors terribilis triste cubile parat.
Ethica torquet eum per costas, et dolor ingens:
Cum male res vadit, vivere fachat eum.
Dixerunt medici, speransa est nulla salutis:
Ethicus in testa vivere pauca potest.
Ante suam mortem voluit parlare per horam
Imperelatori, consiliumque dare.
Scis, Cæsar, stricte nostri groppantur amores,
Namque duas animas corpus utrumque tenet,
Heu! fuge Provensam fortem, fuge littus amarum,
Fac tibi non noceat gloria tanta modo.
TRANSLATION.
But when he returns from boasting Marseilles,
Very ill content, that she had repulsed him,
He found Antonio de Leyva very ill,
For whom terrible death is preparing a sorrowful bed.
Hectic fever tortures him in the ribs, and great pain;
Since things are going ill, he is weary of life.
Before his death he wished to speak an hour
To the emperor, and to give him counsel.
"You know, Cæsar, our affections are closely bound together,
For either body holds the two souls,
Alas! fly Provence the strong, fly the bitter shore,
Take care that your great glory prove not an injury to you."

Thus Leyva goes on to persuade the emperor to abandon his enterprise, and then dies. Arena exults over his death, and over the emperor's grief for his loss, and then proceeds to describe the disastrous retreat of the imperial army, and the glory of France in her king.

Antonius de Arena wrote with vigour and humour, but his verses are tame in comparison with his model, Folengo. The taste for macaronic verse never took strong root in France, and the few obscure writers who attempted to shine in that kind of composition are now forgotten, except by the laborious bibliographer. One named Jean Germain, wrote a macaronic history of the invasion of Provence by the imperialists in rivalry of Arenas. I will not follow the taste for this class of burlesque composition into Spain or Germany, but merely add that it was not adopted in England until the beginning of the seventeenth century, when several authors employed it at about the same time. The most perfect example of these early English macaronics is the "Polemo-Middiana," *i.e.* battle of the dunghill, by the talented and elegant-minded Drummond of Hawthornden. We may take a single example of the English macaronic from this poem, which will not need an English translation. One of the female characters in the dunghill war, calls, among others, to her aid—

Hunc qui dirtiferas tersit cum dishclouty dishras,
Hunc qui gruelias scivit bene lickere plettas,
Et saltpannifumos, et widebricatos fisheros,
Hellæosque etiam salteros duxit ab antris,
Coalheughos nigri girnantes more divelli;
Lifeguardamque sibi sævas vocat improba lassas,
Maggyam magis doctam milkare covœas,

Et doctam suepare flouras, et sternere beddas,
Quæque novit spinnare, et longas ducere threddas;
Nansyam, claves bene quæ keepaverat omnes,
Quæque lanam cardare solet greasy-fingria Betty.

Perhaps before this was written, the eccentric Thomas Coryat had published in the volume of his Crudities, printed in 1611, a short piece of verse, which is perfect in its macaronic style, but in which Italian and other foreign words are introduced, as well as English. The celebrated comedy of "Ignoramus," composed by George Ruggle in 1615, may also be mentioned as containing many excellent examples of English macaronics.

While Italy was giving birth to macaronic verse, the satire upon the ignorance and bigotry of the clergy was taking another form in Germany, which arose from some occurrences which it will be necessary to relate. In the midst of the violent religious agitation at the beginning of the sixteenth century in Germany, there lived a German Jew named Pfeffercorn, who embraced Christianity, and to show his zeal for his new faith, he obtained from the emperor an edict ordering the Talmud and all the Jewish writings which were contrary to the Christian faith to be burnt. There lived at the same time a scholar of distinction, and of more liberal views than most of the scholastics of his time, named John Reuchlin. He was a relative of Melancthon, and was secretary to the palsgrave, who was tolerant like himself. The Jews, as might be expected, were unwilling to give up their books to be burnt, and Reuchlin wrote in their defence, under the assumed name of Capnion, which is a Hebrew translation of his own name of Reuchlin, meaning smoke, and urged that it was better to refute the books in question than to burn them. The converted Pfeffercorn replied in a book entitled "Speculum Manuale," in answer to which Reuchlin wrote his "Speculum Oculare." The controversy had already provoked much bigoted ill-feeling against Reuchlin. The learned doctors of the university of Cologne espoused the cause of Pfeffercorn, and the principal of the university, named in Latin Ortuinus Gratius, supported by the Sorbonne in Paris, lent himself to be the violent organ of the intolerant party. Hard pressed by his bigoted opponents, Reuchlin found good allies, but one of the best of these was a brave baron named Ulric von Hutten, of an old and noble family, born in 1488 in the castle of Staeckelberg, in Franconia. He had studied in the schools at Fulda, Cologne, and Frankfort on the Oder, and distinguished himself so much as a scholar, that he obtained the degree of Master of Arts before the usual age. But Ulric possessed an adventurous and chivalrous spirit, which led him to embrace the profession of a soldier, and he served in the wars in Italy, where he was distinguished by his bravery. He was at Rome in 1516, and defended Reuchlin against the Dominicans. The same year appeared the first edition of that marvellous book, the "Epistolæ Obscurorum Virorum," one of the most remarkable satires that the world has yet seen. It is believed that this book came entirely from the pen of Ulric von Hutten; and the notion that Reuchlin himself, or any others of his friends, had a share in it appears to be without foundation. Ulric was in the following year made poet-laureat. Nevertheless, this book greatly incensed the monks against him, and he was often threatened with assassination. Yet he boldly advocated the cause and embraced the opinions of Luther, and was one of the staunch supporters of Lutheranism. After a very turbulent life, Ulric von Hutten died in the August of the year 1523.

The "Epistolæ Obscurorum Virorum," or letters of obscure men, are supposed to be addressed to Ortuinus Gratius, mentioned above, by various individuals, some his scholars, others his friends, but all belonging to the bigoted party opposed to Reuchlin, and they were designed to throw ridicule on the ignorance, bigotry, and immorality of the clergy of the Romish church. The old scholastic learning had become debased into a heavy and barbarous system of theology, literary composition consisted in writing a no less barbarous Latin, and even the few classical writers who were admitted into the schools, were explained and commented upon in a strange half-theological fashion. These old scholastics were bitterly opposed to the new learning, which had taken root in

Italy, and was spreading abroad, and they spoke contemptuously of it as "secular." The letters of the obscure individuals relate chiefly to the dispute between Reuchlin and Pfeffercorn, to the rivalry between the old scholarship and the new, and to the low licentious lives of the theologists; and they are written in a style of Latin which is intended for a parody on that of the latter, and which closely resembles that which we call "dog-Latin."[97] They are full of wit and humour of the most exquisite description, but they too often descend into details, treated in terms which can only be excused by the coarse and licentious character of the age. The literary and scientific questions discussed in these letters are often very droll. The first in order of the correspondents of Ortuinus Gratius, who boasts of the rather formidable name, Thomas Langschneiderius, and addresses master Ortuinus as "poet, orator, philosopher, and theologist, and more if he would," propounds to him a difficult question:—

"There was here one day an Aristotelian dinner, and doctors, licenciates, and masters too, were very jovial, and I was there too, and we drank at the first course three draughts of Malmsey, ... and then we had six dishes of flesh and chickens and capons, and one of fish, and as we passed from one dish to another, we continually drunk wine of Kotzburg and the Rhine, and ale of Embeck, and Thurgen, and Neuburg. And the masters were well satisfied, and said that the new masters had acquitted themselves well and with great honour. Then the masters in their hilarity began to talk learnedly on great questions, and one asked whether it were correct to say *magister nostrandus*, or *noster magistrandus*, for a person fit to be made doctor in theology.... And immediately Master Warmsemmel, who is a subtle Scotist, and has been master eighteen years, and was in his time twice rejected and thrice delayed for the degree of master, and he went on offering himself, until he was promoted for the honour of the university, ... spoke, and held that we should say *noster magistrandus*.... Then Master Andreas Delitsch, who is very subtle, and half poet, half artist (*i.e.* one who professed in the faculty of arts), physician, and jurist; and now he reads ordinarily 'Ovid on the Metamorphoses,' and expounds all the fables allegorically and literally, and I was his hearer, because he expounds very fundamentally, and he also reads at home Quintillian and Juvencus, and he held the opposite to Master Warmsemmel, and said that we ought to say *magister nostrandus*. For as there is a difference between *magister noster* and *noster magister*, so also there is a difference between *magister nostrandus* and *noster magistrandus*; for a doctor in theology is called *magister noster*, and it is one word, but *noster magister* are two words, and it is taken for any master; and he quoted Horace in support of this. Then the masters much admired his subtlety, and one drank to him a cup of Neuburg ale. And he said, 'I will wait, but spare me,' and touched his hat, and laughed heartily, and drank to Master Warmsemmel, and said, 'There, master, don't think I am an enemy,' and he drank it off at one draught, and Master Warmsemmel replied to him with a strong draught. And the masters were all merry till the bell rang for Vespers."

Master Ortuin is pressed for his judgment on this weighty question. A similar scene described in another letter ends less peacefully. The correspondent on this occasion is Magister Bornharddus Plumilegus, who addresses Ortuinus Gratius as follows:—

"Wretched is the mouse which has only one hole for a refuge! So also I may say of myself, most venerable sir, for I should be poor if I had only one friend, and when that one should fail me, then I should not have another to treat me with kindness. As is the case now with a certain poet here, who is called George Sibutus, and he is one of the secular poets, and reads publicly in poetry, and is in other respects a good fellow (*bonus socius*). But as you know these poets, when they are not theologists like you, will always reprehend others, and despise the theologists. And once in a drinking party in his house, when we were drinking Thurgen ale, and sat until the hour of tierce, and I was moderately drunk, because that ale rose into my head, then there was one who was not before friendly with me, and I drank to him half a cup, and he accepted it. But afterwards he would not return the compliment. And thrice I cautioned him, and he would not reply, but sat in silence and said nothing. Then I thought to myself, Behold this man treats thee with contempt, and is proud, and always wants to confound you. And I was stirred in my anger, and took the cup, and threw it at his head. Then that poet was angry at me, and said that I had caused a disturbance in his house, and said I should go out of his house in the devil's name. Then I replied, 'What matter is it if you are my enemy? I have had as bad enemies as you, and yet I have stood in spite of them. What matters it if you are a poet? I have other poets who are my friends, and they are quite as good as you, *ego bene merdarem in vestram poetriam*! Do you think I am a fool, or that I was born under a tree like apples?' Then he called me an ass, and said that I never saw a poet. And I said, 'You are an ass in your skin, I have seen many more poets than you.' And I spoke of you.... Wherefore I ask you very earnestly to write me one piece of verse, and then I will show it to this poet and others, and I will boast that you are my friend, and you are a much better poet than he."

The war against the secular poets, or advocates of the new learning, is kept up with spirit through this ludicrous correspondence. One correspondent presses Ortuinus Gratius to "write to me whether it be necessary for eternal salvation that scholars learn grammar from the secular poets, such as Virgil, Tullius, Pliny, and others; for," he adds, "it seems to me that this is not a good method of studying." "As I have often written to you," says another, "I am grieved that this ribaldry (*ista ribaldria*), namely, the faculty of poetry, becomes common, and is spread through all provinces and regions. In my time there was only one poet, who was called Samuel; and now, in this city alone, there are at least twenty, and they vex us all who hold with the ancients. Lately I thoroughly defeated one, who said that *scholaris* does not signify a person who goes to the school for the purpose of learning; and I said, 'Ass! will you correct the holy doctor who expounded this word?'" The new learning was, of course, identified with the supporters of Reuchlin. "It is said here," continues the same correspondent, "that all the poets will side with doctor Reuchlin against the theologians. I wish all the poets were in the place where pepper grows, that they might let us go in peace!"

Master William Lamp, "master of arts," sends to Master Ortuinus Gratius, a narrative of his adventures in a journey from Cologne to Rome. First he went to Mayence, where his indignation was moved by the open manner in which people spoke in favour of Reuchlin, and when he hazarded a contrary opinion, he was only laughed at, but he held his tongue, because his opponents all carried arms and looked fierce. "One of them is a count, and is a long man, and has white hair; and they say that he takes a man in armour in his hand, and throws him to the ground, and he has a sword as long as a giant; when I saw him, then I held my tongue." At Worms, he found things no better, for the "doctors" spoke bitterly against the theologians, and when he attempted to expostulate, he got foul words as well as threats, a learned doctor in medicine affirming "*quod merdaret super nos omnes.*" On leaving Worms, Lamp and his companion, another theologist, fell in with plunderers who made them pay two florins to drink, "and I said *occulte*, Drink what may the devil bless to you!" Subsequently they fell into low amours at country inns, which are described coarsely, and then they reached Insprucken, where they found the emperor, and his court and army, with whole manners and proceedings Magister Lamp became sorely disgusted. I pass over other adventures till they reach Mantua, the birthplace of Virgil, and of a late mediæval Latin poet, named from it Baptista Mantuanus. Lamp, in his hostile spirit towards the "secular poets," proceeds,—"And my companion said, 'Here Virgil was born.' I replied, 'What do I care for that pagan? We will go to the Carmelites, and see Baptista Mantuanus, who is twice as good as Virgil, as I have heard full ten times from Ortuinus;' and I told him how you once reprehended Donatus, when he says, 'Virgil was the most learned of poets, and the best;' and you said, 'If Donatus were here, I would tell him to his face that he lies, for Baptista Mantuanus is above Virgil.' And when we came to the monastery of the Carmelites, we were told that Baptista Mantuanus was dead; then I said, 'May he rest in peace!'" They continued their journey by Bologna, where they found the inquisitor Jacob de Hochstraten, and Florence, to Siena. "After this there are small towns, and one is called Monte-flascon, where we drunk excellent wine, such as I never drank in my life. And I asked the host what that wine is called, and he replied that it is lachryma Christi. Then said my companion, 'I wish Christ would cry in our country!' And so we drank a good bout, and two days after we entered Rome."

In the course of these letters the theologists, the poets especially, the character of the clergy, and particularly Reuchlin and Pfeffercorn, afford continual subjects for dispute and pleasantry. The last mentioned individual, in the opinion of some, had merited hanging for theft, and it was pretended that the Jews had expelled him from their society for his wicked courses. One argued that all Jews stink, and as it was well known that Pfeffercorn continued to stink like a Jew, it was quite evident that he could not be a good Christian. Some of Ortuinus's correspondents consult him on difficult theological questions. Here is an example in a letter from one Henricus Schaffmulius, another of his scholars who had made the journey to Rome:—

"Since, before I journeyed to the Court, you said to me that I am to write often to you, and that sometimes I am to send you any theological questions, which you will solve for me better than the courtiers of Rome, therefore now I ask your mastership what you hold as to the case when any one on a Friday, or any other fast day, eats an egg, and there is a chicken inside. Because the other day we sat in a tavern in the Campo-flore, and made a collation, and eat eggs, and I, opening an egg, saw that there was a young chicken in it, which I showed to my companion, and then he said, 'Eat it quickly before the host sees it, for if he sees it, then you will be obliged to give a carlino or a julio for a hen, because it is the custom here that, when the host places anything on the table, you must pay for it, for they will not take it back. And when he sees there is a young hen in the egg, he will say, Pay me for the hen, because he reckons a small one the same as a large one.' And I immediately sucked up the egg, and with it the chicken, and afterwards I bethought me that it was Friday, and I said to my companion. 'You have caused me to commit a mortal sin, in eating flesh on Friday.' And he said that it is not a mortal sin, nor even a venial sin, because that embryo of a chicken is not reckoned other than an egg till it is born; and he told me that it is as in cheeses, in which there are sometimes worms, and in cherries, and fresh peas and beans, yet they are eaten on Fridays, and also in the vigils of the apostles. But the hosts are such rogues, that they say that they are flesh, that they may have more money. Then I went away, and thought about it. And, *per Deum*! Magister Ortuinus, I am much troubled, and I know not how I ought to rule myself. If I went to ask advice of a courtier [of the papal court], I know that they have not good consciences. It seems to me that these young hens in the eggs are flesh, because the matter is already formed and figured in members and bodies of an animal, and it has life; it is otherwise with worms in cheeses and other things, because worms are reputed for fishes, as I have heard from a physician, who is a very good naturalist. Therefore I ask you very earnestly, that you will give me your reply on this question. Because if you hold that it is a mortal sin, then I will purchase an absolution here, before I return to Germany. Also you must know that our master Jacobus de Hochstraten has obtained a thousand florins from the bank, and I think that with these he will gain his cause, and the devil confound that John Reuchlin, and the other poets and jurists, because they will be against the church of God, that is, against the theologists, in whom is founded the church, as Christ said: Thou art Peter, and upon this rock I will build my church. And so I commend you to the Lord God. Farewell. Given from the city of Rome."

While in Italy macaronic literature was reaching its greatest perfection, there arose in the very centre of France a man of great original genius, who was soon to astonish the world by a new form of satire, more grotesque and more comprehensive than anything that had been seen before. Teofilo Folengo may fairly be considered as the precursor of Rabelais, who appears to have taken the Italian satirist as his model. What we know of the life of François Rabelais is rather obscure at best, and is in some parts no doubt fabulous. He was born at Chinon in Touraine, either in 1483 or in 1487, for this seems to be a disputed point, and some doubt has been thrown on the trade or profession of his father, but the most generally received opinion is that he was an apothecary. He is said to have shown from his youth a disposition more inclined to gaiety than to serious pursuits, yet at an early age he had made great proficiency in learning, and is said to have acquired a very sufficient knowledge of Latin, Greek, and Hebrew, two of which, at least, were not popular among the popish clergy, and not only of the modern languages and literature of Italy, Germany, and Spain, but even of Arabic. Probably this estimate of his acquirements in learning is rather exaggerated. It is not quite clear where the young Rabelais gained all this knowledge, for he is said to have been educated in convents and among monks, and to have become at a rather early age a Franciscan friar in the convent of Fontenai-le-Compte, in Lower Poitou, where he became an object of jealousy and ill-feeling to the other friars by his superior acquirements. It was a tradition, at least, that the conduct of Rabelais was not very strictly conventual, and that he had so far shown his contempt for monastic rule, and for the bigotry of the Romish church, that he was condemned to the prison of his monastery, upon a diet of bread and water, which, according to common report, was very uncongenial with the tastes of this jovial friar. Out of this difficulty he is said to have been helped by his friend the bishop of Maillezais, who obtained for him the pope's licence to change the order of St. Francis for the much more easy and liberal order of St. Benedict, and he became a member of the bishop's own chapter in the abbey of Maillezais. His unsteady temper, however, was not long satisfied with this retreat, which he left, and, laying aside the regular habit, assumed that of a secular priest. In this character he wandered for some time, and then settled at Montpellier, where he took a degree as doctor in medicine, and practised for some time with credit. There he published in 1532 a translation of some works of Hippocrates and Galen, which he dedicated to his friend the bishop of Maillezais. The circumstances under which he left Montpellier are not known, but he is supposed to have gone to Paris upon some business of the university, and to have remained there. He found there a staunch friend in Jean de Bellay, bishop of Paris, who soon afterwards was raised to the rank of cardinal. When the cardinal de Bellay went as ambassador to Rome from the court of France, Rabelais accompanied him, it is said in the character of his private medical adviser, but during his stay in the metropolis of Christendom, as Christendom was understood in those days by the Romish church, Rabelais obtained, on the 17th of January, 1536 the papal absolution for all his transgressions, and licence to return to Maillezais, and practise medicine there and elsewhere as an act of charity. Thus he became again a Benedictine monk. He, however, changed again, and became a secular canon, and finally settled down as the curé of Meudon, near Paris, with which he also held a fair number of ecclesiastical benefices. Rabelais died in 1553, according to some in a very religious manner, but others have given strange accounts of his last moments, representing that, even when dying, he conversed in the same spirit of mockery, not only of Romish forms and ceremonies, but of all religions whatever, which was ascribed to him during his life, and which are but too openly manifested in the extraordinary satirical romance which has given so much celebrity to his name.

During the greater part of his life, Rabelais was exposed to troubles and persecutions. He was saved from the intrigues of the monks by the friendly influence of popes and cardinals; and the favour of two successive kings, François I. and Henri II., protected him against the still more dangerous hostility of the Sorbonne and the parliament of Paris. This high protection has been advanced as a reason for rejecting the anecdotes and accounts which have been commonly received relating to the personal character of Rabelais, and his irregularities may possibly have been exaggerated by the hatred which he had drawn upon himself by his writings. But nobody, I think, who knows the character of society at that time, who compares what we know of the lives of the other satirists, and who has read the history of Gargantua and Pantagruel, will consider such an argument of much weight against the deliberate statements of those who were his contemporaries, or be inclined to doubt that the writer of this history was a man of jovial character, who loved a good bottle and a broad joke, and perhaps other things that were equally objectionable. His books present a sort of wild riotous orgy, without much order or plan, except the mere outline of the story, in which is displayed an extraordinary extent of reading in all classes of literature, from the most learned to the most popular, with a wonderful command of language, great imagination, and some poetry, intermixed with a perhaps larger amount of downright obscene ribaldry, than can be found in the macaronics of Folengo, in the "Epistolæ Obscurorum Virorum," or in the works of any of the other satirists who had preceded him, or were his contemporaries. It is a broad caricature, poor enough in its story, but enriched with details, which are brilliant with imagery, though generally coarse, and which are made the occasions for turning to ridicule everything that existed. The five books of this romance were published separately and at different periods, apparently without any fixed intention of continuing them. The earlier editions of the first part were published without date, but the earliest editions with dates belong to the year 1535, when it was several times reprinted. It appeared as the life of Gargantua. This hero is supposed to have flourished in the first half of the fifteenth century, and to have been the son of Grandgousier, king of Utopia, a country which lay somewhere in the direction of Chinon, a prince of an ancient dynasty, but a jovial fellow, who loved good eating and drinking better than anything else. Grandgousier married Gargamelle, daughter of the king of the Parpaillos, who became the mother of Gargantua. The first chapters relate rather minutely how the child was born, and came out at its mother's ear, why it was called Gargantua, how it was dressed and treated in infancy, what were its amusements and disposition, and how Gargantua was put to learning under the sophists, and made no progress. Thereupon Grandgousier sent his son to Paris, to seek instruction there, and he proceeds thither mounted on an immense mare, which had been sent as a present by the king of Numidia—it must be borne in mind that the royal race of Utopia were all giants. At Paris the populace assembled tumultuously to gratify their curiosity in looking at this new scholar; but Gargantua, besides treating them in a very contemptuous manner, carried off the great bells of Notre Dame to suspend at the neck of his mare. Great was the indignation caused by this theft. "All the city was risen up in sedition, they being, as you know, upon any slight occasions, so ready to uproars and insurrections, that foreign nations wonder at the patience of the kings of France, who do not by good justice restrain them from such tumultuous courses." The citizens take counsel, and resolve on sending one of the great orators of the university, Master Janotus de Bragmardo, to expostulate with Gargantua, and obtain the restoration of the bells. The speech which this worthy addresses to Gargantua, in fulfilment of his mission, is an amusing parody on the pedantic style of Parisian oratory. The bells, however, are recovered, and Gargantua, under skilful instructors, pursues his studies with credit, until he is suddenly called home by a letter from his father. In fact, Grandgousier was suddenly involved in a war with his neighbour Picrocole, king of Lerné, caused by a quarrel about cakes between some cake-makers of Lerné and Grandgousier's shepherds, in consequence of which Picrocole had invaded the dominions of Grandgousier, and was plundering and ravaging them. His warlike humour is stirred up by the counsels of his three lieutenants, who persuade him that he is going to become a great conqueror, and that they will make him master of the whole world. It is not difficult to see, in the circumstances of the time, the general aim of the satire contained in the history of this war. It ends in the entire defeat and disappearance of king Picrocole. A sensual and jovial monk named brother Jean des Entommeurs, who has first distinguished himself by his prowess and strength in defending his own abbey against the invaders, contributes largely to the victory gained by Gargantua against his father's enemies, and Gargantua rewards him by founding for him that pleasant abbey of Thélème, a grand establishment, stored with everything which could contribute to terrestrial happiness, from which all hypocrites and bigots were to be excluded, and the rule of which was comprised in the four simple words, "Do as you like."

Such is the history of Gargantua, which was afterwards formed by Rabelais into the first book of his great comic romance. It was published anonymously, the author merely describing himself as "l'abstracteur de quinte essence;" but he afterwards adopted the pseudonyme of Alcofribas Nasier, which is merely an anagram of his own name, François Rabelais. A very improbable story has been handed down to us relating to this book. It is pretended that, having published a book of medical science which had no sale, and the publisher complaining that he had lost money by it, Rabelais promised to make amends for his loss, and immediately wrote the history of Gargantua, by which the same book-seller made his fortune. There can be no doubt that this remarkable satire had a deeper origin than any casual accident like this; but it was exactly suited to the taste and temper of the age. It was quite original in its form and style, and it met with immediate and great success. Numerous editions followed each other rapidly, and its author, encouraged by its popularity, very soon afterwards produced a second romance, in continuation, to which he gave the title of Pantagruel. The caricature in this second romance is bolder even than in the first, the humour broader, and the satire more pungent. Grandgousier has disappeared from the scene, and his son, Gargantua, is king, and has a son named Pantagruel, whose kingdom is that of the Dipsodes. The first part of this new romance is occupied chiefly with Pantagruel's youth and education, and is a satire on the university and on the lawyers, in which the parodies on their style of pleading as then practised is admirable. In the latter part, Pantagruel, like his father Gargantua, is engaged in great wars. It was perhaps the continued success of this new production of his pen which led Rabelais to go on with it, and form the design of making these two books part only of a more extensive romance. During his studies in Paris, Pantagruel has made the acquaintance of a singular individual named Panurge, who becomes his attached friend and constant companion, holding somewhat the position of brother Jean in the first book, but far more crafty and versatile. The whole subject of the third book arises out of Pantagreul's desire to marry, and its various amusing episodes describe the different expedients which, at the suggestion of Panurge, he adopts to arrive at a solution of the question whether his marriage would be fortunate or not.

In publishing his fourth book, Rabelais complains that his writings had raised him enemies, and that he was accused of having at least written heresy. In fact, he had bitterly provoked both the monks and the university and parliament; and, as the increasing reaction of Romanism in France gave more power of persecution to the two latter, he was not writing without some degree of danger, yet the satire of each successive book became bolder and more direct. The fifth, which was left unfinished at his death, and which was published posthumously, was the most severe of them all. The character of Gargantua, indeed, was almost forgotten in that of Pantagruel, and Pantagruelism became an accepted name for the sort of gay, reckless satire of which he was looked upon as the model. He described it himself as a *certaine gaieté d'esprit confite en mépris des choses fortuites*, in fact, neither Romanism nor Protestantism, but simply a jovial kind of Epicurianism. All the gay wits of the time aspired to be Pantagruelists, and the remainder of the sixteenth century abounded in wretched imitations of the style of Rabelais, which are now consigned as mere rarities to the shelves of the bibliophilist.

Among the dangers which began to threaten them in France in the earlier part of the sixteenth century, liberal opinions found an asylum at the court of a princess who was equally distinguished by her beauty, by her talents and noble sentiments, and by her accomplishments. Marguerite d'Angoulême, queen of Navarre, was the only sister of François I., who was her junior by two years, and was affectionately attached to her. She was born on the 11th of April, 1492. She had married, first, that unfortunate duke d'Alençon, whose misconduct at Pavia was the cause of the disastrous defeat of the French, and the captivity of their king. The duke died, it was said of grief at his misfortune, in 1525; and two years afterwards, on the 24th of January, 1527, she married Henri d'Albret, king of Navarre. Their daughter, Jeanne d'Albret, carried this petty royalty to the house of Bourbon, and was the mother of Henri IV.

Marguerite held her court in true princely manner in the castle of Pau or at Nérac, and she loved to surround herself with a circle of men remarkable for their character and talents, and ladies distinguished by beauty and accomplishments, which made it rival in brilliance even that of her brother François. She placed nearest to her person, under the character of her *valets-de-chambre*, the principal poets and *beaux-esprits* of her time, such as Clement Marot, Bonaventure des Periers, Claude Gruget, Antoine du Moulin, and Jean de la Haye, and admitted them to such a tender familiarity of intercourse, as to excite the jealousy of the king her husband, from whose ill-treatment she was only protected by her brother's interference. The poets called her chamber a "veritable Parnassus." Hers was certainly a great mind, greedy of knowledge, dissatisfied with what was, and eager for novelties, and therefore she encouraged all who sought for them. It was in this spirit, combined with her earnest love for letters, that she threw her protection over both the sceptics and the religious reformers. At the beginning of the persecutions, as early as 1523, she openly declared herself the advocate of the Protestants. When Clement Marot was arrested by order of the Sorbonne and the Inquisitor on the charge of having eaten bacon in Lent, Marguerite caused him to be liberated from prison, in defiance of his persecutors. Some of the purest and ablest of the early French reformers, such as Roussel and Le Fèvre d'Etaples, and Calvin himself, found a safe asylum from danger in her dominions. As might be supposed, the bigoted party were bitterly incensed against the queen of Navarre, and were not backward in taking advantage of an opportunity for showing it. A moral treatise, entitled "Le Miroir de l'Ame Pécheresse," of which Marguerite was the author, was condemned by the Sorbonne in 1533, but the king compelled the university, in the person of its rector, Nicolas Cop, to disavow publicly the censure. This was followed by a still greater act of insolence, for, at the instigation of some of the more bigoted papists, the scholars of the college of Navarre, in concert with their regents, performed a farce in which Marguerite was transformed into a fury of hell. François I., greatly indignant, sent his archers to arrest the offenders, who further provoked his anger by resistance, and only obtained their pardon through the generous intercession of the princess whom they had so grossly insulted.

Marguerite was herself a poetess, and she loved above all things those gay, and seldom very delicate, stories, the telling of which was at that time one of the favourite amusements of the evening, and one in which she was known to excel. Her poetical writings were collected and printed, under her own authority, in 1547, by her then *valet-de-chambre*, Jean de la Haye, who dedicated the volume to her daughter. They are all graceful, and some of them worthy of the best poets of her time. The title of this collection was, punning upon her name, which means a pearl, "Marguerites de la Marguerite des princesses, très illustre reyne de Navarre." Marguerite's stories (*nouvelles*) were more celebrated than her verses, and are said to have been committed to writing under her own dictation. All the ladies of her court possessed copies of them in writing. It is understood to have been her intention to form them into ten days' tales, of ten in each day, so as to resemble the "Decameron" of Boccaccio, but only eight days were finished at the time of her death, and the imperfect work was published posthumously by her *valet-de-chambre*, Claude Gruget, under the title of "L'Heptameron, ou Histoire des Amants Fortunés." It is by far the best collection of stories of the sixteenth century. They are told charmingly, in language which is a perfect model of French composition of that age, but they are all tales of gallantry such as could only be repeated in polite society in an age which was essentially licentious. Queen Marguerite died on the 21st of December, 1549, and was buried in the cathedral of Pau. Her death was a subject of regret to all that was good and all that was poetic, not only in France, but in Europe, which had been accustomed to look upon her as the tenth Muse and the fourth Grace:—

Musarum decima et Charitum quarta, inclyta regum
Et soror et conjux, Marguaris illa jacet.

Before Marguerite's death, her literary circle had been broken up by the hatred of religious persecutors. Already, in 1536, the imprudent boldness of Marot had rendered it impossible to protect him any longer, and he had been obliged to retire to a place of concealment, from whence he sometimes paid a stealthy visit to her court. His place of *valet-de-chambre* was given to a man of talents, even more remarkable, and who shared equally the personal esteem of the queen of Navarre, Bonaventure des Periers. Marot's successor paid a graceful compliment to him in a short poem entitled "L'Apologie de Marot absent," published in 1537. The earlier part of the year following witnessed the publication of the most remarkable work of Bonaventure des Periers, the "Cymbalum Mundi," concerning the real character of which writers are still divided in opinion. In it Des Periers introduced a new form of satire, imitated from the dialogues of Lucian. The book consists of four dialogues, written in language which forms a model of French composition, the personages introduced in them intended evidently to represent living characters, whose names are concealed in anagrams and other devices, among whom was Clement Marot. It was the boldest declaration of scepticism which had yet issued from the Epicurean school represented by Rabelais. The author sneers at the Romish church as an imposture, ridicules the Protestants as seekers after the philosopher's stone, and shows disrespect to Christianity itself. Such a book could hardly be published in Paris with impunity, yet it was printed there, secretly, it is said, by a well-known bookseller, Jean Morin, in the Rue St. Jacques, and therefore in the immediate vicinity of the persecuting Sorbonne. Private information had been given of the character of this work, possibly by the printer himself or by one of his men, and on the 6th of March, 1538, when it was on the eve of publication, the whole impression was seized at the printer's, and Morin himself was arrested and thrown into prison. He was treated rigorously, and is understood to have escaped only by disavowing all knowledge of the character of the book, and giving up the name of the author. The first edition of the "Cymbalum Mundi" was burnt, and Bonaventure des Periers, alarmed by the personal dangers in which he was thus involved, retired from the court of the queen of Navarre, and took refuge in the city of Lyons, where liberal opinions at that time found a greater degree of tolerance than elsewhere. There he printed a second edition of the "Cymbalum Mundi," which also was burnt, and copies of either edition are now excessively rare.[98] Bonaventure des Periers felt so much the weight of the persecution in which he had now involved himself, that, in the year 1539, as far as can be ascertained, he put an end to his own existence. This event cast a gloom over the court of the queen of Navarre, from which it seems never to have entirely recovered. The school of scepticism to which Des Periers belonged had now fallen into equal discredit with Catholics and Protestants, and the latter looked upon Marguerite herself, who had latterly conformed outwardly with Romanism, as an apostate from their cause. Henri Estienne, in his "Apologie pour Herodote," speaks of the "Cymbalum Mundi" as an infamous book.

Bonaventure des Periers left behind him another work more amusing to us at the present day, and more characteristic of the literary tastes of the court of Marguerite of Navarre. This is a collection of facetious stories, which was published several years after the death of its author, under the title of "Les Contes, ou Les Nouvelles Récréations et Joyeux Devis de Bonaventure des Periers." They have some resemblance in style to the stories of the Heptameron, but are shorter, and rather more facetious, and are characterised by their bitter spirit of satire against the monks and popish clergy. Some of these stories remind us, in their peculiar character and tone, of the "Epistolæ Obscurorum Virorum," as, for an example, the following, which is given as an anecdote of the curé de Brou:—

"This curé had a way of his own to chant the different offices of the church, and above all he disliked the way of saying the Passion in the manner it was ordinarily said in churches, and he chanted it quite differently. For when our Lord said anything to the Jews, or to Pilate, he made him talk high and loud, so that everybody could hear him, and when it was the Jews or somebody else who spoke, he spoke so low that he could hardly be heard at all. It happened that a lady of rank and importance, on her way to Châteaudun, to keep there the festival of Easter, passed through Brou on Good Friday, about ten o'clock in the morning, and, wishing to hear service, she went to the church where the curé was officiating. When it came to the Passion, he said it in his own manner, and made the whole church ring again when he said *Quem quæritis?* But when it came to the reply, *Jesum Nazarenum,* he spoke as low as he possibly could. And in this manner he continued the Passion. The lady, who was very devout, and, for a woman, well informed in the holy scriptures, and attentive to the ecclesiastical ceremonies, felt scandalised at this mode of chanting, and wished she had never entered the church. She had a mind to speak to the curé, and tell him what she thought of it; and for this purpose sent for him to come to her after the service. When he came, she said to him, 'Monsieur le Curé, I don't know where you learnt to officiate on a day like this, when the people ought to be all humility; but to hear you perform the service, is enough to drive away anybody's devotion.' 'How so, madame?' said the curé. 'How so?' said she, 'you have said a Passion contrary to all rules of decency. When our Lord speaks, you cry as if you were in the town-hall; and when it is a Caiaphas, or Pilate, or the Jews, you speak softly like a young bride. Is this becoming in one like you? are you fit to be a curé? If you had what you deserve, you would be turned out of your benefice, and then you would be made to know your fault!' When the curé had very attentively listened to her, he said, 'Is this what you had to say to me, madame? By my soul! it is very true, what they say; and the truth is, that there are many people who talk of things which they do not understand. Madame, I believe that I know my office as well as another, and I beg all the world to know that God is as well served in this parish according to its condition, as in any place within a hundred leagues of it. I know very well that the other curés chant the Passion quite differently; I could easily chant it like them if I would; but they do not understand their business at all. I should like to know if it becomes those rogues of Jews to speak as loud as our Lord! No, no, madame; rest assured that in my parish it is my will that God be the master, and He shall be as long as I live; and let the others do in their parishes according to their understanding.'"

Another story, equally worthy of Ulric von Hutten, is satirical enough on priestly pedantry:—

"There was a priest of a village who was as proud as might be, because he had seen a little more than his Cato; for he had read *De Syntaxi*, and his *Fauste precor gelida* [the first eclogue of Baptista Mantuanus]. And this made him set up his feathers, and talk very grand, using words that filled his mouth, in order to make people think him a great doctor. Even at confession, he made use of terms which astonished the poor people. One day he was confessing a poor working man, of whom he asked, 'Here, now, my friend, tell me, art thou ambitious?' The poor man said 'No,' thinking this was a word which belonged to great lords, and almost repented of having come to confess to this priest; for he had already heard that he was such a great clerk, and that he spoke so grandly, that nobody understood him, which he now knew by this word *ambitious*; for although he might have heard it somewhere, yet he did not know at all what it was. The priest went on to ask 'Art thou not a fornicator?' 'No,' said the labourer, who understood as little as before. 'Art thou not a gourmand?' said the priest. 'No.' 'Art thou not superbe [*proud*]?' 'No.' 'Art thou not iracund?' 'No.' The priest seeing the man answer always 'No,' was somewhat surprised. 'Art thou not concupiscent?' 'No.' 'And what art thou, then?' said the priest. 'I am,' said he, 'a mason; here is my trowel!'"

At this time "Pantagruelism" had mixed itself more or less largely in all the satirical literature of France. It is very apparent in the writings of Bonaventure des Periers, and in a considerable number of satirical publications which now issued, many of them anonymously, or under the then fashionable form of anagrams, from the press in France. Among these writers were a few who, though far inferior to Rabelais, may be considered as not unequal to Des Periers himself. One of the most remarkable of these was a gentleman of Britany, Noel du Fail, lord of La Hérissaye, who was, like so many of these satirists, a lawyer, and who died, apparently at an advanced age, at the end of 1585, or beginning of 1586. In his publications, according to the fashion of that age, he concealed his name under an anagram, and called himself Leon Ladulfil (doubling the *l* in the name Fail). Noel du Fail has been called the ape of Rabelais, though the mere imitation is not very apparent. He published (as far as has been ascertained), in 1548, his "Discours d'aucuns propos ruftiques facétieux, et de singulière récréation." This was followed immediately by a work entitled

"Baliverneries, ou Contes Nouveaux d'Eutrapel;" but his last, and most celebrated book, the "Contes et Discours d'Eutrapel," was not printed until 1586, after the death of its author. The writings of Noel du Fail are full of charming pictures of rural life in the sixteenth century, and, though sufficiently free, they present less than most similar books of that period of the coarseness of Rabelais. I cannot say the same of a book which is much more celebrated than either of these, and the history of which is still enveloped in obscurity. I mean the "Moyen de Parvenir." This book, which is full of wit and humour, but the licentiousness of which is carried to a degree which renders it unreadable at the present day, is now ascribed by bibliographers, in its present form, to Béroalde de Verville, a gentleman of a Protestant family who had embraced Catholicism, and obtained advancements in the church, and it was not printed until 1610, but it is supposed that in its present form it is only a revision of an earlier composition, perhaps even an unacknowledged work of Rabelais himself, which had been preserved in manuscript in Beroald's family.

Pantagruelism, or, if you like, Rabelaism, did not, during the sixteenth century, make much progress beyond the limits of France. In the Teutonic countries of Europe, and in England, the sceptical sentiment was small in comparison with the religious feeling, and the only satirical work at all resembling those we have been describing, was the "Utopia" of Sir Thomas More, a work comparatively spiritless, and which produced a very slight sensation. In Spain, the state of social feeling was still less favourable to the writings of Rabelais, yet he had there a worthy and true representative in the author of Don Quixote. It was only in the seventeenth century that the works of Rabelais were translated into English; but we must not forget that our satirists of the last century, such as Swift and Sterne, derived their inspiration chiefly from Rabelais, and from the Pantagruelistic writers of the latter half of the sixteenth century. These latter were most of them poor imitators of their original, and, like all poor imitators, pursued to exaggeration his least worthy characteristics. There is still some humour in the writings of Tabourot, the sieur des Accords, especially in his "Bigarrures," but the later productions, which appeared under such names as Bruscambille and Tabarin, sink into mere dull ribaldry.

There had arisen, however, by the side of this satire which smelt somewhat too much of the tavern, another satire, more serious, which still contained a little of the style of Rabelais. The French Protestants at first looked upon Rabelais as one of their towers of strength, and embraced with gratitude the powerful protection they received from the graceful queen of Navarre; but their gratitude failed them, when Marguerite, though she never ceased to give them her protection, conformed outwardly, from attachment to her brother, to the forms of the Catholic faith, and they rejected the school of Rabelais as a mere school of Atheists. Among them arose another school of satire, a sort of branch from the other, which was represented in its infancy by the celebrated scholar and printer, Henri Estienne, better known among us as Henry Stephens.

The remarkable book called an "Apologie pour Herodote," arose out of an attack upon its writer by the Romanists. Henri Estienne, who was known as a staunch Protestant, published, at great expense, an edition of Herodotus in Greek and Latin, and the zealous Catholics, out of spite to the editor, decried his author, and spoke of Herodotus as a mere collector of monstrous and incredible tales. Estienne, in revenge, published what, under the form of an apology for Herodotus, was really a violent attack on the Romish church. His argument is that all historians must relate transactions which appear to many incredible, and that the events of modern times were much more incredible, if they were not known to be true, than anything which is recorded by the historian of antiquity. After an introductory dissertation on the light in which we ought to regard the fable of the Golden Age, and on the moral character of the ancient peoples, he goes on to show that their depravity was much less than that of the middle ages and of his own time, indeed of all periods during which people were governed by the Church of Rome. Not only did this dissoluteness of morals pervade lay society, but the clergy were more vicious even than the people, to whom they ought to serve as an example. A large part of the book is filled with anecdotes of the immoral lives of the popish clergy of the sixteenth century, and of their ignorance and bigotry; and he describes in detail the methods employed by the Romish church to keep the mass of the people in ignorance, and to repress all attempts at inquiry. Out of all this, he says, had risen a school of atheists and scoffers, represented by Rabelais and Bonaventure des Periers, both of whom he mentions by name.

As we approach the end of the sixteenth century, the struggle of parties became more political than religious, but not less bitter than before. The literature of the age of that celebrated "Ligue," which seemed at one time destined to overthrow the ancient royalty of France, consisted chiefly of libellous and abusive pamphlets, but in the midst of them there appeared a work far superior to any purely political satire which had yet been seen, and the fame of which has never passed away. Its object was to turn to ridicule the meeting of the Estates of France, convoked by the duke of Mayenne, as leader of the Ligue, and held at Paris on the 10th of February, 1503. The grand object of this meeting was to exclude Henri IV. from the throne; and the Spanish party proposed to abolish the Salic law, and proclaim the infanta of Spain queen of France. The French ligueurs proposed plans hardly less unpatriotic, and the duke of Mayenne, indignant at the small account made of his own personal pretensions, prorogued the meeting, and persuaded the two parties to hold what proved a fruitless conference at Suresne. It was the meeting of the Estates in Paris which gave rise to that celebrated *Satyre Ménippée*, of which it was said, that it served the cause of Henri IV. as much as the battle of Ivry itself.

This satire originated among a party of friends, of men distinguished by learning, wit, and talent, though most of their names are obscure, who used to meet in an evening in the hospitable house of one of them, Jacques Gillot, on the Quai des Orfèvres in Paris, and there talk satirically over the violence and insolence of the ligueurs. They all belonged either to the bar or to the university, or to the church. Gillot himself, a Burgundian, born about the year 1560, had been a dean in the church of Langres, and afterwards canon of the Sainte Chapelle in Paris, and was at this time conseiller-clerc to the parliament of Paris. In 1589 he was committed to the Bastille, but was soon afterwards liberated. Nicolas Rapin, one of his friends, was born in 1535, and was said to have been the son of a priest, and therefore illegitimate. He was a lawyer, a poet, and a soldier, for he fought bravely in the ranks of Henri IV. at Ivry, and his devotion to that prince was so well known, that he was banished from Paris by the ligueurs, but had returned thither before the meeting of the Estates in 1593. Jean Passerat, born in 1534, was also a poet, and a professor in the Collège Royal. Florent Chrestien, born at Orleans in 1540, had been the tutor of Henri IV., and was well known as a man of sound learning. The most learned of the party was Pierre Pithou, born at Troyes in 1539, who had abjured Calvinism to return to Romanism, and who held a distinguished position at the French bar. The last of this little party of men of letters was a canon of Rouen named Pierre le Roy, a patriotic ecclesiastic, who held the office of almoner to the cardinal de Bourbon. It was Le Roy who drew up the first sketch of the "Satyre Ménippée," each of the others executed his part in the composition, and Pithou finally revised it. For several years this remarkable satire circulated only secretly, and in manuscript, and it was not printed until Henri IV. was established on the throne.

The satire opens with an account of the virtues of the "Catholicon," or nostrum for curing all political diseases, or the *higuiero d'infierno*, which had been so effective in the hands of the Spaniards, who invented it. Some of these are extraordinary enough. If, we are told, the lieutenant of Don Philip "have some of this Catholicon on his flags, he will enter without a blow into an enemy's country, and they will meet him with crosses and banners, legates and primates; and though he ruin, ravage, usurp, massacre, and sack everything, and carry away, ravish, burn, and reduce everything to a desert, the people of the country will say, 'These are our friends, they are good Catholics; they do it for our peace, and for our mother holy church.'" "If an indolent king amuse himself with refining this drug in his escurial, let him write a word into Flanders to Father

Ignatius, sealed with the Catholicon, he will find him a man who (*salva conscientia*) will assassinate his enemy whom he has not been able to conquer by arms in twenty years." This, of course, is an allusion to the murder of the prince of Orange. "If this king proposes to assure his estates to his children after his death, and to invade another's kingdom at little expense, let him write a word to Mendoza, his ambassador, or to Father Commelet (one of the most seditious orators of the Ligue), and if he write with the *higuiero del infierno*, at the bottom of his letter, the words *Yo el Rey*, they will furnish him with an apostate monk, who will go under a fair semblance, like a Judas, and assassinate in cold blood a great king of France, his brother-in-law, in the middle of his camp, without fear of God or men; they will do more, they will canonise the murderer, and place this Judas above St. Peter, and baptise this prodigious and horrible crime with the name of a providential event, of which the godfathers will be cardinals, legates, and primates." The allusion here is to the assassination of Henri III. by Jacques Clement. These are but a few of the marvellous properties of the political drug, after the enumeration of which the report of the meeting of the Estates is introduced by a burlesque description of the grand procession which preceded it. Then we are introduced to the hall of assembly, and different subjects pictured on the tapestries which cover its walls, all having reference to the politics of the Ligue, are described fully. Then we come to the report of the meeting, and to the speeches of the different speakers, each of which is a model of satire. It is not known which of the little club of satirists wrote the open speech of the duke of Mayenne, but that of the Roman legate is known to be the work of Gillot, and that of the cardinal de Pelvé, a masterpiece of Latin in the style of the "Epistolæ Obscurorum Virorum," was written by Florent Chrestien. Nicolas Rapin composed the "harangue" placed in the mouth of the archbishop of Lyons, as well as that of Rose, the rector of the university; and the long speech of Claude d'Aubray was by Pithou. Passerat composed most of the verses which are scattered through the book, and it is understood that Pithou finally revised the whole. This mock report of the meeting of the Estates closes with a description of a series of political pictures which are arranged on the wall of the staircase of the hall.

These pictures, as well as those on the tapestries of the hall of meeting, are simply so many caricatures, and the same may be said of another set of pictures, of which a description is given in one of the satirical pieces which followed the "Satyre Ménippée," on the same side, entitled, "Histoire des Singeries de la Ligue." It was amid the political turmoil of the sixteenth century in France that modern political caricature took its rise.

CHAPTER XX.

POLITICAL CARICATURE IN ITS INFANCY.—THE REVERS DU JEU DES SUYSSES.—CARICATURE IN FRANCE.—THE THREE ORDERS.—PERIOD OF THE LEAGUE; CARICATURES AGAINST HENRI III.—CARICATURES AGAINST THE LEAGUE.—CARICATURE IN FRANCE IN THE SEVENTEENTH CENTURY.—GENERAL GALAS.—THE QUARREL OF AMBASSADORS.—CARICATURE AGAINST LOUIS XIV.; WILLIAM OF FÜRSTEMBERG.

It has been already remarked that political caricature, in the modern sense of the word, or even personal caricature, was inconsistent with the state of things in the middle ages, until the arts of engraving and printing became sufficiently developed, because it requires the facility of quick and extensive circulation. The political or satirical song was carried everywhere by the minstrel, but the satirical picture, represented only in some solitary sculpture or illumination, could hardly be finished before it had become useless even in the small sphere of its influence, and then remained for ages a strange figure, with no meaning that could be understood. No sooner, however, was the art of printing introduced, than the importance of political caricature was understood and turned to account. We have seen what a powerful agent it became in the Reformation, which in spirit was no less political than religious; but even before the great religious movement had begun, this agent had been brought into activity. One of the earliest engravings which can be called a caricature—perhaps the oldest of our modern caricatures known—is represented in our cut No. 171, is no doubt French, and belongs to the year 1499. It is sufficiently explained by the history of the time.

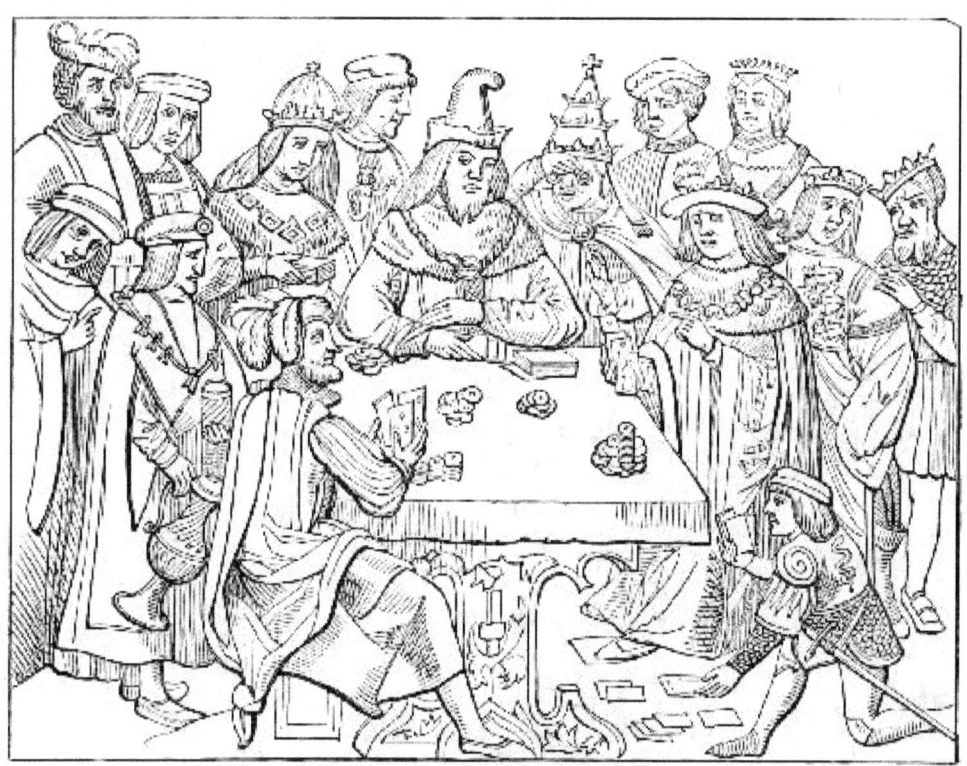

No. 171. The Political Game of Cards.

At the date just mentioned, Louis XII. of France, who had been king less than twelve months, was newly married to Anne of Britany, and had resolved upon an expedition into Italy, to unite the crown of Naples with that of France. Such an expedition affected many political interests and Louis had to employ a certain amount of diplomacy with his neighbours, several of whom were strongly opposed to his projects of ambition, and among those who acted most openly were the Swiss, who were believed to have been secretly supported by England and the Netherlands. Louis, however, overcame their opposition, and obtained a renewal of the alliance which had expired with his predecessor Charles VIII. This temporary difficulty with the Swiss is the subject of our caricature, the original of which bears the title "Le Revers du Jeu des Suysses" (the defeat of the game of the Swiss). The princes most interested are assembled round a card-table, at which are seated the king of France to the right, opposite him the Swiss, and in front the doge of Venice, who was in alliance with the French against Milan. At the moment represented, the king of France is announcing that he has a flush of cards, the Swiss acknowledges the weakness of his hand, and the doge lays down his cards—in fact, Louis XII. has won the game. But the point of the caricature lies principally in the group around. To the extreme right the king of England, Henry VII., distinguished by his three armorial lions, and the king of Spain, are engaged in earnest conversation. Behind the former stands the infanta Margarita, who is evidently winking at the Swiss to give him information of the state of the cards of his opponents. At her side stands the duke of Wirtemberg, and just before him the pope, the infamous Alexander VI. (Borgia), who, though in alliance with Louis, is not able, with all his efforts, to read the king's game, and looks on with evident anxiety. Behind the doge of Venice stands the Italian refugee, Trivulci, an able warrior, devoted to the interests of France; and at the doge's right hand, the emperor, holding in his hands another pack of cards, and apparently exulting in the belief that he has thrown confusion into the king of France's game. In the background to the left are seen the count Palatine and the marquis of Montserrat, who also look uncertain about the result; and below the former appears the duke of Savoy, who was giving assistance to the French designs. The duke of Lorraine is serving drink to the gamblers, while the duke of Milan, who was at this time playing rather a double part, is gathering up the cards which have fallen to the ground, in order to make a game for himself. Louis XII. carried his designs into execution; the duke of Milan, Ludovico Sforza, nick-named the Moor, played his cards badly, lost his duchy, and died in prison.

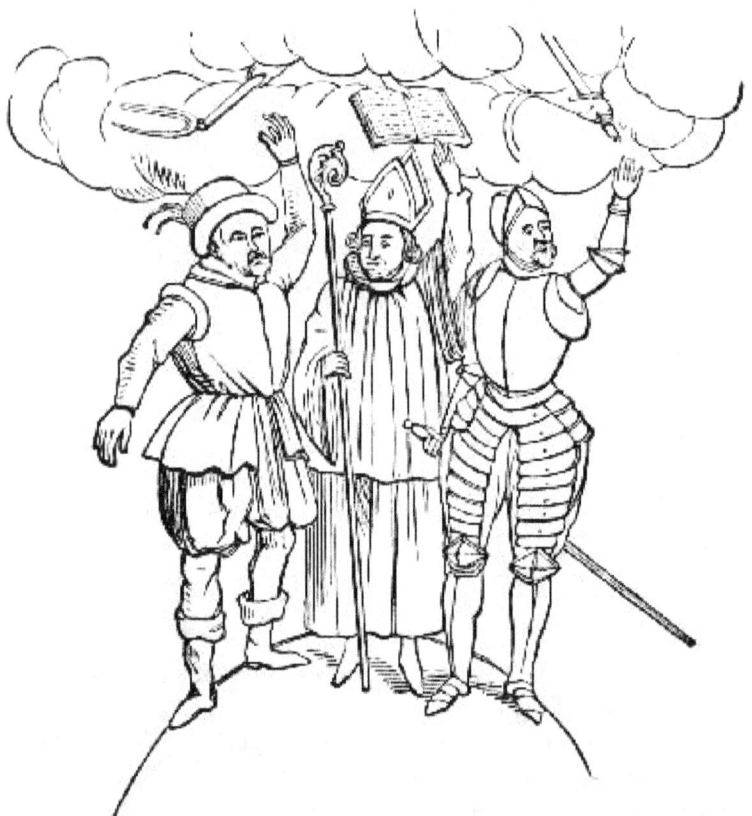

No. 172. The Three Orders of the State.

Such is this earliest of political caricatures—and in this case it was purely political—but the question of religion soon began not only to mix itself up with the political question, but almost to absorb it, as we have seen in the review of the history of caricature under the Reformation. Before this period, indeed, political caricature was only an affair between crowned heads, or between kings and their nobles, but the religious agitation had originated a vast social movement, which brought into play popular feelings and passions: these gave caricature a totally new value. Its power was greatest on the middle and lower classes of society, that is, on the people, the *tiers état*, which was now thrown prominently forward. The new social theory is proclaimed in a print, of which a fac-simile will be found in the "Musée de la Caricature," by E. J. Jaime, and which, from the style and costume, appears to be German. The three orders, the church, the lord of the land, and the people, represented respectively by a bishop, a knight, and a cultivator, stand upon the globe in an honourable equality, each receiving direct from heaven the emblems or implements of his duties. To the bishop is delivered his bible, to the husbandman his mattock, and to the knight the sword with which he is to protect and defend the others. This print—see cut No. 172—which bears the title, in Latin, "Quis te prætulit?" (Who chose thee?) belongs probably to the earlier half of the sixteenth century. A painting in the Hôtel de Ville of Aix, in Provence, represents the same subject much more satirically, intending to delineate the three orders as they were, and not as they ought to be. The divine hand is letting down from heaven an immense frame in the form of a heart, in which is a picture representing a king kneeling before the cross, intimating that the civil power was to be subordinate to the ecclesiastical. The three orders are represented by a cardinal, a noble, and a peasant, the latter of whom is bending under the burthen of the heart, the whole of which is thrown upon his shoulders, while the cardinal and the noble, the latter dressed in the fashionable attire of the court minions of the day, are placing one hand to the heart on each side, in a manner which shows that they support none of the weight.

Amid the fierce agitation which fell upon France in the sixteenth century, for a while we find but few traces of the employment of caricature by either party. The religious reformation there was rather aristocratic than popular, and the reformers sought less to excite the feelings of the multitude, which, indeed, went generally in the contrary direction. There was, moreover, a character of gloom in the religion of Calvin, which contracted strongly with the joyousness of that of the followers of Luther; and the factions in France sought to slaughter, rather than to laugh at, each other. The few caricatures of this period which are known, are very bitter and coarse. As far as I am aware, no early Huguenot caricatures are known, but there are a few directed against the Huguenots. It was, however, with the rise of the Ligue that the taste for political caricature may be said to have taken root in France, and in that country it long continued to flourish more than anywhere else. The first caricatures of the ligueurs were directed against the person of the king, Henri de Valois, and possess a brutality almost beyond description. It was now an object to keep up the bitterness of spirit of the fanatical multitude. In one of these caricatures a demon is represented waiting on the king to summon him to a meeting of the "Estates" in hell; and in the distance we see another demon flying away with him. Another relates to the murder of the Guises, in 1588, which the ligueurs professed to ascribe to the councils of M. d'Epernon, one of his favourites, on whom they looked with great hatred. It is entitled, "Soufflement et Conseil diabolique de d'Epernon à Henri de Valois pour faccager les Catholiques." In the middle of the picture stands the king, and beside him D'Epernon, who is blowing into his ear with a bellows. On the ground before them lie the headless corpses of the *deux frères Catholiques*, the duke of Guise, and his brother the cardinal, while the executioner of royal vengeance is holding up their heads by the hair. In the distance is seen the castle of Blois, in which this tragedy took place; and on the left of the picture appear the cardinal de Bourbon, the archbishop of Blois, and other friends of the Guises, expressing their horror at the deed. Henri III. was himself murdered in the year following, and the caricatures against him became still more brutal during the period in which the ligueurs tried to set up a king of their own in his place. In one caricature, which has more of an emblematical character than most of the others, he is pictured as "Henri le Monstrueux;" and in others, entitled "Les Hermaphrodites," he is exhibited under forms which point at the infamous vices with which he was charged.

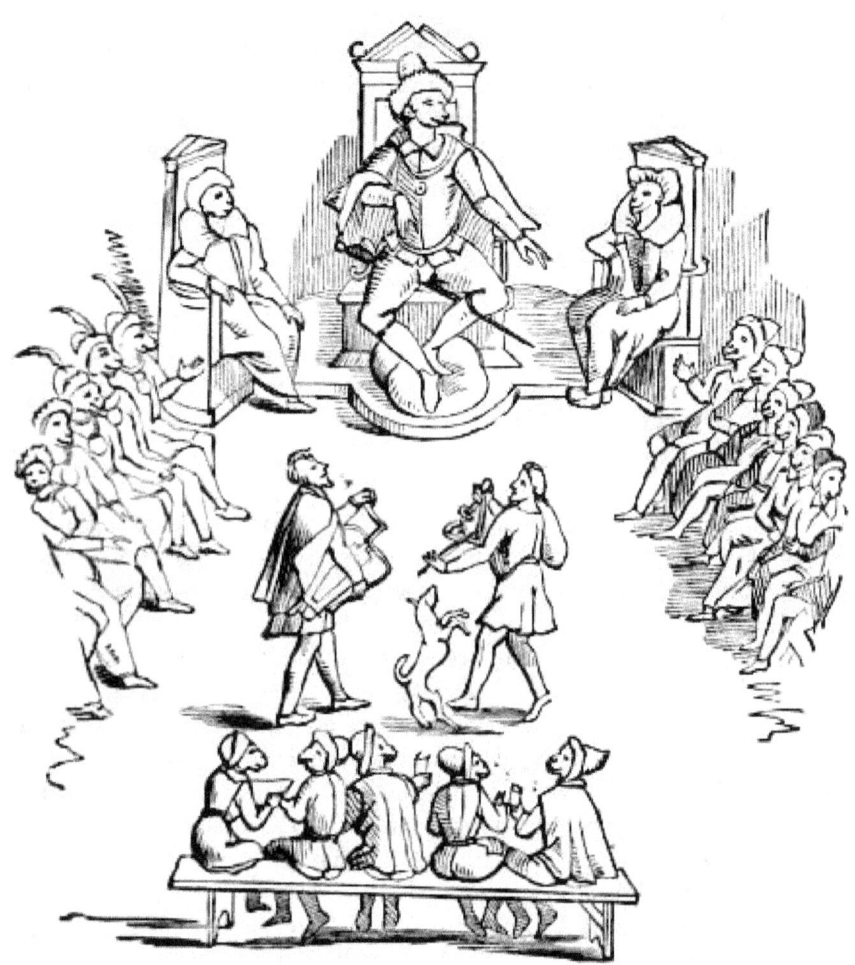

No. 173. The Assembly of Apes.

The tide of caricature, however, soon turned in the contrary direction, and the coarse, unprincipled abuse employed by the ligueurs found a favourable contrast in the powerful wit and talent of the satirists and caricaturists who now took up pen and pencil in the cause of Henri IV. The former was, on the whole, the more formidable weapon, but the latter represented to some eyes more vividly in picture what had already been done in type. This was the case on both sides; the caricature last mentioned was founded upon a very libellous satirical pamphlet against Henri III., entitled "L'Isle des Hermaphrodites." It is the case also with the first caricatures against the ligueurs, which I have to mention. The Estates held in Paris by the duke of Mayenne and the ligueurs for the purpose of electing a new king in opposition to Henri of Navarre, were made the subject of the celebrated "Satyre Ménippée," in which the proceedings of these Estates were turned to ridicule in the most admirable manner. Four large editions were sold in less than as many months. Several caricatures arose out of or accompanied this remarkable book. One of these is a rather large print, entitled "La Singerie des Estats de la Ligue, l'an 1593," in which the members of the Estates and the ligueurs are pictured with the heads of monkeys. The central part represents the meeting of the Estates, at which the lieutenant-general of the kingdom, the duke of Mayenne, seated on the throne, presides. Above him is suspended a large portrait of the infanta of Spain, *L'Espousée de la Ligue*, as she is called in the satire, ready to marry any one whom the Estates shall declare king of France. In chairs, on each side of Mayenne, are the two "ladies of honour" of the said future spouse. To the left are seated in a row the celebrated council of sixteen (*les seize*), reduced at this time to twelve, because the duke of Mayenne, to check their turbulence, had caused four of them to be hanged. They wear the favours of the future spouse. Opposite to them are the representatives of the three orders, all, we are told, devoted to the service of "the said lady." Before the throne are the two musicians of the Ligue, one described as Phelipottin, the blind performer on the viel, or hurdy-gurdy, to the Ligue, and his subordinate, the player on the triangle, "kept at the expense of the future spouse." These were to entertain the assembly during the pauses between the orations of the various speakers. All this is a satire on the efforts of the king of Spain to establish a monarch of his own choice. On the bench behind the musicians sit the deputies from Lyons, Poitiers, Orleans, and Rheims, cities where the influence of the Ligue was strong, discussing the question as to who should be king. Thus much of this picture is represented in our cut No. 173. There are other groups of figures in the representation of the assembly of the Estates; and there are two side compartments—that on the left representing a forge, on which the fragments of a broken king are laid to be refounded, and a multitude of apes, with hammers and an anvil, ready to work him into a new king; the other side of the picture represents the circumstances of a then well-known act of tyranny perpetrated by the Estates of the Ligue. Another large and well-executed engraving, published at Paris in 1594, immediately after Henri IV. had obtained possession of his capital, also represents the grand procession of the Ligue as described at the commencement of the "Satyre Ménippée," and was intended to hold up to ridicule the warlike temper of the French Catholic clergy. It is entitled, "La Procession de la Ligue."

Henri's triumph over the Ligue was made the subject of a series of three caricatures, or perhaps, more correctly, of a caricature in three divisions. The first is entitled the "Naissance de la Ligue," and represents it under the form of a monster with three heads, severally those of a wolf, a fox, and a serpent, issuing from hell-mouth. Under it are the following lines:—

L'enfer, pour asservir soubs ses loix tout le monde,
Vomit ce monstre hideux, fait d'un loup ravisseur,
D'un renard enveilly, et d'un serpent immonde,
Affublé d'un manteau propre à toute couleur.

The second division, the "Declin de la Ligue," representing its downfall, is copied in our cut No. 174. Henri of Navarre, in the form of a lion, has pounced fiercely upon it, and not too soon, for it had already seized the crown and sceptre. In the distance, the sun of national prosperity is seen rising over the country. The third picture, the "Effets de la Ligue," represents the destruction of the kingdom and the slaughter of the people, of which the Ligue had been the cause.

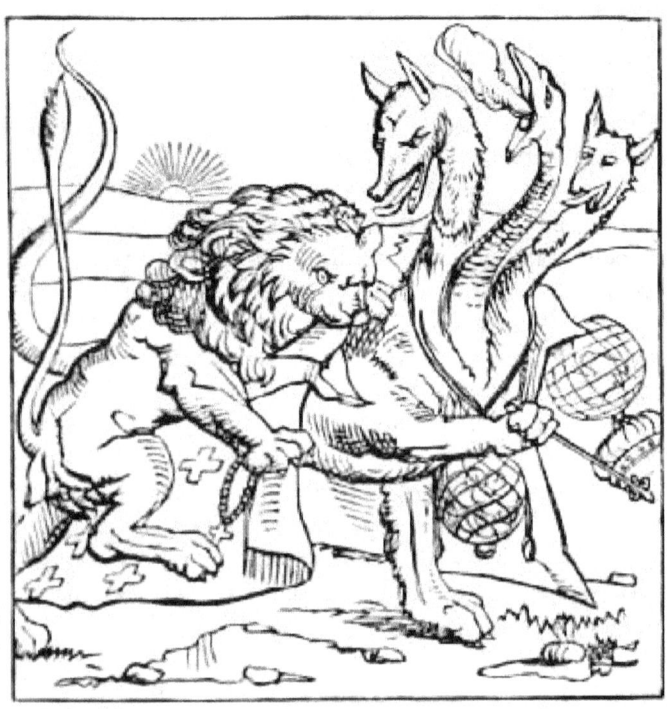

No. 174. The Destruction of the Ligue.

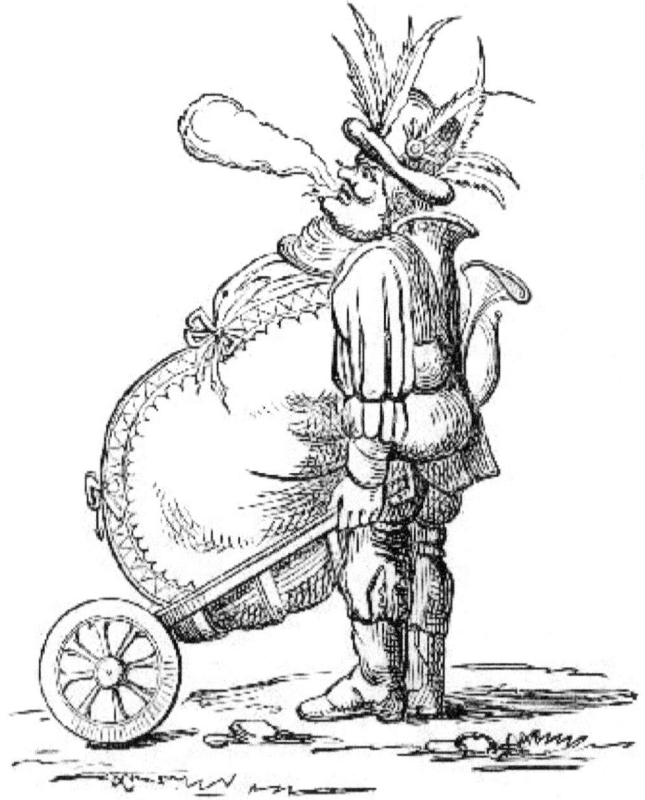

No. 175. General Galas.

The caricatures in France became more numerous during the seventeenth century, but they are either so elaborate or so obscure, that each requires almost a dissertation to explain it, and they often relate to questions or events which have little interest for us at the present day. Several rather spirited ones appeared at the time of the disgrace of the mareschal d'Ancre and his wife; and the inglorious war with the Netherlands, in 1635, furnished the occasion for others, for the French, as usual, could make merry in their reverses as well as in their successes. The imperialist general Galas inflicted serious defeat on the French armies, and compelled them to a very disastrous retreat from the countries they had invaded, and they tried to amuse themselves at the expense of their conqueror. Galas was rather remarkable for obesity, and the French caricaturists of the day made this circumstance a subject for their satire. Our cut No. 175 is copied from a print in which the magnitude of the stomach of General Galas is certainly somewhat exaggerated. He is represented, not apparently with any good reason, as puffed up with his own importance, which is evaporating in smoke; and along with the smoke thus issuing from his mouth, he is made to proclaim his greatness in the following rather doggrel verses:—

Je suis ce grand Galas, autrefois dans l'armée
La gloire de l'Espagne et de mes compagnons;
Maintenant je ne suis qu'un corps plein de fumée,
Pour avoir trop mangé de raves et d'oignons.
Gargantua jamais n'eut une telle panse, &c.

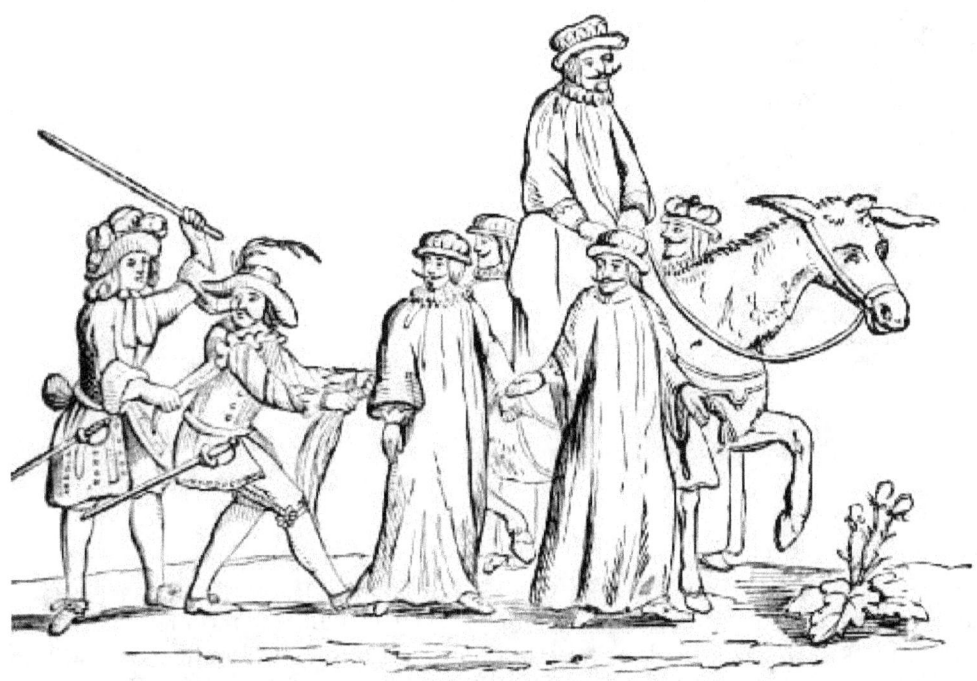

No. 176. Batteville Humiliated.

Caricatures in France began to be tolerably abundant during the middle of the seventeenth century, but under the crushing tyranny of Louis XIV., the freedom of the press, in all its forms, ceased to exist, and caricatures relating to France, unless they came from the court party, had to be published in other countries, especially in Holland. It will be sufficient to give two examples from the reign of Louis XIV. In the year 1661, a dispute arose in London between the ambassador of France, M. D'Estrades, and the Spanish ambassador, the baron de Batteville, on the question of precedence, which was carried so far as to give rise to a tumult in the streets of the English capital. At this very moment, a new Spanish ambassador, the marquis de Fuentes, was on his way to Paris, but Louis, indignant at Batteville's behaviour in London, sent orders to stop Fuentes on the frontier, and forbid his further advance into his kingdom. The king of Spain disavowed the act of his ambassador in England, who was recalled, and Fuentes received orders to make an apology to king Louis. This event was made the subject of a rather boasting caricature, the greater portion of which is given in our cut No. 176. It is entitled "Batteville vient adorer le Soliel" (Batteville comes to worship the sun). In the original the sun is seen shining in the upper corner of the picture to the right, and presenting the juvenile face of Louis XIV., but the caricaturist appears to have substituted Batteville in the place of Fuentes. Beneath the whole are the following boastful lines:—

On ne va plus à Rome, on vient de Rome en France,
Mériter le pardon de quelque grande offence.
L'Italie tout entière est soumise à ces loix;
Un Espagnol s'oppose à ce droit de nos rois.
Mais un Français puissant joua des bastonnades,
Et punit l'insolent de ses rodomontades.

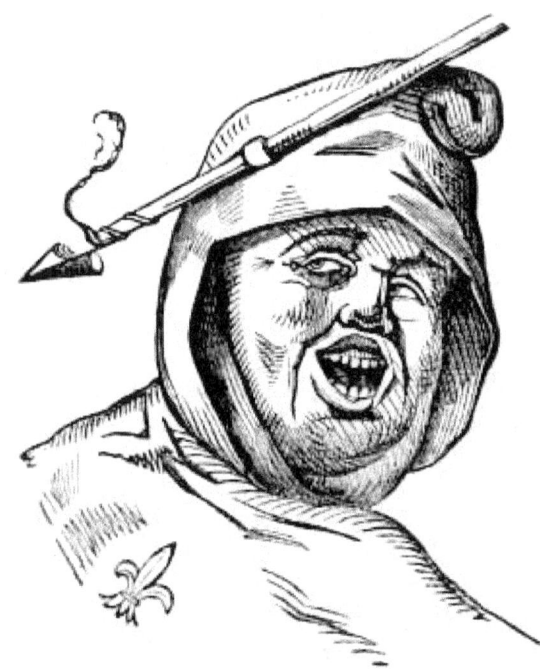

No. 177. William of Fürstemberg.

From this time there sprung up many caricatures against the Spaniards; but the most ferocious caricature, or rather book of caricatures, of the reign of Louis XIV., came from without, and was directed against the king and his ministers and courtiers. The revocation of the edict of Nantes took place in October, 1685, and was preceded and followed by frightful persecutions of the Protestants, which drove away in thousands the earnest, intelligent, and industrious part of the population of France. They carried with them a deep hatred to their oppressors, and sought refuge especially in the countries most hostile to Louis XIV.—England and Holland. The latter country, where they then enjoyed the greatest freedom of action, soon sent forth numerous satirical books and prints against the French king and his ministers, of which the book just alluded to was one of the most remarkable. It is entitled "Les Heros de la Ligue, ou la Procession Monacale conduite par Louis XIV. pour la Conversion des Protestans de son Royaume," and consists of a series of twenty-four most grotesque faces, intended to represent the ministers and courtiers of the "grand roi" most odious to the Calvinists. It must have provoked their wrath exceedingly. I give one example, and as it is difficult to select, I take the first in the list, which represents William of Fürstemberg, one of the German princes devoted to Louis XIV., who, by his intrigues, had forced him into the archbishopric of Cologne, by which he became an elector of the empire. For many reasons William of Fürstemberg was hated by the French Protestants, but it is not quite clear why he is here represented in the character of one of the low merchants of the Halles. Over the picture, in the original, we read, *Guillaume de Furstemberg, crie, ite, missa est*, and beneath are the four lines:—

J'ay quitté mon pais pour servir à la France,
Soit par ma trahison, soit par ma lacheté;
J'ay troublé les états par ma méchanceté,
Une abbaye est ma recompense.

CHAPTER XXI.

EARLY POLITICAL CARICATURE IN ENGLAND.—THE SATIRICAL WRITINGS AND PICTURES OF THE COMMONWEALTH PERIOD.—SATIRES AGAINST THE BISHOPS; BISHOP WILLIAMS.—CARICATURES ON THE CAVALIERS; SIR JOHN SUCKLING.— THE ROARING BOYS; VIOLENCE OF THE ROYALIST SOLDIERS.—CONTEST BETWEEN THE PRESBYTERIANS AND INDEPENDENTS.—GRINDING THE KING'S NOSE.—PLAYING-CARDS USED AS THE MEDIUM FOR CARICATURE; HASELRIGGE AND LAMBERT.—SHROVETIDE.

During the sixteenth century caricature can hardly be said to have existed in England, and it did not come much into fashion, until the approach of the great struggle which convulsed our country in the century following. The popular reformers have always been the first to appreciate the value of pictorial satire as an offensive weapon. Such was the case with the German reformers in the age of Luther; as it was again with the English reformers in the days of Charles I., a period which we may justly consider as that of the birth of English political caricature. From 1640 to 1661 the press launched forth an absolute deluge of political pamphlets, many of which were of a satirical character, scurrilous in form and language, and, on whatever side they were written, very unscrupulous in regard to the truth of their statements. Among them appeared a not unfrequent engraving, seldom well executed, whether on copper or wood, but displaying a coarse and pungent wit that must have told with great effect on those for whom it was intended. The first objects of attack in these caricatures were the Episcopalian party in the church and the profaneness and insolence of the cavaliers. The Puritans or Presbyterians who took the lead in, and at first directed, the great political movement, looked upon Episcopalianism as differing in little from popery, and, at all events, as leading direct to it. Arminianism was with them only another name for the same thing, and was equally detested. In a caricature published in 1641, Arminius is represented supported on one side by Heresy, wearing the triple crown, while on the other side Truth is turning away from him, and carrying with her the Bible. It was the indiscreet zeal of archbishop Laud which led to the triumph of the Puritan party, and the downfall of the episcopal church government, and Laud became the butt for attacks of all descriptions, in pamphlets, songs and satirical prints, the latter usually figuring in the titles of the pamphlets. Laud was especially obnoxious to the Puritans for the bitterness with which he had persecuted them.

In 1640 Laud was committed to the Tower, an event which was hailed as the first grand step towards the overthrow of the bishops. As an example of the feeling of exultation displayed on this occasion by his enemies, we may quote a few lines from a satirical song, published in 1641, and entitled "The Organs Eccho. To the Tune of the Cathedrall Service." It is a general attack on the prelacy, and opens with a cry of triumph over the fall of William Laud, of whom the song says—

As he was in his braverie,
And thought to bring us all in slaverie,
The parliament found out his knaverie;
And so fell William.
Alas! poore William!
His pope-like domineering,
And some other tricks appearing,
Provok'd Sir Edward Deering
To blame the old prelate.
Alas! poore prelate!
Some say he was in hope
To bring England againe to th' pope;
But now he is in danger of an axe or a rope.
Farewell, old Canterbury.
Alas! poore Canterbury!

Wren, bishop of Ely, was another of the more obnoxious of the prelates, and there was hardly less joy among the popular party when he was committed to the Tower in the course of the year 1641. Another song, in verse similar to the last, contains a general review of the demerits of the members of the prelacy, under the title of "The Bishops Last Good-night." At the head of the broadside on which it is printed stand two satirical woodcuts, but it must be confessed that the words of the song are better than the engraving. The bishop of Ely, we are told, had just gone to join his friend Laud in the Tower—

Ely, thou hast alway to thy power
Left the church naked in a storme and showre,
And now for 't thou must to thy old friend i' th' Tower.
To the Tower must Ely;
Come away, Ely.

A third obnoxious prelate was bishop Williams. Williams was a Welshman who had been high in favour with James I., but he had given offence to the government of Charles I., and been imprisoned in the Tower during the earlier part of that king's reign. He was released by the parliament in 1640, and so far regained the favour of king Charles, that he was raised to the archbishopric of York in the year following. When the civil war began, he retired into Wales, and garrisoned Conway for the king. Williams's warlike behaviour was the source of much mirth among the Roundheads. In 1642 was published a large caricature on the three classes to whom the parliamentarians were especially hostile—the royalist judges, the prelates, and the ruffling cavaliers; represented here, as we are told in writing in the copy among the king's pamphlets, by judge Mallet, bishop Williams, and colonel Lunsford. These three figures are placed in as many compartments with doggrel verses under each. That of bishop Williams is copied in our cut No. 178. The bishop is armed cap-à-pie, and in the distance behind him are seen on one side his cathedral church, and on the other his war-horse. The verses beneath it contain an allusion to this prelate's Welsh extraction in the orthography of some of the words:—

Oh, sir, I'me ready, did you never heere
How forward I have byn t'is many a yeare,
T'oppose the practice dat is now on foote,
Which plucks my brethren up both pranch and roote?
My posture and my hart toth well agree
To fight; now plud is up: come, follow mee.

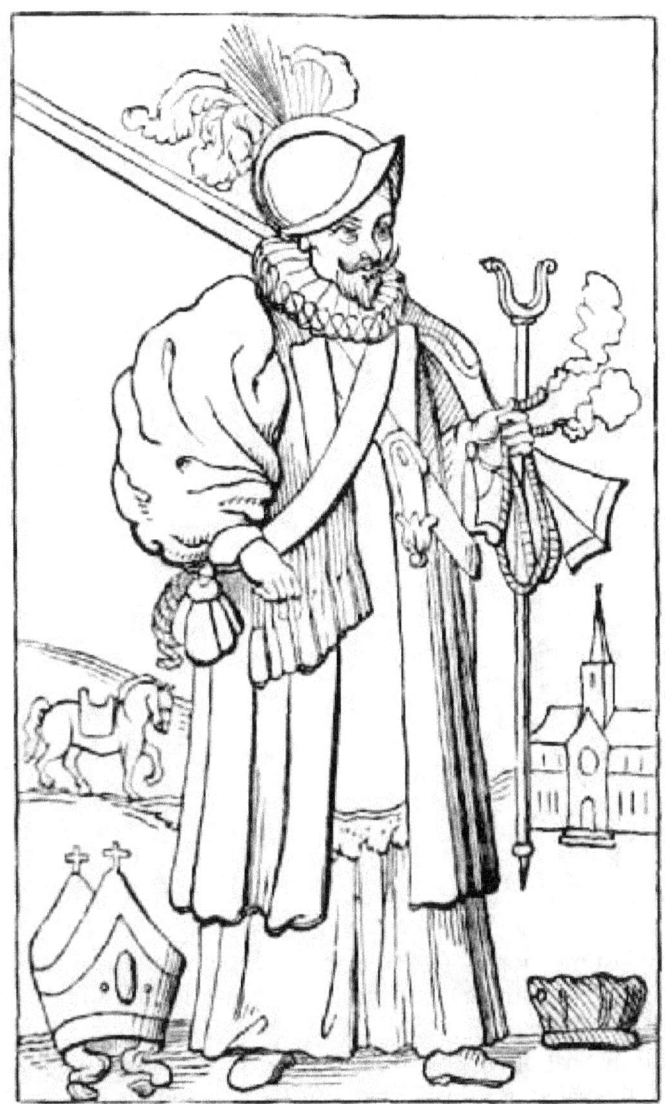

No. 178. The Church Militant.

The country had now begun to experience the miseries of war, and to smart under them; and the cavaliers were especially reproached for the cruelty with which they plundered and ill-treated people whenever they gained the mastery. Colonel Lunsford was especially notorious for the barbarities committed by himself and his men—to such a degree that he was popularly accused of eating children, a charge which is frequently alluded to in the popular songs of the time. Thus one of these songs couples him with two other obnoxious royalists:—

From Fielding, and from Vavasour,
Both ill-affected men,
From Lunsford eke deliver us,
Who eateth up children.

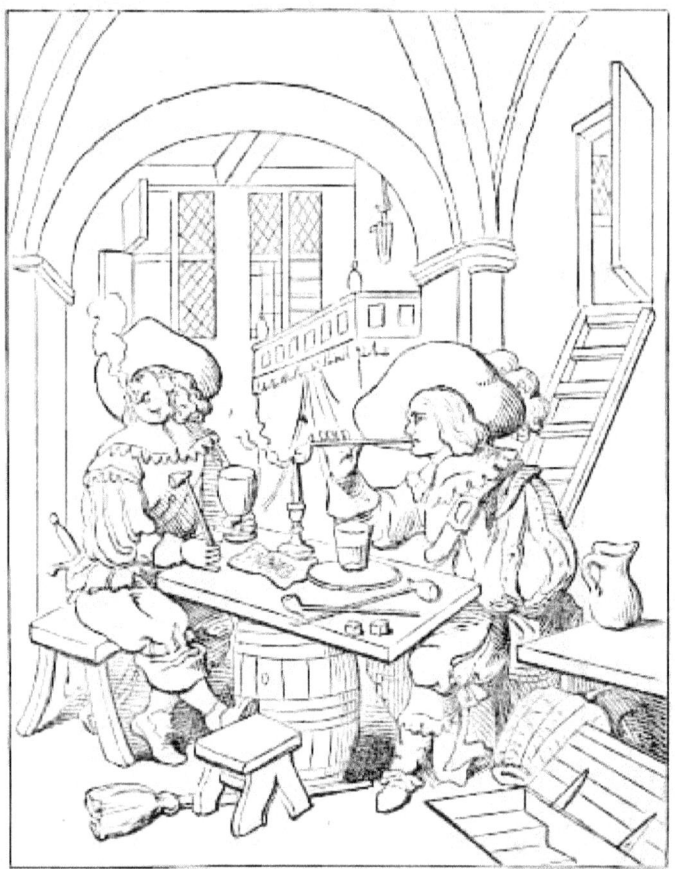

No. 179. The Sucklington Faction.

In the third compartment of the caricature just mentioned, we see in the background of the picture, behind colonel Lunsford, his soldiers occupied in burning towns, and massacring women and children. The model of the gay cavalier of the earlier period of this great revolution, before the war had broken out in its intensity, was the courtly Sir John Suckling, the poet of the drawing-room and tavern, the admired of "roaring boys," and the hated of rigid Puritans. Sir John outdid his companions in extravagance in everything which was fashionable, and the display of his zeal in the cause of royalty was not calculated to conciliate the reformers. When the king led an army against the Scottish Covenanters in 1639, Suckling raised a troop of a hundred horse at his own expense; but they gained more reputation by their extraordinary dress than by their courage, and the whole affair was made a subject of ridicule. From this time the name of Suckling became identified with that gay and profligate class who, disgusted by the outward show of sanctity which the Puritans affected, rushed into the other extreme, and became notorious for their profaneness, their libertinism, and their indulgence in vice, which threw a certain degree of discredit upon the royalist party. There is a large broadside among the King's Pamphlets in the British Museum, entitled, "The Sucklington Faction; or (Sucklings) Roaring Boys." It is one of those satirical compositions which were then fashionable under the title of "Characters," and is illustrated by an engraving, from which our cut No. 179 is copied. This engraving, which from its superior style is perhaps the work of a foreign artist, represents the interior of a chamber, in which two of the Roaring Boys are engaged in drinking and smoking, and forms a curious picture of contemporary manners. Underneath the engraving we read the following lines:—

Much meate doth gluttony produce,
And makes a man a swine;

But hee's a temperate man indeed
That with a leafe can dine.
Hee needes no napkin for his handes,
His fingers for to wipe;
He hath his kitchin in a box,
His roast meate in a pipe.

When the war spread itself over the country, many of these Roaring Boys became soldiers, and disgraced the profession by rapacity and cruelty. The pamphlets of the parliamentarians abound with complaints of the outrages perpetrated by the Cavaliers, and the evil appears to have been increased by the ill-conduct of the auxiliaries brought over from Ireland to serve the king, who were especially objects of hatred to the Puritans. A broadside among the king's pamphlets is adorned by a satirical picture of "The English Irish Souldier, with his new discipline, new armes, old stomacke, and new taken pillage; who had rather eat than fight." It was published in 1642. The English Irish soldier is, as may be supposed, heavily laden with plunder. In 1646 appeared another caricature, which is copied in our cut No. 180. It represents "England's Wolfe with Eagles clawes: the cruell impieties of bloud-thirsty royalists and blasphemous anti-parliamentarians, under the command of that inhumane prince Rupert, Digby, and the rest, wherein the barbarous crueltie of our civill uncivill warres is briefly discovered." England's wolf, as will be seen, is dressed in the high fashion of the gay courtiers of the time.

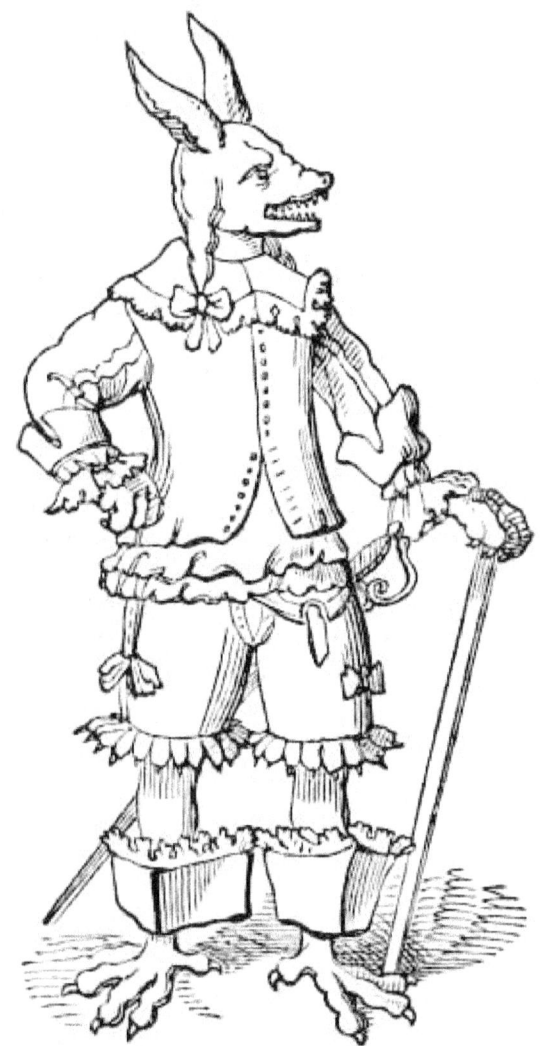

No. 180. "England's Wolf."

A few large caricatures, embodying satire of a more comprehensive description, appeared from time to time, during this troubled age. Such is a large emblematical picture, published on the 9th of November, 1642, and entitled "Heraclitus' Dream," for the scene is supposed to be manifested to the philosopher in a vision. In the middle of the picture the sheep are seen shearing their shepherd; while one cuts his hair, another treats his beard in the same manner. Under the picture we read the couplet—

The flocke that was wont to be shorne by the herd,
Now polleth the shepherd in spight of his beard.

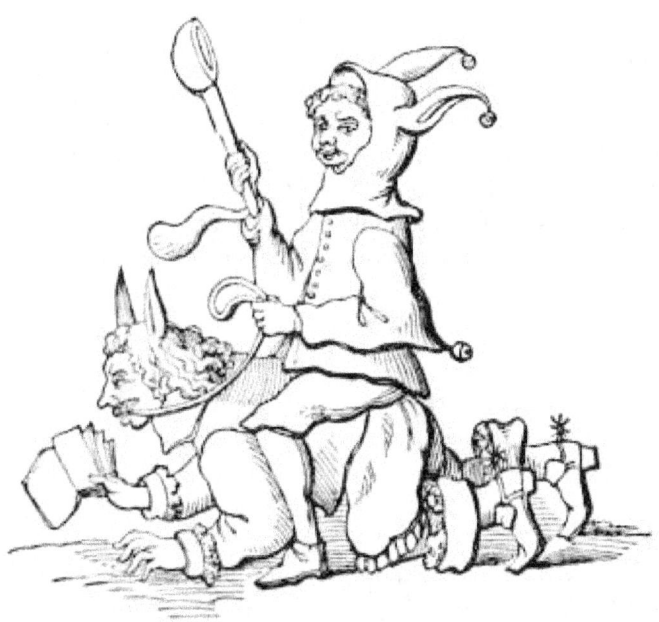

No. 181. Folly Uppermost.

On the 19th of January, 1647, a caricature appeared under the title "An Embleme of the Times." On one side War, represented as a giant in armour, is seen standing upon a heap of dead and mutilated bodies, while Hypocrisy, in the form of a woman with two faces, is flying towards a distant city. "Libertines," "anti-sabbatarians," and others, are hastening in the same direction; and the angel of pestilence, hovering over the city, is ready to pounce upon it.

The party of the parliament was now triumphant, and the question of religion again became the subject of dispute. The Presbyterians had been establishing a sort of tyranny over men's minds, and sought to proscribe all other sects, till their intolerance gradually raised up a strong and general feeling of resistance. Since 1643 a brisk war of political pamphlets had been carried on between the Presbyterians and their opponents, when, in 1647, the Independents, whose cause had been espoused by the army, gained the mastery. "Sir John Presbyter" or to use the more familiar phrase, "Jack Presbyter," furnished a subject for frequent satire, and the Presbyterians were not slow in returning the blow. In the collection in the British Museum we find a caricature which must have come from the Presbyterian party, entitled "Reall Persecution, or the Foundation of a general Toleration, displaied and portrayed by a proper emblem, and adorned with the same flowers wherewith the scoffers of this last age have strowed their libellous pamphlets." The group which occupies the middle part of this broadside, is copied in our cut No. 181. It has its separate title, "The Picture of an English Persecutor, or a foole-ridden ante-Presbeterian sectary." (I give the spelling as in the original.) Folly is riding on the sectarian, whom he holds with a bridle, the sectarian having the ears of an ass. The following homely rhymes are placed in the mouth of Folly,—

Behould my habit, like my witt,
Equalls his on whom sitt.

Anti-Presbyterian is, as will be seen, dressed in the height of the fashion, and says—

My cursed speeches against Presbetry
Declares unto the world my foolery.

The mortification of the Presbyterians led in Scotland to the proclamation of Charles II. as king, and to the ill-fated expedition which ended in the battle of Worcester in 1651, when satirical pamphlets, ballads, and caricatures against the Scottish Presbyterians became for a while very popular. One of the best of the latter is represented in our cut No. 182. Its object is to ridicule the conditions which the Presbyterians exacted from the young prince before they offered him the crown. It is printed in the middle of the broadside, in prose, published on the 14th of July, 1651, with the general title, "Old Sayings and Predictions verified and fulfilled, touching the young King of Scotland and his gude subjects." The picture has its separate title, "The Scots holding their young kinges nose to the grinstone." followed by the lines—

Come to the grinstone, Charles, 'tis now to late
To recolect, 'tis presbiterian fate,
You covinant pretenders, must I bee
The subject of youer tradgie-comedie?

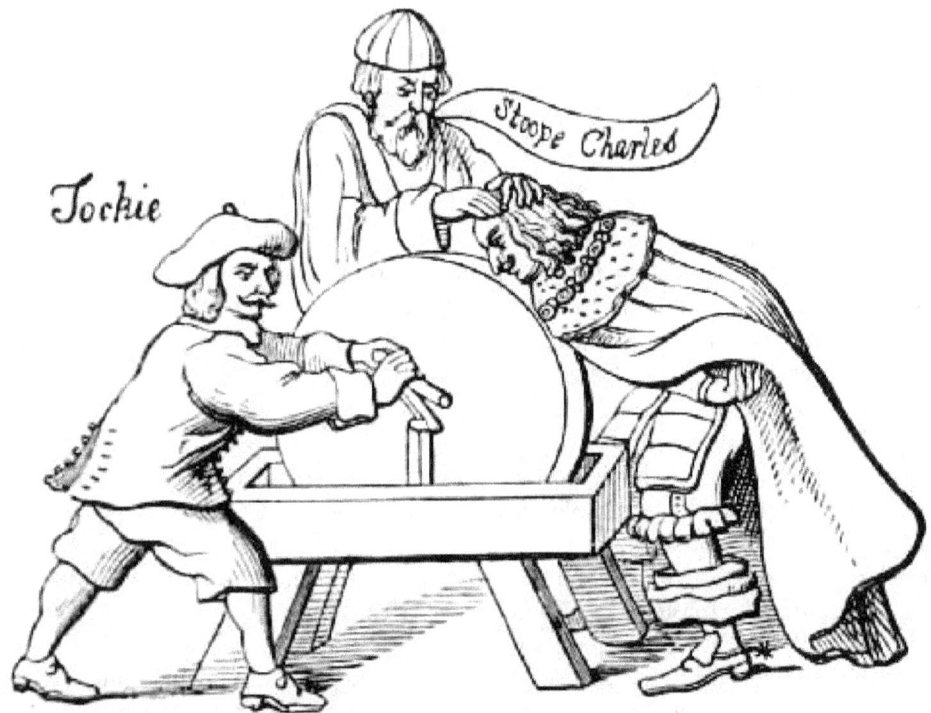

No. 182. Conditions of Royalty.

In fact, the picture represents Presbyterianism—Jack Presbyter—holding the young king's nose to the grindstone, which is turned by the Scots, personified as Jockey. The following lines are put into the mouths of the three actors in this scene:—

Jockey.—I, Jockey, turne the stone of all your plots,
For none turnes faster than the turne-coat Scots.
Presbyter.—We for our ends did make thee king, be sure,
Not to rule us, we will not that endure.
King.—You deep dissemblers, I kow what you doe,
And, for revenges sake, I will dissemble too.

Charles's defeat and flight from Worcester furnished materials for a much more elaborate caricature than most of the similar productions of this period, and of a somewhat singular design. It was published on the 6th of November, 1651, and bears the title "A Mad Designe; or a Description of the king of Scots marching in his disguise, after the Rout at Worcester." A long, and not unnecessary, explanation of the several groups forming this picture, enables us to understand it. On the left Charles is seated on the globe "in a melancholy posture." A little to the right, and nearly in front, the bishop of Clogher is performing mass, at which lords Ormond and Inchquin, in the shapes of strange animals, hold torches, and the lord Taaf, in the form of a monkey, holds up the bishop's train. The Scottish army is seen marching up, consisting, according to the description, of papists, prelatical malignants, Presbyterians, and old cavaliers; the latter of whom are represented by the "fooles head upon a pole in the rear." The next group consists of two monkeys, one with a fiddle, the other carrying a long staff with a torch at the end, concerning which we learn that "The two ridiculous anticks, one with a fiddle, and the other with a torch, set forth the ridiculousness of their condition when they marched into England, carried up with high thoughts, yet altogether in the darke, having onely a fooles bawble to be their light to walke by, mirth of their own whimsies to keep up their spirits, and a sheathed sword to truste in." Next come a troop of women, children, and papists, lamenting over their defeat. Two monkeys on foot, and one on horseback, follow, the latter riding with his face turned to the horse's tail, and carrying in his hand a spit with provisions on it. It is explained as "The Scots Kings flight from Worcester, represented by the foole on horseback, riding backward, turning his face every way in feares, ushered by duke Hambleton and the lord Wilmot." Lastly, a crowd of women with flags bring up the rear. It cannot be said that the wit displayed in this satire is of the very highest order.

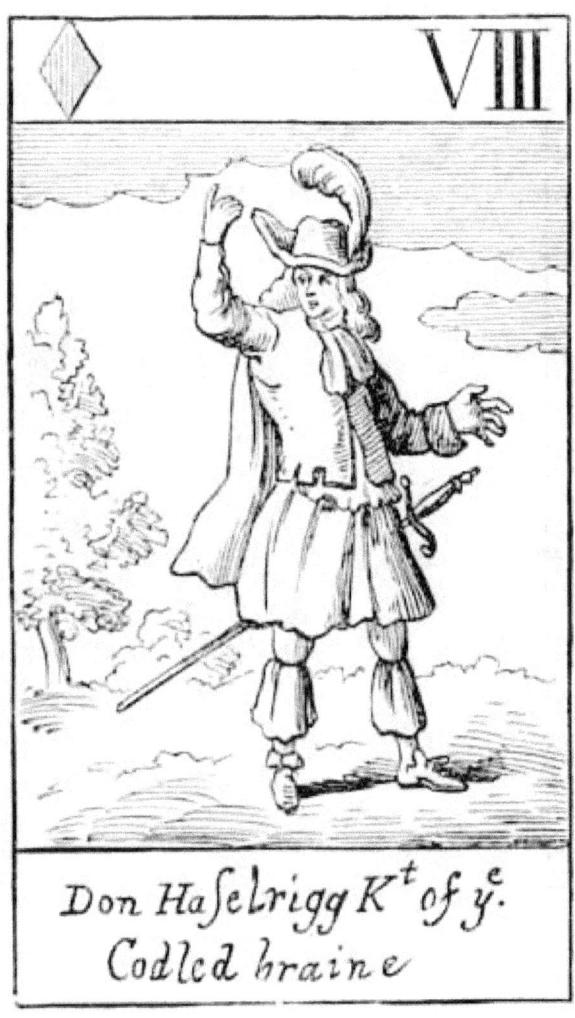

No. 183. Arthur Haselrigg.

After this period we meet with comparatively few caricatures until the death of Cromwell, and the eve of the Restoration, when there came a new and fierce struggle of political parties. The Dutch were the subject of some satirical prints and pamphlets in 1652; and we find a small number of caricatures on the social evils, such as drunkenness and gluttony, and on one or two subjects of minor agitation. With the close of the Commonwealth a new form of caricature came in. Playing cards had, during this seventeenth century, been employed for various purposes which were quite alien to their original character. In France they were made the means of conveying instruction to children. In England, at the time of which we are speaking, they were adopted as the medium for spreading political caricature. The earliest of these packs of cards known is one which appears to have been published at the very moment of the restoration of Charles II., and which was, perhaps, engraved in Holland. It contains a series of caricatures on the principal acts of the Commonwealth, and on the parliamentary leaders. Among other cards of a similar character which have been preserved is a pack relating to the popish plot, another relating to the Rye House conspiracy, one on the Mississippi scheme, published in Holland, and one on the South Sea bubble.

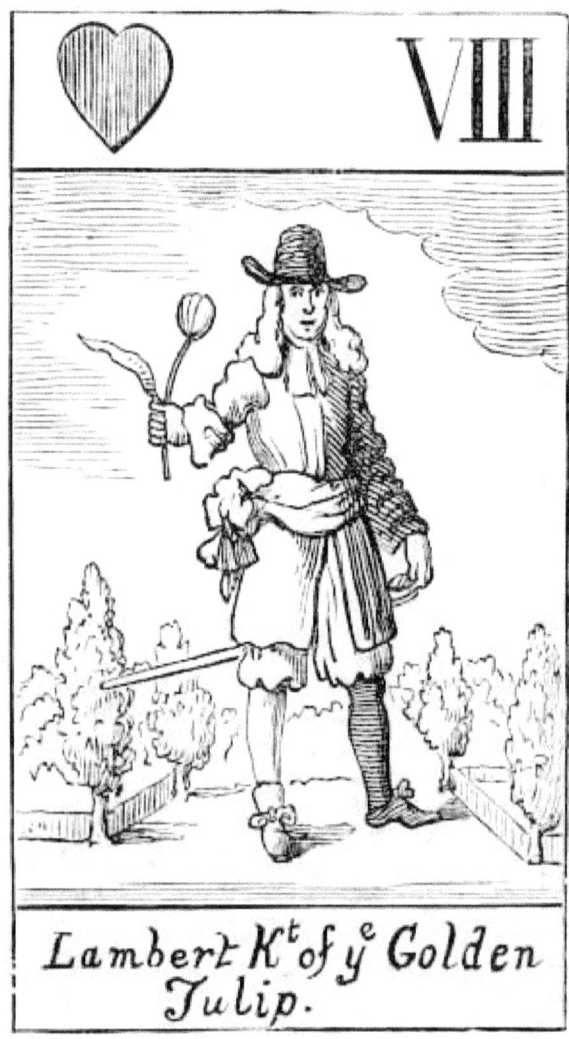

No. 184. General Lambert.

The earliest of these packs of satirical cards, that on the Commonwealth, belonged a few years ago to a lady of the name of Prest, and is very fully described in a paper by Mr. Pettigrew, printed in the "Journal of the British Archæological Association." Each of the fifty-two cards presents a picture with a satirical title. Thus the ace of diamonds represents "The High Court of Justice, or Oliver's Slaughter House." The eight of diamonds is represented in our cut No. 183; its subject is "Don Haselrigg, Knight of the Codled Braine." It is hardly necesiary to say that Sir Arthur Haselrigg acted a very prominent and remarkable part during the whole of the Commonwealth period, and that his manners were impetuous and authoritative, which was probably the meaning of the epithet here given to him. The card of the king of diamonds represents rather unequivocally the subject indicated by its title, "Sir H. Mildmay solicits a citizen's wife, for which his owne corrects him." It is an allusion to one of the petty scandals of the republican period. The eight of hearts is a satire on major-general Lambert. This able and distinguished man was remarkably fond of flowers, took great pleasure in cultivating them, and was skilful in drawing them, which was one of his favourite amusements. He withdrew to Amsterdam during the Protectorate, and there gave full indulgence to this love of flowers, and I need hardly say that it was the age of the great tulip mania in Holland. When, after the Restoration, he was involved in the fate of the regicides, but had his sentence commuted for thirty years of imprisonment, he alleviated the dulness of his long confinement in the isle of Guernsey by the same amusement. In the card we have engraved, Lambert is represented in his garden, holding a large tulip in his hand; and it is no doubt in allusion to this innocent taste that he is here entitled "Lambert, Knight of the Golden Tulip."

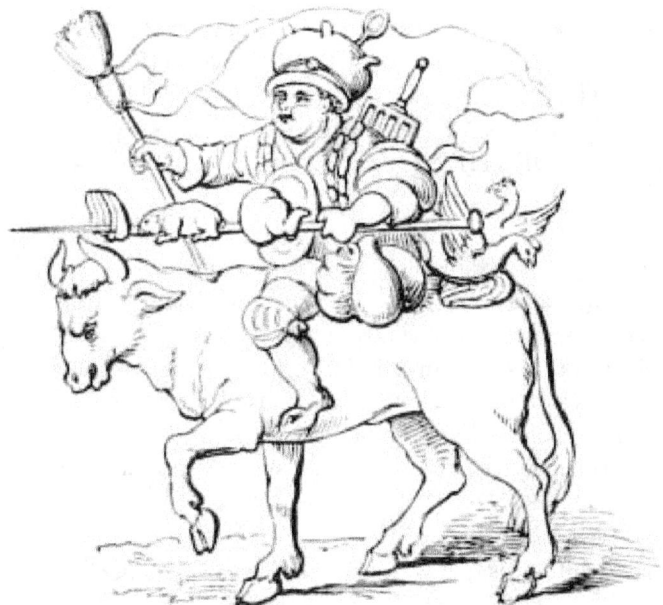

No. 185. Shrovetide.

The Restoration furnished better songs than prints, and many years passed before any caricatures worthy of notice appeared in England. Even burlesque subjects of any merit occur but rarely, and I hardly know of one which is worth describing here. Among the best of those I have met with, is a pair of plates, published in 1660, representing Lent and Shrovetide, and these, I believe, are copied or imitated from foreign prints. Lent is come as a thin miserable-looking knight-errant, appropriately armed and mounted, ready to give battle to Shrovetide, whose good living is pernicious to the whole community, and he abuses his opponent in good round terms. In the companion print, of which our cut No. 185 is a copy, Shrovetide appears as a jolly champion, quite ready to meet his enemy. He is best described in the following lines, extracted from the verses which accompany the prints:—

Fatt Shrovetyde, mounted on a good fatt oxe,
Supposd that Lent was mad, or caught a foxe,[99]
Armed cap-a-pea from head unto the heel,
A spit his long sword, somewhat worse than steale,
(Sheath'd in a fatt pigge and a peece of porke),
His bottles fild with wine, well stopt with corke;
The two plump capons fluttering at his crupper;
And 's shoulders lac'd with sawsages for supper;
The gridir'n (like a well strung instrument)
Hung at his backe, and for the turnament
His helmet is a brasse pott, and his flagge
A cookes foule apron, which the wind doth wagg,
Fixd to a broome: thus bravely he did ride,
And boldly to his foe he thus replied.

CHAPTER XXII.

ENGLISH COMEDY.—BEN JONSON.—THE OTHER WRITERS OF HIS SCHOOL.—
INTERRUPTION OF DRAMATIC PERFORMANCES.—COMEDY AFTER THE
RESTORATION.—THE HOWARDS BROTHERS; THE DUKE OF BUCKINGHAM; THE
REHEARSAL.—WRITERS OF COMEDY IN THE LATTER PART OF THE
SEVENTEENTH CENTURY.—INDECENCY OF THE STAGE.—COLLEY CIBBER.—
FOOTE.

In England, as in Athens of old, perfect comedy arose gradually out of the personalities of the rude dramatic attempts of an earlier period. Such productions as Ralph Roister Doister and Gammer Gurton's Needle were mere imperfect attempts at, we may perhaps rather say feelers towards, comedy itself—that drama, the object of which was to caricature, and thus to dissect and apply correctives to, the vices and weaknesses of contemporary society. The genius of Shakespeare was far too exquisitely poetical to qualify him for a task like this; it wanted some one who could use the lancet and scalpel skilfully, but soberly, and who was not liable to be led astray by too much vigour of imagination.

Such a one was Ben Jonson, whom we may rightly consider as the father of English comedy. "Bartholomew Fair," first performed at the Hope Theatre, on Bankside, London, on the 31st of October, 1614, is the most perfect and most remarkable example of the truly English comedy, remarkable, among many other things, for the extraordinary number of characters who were brought upon the stage in one piece, and who are all at the same time grouped and individualised with a skill that reminds us of the pictorial triumphs of a Callot or a Hogarth. London life is placed before us in all its more popular forms in one grand tableau, the one in which it would show itself in its more grotesque attitudes; the London citizen, his vain or easy wife, sharpers of every description, and their victims no less varied in character, the petty city officers, all come in for their share of satire. The different groups are distributed so naturally, that it is difficult to say who is the principal character of the piece—and who ever was the principal character in Bartholomew Fair? Perhaps the character of Cokes, the young booby squire from Harrow—for in those times even so near London as Harrow, a young squire was considered to be in all probability but a young country booby—strikes us most. It is said to have been at a later period the favourite character of Charles II. Among the other principal characters of the play are a proctor of the Arches Court named Littlewit, who imagines himself to be a *bel esprit* of the first order; his wife, and her mother, dame Purecraft, who is a widow; Justice Overdo, a London magistrate, to whose ward, Grace Wellborn, Cokes is affianced in marriage; a zealous Puritan, named Zeal-of-the-land Busy, who is a suitor to the widow Purecraft, herself also a Puritan; Winwife, Busy's rival; and a gamester named Tom Quarlous, who figures as Winwife's friend and companion. All these meet in town, on the morning of the fair, Cokes under the care of a sort of steward or upper servant, named Waspe, who was of a quarrelsome disposition, and separate in groups among the crowd which filled Smithfield and its vicinity, each having their separate adventures, but meeting from time to time, and reassembling at the end. Cokes behaves as a simpleton from the country, longs for everything, and wonders at everything, buys up toys and gingerbread, is separated from all his companions, robbed of his money and even of his outer garments, and in this condition finally settles down at a puppet-show. Meanwhile the Puritan Busy, by his zeal against the "heathen abominations" of the fair on one hand, and Waspe, by his quarrelsome temper on the other, fall into a series of scrapes, which end in both being carried to the stocks. They are there joined by another important personage. Justice Overdo, who is distinguished by an extraordinary zeal for the right administration of justice and the suppression of social vices of all kinds, has come into the fair in disguise, in order to make himself acquainted with its various abuses, and he passes among them unknown; and his inquisitive intermeddling brings him into a variety of mishaps, in the course of which he also is seized by the constable, and allows himself to be taken to the stocks, rather than betray his identity. Thus all three, Busy, Waspe, and Overdo, are placed in the stocks at the same time; but Waspe, by a clever trick, escapes, and leaves the Puritan and the justice confined together, the one looking upon himself as a martyr for religion's sake, the other rather glorying in suffering through his disinterested zeal for the common good. They, too, after a while make their escape through an accidental oversight of their keepers, and mix again with the mob. The women, likewise, have been separated from their male companions, have fallen among sharpers and bullies, been made drunk, and escaped but narrowly from still worse disasters. They all finally meet before the puppet-show, which has fixed the attention of Cokes, and there justice Overdo discovers himself. Such are the materials of Ben Jonson's "Bartholomew Fair," the busiest and most amusing of plays. It is said, when first acted, to have given great satisfaction to king James, by the ridicule thrown upon the Puritans, and it continued to be a favourite comedy when revived after the Restoration.

"The Alchemist," by the same author, preceded "Bartholomew Fair," by four years, and was designed as a satire upon a class of impostors who, in that age, were among the greatest pests of society, and were instruments, one way or other, in the greatest crimes of the day. "The Alchemist" belongs, also, to the pure English comedy, but its plot is more simple and distinct than that of "Bartholomew Fair." It involves events which may have occurred frequently, at periods when the metropolis was from time to time exposed to the vicissitudes of the plague. On one of these occasions, Lovewit, a London gentleman, obliged to quit the metropolis in order to avoid the plague, leaves his town house to the charge of one man-servant, Face, who proves dishonest, associates himself with a rogue named Subtle, and an immoral woman named Dol Common, and introduces them into the house, which is made the basis for their subsequent operations. Subtle assumes the character of a magician and alchemist, while Dol acts various female parts, and Face goes about alluring people into their snares. Among their dupes are a knight who lives upon the town, two English Puritans from Amsterdam, a lawyer's clerk, a tobacco man, a young country squire, and his sister dame Pliant, a widow. The various intrigues in which these individuals are involved, show us the way in which the pretended conjurers and alchemists contributed to all the vices of the town. At length their base dealings are on the point of being exposed by the cunning of one upon whom they had attempted to impose, when Truewit, the master of the house, returns unexpectedly, and all is discovered, but the alchemist and his female associate contrive to escape.

The object of their last intrigue had been to entrap dame Pliant, who was rich, into a marriage with a needy sharper; and Lovewit, finding the lady in the house, and liking her, marries her himself, and, in consideration of the satisfaction he has thus procured, forgives his unfaithful servant. Many have considered the Alchemist to be the best of Jonson's dramas. "Epicœne, or the Silent Woman," which belongs to the year 1609, is another satirical picture of London society, in which the same class of characters appear. Morose, an eccentric gentleman of fortune, who has a great horror for noise, and even obliges his servants to communicate with him by signs, has a nephew, a young knight named Sir Dauphine Eugenie, with whom he is dissatisfied, and he refuses to allow him money for his support. A plot is laid by his friends, whereby the uncle is led into a marriage with a supposed silent woman, named Epicœne, but she only sustains the character until the wedding formalities are completed, and these are followed by a scene of noise and riot, which completely horrifies Morose, and leads to a reconciliation with his nephew, to whom he makes over half his fortune. The earliest of Ben Jonson's comedies, "Every Man in his Humour," was composed in its present form in 1598, and is the first of these dramatic satires on the manners and character of the citizens of London, of whom it was fashionable at the courts of James I. and Charles I. to speak contemptuously. Kno'well, an old gentleman of respectability, is highly displeased with his son Edward, because the latter has taken to writing poetry, and has formed a friendship with another gentleman of his own age, who loves poetry and frequents the rather gay society of the poets and wits of the town. Wellbred has a half-brother, a "plain squire," named Downright, and a sister married to a rich city merchant named Kitely. Kitely, the merchant, who is extremely jealous of his wife, has a great desire to reform Wellbred, and draw him to a steadier line of life, a sentiment in which Downright heartily joins. Kitely's jealousy, and the steps taken to reform Wellbred, lead to the most comic parts of the play, which concludes with the marriage of young Kno'well to Kitely's daughter, Miss Bridget, and his reconciliation with his father. Among the other characters in the piece are captain Bobadil, "a blustering coward," justice Clement, "an old merry magistrate," his clerk, Roger Formal, and a country gull and a town gull.

These comedies of London life became popular, and continued so during this and the following reign—in fact, the mass of those who attended the theatres could understand and appreciate them better than any others, and, what was more, they felt them. Among Jonson's contemporaries in the literature of this English comedy were Middleton and Thomas Heywood, both very prolific writers, Chapman, and Marston. Certain classes of characters are continually repeated in this comedy, because they belonged especially to the London society of the time, but the employment and distribution of these characters admitted of great variations, and they perhaps often had at the time a special interest, as representing known individuals, or as being combined in a plot which was built upon real incidents in London life. Among these were usually a country gentleman of fortune, who was very avaricious, and had a spendthrift son, or who had a daughter, a rich heiress, who was the object of the intrigues of spendthrift suitors; young heirs, who have just come to their estates, and are spending them in London; young country squires who are easy victims; a needy knight, as poor in principles as in money, who lived upon the public in every way he could; designing and unscrupulous women; bullies and sharpers of every description. In fact, we seem to be always in the smell of the tavern, and in the midst of dissipation. Then there are fat, sleek, and wealthy citizens, whole souls are entirely wrapt up in their merchandise, who are proud, nevertheless, of their position; and easy, credulous city wives, who are fond of finery and of praise, eager for gaiety and display, impatient of the rule of husbands, or of the dulness of home, and very ready to listen to the advances of the gay gallants from the court end of the town, or from the tavern. The city tradesman has generally an apprentice or two, sometimes very sober but perhaps more frequently dissipated, who play their parts in the piece; and often a daughter, who is either a model of modesty and all the domestic virtues, and is finally the reward of some hero of good principles, who has been temporarily led astray, and his character misinterpreted, or who is gay and intriguing, and comes to disgrace. But the favourite idea of excellence, or, to use a technical phrase, the *beau ideal* of this comedy, appears to have been a wild youth, who goes through every scene of dissipation, in a gentlemanly manner (as the term was then understood), and comes out at the end of the play as an honest, virtuous man, and receives the reward for qualities which he had not previously displayed.

Sometimes the writers of this comedy indulged in personal, or even in political, allusions which brought them into trouble. In the year 1605, Ben Jonson, George Chapman, and John Marston, wrote jointly a comedy entitled "Eastward Hoe." It is a very excellent and amusing comedy, and was very popular. Touchstone, an honest goldsmith in the city, has two apprentices, Golding, a sober and industrious youth, and Quicksilver, who is an irreclaimable rake. Touchstone has also two daughters, the eldest of whom, Gertrude, affects the fine lady, and is ambitious of finding a husband in the fashionable world, while her younger sister, Mildred, is all virtue and humility. An attachment arises between Golding and Mildred. Another character in this drama is a needy, scheming knight, who lives upon the town, and rejoices in the name of Sir Petronel Flash. Sir Petronel is attracted by the rich dowry which the young lady, Gertrude, had to expect, pays his court to her, and easily works upon her vanity; and, her mother encouraging her, they are hastily married, contrary to the wishes of her father. The knight is supposed to possess a magnificent castle somewhere to the east of London, and the young bride and her mother proceed in search of this, from which the comedy derives its title of "Eastward Hoe," but they are involved in various disagreeable adventures in the search, which ends in the conviction that it is all a fable. Another character in the play is a greedy and unprincipled usurer, who is so jealous of his young and pretty wife, that he keeps her under lock and key; and this man is deeply involved in money-lending with Sir Petronel Flash, and they are engaged in a series of unprincipled transactions, which lead to the disgrace of them all, and in the course of which the virtue of the usurer's wife falls a sacrifice. Meanwhile the fortunes of the two apprentices have been advancing in directly opposite directions. Quicksilver, the unworthy apprentice, leaves his master, proceeds from bad to worse, and finally is committed to prison, for a crime the punishment of which was death. On the other hand, Golding has not only gained his master's esteem and married his daughter Mildred, and been adopted as the heir to his wealth, but he has merited the respect of his fellow-citizens, and has been promoted in municipal rank. It becomes Golding's duty to preside over the trial of his old fellow apprentice Quicksilver, but the latter escapes through Golding's generosity.

There is some sound morality in the spirit of this comedy, and a very large amount of immorality in the text. There was, indeed, a coarse licence in the relations of society at this period, which are but too faithfully represented in its literature. But there are two circumstances, accidentally attached to this drama, which give it a peculiar interest. When brought out upon the stage it contained reflections upon Scotchmen which provoked the anger of king James I. to such a degree, that all the authors were seized and thrown into prison, and narrowly escaped the loss of their ears and noses, but they obtained their release with some difficulty, and only through powerful intercession. In the copy which has been brought down to us through the press, we find no reflections whatever upon Scotchmen, so that it must have been altered from the original text. When we consider that, at this time, the English court and capital were crowded with needy Scottish adventurers, who were looked upon with great jealousy, it is not improbable that in the original form of the comedy, Sir Petronel Flash may have been a Scotchman, and intended not only as a satire upon the Scottish adventurers in general, but to have been designed for some one in particular who had the means of bringing upon the authors the extreme displeasure of the court.

The other circumstance which has given celebrity to this comedy, is one of still greater interest. After the Restoration, it was new modelled by Nicholas Tate, and brought again upon the stage under the title of "Cuckold's Haven." Perhaps through this remodelled edition, Hogarth took from the comedy of "Eastward Hoe," the idea of his series of plates of the history of the Idle and Industrious Apprentices.

When we consider the ridicule which was continually thrown upon them in this earlier period of the English comedy, we can easily understand the bitterness with which the Puritans regarded the stage and the drama. When they obtained power, the stage, as might be expected, was suppressed, and for some years England was without a theatre. At the Restoration, however, the theatres were opened again, and with greater freedom than ever. At first the old comedies of the days of James I. and Charles I. were revived, and many of them, modified and adapted to the new circumstances, were again brought upon the stage. The original comedies which appeared immediately after the Restoration, were often marked with a political tinge; as the stage saw its natural protectors in the court, and in the court party, it embraced their politics; and Puritans, Roundheads, Whigs, all whose principles were supposed to be contrary to royalty and arbitrary power, fell under its satire. Such was the character of the comedy of "The Cheats," by a play-writer of some repute named Wilson, which was brought out in 1662. The object of this play appears to have been, in the first place, to satirise the Nonconformists or Puritanical clergy—with whom were classed the astrologers and conjurers, who had increased in number during the Commonwealth time, and infested society more than ever—and the city magistrates, who were not looked upon as being generally over-loyal. The three cheats who are the heroes of this comedy, are Scruple, the Nonconformist, Mopus, a pretender to physic and astrology, and alderman Whitebroth. Direct personal attacks had been introduced into the comedy of the Restoration, and it is probable that somebody of influence was satirised under the name of Scruple, for the play was suppressed by authority, and at a later period, when it was revived, the prologue announces this fact in the following words:—

Sad news, my masters; and too true, I fear,
For us—Scruple's a silenc'd minister.
Would ye the cause? The brethren snivel, and say,
'Tis scandalous that any cheat but they.

Many of the dramatists of the Restoration were men of good and aristocratic families, witty and profligate cavaliers, who had returned from exile with their king. The family of the earl of Berkshire produced no less than four writers of comedy, all brothers, Edward Howard, colonel Henry Howard, sir Robert Howard, and James Howard, while their sister, the lady Elizabeth Howard, was married to the poet Dryden. Edward Howard's first dramatic piece was a tragi-comedy entitled "The Usurper," which came out in 1668, and was intended as a satire upon Cromwell. His best known comedies were "The Man of Newmarket," and "Woman's Conquest." Colonel Henry Howard composed a comedy entitled "United Kingdoms," which appears not to have been printed. To James Howard, the youngest of the brothers, the play-going public, even then rather a large one, owed "The English Mounsieur," and "All Mistaken, or the Mad Couple." Sir Robert Howard was the best writer of the four, and wrote both tragedies and comedies, which were afterwards published collectively. The best of his comedies is "The Committee," which was first brought on the stage in 1665, and through some chance, certainly not by its merit, continued to be an acting play during the whole of the last century.

"The Committee" is by far the best of the dramatic writings of the Howards. Its design was to turn to ridicule the Commonwealth men and the Puritans. Colonel Blunt and colonel Careless are two royalists, whose estates are in the hands of the committee of sequestrations, and who repair to London for the purpose of compounding for them. The chairman of the committee is a Mr. Day, a worldly-minded and sufficiently selfish Puritan, but who is ruled by his more crafty and still less scrupulous wife, a designing and very talkative woman. Both are of low origin, for Mrs. Day had been a kitchen-woman, and both are very proud and very tyrannical. Among the other principal characters are Abel Day, their son, Obadiah, the clerk to the committee, a man in the interest of the Days, and an Irish servant named Teague, who had been the servant of Careless's dear friend, a royalist officer killed in battle, and whom the colonel finds in great distress, and takes into his own service out of charity. The character of Teague is a very poor caricature upon an Irishman, and his blunders and bulls are of a very spiritless description. Here is an example. Teague has overheard the two colonels state that they should be obliged to take the Covenant, and express their reluctance to do it, and in his inconsiderate zeal, he hurries away to try if he cannot take the covenant for them, and thus save them a disagreeable operation. In the street he meets a wandering bookseller—a class of pedlars who were then common—and a scene takes place which is best given in the words of the original:—

Bookseller.—New books, new books! A Desperate Plot and Engagement of the Bloody Cavaliers! Mr. Saltmarshe's Alarum to the Nation, after having been three days dead! Mercurius Britannicus—

Teague.—How's that? They cannot live in Ireland after they are dead three days!

Book.—Mercurius Britannicus, or the Weekly Post, or the Solemn League and Covenant!

Teag.—What is that you say? Is it the Covenant you have?

Book.—Yes; what then, sir?

Teag.—Which is that Covenant?

Book.—Why, this is the Covenant.

Teag.—Well, I must take that Covenant.

Book.—You take my commodities?

Teag.—I must take that Covenant, upon my soul, now.

Book.—Stand off, sir, or I'll set you further!

Teag.—Well, upon my soul, now, I will take the Covenant for my master.

Book.—Your master must pay me for't, then!

Teag.—I must take it first, and my master will pay you afterwards.

Book.—You must pay me now.

Teag.—Oh! that I will [*Knocks him down*]. Now you're paid, you thief of the world. Here's Covenants enough to poison the whole nation.

[*Exit.*

Book.—What a devil ails this fellow? [*Crying*]. He did not come to rob me, certainly; for he has not taken above two-pennyworth of lamentable ware away; but I feel the rascal's fingers. I may light upon my wild Irishman again, and, if I do, I will fix him with some catchpole, that shall be worse than his own country bogs.

[*Exit.*

In the sequel, Teague is caught by the constables, and is liberated at the interference of his master, who pays twopence for the book. The plot of the comedy is but a simple one, and is neither skilfully nor naturally carried out. Colonel Blunt comes to London from Reading in the inside of a stage-coach, having for his travelling companions Mrs. Day, her supposed daughter Ruth, and Arabella, a young lady whose father is recently dead, leaving his estates in the hands of the committee of sequestrations. Ruth is, in truth, a young lady whose estates the Days have, under similar circumstances, robbed her of, and it is their design to treat Arabella in the same manner, under disguise of forcing her to marry their son Abel, a vain silly lad. To effect this, as the committee itself requires some influencing to engage them in the selfish plans of their chairman, Day and his wife forge a letter from the exiled king, complimenting the former on his great power and influence and talents as a statesman, and offering him great rewards if he will secretly promote his cause. Day communicates this to the committee under the pretext that it is his duty to make them acquainted with all such perfidious designs that might come to his knowledge, and they, convinced of his honesty and value to them, give up Arabella's estates to the Days, and she falls entirely under their power. Meanwhile, on the one hand, Arabella has gained the confidence of Ruth, who makes her acquainted with the whole plot against her and her estates, and on the other, Ruth falls in love with colonel Careless, and colonel Blunt is smitten with the charms of Arabella, and all this takes place in the committee room. Various incidents follow, which seem not very much to the purpose, but at last, as the marriage of Arabella to Abel Day is pressed forward, the two young ladies, although as yet they have hardly had an interview with the colonels, resolve to make their escape from the house of the chairman of the committee, and fly to their lovers for protection. A short absence from the house of Mr. and Mrs. Day and their son together, presents the desired opportunity, and Day having accidentally left his keys behind him, the idea suggests itself to Ruth to open his cabinet, and gain possession of the deeds and papers of her own estates and those of Arabella. As she had before this secretly observed the private drawer in which they were placed, she met with no difficulty in effecting her purpose, and not only found these documents, but also with them the forged letter from the king, and some letters addressed to Day by young women whom he was secretly keeping, and who demanded money for the support of children they had by him, and alluded to matters of a still more serious character. Ruth takes possession of all these, and thus laden, the two damsels hurry away, and reach without interruption the house where they were to meet the colonels. The Days return home immediately after the departure of their wards, and at once suspect the real state of affairs, which is fully confirmed, when Mr. Day finds that his most private drawer has been opened, and his most important papers carried off. They immediately proceed in search of the fugitives, having sent orders for a detachment of soldiers to assist them, and the house in which the lovers have taken refuge is surrounded before they have had time to escape. Finding it useless to attempt resistance by force, the besieged call for a parley, and then Ruth frightens Day by acquainting him with the contents of the private letters she has become possessed of, and his wife by the knowledge she has obtained of the forged letter, which also she has in her possession. The Days are thus overreached, and the play ends with a general reconciliation. The ladies are left with the titles of their estates, and with their lovers, and we are left to suppose that they afterwards married, and were happy.

The plot of "The Committee," it will be seen, is not a very capital one, but the manner in which it is worked out is still worse. The dialogue is extremely tame, and the incidents are badly interwoven. When I say that the example of wit given above is the best in the play, and that there are not many attempts at wit in it, it will hardly be thought that it could be amusing, and we cannot but feel astonished at the popularity which it once enjoyed. This popularity, indeed, is only explained by the fashion of ridiculing the Puritans, which then prevailed so strongly; and it perhaps retained its place on the stage during the last century chiefly from the circumstance of its wanting the objectionable qualities which characterised the written plays of the latter half of the seventeenth century.

"The Committee" is, after all, one of the very best comedies of the school of dramatists represented by the brothers Howard. Contemporary with this school of flat comedies, there was a school of equally inflated tragedy, and both soon became objects of ridicule to the satirists of the day. Of these, one of the boldest was George Villiers, duke of Buckingham, the son of the favourite of king James I., and equally celebrated for his talents and his profligacy. Buckingham is said to have planned and begun his satirical comedy of "The Rehearsal" as early as the year 1663, and to have had it ready for representation towards the December of 1665, when the breaking out of the great plague caused the theatres to be closed. After this interruption its author, who was a desultory writer, appears to have laid it aside for some time and then, new objects for satire having presented themselves, he altered and modified it, and it was finally completed in 1671, when it was brought out at the Theatre Royal in Covent Garden. It is said that Buckingham was assisted in the composition of this satire, but it is not stated in what manner, by Butler, and by Martin Clifford, of the Charter-house. It is understood that, in the first form of his satire, Buckingham had chosen the Hon. Edward Howard for its hero, and that he afterwards exchanged him for Sir William Davenant, but he finally fixed upon Dryden, whose tragedies and comedies are certainly not the best of his writings—possibly some personal pique may have had an influence in the selection. Nevertheless, with Dryden, the Howards, Davenant, and one or two other writers of comedy, come in for their share of ridicule. Dryden, under the name of Bayes, has composed a new drama, and a friend named Johnson goes to witness the rehearsal of this play, taking with him a country friend of the name of Smith. The play itself is a piece of mockery throughout, made up of parodies, often very happy, on the different play-writers of the day, and especially upon Dryden; and it is mixed up with a running conversation between Bayes, the author, and his two visitors, which is full of satirical humour. The first part of the prologue explains to us sufficiently the spirit in which this satire was written.

We might well call this short mock-play of ours
A posie made of weeds instead of flowers;
Yet such have been presented to your noses,
And there are such, I fear, who thought 'em roses.
Would some of 'em were here, to see this night
What stuff it is in which they took delight.
Here, brisk, insipid rogues, for wit, let fall
Sometimes dull sense, but oft'ner none at all;
There, strutting heroes, with a grim-fac'd train,
Shalt brave the gods, in king Cambyses vein.
For (changing rules, of late, as if men writ
In spite of reason, nature, art, and wit)
Our poets make us laugh at tragedy,
And with their comedies they make us cry.

A short account of this satire will, perhaps, be best understood, if I explain that the antagonism of two contending kings of Granada having been a favourite idea of Dryden in his tragedies, Buckingham is said to have designed to ridicule him in making two, not rival, but associate kings of Brentford, though others say that these two kings of Brentford were intended for a sneer upon king Charles II. and the duke of York. These two kings are the heroes of Bayes's play. The first act of "The Rehearsal" consists of a discussion between Bayes, Johnson, and Smith, on the general character of the play, in which Bayes exhibits a large amount of vanity and self-confidence, said to have been a characteristic of all these play-writers of the earlier period of the Restoration, and he informs them that he has "made a prologue and an epilogue, which may both serve for either; that is, the prologue for the epilogue, or the epilogue for the prologue, (do you mark!) nay, they may both serve, too, 'egad, for any other play as well as this." Smith observes, "That's indeed artificial." Finally Bayes explains, that as other authors, in their prologues, sought to flatter and propitiate their audience, in order to gain their favourable opinion of the plot, he, on the contrary, intended to force their applause out of them by mere dint of terror, and for that purpose, he had introduced as speakers of his prologue, no less personages than Thunder and Lightning. This prologue, disengaged from the remarks of Bayes and his friends, runs as follows:—

Enter Thunder *and* Lightning.

Thun.—I am the bold Thunder.
Light.—The brisk Lightning I.
Thun.—I am the bravest Hector of the sky.
Light.—And I fair Helen, that made Hector die.
Thun.—I strike men down.
Light.—I fire the town.
Thun.—Let critics take heed how they grumble,
For then I begin for to rumble.
Light.—Let the ladies allow us their graces,
Or I'll blast all the paint on their faces,
And dry up their peter to soot.
Thun.—Let the critics look to't.
Light.—Let the ladies look to't.
Thun.—For the Thunder will do't.
Light.—For the Lightning will shoot.
Thun.—I'll give you dash for dash.
Light.—I'll give you flash for flash.
Gallants, I'll singe your feather.
Thun.—I'll Thunder you together.
Both.—Look to't, look to't; we'll do't, we'll do't; look to't; we'll do't.
[*Twice or thrice repeated.*

Bayes calls this "but a slash of a prologue," in reply to which, Smith observes, "Yes; 'tis short, indeed, but very terrible." It is a parody on a scene in "The Slighted Maid," a play by Sir Robert Stapleton, where Thunder and Lightning were introduced, and their conversation begins in the same words. But the poet has another difficulty on which he desires the opinion of his visitors. "I have made," he says, "one of the most delicate, dainty similes in the whole world, 'egad, if I knew how to apply it. 'Tis," he adds, "an allusion to love." This is the simile—

So boar and sow, when any storm is nigh
Snuff up, and smell it gathering in the sky;
Boar beckons sow to trot in chesnut groves,
And there consummate their unfinished loves:
Pensive in mud they wallow all alone,
And snore and gruntle to each others moan.

It is a rather coarse, but clever parody on a simile in Dryden's "Conquest of Granada," part ii.:—

So two kind turtles, when a storm is nigh,

Look up, and see it gathering in the sky;
Each calls his mate to shelter in the groves,
Leaving, in murmurs, their unfinished loves;
Perch'd on some dropping branch, they sit alone,
And coo, and hearken to each other's moan.

It is decided that the simile should be added to the prologue, for, as Johnson remarks to Bayes, "Faith, 'tis extraordinary fine, and very applicable to Thunder and Lightning, methinks, because it speaks of a storm." In the second act we come to the opening of the play, the first scene consisting of whispering, in ridicule of a scene in Davenant's "Play-house to Let," where Drake senior says—

Draw up your men,
And in low whispers give your orders out.

In fact, the Gentleman-Usher and the Physician of the two kings of Brentford appear upon the scene alone, and discuss a plot to dethrone the two kings of Brentford, which they communicate by whispers into each other's ears, which are totally inaudible. In Scene ii., "Enter the two kings, hand in hand," and Bayes remarks to his visitors, "Oh! these are now the two kings of Brentford; take notice of their style—'twas never yet upon the stage; but, if you like it, I could make a shift, perhaps, to show you a whole play, writ all just so." The kings begin, rather familiarly, because, as Bayes adds, "they are both persons of the same quality:"—

1st King.—Did you observe their whispers, brother king?
2nd King.—I did, and heard, besides, a grave bird sing,
That they intend, sweetheart, to play us pranks.
1st King.—If that design appears,
I'll lay them by the ears,
Until I make 'em crack.
2nd King.—And so will I, i' fack!
1st King.—You must begin, *mon foi.*
2nd King.—Sweet sir, *pardonnez moi.*

Bayes observes that he makes the two kings talk French in order "to show their breeding." In the third act, Bayes introduces a new character, prince Prettyman, a parody upon the character of Leonidas, in Dryden's "Marriage-a-la-Mode." The prince falls asleep, and then his beloved Cloris comes in, and is surprised, upon which Bayes remarks, "Now, here she must make a simile." "Where's the necessity of that, Mr. Bayes?" asks the critical Mr. Smith. "Oh," replies Bayes, "because she's surprised. That's a general rule. You must ever make a simile when you are surprised; 'tis a new way of writing." Now we have another parody upon one of Dryden's similes. In the fourth scene, the Gentleman-Usher and Physician appear again, discussing the question whether their whispers had been heard or not, a discussion which they conclude by seizing on the two thrones, and occupying them with their drawn swords in their hands. Then they march out to raise their forces, and a battle to music takes place, four soldiers on each side, who are all killed. Next we have a scene between prince Prettyman and his tailor, Tom Thimble, which involves a joke upon the princely principle of non-payment. A scene or two follows in a similar tone, without at all advancing the plot; although it appears that another prince, Volscius, who, we are to suppose, supports the old dynasty of Brentford, has made his escape to Piccadilly, while the army which he is to lead has assembled, and is concealed, at Knightsbridge. This incident produces a discussion between Mr. Bayes and his friends:—

Smith.—But pray, Mr. Bayes, is not this a little difficult, that you were saying e'en now, to keep an army thus concealed in Knightsbridge?

Bayes.—In Knightsbridge?—stay.

Johnson.—No, not if inn-keepers be his friends.[100]

Bayes.—His friends? Ay, sir, his intimate acquaintance; or else, indeed, I grant it could not be.

Smith.—Yes, faith, so it might be very easy.

Bayes.—Nay, if I don't make all things easy, 'egad, I'll give 'em leave to hang me. Now you would think that he is going out of town; but you will see how prettily I have contrived to stop him, presently.

Accordingly, prince Volscius yields to the influence of a fair *demoiselle,* who bears the classical name of Parthenope, and after various exhibitions of hesitation, he does not leave town. Another scene or two, with little meaning, but full of clever parodies on the plays of Dryden, the Howards, and their contemporaries. The first scene of the fourth act opens with a funeral, a parody upon colonel Henry Howard's play of the "United Kingdoms." Pallas interferes, brings the lady who is to be buried to life, gets up a dance, and furnishes a very extempore feast. The princes Prettyman and Volscius dispute about their sweethearts. At the commencement of the fifth act the two usurping kings appear in state, attended by four cardinals, the two princes, all the lady-loves, heralds, and sergeants-at-arms, &c In the middle of all this state, "the two right kings of Brentford descend in the clouds, singing, in white garments, and three fiddlers sitting before them in green." "Now," says Bayes to his friends, "because the two right kings descend from above, I make 'em sing to the tune and style of our modern spirits." And accordingly they proceeded in a continuous parody:—

1st King.— Haste, brother king, we are sent from above.
2nd King.—Let us move, let us move;
Move, to remove the fate
Of Brentford's long united state.
1st King.— Tara, tan, tara!—full east and by south.
2nd King.—We sail with thunder in our mouth.
In scorching noon-day, whilst the traveller stays,
Busy, busy, busy, busy, we bustle along,
Mounted upon warm Phœbus's rays,
Through the heavenly throng,
Hasting to those
Who will feast us at night with a pig's pettytoes.
1st King.— And we'll fall with our plate
In an olio of hate
2nd King.—But, now supper's done, the servitors try,
Like soldiers, to storm a whole half-moon pie.
1st King.— They gather, they gather, hot custards in spoons:
But, alas! I must leave these half-moons,
And repair to my trusty dragoons.
2nd King.—O stay! for you need not as yet go astray;
The tide, like a friend, has brought ships in our way,
And on their high ropes we will play;

Like maggots in filberts, we'll snug in our shell,
We'll frisk in our shell,
We'll firk in our shell,
And farewell.
1st King.— But the ladies have all inclination to dance,
And the green frogs croak out a coranto of France.

All this is quite Aristophanic. It is interrupted by a discussion between Bayes and his visitors on the music and the dance, and then the two kings continue:—

2nd King.—Now mortals, that hear
How we tilt and career,
With wonder, will fear
The event of such things as shall never appear.
1st King.—Stay you to fulfil what the gods have decreed.
2nd King.—Then call me to help you, if there shall be need.
1st King.— So firmly resolved is a true Brentford king,
To save the distressed, and help to 'em bring,
That, ere a full pot of good ale you can swallow,
He's here with a whoop, and gone with a halloo.

The rather too inquisitive Smith wonders at all this, and complains that, to him, the sense of this is "not very plain." "Plain!" exclaims Bayes, "why, did you ever hear any people in the clouds speak plain? They must be all for flight of fancy, at its full range, without the least check or control upon it. When once you tie up sprites and people in clouds to speak plain, you spoil all." The two kings of Brentford now "light out of the clouds, and step into the throne," continuing the same *dignified* conversation:—

1st King.—Come, now to serious council we'll advance.
2nd King.—I do agree; but first, let's have a dance.

This confidence of the two kings of Brentford is suddenly disturbed by the sound of war. Two heralds announce that the army, that of Knightsbridge, had come to protect them, and that it had come *in disguise*, an arrangement which puzzles the author's two visitors:—

1st King.—What saucy groom molests our privacies?
1st Herald.— The army's at the door, and, in disguise,
Desires a word with both your majesties.
2nd Herald.—Having from Knightsbridge hither march'd by stealth.
2nd King.—Bid 'em attend a while, and drink our health.
Smith.—How, Mr. Bayes? The army in disguise!
Bayes.—Ay, sir, for fear the usurpers might discover them, that went out but just now.

War itself follows, and the commanders of the two armies, the general and the lieutenant-general, appear upon the stage in another parody upon the opening scenes of Dryden's "Siege of Rhodes:"—

Enter, at several doors, the General *and* Lieutenant-general, *armed cap-à-pie, with each a lute in his hand, and his sword drawn, and hung with a scarlet riband at the wrist.*

Lieut.-Gen.—Villain, thou liest.

Gen.—Arm, arm, Gonsalvo, arm. What! ho!
The lie no flesh can brook, I trow.
Lieut.-Gen.—Advance from Acton with the musqueteers.
Gen.—Draw down the Chelsea cuirassiers.
Lieut.-Gen.— The band you boast of, Chelsea cuirassiers,
Shall in my Putney pikes now meet their peers.
Gen.—Chiswickians, aged, and renowned in fight,
Join with the Hammersmith brigade.
Lieut.-Gen.— You'll find my Mortlake boys will do them right,
Unless by Fulham numbers over-laid.
Gen.—Let the left wing of Twick'n'am foot advance,
And line that eastern hedge.
Lieut.-Gen.— The horse I raised in Petty France
Shall try their chance,
And scour the meadows, overgrown with sedge.
Gen.—Stand: give the word.
Lieut.-Gen.—Bright sword.
Gen.—That may be thine,
But 'tis not mine.
Lieut.-Gen.— Give fire, give fire, at once give fire,
And let those recreant troops perceive mine ire.
Gen.—Pursue, pursue; they fly,
That first did give the lie!
[*Exeunt.*

Thus the battle is carried on in talk between two individuals. Bayes alleges, as an excuse for introducing these trivial names of places, that "the spectators know all these towns, and may easily conceive them to be within the dominions of the two kings of Brentford." The battle is finally stopped by an eclipse, and three personages, representing the sun, moon, and earth, advance upon the stage, and by dint of singing and manœuvring, one gets in a line between the other two, and this, according to the strict rules of astronomy, constituted the eclipse. The eclipse is followed by another battle of a more desperate character, to which a stop is put in an equally extraordinary manner, by the entrance of the furious hero Drawcansir, who slays all the combatants on both sides. The marriage of prince Prettyman was to form the subject of the fifth act, but while Bayes, Johnson, and Smith withdraw temporarily, all the players, in disgust, run away to their dinners, and thus ends "The Rehearsal" of Mr. Bayes's play. The epilogue returns to the moral which the play was designed to inculcate:—

The play is at an end, but where's the plot?
That circumstance the poet Bayes forgot.
And we can boast, though 'tis a plotting age,
No place is freer from it than the stage.

Formerly people sought to write so that they might be understood, but "this new way of wit" was altogether incomprehensible:—

Wherefore, for ours, and for the kingdom's peace,
May this prodigious way of writing cease;
Let's have, at least once in our lives, a time
When we may hear some reason, not all rhyme.
We have this ten years felt its influence;

Pray let this prove a year of prose and sense.

English comedy was certainly greatly reformed, in some senses of the word reform, during the period which followed the publication of "The Rehearsal," and, in the hands of writers like Wycherley, Shadwell, Congreve, and D'Urfey, the dulness of the Howards was exchanged for an extreme degree of vivacity. The plot was as little considered as ever—it was a mere peg on which to hang scenes brilliant with wit and *repartee*. The small intrigue is often but a frame for a great picture of society in its forms then most open to caricature, with all the petty intrigues inseparable from it. "Epsom Wells," one of Shadwell's earlier comedies, and perhaps his best, will bear comparison with Jonson's "Bartholomew Fair." The personages represented in it are exactly those which then shone in such society—three "men of wit and pleasure," one of the class of country squires whom the wits of London loved to laugh at, and who is described as "a country justice, a public spirited, politick, discontented fop, an immoderate hater of London, and a lover of the country above measure, a hearty true English coxcomb." Then we have "two cheating, sharking, cowardly bullies." The citizens of London are represented by Bisket, "a comfit-maker, a quiet, humble, civil cuckold, governed by his wife, whom he very much fears and loves at the same time, and is very proud of," and Fribble, "a haberdasher, a surly cuckold, very conceited, and proud of his wife, but pretends to govern and keep her under," and their wives, the first "an impertinent, imperious strumpet," and the other, "an humble, submitting wife, who jilts her husband that way, a very ——." One or two other characters of the same stamp, with "two young ladies of wit, beauty, and fortune," who behave themselves not much better than the others, and a full allowance of "parsons, hectors, constables, watchmen, and fiddlers," complete the *dramatis personæ* of "Epsom Wells." With such materials anybody will understand the character of the piece, which was brought out on the stage in 1672. "The Squire of Alsatia," by the same author, brought upon the stage in the eventful year 1688, is a vivid picture of one of the wildest phases of London life in those still rather primitive times. Alsatia, as every reader of Walter Scott knows, was a cant name for the White Friars, in London, a locality which, at that time, was beyond the reach of the law and its officers, a refuge for thieves and rogues, and especially for debtors, where they could either resist with no great fear of being overcome, or, when resistance was no longer possible, escape with ease. With such a scene, and such people for characters, we are not surprised that the printed edition of this play is prefaced by a vocabulary of the cant words employed in it. The principal characters in the play are of the same class with those which form the staple of all these old comedies. First there is a country father or uncle, who is rich and severe upon the vices of youth, or arbitrary, or avaricious. He is here represented by sir William Belfond, "a gentleman of about £3000 per annum, who in his youth had been a spark of the town; but married and retired into the country, where he turned to the other extreme—rigid, morose, most sordidly covetous, clownish, obstinate, positive, and forward." He must have a London brother, or near relative, endowed with exactly contrary qualities, here represented by sir Edward Belfond, sir William's brother, "a merchant, who by lucky hits had gotten a great estate, lives single with ease and pleasure, reasonably and virtuously, a man of great humanity and gentleness and compassion towards mankind, well read in good books, possessed with all gentlemanlike qualities." Sir William Belfond has two sons. Belfond senior, the eldest, is "bred after his father's rustic, swinish manner, with great rigour and severity, upon whom his father's estate is entailed, the confidence of which makes him break out into open rebellion to his father, and become lewd, abominably vicious, stubborn, and obstinate." The younger Belfond, Sir William's second son, had been "adopted by Sir Edward, and bred from his childhood by him, with all the tenderness and familiarity, and bounty, and liberty that can be;" he was "instructed in all the liberal sciences, and in all gentleman-like education; somewhat given to women, and now and then to good fellowship; but an ingenious, well-accomplished gentleman; a man of honour, and of excellent disposition and temper." Then we have some of the leading heroes of Alsatia, and first Cheatly, who is described as "a rascal, who by reason of debts, dares not stir out of Whitefryers, but there inveigles young heirs in tail; and helps 'em to goods and money upon great disadvantages; is bound for them, and shares with them, till he undoes them; a lewd, impudent, debauched fellow, very expert in the cant about the town." Shamwell is "cousin to the Belfonds, an heir, who, being ruined by Cheatly, is made a decoy-duck for others; not daring to stay out of Alsatia, where he lives; is bound with Cheatly for heirs, and lives upon them, a dissolute, debauch'd life." Another of these characters is captain Hackum, "a block-headed bully of Alsatia; a cowardly, impudent, blustering fellow; formerly a sergeant in Flanders, run from his colours, retreating into Whitefryers for a very small debt; where by the Alsatians he is dubb'd a captain; marries one that lets lodgings, sells cherry-brandy, and is a bawd." Nor is Alsatia without a representative of the Puritanical part of society, in Scrapeall, "a hypocritical, repeating, praying, psalm-singing, precise fellow, pretending to great piety; a godly knave, who joins with Cheatly, and supplies young heirs with goods and money." A rather large number of inferior characters fill up the canvas; and the females, with two exceptions, belong to the same class. The plot of this play is very simple. The elder son of sir William Belfond has taken to Alsatia, but sir William, on his return from abroad, hearing talk of the fame of a squire Belfond among the Alsatians, imagines that it is his younger son, and out of this mistake a considerable amount of misunderstanding arises. At last sir William discovers his error, and finds his eldest son in Whitefryers, but the youth sets him at defiance. The father, in great anger, brings tipstaff constables, to take away his son by force; but the Alsatians rise in force, the officers of the law are beaten, and sir William himself taken prisoner. He is rescued by the younger Belfond, and in the conclusion the elder brother becomes penitent, and is reconciled with his father. There is an underplot, far from moral in its character, which ends in the marriage of Belfond junior. It is a busy, noisy play, and was a great favourite on the stage; but it is now chiefly interesting as a vivid picture of London life in the latter half of the seventeenth century. "Bury Fair," by Shadwell, is another comedy of the same description; with little interest in the plot, but full of life and movement. If "The Squire of Alsatia" was noisy, "The Scowrers," another comedy by the same author, first brought on the stage in 1691, was still more so. The wild and riotous gallants who, in former times of inefficient police regulation, infested the streets at night, and committed all sorts of outrages, were known at different periods by a variety of names. In the reign of James I. and Charles I. they were the "roaring boys;" in the time of Shadwell, they were called the "scowrers," because they scowered the streets at night, and rather roughly cleared them of all passengers; a few years later they took the name of Mohocks, or Mohawks. During the night London lay at the mercy of these riotous classes, and the streets witnessed scenes of brutal violence, which, at the present day, we can hardly imagine. This state of things is pictured in Shadwell's comedy. Sir William Rant, Wildfire, and Tope, are noted scowrers, well known in the town, whose fame has excited emulation in men of less distinction in their way, Whachum, "a city wit and scowrer, imitator of sir William," and "two scoundrells," his companions, Bluster and Dingboy. Great enmity arises between the two parties of rival scowrers. The more serious characters in the play are Mr. Rant, sir William Rant's father, and sir Richard Maggot, "a foolish Jacobite alderman" (it must be remembered that we are now in the reign of king William). Sir Richard's wife, lady Maggot, like the citizen's wives of the comedy of the Restoration generally, is a lady rather wanting in virtue, ambitious of mixing with the gay and fashionable world, and somewhat of a tyrant over her husband. She has two handsome daughters, whom she seeks to keep confined from the world, lest they should become her rivals. There are low characters of both sexes, who need not be enumerated. Much of the play is taken up with street rows, capital satirical pictures of London life. The play ends with marriages, and with the reconciliation of sir William Rant with his father, the serious old gentleman of the play. Shadwell excelled in these busy comedies. One of the nearest approaches to him is Mountfort's comedy of "Greenwich Park," which is another striking satire on the looseness of London life at that time. As in the others, the plot is simply nothing. The play consists of a number of intrigues, such as may be imagined, at a time when morality was little respected, in places of fashionable resort like Greenwich Park and Deptford Wells.

An element of satire was now introduced into English comedy which does not appear to have belonged to it before—this was mimicry. Although the principal characters in the play bore conventional names, they appear often to have been intended to represent individuals then well known in society, and these individuals were caricatured in their dress, and mimicked in their language and manners. We are told that this mimicry contributed greatly to the success of "The Rehearsal," the duke of Buckingham having taken incredible pains to make Lacy, who acted the part of Bayes, perfect in imitating the voice and manner of Dryden, whose dress and gait were minutely copied. This personal satire was not always performed with impunity. On the 1st of February, 1669, Pepys went to the Theatre Royal to see the performance of "The Heiress," in which it appears that sir Charles Sedley was personally caricatured, and the secretary of king Charles's admiralty has left in his diary the following entry:—"To the king's house, thinking to have seen the Heyresse, first acted on Saturday, but when we come thither we find no play there; Kynaston, that did act a part therein in abuse to sir Charles Sedley, being last night exceedingly beaten with sticks by two or three that saluted him, so as he is mightily bruised, and forced to keep his bed." It is said that Dryden's comedy of "Limberham," brought on the stage in 1678, was prohibited after the first night, because the character of Limberham was considered to be too open a satire on the duke of Lauderdale.

Another peculiarity in the comedies of the age of the Restoration was their extraordinary indelicacy. The writers seemed to emulate each other in presenting upon the stage scenes and language which no modest ear or pure mind could support. In the earlier period coarseness in conversation was characteristic of an unpolished age—the language put in the mouths of the actors, as remarked before, smelt of the tavern; but under Charles II. the tone of fashionable society, as represented on the stage, is modelled upon that of the brothel. Even the veiled allusion is no longer resorted to, broad and direct language is substituted in its place. This open profligacy of the stage reached its greatest height between the years 1670 and 1680. The staple material of this comedy may be considered to be the commission of adultery, which is presented as one of the principal ornaments in the character of the well-bred gentleman, varied with the seducing of other men's mistresses, for the keeping of mistresses appears as the rule of social life. The "Country Wife," one of Wycherley's comedies, which is supposed to have been brought on the stage perhaps as early as 1672, is a mass of gross indecency from beginning to end. It involves two principal plots, that of a voluptuary who feigns himself incapable of love and insensible to the other sex, in order to pursue his intrigues with greater liberty; and that of a citizen who takes to his wife a silly and innocent country girl, whose ignorance he believes will be a protection to her virtue, but the very means he takes to prevent her, lead to her fall. The "Parson's Wedding," by Thomas Killigrew, first acted in 1673, is equally licentious. The same at least may be said of Dryden's "Limberham, or the Kind Keeper," first performed in 1678, which, according to the author's own statement, was prohibited on account of its freeness, but more probably because the character of Limberham was believed to be intended for a personal satire on the unpopular earl of Lauderdale. Its plot is simple enough; it is the story of a debauched old gentleman, named Aldo, whose son, after a rather long absence on the Continent, returns to England, and assumes the name of Woodall, in order to enjoy freely the pleasures of London life before he makes himself known to his friends. He takes a lodging in a house occupied by some loose women, and there meets with his father, but, as the latter does not recognise his son, they become friends, and live together licentiously so long, that when the son at length discovers himself, the old man is obliged to overlook his vices. Otway's comedy of "Friendship in Fashion," performed the same year, was not a whit more moral. But all these are far outdone by Ravenscroft's comedy of "The London Cuckolds," first brought out in 1682, which, nevertheless, continued to be acted until late in the last century. It is a clever comedy, full of action, and consisting of a great number of different incidents, selected from the less moral tales of the old story-tellers as they appear in the "Decameron" of Boccaccio, among which that of the ignorant and uneducated young wife, similar to the plot of Wycherley's "Country Wife," is again introduced.

The corruption of morals had become so great, that when women took up the pen, they exceeded in licentiousness even the other sex, as was the case with Mrs. Behn. Aphra Behn is understood to have been born at Canterbury, but to have passed some part of her youth in the colony of Surinam, of which her father was governor. She evidently possessed a disposition for intrigue, and she was employed by the English government, a few years after the Restoration, as a political spy at Antwerp. She subsequently settled in London, and gained a living by her pen, which was very prolific in novels, poems, and plays. It would be difficult to point out in any other works such scenes of open profligacy as those presented in Mrs. Behn's two comedies of "Sir Patient Fancy" and "The City Heiress, or Sir Timothy Treat-all," which appeared in 1678 and 1681. Concealment of the slightest kind is avoided, and even that which cannot be exposed to view, is tolerably broadly described.

It appears that the performance of the "London Cuckolds" had been the cause of some scandal, and there were, even among play-goers, some who took offence at such outrages on the ordinary feelings of modesty. The excess of the evil had begun to produce a reaction. Ravenscroft, the author of that comedy, produced on the stage, in 1684, a comedy, entitled "Dame Dobson, or the Cunning Woman," which was intended to be a modest play, but it was unceremoniously "damned" by the audience. The prologue to this new comedy intimates that the "London Cuckolds" had pleased the town and diverted the court, but that some "squeamish females" had taken offence at it, and that he had now written a "dull, civill" play to make amends. They are addressed, therefore, in such terms as these:—

In you, chaste ladies, then we hope to-day,
This is the poet's recantation play.
Come often to 't, that he at length may see
'Tis more than a pretended modesty.
Stick by him now, for if he finds you falter,
He quickly will his way of writing alter;
And every play shall send you blushing home,
For, though you rail, yet then we're sure you'll come.

And it is further intimated,—

A naughty play was never counted dull—
Nor modest comedy e'er pleased you much.

"I remember," says Colley Cibber in his "Apology," looking back to these times, "I remember the ladies were then observed to be decently afraid of venturing bare-faced to a new comedy, till they had been assured they might do it without the risk of an insult to their modesty; or if their curiosity were too strong for their patience, they took care at least to save appearances, and rarely came upon the first days of acting but in masks (then daily worn, and admitted in the pit, the side boxes, and gallery), which custom, however, had so many ill consequences attending it, that it has been abolished these many years." According to the *Spectator*, ladies began now to desert the theatre when comedies were brought out, except those who "never miss the first day of a new play, lest it should prove too luscious to admit of their going with any countenance to the second."

In the midst of this abuse, there suddenly appeared a book which created at the time a great sensation. The comedies of the latter half of the seventeenth century were not only indecent, but they were filled with profane language, and contained scenes in which religion itself was treated with contempt. At that time there lived a divine of the Church of England, celebrated for his

Jacobitism—for I am now speaking of the reign of king William—for his talents as a controversial writer, and for his zeal in any cause which he undertook. This was Jeremy Collier, the author of several books of some merit, which are seldom read now, and who suffered for his zeal in the cause of king James, and for his refusal to take the oath of allegiance to king William. In the year 1698 Collier published his "Short View of the Immorality and Profaneness of the English stage," in which he boldly attacked the licentiousness of the English comedy. Perhaps Collier's zeal carried him a little too far; but he had offended the wits, and especially the dramatic poets, on all sides, and he was exposed to attacks from all quarters, in which Dryden himself took an active part. Collier showed himself fully capable of dealing with his opponents, and the controversy had the effect of calling attention to the immoralities of the stage, and certainly contributed much towards reforming them. They were become much less frequent and less gross at the opening of the eighteenth century.

Towards the end of the reign of king Charles II., the stage was more largely employed as a political agent, and under his successor, James II., the Puritans and the Whigs were constantly held up to scorn. After the Revolution, the tables were turned, and the satire of the stage was often aimed at Tories and Non-jurors. "The Non-juror," by Colley Cibber, which appeared in 1717, at a very opportune moment, gained for its author a pension and the office of poet-laureate. It was founded upon the "Tartuffe" of Molière, for the English comedy writers borrowed much from the foreign stage. A disguised priest, who passes under the name of Dr. Wolf, and who had been engaged in the rebellion of 1715, has insinuated himself into the household of a gentleman of fortune, of not very strong judgment, Sir John Woodvil, whom, under the title of a Non-juror, he has not only induced to become an abettor of rebels, but he has persuaded him to disinherit his son, and he labours to seduce his wife and to deceive his daughter. His baseness is exposed only just soon enough to defeat his designs. Such a production as this could not fail to give great offence to all the Jacobite party, of whatever shade, who were then rather numerous in London, and Cibber assures us that his reward was a considerable amount of adverse criticism in every quarter where the Tory influence reached. His comedies were inferior in brilliance of dialogue to those of the previous age, but the plots were well imagined and conducted, and they are generally good acting plays.

To Samuel Foote, born in 1722, we owe the last change in the form and character of English comedy. A man of infinite wit and humour, and possessed of extraordinary talent as a mimic, Foote made mimicry the principal instrument of his success on the stage. His plays are above all light and amusing; he reduced the old comedy of five acts to three acts, and his plots were usually simple, the dialogue full of wit and humour; but their peculiar characteristic was their open boldness of personal satire. It is entirely a comedy of his own. He sought to direct his wit against all the vices of society, but this he did by holding up to ridicule and scorn the individuals who had in some way or other made themselves notorious by the practice of them. All his principal characters were real characters, who were more or less known to the public, and who were so perfectly mimicked on the stage in their dress, gait, and speech, that it was impossible to mistake them. Thus, in "The Devil upon Two Sticks," which is a general satire on the low condition to which the practice of medicine had then fallen, the personages introduced in it all represented quacks well known about the town. "The Maid of Bath" dragged upon the stage scandals which were then the talk of Bath society. The nabob of the comedy which bears that title, had also his model in real life. "The Bankrupt" may be considered as a general satire on the baseness of the newspaper press of that day, which was made the means of propagating private scandals and libellous accusations in order to extort money, yet the characters introduced are said to have been all portraits from the life; and the same statement is made with regard to the comedy of "The Author."

It is evident that a drama of this inquisitorial character is a dangerous thing, and that it could hardly be allowed to exist where the rights of society are properly defined; and we are not surprised if

Foote provoked a host of bitter enemies. But in some cases the author met with punishment of a heavier and more substantial description. One of the individuals introduced into "The Maid of Bath," extorted damages to the amount of £3,000. One of the persons who figured in "The Author," obtained an order from the lord chamberlain for putting a stop to the performance after it had had a short run; and the consequences of "The Trip to Calais," were still more disastrous. It is well known that the character of lady Kitty Crocodile in that play was a broad caricature on the notorious duchess of Kingston. Through the treachery of some of the people employed by Foote, the duchess obtained information of the nature of this play before it was ready for representation, and she had sufficient influence to obtain the lord chamberlain's prohibition for bringing it on the stage. Nor was this all, for as the play was printed, if not acted,—and it was subsequently brought out in a modified form, with omission of the part of lady Kitty Crocodile, though the characters of some of her agents were still retained,—infamous charges were got up against Foote, in retaliation, which caused him so much trouble and grief, that they are said to have shortened his days.

The drama which Samuel Foote had invented did not outlive him; its caricature was itself transferred to the caricature of the print-shop.

CHAPTER XXIII.

CARICATURE IN HOLLAND.—ROMAIN DE HOOGHE.—THE ENGLISH REVOLUTION.—CARICATURES ON LOUIS XIV. AND JAMES II.—DR. SACHEVERELL.—CARICATURE BROUGHT FROM HOLLAND TO ENGLAND.— ORIGIN OF THE WORD "CARICATURE."—MISSISSIPPI AND THE SOUTH SEA; THE YEAR OF BUBBLES.

Modern political caricature, born, as we have seen, in France, may be considered to have had its cradle in Holland. The position of that country, and its greater degree of freedom, made it, in the seventeenth century, the general place of refuge to the political discontents of other lands, and especially to the French who fled from the tyranny of Louis XIV. It possessed at that time some of the most skilful artists and best engravers in Europe, and it became the central spot from which were launched a multitude of satirical prints against that monarch's policy, and against himself and his favourites and ministers. This was in a great measure the cause of the bitter hatred which Louis always displayed towards that country. He feared the caricatures of the Dutch more than their arms, and the pencil and graver of Romain de Hooghe were among the most effective weapons employed by William of Nassau.

The marriage of William with Mary, daughter of the duke of York, in 1677, naturally gave the Dutch a greater interest than they could have felt before in the domestic affairs of Great Britain, and a new stimulus to their zeal against Louis of France, or, which was the same thing, against arbitrary power and Popery, both of which had been rendered odious under his name. The accession of James II. to the throne of England, and his attempt to re-establish Popery, added religious as well as political fuel to these feelings, for everybody understood that James was acting under the protection of the king of France. The very year of king James's accession, in 1685, the caricature appeared which we have copied in our cut No. 186, and which, although the inscription is in English, appears to have been the work of a foreign artist. It was probably intended to represent Mary of Modena, the queen of James II., and her rather famous confessor, father Petre, the latter under the character of the wolf among the sheep. Its aim is sufficiently evident to need no explanation. At the top, in the original, are the Latin words, *Converte Angliam,* "convert England," and beneath, in English, "It is a foolish sheep that makes the wolf her confessor."

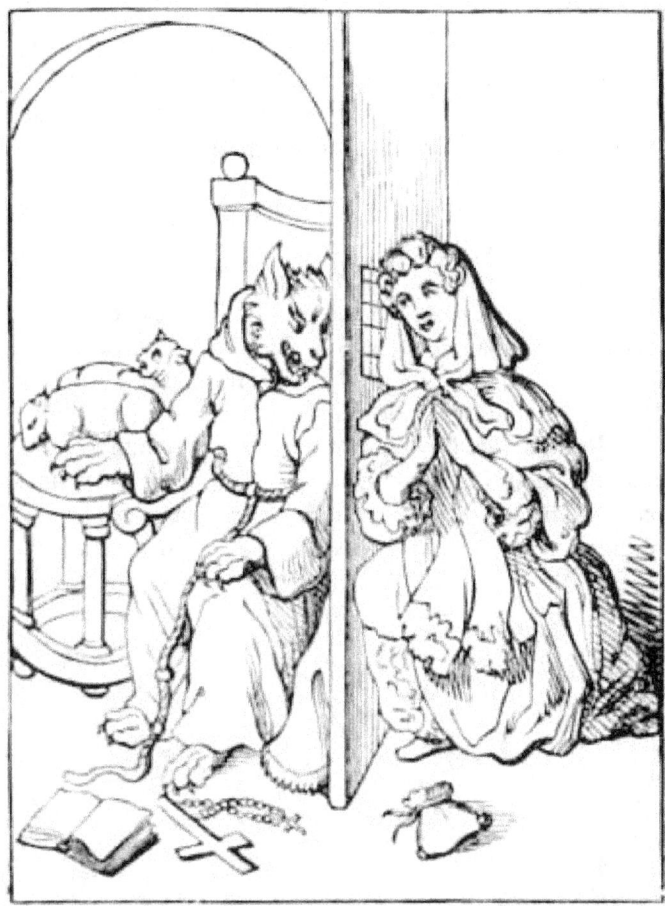

No. 186. A Dangerous Confessor.

The period during which the Dutch school of caricature flourished, extended through the reign of Louis XIV., and into the regency in France, and two great events, the revolution of 1688 in England, and the wild money speculations of the year 1720, exercised especially the pencils of its caricaturists. The first of these events belongs almost entirely to Romain de Hooghe. Very little is known of the personal history of this remarkable artist, but he is believed to have been born towards the middle of the seventeenth century, and to have died in the earlier years of the eighteenth century. The older French writers on art, who were prejudiced against Romain de Hooghe for his bitter hostility to Louis XIV., inform us that in his youth he employed his graver on obscene subjects, and led a life so openly licentious, that he was banished from his native town of Amsterdam, and went to live at Haerlem. He gained celebrity by the series of plates, executed in 1672, which represented the horrible atrocities committed in Holland by the French troops, and which raised against Louis XIV. the indignation of all Europe. It is said that the prince of Orange (William III. of England), appreciating the value of his satire as a political weapon, secured it in his own interests by liberally patronising the caricaturist; and we owe to Romain de Hooghe a succession of large prints in which the king of France, his *protégé* James II., and the adherents of the latter, are covered with ridicule. One, published in 1688, and entitled "Les Monarches Tombants," commemorates the flight of the royal family from England. Another, which appeared at the same date, is entitled, in French, "Arlequin fur l'hypogryphe à la croisade Loioliste," and in Dutch, "Armeé van de Heylige League voor der Jesuiten Monarchy" (*i.e.* "the army of the holy league for establishing the monarchy of the Jesuits"). Louis XIV. and James II. were represented under the characters of Arlequin and Panurge, who are seated on the animal here called a "hypogryphe," but which is really a wild ass. The two kings have their heads joined together under one Jesuit's cap. Other figures, forming part of this army of Jesuitism, are distributed over the field, the most grotesque of which is that given in our cut No. 187. Two personages introduced in some ridiculous position or other, in most of these caricatures, are father Petre, the Jesuit, and the infant prince of Wales, afterwards the old Pretender. It was pretended that this infant was in fact the child of a miller, secretly introduced into the queen's bed concealed in a warming-pan; and that this ingenious plot was contrived by father Petre. Hence the boy was popularly called Peterkin, or Perkin, *i.e.* little Peter, which was the name given afterwards to the Pretender in songs and satires at the time of his rebellion; and in the prints a windmill was usually given to the child as a sign of its father's trade. In the group represented in our cut, father Petre, with the child in his arms, is seated on a rather singular steed, a lobster. The young prince here carries the windmill on his head. On the lobster's back, behind the Jesuit, are carried the papal crown, surmounted by a fleur-de-lis, with a bundle of relics, indulgences, &c, and it has seized in one claw the English church service book, and in the other the book of the laws of England. In the Dutch description of this print, the child is called "the new born Antichrist." Another of Romain de Hooghe's prints, entitled "Panurge secondé par Arlequin Deodaat à la croisade d'Irlande, 1689," is a satire on king James's expedition to Ireland, which led to the memorable battle of the Boyne. James and his friends are proceeding to the place of embarkation, and, as represented in our cut No. 188, father Petre marches in front, carrying the infant prince in his arms.

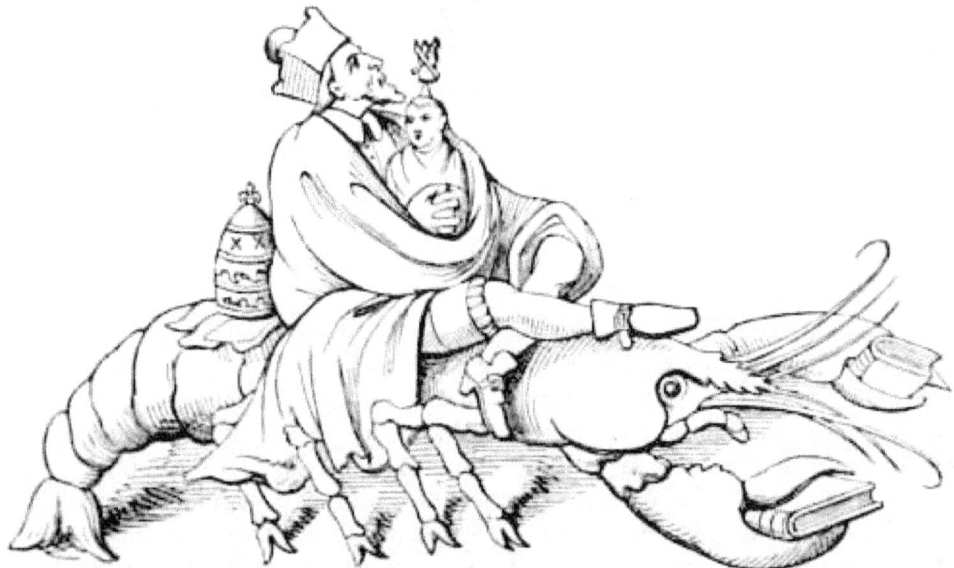

No. 187. A Jesuit well Mounted.

The drawing of Romain de Hooghe is not always correct, especially in his larger subjects, which perhaps may be ascribed to his hasty and careless manner of working; but he displays great skill in grouping his figures, and great power in investing them with a large amount of satirical humour. Most of the other caricatures of the time are poor both in design and execution. Such is the case with a vulgar satirical print which was published in France in the autumn of 1690, on the arrival of a false rumour that king William had been killed in Ireland. In the field of the picture the corpse of the king is followed by a procession consisting of his queen and the principal supporters of his cause. The lower corner on the left hand is occupied by a view of the interior of the infernal regions, and king William introduced in the place allotted to him among the flames. In different parts of the picture there are several inscriptions, all breathing a spirit of very insolent exultation. One of them is the—

Billet d'Enterrement.

Vous estes priez d'assister au convoy, service, et enterrement du tres haut, tres grand, et tres infame Prince infernal, grand stadouter, des Armés diaboliques de la ligue d'Ausbourg, et insigne usurpateur des Royaumes d'Angleterre, d'Eccosse, et d'Irlande, décédé dans l'Irlande au mois d'Aoust 1690, qui se fera le dit mois, dans sa paroisse infernale, ou assisteront Dame Proserpine, Radamonte, et les Ligueurs.

Les Dames lui diront s'il leur plaist des injures.

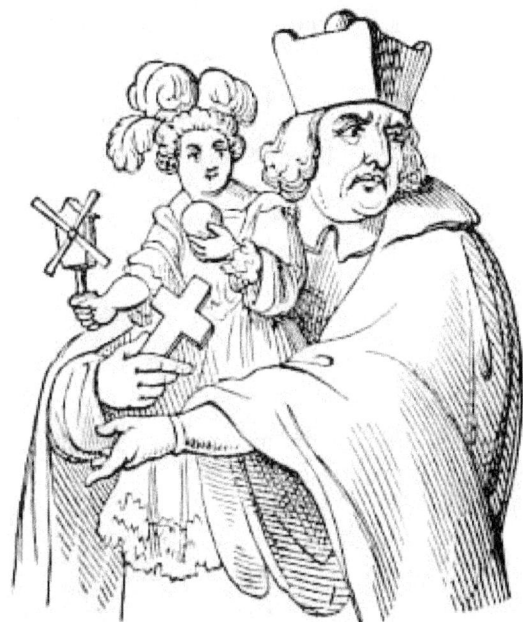

No. 188. Off to Ireland.

The prints executed in England at this time were, if possible, worse than those published in France. Almost the only contemporary caricature on the downfall of the Stuarts that I know, is an ill-executed print, published immediately after the accession of William III., under the title, "England's Memorial of its wonderful deliverance from French Tyranny and Popish Oppression." The middle of the picture is occupied by "the royal orange tree," which flourishes in spite of all the attempts to destroy it. At the upper corner, on the left side, is a representation of the French king's "council," consisting of an equal number of Jesuits and devils, seated alternately at a round table.

The circumstance that the titles and inscriptions of nearly all these caricatures are in Dutch, seems to show that their influence was intended to be exercised in Holland rather than elsewhere. In two or three only of them these descriptions were accompanied with translations in English or French; and after a time, copies of them began to be made in England, accompanied with English descriptions. A curious example of this is given in the fourth volume of the "Poems on State Affairs," printed in 1707. In the preface to this volume the editor takes occasion to inform the reader—"That having procur'd from beyond sea a Collection of Satyrical Prints done in Holland and elsewhere, by Rom. de Hoog, and other the best masters, relating to the French King and his

Adherents, since he unjustly begun this war, I have persuaded the Bookseller to be at the expense of ingraving several of them; to each of which I have given the Explanation in English verse, they being in Dutch, French, or Latin in the originals." Copies of seven of these caricatures are accordingly given at the end of the volume, which are certainly inferior in every respect to those of the best period of Romain de Hooghe. One of them commemorates the eclipse of the sun on the 12th of May, 1706. The sun, as it might be conjectured, is Louis XIV., eclipsed by queen Anne, whose face occupies the place of the moon. In the foreground of the picture, just under the eclipse, the queen is seated on her throne under a canopy, surrounded by her counsellors and generals. With her left arm she holds down the Gallic cock, while with the other hand she clips one of its wings (see our cut No. 189). In the upper corner on the right, is inserted a picture of the battle of Ramillies, and in the lower corner on the left, a sea-fight under admiral Leake, both victories gained in that year. Another of these copies of foreign prints is given in our cut No. 190. We are told that "these figures represent a French trumpet and drum, sent by Louis le Grand to enquire news of several citys lost by the Mighty Monarch last campaign." The trumpeter holds in his hand a list of lost towns, and another is pinned to the breast of the drummer; the former list is headed by the names of "Gaunt, Brussels, Antwerp, Bruges," the latter by "Barcelona."

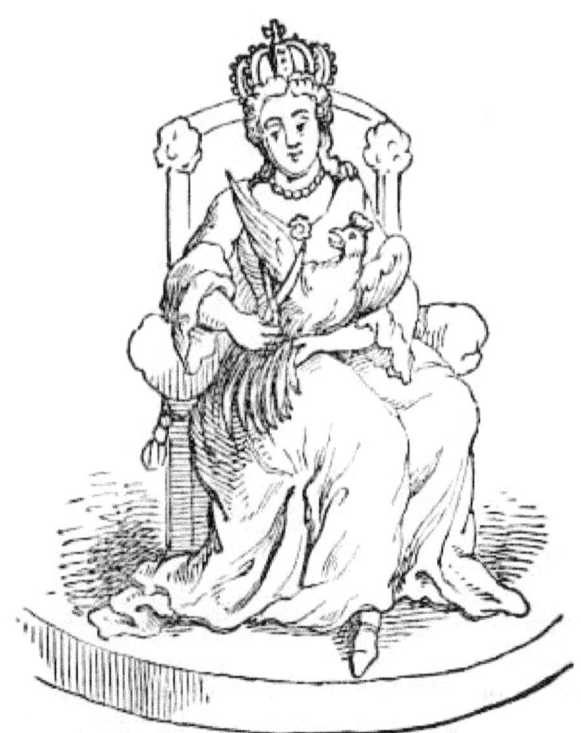

No. 189. Clipping the Cock's Wings.

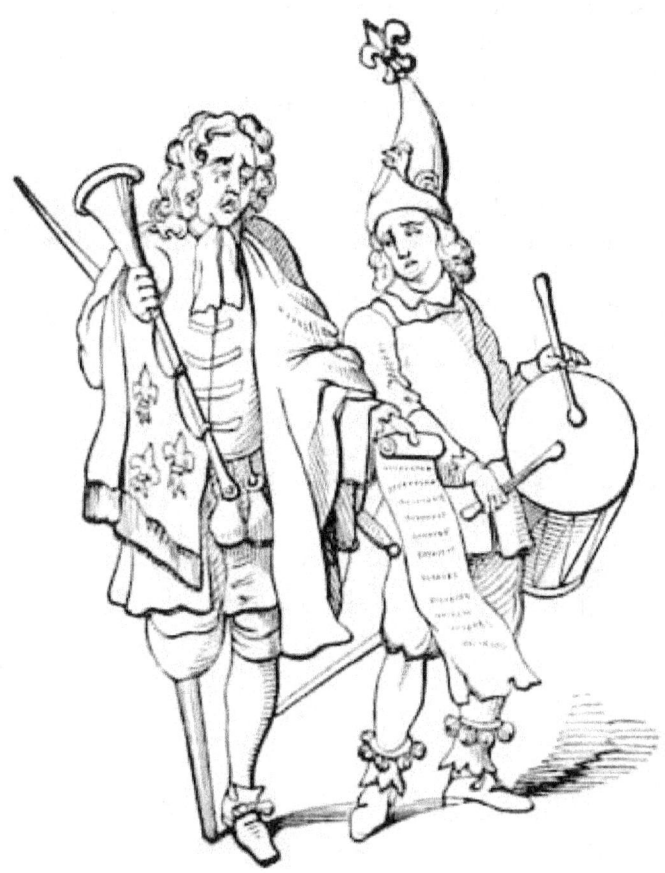

No. 190. Trumpet and Drum.

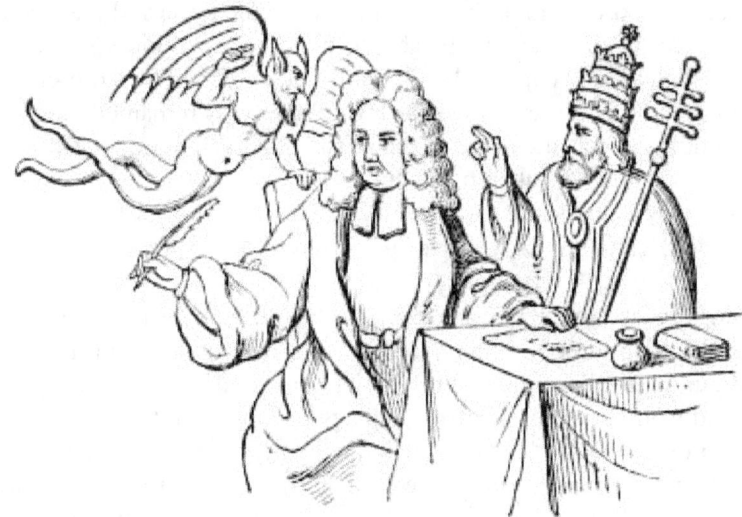

No. 191. The Three False Brethren.

The first remarkable outburst of caricatures in England was caused by the proceedings against the notorious Dr. Sacheverell in 1710. It is somewhat curious that Sacheverell's partisans speak of caricatures as things brought recently from Holland, and new in England, and ascribe the use of them as peculiar to the Whig party. The writer of a pamphlet, entitled "The Picture of Malice, or a true Account of Dr. Sacheverell's Enemies, and their behaviour with regard to him," informs us that "the chief means by which all the lower order of that sort of men call'd Whigs, shall ever be found to act for the ruin of a potent adversary, are the following three—by the Print, the Canto or Doggrell Poem, and by the Libell, grave, calm, and cool, as the author of the 'True Answer' describes it. These are not all employed at the same time, any more than the ban and arierban of a kingdom is raised, unless to make sure work, or in cases of great exigency and imminent danger." "The Print," he goes on to say, "is originally a Dutch talisman (bequeathed to the ancient Batavians by a certain Chinese necromancer and painter), with a virtue far exceeding that of the Palladium, not only of guarding their cities and provinces, but also of annoying their enemies, and preserving a due balance amongst the neighbouring powers around." This writer warms up so much in his indignation against this new weapon of the Whigs, that he breaks out in blank verse to tell us how even the mysterious power of the magician did not destroy its victims—

Swifter than heretofore the Print effac'd
The pomp of mightiest monarchs, and dethron'd
The dread idea of royal majesty;
Dwindling the prince below the pigmy size.
Witness the once Great Louis in youthful pride,
And Charles of happy days, who both confess'd
The magic power of mezzotinto[101] shade,
And form grotesque, in manifestoes loud
Denouncing death to boor and burgomaster.
Witness, ye sacred popes with triple crown,
Who likewise victims fell to hideous print,
Spurn'd by the populace who whilome lay
Prostrate, and ev'n adored before your thrones.

We are then told that "this, if not the first, has yet been the chief machine which his enemies have employ'd against the doctor; they have exposed him in the same piece with the pope and the devil, and who now could imagine that any simple priest should be able to stand before a power which had levelled popes and monarchs?" At least one copy of the caricature here alluded to is preserved, although a great rarity, and it is represented in our cut No. 191. Two of the party remained long associated together in the popular outcry, and as the name of the third fell into contempt and oblivion, the doctor's place in this association was taken by a new cause of alarm, the Pretender, the child whom we have just seen so joyously brandishing his windmill. It is evident, however, that this caricature greatly exasperated Sacheverell and the party which supported him.

It will have been noticed that the writer just quoted, in using the term "print," ignores altogether that of caricature, which, however, was about this time beginning to come into use, although it is not found in the dictionaries, I believe, until the appearance of that of Dr. Johnson, in 1755. *Caricature* is, of course, an Italian word, derived from the verb *caricare*, to charge or load; and therefore, it means a picture which is charged, or exaggerated (the old French dictionaries say, "*c'est la même chose que charge en peinture*"). The word appears not to have come into use in Italy until the latter half of the seventeenth century, and the earliest instance I know of its employment by an English writer is that quoted by Johnson from the "Christian Morals" of Sir Thomas Brown, who died in 1682, but it was one of his latest writings, and was not printed till long after his death:—"Expose not thyself by four-footed manners unto monstrous draughts (*i.e.* drawings) and *caricatura* representations." This very quaint writer, who had passed some time in Italy, evidently uses it as an exotic word. We find it next employed by the writer of the Essay No. 537, of the "Spectator," who, speaking of the way in which different people were led by feelings of jealousy and prejudice to detract from the characters of others, goes on to say, "From all these hands we have such draughts of mankind as are represented in those burlesque pictures which the Italians call *caricaturas*, where the art consists in preserving, amidst distorted proportions and aggravated features, some distinguishing likeness of the person, but in such a manner as to transform the most agreeable beauty into the most odious monster." The word was not fully established in our language in its English form of *caricature* until late in the last century.

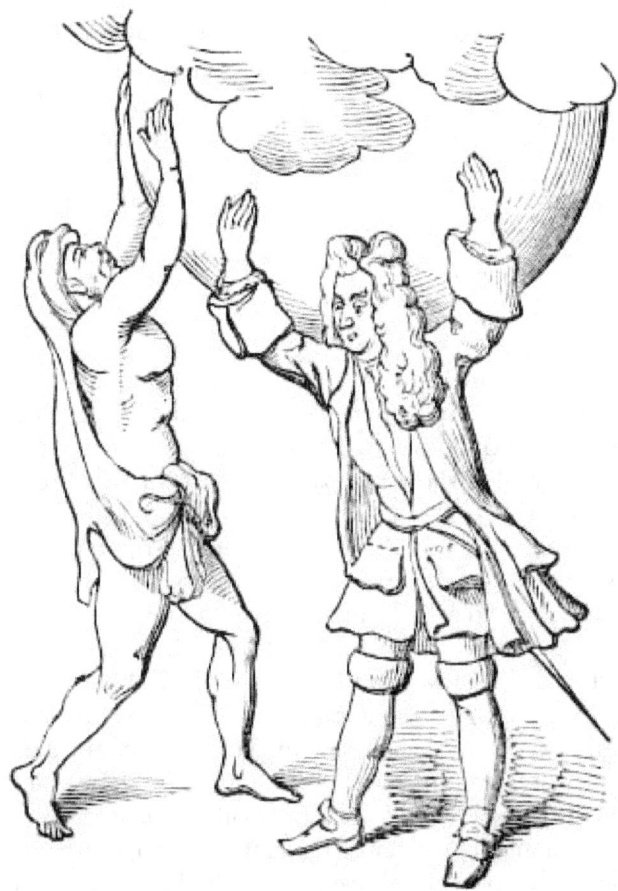

No. 192. Atlas.

The subject of agitation which produced a greater number of caricatures than any previous event was the wild financial scheme introduced into France by the Scottish adventurer, Law, and imitated in England in the great South Sea Bubble. It would be impossible here, within our necessary limits, to attempt to trace the history of these bubbles, which all burst in the course of the year 1720; and, in fact, it is a history of which few are ignorant. On this, as on former occasions, the great mass of the caricatures, especially those against the Mississippi scheme, were executed in Holland, but they are much inferior to the works of Romain de Hooghe. In fact, so great was the demand for these caricatures, that the publishers, in their eagerness for gain, not only deluged the world with plates by artists of no talent, which were without point or interest, but they took old plates of any subject in which there was a multitude of figures, put new titles to them, and published them as satires on the Mississippi scheme; for people were ready to take anything which represented a crowd as a satire on the eagerness with which Frenchmen rushed into the share-market. One or two curious instances of this deception might be pointed out. Thus, an old picture, evidently intended to represent the meeting of a king and a nobleman, in the court of a palace, surrounded by a crowd of courtiers, in the costume probably of the time of Henri IV., was republished as a picture of people crowding to the grand scene of stock-jobbing in Paris, the Rue Quinquenpoix; and the old picture of the battle between Carnival and Lent came out again, a little re-touched, under the Dutch title, "Stryd tuszen de smullende Bubbel-Heeren en de aanstaande Armoede," *i.e.*, "The battle between the good-living bubble-lords and approaching poverty."

Besides being issued singly, a considerable number of these prints were collected and published in a volume, which is still met with not unfrequently, under the title "Het groote Tafereel der Dwaasheid," "The great picture of folly." One of this set of prints represents a multitude of persons, of all ages and sexes, acting the part of Atlas in supporting on their backs globes, which, though made only of paper, had become, through the agitation of the stock exchange, heavier than gold. Law himself (see our cut No. 192) stands foremost, and requires the assistance of Hercules to support his enormous burthen. In the French verses accompanying this print, the writer says—

Ami Atlas, on voit (sans conter vous et moi)
Faire l'Atlas partout des divers personnages,
Riche, pauvre, homme, femme, et sot et quasi-sage,
Valet, et paisan, le gueux s'eleve en roi.

Another of these caricatures represents Law in the character of Don Quixote, riding upon Sancho's donkey. He is hastening to his Dulcinia, who waits for him in the *actie huis* (action or share-house), towards which people are dragging the animal on which he is seated. The devil (see our cut No. 193), sits behind Law, and holds up the ass's tail, while a shower of paper, in the form of shares in companies, is scattered around, and scrambled for by the eager *actionnaires*. In front, the animal is laden with the money into which this paper has been turned,—the box bears the inscription, "*Bombarioos Geldkist,* 1720," "Bombario's (Law's) gold chest;" and the flag bears the inscription, "*Ik koom, ik koom, Dulcinia,*" "I come, I come, Dulcinia." The best, perhaps, of this lot of caricatures is a large engraving by the well-known Picart, inserted among the Dutch collection with explanations in Dutch and French, and which was re-engraved in London, with English descriptions and applications. It is a general satire on the madness of the memorable year 1720. Folly appears as the charioteer of Fortune, whose car is drawn by the representatives of the numerous companies which had sprung up at this time, most of which appear to be more or less unsound. Many of these agents have the tails of foxes, "to show their policy and cunning," as the explanation informs us. The devil is seen in the clouds above, blowing bubbles of soap, which mix with the paper which Fortune is distributing to the crowd. The picture is crowded with figures, scattered in groups, who are employed in a variety of occupations connected with the great folly of the day, one of which, as an example, is given in our cut No. 194. It is a transfer of stock, made through the medium of a Jew broker.

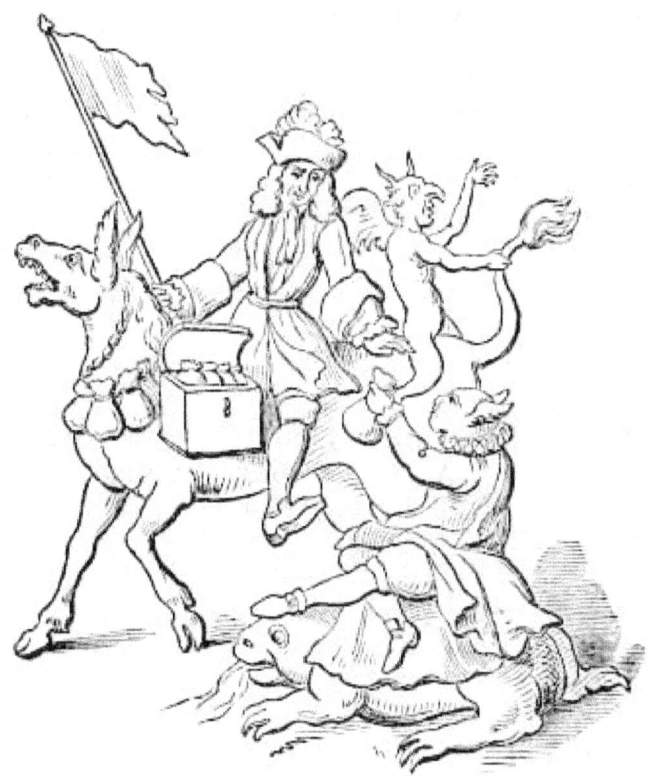

No. 193. The Don Quixote of Finance.

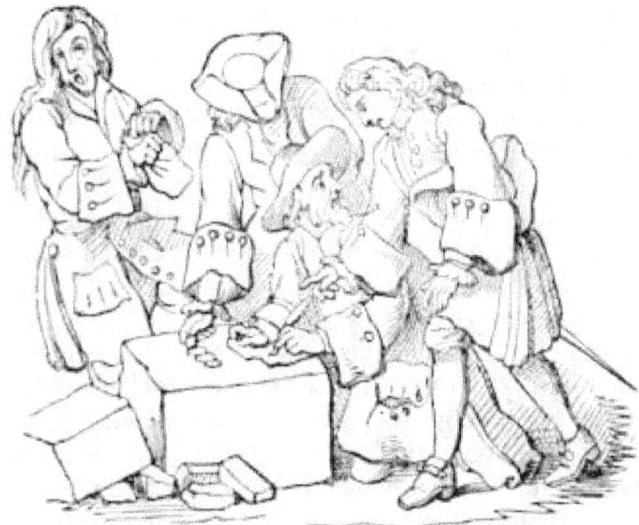

No. 194. Transfer of Stock.

It was in this bubble agitation that the English school of caricature began, and a few specimens are preserved, though others which are advertised in the newspapers of that day, seem to be entirely lost. In fact, a very considerable portion of the caricature literature of a period so comparatively recent as the first half of the last century, appears to have perished; for the interest of these prints was in general so entirely temporary that few people took any care to preserve them, and few of them were very attractive as pictures. As yet, indeed, these English prints are but poor imitations of the works of Picart and other continental artists. A pair of English prints, entitled "The Bubbler's Mirrour," represents, one a head joyful at the rise in the value of stock, the other, a similar head sorrowful at its fall, surrounded in each case with lists of companies and epigrams upon them. They are engraved in mezzotinto, a style of art supposed to have been invented in England—its invention was ascribed to Prince Rupert—and at this time very popular. In the imprint of these last-mentioned plates, we are informed that they were "Printed for Carington Bowles, next yᵉ Chapter House, in St. Paul's Ch. Yard, London," a well-known name in former years, and even now one quite familiar to collectors, of this class of prints, especially. Of Carington Bowles we shall have more to say in the next chapter. With him begins the long list of celebrated English printsellers.

CHAPTER XXIV.

ENGLISH CARICATURE IN THE AGE OF GEORGE II.—ENGLISH PRINTSELLERS.—
ARTISTS EMPLOYED BY THEM.—SIR ROBERT WALPOLE'S LONG MINISTRY.—THE
WAR WITH FRANCE.—THE NEWCASTLE ADMINISTRATION.—OPERA INTRIGUES.—
ACCESSION OF GEORGE III., AND LORD BUTE IN POWER.

With the accession of George II., the taste for political caricatures increased greatly, and they had become almost a necessity of social life. At this time, too, a distinct English school of political caricature had been established, and the print-sellers became more numerous, and took a higher position in the commerce of literature and art. Among the earliest of these printsellers the name of Bowles stands especially conspicuous. Hogarth's burlesque on the Beggar's Opera, published in 1728, was "printed for John Bowles, at the Black Horse, in Cornhill." Some copies of "King Henry the Eighth and Anna Bullen," engraved by the same great artist in the following year, bear the imprint of John Bowles; and others were "printed for Robert Wilkinson, Cornhill, Carington Bowles, in St. Paul's Church Yard, and R. Sayer, in Fleet Street." Hogarth's "Humours of Southwark Fair" was also published, in 1733, by Carington and John Bowles. This Carington Bowles was, perhaps, dead in 1755, for in that year the caricature entitled "British Resentment" bears the imprint, "Printed for T. Bowles, in St. Paul's Church Yard, and Jno. Bowles & Son, in Cornhill." John Bowles appears to have been the brother of the first Carington Bowles in St. Paul's Churchyard, and a son named Carington succeeded to that business, which, under him and his son Carington, and then as the establishment of Bowles and Carver, has continued to exist within the memory of the present generation. Another very celebrated printshop was established in Fleet Street by Thomas Overton, probably as far back as the close of the seventeenth century. On his death his business was purchased by Robert Sayers, a mezzotinto engraver of merit, whose name appears as joint publisher of a print by Hogarth in 1729. Overton is said to have been a personal friend of Hogarth. Sayers was succeeded in the business by his pupil in mezzotinto engraving, named Laurie, from whom it descended to his son, Robert H. Laurie, known in city politics, and it became subsequently the firm of Laurie and Whittle. This business still exists at 53, Fleet Street, the oldest establishment in London for the publication of maps and prints. During the reign of the second George, the number of publishers of caricatures increased considerably, and among others, we meet with the names of J. Smith, "at Hogarth's Head, Cheapside," attached to a caricature published August, 1756; Edwards and Darly, "at the Golden Acorn, facing Hungerford, Strand," who also published caricatures during the years 1756-7; caricatures and burlesque prints were published by G. Bickham, May's Buildings, Covent Garden, and one, directed against the employment of foreign troops, and entitled "A Nurse for the Hessians," is stated to have been "sold in May's Buildings, Covent Garden, where is 50 more;" "The Raree Show," published in 1762, was "sold at Sumpter's Political Print-shop, Fleet Street," and many caricatures on contemporary costume, especially on the Macaronis, about the year 1772, were "published by T. Bowen, opposite the Haymarket, Piccadilly." Sledge, "printseller, Henrietta Street, Covent Garden," is also met with about the middle of the last century. Among other burlesque prints, Bickham, of May's Buildings, issued a series of figures representing the various trades, made up of the different tools, &c, used by each. The house of Carington Bowles, in St. Paul's Churchyard, produced an immense number of caricatures, during the last century and the present, and of the most varied character, but they consisted more of comic scenes of society than of political subjects, and many of them were engraved in mezzotinto, and rather highly coloured. Among them were caricatures on the fashions and foibles of the day, amusing accidents and incidents, common occurrences of life, characters, &c., and they are frequently aimed at lawyers and priests, and especially at monks and friars, for the anti-Catholic feeling was strong in the last century. J. Brotherton, at No. 132, New Bond Street, published many of Bunbury's caricatures; while the house of Laurie and Whittle gave employment especially to the Cruikshanks. But perhaps the most extensive publisher of caricatures of them all was S. W. Fores, who dwelt first at No. 3, Piccadilly, but afterwards established himself at No. 50, the corner of Sackville Street, where the name still remains. Fores seems to have been most fertile in ingenious expedients for the extension of his business. He formed a sort of library of caricatures and other prints, and charged for admission to look at them; and he afterwards adopted a system of lending them out in portfolios for evening parties, at which these portfolios of caricatures became a very fashionable amusement in the latter part of the last century. At times, some remarkable curiosity was employed to add to the attractions of his shop. Thus, on caricatures published in 1790, we find the statement that, "In Fores' Caricature Museum is the completest collection in the kingdom. Also *the head and hand of Count Struenzee*. Admittance, 1*s*." Caricatures against the French revolutionists, published in 1793, bear imprints stating that they were "published by S. W. Fores, No. 3, Piccadilly, where may be seen *a complete Model of the Guillotine*—admittance, one shilling." In some this model is said to be six feet high.

Among the artists employed by the print-publishers of the age of George II., we still find a certain number of foreigners. Coypel, who caricatured the opera in the days of Farinelli, and pirated Hogarth, belonged to a distinguished family of French painters. Goupy, who also caricatured the *artistes* of the opera (in 1727), and Boitard, who worked actively for Carington Bowles from 1750 to 1770, were also Frenchmen. Liotard, another caricaturist of the time of George II., was a native of Geneva. The names of two others, Vandergucht and Vanderbank, proclaim them Dutchmen. Among the English caricaturists who worked for the house of Bowles, were George Bickham, the brother of the printseller, John Collet, and Robert Dighton, with others of less repute. R. Attwold, who published caricatures against admiral Byng in 1750, was an imitator of Hogarth. Among the more obscure caricaturists of the latter part of the half-century, were MacArdell—whose print of "The Park Shower," representing the confusion raised among the fashionable company in the Mall in St. James's Park by a sudden fall of rain, is so well known—and Darley. Paul Sandby, who was patronised by the duke of Cumberland, executed caricatures upon Hogarth. Many of these artists of the earlier period of the English school of caricature appear to have been very ill paid—the first of the family of Bowles is said to have boasted that he bought many of the plates for little more than their value as metal. The growing taste for caricature had also brought forward a number of amateurs, among whom were the countess of Burlington, and general, afterwards marquis, Townshend. The former, who was the lady of that earl who built Burlington House, in Piccadilly, was the leader of one of the factions in the opera disputes at the close of the reign of George I., and is understood to have designed the well-known caricature upon Cuzzoni, Farinelli, and Heidegger, which was etched by Goupy, whom she patronised. It must not be forgotten that Bunbury himself, as well as Sayers, were amateurs; and among other amateurs I may name captain Minthull, captain Baillie, and John Nixon. The first of these published caricatures against the Macaronis (as the dandies of the earlier part of the reign of George III. were called), one of which, entitled "The Macaroni Dressing-Room," was especially popular.

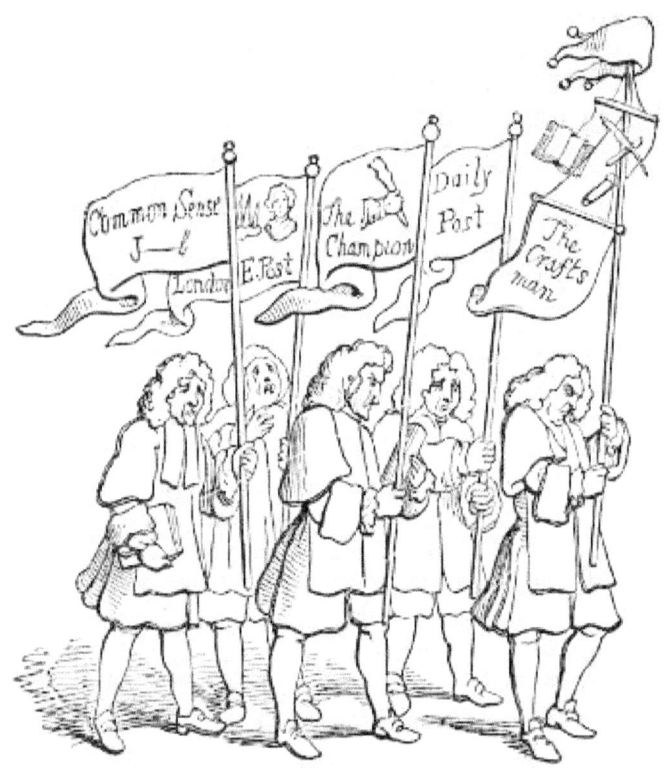

No. 195. A Party of Mourners.

English political caricature came into its full activity with the ministry of Sir Robert Walpole, which, beginning in 1721, lasted through the long period of twenty years. In the previous period the Whigs were accused of having invented caricature, but now the Tories certainly took the utmost advantage of the invention, for, during several years, the greater number of the caricatures which were published were aimed against the Whig ministry. It is also a rather remarkable characteristic of society at this period, that the ladies took so great an interest in politics, that the caricatures were largely introduced upon fans, as well as upon other objects of an equally personal character. Moreover, the popular notion of what constituted a caricature was still so little fixed, that they were usually called *hieroglyphics*, a term, indeed, which was not ill applied, for they were so elaborate, and so filled with mystical allusions, that now it is by no means easy to understand or appreciate them. Towards the year 1739, there was a marked improvement in the political caricatures—they were better designed, and displayed more talent, but still they required rather long descriptions to render them intelligible. One of the most celebrated was produced by the motion in the House of Commons, Feb. 13, 1741, against the minister Walpole. It was entitled "The Motion," and was a Whig satire upon the opposition, who are represented as driving so hurriedly and inconsiderately to obtain places, that they are overthrown before they reach their object. The party of the opposition retaliated by a counter-caricature, entitled, "The Reason," which was in some respects a parody upon the other, to which it was inferior in point and spirit. At the same time appeared another caricature against the ministry, under the title of "The Motive." These provoked another, entitled, "A Consequence of the Motion;" which was followed the day after its publication by another caricature upon the opposition, entitled, "The Political Libertines; or, Motion upon Motion;" while the opponents of the government also brought out a caricature, entitled, "The Grounds," a violent and rather gross attack upon the Whigs. Among other caricatures published on this occasion, one of the best was entitled, "The Funeral of Faction," and bears the date of March 26, 1741. Beneath it are the words, "Funerals performed by Squire S——s," alluding to Sandys, who was the motion-maker in the House of Commons, and who thus brought on his party a signal defeat. Among the chief mourners on this occasion are seen the opposition journals, *The Craftsman*, the creation of Bolingbroke and Pulteney, the still more scurrilous *Champion*, *The Daily Post*, *The London and Evening Post*, and *The Common Sense Journal*. This mournful group is reproduced in our cut No. 195.

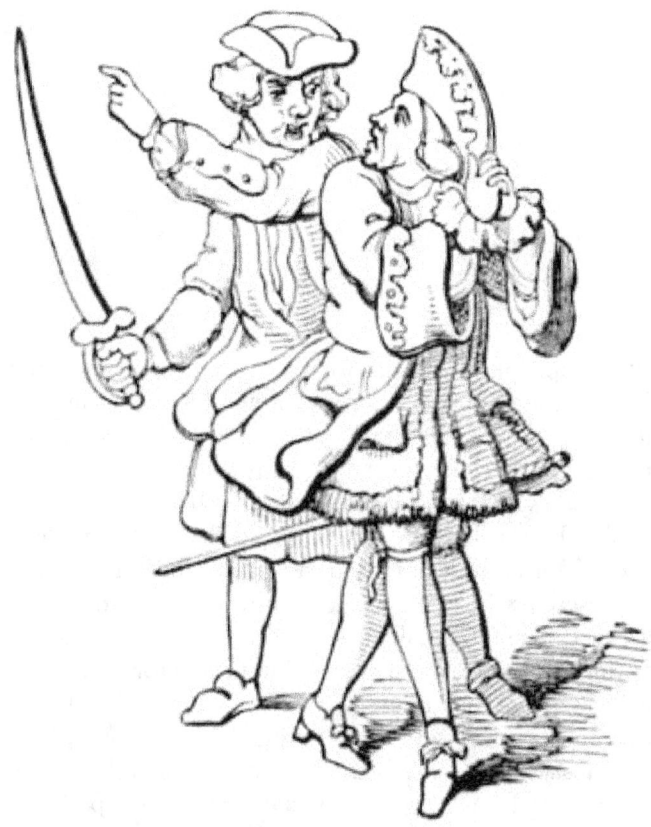

No. 196. British Resentment.

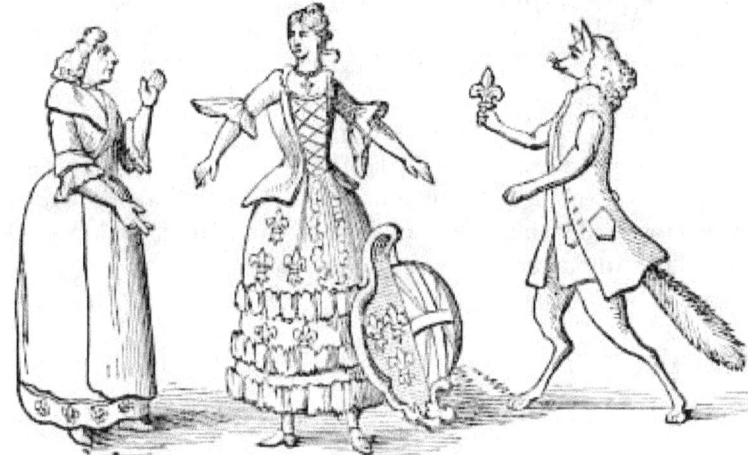

No. 197. Britannia in a New Dress.

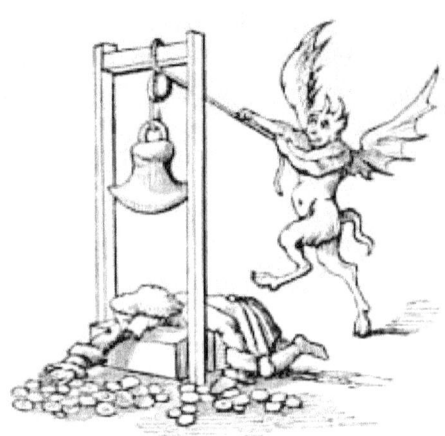

No. 198. Caught by a Bait.

From this time there was no falling off in the supply of caricatures, which, on the contrary, seemed to increase every year, until the activity of the pictorial satirists was roused anew by the hostilities with France in 1755, and the ministerial intrigues of the two following years. The war, accepted by the English government reluctantly, and ill prepared for, was the subject of much discontent, although at first hopes were given of great success. One of the caricatures, published in the middle of these early hopes, at a time when an English fleet lay before Louisbourg, in Canada, is entitled, "British Resentment, or the French fairly coop'd at Louisbourg," and came from the pencil of the French artist Boitard. One of its groups, representing the courageous English sailor and the despairing Frenchman, is given in our cut No. 196, and may serve as an example of Boitard's style of drawing. It became now the fashion to print political caricatures, in a diminished form, on cards, and seventy-five of these were formed into a small volume, under the title of "A Political and Satirical History of the years 1756 and 1757. In a series of seventy-five humorous and entertaining Prints, containing all the most remarkable Transactions, Characters, and Caricaturas of those two memorable years.... London: printed for E. Morris, near St. Paul's." The imprints of the plates, which bear the dates of their several publications, inform us that they came from the well-known shop of "Darly and Edwards, at the Acorn, facing Hungerford, Strand." These caricatures begin with our foreign relations, and express the belief that the ministers were sacrificing English interests to French influence. In one of them (our cut No. 197), entitled, "England made odious, or the French Dressers," the minister, Newcastle, in the garb of a woman, and his colleague, Fox, have dressed Britannia in a new French robe, which does not fit her. She exclaims, "Let me have my own cloathes. I cannot stir my arms in these; besides, everybody laughs at me." Newcastle replies, rather imperiously, "Hussy, be quiet, you have no need to stir your arms—why, sure! what's here to do?" While Fox, in a more insinuating tone, offers her a fleur-de-lis, and says, "Here, madam, stick this in your bosom, next your heart." The two pictures which adorn the walls of the room represent an axe and a halter; and underneath we read the lines,—

And shall the substitutes of power
Our genius thus bedeck?
Let them remember there's an hour
Of quittance—then, ware neck.

In another print of this series, this last idea is illustrated more fully. It is aimed at the ministers, who were believed to be enriching themselves at the expense of the nation, and is entitled, "The Devil turned Bird-catcher." On one side, while Fox is greedily scrambling for the gold, the fiend has caught him in a halter suspended to the gallows; on the other side another demon is letting down the fatal axe on Newcastle, who is similarly employed. The latter (see our cut No. 198) is described as a "Noddy catching at the bait, while the bird-catcher lets drop an axe." This implement of execution is a perfect picture of a guillotine, long before it was so notoriously in use in France.

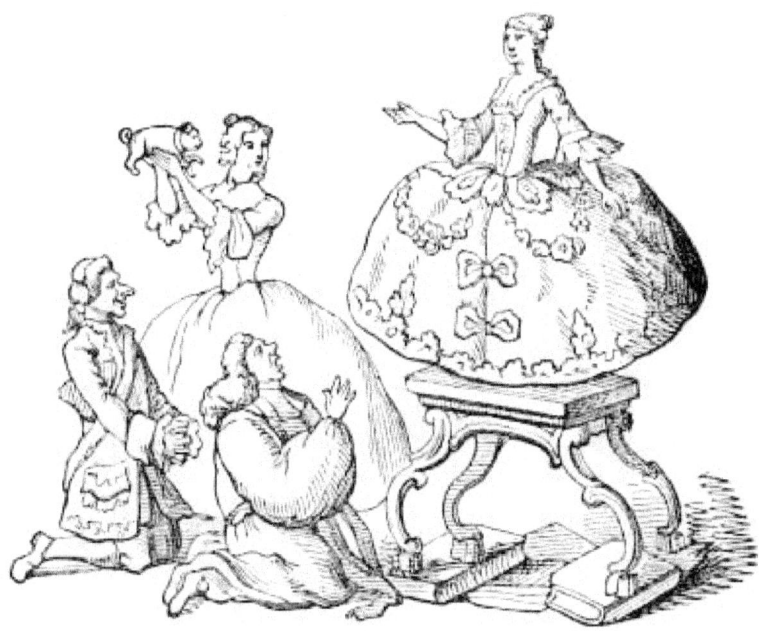

No. 199. British Idolatry.

The third example of these caricatures which I shall quote is entitled "The Idol," and has for its subject the extravagancies and personal jealousies connected with the Italian opera. The rivalry between Mingotti and Vanneschi was now making as much noise there as that of Cuzzoni and Faustina some years before. The former acted arbitrarily and capriciously, and could with difficulty be bound to sing a few times during the season for a high salary: it is said, £2,000 for the season. In the caricature to which I allude, this lady appears raised upon a stool, inscribed "£2,000 per annum," and is receiving the worship of her admirers. Immediately before her an ecclesiastic is seen on his knees, exclaiming, "Unto thee be praise now and for evermore!" In the background a lady appears, holding up her pug-dog, then the fashionable pet, and addressing the opera favourite, "'Tis only pug and you I love." Other men are on their knees behind the ecclesiastic, all persons of distinction; and last comes a nobleman and his lady, the former holding in his hand an order for £2,000, his subscription to the opera, and remarking, "We shall have but twelve songs for all this money." The lady replies, with an air of contempt, "Well, and enough too, for the paltry trifle." The idol, in return for all this homage, sings rather contemptuously—

Ra, ru, ra, rot ye,
My name is Mingotti,
If you worship me notti,
You shall all go to potti.

The closing years of the reign of George II., under the vigorous administration of the first William Pitt, witnessed a calm in the domestic politics of the country, which presented a strange contrast to the agitation of the previous period. Faction seemed to have hidden its head, and there was comparatively little employment for the caricaturist. But this calm lasted only a short time after that king's death, and the new reign was ushered in by indications of approaching political agitation of the most violent description, in which satirists who had hitherto contented themselves with other subjects were tempted to embark in the strife of politics. Among these was Hogarth, whose discomforts as a political caricaturist we shall have to describe in our next chapter.

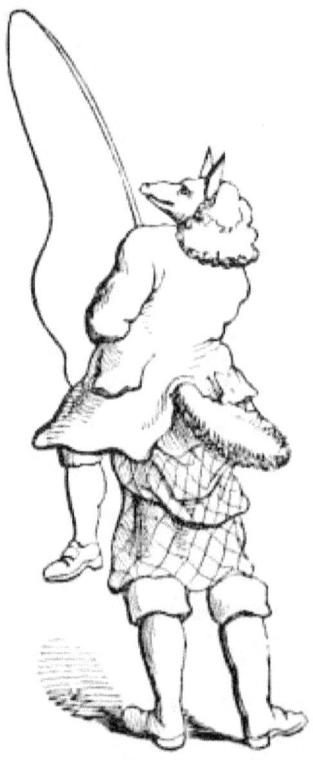

No. 200. Fox on Boots.

Perhaps no name ever provoked a greater amount of caricature and satirical abuse than that of Lord Bute, who, through the favour of the Princess of Wales, ruled supreme at court during the first period of the reign of George III. Bute had taken into the ministry, as his confidential colleague, Fox—the Henry Fox who became subsequently the first Lord Holland, a man who had enriched himself enormously with the money of the nation, and these two appeared to be aiming at the establishment of arbitrary power in the place of constitutional government. Fox was usually represented in the caricatures with the head and tail of the animal represented by his name rather strongly developed; while Bute was drawn, as a very bad pun upon his name, in the garb of a Scotchman, wearing two large boots, or sometimes a single boot of still greater magnitude. In these caricatures Bute and Fox are generally coupled together. Thus, a little before the resignation of the duke of Newcastle in 1762, there appeared a caricature entitled "The State Nursery," in which the various members of the ministry, as it was then formed under Lord Bute's influence, are represented as engaged in childish games. Fox, as the whipper-in of parliamentary majorities, is riding, armed with his whip, on Bute's shoulders (see our cut No. 200), while the duke of Newcastle performs the more menial service of rocking the cradle. In the rhymes which accompany this caricature, the first of these groups is described as follows (Fox was commonly spoken of in satire by the title of Volpone)—

First you see old sly Volpone-y,
Riding on the shoulders brawny
Of the muckle favourite Sawny;
Doodle, doodle, doo.

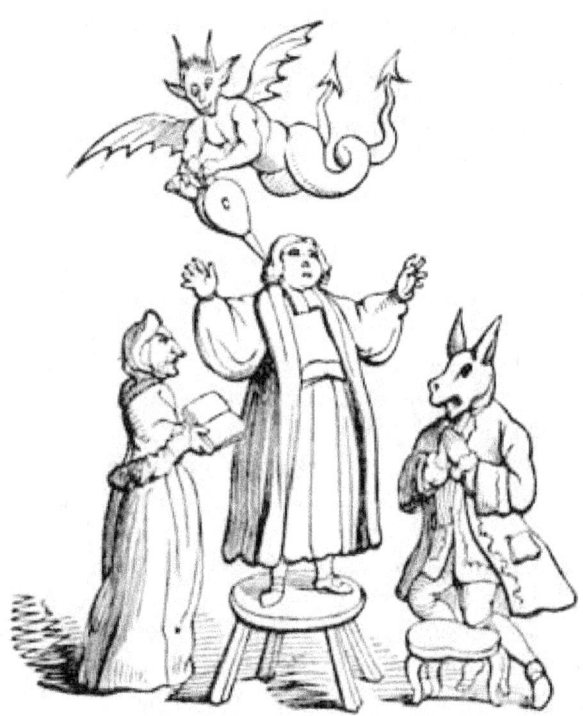

No. 201. Fanaticism in another Shape.

The number of caricatures published at this period was very great, and they were almost all aimed in one direction, against Bute and Fox, the Princess of Wales, and the government they directed. Caricature, at this time, ran into the least disguised licence, and the coarsest allusions were made to the supposed secret intercourse between the minister and the Princess of Wales, of which perhaps the most harmless was the addition of a petticoat to the boot, as a symbol of the influence under which the country was governed. In mock processions and ceremonies a Scotchman was generally introduced carrying the standard of the boot and petticoat. Lord Bute, frightened at the amount of odium which was thus heaped upon him, fought to stem the torrent by employing satirists to defend the government, and it is hardly necessary to state that among these mercenary auxiliaries was the great Hogarth himself, who accepted a pension, and published his caricature entitled, "The Times, Nov. 1," in the month of September, 1762. Hogarth did not excel in political caricature, and there was little in this print to distinguish it above the ordinary publications of a similar character. It was the moment of negotiations for Lord Bute's unpopular peace, and Hogarth's satire is directed against the foreign policy of the great ex-minister Pitt. It represents Europe in a state of general conflagration, and the flames already communicating to Great Britain. While Pitt is blowing the fire, Bute, with a party of soldiers and sailors zealously assisted by his favourite Scotchmen, is labouring to extinguish it. In this he is impeded by the interference of the duke of Newcastle, who brings a wheelbarrow full of *Monitors* and *North Britons,* the violent opposition journals, to feed the flames. The advocacy of Bute's mercenaries, whether literary or artistic, did little service to the government, for they only provoked increased activity among its opponents. Hogarth's caricature of "The Times," drew several answers, one of the best of which was a large print entitled "The Raree Show: a political contrast to the print of 'The Times,' by William Hogarth." It is the house of John Bull which is here on fire, and the Scots are dancing and exulting at it. In the centre of the picture appears a great actors' barn, from an upper window of which Fox thrusts out his head and points to the sign, representing Æneas and Dido entering the cave together, as the performance which was acting within. It is an allusion to the scandal in general circulation relating to Bute and the princess, who, of course, were the Æneas and Dido of the piece, and appear in those characters on the scaffold in front, with two of Bute's mercenary writers, Smollett, who edited the *Briton,* and

Murphy, who wrote in the *Auditor*, one blowing the trumpet and the other beating the drum. Among the different groups which fill the picture, one, behind the actors' barn (see our cut No. 201), is evidently intended for a satire on the spirit of religious fanaticism which was at this time spreading through the country. An open-air preacher, mounted on a stool, is addressing a not very intellectual-looking audience, while his inspiration is conveyed to him in a rather vulgar manner by the spirit, not of good, but of evil.

The violence of this political warfare at length drove Lord Bute from at least ostensible power. He resigned on the 6th of April, 1763. One of the popular favourites at this time was the duke of Cumberland, the hero of Culloden, who was regarded as the leader of the opposition in the House of Lords. People now believed that it was the duke of Cumberland who had overthrown "the boot," and his popularity increased on a sudden. The triumph was commemorated in several caricatures. One of these is entitled, "The Jack-Boot kick'd down, or English Will triumphant: a Dream." The duke of Cumberland, whip in hand, has kicked the boot out of the house, exclaiming to a young man in tailor's garb who follows him, "Let me alone, Ned; I know how to deal with Scotsmen. Remember Culloden." The youth replies, "Kick hard, uncle, keep him down. Let me have a kick too." Nearly the same group, using similar language, is introduced into a caricature of the same date, entitled, "The Boot and the Blockhead." The youthful personage is no doubt intended for Cumberland's nephew, Edward, duke of York, who was a sailor, and was raised to the rank of rear-admiral, and who appears to have joined his uncle in his opposition to Lord Bute. The "boot," as seen in our cut No. 202, is encircled with Hogarth's celebrated "line of beauty," of which I shall have to speak more at length in the next chapter.

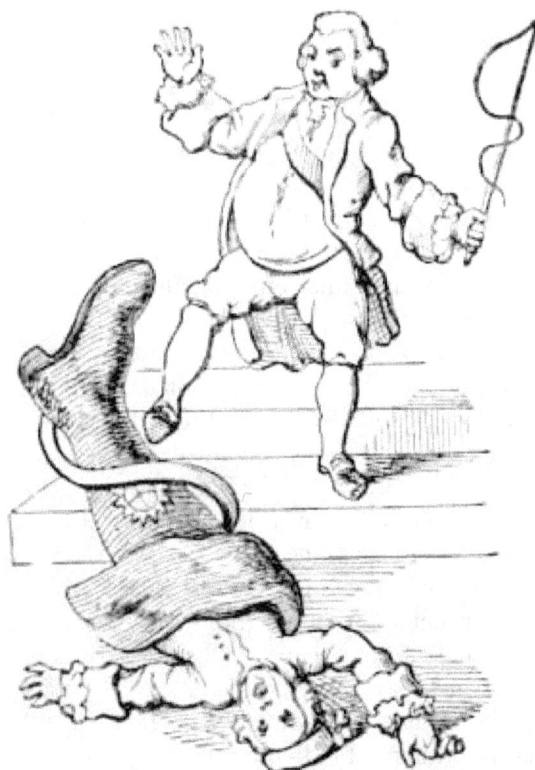

No. 202. The Overthrow of the Boot.

With the overthrow of Bute's ministry, we may consider the English school of caricature as completely formed and fully established. From this time the names of the caricaturists are better known, and we shall have to consider them in their individual characters. One of these, William Hogarth, had risen in fame far above the group of the ordinary men by whom he was surrounded.

CHAPTER XXV.

HOGARTH.—HIS EARLY HISTORY.—HIS SETS OF PICTURES.—THE HARLOT'S PROGRESS.—THE RAKE'S PROGRESS.—THE MARRIAGE A LA MODE.—HIS OTHER PRINTS.—THE ANALYSIS OF BEAUTY, AND THE PERSECUTION ARISING OUT OF IT.—HIS PATRONAGE BY LORD BUTE.—CARICATURE OF THE TIMES.—ATTACKS TO WHICH HE WAS EXPOSED BY IT, AND WHICH HASTENED HIS DEATH.

On the 10th of November, 1697, William Hogarth was born in the city of London. His father, Richard Hogarth, was a London schoolmaster, who laboured to increase the income derived from his scholars by compiling books, but with no great success. From his childhood, as he tells us in his "Anecdotes" of himself, the young Hogarth displayed a taste for drawing, and especially for caricature; and, out of school, he appears to have been seldom without a pencil in his hand. The limited means of Richard Hogarth compelled him to take the boy from school at an early age, and bind him apprentice to a steel-plate engraver. But this occupation proved little to the taste of one whose ambition rose much higher; and when the term of his apprenticeship had expired, he applied himself to engraving on copper; and, setting up on his own account, did considerable amount of work, first in engraving arms and shop-bills, and afterwards in designing and engraving book illustrations, none of which displayed any superiority over the ordinary run of such productions. Towards 1728 Hogarth began to practice as a painter, and he subsequently attended the academy of sir James Thornhill, in Covent Garden, where he became acquainted with that painter's only daughter, Jane. The result was a clandestine marriage in 1730, which met the disapproval and provoked the anger of the lady's father. Subsequently, however, sir James became convinced of the genius of his son-in-law, and a reconciliation was effected through the medium of lady Thornhill.

At this time Hogarth had already commenced that new style of design which was destined to raise him soon to a degree of fame as an artist few men have ever attained. In his "Anecdotes" of himself, the painter has given us an interesting account of the motives by which he was guided. "The reasons," he says, "which induced me to adopt this mode of designing were, that I thought both writers and painters had, in the historical style, totally overlooked that intermediate species of subjects which may be placed between the sublime and the grotesque. I therefore wished to compose pictures on canvas similar to representations on the stage; and further hope that they will be tried by the same test, and criticised by the same criterion. Let it be observed, that I mean to speak only of those scenes where the human species are actors, and these, I think, have not often been delineated in a way of which they are worthy and capable. In these compositions, those subjects that will both entertain and improve the mind bid fair to be of the greatest public utility, and must therefore be entitled to rank in the highest class. If the execution is difficult (though that is but a secondary merit), the author has claim to a higher degree of praise. If this be admitted, comedy, in painting as well as writing, ought to be allotted the first place, though *the sublime*, as it is called, has been opposed to it. Ocular demonstration will carry more conviction to the mind of a sensible man than all he would find in a thousand volumes, and this has been attempted in the prints I have composed. Let the decision be left to every unprejudiced eye; let the figures in either pictures or prints be considered as players dressed either for the sublime, for genteel comedy or farce, for high or low life. I have endeavoured to treat my subjects as a dramatic writer: my picture is my stage, and men and women my players, who, by means of certain actions and gestures, are to exhibit *a dumb-show.*"

The great series of pictures, indeed, which form the principal foundation of Hogarth's fame, are comedies rather than caricatures, and noble comedies they are. Like comedies, they are arranged, by a series of successive plates, in acts and scenes; and they represent contemporary society pictorially, just as it had been and was represented on the stage in English comedy. It is not by delicacy or excellence of drawing that Hogarth excels, for he often draws incorrectly; but it is by his extraordinary and minute delineation of character, and by his wonderful skill in telling a story thoroughly. In each of his plates we see a whole act of a play, in which nothing is lost, nothing glossed over, and, I may add, nothing exaggerated. The most trifling object introduced into the picture is made to have such an intimate relationship with the whole, that it seems as if it would be imperfect without it. The art of producing this effect was that in which Hogarth excelled. The first of Hogarth's great *suites* of prints was "The Harlot's Progress," which was the work of the years 1733 and 1734. It tells a story which was then common in London, and was acted more openly in the broad face of society than at the present day; and therefore the effect and consequent success were almost instantaneous. It had novelty, as well as excellence, to recommend it. This series of plates was followed, in 1735, by another, under the title of "The Rake's Progress." In the former, Hogarth depicted the shame and ruin which attended a life of prostitution; in this, he represented the similar consequences which a life of profligacy entailed on the other sex. In many respects it is superior to the "Harlot's Progress," and its details come more home to the feelings of people in general, because those of the prostitute's history are more veiled from the public gaze. The progress of the spendthrift in dissipation and riot, from the moment he becomes possessed of the fruits of paternal avarice, until his career ends in prison and madness, forms a marvellous drama, in which every incident presents itself, and every agent performs his part, so naturally, that it seems almost beyond the power of acting. Perhaps no one ever pictured despair with greater perfection than it is shown in the face and bearing of the unhappy hero of this history, in the last plate but one of the series, where, thrown into prison for debt, he receives from the manager of a theatre the announcement that the play which he had written in the hope of retrieving somewhat of his position—his last resource—has been refused. The returned manuscript and the manager's letter lie on the wretched table (cut No. 203); while on the one side his wife reproaches him heartlessly with the deprivations and sufferings which he has brought upon her, and on the other the jailer is reminding him of the fact that the fees exacted for the slight indulgence he has obtained in prison are unpaid, and even the pot-boy refuses to deliver him his beer without first receiving his money. It is but a step further to Bedlam, which, in the next plate, closes his unblessed career.

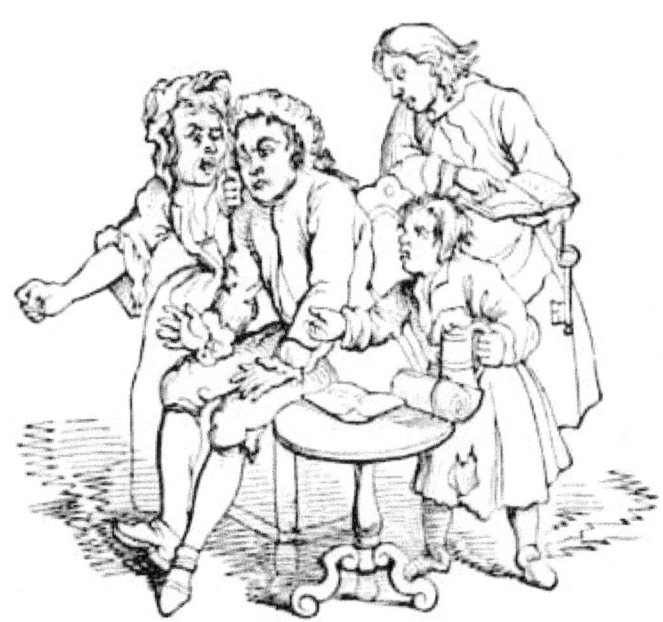

No. 203. Despair.

Ten years almost from this time had passed away before Hogarth gave to the world his next grand series of what he called his "modern moral subjects." This was "The Marriage *à la mode*," which was published in six plates in 1745, and which fully sustained the reputation built upon the "Harlot's Progress" and the "Rake's Progress." Perhaps the best plate of the "Marriage *à la mode*," is the fourth—the music scene—in which one principal group of figures especially arrests the attention. It is represented in our cut No. 204. William Hazlitt has justly remarked upon it that, "the preposterous, overstrained admiration of the lady of quality; the sentimental, insipid, patient delight of the man with his hair in papers, and sipping his tea; the pert, smirking, conceited, half-distorted approbation of the figure next to him; the transition to the total insensibility of the round face in profile, and then to the wonder of the negro boy at the rapture of his mistress, form a perfect whole."

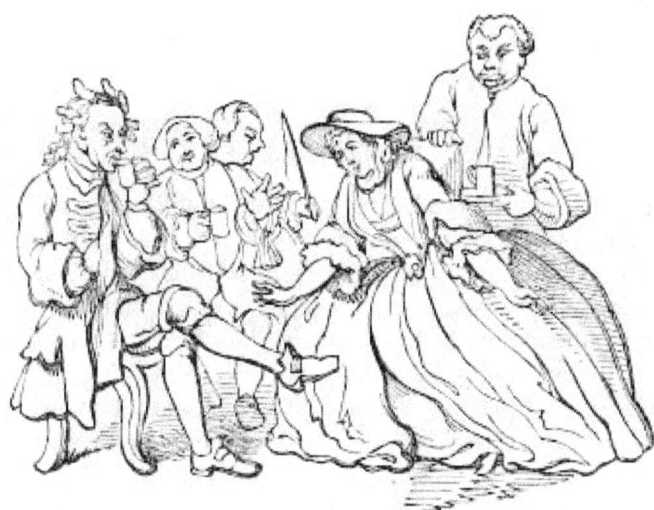

No. 204. Fashionable Society.

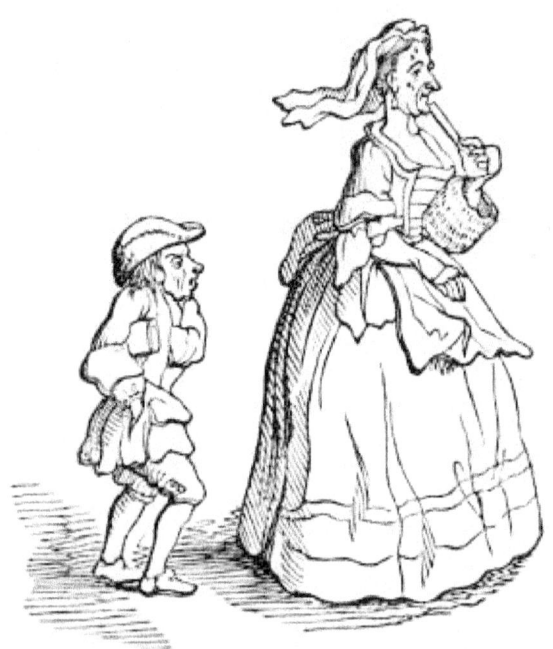

No. 205. An Old Maid and her Page.

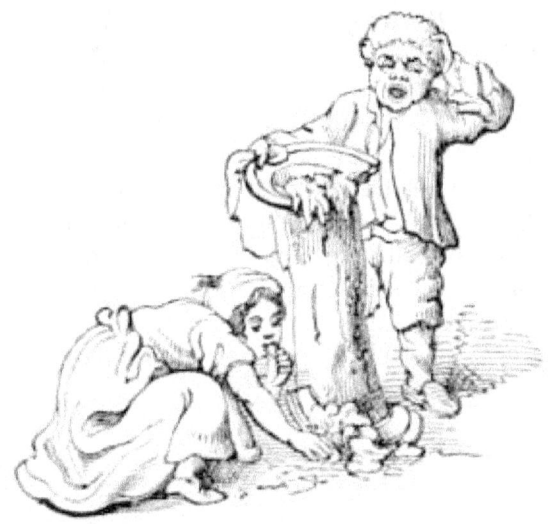

No. 206. Loss and Gain.

In the interval between these three great monuments of his talent, Hogarth had published various other plates, belonging to much the same class of subjects, and displaying different degrees of excellence. His engraving of "Southwark Fair," published in 1733, which immediately preceded the "Harlot's Progress," may be regarded almost as an attempt to rival the fairs of Gallot. "The Midnight Modern Conversation" appeared in the interval between the "Harlot's Progress" and the "Rake's Progress;" and three years after the series last mentioned, in 1738, the engraving, remarkable equally in design and execution, of the "Strolling Actresses in a Barn," and the four plates of "Morning," "Noon," "Evening," and "Night," all full of choicest bits of humour. Such is the group of the old maid and her footboy in the first of this series (cut No. 205)—the former stiff and prudish, whose religion is evidently not that of charity; while the latter crawls after, shrinking at the same time under the effects of cold and hunger, which he sustains in consequence of the hard, niggardly temper of his mistress. Among the humorous events which fill the plate of "Noon," we may point to the disaster of the boy who has been sent to the baker's to fetch home the family dinner, and who, as represented in our cut No. 206, has broken his pie-dish, and spilt its contents on the ground; and it is difficult to say which is expressed with most fidelity to nature—the terror and shame of the unfortunate lad, or the feeling of enjoyment in the face of the little girl who is feasting on the fragments of the scattered meal. In 1741 appeared the plate of "The Enraged Musician." During this period Hogarth appears to have been hesitating between two subjects for his third grand pictorial drama. Some unfinished sketches have been found, from which it would seem that, after depicting the miseries of a life of dissipation in either sex, he intended to represent the domestic happiness which resulted from a prudent and well-assorted marriage; but for some reason or other he abandoned this design, and gave the picture of wedlock in a less amiable light, in his "Marriage *à la mode*." The title was probably taken from that of Dryden's comedy. In 1750 appeared "The March to Finchley," in many respects one of Hogarth's best works. It is a striking exposure of the want of discipline, and the low *morale* of the English army under George II. Many amusing groups fill this picture, the scene of which is laid in Tottenham Court Road, along which the guards are supposed to be marching to encamp at Finchley, in consequence of rumours of the approach of the Pretender's army in the Rebellion of '45. The soldiers in front are moving on with some degree of order, but in the rear we see nothing but confusion, some reeling about under the effects of liquor, and confounded by the cries of women and children, camp-followers, ballad-singers, plunderers, and the like. One of the latter, as represented in our cut No. 207, is assisting a fallen soldier with an additional dose of liquor, while his pilfering propensities are betrayed by the hen screaming from his wallet, and by the chickens following distractedly the cries of their parent.

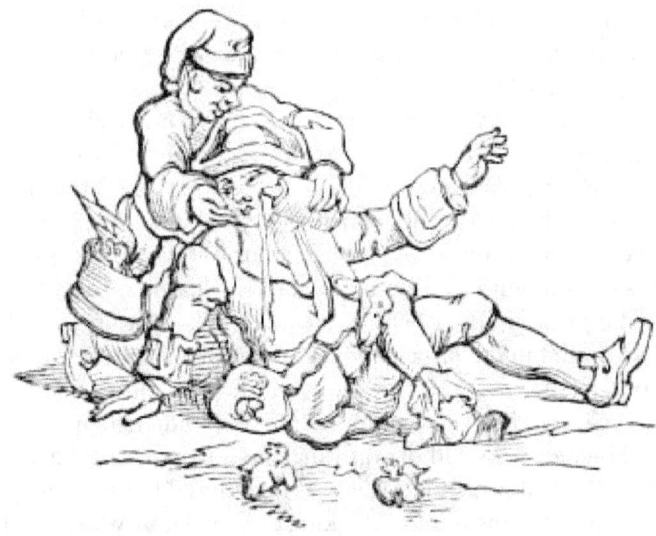

No. 207. A brave Soldier.

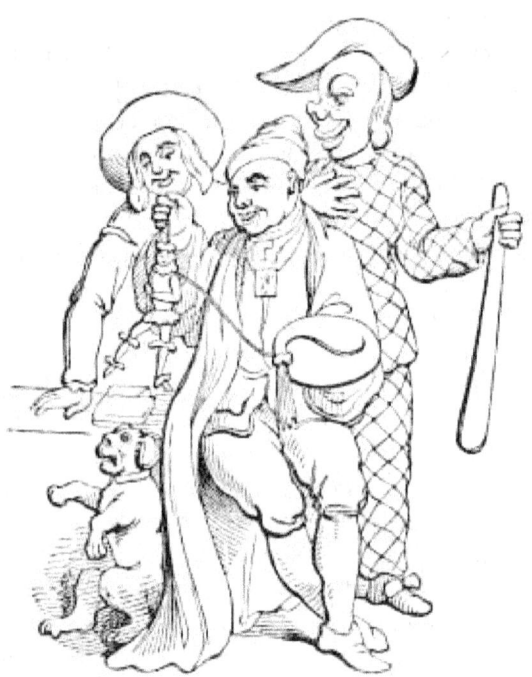

No. 208. A Painter's Amusements.

Hogarth presents a singular example of a satirist who suffered under the very punishment which he inflicted on others. He made many personal enemies in the course of his labours. He had begun his career with a well-known personal satire, entitled "The Man of Taste," which was a caricature on Pope, and the poet is said never to have forgiven it. Although the satire in his more celebrated works appears to us general, it told upon his contemporaries personally; for the figures which act their parts in them were so many portraits of individuals who moved in contemporary society, and who were known to everybody, and thus he provoked a host of enemies. It was like Foote's mimicry. He was to an extraordinary degree vain of his own talent, and jealous of that of others in the same profession; and he spoke in terms of undisguised contempt of almost all artists, past or present. Thus, the painter introduced into the print of "Beer Street," is said to be a caricature upon John Stephen Liotard, one of the artists mentioned in the last chapter. He thus provoked the hostility of the greatest part of his contemporaries in his own profession, and in the sequel had to support the full weight of their anger. When George II., who had more taste for soldiers than pictures, saw the painting of the "March to Finchley," instead of admiring it as a work of art, he is said to have expressed himself with anger at the insult which he believed was offered to his army; and Hogarth not only revenged himself by dedicating his print to the king of Prussia, by which it did become a satire on the British army, but he threw himself into the faction of the prince of Wales at Leicester House. The first occasion for the display of all these animosities was given in the year 1753, at the close of which he published his "Analysis of Beauty." Though far from being himself a successful painter of beauty, Hogarth undertook in this work to investigate its principles, which he referred to a waving or serpentine line, and this he termed the "line of beauty." In 1745 Hogarth had published his own portrait as the frontispiece to a volume of his collected works, and in one corner of the plate he introduced a painter's palette, on which was this waving line, inscribed "The line of beauty." For several years the meaning of this remained either quite a mystery, or was only known to a few of Hogarth's acquaintances, until the appearance of the book just mentioned. Hogarth's manuscript was revised by his friend, Dr. Morell, the compiler of the "Thesaurus," whose name became thus associated with the book. This work exposed its author to a host of violent attacks, and to unbounded ridicule, especially from the whole tribe of offended artists. A great number of caricatures upon Hogarth and his line of beauty appeared during the year 1754, which show the bitterness of the hatred he had provoked; and to hold still further their terror over his head, most of them are inscribed with the words, "To be continued." Among the artists who especially signalised themselves by their zeal against him, was Paul Sandby, to whom we owe some of the best of these anti-Hogarthian caricatures. One of these is entitled, "A New Dunciad, done with a view of [fixing] the fluctuating ideas of taste." In the principal group (which is given in our cut No. 208), Hogarth is represented playing with a *pantin*, or figure which was moved into activity by pulling a string. The string takes somewhat the form of the line of beauty, which is also drawn upon his palette. This figure is described underneath the picture as "a painter at the proper exercise of his taste." To his breast is attached a card (the knave of hearts), which is described by a very bad pun as "the fool of arts." On one side "his genius" is represented in the form of a black harlequin; while behind appears a rather jolly personage (intended, perhaps, for Dr. Morell), who, we are told, is one of his admirers. On the table are the foundations, or the remains, of "a house of cards." Near him is Hogarth's favourite dog, named Trump, which always accompanies him in these caricatures. Another caricature which appeared at this time represents Hogarth on the stage as a quack doctor, holding in his hand the line of beauty, and recommending its extraordinary qualities. This print is entitled "A Mountebank Painter demonstrating to his admirers and subscribers that crookedness is yᵉ most beautifull." Lord Bute, whose patronage at Leicester House Hogarth now enjoyed, is represented fiddling, and the black harlequin serves as "his puff." In the front a crowd of deformed and hump-backed people are pressing forwards (see our cut No. 209), and the line of beauty fits them all admirably.

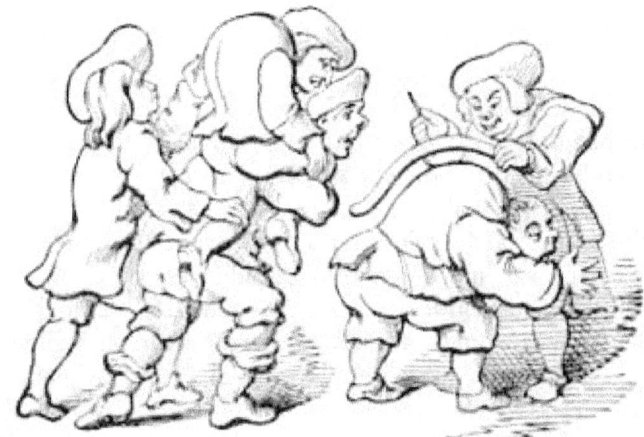

No. 209. The Line of Beauty exemplified.

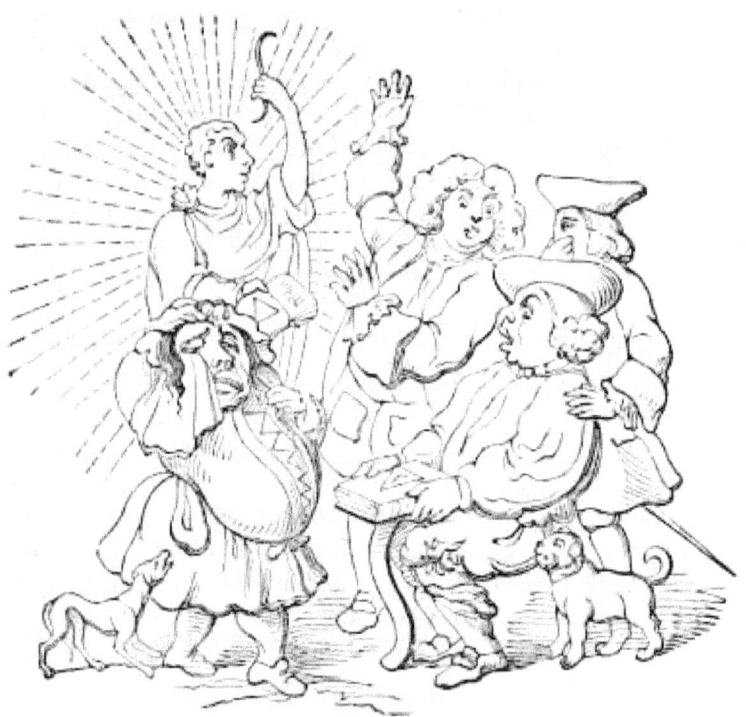

No. 210. Piracy Exposed.

Much as this famous line of beauty was ridiculed, Hogarth was not allowed to retain the small honour which seemed to arise from it undisputed. It was said that he had stolen the idea from an Italian writer named Lomazzo, Latinised into Lomatius, who had enounced it in a treatise on the Fine Arts, published in the sixteenth century.[102] In another caricature by Paul Sandby, with a vulgar title which I will not repeat, Hogarth is visited, in the midst of his glory, by the ghost of Lomazzo, carrying in one hand his treatise on the arts, and with his other holding up to view the line of beauty itself. In the inscriptions on the plate, the principal figure is described as "An author sinking under the weight of his saturnine analysis;" and, indeed, Hogarth's terror is broadly painted, while the volume of his analysis is resting heavily upon "a strong support bent in the line of beauty by the mighty load upon it." Beside Hogarth stands "his faithful pug," and behind him "a friend of the author endeavouring to prevent his sinking to his natural lowness." On the other side stands Dr. Morell, or, perhaps, Mr. Townley, the master of Merchant Taylors' School, who continued his service in preparing the book for the press after Morell's death, described as "the author's friend and corrector," astonished at the sight of the ghost. The ugly figure on the left hand of the picture is described as "Deformity weeping at the condition of her darling son," while the dog is "a greyhound bemoaning his friend's condition." This group is represented in our cut No. 210. The other caricatures which appeared at this time were two numerous to allow us to give a particular description of them. The artist is usually represented, under the influence of his line of beauty, painting ugly pictures from deformed models, or attempting historical pictures in a style bordering on caricature, or, on one occasion, as locked up in a mad-house, and allowed only to exercise his skill upon the bare walls. One of these caricatures is entitled, in allusion to the title of one of his most popular prints, "The Painter's March through Finchley, dedicated to the king of the gipsies, as an encourager of arts, &c" Hogarth appears in full flight through the village, closely pursued by women and children, and animals in great variety, and defended only by his favourite dog.

With the "Marriage *à la mode*," Hogarth may be considered as having reached his highest point of excellence. The set of "Industry and Idleness" tells a good and useful moral story, but displays inferior talent in design. "Beer Street" and "Gin Lane" disgust us by their vulgarity, and the "Four Stages of Cruelty" are equally repulsive to our feelings by the unveiled horrors of the scenes which are too coarsely depicted in them. In the four prints of the proceedings at an election, which are the last of his pictures of this description, published in 1754, Hogarth rises again, and approaches in some degree to his former elevation.

In 1757, on the death of his brother-in-law, John Thornhill, the office of sergeant-painter of all his Majesty's works became vacant, and it was bestowed upon Hogarth, who, according to his own account, received from it an income of about £200 a-year. This appointment caused another display of hostility towards him, and his enemies called him jeeringly the king's chief panel painter. It was at this moment that a plan for the establishment of an academy of the fine arts was agitated, which, a few years later, came into existence under the title of the Royal Academy, and Hogarth proclaimed so loud an opposition to this project, that the old cry was raised anew, that he was jealous and envious of all his profession, and that he sought to stand alone as superior to them all. It was the signal for a new onslaught of caricatures upon himself and his line of beauty. Hitherto his assailants had been found chiefly among the artists, but the time was now approaching when he was destined to thrust himself into the midst of a political struggle, where the attacks of a new class of enemies carried with them a more bitter sting.

George II. died on the 17th of October, 1760, and his grandson succeeded him to the throne as George III. It appears evident that before this time Hogarth had gained the favour of lord Bute, who, by his interest with the princess of Wales, was all-powerful in the household of the young prince. The painter had hitherto kept tolerably clear of politics in his prints, but now, unluckily for himself, he suddenly rushed into the arena of political caricature. It was generally said that Hogarth's object was, by displaying his zeal in the cause of his patron, lord Bute, to obtain an increase in his pension; and he acknowledges himself that his object was gain. "This," he says, "being a period when war abroad and contention at home engrossed every one's mind, prints were thrown into the background; and the stagnation rendered it necessary that I should do some *timed thing* [the italics are Hogarth's] to recover my lost time, and stop a gap in my income." Accordingly he determined to attack the great minister, Pitt, who had then recently been compelled to resign his office, and had gone over to the opposition. It is said that John Wilkes, who had previously been Hogarth's friend, having been privately informed of his design, went to the painter, expostulated with him, and, as he continued obstinate, threatened him with retaliation. In September, 1762, appeared the print entitled "The Times, No. I," indicating that it was to be followed by a second caricature. The principal features of the picture are these: Europe is represented in flames, which are communicating to Great Britain, but lord Bute, with soldiers and sailors, and the assistance of Highlanders, is labouring to extinguish them, while Pitt is blowing the fire, and the duke of Newcastle brings a barrowful of *Monitors* and *North Britons*, the violent journals of the popular party, to feed it. There is much detail in the print which it is not necessary to describe. In fulfilment of his threat, Wilkes, in the number of the *North Briton* published on the Saturday immediately following the publication of this print, attacked Hogarth with extraordinary bitterness, casting cruel reflections upon his domestic as well as his professional character. Hogarth, stung to the quick, retaliated by publishing the well-known caricature of Wilkes. Thereupon Churchill, the poet, Wilkes's friend, and formerly the friend of Hogarth also, published a bitter invective in verse against the painter, under the title of an "Epistle to William Hogarth." Hogarth retaliated again: "Having an old plate by me," he tells us, "with some parts ready, such as a background and a dog, I began to consider how I could turn so much work laid aside to some account, so patched up a print of Master Churchill in the character of a bear." The unfinished picture was intended to be a portrait of Hogarth himself; the canonical bear, which represented Churchill, held a pot of porter in one hand, and in the other a knotted club, each knot labelled "lie 1," "lie 2," &c The painter, in his "Anecdotes," exults over the pecuniary profit he derived from the extensive sale of these two prints.

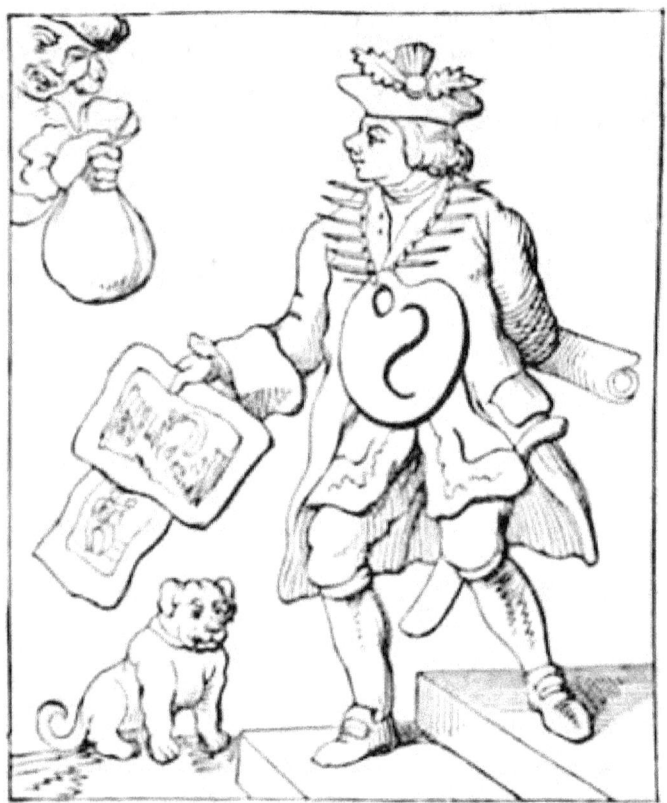

No. 211. An Independent Draughtsman.

The virulence of the caricaturists against Hogarth became on this occasion greater than ever. Parodies on his own works, sneers at his personal appearance and manners, reflections upon his character, were all embodied in prints which bore such names as Hogg-ass, Hoggart, O'Garth, &c Our cut No. 211 represents one of the caricature portraits of the artist. It is entitled "Wm. Hogarth, Esq., drawn from the Life." Hogarth wears the thistle on his hat, as the sign of his dependence on lord Bute. At his breast hangs his palette, with the line of beauty inscribed upon it. He holds behind his back a roll of paper inscribed "Burlesque on L—d B—t." In his right hand he presents to view two pictures, "The Times," and the "Portrait of Wilkes." At the upper corner to the left is the figure of Bute, offering him in a bag a pension of "£300 per ann." Some of the allusions in this picture are now obscure, but they no doubt relate to anecdotes well known at the time. They receive some light from the following mock letters which are written at the foot of the plate:—

"*Copy of a Letter from Mr. Hog-garth to Lord Mucklemon, wth his Lordship's Answer.*

"My Lord,—The enclosed is a design I intend to publish; you are sensible it will not redound to your honour, as it will expose you to all the world in your proper colours. You likewise know what induced me to do this; but it is in y^r power to prevent it from appearing in publick, which I would have you do immediately.

"Willm Hog-garth.

"Mais^r Hog-garth,—By my saul, mon, I am sare troobled for what I have done; I did na ken y^r muckle merit till noow; say na mair aboot it; I'll mak au things easy to you, & gie you bock your Pension.

"Sawney Mucklemon."

In an etching without a title, published at this time, and copied in our cut No. 212, the Hogarthian dog is represented barking from a cautious distance at the canonical bear, who appears to be meditating further mischief. Pugg stands upon his master's palette and the line of beauty, while Bruin rests upon the "Epistle to Wm. Hogarth," with the pen and ink by its side. On the left, behind the dog, is a large frame, with the words "Pannel Painting" inscribed upon it.

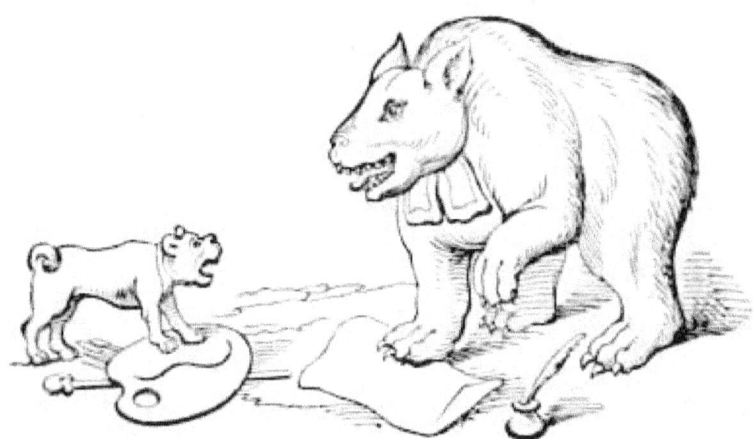

No. 212. Beauty and the Bear.

The article by Wilkes in the *North Briton*, and Churchill's metrical epistle, irritated Hogarth more than all the hostile caricatures, and were generally believed to have broken his heart. He died on the 26th of October, 1764, little more than a year after the appearance of the attack by Wilkes, and with the taunts of his political as well as his professional enemies still ringing in his ears.

CHAPTER XXVI.

THE LESSER CARICATURISTS OF THE REIGN OF GEORGE III.—PAUL SANDBY.— COLLET; THE DISASTER, AND FATHER PAUL IN HIS CUPS.—JAMES SAYER; HIS CARICATURES IN SUPPORT OF PITT, AND HIS REWARD.—CARLO KHAN'S TRIUMPH.—BUNBURY; HIS CARICATURES ON HORSEMANSHIP.—WOODWARD; GENERAL COMPLAINT.—ROWLANDSON'S INFLUENCE ON THE STYLE OF THOSE WHOSE DESIGNS HE ETCHED.—JOHN KAY OF EDINBURGH: LOOKING A ROCK IN THE FACE.

The school of caricature which had grown amid the political agitation of the reigns of the two first Georges, gave birth to a number of men of greater talent in the same branch of art, who carried it to its highest degree of perfection during that of George III. Among them are the three great names of Gillray, Rowlandson, and Cruikshank, and a few who, though second in rank to these, are still well remembered for the talent displayed in their works, or with the effect they produced on contemporaries. Among these the principal were Paul Sandby, John Collet, Sayer, Bunbury, and Woodward.

Sandby has been spoken of in the last chapter. He was not by profession a caricaturist, but he was one of those rising artists who were offended by the sneering terms in which Hogarth spoke of all artists but himself, and he was foremost among those who turned their satire against him. Examples of his caricatures upon Hogarth have already been given, sufficient to show that they display skill in composition as well as a large amount of wit and humour. After his death, they were republished collectively, under the title, "Retrospective Art, from the Collection of the late Paul Sandby, Esq., R.A." Sandby was, indeed, one of the original members of the Royal Academy. He was an artist much admired in his time, but is now chiefly remembered as a topographical draughtsman. He was a native of Nottingham, where he was born in 1725,[103] and he died on the 7th of November, 1809.[104]

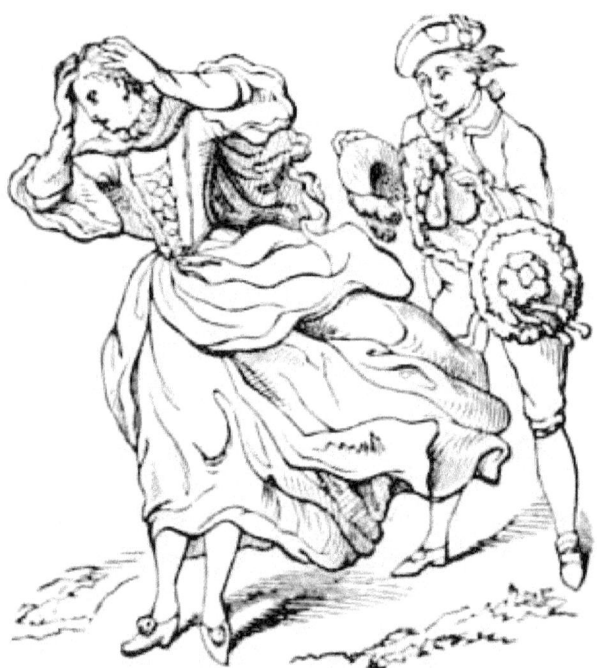

No. 213. A Disaster.

John Collet, who also has been mentioned in a previous chapter, was born in London in 1725, and died there in 1780. Collet is said to have been a pupil of Hogarth, and there is a large amount of Hogarthian character in all his designs. Few artists have been more industrious and produced a greater number of engravings. He worked chiefly for Carrington Bowles, in St. Paul's Churchyard, and for Robert Sayers, at 53, Fleet Street. His prints published by Bowles were engraved generally in mezzotinto, and highly coloured for sale; while those published by Sayers were usually line engravings, and sometimes remarkably well executed. Collet chose for his field of labour that to which Hogarth had given the title of comedy in art, but he did not possess Hogarth's power of delineating whole acts and scenes in one picture, and he contented himself with bits of detail and groups of characters only. His caricatures are rarely political—they are aimed at social manners and social vanities and weaknesses, and altogether they form a singularly curious picture of society during an important period of the last century. The first example I give (No. 213) is taken from a line engraving, published by Sayers in 1776. At this time the natural adornments of the person in both sexes had so far yielded to artificial ornament, that even women cut off their own hair in order to replace it by an ornamental *peruque*, supporting a head-dress, which varied from time to time in form and in extravagance. Collet has here introduced to us a lady who, encountering a sudden and violent wind, has lost all her upper coverings, and wig, cap, and hat are caught by her footman behind. The lady is evidently suffering under the feeling of shame; and hard by, a cottager and his wife, at their door, are laughing at her discomfiture. A bill fixed against a neighbouring wall announces "A Lecture upon Heads."

At this time the "no-popery" feeling ran very high. Four years afterwards it broke out violently in the celebrated lord Gordon riots. It was this feeling which contributed greatly to the success of Sheridan's comedy of "The Duenna," brought out in 1775. Collet drew several pictures founded upon scenes in this play, one of which is given in our cut No. 214. It forms one of Carington Bowles's rather numerous series of prints from designs by Collet, and represents the well-known drinking scene in the convent, in the fifth scene of the third act of "The Duenna." The scene, it will be remembered, is "a room in the priory," and the excited monks are toasting, among other objects of devotion, the abbess of St. Ursuline and the blue-eyed nun of St. Catherine's. The "blue-eyed nun" is, perhaps, the lady seen through the window, and the patron saint of her convent is represented in one of the pictures on the wall. There is great spirit in this picture, which is entitled "Father Paul in his Cups, or the Private Devotions of a Convent." It is accompanied with the following lines:—

See with these friars how religion thrives,
Who love good living better than good lives;
Paul, the superior father, rules the roast,
His god's the glass, the blue-eyed nun his toast.
Thus priests consume what fearful fools bestow,
And saints' donations make the bumpers flow.
The butler sleeps—the cellar door is free—
This is a modern cloister's piety.

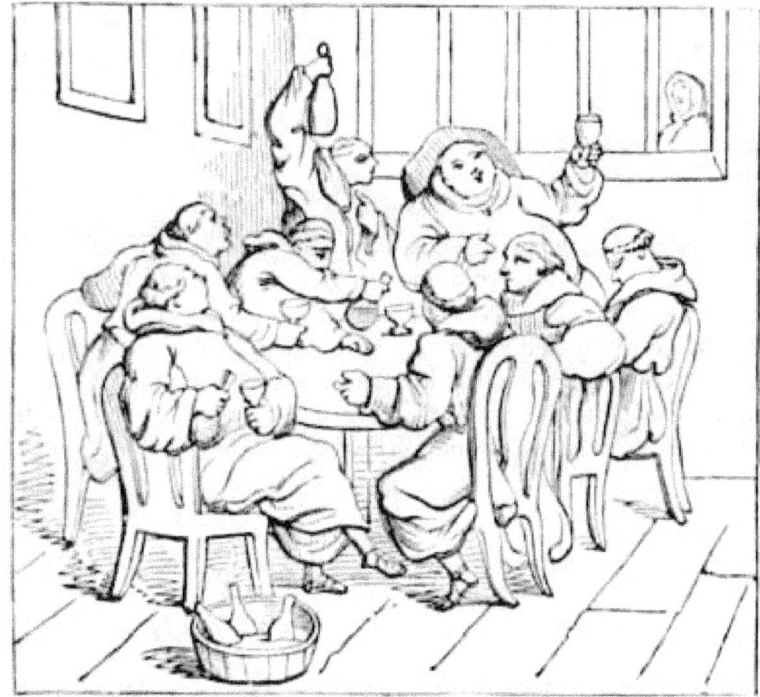

No. 214. Father Paul in his Cups.

From Collet to Sayer we rush into the heat—I may say into the bitterness—of politics, for James Sayer is known, with very trifling exceptions, as a political caricaturist. He was the son of a captain of a merchant ship at Great Yarmouth, but was himself put to the profession of an attorney. As, however, he was possessed of a moderate independence, and appears to have had no great taste for the law, he neglected his business, and, with considerable talent for satire and caricature, he threw himself into the political strife of the day. Sayer was a bad draughtsman, and his pictures are produced more by labour than by skill in drawing, but they possess a considerable amount of humour, and were sufficiently severe to obtain popularity at a time when this latter character excused worse drawing even than that of Sayer. He made the acquaintance and gained the favour of the younger William Pitt, when that statesman was aspiring to power, and he began his career as a caricaturist by attacking the Rockingham ministry in 1782—of course in the interest of Pitt. Sayer's earliest productions which are now known, are a series of caricature portraits of the Rockingham administration, that appear to have been given to the public in instalments, at the several dates of April 6, May 14, June 17, and July 3, 1782, and bear the name of C. Bretherton as publisher. He published his first veritable caricature on the occasion of the ministerial changes which followed the death of lord Rockingham, when lord Shelburne was placed at the head of the cabinet, and Fox and Burke retired, while Pitt became chancellor of the exchequer. This caricature, which bears the title of "Paradise Lost," and is, in fact, a parody upon Milton, represents the once happy pair, Fox and Burke, turned out of their paradise, the Treasury, the arch of the gate of which is ornamented with the heads of Shelburne, the prime minister, and Dunning and Barré, two of his staunch supporters, who were considered to be especially obnoxious to Fox and Burke. Between these three heads appear the faces of two mocking fiends, and groups of pistols, daggers, and swords. Beneath are inscribed the well-known lines of Milton—

To the eastern side
Of Paradise, so late their happy seat,
Waved over by that flaming brand; the gate
With dreadful faces thronged and fiery arms!
Some natural tears they dropt, but wiped them soon.
The world was all before them, where to choose
Their place of rest, and providence their guide.
They, arm in arm, with wand'ring steps, and slow,
Thro' Eden took their solitary way.

Nothing can be more lugubrious than the air of the two friends, Fox and Burke, as they walk away, arm in arm, from the gate of the ministerial paradise. From this time Sayer, who adopted all Pitt's virulence towards Fox, made the latter a continual subject of his satire. Nor did this zeal pass unrewarded, for Pitt, in power, gave the caricaturist the not unlucrative offices of marshal of the court of exchequer, receiver of the sixpenny duties, and cursitor. Sayer was, in fact, Pitt's caricaturist, and was employed by him in attacking successively the coalition under Fox and North, Fox's India Bill, and even, at a later period, Warren Hastings on his trial.

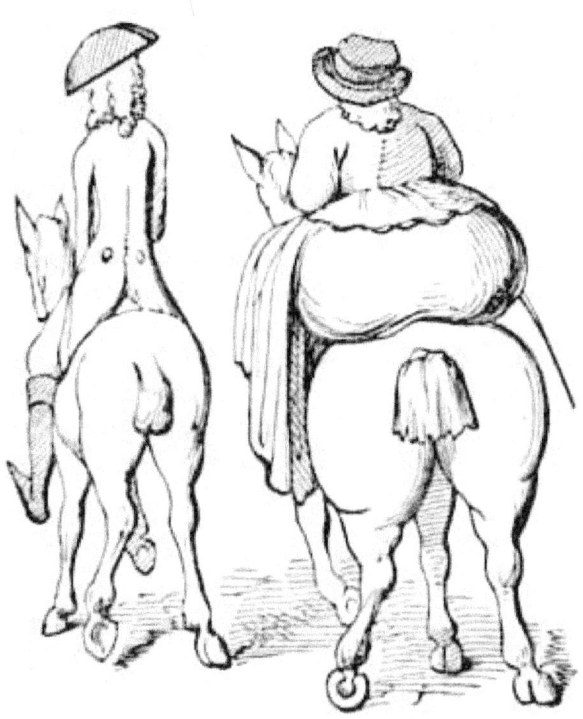

No. 215. A Contrast.

I have already remarked that Sayer was almost exclusively a political caricaturist. The exceptions are a few prints on theatrical subjects, in which contemporary actors and actresses are caricatured, and a single subject from fashionable life. A copy of the latter forms our cut No. 215. It has no title in the original, but in a copy in my possession a contemporary has written on the margin in pencil that the lady is Miss Snow and the gentleman Mr. Bird, no doubt well-known personages in contemporary society. It was published on the 19th of July, 1783.

One of Sayer's most successful caricatures, in regard to the effect it produced on the public, was that on Fox's India Bill, published on the 5th of September, 1783. It was entitled "Carlo Khan's Triumphal Entry into Leadenhall Street," Carlo Khan being personified by Fox, who is carried in triumph to the door of the India House on the back of an elephant, which presents the face of lord North. Burke, who had been the principal supporter of the bill in debate, appears in the character of the imperial trumpeter, and leads the elephant on its way. On a banner behind Carlo, the old inscription, "The Man of the People," the title popularly given to Fox, is erased, and the two Greek words, ΒΑΣΙΛΕΥΣ ΒΑΣΙΛΕΩΝ "king of kings," substituted in its place. From a chimney above, the bird of ill omen croaks forth the doom of the ambitious minister, who, it was pretended, aimed at making himself more powerful than the king himself; and on the side of the house just below we read the words—

The night-crow cried foreboding luckless time.—Shakespeare.

Henry William Bunbury belonged to a more aristocratic class in society than any of the preceding. He was the second son of sir William Bunbury, Bart., of Mildenhall, in the county of Suffolk, and was born in 1750. How he first took so zealously to caricature we have no information, but he began to publish before he was twenty-one years of age. Bunbury's drawing was bold and often good, but he had little skill in etching, for some of his earlier prints, published in 1771, which he etched himself, are coarsely executed. His designs were afterwards engraved by various persons, and his own style was sometimes modified in this process. His earlier prints were etched and sold by James Bretherton, who has been already mentioned as publishing the works of James Sayer. This Bretherton was in some esteem as an engraver, and he also had a print-shop at 132, New Bond Street, where his engravings were published. James had a son named Charles, who displayed great talent at an early age, but he died young. As early as 1772, when the macaronis (the dandies of the eighteenth century) came into fashion, James Bretherton's name appears on prints by Bunbury as the engraver and publisher, and it occurs again as the engraver of his print of "Strephon and Chloe" in 1801, which was published by Fores. At this and a later period some of his designs were engraved by Rowlandson, who always transferred his own style to the drawings he copied. A remarkable instance of this is furnished by a print of a party of anglers of both sexes in a punt, entitled "Anglers of 1811" (the year of Bunbury's death). But for the name, "H. Bunbury, del.," very distinctly inscribed upon it, we should take this to be a genuine design by Rowlandson; and in 1803 Rowlandson engraved some copies of Bunbury's prints on horsemanship for Ackermann, of the Strand, in which all traces of Bunbury's style are lost. Bunbury's style is rather broadly burlesque.

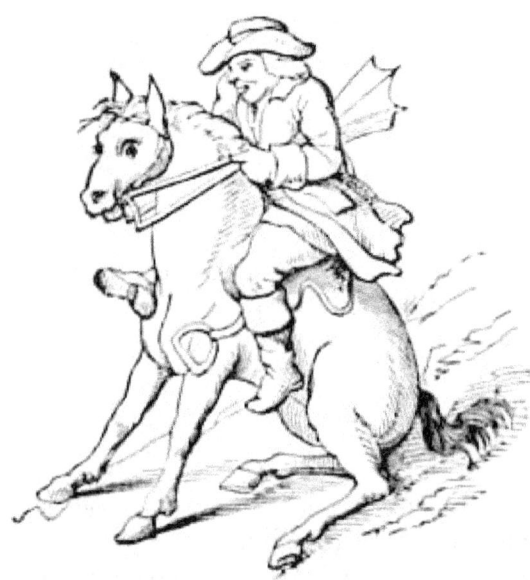

No. 216. How to Travel on Two Legs in a Frost.

Bunbury had evidently little taste for political caricature, and he seldom meddled with it. Like Collet, he preferred scenes of social life, and humorous incidents of contemporary manners, fashionable or popular. He had a great taste for caricaturing bad or awkward horsemanship or unmanageable horses, and his prints of such subjects were numerous and greatly admired. This taste for equestrian pieces was shown in prints published in 1772, and several droll series of such subjects appeared at different times, between 1781 and 1791, one of which was long famous under the title of "Geoffrey Gambado's Horsemanship." An example of these incidents of horsemanship is copied in our cut No. 216, where a not very skilful rider, with a troublesome horse, is taking advantage of the state of the ground for accelerating locomotion. It is entitled, "How to travel on Two Legs in a Frost," and is accompanied with the motto, in Latin, " *Ostendunt terris hunc tantum fata, neque ultra esse sinent.*"

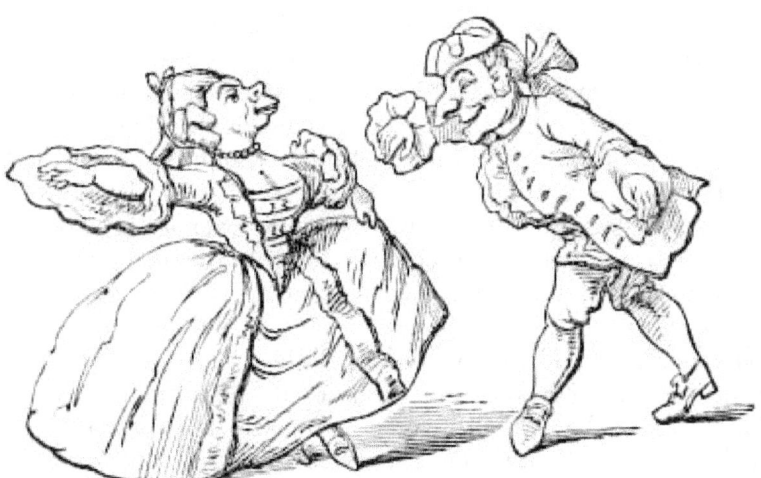

No. 217. Strephon and Chloe.

Occasionally Bunbury drew in a broader style of caricature, especially in some of his later works. Of our examples of this broader style, the first cut, No. 217, entitled "Strephon and Chloe," is dated the 1st of July, 1801. It is the very acme of sentimental courtship, expressed in a spirit of drollery which could not easily be excelled. The next group (cut No. 218), from a similar print published on the 21st of July in the same year, is a no less admirable picture of overstrained politeness. It is entitled in the original, "The Salutation Tavern," probably with a temporary allusion beyond the more apparent design of the picture. Bunbury, as before stated, died in 1811. It is enough to say that sir Joshua Reynolds used to express a high opinion of him as an artist.

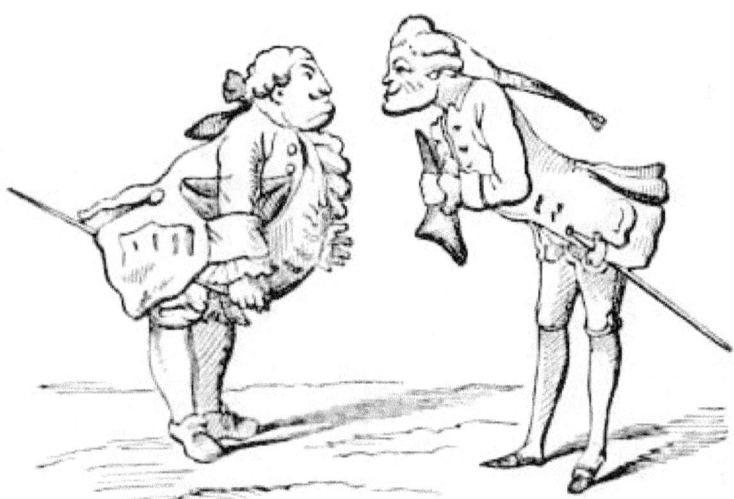

No. 218. A Fashionable Salutation.

Bunbury's prints rarely appeared without his name, and, except when they had passed through the engraving of Rowlandson, are easily recognised. No doubt his was considered a popular name, which was almost of as much importance as the print itself. But a large mass of the caricatures published at the latter end of the last century and the beginning of the present, appeared anonymously, or with imaginary names. Thus a political print, entitled "The Modern Atlas," bears the inscription "Mas.ʳ Hook fecit;" another entitled "Farmer George delivered," has that of "Poll Pitt del." "Everybody delinᵗ.," is inscribed on a caricature entitled "The Lover's Leap;" and one which appeared under the title of "Veterinary Operations," is inscribed "Giles Grinagain fect." Some of these were probably the works of amateurs, for there appear to have been many amateur caricaturists in England at that time. In a caricature entitled "The Scotch Arms," published by Fores on the 3rd of January, 1787, we find the announcement, "Gentlemen's designs executed gratis," which means, of course, that Fores would publish the caricatures of amateurs, if he approved them, without making the said amateurs pay for the engraving. But also some of the best caricaturists of the day published much anonymously, and we know that this was the case to a very great extent with such artists as Cruikshank, Woodward, &c, at all events until such time as their names became sufficiently popular to be a recommendation to the print. It is certain that many of Woodward's designs were published without his name. Such was the case with the print of which we give a copy in our cut No. 219, which was published on the 5th of May, 1796, and which bears strongly the marks of Woodward's style. The spring of this year, 1796, witnessed a general disappointment at the failure of the negociations for peace, and therefore the necessity of new sacrifices for carrying on the war, and of increased taxation. Many clever caricatures appeared on this occasion, of which this by Woodward was one. Of course, when war was inevitable, the question of generals was a very important one, and the caricaturist pretends that the greatest general of the age was "General Complaint." The general appears here with an empty purse in his right hand, and in his left a handful of papers containing a list of bankrupts, the statement of the budget, &c Four lines beneath, in rather doggrel verse, explain the situation as follows:—

Don't tell me of generals raised from mere boys,
Though, believe me, I mean not their laurel to taint;
But the general, I'm sure, that will make the most noise,
If the war still goes on, will be General Complaint.

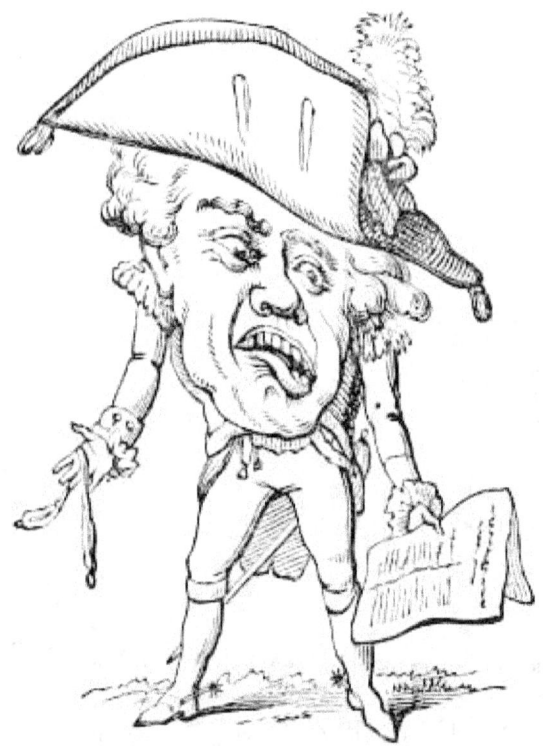

No. 219. General Complaint.

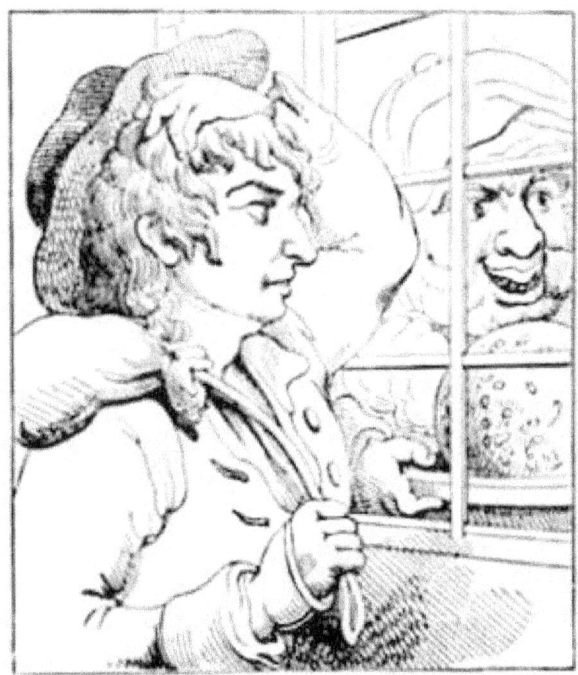

No. 220. Desire.

There was much of Bunbury's style in that of Woodward, who had a taste for the same broad caricatures upon society, which he executed in a similar spirit. Some of the *suites* of subjects of this description that he published, such as the series of the "Symptoms of the Shop," those of "Everybody out of town" and "Everybody in Town," and the "Specimens of Domestic Phrensy," are extremely clever and amusing. Woodward's designs were also not unfrequently engraved by Rowlandson, who, as usual, imprinted his own style upon them. A very good example of this practice is seen in the print of which we give a copy in our cut No. 220. Its title, in the original, is "Desire," and the passion is exemplified in the case of a hungry schoolboy watching through a window a jolly cook carrying by a tempting plum-pudding. We are told in an inscription underneath: "Various are the ways this passion might be depicted; in this delineation the subjects chosen are simple—a hungry boy and a plum-pudding." The design of this print is stated to be Woodward's; but the style is altogether that of Rowlandson, whose name appears on it as the etcher. It was published by R. Ackermann, on the 20th of January, 1800. Woodward is well known by his prolific pencil, but we are so little acquainted with the man himself, that I cannot state the date either of his birth or of his death.

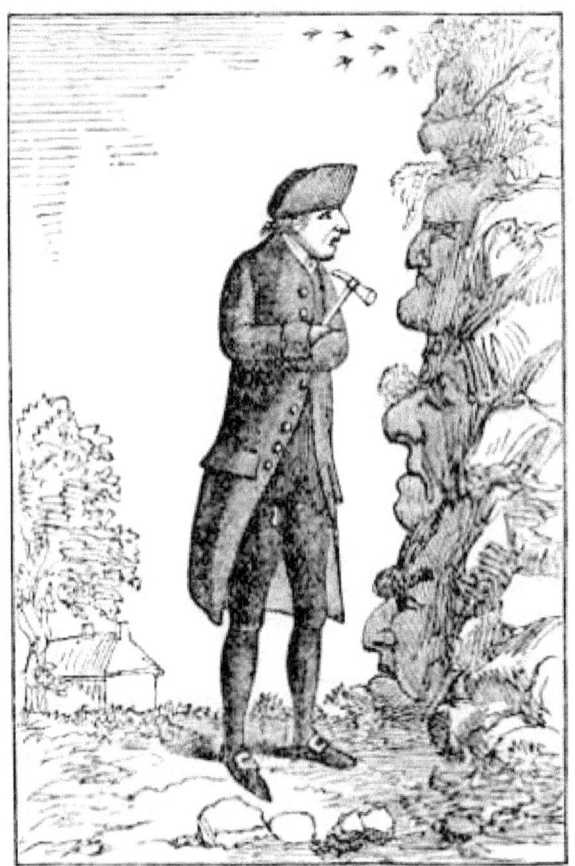

No. 221. Looking a Rock in the Face.

There lived at this time in Edinburgh an engraver of some eminence in his way, but whose name is now nearly forgotten, and, in fact, it does not occur in the last edition of Bryan's "Dictionary of Engravers." This name was John Kay, which is found attached to prints, of which about four hundred are known, with dates extending from 1784 to 1817. As an engraver, Kay possessed no great talent, but he had considerable humour, and he excelled in catching and delineating the striking points in the features and gait of the individuals who then moved in Edinburgh Society. In fact, a large proportion of his prints consist of caricature portraits, often several figures on the same plate, which is usually of small dimensions. Among them are many of the professors and other distinguished members of the university of Edinburgh. Thus one, copied in our cut No. 221, represents the eminent old geologist, Dr. James Hutton, rather astonished at the shapes which his favourite rocks have suddenly taken. The original print is dated in 1787, ten years before Dr. Hutton's death. The idea of giving faces to rocks was not new in the time of John Kay, and it has been frequently repeated. Some of these caricature portraits are clever and amusing, and they are at times very satirical. Kay appears to have rarely ventured on caricature of any other description, but there is one rare plate by him, entitled "The Craft in Danger," which is stated in a few words pencilled on the copy I have before me, to have been aimed at a cabal for proposing Dr. Barclay for a professorship in the university of Edinburgh. It displays no great talent, and is, in fact, now not very intelligible. The figures introduced in it are evidently intended for rather caricatured portraits of members of the university engaged in the cabal, and are in the style of Kay's other portraits.[105]

CHAPTER XXVII.

GILLRAY.—HIS FIRST ATTEMPTS.—HIS CARICATURES BEGIN WITH THE
SHELBURNE MINISTRY.—IMPEACHMENT OF WARREN HASTINGS.—CARICATURES
ON THE KING; "NEW WAY TO PAY THE NATIONAL DEBT."—ALLEGED REASON
FOR GILLRAY'S HOSTILITY TO THE KING.—THE KING AND THE APPLE-
DUMPLINGS.—GILLRAY'S LATER LABOURS.—HIS IDIOTCY AND DEATH.

In the year 1757 was born the greatest of English caricaturists, and perhaps of all caricaturists of modern times whose works are known—James Gillray. His father, who was named like himself, James, was a Scotchman, a native of Lanark, and a soldier, and, having lost one arm at the battle of Fontenoy, became an out-pensioner of Chelsea Hospital. He obtained also the appointment of sexton at the Moravian burial-ground at Chelsea, which he held forty years, and it was at Chelsea that James Gillray the younger was born. The latter, having no doubt shown signs of artistic talent, was put apprentice to letter-engraving; but after a time, becoming disgusted with this employment, he ran away, and joined a party of strolling players, and in their company passed through many adventures, and underwent many hardships. He returned, however to London, and received some encouragement as a promising artist, and obtained admission as a student in the Royal Academy— the then young institution to which Hogarth had been opposed. Gillray soon became known as a designer and engraver, and worked in these capacities for the publishers. Among his earlier productions, two illustrations of Goldsmith's "Deserted Village" are spoken of with praise, as displaying a remarkable freedom of effect. For a long time after Gillray became known as a caricaturist he continued to engrave the designs of other artists. The earliest known caricature which can be ascribed to him with any certainty, is the plate entitled "Paddy on Horseback," and dated in 1779, when he was twenty-two years of age. The "horse" on which Paddy rides is a bull; he is seated with his face turned to the tail. The subject of satire is supposed to be the character then enjoyed by the Irish as fortune-hunters. The point, however, is not very apparent, and indeed Gillray's earliest caricatures are tame, although it is remarkable how rapidly he improved, and how soon he arrived at excellence. Two caricatures, published in June and July, 1782, on the occasion of admiral Rodney's victory, are looked upon as marking his first decided appearance in politics.

A distinguishing characteristic of Gillray's style is, the wonderful tact with which he seizes upon the points in his subject open to ridicule, and the force with which he brings those points out. In the fineness of his design, and in his grouping and drawing, he excels all the other caricaturists. He was, indeed, born with all the talents of a great historical painter, and, but for circumstances, he probably would have shone in that branch of art. This excellence will be the more appreciated when it is understood that he drew his picture with the needle on the plate, without having made any previous sketch of it, except sometimes a few hasty outlines of individual portraits or characters scrawled on cards or scraps of paper as they struck him.

Soon after the two caricatures on Rodney's naval victory, the Rockingham administration was broken up by the death of its chief, and another was formed under the direction of Lord Shelburne, from which Fox and Burke retired, leaving in it their old colleague, Pitt, who now deserted the Whig party in parliament. Fox and Burke became from this moment the butt of all sorts of abuse and scornful satire from the caricaturists, such as Sayer, and newspaper writers in the pay of their opponents; and Gillray, perhaps because it offered at that moment the best chance of popularity and success, joined in the crusade against the two ex-ministers and their friends. In one of his caricatures, which is a parody upon Milton, Fox is represented in the character of Satan, turning his back upon the ministerial Paradise, but looking enviously over his shoulder at the happy pair (Shelburne and Pitt) who are counting their money on the treasury table:—

Aside he turned
For envy, yet with jealous leer malign
Eyed them askance.

Another, also by Gillray, is entitled "Guy Faux and Judas Iscariot," the former represented by Fox, who discovers the desertion of his late colleague, lord Shelburne, by the light of his lantern, and recriminates angrily, "Ah! what, I've found you out, have I? Who arm'd the high priests and the people? Who betray'd his mas—?" At this point he is interrupted by a sneering retort from Shelburne, who is carrying away the treasury bag with a look of great self-complacency, "Ha, ha! poor Gunpowder's vexed! He, he, he!—Shan't have the bag, I tell you, old Goosetooth!" Burke was usually caricatured as a Jesuit; and in another of Gillray's prints of this time (published Aug. 23, 1782), entitled "Cincinnatus in Retirement," Burke is represented as driven into the retirement of his Irish cabin, where he is surrounded by Popish relics and emblems of superstition, and by the materials for drinking whisky. A vessel, inscribed "Relick No. 1., used by St. Peter," is filled with boiled potatoes, which Jesuit Burke is paring. Three imps are seen dancing under the table.

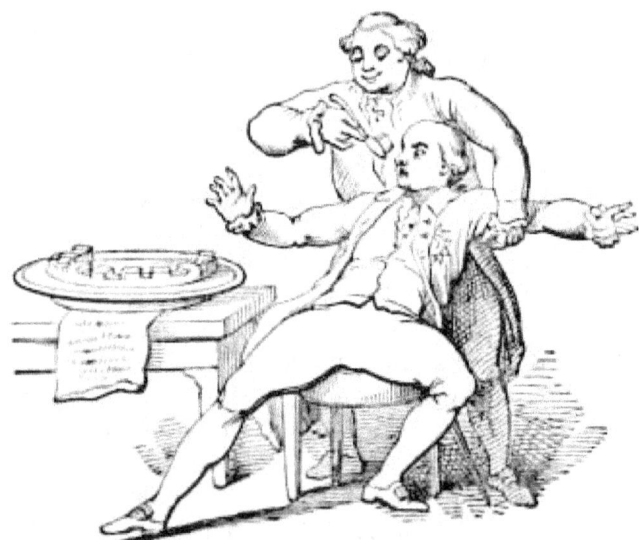

No. 222. A Strong Dose.

In 1783 the Shelburne ministry itself was dissolved, and succeeded by the Portland ministry, in which Fox was secretary of state for foreign affairs, and Burke, paymaster of the forces, and Lord North, who had joined the Whigs against lord Shelburne, now obtained office as secretary for the home department. Gillray joined warmly in the attacks on this coalition of parties, and from this time his great activity as a caricaturist begins. Fox, especially, and Burke, still under the character of a Jesuit, were incessantly held up to ridicule in his prints. In another year this ministry also was overthrown, and young William Pitt became established in power, while the ex-ministers, now the opposition, had become unpopular throughout the country. The caricature of Gillray followed them, and Fox and Burke constantly appeared under his hands in some ridiculous situation or other. But Gillray was not a hired libeller, like Sayer and some of the lower caricaturists of that time; he evidently chose his subjects, in some degree independently, as those which offered him the best mark for ridicule; and he had so little respect for the ministers or the court, that they all felt his satire in turn. Thus, when the plan of national fortifications—brought forward by the duke of Richmond, who had deserted the Whigs to be made a Tory minister, as master-general of the ordnance—was defeated in the House of Commons in 1787, the best caricature it provoked was one by Gillray, entitled "Honi soit qui mal y pense," which represents the horror of the duke of

Richmond at being so unceremoniously compelled to swallow his own fortifications (cut No. 222). It is lord Shelburne, who had now become marquis of Lansdowne, who is represented as administering the bitter dose. Some months afterwards, in the famous impeachment against Warren Hastings, Gillray sided warmly against the impeachers, perhaps partly because these were Burke and his friends; yet several of his caricatures on this affair are aimed at the ministers, and even at the king himself. Lord Thurlow, who was a favourite with the king, and who supported the cause of Warren Hastings with firmness, after he had been deserted by Pitt and the other ministers, was especially an object of Gillray's satire. Thurlow, it will be remembered, was rather celebrated for profane swearing, and was sometimes spoken of as the thunderer. One of the finest of Gillray's caricatures at this period, published on the 1st of March, 1788, is entitled "Blood on Thunder fording the Red Sea," and represents Warren Hastings carried on chancellor Thurlow's shoulders through a sea of blood, strewed with the mangled corpses of Hindoos. As will be seen in our copy of the most important part of this print (cut No. 223), the "saviour of India," as he was called by his friends, has taken care to secure his gains. A remarkably bold caricature by Gillray against the government appeared on the 2nd of May in this year. It is entitled "Market-Day—every man has his price," and represents a scene in Smithfield, where the horned cattle exposed for sale are the supporters of the king's ministry. Lord Thurlow, with his characteristic frown, appears as the principal purchaser. Pitt, and his friend and colleague Dundas, are represented drinking and smoking jovially at the window of a public-house. On one side Warren Hastings is riding off with the king in the form of a calf, which he has just purchased, for Hastings was popularly believed to have worked upon king George's avarice by rich presents of diamonds. On another side, the overwhelming rush of the cattle is throwing over the van in which Fox, Burke, and Sheridan are driving. This plate deserves to be placed among Gillray's finest works.

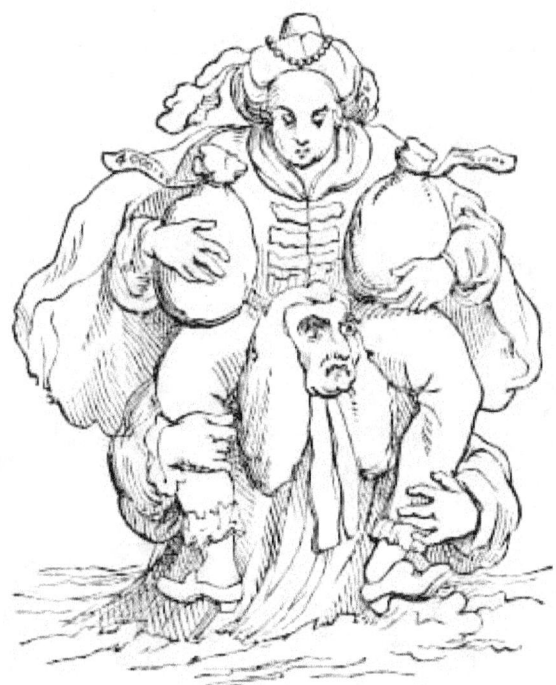

No. 223. Blood on Thunder.

Gillray caricatured the heir to the throne with bitterness, perhaps because his dissipation and extravagance rendered him a fair subject of ridicule, and because he associated himself with Fox's party in politics; but his hostility to the king is ascribed in part to personal feelings. A large and very remarkable print by our artist, though his name was not attached to it, and one which displays in a special manner the great characteristics of Gillray's style, appeared on the 21st of April, 1786, just after an application had been made to the House of Commons for a large sum of money to pay off the king's debts, which were very great, in spite of the enormous income then attached to the crown. George was known as a careful and even a parsimonious man, and the queen was looked upon generally as a mean and very avaricious woman, and people were at a loss to account for this extraordinary expenditure, and they tried to explain it in various ways which were not to the credit of the royal pair. It was said that immense sums were spent in secret corruption to pave the way to the establishment of arbitrary power; that the king was making large savings, and hoarding up treasures at Hanover; and that, instead of spending money on his family, he allowed his eldest son to run into serious difficulties through the smallness of his allowance, and thus to become an object of pity to his French friend, the wealthy duc d'Orleans, who had offered him relief. The caricature just mentioned, which is extremely severe, is entitled "A new way to pay the National Debt." It represents the entrance to the treasury, from which king George and his queen, with their band of pensioners, are issuing, their pockets, and the queen's apron, so full of money, that the coins are rolling out and scattering about the ground. Nevertheless, Pitt, whose pockets also are full, adds to the royal treasures large bags of the national revenue, which are received with smiles of satisfaction. To the left, a crippled soldier sits on the ground, and asks in vain for relief; while the wall above is covered with torn placards, on some of which may be read, "God save the King;" "Charity, a romance;" "From Germany, just arrived a large and royal assortment...;" and "Last dying speech of fifty-four malefactors executed for robbing a hen-roost." The latter is a satirical allusion to the notorious severity with which the most trifling depredators on the king's private farm were prosecuted. In the background, on the right hand side of the picture, the prince appears in ragged garments, and in want of charity no less than the cripple, and near him is the duke of Orleans, who offers him a draft for £200,000. On the placards on the walls here we read such announcements as "Economy, an old song;" "British property, a farce;" and "Just published, for the benefit of posterity, the dying groans of Liberty;" and one, immediately over the prince's head, bears the prince's feathers, with the motto, "Ich starve." Altogether this is one of the most remarkable of Gillray's caricatures.

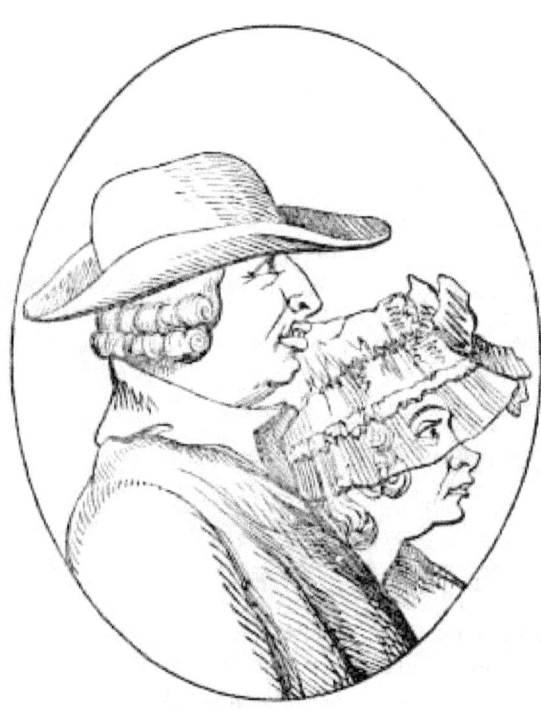

No. 224. Farmer George and his Wife.

The parsimoniousness of the king and queen was the subject of caricatures and songs in abundance, in which these illustrious personages appeared haggling with their tradesmen, and making bargains in person, rejoicing in having thus saved a small sum of money. It was said that George kept a farm at Windsor, not for his amusement, but to draw a small profit from it. By Peter Pindar he is described as rejoicing over the skill he has shown in purchasing his live stock as bargains. Gillray seized greedily all these points of ridicule, and, as early as 1786, he published a print of "Farmer George and his Wife" (see our cut No. 224), in which the two royal personages are represented in the very familiar manner in which they were accustomed to walk about Windsor and its neighbourhood. This picture appears to have been very popular; and years afterwards, in a caricature on a scene in "The School for Scandal," where, in the sale of the young profligate's effects, the auctioneer puts up a family portrait, for which a broker offers five shillings, and Careless, the auctioneer, says, "Going for no more than one crown," the family piece is the well-known picture of "Farmer George and his Wife," and the ruined prodigal is the prince of Wales, who exclaims, "Careless, knock down the farmer."

Many caricatures against the undignified meanness of the royal household appeared during the years 1791 and 1792, when the king passed much of his time at his favourite watering-place, Weymouth; and there his domestic habits had become more and more an object of remark. It was said that, under the pretence of Weymouth being an expensive place, and taking advantage of the obligations of the royal mail to carry parcels for the king free, he had his provisions brought to him by that conveyance from his farm at Windsor. On the 28th of November, 1791, Gillray published a caricature on the homeliness of the royal household, in two compartments, in one of which the king is represented, in a dress which is anything but that of royalty, toasting his muffins for breakfast; and in the other, queen Charlotte, in no less homely dress, though her pocket is overflowing with money, toasting sprats for supper. In another of Gillray's prints, entitled "Anti-saccharites," the king and queen are teaching their daughters economy in taking their tea without sugar; as the young princesses show some dislike to the experiment, the queen admonishes them, concluding with the remark, "Above all, remember how much expense it will save your poor papa!"

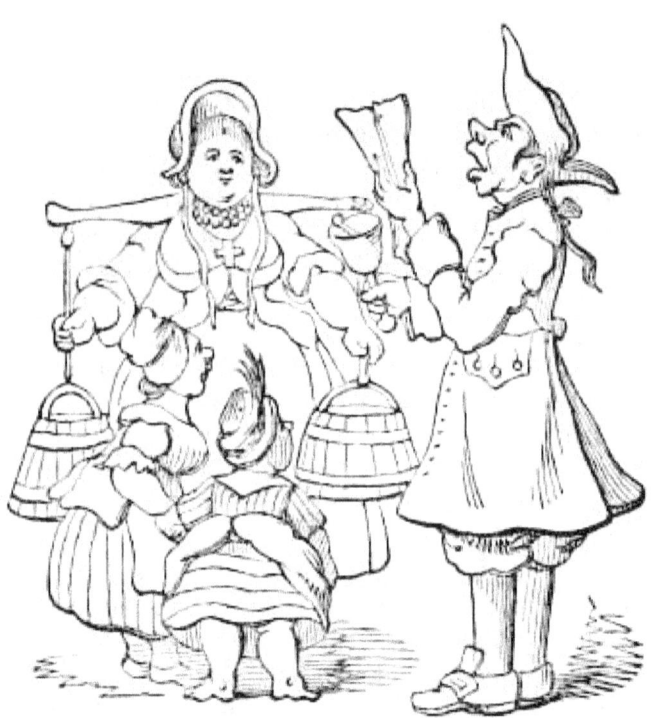

No. 225. A Flemish Proclamation.

According to a story which seems to be authentic, Gillray's dislike of the king was embittered at this time by an incident somewhat similar to that by which George II. had provoked the anger of Hogarth. Gillray had visited France, Flanders, and Holland, and he had made sketches, a few of which he engraved. Our cut No. 225 represents a group from one of these sketches, which explains itself, and is a fair example of Gillray's manner of drawing such subjects. He accompanied the painter Loutherbourg, who had left his native city of Strasburg to settle in England, and become the king's favourite artist, to assist him in making sketches for his great painting of "The Siege of Valenciennes," Gillray sketching groups of figures while Loutherbourg drew the landscape and buildings. After their return, the king expressed a desire to see their sketches, and they were placed before him. Loutherbourg's landscapes and buildings were plain drawings, and easy to understand, and the king expressed himself greatly pleased with them. But the king's mind was already prejudiced against Gillray for his satirical prints, and when he saw his hasty and rough, though spirited sketches, of the French soldiers, he threw them aside contemptuously, with the remark, "I don't understand these caricatures." Perhaps the very word he used was intended as a sneer upon Gillray, who, we are told, felt the affront deeply, and he proceeded to retort by a caricature, which struck at once at one of the king's vanities, and at his political prejudices. George III. imagined himself a great connoisseur in the fine arts, and the caricature was entitled "A Connoisseur examining a Cooper." It represented the king looking at the celebrated miniature of Oliver Cromwell, by the English painter, Samuel Cooper. When Gillray had completed this print, he is said to have exclaimed, "I wonder if the royal connoisseur will understand this!" It was published on the 18th of June, 1792, and cannot have failed to produce a sensation at that period of revolutions. The king is made to exhibit a strange mixture of alarm with astonishment in contemplating the features of this great overthrower of kingly power, at a moment when all kingly power was threatened. It will be remarked, too, that the satirist has not overlooked the royal character for domestic economy, for, as will be seen in our cut No. 226, the king is looking at the picture by the light of a candle-end stuck on a "save-all."

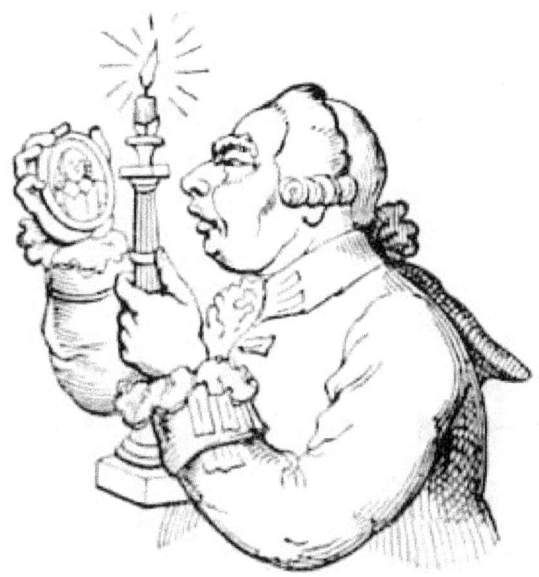

No. 226. A Connoisseur in Art.

From this time Gillray rarely let pass an opportunity of caricaturing the king. Sometimes he pictured his awkward and undignified gait, as he was accustomed to shuffle along the esplanade at Weymouth; sometimes in the familiar manner in which, in the course of his walks in the neighbourhood of his Windsor farm, he accosted the commonest labourers and cottagers, and overwhelmed them with a long repetition of trivial questions—for king George had a characteristic manner of repeating his questions, and of frequently giving the reply to them himself.

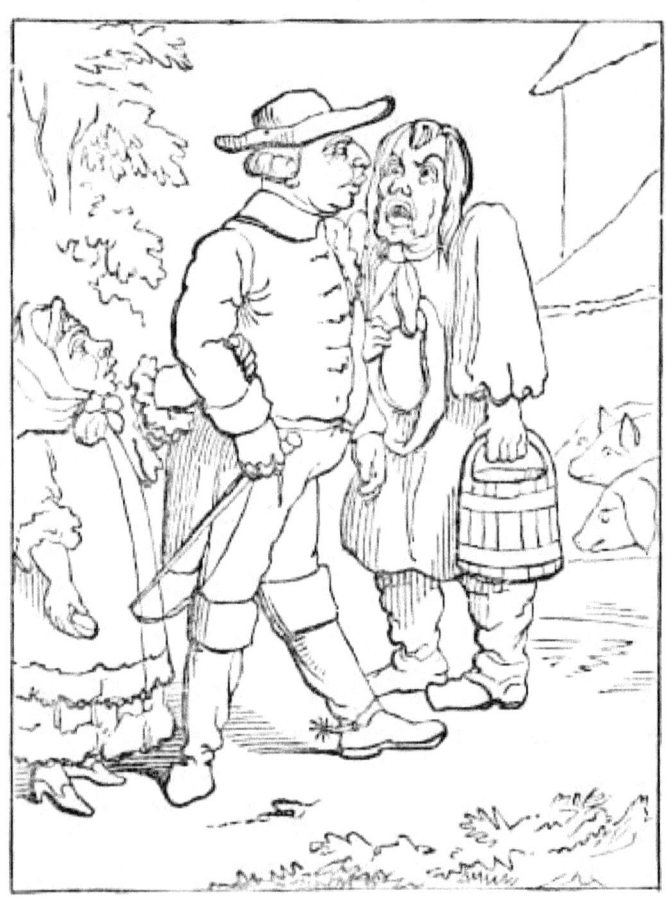

No. 227. Royal Affability.

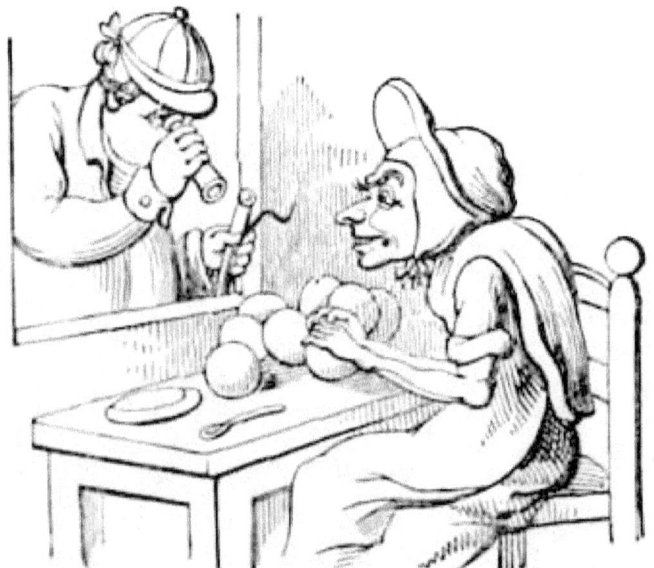

No. 228. A Lesson in Apple Dumplings.
Then asks the farmer's wife, or farmer's maid,
How many eggs the fowls have laid;
What's in the oven, in the pot, the crock;
Whether 'twill rain or no, and what's o'clock;

Thus from poor hovels gleaning information,
To serve as future treasure for the nation.

So said Peter Pindar; and in this *rôle* king George was represented not unfrequently in satirical prints. On the 10th of February Gillray illustrated the quality of "Affability" in a picture of one of these rustic encounters. The king and queen, taking their walk, have arrived at a cottage, where a very coarse example of English peasantry is feeding his pigs with wash. The scene is represented in our cut No. 227. The vacant stare of the countryman betrays his confusion at the rapid succession of questions—"Well, friend, where a' you going, hay?—What's your name, hay?—Where do you live, hay?—hay?" In other prints the king is represented running into ludicrous adventures while hunting, an amusement to which he was extremely attached. One of the best known of these has been celebrated equally by the pen of Peter Pindar and by the needle of Gillray. It was said that one day while king George was following the chase, he came to a poor cottage, where his usual curiosity was rewarded by the discovery of an old woman making apple dumplings. When informed what they were, he could not conceal his astonishment how the apples could have been introduced without leaving a seam in their covering. In the caricature by Gillray, from which we take our cut No. 228, the king is represented looking at the process of dumpling making through the window, inquiring in astonishment, "Hay? hay? apple dumplings?—how get the apples in?—how? Are they made without seams?" The story is told more fully in the following verses of Peter Pindar, which will serve as the best commentary on the engraving:—

THE KING AND THE APPLE DUMPLING.

Once on a time a monarch, tired with whooping,
Whipping and spurring,
Happy in worrying
A poor, defenceless, harmless buck
(The horse and rider wet as muck),
From his high consequence and wisdom stooping,
Enter'd through curiosity a cot,
Where sat a poor old woman and her pot.
The wrinkled, blear-eyed, good old granny,
In this same cot, illum'd by many a cranny.
Had finish'd apple dumplings for her pot.
In tempting row the naked dumplings lay,
When lo! the monarch in his usual way
Like lightning spoke, "What this? what this? what? what?"
Then taking up a dumpling in his hand,
His eyes with admiration did expand,
And oft did majesty the dumpling grapple.
"'Tis monstrous, monstrous hard, indeed?" he cried;
"What makes it, pray, so hard?"—The dame replied,
Low curtseying, "Please your majesty, the apple."
"Very astonishing, indeed! strange thing!"
Turning the dumpling round, rejoined the king;
"'Tis most extraordinary then, all this is—
It beats Pinetti's conjuring all to pieces—
Strange I should never of a dumpling dream!
But, Goody, tell me where, where, where's the seam?"
"Sir, there's no seam," quoth she, "I never knew
That folks did apple dumplings sew."

"No!" cried the staring monarch with a grin,
"How, how the devil got the apple in?"
On which the dame the curious scheme reveal'd
By which the apple lay so sly conceal'd,
Which made the Solomon of Britain start;
Who to the palace with full speed repair'd
And queen, and princesses so beauteous, scared,
All with the wonders of the dumpling art.
There did he labour one whole week, to show
The wisdom of an apple dumpling maker;
And lo! so deep was majesty in dough,
The palace seem'd the lodging of a baker!

Gillray was not the only caricaturist who turned the king's weaknesses to ridicule, but none caricatured them with so little gentleness, or evidently with so good a will. On the 7th of March, 1796, the princess of Wales gave birth to a daughter, so well known since as the princess Charlotte. The king is said to have been charmed with his grandchild, and this sentiment appears to have been anticipated by the public, for on the 13th of February, when the princess's accouchment was looked forward to with general interest, a print appeared under the title of "Grandpapa in his Glory." In this caricature, which is given in our cut No. 229, king George, seated, is represented nursing and feeding the royal infant in an extraordinary degree of homeliness. He is singing the nursery rhyme—

There was a laugh and a craw,
There was a giggling honey,
Goody good girl shall be fed,
But naughty girl shall have noney.

This print bears no name, but it is known to be by Woodward, though it betrays an attempt to imitate the style of Gillray. Gillray was often imitated in this manner, and his prints were not unfrequently copied and pirated. He even at times copied himself, and disguised his own style, for the sake of gaining money.

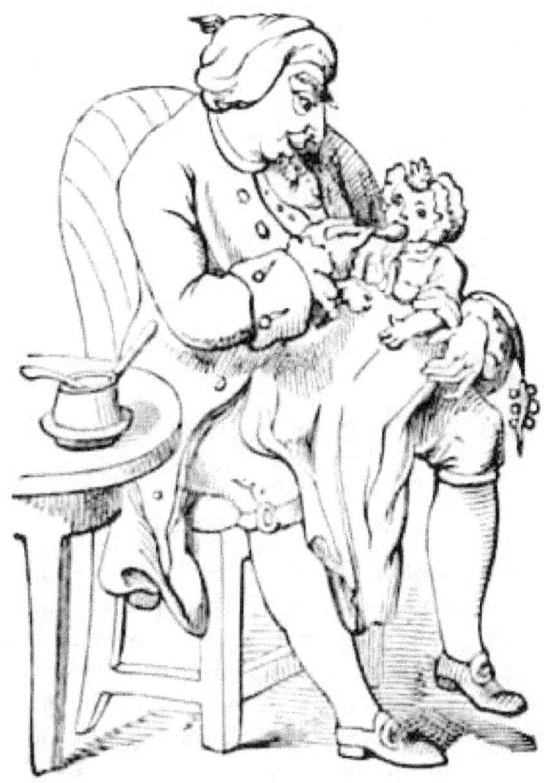

No. 229. Grandfather George.

At the period of the regency bill in 1789, Gillray attacked Pitt's policy in that affair with great severity. In a caricature published on the 3rd of January, he drew the premier in the character of an over-gorged vulture, with one claw fixed firmly on the crown and sceptre, and with the other seizing upon the prince's coronet, from which he is plucking the feathers. Among other good caricatures on this occasion, perhaps the finest is a parody on Fuseli's picture of "The Weird Sisters," in which Dundas, Pitt, and Thurlow, as the sisters, are contemplating the moon, the bright side of whose disc represents the face of the queen, and the other that of the king, overcast with mental darkness. Gillray took a strongly hostile view of the French revolution, and produced an immense number of caricatures against the French and their rulers, and their friends, or supposed friends, in this country, during the period extending from 1790 to the earlier years of the present century. Through all the changes of ministry or policy, he seems to have fixed himself strongly on individuals, and he seldom ceased to caricature the person who had once provoked his attacks. So it was with the lord chancellor Thurlow, who became the butt of savage satire in some of his prints which appeared in 1792, at the time when Pitt forced him to resign the chancellorship. Among these is one of the boldest caricatures which he ever executed. It is a parody, fine almost to sublimity, on a well-known scene in Milton, and is entitled, "Sin, Death, and the Devil." The queen, as Sin, rushes to separate the two combatants, Death (in the semblance of Pitt) and Satan (in that of Thurlow). During the latter part of the century Gillray caricatured all parties in turn, whether ministerial or opposition, with indiscriminate vigour; but his hostility towards the party of Fox, whom he persisted in regarding, or at least in representing, as unpatriotic revolutionists, was certainly greatest. In 1803 he worked energetically against the Addington ministry; and in 1806 he caricatured that which was known by the title of "All the Talents;" but during this later period of his life his labours were more especially aimed at keeping up the spirit of his countrymen against the threats and designs of our foreign enemies. It was, in fact, the caricature which at that time met with the greatest encouragement.

In his own person, Gillray had lived a life of great irregularity, and as he grew older, his habits of dissipation and intemperance increased, and gradually broke down his intellect. Towards the year 1811 he ceased producing any original works; the last plate he executed was a drawing of Bunbury's, entitled "A Barber's Shop in Assize Time," which is supposed to have been finished in the January of that year. Soon afterwards his mind sank into idiotcy, from which it never recovered. James Gillray died in 1815, and was buried in St. James's churchyard, Piccadilly, near the rectory house.

CHAPTER XXVIII.

GILLRAY'S CARICATURES ON SOCIAL LIFE.—THOMAS ROWLANDSON.—HIS EARLY LIFE.—HE BECOMES A CARICATURIST.—HIS STYLE AND WORKS.—HIS DRAWINGS.—THE CRUIKSHANKS.

Gillray was, beyond all others, the great political caricaturist of his age. His works form a complete history of the greater and more important portion of the reign of George III. He appears to have had less taste for general caricature, and his caricatures on social life are less numerous, and with a few exceptions less important, than those which were called forth by political events. The exceptions are chiefly satires on individual characters, which are marked by the same bold style which is displayed in his political attacks. Some of his caricatures on the extravagant costume of the time, and on its more prominent vices, such as the rage for gambling, are also fine, but his social sketches generally are much inferior to his other works.

This, however, was not the case with his contemporary, Thomas Rowlandson, who doubtlessly stands second to Gillray, and may, in some respects, be considered his equal. Rowlandson was born in the Old Jewry in London, the year before that of the birth of Gillray, in the July of 1756. His father was a city merchant, who had the means to give him a good education, but embarking rashly in some unsuccessful speculations, he fell into reduced circumstances, and the son had to depend upon the liberality of a relative. His uncle, Thomas Rowlandson, after whom probably he was named, had married a French lady, a Mademoiselle Chatelier, who was now a widow, residing in Paris, with what would be considered in that capital a handsome fortune, and she appears to have been attached to her English nephew, and supplied him rather freely with money. Young Rowlandson had shown at an early age great talent for drawing, with an especial turn for satire. As a schoolboy, he covered the margins of his books with caricatures upon his master and upon his fellow-scholars, and at the age of sixteen he was admitted a student in the Royal Academy in London, then in its infancy. But he did not profit immediately by this admission, for his aunt invited him to Paris, where he began and followed his studies in art with great success, and was remarked for the skill with which he drew the human body. His studies from nature, while in Paris, are said to have been remarkably fine. Nor did his taste for satirical design fail him, for it was one of his greatest amusements to caricature the numerous individuals, and groups of individuals, who must in that age have presented objects of ridicule to a lively Englishman. During this time his aunt died, leaving him all her property, consisting of about £7,000 in money, and a considerable amount in plate and other objects. The sudden possession of so much money proved a misfortune to young Rowlandson. He appears to have had an early love for gaiety, and he now yielded to all the temptations to vice held out by the French metropolis, and especially to an uncontrollable passion for gambling, through which he soon dissipated his fortune.

Before this, however, had been effected, Rowlandson, after having resided in Paris about two years, returned to London, and continued his studies in the Royal Academy. But he appears for some years to have given himself up entirely to his dissipated habits, and to have worked only at intervals, when he was driven to it by the want of money. We are told by one who was intimate with him, that, when reduced to this condition, he used to exclaim, holding up his pencil, "I have been playing the fool, but here is my resource!" and he would then produce—with extraordinary rapidity—caricatures enough to supply his momentary wants. Most of Rowlandson's earlier productions were published anonymously, but here and there, among large collections, we meet with a print, which, by companion of the style with that of his earliest known works, we can hardly hesitate in ascribing to him; and from these it would appear that he had begun with political caricature, because, perhaps, at that period of great agitation, it was most called for, and, therefore, most profitable. Three of the earliest of the political caricatures thus ascribed to Rowlandson belong to the year 1784, when he was twenty-eight years of age, and relate to the dissolution of parliament in that year, the result of which was the establishment of William Pitt in power. The first, published on the 11th of March, is entitled "The Champion of the People." Fox is represented under this title, armed with the sword of Justice and the shield of Truth, combating the many-headed hydra, its mouths respectively breathing forth "Tyranny," "Assumed Prerogative," "Despotism," "Oppression," "Secret Influence," "Scotch Politics," "Duplicity," and "Corruption." Some of these heads are already cut off. The Dutchman, Frenchman, and other foreign enemies are seen in the background, dancing round the standard of "Sedition." Fox is supported by numerous bodies of English and Irishmen, the English shouting, "While he protects us, we will support him." The Irish, "He gave us a free trade and all we asked; he shall have our firm support." Natives of India, in allusion to his unsuccessful India Bill, kneel by his side and pray for his success. The second of these caricatures was published on the 26th of March, and is entitled "The State Auction." Pitt is the auctioneer, and is represented as knocking down with the hammer of "prerogative" all the valuable articles of the constitution. The clerk is his colleague, Henry Dundas, who holds up a weighty lot, entitled, "Lot 1. The Rights of the People." Pitt calls to him, "Show the lot this way, Harry—a'going, a'going—speak quick, or it's gone—hold up the lot, ye Dund-ass!" The clerk replies in his Scottish accent, "I can hould it na higher, sir." The Whig members, under the title of the "chosen representers," are leaving the auction room in discouragement, with reflections in their mouths, such as, "Adieu to Liberty!" "Despair not!" "Now or never!" While Fox stands firm in the cause, and exclaims—"I am determined to bid with spirit for Lot 1; he shall pay dear for it that outbids me!" Pitt's Tory supporters are ranged under the auctioneer, and are called the "hereditary virtuosis;" and their leader, who appears to be the lord chancellor, addresses them in the words, "Mind not the nonsensical biddings of those common fellows." Dundas remarks, "We shall get the supplies by this sale." The third of these caricatures is dated on the 31st of March, when the elections had commenced, and is entitled, "The Hanoverian Horse and British Lion—a Scene in a new Play, lately acted in Westminster, with distinguished applause. Act 2nd, Scene last." At the back of the picture stands the vacant throne, with the intimation, "We shall resume our situation here at pleasure, *Leo Rex.*" In front, the Hanoverian horse, unbridled, and without saddle, neighs "pre-ro-ro-ro-ro-rogative," and is trampling on the safeguard of the constitution, while it kicks out violently the "faithful commons" (alluding to the recent dissolution of parliament). Pitt, on the back of the horse, cries, "Bravo!—go it again!—I love to ride a mettled steed; send the vagabonds packing!" Fox appears on the other side of the picture, mounted on the British lion, and holding a whip and bridle in his hand. He says to Pitt, "Prithee, Billy, dismount before ye get a fall, and let some abler jockey take your seat;" and the lion observes, indignantly, but with gravity, "If this horse is not tamed, he will soon be absolute king of our forest."

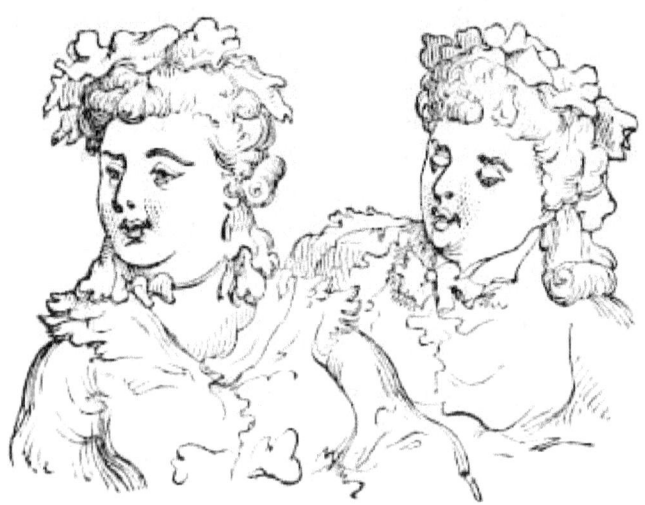

No. 230. Opera Beauties.

If these prints are correctly ascribed to Rowlandson, we see him here fairly entered in the lists of political caricature, and siding with Fox and the Whig party. He displays the same boldness in attacking the king and his ministers which was displayed by Gillray—a boldness that probably did much towards preserving the liberties of the country from what was no doubt a resolute attempt to trample upon them, at a time when caricature formed a very powerful weapon. Before this time, however, Rowlandson's pencil had become practised in those burlesque pictures of social life for which he became afterwards so celebrated. At first he seems to have published his designs under fictitious names, and one now before me, entitled "The Tythe Pig," bears the early date of 1786, with the name of "Wigstead," no doubt an assumed one, which is found on some others of his early prints. It represents the country parson, in his own parlour, receiving the tribute of the tithe pig from an interesting looking farmer's wife. The name of Rowlandson, with the date 1792, is attached to a very clever and humorous etching which is now also before me, entitled "Cold Broth and Calamity," and representing a party of skaters, who have fallen in a heap upon the ice, which is breaking under their weight. It bears the name of Fores as publisher. From this time, and especially toward the close of the century, Rowlandson's caricatures on social life became very numerous, and they are so well known that it becomes unnecessary, nor indeed would it be easy, to select a few examples which would illustrate all his characteristic excellencies. In prints published by Fores at the beginning of 1794, the address of the publisher is followed by the words, "where may be had all Rowlandson's works," which shows how great was his reputation as a caricaturist at that time. It may be stated briefly that he was distinguished by a remarkable versatility of talent, by a great fecundity of imagination, and by a skill in grouping quite equal to that of Gillray, and with a singular ease in forming his groups of a great number of figures. Among those of his contemporaries who spoke of him with the highest praise were sir Joshua Reynolds and Benjamin West. It has been remarked, too, that no artist ever possessed the power of Rowlandson of expressing so much with so little effort. We trace a great difference in style between Rowlandson's earlier and his later works; although there is a general identity of character which cannot be mistaken. The figures in the former show a taste for grace and elegance that is rare in his later works, and we find a delicacy of beauty in his females which he appears afterwards to have entirely laid aside. An example of his earlier style in depicting female faces is furnished by the pretty farmer's wife, in the print of "The Tythe Pig," just alluded to; and I may quote as another example, an etching published on the 1st of January, 1794, under the title of "English Curiosity; or, the foreigner stared out of countenance." An individual, in a foreign costume, is seated in the front row of the boxes of a theatre, probably intended for the opera, where he has become the object of curiosity of the whole audience, and all eyes are eagerly directed upon him. The faces of the men are rather coarsely grotesque, but those of the ladies, two of which are given in our cut No. 230, possess a considerable degree of refinement. He appears, however, to have been naturally a man of no real refinement, who easily gave himself up to low and vulgar tastes, and, as his caricature became more exaggerated and coarse, his females became less and less graceful, until his model of female beauty appears to have been represented by something like a fat oyster-woman. Our cut No. 231, taken from a print in the possession of Mr. Fairholt, entitled, "The Trumpet and Bassoon," presents a good example of Rowlandson's broad humour, and of his favourite models of the human face. We can almost fancy we hear the different tones of this brace of snorers.

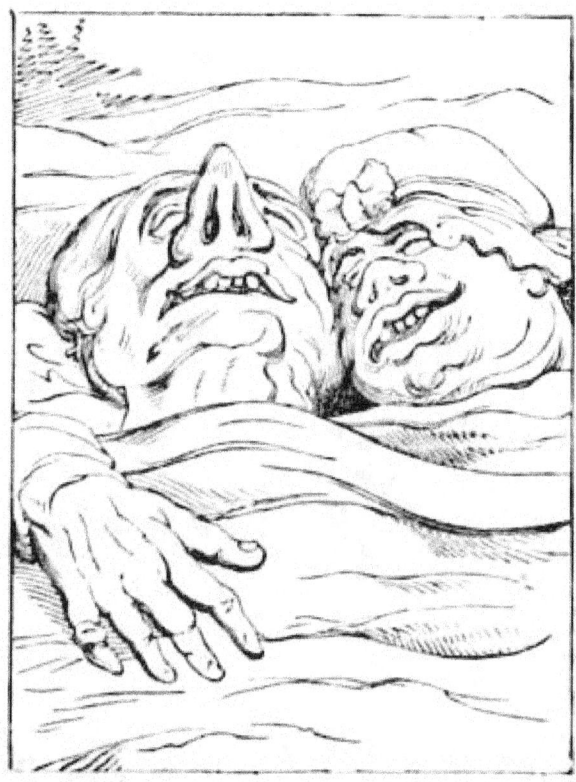

No. 231. The Trumpet and Bassoon.

A good example of Rowlandson's grotesques of the human figure is given in our cut No. 232, taken from a print published on the 1st of January, 1796, under the title of "Anything will do for an Officer." People complained of the mean appearance of the officers in our armies, who obtained their rank, it was pretended, by favour and purchase rather than by merit; and this caricature is explained by an inscription beneath, which informs us how "Some school-boys, who were playing at soldiers, found one of their number so ill-made, and so much under size, that he would have disfigured the whole body if put into the ranks. 'What shall we do with him?' asked one. 'Do with him?' says another, 'why make an officer of him.'" This plate is inscribed with his name, "Rowlandson fecit."

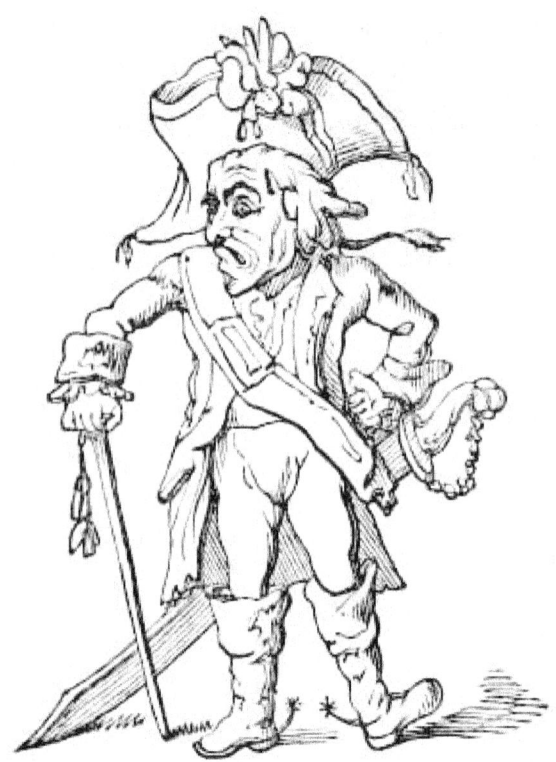

No. 232. A Model Officer.

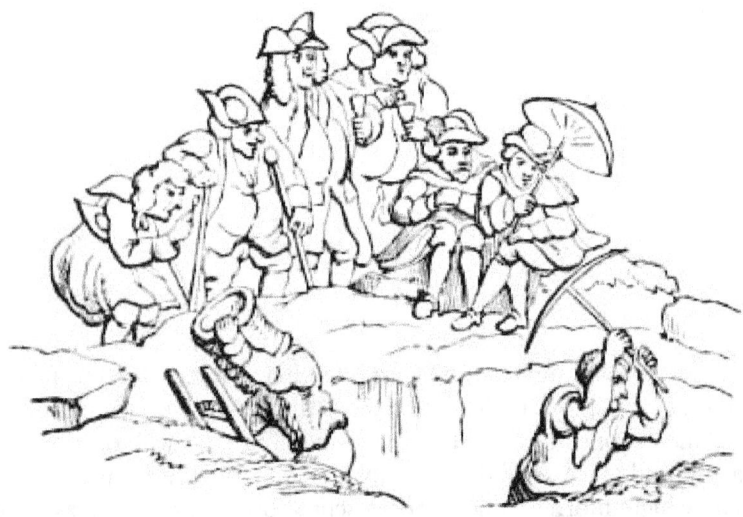

No. 233. Antiquaries at Work.

At this time Rowlandson still continued to work for Fores, but before the end of the century we find him working for Ackermann, of the Strand, who continued to be his friend and employer during the rest of his life, and is said to have helped him generously in many difficulties. In these, indeed, he was continually involved by his dissipation and thoughtlessness. Ackermann not only employed him in etching the drawings of other caricaturists, especially of Bunbury, but in furnishing illustrations to books, such as the several series of Dr. Syntax, the "New Dance of Death," and others. Rowlandson's illustrations to editions of the older standard novels, such as "Tom Jones," are remarkably clever. In transferring the works of other caricaturists to the copper,

Rowlandson was in the habit of giving his own style to them to such a degree, that nobody would suspect that they were not his own, if the name of the designer were not attached to them. I have given one example of this in a former chapter, and another very curious one is furnished by a print now before me, entitled "Anglers of 1811," which bears only the name "H. Bunbury del.," but which is in every particular a perfect example of the style of Rowlandson. During the latter part of his life Rowlandson amused himself with making an immense number of drawings which were never engraved, but many of which have been preserved and are still found scattered through the portfolios of collectors. These are generally better finished than his etchings, and are all more or less burlesque. Our cut No. 233 is taken from one of these drawings, in the possession of Mr. Fairholt; it represents a party of antiquaries engaged in important excavations. No doubt the figures were intended for well-known archæologists of the day.

Thomas Rowlandson died in poverty, in lodgings in the Adelphi, on the 22nd of April, 1827.

Among the most active caricaturists of the beginning of the present century we must not overlook Isaac Cruikshank, even if it were only because the name has become so celebrated in that of his more talented son. Isaac's caricatures, too, were equal to those of any of his contemporaries, after Gillray and Rowlandson. One of the earliest examples which I have seen bearing the well-known initials, I. C., was published on the 10th of March, 1794, the year in which George Cruikshank was born, and probably, therefore, when Isaac was quite a young man. It is entitled "A Republican Belle," and is an evident imitation of Gillray. In another, dated the 1st of November, 1795, Pitt is represented as "The Royal Extinguisher," putting out the flame of "Sedition." Isaac Cruikshank published many prints anonymously, and among the numerous caricatures of the latter end of the last century we meet with many which have no name attached to them, but which resemble so exactly his known style, that we can hardly hesitate in ascribing them to him. It will be remarked that in his acknowledged works he caricatures the opposition; but perhaps, like other caricaturists of his time, he worked privately for anybody who would pay him, and was as willing to work against the government as for it, for most of the prints which betray their author only by their style are caricatures on Pitt and his measures. Such is the group given in our cut No. 234, which was published on the 15th of August, 1797, at a time when there were loud complaints against the burthen of taxation. It is entitled "Billy's Raree-Show; or, John Bull En-lighten'd," and represents Pitt, in the character of a showman, exhibiting to John Bull, and picking his pocket while his attention is occupied with the show. Pitt, in a true showman's style, says to his victim, "Now, pray lend your attention to the enchanting prospect before you,—this is the prospect of peace—only observe what a busy scene presents itself—the ports are filled with shipping, the quays loaded with merchandise, riches are flowing in from every quarter—this prospect alone is worth all the money you have got about you." Accordingly, the showman abstracts the same money from his pocket, while John Bull, unconscious of the theft exclaims with surprise, "Mayhap it may, master showman, but I canna zee ony thing like what you mentions,—I zees nothing but a woide plain, with some mountains and molehills upon't—as sure as a gun, it must be all behoind one of those!" The flag of the show is inscribed, "Licensed by authority, Billy Hum's grand exhibition of moving mechanism; or, deception of the senses."

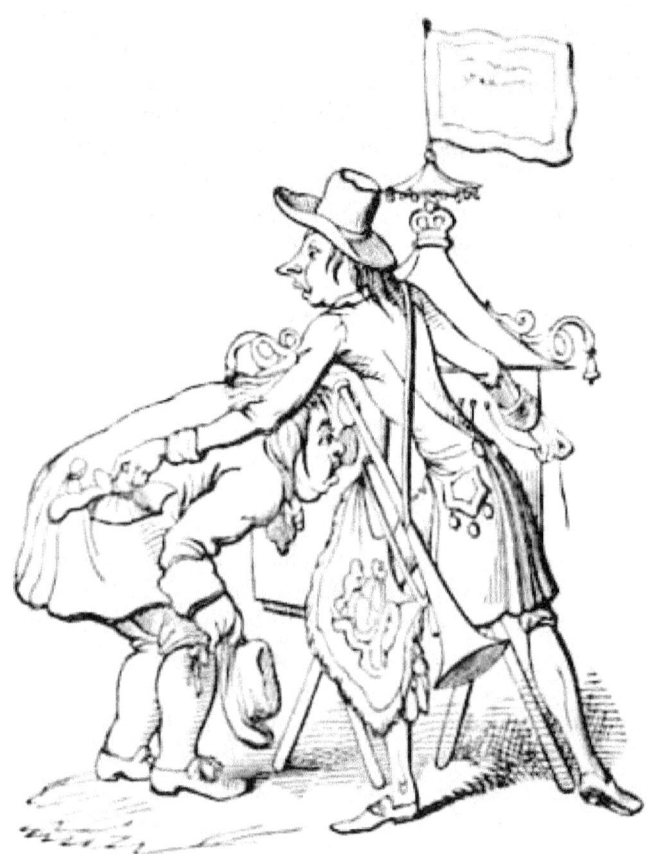

No. 234. The Raree-Show.

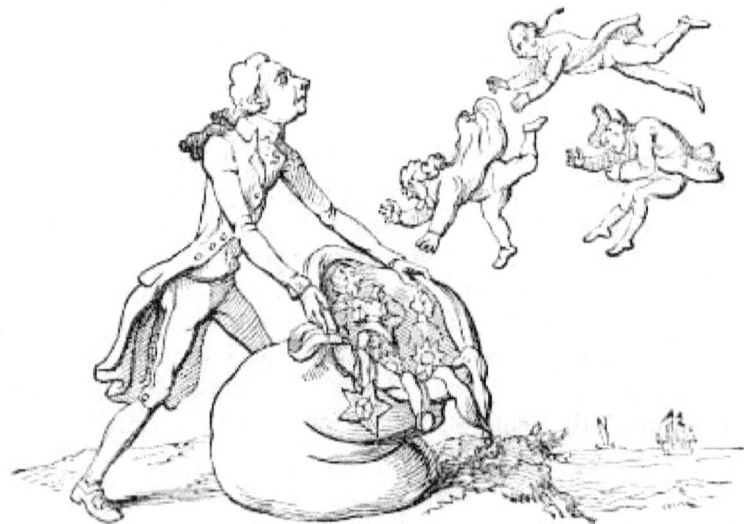

No. 235. Flight across the Herring Pond.

In a caricature with the initials of I. C., and published on the 20th of June, 1797, Fox is represented as "The Watchman of the State," ironically, of course, for he is betraying the truth which he had ostentatiously assumed, and absenting himself at the moment when his agents are putting the match to the train they have laid to blow up the constitution. Yet Cruikshank's caricatures on the Irish union were rather opposed to ministers. One of these, published on the 20th of June, 1800, is full of humour. It is entitled "A Flight across the Herring Pond." England and Ireland are separated by a rough sea, over which a crowd of Irish "patriots" are flying, allured by the prospect of honours and rewards. On the Irish shore, a few wretched natives, with a baby and a dog, are in an attitude of prayer, expostulating with the fugitives,—"Och, och! do not leave us—consider your old house, it will look like a big wallnut-shell without a kernel." On the English shore, Pitt is holding open the "Imperial Pouch," and welcoming them,—"Come on, my little fellows, there's plenty of room for you all—the budget is not half full." Inside the "pouch" appears a host of men covered with honours and dignities, one of whom says to the foremost of the Irish candidates for favour, "Very snug and convenient, brother, I allure you." Behind Pitt, Dundas, seated on a pile of public offices united in his person, calls out to the immigrants, "If you've ony consciences at a', here's enugh to satisfy ye a'." A portion of this clever caricature is represented in our cut No. 235.

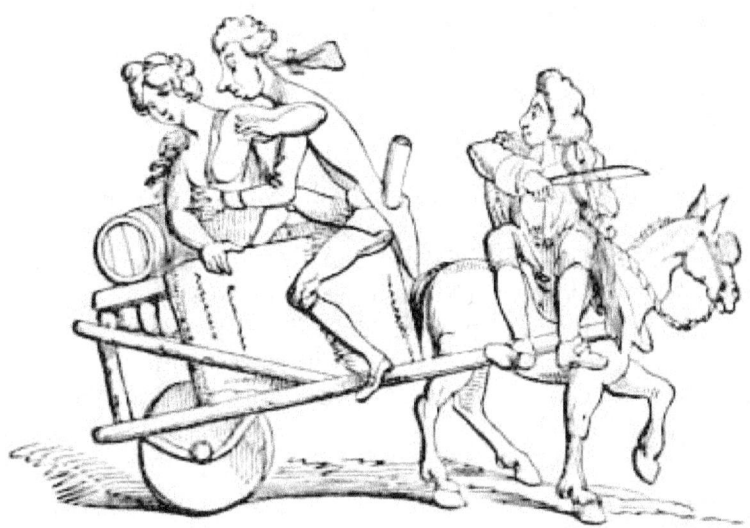

No. 236. A Case of Abduction.

There is a rare caricature on the subject of the Irish union, which exhibits a little of the style of Isaac Cruikshank, and a copy of which is in the possession of Mr. Fairholt. From this I have taken merely the group which forms our cut No. 236. It is a long print, dated on the 1st of January, 1800, and is entitled "The Triumphal entry of the Union into London." Pitt, with a paper entitled "Irish Freedom" in his pocket, is carrying off the young lady (Ireland) by force, with her natural accompaniment, a keg of whisky. The lord chancellor of Ireland (lord Clare) sits on the horse and performs the part of fiddler. In advance of this group are a long rabble of radicals, Irishman, &c, while close behind comes Grattan, carried in a sedan-chair, and earnestly appealing to the lady, "Ierne, Ierne! my sweet maid, listen not to him—he's a false, flattering, gay deceiver." Still farther in the rear follows St. Patrick, riding on a bull, with a sack of potatoes for his saddle, and playing on the Irish harp. An Irishman expostulates in the following words—"Ah, long life to your holy reverence's memory, why will you lave your own nate little kingdom, and go to another where they will tink no more of you then they would of an old brogue? Shure, of all the saints in the red-letter calendar, we give you the preference! och hone! och hone!" Another Irishman pulls the bull by the tail, with the lament, "Ah, masther, honey, why will you be after leaving us? What will become of poor Shelagh and all of us, when you are gone?" It is a regular Irish case of abduction.

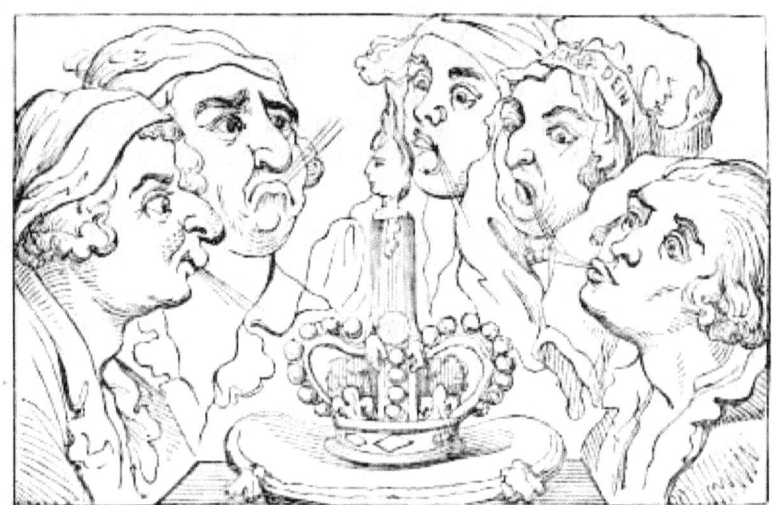

No. 237. The Farthing Rushlight.

The last example I shall give of the caricatures of Isaac Cruikshank is the copy of one entitled "The Farthing Rushlight," which, I need hardly say, is a parody on the subject of a well-known song. The rushlight is the poor old king, George, whom the prince of Wales and his Whig associates, Fox, Sheridan, and others, are labouring in vain to blow out. The latest caricature I possess, bearing the initials of Isaac Cruikshank, was published by Fores, on the 19th of April, 1810, and is entitled, "The Last Grand Ministerial Expedition (on the Street, Piccadilly)." The subject is the riot on the arrest of sir Francis Burdett, and it shows that Cruikshank was at this time caricaturing on the radical side in politics.

Isaac Cruikshank left two sons who became distinguished as caricaturists, George, already mentioned, and Robert. George Cruikshank, who is still amongst us, has raised caricature in art to perhaps the highest degree of excellence it has yet reached. He began as a political caricaturist, in imitation of his father Isaac—in fact the two brothers are understood to have worked jointly with their father before they engraved on their own account. I have in my own possession two of his earliest works of this class, published by Fores, of Piccadilly, and dated respectively the 3rd and the 19th of March, 1815. George was then under twenty-one years of age. The first of these prints is a caricature on the restrictions laid upon the trade in corn, and is entitled "The Blessings of Peace, or, the Curse of the Corn Bill." A foreign boat has arrived, laden with corn at a low price—one of the foreign traders holds out a sample and says, "Here is de best for 50s." A group of bloated aristocrats and landholders stand on the shore, with a closed storehouse, filled with corn behind them; the foremost, warning the boat away with his hand, replies to the merchant, "We won't have it at any price—we are determined to keep up our own to 80s., and if the poor can't buy at that price, why they must starve. We love money too well to lower our rents again; the income tax is taken off." One of his companions exclaims, "No, no, we won't have it at all." A third adds, "Ay, ay, let 'em starve, and be d— to 'em." Upon this another of the foreign merchants cries, "By gar, if they will not have it at all, we must throw it overboard!" and a sailor is carrying this alternative into execution by emptying a sack into the sea. Another group stands near the closed storehouse—it consists of a poor Englishman, his wife with an infant in the arms, and two ragged children, a boy and a girl. The father is made to say, "No, no, masters, I'll not starve; but quit my native country, where the poor are crushed by those they labour to support, and retire to one more hospitable, and where the arts of the rich do not interpose to defeat the providence of God." The corn bill was passed in the spring of 1815, and was the cause of much popular agitation and rioting. The second of these caricatures, on the same subject, is entitled, "The Scale of Justice reversed," and represents the rich exulting over the disappearance of the tax on property, while the poor are crushed under the weight of taxes which bore only upon them. These two caricatures present unmistakable traces of the peculiarities of style of George Cruikshank, but not as yet fully developed.

George Cruikshank rose into great celebrity and popularity as a political caricaturist by his illustrations to the pamphlets of William Houe, such as "The Political House that Jack built," "The Political Showman at Home," and others upon the trial of queen Caroline; but this sort of work suited the taste of the public at that time, and not that of the artist, which lay in another direction. The ambition of George Cruikshank was to draw what Hogarth called moral comedies, pictures of society carried through a series of acts and scenes, always pointed with some great moral; and it must be confessed that he has, through a long career, succeeded admirably. He possesses more of the true spirit of Hogarth than any other artist since Hogarth's time, with greater skill in drawing. He possesses, even to a greater degree than Hogarth himself, that admirable talent of filling a picture with an immense number of figures, every one telling a part of the story, without which, however minute, the whole picture would seem to us incomplete. The picture of the "Camp at Vinegar Hill," and one or two other illustrations to Maxwell's "History of the Irish Rebellion in 1798," are equal, if not superior, to anything ever produced by Hogarth or by Callot.

The name of George Cruikshank forms a worthy conclusion to the "History of Caricature and Grotesque." He is the last representative of the great school of caricaturists formed during the reign of George III. Though there can hardly be said to be a school at the present day, yet our modern artists in this field have been all formed more or less under his influence; and it must not be forgotten that we owe to that influence, and to his example, to a great degree, the cleansing of this branch of art from the objectionable characteristics of which I have on more than one occasion been obliged to speak. May he still live long among the friends who not only admire him for his talents, but love him for his kindly and genial spirit; and none among them love and admire him more sincerely than the author of the present volume.

FINIS.

www.ingramcontent.com/pod-product-compliance
Lightning Source LLC
Chambersburg PA
CBHW081715220526
45468CB00008B/1855